Consumer Credit and

the American Economy

FINANCIAL MANAGEMENT ASSOCIATION
Survey and Synthesis Series

Asset Management: A Systematic Approach to Factor Investing
Andrew Ang

Asset Pricing and Portfolio Choice Theory
Kerry E. Back

Beyond Greed and Fear: Understanding Behavioral Finance and the Psychology of Investing
Hersh Shefrin

Beyond the Random Walk: A Guide to Stock Market Anomalies and Low-Risk Investing
Vijay Singal

Debt Management: A Practitioner's Guide
John D. Finnerty and Douglas R. Emery

Dividend Policy: Its Impact on Firm Value
Ronald C. Lease, Kose John, Avner Kalay, Uri Loewenstein, and Oded H. Sarig

Efficient Asset Management: A Practical Guide to Stock Portfolio Optimization and Asset Allocation [title], 2nd Edition
Richard O. Michaud and Robert O. Michaud

Last Rights: Liquidating a Company
Dr. Ben S. Branch, Hugh M. Ray, and Robin Russell

Managing Pension and Retirement Plans: A Guide for Employers, Administrators, and Other Fiduciaries
August J. Baker, Dennis E. Logue, and Jack S. Rader

Managing Pension Plans: A Comprehensive Guide to Improving Plan Performance
Dennis E. Logue and Jack S. Rader

Mortgage Valuation Models: Embedded Options, Risk, and Uncertainty
Andrew Davidson and Alex Levin

Real Estate Investment Trusts: Structure, Performance, and Investment Opportunities
Su Han Chan, John Erickson, and Ko Wang

Real Options: Managing Strategic Investment in an Uncertain World
Martha Amram and Nalin Kulatilaka

Real Options in Theory and Practice
Graeme Guthrie

Slapped by the Invisible Hand: The Panic of 2007
Gary B. Gorton

Survey Research in Corporate Finance: Bridging the Gap between Theory and Practice
H. Kent Baker, J. Clay Singleton, and E. Theodore Veit

The Financial Crisis of Our Time
Robert W. Kolb

The Search for Value: Measuring the Company's Cost of Capital
Michael C. Ehrhardt

Too Much Is Not Enough: Incentives in Executive Compensation
Robert W. Kolb

Trading and Exchanges: Market Microstructure for Practitioners
Larry Harris

Truth in Lending: Theory, History, and a Way Forward
Thomas A. Durkin and Gregory Elliehausen

Value Based Management with Corporate Social Responsibility [title], 2nd Edition
John D. Martin, J. William Petty, and James S. Wallace

Valuing the Closely Held Firm
Michael S. Long and Thomas A. Bryant

Working Capital Management
Lorenzo Preve and Virginia Sarria-Allende

Consumer Credit and the American Economy

THOMAS A. DURKIN,

GREGORY ELLIEHAUSEN,

MICHAEL E. STATEN,

AND

TODD J. ZYWICKI

OXFORD
UNIVERSITY PRESS

Oxford University Press is a department of the University of Oxford.
It furthers the University's objective of excellence in research,
scholarship, and education by publishing worldwide.

Oxford   New York
Auckland   Cape Town   Dar es Salaam   Hong Kong   Karachi
Kuala Lumpur   Madrid   Melbourne   Mexico City   Nairobi
New Delhi   Shanghai   Taipei   Toronto

With offices in
Argentina   Austria   Brazil   Chile   Czech Republic   France   Greece
Guatemala   Hungary   Italy   Japan   Poland   Portugal   Singapore
South Korea   Switzerland   Thailand   Turkey   Ukraine   Vietnam

Oxford is a registered trademark of Oxford University Press
in the UK and certain other countries.

Published in the United States of America by
Oxford University Press
198 Madison Avenue, New York, NY 10016

Library of Congress Cataloging-in-Publication Data
Durkin, Thomas A.
Consumer credit and the American economy / Thomas A. Durkin, Gregory Elliehausen,
Michael E. Staten, and Todd J. Zywicki.
    pages cm.—(Financial Management Association survey and synthesis series)
Includes bibliographical references.
ISBN 978–0–19–516992–8 (alk. paper)   1. Consumer credit—United States.
2. Consumer credit—Government policy—United States.   3. United States—Economic
conditions   I. Title.
HG3756.U54D865 2014
332.7'43—dc23
2014006801

9 8 7 6 5 4 3 2
Printed in the United States of America
on acid-free paper

Dedicated to pioneer researchers in this field,
from whom we have learned so much:
John M. Chapman (1887–1970)
Robert W. Johnson (1923–2009)
F. Thomas Juster (1926–2010)
George Katona (1901–1981)
Edwin R. A. Seligman (1861–1939)
Robert P. Shay (1922–2001)

CONTENTS

LIST OF TABLES AND FIGURES

TABLES

FIGURES

To the four of us, writing about consumer credit in the American economy seems like the most natural and logical thing in the world. First of all, each of us underwent full immersion in the study of this field early in graduate school, and we have pursued it in a variety of ways throughout our professional careers. We have watched the markets grow, as product offerings expanded and more people used them. We also have had the opportunity over the years to meet and come to know many of the individuals who developed the field, including the business figures who grew it, the academics and others who wrote about it, and the government officials who regulated it. We have been thinking about this area for our entire adult lifetimes; frankly, we find the subject of consumer credit—its use, users, entrepreneurs, institutions, and regulation—more than fascinating (believe it or not).

Second, what other common consumer product or service is so widely used today but apparently so little known about or really understood, even by its users? We all think we know about credit, but do we? Do most of us even have the patience to look at credit very closely or read all the disclosures we get in a credit contract or in the mail? At least one close observer, cultural historian Lendol Calder, has mused that consumer credit is not intellectually interesting to the masses (despite being frequently used, sometimes misused, and occasionally strongly condemned), in part because there has been so little human personality associated with the story of its origin and manufacture. There has been no Henry Ford, Henry Kissinger, Henry Aaron, Henry VIII, or any other bigger-than-life individual to personalize and popularize its story. Although there have been many colorful characters involved with creating the modern consumer credit industry and institutions we know today, few of these individuals have been very well known outside the immediate spheres of their business or regulatory influence.

It seems to us, however, as it did to Calder, that the story of modern consumer credit really *is* interesting. We believe its current place in society deserves a fuller telling, as Calder has done so well with its domestic cultural origins and background. If it is not bigger than life, it certainly is *part* of life: virtually all American consumers use consumer credit at some point in their financial lifetimes. But does this make it interesting? The basics of consumer credit certainly appear straightforward enough: you borrow money or purchase something "on time" and make the payments over a period of months or years. What could be simpler or more straightforward? Why is it so interesting?

We contend that the subject really amounts to a lot more than that, and this book tells this larger story. Economists and moral philosophers actually have studied and commented on personal credit use for centuries. More recently, so have sociologists, educators, psychologists, finance specialists, historians, counselors, journalists, politicians, legal experts, political activists, judges, and many others; even theologians have examined personal credit use. These specialists have looked at consumer credit from many viewpoints and have written about it in a range of both widely disseminated and obscure sources. The diversity of their efforts, along with the extent of the subject matter, practically begs for a more comprehensive review.

There is also a third reason we decided to write this book: there simply are no similar books, that is, works that start at the beginning of consumer credit and examine it in one place from all of these possible directions. There are, to be sure, histories of consumer credit, legal treatises, and even textbooks. There certainly also are consumer self-help handbooks on the subject, with variations of attention-grabbing titles such as "How to Get Out of Debt and Improve Your Health and Well-Being." Undoubtedly, such works are useful to those who need them. But nowhere has there been a comprehensive look at consumer credit as an American economic and cultural institution, born elsewhere in antiquity; nurtured and fought over in many places through the centuries by entrepreneurs, politicians, regulators, and churches; and loved or hated by them and their constituents of all sorts in the past and now. Such a comprehensive review is the purpose of this undertaking.

Our personal backgrounds and training as economists naturally color our approach to this effort and, for that matter, to our examining or thinking about any subject. Therefore, first and foremost, we report here on the fundamental economics of consumer credit, but this is not our sole intent. While our thought processes are certainly influenced by our basic discipline and training, we try not to slight the psychological, sociological, historical, and especially legal traditions that go into fully understanding what consumer credit is today. The interaction of all these fields is a good part of what makes consumer credit so fascinating to us.

In our exploration of consumer credit, we examine demand, supply, trends, growth, technological changes, regulatory structure, and other market and institutional phenomena and developments. Our motivation is to look analytically at the underlying reasons that explain *why* consumer credit has become such a widespread phenomenon that it has attracted the attention of analysts from journalists to theologians. Although we cast about widely in our analytic rendering, we believe our approach is well within the boundaries and traditions of mainstream positive economic analysis.

As we were contemplating a comprehensive work on modern consumer credit in the United States, the editorial committee of the Survey and Synthesis Series of the Financial Management Association, the largest association of financial professionals, saw the same need. Without going into detail here with the background about how we got together on this project, suffice it to say that their interests and ours became known to each other, and we joined forces. We are very grateful for their interest and encouragement.

As a "survey and synthesis" covering broad background, development, economics, behavioral science, institutions, public policy, and legal issues, this work contains many references and footnotes. The book is not intended specifically as a textbook, but it could serve as one in specialized courses in this area; for this reason, it begins with general matters and moves onward to more concentrated ones, including modern policy issues. We hope it serves as a useful guide to the major concerns in the latter area and to the underlying general principles associated with the basics of consumer credit.

Because we hope this work will be of interest to a reasonably wide variety of potential readers, we purposely try to stay away from too much jargon from any of the underlying academic specialties. We include tables and graphs as we think them useful, but we specifically try to avoid dependence on mathematical language for the most part. For those especially interested in more rigorous presentation employing mathematical and statistical methodologies, we point out many useful sources through footnotes and references.

ACKNOWLEDGMENTS

We are personally indebted to countless individuals with whom we have had even more countless conversations about these and other credit-related matters over the years, learning a little bit more each time about how the system works. We cannot individually thank all of you, but we remember each of you and how you helped and inspired us. In this context, we would be remiss, though, if we did not mention some special individuals. First are the finance professors who introduced us to the field of finance in the first place: the late Robert P. Shay of Columbia University and Robert W. Johnson of Purdue University, retired John "Russ" Ezzell and George Philippatos at Penn State, and John Umbeck at Purdue. Another important influence was the late George Benston of Emory University.

Certainly many individuals from the business community have also provided insights and encouragement over the years, but some now retired must be mentioned: Dennis Young of Wells Fargo Financial, the "finance guy" who presided for years over the strong balance sheet of that company and its predecessors; Randy Lively of Sears, Roebuck & Co. and later the American Financial Services Association, who has seen it all; James Smith, also of Sears and later the University of North Carolina, whose upbeat analyses of the implications of consumer credit for economic growth always keep audiences coming back for more; David Wesselink, a research director with an academic mind who made good as chief financial officer and CEO of a number of important companies; the late James Browne, accountant, tax guy, CEO of Chrysler First Financial, who really understood consumer lending; Gary Chandler, college professor, credit scoring pioneer, and cofounder of Management Decision Systems, who never lost his academic curiosity even as the mathematical scoring business prospered; Ted Spurlock, retired general credit manager of the J. C. Penney Company, a leader in business and a genuinely nice guy; Mort Schwartz of Citibank, a pioneer and brilliant authority on credit cards; Walter Kurth, retired as leader of Associated Credit Bureaus but not retired as a leader of the community at large; William Burfeind, longtime leader of the Consumer Credit Insurance Association (later the Consumer Credit Industry Association) and a real authority on credit insurance and debt protection products. Among many individuals still active in the field, we also single out Chris Stinebert and Bill Himpler of the American Financial Services Association, who are always willing to answer our questions.

From the legal side, a few retired or semiretired individuals also must be mentioned specially: Ralph Rohner of Catholic University Law School, a true academic authority on federal consumer credit law; Neil Butler, private practitioner in Washington, DC, and lifelong colorful character in consumer credit, and Joe Crouse, formerly of MBNA America Bank and Maryland Banking Commissioner, both of whom are former colleagues at the Federal Reserve and always willing to answer questions, no matter how complicated the question or obvious the answer; and Neal Petersen, formerly general counsel of the Federal Reserve Board and now in private practice, a loquacious advice giver and good friend. There are many other legal experts in various trade associations and law schools who have generously responded to our many information requests. They include Steven Zeisel, for many years a legal fixture at the Consumer Bankers Association, and Robert McKew, past general counsel of the American Financial Services Association, both equally willing to entertain and answer any vexing query; Scott Cipinko of the Consumer Credit Industry Association; Robert Weinberger of H&R Block; Vicki Woodward of the Consumer Financial Services Association; Hilary Miller, in private practice; and Sarah Hughes of the Indiana University Law School.

In addition, we have benefited from many conversations with other supporters of consumer credit research. They include David Walker of Georgetown University; Edward Lawrence of the University of Missouri at St. Louis; Fran Smith, formerly of Consumer Alert, and her husband, Fred Smith, of the Competitive Enterprise Institute, both irrepressible spokespersons for clear thinking in economics; Winthrop Hambley, former director of the Federal Reserve's Congressional Affairs Office and now special assistant to the Board, not exactly an academic but someone who exhibits the same thoughtfulness as the best of that profession; Charlie Luckett, retired senior economist of the Federal Reserve's Research Division, where he was both "Mr. Debt Burden Statistics" and keeper of the Fed's sense of humor; William Dunkelberg, former dean of Temple University's business school and another of the lifelong characters of consumer (and business) credit; and Richard Curtin of the University of Michigan, who helped us so much with finding out how to learn about consumer experiences through surveys.

Other colleagues on the economics side of government agencies who deserve special mention for ongoing helpful conversations, ideas, thoughts, and guidance at various stages of our careers include (in alphabetical order) Robert Avery, Kenneth Brevoort, Glenn Canner, Joe Cleaver, Robert Eisenbeis, Robert Fisher, Simona Hannon, Kathleen Johnson, James Lacko, Geng Li, Barbara Lowrey, Janis Pappalardo, and Stephanie Wilshusen; and from the legal side, Jane Ahrens, Krista Ayoub, Leonard Chanin, Griffith Garwood, Glenn Loney, Ellen Maland, James Michaels, Daniel Sokolov, David Stein, Ky Tran-Trong, and John Wood. None of these individuals is responsible for any errors of fact, judgment, or understanding that remain in what we have produced.

Many research assistants and junior partners over the years have also been more than important in the compilation of information, statistics, references, and details of projects that made what went into this work possible. These individuals include (in chronological order) Julie Rochlin, Julia Springer, Dale Griffa, Ysabel

Burns McAleer, her irrepressible brother Ian Burns, Matt (now Dr.) Maciejewski, Kim (now Dr.) Cole, Zach (now Dr.) Jonasson, Nicole Price, Christy Thomas, Chris Reynolds, Rachel Janke, and Jessica Zehel. All have been helpful in many ways, especially by continually asking questions when our answers to the last ones were not yet satisfactorily clear.

Todd Zywicki would like personally to thank George Mason University School of Law and especially Dean Dan Polsby, who has been a sincere and enthusiastic supporter of this project and others. Henry Butler and the Law and Economics Center at George Mason University have provided not only research support but many ideas that found their way into this book through the lecture series of the Law and Economics Center. He also would like to thank the Searle Foundation for providing sponsorship as a Searle Fellow and the Hoover Institution at Stanford University for a congenial home to spend some time in as a National Fellow. He also thanks friends and colleagues at George Mason Law School, especially Joshua Wright, who have patiently humored and encouraged him while being regaled with endless conversations about credit cards, payday lenders, loan sharks, and other credit sources. He adds that he has been immensely blessed with an extraordinary set of smart, friendly, and intellectually honest colleagues there and that no scholar could ask for a more welcoming and inspiring intellectual environment. Finally, he thanks his parents, Henry and Jo Ann Zywicki, "who taught me the virtues of hard work and financial responsibility and have supported me with all of my adventures in life."

Finally, but not by any means least, we express our thanks to the staff at Oxford University Press. They have been immensely helpful and understanding as the creative process has gone forward, but more important, they have been patient. We thank them especially for their ongoing understanding of the delays that have been our responsibility.

Introduction and Overview of Consumer Credit

Development, Uses, Kinds, and Policy Issues

Without question, the post–World War II decades have witnessed many significant changes to the American economy; not the least of them is the ongoing revolution in the money management habits of the large and growing middle class. In the early years after the war, the range of financial decisions for most people seems simple by today's standards: what proportion of savings to hold in government savings bonds versus deposits, how to choose depository institutions to open savings and checking accounts, and where to obtain loans, either for split-level homes in the developing subdivisions or for the new car models finally available after the end of wartime restrictions. Most of these financial decisions required relatively little investigation or intellectual effort for most people.

By contrast, today the variety and use of financial services have grown sufficiently to become a staple of discussion, even on talk radio and at lunchtime and evening seminars. Stock markets, mutual funds, exchange traded funds, variable annuities, IRAs, 401(k)s, 529s, tax-exempt bonds, defined benefit and contribution pension plans, health savings accounts, universal life insurance, and even formerly exotic products such as put and call options now are commonplace discussion topics. On the household liability side, consumers must contend with adjustable-rate mortgages, balloon mortgages, subprime mortgages, home equity credit lines, other secured loans, unsecured credit lines, other unsecured loans, and even thin plastic devices that access credit accounts usable worldwide. Today it is possible to transact in these and other asset and debt instruments not only at the office of a financial institution or broker, in person or over the telephone, but also impersonally in one's own den on a computer or almost anywhere else using a computer or cell-phone wireless link. Consumer sector financial management even became a staple of the nightly television news during the financial crisis of 2008–2009. For some people, the understanding and management of personal finances has become a hobby; for others, it is a nightmare.

Within the breadth of new and redesigned consumer financial products and services, none is more ubiquitous (or more controversial) than the various types of products known as consumer credit. Obviously, loans of various kinds to finance real estate purchases are common today (and even provoked the worldwide financial crisis beginning in 2008), but even more common are smaller extensions of credit. Specifically, the term *consumer credit* as used here refers to all kinds of credit employed by individuals that are not collateralized by real estate (that is, not home loans and home equity credit, which are *mortgage credit*) or by specific financial assets such as stocks and bonds and that are not used for business purposes. Typical auto loans, home improvement loans, appliance and recreational goods credit, unsecured cash loans, mobile home loans, student loans, and credit card credit all fall into the consumer credit category. From its origin as a small grouping of financial services used typically by the lower- to middle-income segments of the middle class between the world wars (and actually restricted by federal controls during World War II and the Korean War), modern consumer credit has grown so much that virtually all consumers are users at some point in their financial lives; certainly, almost all are at least aware of its benefits and risks.

What has caused consumer credit to move so far into the mainstream? Providers of financial services would probably answer with something about the demands of customers. Consumers would probably reply about the growth of useful product offerings by suppliers. Both would be right, of course, since it always takes both demand and supply to make a market. But these are simple answers, and, like so many easy responses, they are only part of a larger, more interesting, and arguably more important story. It is a truism that markets develop where demand meets supply, but consumer credit has grown so much, and the available financial products are now so numerous and their distribution system so extensive and diverse, that there must be a lengthier tale.

This book explores that part of the consumer indebtedness story not explicitly related to credit based on real estate collateral, related to stocks and bonds or other financial collateral, or used for business purposes. In other words, it examines the domain of consumer credit. It is the saga of wealth creation in the middle class over time that has led to demand for a wider range of financial products, including completely new forms of credit. It is also the story of the evolution and regulation of financial institutions that have grown to supply those needs and desires. It is simultaneously a tale of growth and competition among these financial providers and of the consequent pressures to attract customers while reducing production costs. Today these competitive forces continue to contribute to the ongoing revolution in product offerings. Innovations such as credit scoring, risk-based pricing, automated electronic credit reporting systems, product delivery through automated teller machines (ATMs) and more recently the Internet, and virtually instantaneous access to billions of dollars of credit worldwide illustrate a progression without an ending, as markets continue to evolve and as institutions plan and implement new financial services and delivery mechanisms. Even periodic financial crises are unlikely to slow this long-term trend very much.

CONSUMERS AND THEIR CREDIT

The idea of credit for households is certainly not new; in fact, there are well-known negative views of lending and personal debt in the Bible (Exodus, Leviticus, Deuteronomy), *Hamlet*, *Poor Richard's Almanac*, and *David Copperfield*, among many others from long ago.[1] For years, consumer debt as we know it today did not cause too many widespread domestic worries, however; debt growth for what today are common consumer purposes was almost unknown through much of American history before the late nineteenth century.

A Modern Phenomenon with Distant Roots

From colonial times until the Civil War, most free Americans lived on farms and plantations or in small villages among extended families. Families typically built their own farmhouses or bartered for construction help, and family members provided aid directly to children, siblings, and cousins in emergency situations. There was use of credit, to be sure, but largely as a substitute for circulating coin money that often was in short supply. For example, farmers often purchased store goods on credit while they awaited harvest time and the barter or sale of farm products that followed. Artisans of various sorts also extended credit if they, like the shopkeepers, were to sell their services and be paid at all.[2] But without much in the way

---

1. Exodus 22:25 (King James translation): "If thou lend money to my people poor by thee, thou shalt not be to him as an usurer, neither shalt thou lay upon him usury." (Until about the sixteenth century, the term *usury* referred to any taking of interest, not just high rates of interest.) Leviticus 25:35–37: "And if thy brother be waxen poor, and fallen in decay with thee; then thou shalt relieve him; yea, though he be a stranger, or a sojourner; that he may live with thee. Take then no usury of him, or increase; but fear thy God; that thy brother may live with thee." Deuteronomy 23:19–20: "Thou shalt not lend upon usury to thy brother; usury of money, usury of victuals, usury of anything…. Unto a stranger thou mayest lend upon usury; but unto thy brother thou shalt not lend upon usury."

Pronouncements against debt have also produced some of the best-known literary quotations in the English language. In Act 3 of *Hamlet*, Polonius offers his son, Laertes, the famous advice: "Neither a borrower nor a lender be; For loan oft loses both itself and friend, And borrowing dulls the edge of husbandry." Poor Richard has a number of pithy things to say about debt. Among the more memorable is "If you want to know the value of money, go and try to borrow some; for he who goes a borrowing goes a sorrowing…. the borrower is a slave to the lender."

Charles Dickens, who was personally familiar with the difficulties sometimes associated with debts, had his famous debtor Mr. Micawber say to David Copperfield, "My other piece of advice, Copperfield, you know. Annual income twenty pounds, annual expenditure nineteen, nineteen, six, result happiness. Annual income twenty pounds, annual expenditure twenty pounds ought and six, result misery. The blossom is blighted, the leaf is withered, the God of day goes down upon the dreary scene, and in short you are forever floored. As I am!"

2. For example, this author was able to purchase from a historian and antiques dealer a promissory note, dated April 1794, payable to his fifth great-grandfather and carefully signed by him (in three places), agreeing to receive time payment for carpentry work in building a house in the then-small village of Lebanon, Pennsylvania.

of consumer goods to choose from or much of a trade economy anyway, at least compared with today, there was little need for additional household credit beyond purchase-mortgage loans for farms, agricultural credit for planting, and deferred payments to shopkeepers and artisans for a few necessities until the crops came in. Ultimately, farm loans were extensions of business credit by lenders, when available at all, and would not be considered consumer credit then or now.

This is not to say that credit, and especially agricultural loans, was unimportant in the economic or political affairs of the earlier years of the republic. Rather, banking and agriculture were central concerns and divisive political issues up to and throughout the nineteenth century. Controversy over chartering a Bank of the United States instead of only smaller, local banks that would be more closely responsive to the needs of farmers was a major political issue throughout the first five decades of the country's history (see Hammond 1957). The controversial enthusiasm of Alexander Hamilton, an early "eastern financier" and the first US Treasury secretary, for the first Bank of the United States in the late eighteenth century is well known. So is the vehement opposition four decades later of Andrew Jackson, the first western president, to the second Bank of the United States. After Jackson vetoed the renewal of the second bank's national charter in 1832, that bank (rechartered in Pennsylvania as a state bank) became a notable financial failure in the recession and financial collapse that occurred later in that decade.

After the Civil War, there was widespread agrarian unrest over financial matters for the rest of the century. The political centrality of falling prices and associated credit difficulties for farmers (and other debtors) culminated during these years in the Greenback and Free Silver political movements and the final victory of the gold standard in the presidential election of William McKinley in 1896. Agricultural finance, metallic coinage, inflation, deflation, and the role of banks in society continued to be among the most important political issues for decades.[3]

Banking issues have remained vital politically in the twentieth and twenty-first centuries, if mostly not quite so divisive. The early years of the twentieth century witnessed the peak influence of financier J. Pierpont Morgan, whose name still echoes through Wall Street. A financial collapse and panic in 1907 produced extensive public review of finance, leading directly to passage of the Federal Reserve Act in 1913. A bit later, the onset of massive numbers of bank failures associated with depressed economic conditions during the 1930s produced another round of political centrality for banking matters. The Federal Deposit Insurance Corporation (FDIC) and the Securities and Exchange Commission (SEC) both were created during this period. Banking came to the forefront again in the 1980s, with the implosion of much of the network of savings and loan associations. Bankruptcy law changes in 2005 affecting consumer indebtedness and upheavals in the market for subprime mortgage loans in 2008–2009 affecting a whole host of financial institutions brought banking and finance as a highly visible political issue into the twenty-first century.

---

3. See Friedman and Schwartz (1963) for a scholarly treatise on monetary and financial matters during these years and up to 1960.

But compared with the other functions of domestic credit such as commercial lending, government finance, and housing loans, consumer credit as we think of it today is a relatively modern phenomenon. Despite some installment-purchase plans by sellers of furniture, sewing machines, and some other domestic goods and even clothing during the nineteenth century, consumer credit use was nothing like the common experience it is today. There simply were few needs before the 1920s for the auto loans, boat loans, durable goods credit, college tuition credits, and home modernization and repair loans that make up the bulk of consumer credit use today. Much of the demand for consumer credit arose with the development of urbanization, mass production of consumer goods, and growth of the middle class that began slowly in the nineteenth century but mostly came later, especially in the decades after World War II.[4]

There also were few financial institutions in the nineteenth and early twentieth centuries willing to extend credit in the small amounts consumers might need, and credit for households beyond housing debt was generally regarded as somewhat disreputable anyway. To be sure, in the later part of the nineteenth century, some enterprises began to extend credit to households for purchasing their products; for example, the Singer Sewing Machine Company began to offer time payments on its products in the 1850s, and some local sellers also offered time payments on their merchandise. But the development of major household-oriented durable goods industries based on electricity and the internal-combustion engine early in the twentieth century started consumer credit on its way to being the mass-market collection of financial products that it is today. Much of the impetus to consumer credit growth arose from efforts of manufacturing pioneers such as automakers to sell their products on a broader scale by also financing them. As a result, by the 1930s and afterward, household credit began to be more widely understood and appreciated as something beyond home loans, emergency funds for slightly down-and-out individuals, or a convenient way for a few rich people to avoid carrying around cash.[5]

The six decades and more since World War II have witnessed tremendous economic expansion in the United States. Consumer sector income, measured by disposable personal income, which consists of income after transfer payments and taxes, has risen more than seventy-five-fold in nominal dollars from 1945 to 2012 and to more than 600 percent of its 1945 level in inflation-adjusted terms (see table 1.1). Consumer sector total assets have grown even more rapidly over the same period, but consumers' debts have risen faster still, in percentage terms. At the end of 2012, home mortgage credit outstanding measured more than $9 trillion, and consumer credit was more than $2.5 trillion. The rapid growth of installment

---

4. Economic, monetary, financial, and banking history are all sizable areas of scholarship. In the banking area, important works include Redlich (1947), Hammond (1957), Friedman and Schwartz (1963), Fischer (1968), Homer and Sylla (1996), and Bodenhorn (2003). For historical discussion of consumer credit and its institutions, see Michelman (1966), Rogers (1974), Olney (1991), Calder (1999), and Gelpi and Julien-Labruyere (2000).

5. For an especially lively and readable account by a cultural historian of the historical development of consumer credit as a cultural phenomenon in the United States in the nineteenth and early twentieth centuries, see Calder (1999).

credit raises the question of whether debts have risen too fast, an analytical discussion area for consumer credit with a history all its own (see chapter 2).

Demand and Supply

Today, regardless of any concerns over growth trends, most informed observers agree that consumer credit availability in the modern economy provides a number of important economic benefits. First, consumer credit makes engaging in household investment undertakings easier and more timely for many families. In this context, the term *household investments on credit* does not refer to financial investment in such assets as stocks, bonds, or mutual fund shares. Rather, it means making expenditures for high-value goods or services (such as automobiles, appliances, home repairs and furnishings, education, and significant hobby items such as boats and motorcycles) that provide their benefits over a period of time and whose cash purchase does not usually fit comfortably into monthly budgets. By facilitating such investment spending, credit enables consumers to change the timing of their saving and consumption flows to a preferred pattern.

Specifically, rather than postponing the purchase of household investment goods and services and the consumption benefits they provide until funds are

Table 1.1 SELECTED MEASURES OF ASSETS, DEBTS, AND INCOME OF AMERICAN CONSUMERS, SELECTED YEARS, 1945–2012

	1945	1955	1965	1975	1985	1995	2005	2010	2012
	CURRENT DOLLARS (BILLIONS)								
Disposable personal income[a]	152	283	498	1,187	3,079	5,457	9,277	11,127	11,931
Total assets	722	1,534	2,794	5,670	16,071	32,370	71,020	71,070	76,930
Financial assets	559	1,019	1,960	3,679	9,995	21,783	44,903	49,848	54,390
Deposits	106	176	380	924	2,551	3,400	6,217	7,953	9,046
Other financial	454	843	1,580	2,754	7,444	18,384	38,686	41,895	45,345
Total liabilities	30	139	342	740	2,224	4,744	11,586	12,932	12,751
Home mortgages	19	88	219	459	1,450	3,319	8,907	9,890	9,430
Consumer credit	7	43	98	207	611	1,168	2,321	2,442	2,779
Other liabilities	4	9	25	74	164	257	358	500	541
Net worth	692	1,395	2,452	4,930	13,847	27,626	59,434	57,991	64,179

Table 1.1 CONTINUED

	1945	1955	1965	1975	1985	1995	2005	2010	2012
2012 DOLLARS (BILLIONS)									
Disposable personal income[a]	1,941	2,425	3,628	5,067	6,571	8,821	10,907	11,714	11,931
Total assets	9,203	13,143	20,364	24,200	34,292	48,767	83.493	74,817	76,930
Financial assets	7,134	8,727	14,289	15,700	21,327	32,818	52,789	52,476	54,390
Deposits	1,347	1,506	2,771	3,945	5,443	5,122	7,309	8,373	9,046
Other financial	5,787	7,220	11,519	11,754	15,884	27,696	43,480	44,104	45,345
Total liabilities	383	1,199	2,486	3,158	4,746	7,147	13,621	13,614	12,751
Home mortgages	239	753	1,599	1,959	3,093	5,000	10,471	10,411	9,430
Consumer credit	87	368	711	883	1,303	1,760	2,728	2,676	2,779
Other liabilities	51	77	182	316	350	387	421	526	541
Net worth	8,827	11,943	17,880	21,040	29,547	41,620	69,872	61,204	64,179

[a]Measured at annual rate. All other amounts are year-end, not seasonally adjusted.

Adjustments to 2012 dollars are made using the Consumer Price Index for All Urban Consumers (CPI-U). Components may not add exactly to totals because of rounding.

SOURCE: Federal Reserve Statistical Release Z1, "Flow of Funds Accounts of the United States," various issues. Figures shown are year-end, not seasonally adjusted. Table excludes assets but not liabilities of nonprofit organizations, thereby somewhat understating consumer sector net worth.

available from savings (a difficult task for many families, especially in the earlier stages of their earning years), consumers can use credit to purchase the investment goods and services first and pay for them while using them. In effect, they can save for them by making payments while actually using the goods and services. In exchange for this alteration in timing, lenders impose a cost known as interest or finance charge, which provides a return to those making the current resources available. When consumers decide to make such investments, it is reasonable to surmise that at least most of them engage in some sort of economic calculus concerning this cost relative to the associated benefits of using credit rather than waiting. Some elements of this decision are introduced briefly in the next section of this chapter, and it is discussed at greater length in chapters 3 and 4.

A second economic benefit of consumer credit is its substantial contribution to the growth of durable goods industries, where new technologies, mass production, and economies of scale historically have produced employment growth and new wealth. It is simply hard to imagine development of the suburbs or the auto-mobile and appliance industries in this country and worldwide in the twentieth century, or, for that matter, the higher education system as it now exists, without the simultaneous rise of consumer credit to facilitate sale of the output. (This is sometimes known as *moving the metal* in the vernacular of the auto industry, with-out any recognized counterpart phraseology in education.) Little more will be said here about this aspect of economic development in the United States, but the importance of consumer credit in this area cannot go without mention.

Third, consumer credit provides an important outlet for employing finan-cial resources available from net surplus components of the economy (savers), notably from consumers themselves. In fact, if not in common perception, the consumer sector of the American economy taken as a whole actually has always been a net lender in financial markets, not a net borrower. As revealed in the Federal Reserve's Flow of Funds accounting system, net financial lending and equity investment by the economy's consumer sector (either directly or through intermediaries such as banks and pension funds) passed the $1 trillion mark as long ago as 1958 (net of $183 billion of household liabilities at that time) and has continued to rise, mostly steadily, in the years since. Consumer sector *financial* assets totaled more than $54 trillion at the end of 2012 (see table 1.1). At that time, consumers' total liabilities were about $13 trillion. This left household sec-tor *financial* net worth at more than $40 trillion in 2012 dollars. Even so, house-holds obviously continue to borrow large amounts of funds, typically through financial intermediaries, sometimes from the same ones where they hold their reserves.

Ultimately, the source of funds for consumers who borrow is other (or even the same) consumers who have a financial surplus that they can hold as deposits, as life insurance and pension reserves, or as portfolios of securities including bonds, stocks, and mutual fund shares. By holding reserves in financial assets, typically through intermediation of financial institutions, these consumers/financial investors find an available source of financial return arising from the needs of the consumers who borrow. The transfer of resources from surplus to deficit consum-ers may actually take place through multiple intermediaries. Although the pri-mary focus of this book is on the liability side of consumers' balance sheets, it also briefly explores the channels of this transfer of funds from those with a surplus to those with a borrowing need, along with some of the difficulties of effecting this transfer efficiently (chapter 5).

An important element of efficient transfer of these resources is availability of information that lenders can use to reduce default risk. This has led to develop-ment of the automated credit reporting agency (CRA), popularly known as the "credit bureau." The CRAs maintain electronic files on consumers' experiences with credit use so as to help satisfy lenders' need for better information on credit-worthiness of credit applicants. Anyone making an application can claim that he or she is a good credit risk, but the automated files on past experiences confirm it or cast doubt. In this way, those with past success in meeting their obligations can command the lower prices (lower interest rates) that their preferable risk status implies. Those less successful in the past often can still be accommodated, albeit at somewhat higher risk-based price, pending generation of better experience making their status more favorable (chapter 6).

TYPES OF CONSUMER CREDIT

Modern consumer credit is diverse enough that it can be classified in many ways. Probably most familiar in conversation is by intended use of the funds. Common uses include automobile credit, student loans, boat loans, mobile home loans, home improvement loans, furniture credit, debt refinancing, and so on. There are some complications with this familiar form of referring to credit use, however, that go to the very heart of the reasons for using consumer credit in the first place.

Kinds of Consumer Credit, Classified by Usage

For descriptive purposes, it is common to say that consumers use consumer credit for such and such a purpose, including all those mentioned above and others. Many people owe on auto loans, student loans, and other obligations that they acquire as they purchase household assets and education and refinance other debts. Financial institutions widely offer debt products associated with such purchases, and hardly any consumers are unaware of the possibilities. Dealers and stores say that "financing is available." Car loans are trumpeted in television and radio advertisements and in the automobile sections of daily newspapers and on the Internet. Student loans are a topic of conversation in virtually any college cafeteria. Other credit products are just as well known to those who might employ them. Even Harley-Davidson has its own consumer financing subsidiary for its motorcycles, for example.

Nonetheless, a little reflection quickly shows that buying autos, household repairs and furnishings, major hobby items, and education is only part of the fundamental economic behavior that gives rise to these classifications of debt. Rather, it is useful to recall that a significant component of the underlying, basic economic demand motivation for consumer credit is the desire by consumers to change both the size and the timing of their resource inflows and outflows. Credit markets arise to change the lumpiness of the patterns, particularly of the outflows for purchasing housing and durable goods, and to bring household capital investment transactions forward in time to the present instead of far off in the future.

Most purchases on credit could be accomplished by accumulating cash first and then buying the item later, but this often is not the time pattern consumers prefer. For many goods, accumulating cash first could mean doing without the item or paying for more expensive substitute services for a period that might amount to years, both of which are costly. People could walk to work, for example, or they could ride bicycles or take the subway or bus rather than making payments on car loans. They could forgo the pleasures of easily visiting friends and family by car as part of the costs they would bear. They also could use laundromats and scrimp on other appliances and furniture or acquire used equipment. They could put on sweaters and coats if the furnace failed while saving to replace it, or they could live with relatives. Many people do all of these things in lots of places, but with the limited length of lifetimes that often involve children in relatively early years of a family's life cycle, waiting to make these investments is frequently not the preferred option in middle-class societies if there is an alternative. The types of credit we observe in the marketplace in large part come about because they are the least costly ways of providing an acceptable alternative.

In more detail, inflows from wages and salaries that make up the income of most employed workers in a modern economy typically are quite regular, and credit offers the opportunity to smooth the outflows. Lumpiness in outflows can occur during the course of the period between paychecks, but it certainly will occur during the course of longer periods such as a year, within a particular life-cycle stage, or over a consumer's or a family economic unit's whole lifetime. For example, for many families, expenditures increase during selected seasons such as vacation periods, back-to-school time in September, and around the year-end holidays. Then, in some years, there also are bigger, investment-type purchases, such as an automobile or a new home. A few years later, there may be need for another auto or a larger home and later still for college education for children. Purchase of a vacation home or a large recreational item such as a boat may occur once or twice in a lifetime. Credit facilitates all these transactions by enabling households to use future regular inflows to pay for lumpy expenditures made today. Consumers have shown that they are willing to pay a price in the form of interest and finance charges for the possibility of changing the time pattern of expenditures.

This picture of inflow and outflow/expenditure patterns illustrates how it often is not really correct to say that credit arises solely for the purpose of purchasing specific items. The purchases could often be made anyway, just on a different schedule. The accumulating could be done first, although this would also mean postponing the benefits of the investments and often paying for substitutes in the meantime. The correct interpretation in these cases is that credit markets arise to increase consumers' overall well-being by changing the time pattern of investment inflows and outflows to a preferred one.

The problem of classification by usage is especially obvious for an individual purchasing a $35,000 automobile or truck on credit who simultaneously holds $35,000 or more in financial assets. In some significant sense, this individual is not really using credit only to purchase the vehicle. Rather, the underlying motivation for credit use is to avoid some combination of not buying the car or truck now, not giving up some other current purchases either, not paying taxes and penalties for liquidating assets held in retirement accounts, and not reducing reserves stored in other financial assets. Risk-averse consumers may well prefer not to reduce their reserves, which are valuable to them. Credit obviates the need to do things consumers think are disadvantageous, such as running down financial reserves, while matching the pattern of outflows (payments) better to inflows (paychecks).

Certain kinds of credit associated with specific sorts of investment purchases arise because they permit changing the flow pattern in the least costly manner. Credit is often associated with automobile purchase transactions, for example, because the associated expenditure is large and since relatively large amounts of credit at relatively low cost are readily available to those who are willing to offer the auto or truck as collateral for the loan. Such loans are so common that "automobile credit" has become a large industry by itself. Credit generated in the process of making home improvements and buying automobiles, durable goods, education, and a variety of other transactions (including payment of taxes, debt consolidation, etc.) are all well-known types of consumer credit. Advertising for each usage is common, and many financial institutions memorialize these distinctions by separate departments and personnel, even separate subsidiaries.

For the most part, official figures for the volumes of credit for many "uses" are no longer assembled by the government's statistical mills, largely for the conceptual reasons mentioned and because of the practical difficulties of collecting necessary data from creditors to generate meaningful statistical aggregates according to consumers' use of the credit.[6] The only practical way to produce an estimate of consumer credit purpose is to design statistically reliable surveys of consumers, ask them about their credit experiences, and then in some manner extrapolate from their experiences to the broader public.

The Federal Reserve Board has provided the means of doing this with its series of surveys known as the Surveys of Consumer Finances, which began in 1946. The Surveys of Consumer Finances were annual from 1948 to 1970 and then periodic after that date, 1977, 1983, and 1989, before stabilizing on a three-year cycle beginning with the 1989 survey.[7] The surveys, of course, do not follow the fortunes of the same consumers over time as they age. Rather, they look at the financial experiences of representative samples of consumers through successive cross sections. Each survey is designed so that it is individually representative of the entire population at the time the surveying is undertaken.

Fortunately for making comparisons, the structure of the Surveys of Consumer Finances shows substantial similarities from one survey to the next. Over longer periods, as might be expected, the surveys have evolved along with consumer-oriented financial markets and the underlying questions of interest. Shortly after World War II, for instance, a major focus of the surveys was the distribution of holdings of federal savings bonds and other war-related federal debt among consumers. In the 1950s and 1960s, the surveys examined more closely use and holdings of consumer credit. Credit cards made their first significant appearance in the surveys in

6. In the past, the Federal Reserve Board collected information on amounts of consumer credit by usage in its monthly survey of credit volume at granting institutions, but the Board discontinued the usage collection decades ago. Before that time, the monthly surveys asked lending institutions to report credit according to whether it was for automobiles, durable goods, home improvement, or other, but even classifying credit into a few broad categories became increasingly difficult with the advent of open-end credit such as credit cards, where lending institutions knew little or nothing about account uses.

7. There also were limited surveys in 1971, 1978, and 1986 that can be considered part of this series. During the 1960s, the surveys were largely sponsored by private sources, including the Ford Foundation.

1970, and the 1977 survey focused especially on then-new federal consumer protection laws, such as the Truth in Lending Act and the Equal Credit Opportunity Act. In 1983, serious interest in consumer asset holdings returned to the surveys, and examination of the asset side of consumers' balance sheets remained primary in the 1990s and from 2001 to 2010. (Results of the 2013 survey will become available in 2015.) Although these differences within the project are apparent over time, the surveys offer much that is directly comparable.

The surveys show that most households are consumer credit users in recent years (upper panel of table 1.2). Focusing on consumer *installment* credit (encompassing any consumer credit involving multiple payments, which today constitutes by far the bulk of consumer credit), the table shows that about a third of households were users of this kind of credit in 1951, a proportion that rose to half by 1963 and to about three-fifths in 1977 (last line of the upper panel of the table). Since 1977, the fraction of households with consumer installment credit outstanding has fluctuated around 60 to 65 percent.

Employing the Surveys of Consumer Finances to provide further breakdown on the uses of consumer credit shows clearly the importance of credit to household investment spending (lower part of table 1.2). In fact, the bulk of consumer installment credit arises in the course of undertaking household investments that provide a return over time, especially purchase of automobiles, educations, and mobile home housing. The table also shows that *revolving* credit outstanding (defined more fully later but consisting mostly of credit card debt along with some unsecured credit lines not involving a credit card) has fluctuated in the range of one-fifth to approximately one-quarter of consumer credit since the 1983 survey. It is easy enough to see how it appears that this newer form of consumer credit that is especially difficult to classify by purpose has partly replaced older kinds of installment credit classified as nonautomobile durable goods credit, plus home improvement loans and "other" credit. In 1977, these three categories summed to 20 percent of consumer credit, but in 2010, they were only 12 percent. Over the same time, the revolving credit proportion, but without specific usage indicated, rose from 11 percent to 22 percent.[8]

8. Federal Reserve statistical information on consumer credit collected from creditors indicates that at year end 2013, about 28 percent of consumer credit is revolving credit, but this total includes "convenience credit" that is outstanding on credit cards when the monthly survey of institutions is made but is repaid within a month. Because of this rapid repayment, most observers do not consider this "credit" as anything more than a statistical artifact that is impossible to remove from the data. The Surveys of Consumer Finances exclude this credit from its definition of consumer credit outstanding and go to great trouble to try to remove it. The consumer surveys also try to remove credit outstanding on credit cards that is actually used for business purposes, often by owners of small businesses. It is not possible to remove this kind of credit from the totals of consumer credit in the monthly institutional surveys, but the periodic Surveys of Consumer Finances remove it. Both of these differences reduce the proportion of revolving credit in the consumer surveys relative to the institutional surveys. The consumer survey results are probably closer to the correct proportion of revolving credit that is actually used for longer-term consumer uses and within the normally used meaning of the term *consumer credit*. Chapter 2 discusses these statistical issues further.

Table 1.2 Consumer Installment Credit by Purpose of Credit Use, 1951–2010

Type of Credit	1951[a]	1956[b]	1963[b]	1970[c]	1977	1983	1989	1995	2001	2004	2007	2010
Proportions of households using consumer installment credit (percent)												
Closed-end installment credit												
Automobiles	26	21	26	29	34	28	33	31	34	35	34	30
Nonauto durables		30	22		14	10	9	7	5	3	5	4
Home improvement	3	6	6		6	5	3	2	1	1	1	1
Education					2	2	5	12	11	13	15	19
Mobile homes					2	2	2	2	2	2	2	1
Other	7	7	25	37	12	7	7	6	4	4	5	7
Any closed-end installment	32	45	50	49	49	41	44	45	44	46	46	46
Revolving credit account with balance				22	34	37	40	47	44	46	46	39
Closed-end or revolving installment credit	32	45	50	54	59	58	59	64	62	64	65	60

(*Continued*)

Table 1.2 (CONTINUED)

Type of Credit	1951[a]	1956[b]	1963[b]	1970[c]	1977	1983	1989	1995	2001	2004	2007	2010
SHARES OF OUTSTANDING BALANCES ON CONSUMER INSTALLMENT CREDIT, BY PURPOSE (PERCENT OF TOTAL)												
Closed-end installment credit												
Automobiles	67	60	57	53	60	47	55	43	45	41	35	27
Nonauto durables		23	13		5	6	7	4	3	3	5	5
Home improvement	8	8	7		6	8	3	3	1	1	1	1
Education					1	3	5	16	19	21	25	37
Mobile homes					8	9	5	6	7	6	5	3
Other	25	9	23	42	9	5	5	3	2	6	3	6
Revolving credit account with balance				6	11	23	20	26	23	22	27	22
Closed-end or revolving installment credit	100	100	100	100	100	100	100	100	100	100	100	100

[a] In 1951, category "automobiles" also includes nonauto durable goods; category "other" also includes education and mobile homes.

[b] In 1956 and 1963, category "other" also includes education and mobile homes.

[c] In 1970, category "other" also includes nonauto durable goods, home improvements, education, and mobile homes.

SOURCE: Data from the Surveys of Consumer Finances.

Growth of revolving consumer credit has nonetheless been controversial. Some observers have focused on the growth rates of revolving credit alone and have overlooked how much of this growth appears to arise from a substitution process. Much of revolving credit represents favorable consumer response to technological change that has permitted lenders to offer them a more convenient form of consumer credit, specifically, prearranged revolving credit available to them anywhere worldwide that their credit cards are acceptable for payments. The critics have argued instead that the growth of revolving credit has permitted everything from irrational purchasing by consumers to massive increases in consumer bankruptcies. These issues flow through the discussion in many of the chapters that follow, notably those on long-term growth of consumer credit (chapter 2), consumer credit demand and supply (chapters 3 through 6), credit cards (chapter 7), and consumer and market responses to over indebtedness, including the ultimate consumer legal response, consumer bankruptcy (chapter 13).

Regardless of one's views of revolving credit, consumer surveys provide a good look at the question of classification of consumer credit by usage and find that the bulk of consumer credit, including revolving credit, is associated with consumer investment spending for household durable goods and education. It is worth noting again and keeping in mind, however, that the full motivation is not just purchase of investment goods but also smoothing spending outflows to match income inflows and to change the timing of purchasing relative to saving. Surveys show that most consumer credit arises from the process of investment spending and not merely from some sort of consumer profligacy, as is sometimes alleged. A desire to change this timing is not especially surprising, given the limited length of human lifetimes.

Kinds of Consumer Credit, Classified by Flexibility of Repayment Terms

If it is not completely straightforward to categorize consumer credit by reason for borrowing, there still are other useful distinctions. One already alluded to is by flexibility of credit repayment pace. There are many variations, but three basic kinds of consumer credit are classified this way. First is noninstallment consumer credit, where lenders extend credit in a variety of ways but expect repayment in one lump sum (a small enough part of total consumer debt that it is no longer separately reflected in official statistics). Second is nonrevolving, or "closed-end," installment credit, where credit normally is extended at one time and repaid under contract in a series of similarly sized payments sometimes called "installments," typically monthly (automobile credit, for example). Third is revolving, or "open-end," installment credit, where credit is extended in variable amounts and repaid at the consumer's preferred pace through variable monthly installment payments, within contractual limits (credit card credit, for example). These latter two kinds of consumer installment credit were already introduced in table 1.2.

NONINSTALLMENT CREDIT

Noninstallment consumer credit is largely of historical interest today (and so it is left out of table 1.2), but it once was an important factor in consumer credit. At that time, and conceptually even today, it consisted of three components: charge accounts at merchants and dealers, service credit, and single-payment loans.[9]

Charge accounts are credit arrangements owed to retail stores and other purchase outlets that are payable in full at one time, typically at the end of the month or in thirty days. Sometimes goods such as furniture or computers are still sold this way today, and some merchants offer plastic cards known as "charge account cards" or "charge cards" as evidence of an ongoing account relationship. Terminology in this area often is applied loosely, but strictly speaking, charge cards are not the same as "credit cards" that permit payment over a longer period at the customer's option. Most plastic credit devices are credit cards in this sense, but the American Express Green Card is a charge card. Consumers can use Green Cards at a variety of merchants outlets, but payment in full is due at the end of the billing month.[10]

In years past, charge accounts were important at department stores, oil companies, appliance dealers, specialty clothing stores, and other neighborhood retailers. Charge cards are still held and used today, but the majority of retailers have given up their charge account plans in favor of accepting credit cards, either their own or American Express, Discover, MasterCard, and Visa cards offered by third parties. Today the amount of consumer credit outstanding on merchant charge cards and accounts is small, and much of the credit outstanding on the American Express Green Cards is business credit and not consumer credit. For these reasons, the Federal Reserve statisticians who are the scorekeepers in this area have dropped the separate classification of noninstallment credit from the monthly figures on consumer credit outstanding. Today the statisticians have included estimates of remaining charge account consumer credit within revolving installment credit, even though they know this is not strictly correct.

Service credit consists of amounts owed by consumers to service providers such as doctors, dentists, lawyers, plumbers, and other service professionals who do not demand immediate payment on the spot. Again, like charge accounts, service credit has become less common as professionals today typically prefer to accept credit cards for payments to minimize the accounting and record keeping necessary for maintaining their own billing operations. This fact probably improves the estimates of total consumer credit outstanding, since no one

9. Before World War II and during the immediate postwar years, charge accounts were much more important than today. Including them in table 1.2 would raise the proportion of credit users in the earlier years.

10. Until early 2005, another well-known charge card brand was Diners Club, in recent years owned by Citigroup. Diners Club cards were the original multiparty charge cards, but in 2005, Citigroup began to merge its Diners Club brand with its MasterCards. In 2008, Citigroup agreed to sell its Diners Club brand name outside North America to Discover Financial Services, issuer of the Discover Card. In 2010, the Bank of Montreal acquired the rights to the Diners Club brand name in North America.

contends that service credit outstanding was ever estimated very accurately in the aggregate anyway.

Single-payment loans are made directly to individuals by banks, insurance companies, stock brokerage firms, and other institutions to finance a variety of lumpy expenditures, including medical expenses, education, and payment of taxes. Often, such loans are made to individuals with financial assets such as stocks, other securities, or cash-value life insurance policies that can be pledged as collateral for the loan. Yet the conceptual issue arises of whether "loans" with collateral of this sort are really not just economic liquidations of underlying asset positions rather than credit use. For the most part, the answer from the statisticians has been yes, in that credit balances from these sources have not been included in the official statistics on consumer credit. Today most individuals do not employ credit of the latter sort for consumer purposes anyway, although some upscale consumers do have single-payment loans based on stock portfolios through "cash management accounts" and accounts with similar names with their stock brokerage companies.

A few high-rate credit products, including pawn loans, tax refund anticipation loans, and payday loans, are also single-payment loans. These loans are quite small, have short terms to maturity, and are often called fringe products because they are used by consumers who have limited access to mainstream credit products. For Federal Reserve statistical purposes, they are counted within the finance company segment of installment credit lenders. (Chapter 8 discusses these and other fringe credit products in more detail.)

Overall, noninstallment credit has declined in relative importance, as the shares of charge accounts and service credit have diminished relatively and single-payment loans are generally not counted as consumer credit. As consumer credit use has become more widespread, installment credit, especially in the form of revolving lines of credit and credit cards, has taken over many of the former uses of noninstallment credit. As indicated, the main exception to the historical-only nature of most noninstallment consumer credit is the amount of consumer credit due on charge accounts at some merchants and on American Express Green Cards. For all practical purposes, noninstallment consumer credit has disappeared statistically, if not conceptually, since outstanding consumer balances even on these specialized cards are now counted as part of revolving installment credit.

CLOSED-END INSTALLMENT CREDIT

Installment consumer credit is consumer credit repayable in a series of payments, known as installments, usually monthly. There are two basic kinds of installment credit: nonrevolving, or "closed-end," installment credit and revolving, or "open-end," installment credit. Of the two, nonrevolving installment credit still represents the larger segment by volume outstanding, although it grew more slowly in recent decades than revolving/open-end installment credit, until the financial crisis 2008–2009 (first panel of table 1.3).

Nonrevolving installment credit is a very common consumer credit arrangement in which a specified amount of credit is advanced for a certain length of time

Table 1.3 CONSUMER CREDIT OUTSTANDING, END OF SELECTED YEARS, 1945–
2012, IN BILLIONS OF CURRENT DOLLARS

	1945	1955	1965	1975	1985	1995	2005	2010	2012
BY TYPE OF CREDIT									
Nonrevolving	7	43	97	192	479	703	1,464	1,695	1,928
Revolving				15	132	465	857	847	850
Total	7	43	97	207	611	1,168	2,321	2,542	2,778
BY TYPE OF INSTITUTION									
Depository institutions	3	19	49	116	355	542	816	1,186	1,218
Finance companies	1	12	24	33	112	152	517	705	678
Credit unions	*	1	6	26	74	132	229	226	243
Nonfinancial business	3	11	18	33	63	85	60	53	53
Pools of securitized assets						213	610	63	58
Federal government					7	44	90	309	528
Total	7	43	98	207	611	1,168	2,321	2,542	2,778

* Greater than zero but less than 0.5 billion.
Components may not add exactly to totals because of rounding.

SOURCE: Federal Reserve Statistical Release G19, "Consumer Credit," Historical Data.
Figures shown are for December, not seasonally adjusted.

and is repayable in a prearranged number of payments. Three-, four-, and five-year
auto loans are common examples of closed-end installment credit. On a standard
closed-end contract, a certain amount of credit is advanced (automobile purchase
price and fees minus trade-in and down payment, for example), a finance charge
is calculated, and the sum of the two is divided equally by the specified number
of payments. The consumer's obligation is to make this number of payments, normally each month in the same amount. This kind of consumer credit has become
known as closed-end installment credit because the contract is of a "closed" form
once it starts running. There generally are no changes in the contractual amounts,
costs, or payment sizes after the outset until final payoff (or maybe refinancing
with a new closed-end contract). Typical automobile credit offers the most familiar example, but there are many others, including home remodeling contracts,
furniture loans, boat loans, student loans, and cash loan arrangements for a variety of purposes. Mostly, a credit contract associated with a single credit advance
for a single large purchase or purpose is a closed-end contract, although there are
occasional exceptions.

Operationally, there are two kinds of closed-end installment credit. The first is direct credit, where the consumer is the customer of the financial institution. In a common example, a consumer might apply for and obtain an auto loan or a home improvement loan at his or her local bank or credit union. In this case, the consumer would negotiate the credit terms directly with the loan officer in person or electronically and either sign the contract at the office of the lending institution or authorize it electronically. Other examples include small cash installment loans at banks, finance companies, and credit unions.

In contrast, in an indirect credit arrangement, the consumer is the customer of a seller of retail merchandise or services such as an automobile dealer, a furniture store, or a home improvement contractor. The consumer in this case negotiates the credit terms with the seller of the goods or service, who typically presents to the customer the terms offered by its own financial institution (or institutions). When the consumer signs the contract, it is sold by the retail dealer, store, or contractor to the financial institution. Thus, the merchant receives immediate payment from the bank or finance company, and the consumer repays the financial institution over time (with finance charges). This sort of arrangement is known as indirect credit, because the customer never contracts or negotiates the terms with the financing institution directly; arrangements are made through the seller of goods or services. This method of finance is also known as installment financing or sales finance, in contrast to installment lending, because it involves the financing of sales of specific goods or services rather than loan of money.[11]

For many years, the largest indirect lenders were the financing arms or affiliates of the automobile manufacturers, notably the General Motors Acceptance Corporation (GMAC, today Ally Financial), Ford Motor Credit Company, and Chrysler Financial Corporation (Chrysler Financial Services, during 1998–2007 part of Daimler Chrysler Services Group and today part of TD Bank). More recently, other auto financing firms such as Toyota Motor Credit Corporation have added to the list, and the financial crisis of 2008–2009 has caused Ally to become a market partner rather than an owned affiliate of General Motors. But

11. Historically, under the laws of most states, sales finance arrangements legally were not loans but were "retail installment sales" and often were regulated differently from loans of money. The regulatory differences arose because direct and indirect consumer credit developed separately in the United States, and consequently, they had different histories and backgrounds that gave rise to different sorts of regulation. See Rogers (1974) and Calder (1999) for historical discussion of the institutions and Curran (1965) for development of the law.

Because of this legal difference, it is not strictly correct to refer to an installment sale contract as a loan. Rather, such an arrangement is an installment sale of goods on a time contract rather than a loan, which in most jurisdictions in the United States has referred legally to loan of money, at least historically. Consequently, installment *loans* are part of installment *credit*, but not all installment credit is a loan. Because this historical legal distinction is not important to most observers of consumer credit, including even most legal practitioners who are not specialists in this area, the common approach of using the terms *consumer credit* and *consumer loan* or *installment credit* and *installment loan* interchangeably is adopted for the purposes of this book, except where this distinction is important, such as in discussion of usury laws that sometimes have affected the two areas differently (see chapter 11).

the basic role of these companies has not changed. They still stand ready to buy acceptable retail sales contracts from dealers in their affiliated factories' auto lines. (They also are ready to finance the dealers' inventory shipped from the factory, a form of direct business lending known as floor planning.) In addition to the automakers' financing affiliates or partners, there also are many other nonrelated indirect financing sources that buy the credit contracts originated by automobile, furniture, appliance, and home improvement dealers. They include many smaller finance companies and also the "dealer departments" of many small and large banking institutions.

Volume breakdowns are not available for direct versus indirect closed-end consumer credit, but it seems that in recent years, indirect credit has grown relative to direct lending, in large measure because of the increasingly aggressive competitive stance of the automobile finance companies in the era of 0.0 percent financing and other factory-supported credit plans in recent decades. As the automobile companies' financing subsidiaries and affiliates became more vigorous competitors in all ranges of the customer risk scale since the 1980s, they changed the makeup of the indirect market for automobile and truck financing. Finding more attractive rates and terms than previously available in the indirect market, less risky consumers, who in the past often had sought the better terms historically available in the direct market, now found it easier to engage in one-stop shopping and obtain automobiles and financing without ever leaving the dealer's back office. There are still many direct lenders, however, including the direct loan departments of most banks and many finance companies. Credit unions usually are mostly direct lenders.

Other than the convenience of one- versus two-stop shopping, today there is little practical difference from the consumer's viewpoint in the mechanics or costs of obligations taken on in direct versus indirect form for the closed-end installment purchase of big-ticket items such as cars and trucks. In the past, financing rates and charges (pricing), along with other terms on direct auto credit, often were more favorable to the consumer than on indirect auto credit, but this has changed as consumer credit markets have become more competitive overall. Formerly, direct customers tended more to be those with previous favorable credit experience and reputations or with favorable current financial prospects, such as higher income or assets. Through experience, they became familiar customers to their banks or credit unions. They made attractive direct customers for the financial institutions, which often would compete to supply them with a range of financial products, including direct loans.

At that time, indirect auto customers were more likely to include those with weaker credit histories or those with less credit experience who could benefit from the intervention of the dealer in finding a credit source. In some cases, the dealer might even enter into some sort of risk-sharing arrangement with the financial institution, sometimes even including a partial guarantee of the consumer's credit through a recourse (contract buyback) agreement between the goods seller and the financial institution if payment troubles arose. A riskier pool of customers and the possible presence of complicated risk-sharing arrangements meant that the indirect credit often was more costly both for the financing institution and for the customer. Higher risk and higher cost are no longer generally true for indirect credit, at least in the large and competitive market for financing of new automobiles and trucks.

In addition to indirect financing and direct lending for purchase of specific consumer products and services, thousands of banks, credit unions, and finance companies also make direct, closed-end cash loans to creditworthy customers for a wide range of other consumer purposes. Such direct loan uses encompass consolidation of other debts and refinancing of credit card bills, payment of income and property taxes, and even loans to purchase luxuries including art and antiques. Direct cash loans range from very small loans made to less fortunate individuals down on their luck and facing an emergency, such as an illness or an unexpected car repair, to much larger loans to pay for country club memberships without liquidating any of the family stock portfolio. The modern consumer credit system covers a vast multitude of possibilities.

Much of both direct and indirect closed-end installment credit has been generated through a signed credit contract in exchange for a check or an electronic inflow into a deposit account made payable either to a consumer or to a seller or dealer. For example, a bank making a direct auto loan to a consumer typically would give a check to the consumer payable to the dealer or upon sale of a car would advance the funds directly to the dealer in electronic form. Consumers may also institute direct closed-end cash loans with banks, credit unions, or finance companies and receive checks or electronic transfers payable directly to the consumer. In some small direct loans, such as a "payday loan" or a pawn loan, the consumer might even receive cash across the counter.

In an indirect financing arrangement, a consumer would still sign a credit contract, but it would be with the merchant, dealer, home improvement contractor, or other provider of goods and services. The dealer or merchant would then sell this contract to the financer (for example, Ford or Toyota Motor Credit) and receive electronic payment for the contract. The consumer would then make the payments to the financial institution that purchased the contract.

Over the past four decades, the sum of indirect and direct closed-end installment credit has tended to lose ground relative to open-end credit, which grew more rapidly until the financial crisis. This came about as consumers apparently have transferred much of the financing of medium-ticket consumer items such as furniture, appliances, some home repairs, travel, medical expenses, and some taxes and insurance payments to open-end credit cards (this trend is visible in table 1.2 and in figure 2.4 in the next chapter). In earlier times, consumers might have arranged direct, closed-end installment loans or purchase of durable goods using indirect sales credit for many of these transactions. The convenience of prearranged open-end credit lines on credit cards has become attractive to many consumers. When consumers needed additional credit to make purchases a generation or so ago, they would have had to visit their bank, credit union, or finance company for a closed-end loan, or they would have had to negotiate with the credit department of their durable goods retailers. Many consumers find credit cards much more attractive for routine purchases.

OPEN-END INSTALLMENT CREDIT

In the case of revolving or open-end installment credit, both the credit amount used and the size of the monthly payments are at the option of the consumer, as long as the amount does not exceed the credit line or limit and the consumer makes at least some required minimum monthly payment. This sort of credit has become pervasive in recent decades because of its flexibility. Consumers can arrange credit in advance and use it at the pace and in the manner they please. They do not have to negotiate a new contract with a creditor every time they buy a new appliance or hobby item that they would prefer to pay for over a few months or longer. Consumers appear to prefer revolving credit for its convenience, and creditors have been more willing and able to provide it as the needed computer systems, communications hardware, and risk management technology have become more available and affordable over time (chapter 7).

The primary access devices in open-end credit arrangements are the credit card and special checks sometimes referred to as loan checks or, by the issuers, as convenience checks. Credit cards are, of course, pieces of plastic with a strip of magnetic tape or an embedded computer chip that, upon presentation of the plastic (or just the numbers, say, by telephone or over the Internet), activate the consumer's existing line of credit with the credit source. Historically, credit cards were used to generate small amounts of credit and served as substitutes for cash or for small cash loans. More recently, lines of credit attached to credit cards have grown larger in the competitive credit card marketplace, and credit cards have replaced much of closed-end installment credit for medium-ticket consumer purchases. Both the sellers of goods and services (stores and dealers) and financial institutions (banks and credit unions) compete with one another today in issuing credit cards to consumers.

Some banks and other financial institutions also offer open-end credit plans that the consumer activates by writing a check rather than by using a plastic card. In the past, many institutions offered separate accounts with a special book of checks that a consumer could use to access an open-end credit line. Some institutions also permitted overdrafts on normal checking accounts through the regular checks for the account. The overdraft would access a prearranged credit line repayable at the consumer's preferred pace. Both of these kinds of accounts still exist today, but they are less common than in earlier decades. A newer method is distribution of special loan or convenience checks, as already mentioned, that consumers can use as supplements to their plastic cards in accessing their credit card accounts. Credit card issuers frequently distribute such checks by mailing them to consumers in good credit standing as promotions encouraging account holders to put new or larger balances on their card accounts.

INSTITUTIONAL SOURCES OF CONSUMER CREDIT

Another way to classify consumer credit is by the type of institution offering the credit. Thousands of entities have extended consumer credit over the years, but it is possible to classify them into a limited number of institutional categories, although sometimes with some ambiguities. The Federal Reserve Board compiles volume information on consumer credit outstanding according to method of repayment administration (nonrevolving versus revolving credit) and also by institutional source based on type of corporate charter. Some complications naturally arise as markets and operations evolve over the years, and some institutions in one charter category begin to look and act more like those in another category.

Depository Institutions (Especially Commercial Banks)

Consumer credit before World War II was largely the province of retail stores and nonbanking lending companies generally referred to as finance companies. Since the war, the institutional landscape has changed dramatically, as the amount of consumer credit outstanding has risen. Statistics show that in the intervening period, depository institutions have passed the others to become the major source of consumer credit by volume outstanding (second panel of table 1.3). Before statistical revisions the Federal Reserve undertook in 2012, commercial banks and savings depository institutions were reported separately. By that time, however, the share of the savings depositories had declined sufficiently that they were combined that year with the commercial banks that held the lion's share of consumer credit at institutions with depository charters.

In the United States, depository institutions, hereinafter called banks, are companies that obtain necessary banking charters either from the federal government (national banks, regulated by the Office of the Comptroller of the Currency, a branch of the Treasury Department) or from state governments (state banks, regulated by the Federal Reserve System, the Federal Deposit Insurance Corporation, and state government banking departments). These charters allow the institutions to undertake a banking business, which means primarily that they can engage in providing deposit accounts and simultaneously supplying a variety of loans, including business loans. Most banks provide an extensive list of financial services. They offer various kinds of deposit accounts for consumers, businesses, and governments, and they make the deposited funds available as various kinds of loans to individuals, incorporated and unincorporated businesses, governments, and governmental agencies.

Before the development of credit cards, consumer credit lending by the depositories largely consisted of the two kinds of closed-end credit already described: direct closed-end loans, where the consumer approaches the bank directly for the loan, and indirect loans, where the consumer is actually the customer of a store or a dealer in consumer goods or services that subsequently sells the credit account to the bank. Today the largest portion of consumer credit from the banking system is extended through open-end credit card accounts. The cards serve as plastic identifying devices that signify existence of a prearranged amount of open-end credit. As indicated, the consumer can then draw on this credit at will at his or her choice of sellers. In effect, credit cards are a technological innovation whereby direct loans are made by the card issuer but at the point of sale of a third party where the customer uses the card.

The banking institutions that issue credit cards have also changed, to the point where some of the largest providers of credit card credit no longer look like traditional deposit-taking banks. Instead, many of the consumer credit behemoths in the banking industry today are the "monoline" credit card banks that engage largely or completely in credit card credit. The monoline institutions, such as FIA Card Services, are part of large financial conglomerates that include other, full-service commercial banks. The monoline banks that are part of financial conglomerates do not themselves have branch systems or, for the most part, offer much of an array of traditional banking product lines beyond credit cards, even though they are affiliated with institutions that provide other services. Some early monoline card banks, such as Capital One, actually began as freestanding, independent institutions. These independent monolines also grew rapidly in recent decades, but by year end 2006, most of the independents had agreed to merge with other banking companies.[12]

All of the monoline credit card banks are chartered commercial banks, but they operate much like traditional finance companies in that they raise most of their funds in large chunks by issuing securities of various kinds in global financial markets rather than by the traditional banking method of acquiring deposit funds. In statistical compilations, consumer credit at the monoline institutions is counted as depository credit rather than finance company credit because of the nature of their corporate charters, even though in operating terms they are not much like the traditional banking institutions with which they are included.

For most banking organizations other than the monoline credit card banks, consumer credit is only a fraction of the lending portfolio, which also consists of business loans, home mortgage lending, and loans to governments and their agencies, including purchases of federal and state and local government bonds. Most commercial banks typically are active in diverse areas of consumer credit issuance, including direct and indirect closed-end credit associated with automobile and other purchases, other closed-end loans, revolving check credit, and, for some, credit cards.

But consolidation through mergers and portfolio acquisitions, in addition to organic growth, has meant that banking organizations with large portfolios of

---

12. Before the wave of mergers that eliminated most of the independent monoline institutions, some of the independents had begun to expand their product offerings to auto and mortgage lending as a means of diversifying their asset base, becoming a bit less "monoline" in the process. In early 2005, Capital One agreed to acquire a relatively large full-service commercial bank based in New Orleans and with a branch system concentrated in Louisiana and Texas (Hibernia National Bank) as a way of diversifying its activities; the following year, it acquired North Fork Bancorporation of New York for the same reason. In the middle of 2005, the other remaining large independent monolines went the other way and agreed to be acquired by the parent holding companies of full-service banking companies: MBNA America Bank by Bank of America, Providian Financial by Washington Mutual Bank of Seattle (itself later acquired by J. P. Morgan Chase during the 2008 financial crisis), and Metris Companies by HSBC Financial, the American subsidiary of HSBC Holdings (formerly Hong Kong Shanghai Banking Company) of London.

credit card credit are now also the largest banking organizations active in the entire consumer credit field, including consumer credit not generated by credit cards. A list of the largest banking institution providers of consumer credit is highly consistent with the list of largest institutional issuers of credit card credit. In fact, the eleven largest bank providers of consumer credit calculated from reports to regulatory agencies are also the eleven largest card credit issuers, with somewhat different orders. Both lists include some very well-known companies, including Citibank, NA, Bank of America, NA, Wells Fargo Bank, NA, Capital One Bank USA, Discover Bank, and American Express Centurion Bank. (*NA* in a bank's name stands for "National Association," a common way in which federally chartered banks include the required word *national* in their names.) Even though there are thousands of other banking organizations in the consumer credit business, the ranking of the largest banks in the consumer credit industry certainly shows how important the bank credit card business has become within consumer credit.

Finance Companies

Finance companies have long been next in importance to the depository institutions (mostly commercial banks) in providing consumer credit, and, like banks, they also are involved in a variety of areas of consumer finance. The term *finance company* can, of course, be applied to any financial institution, but for purposes of classifying consumer credit issuers, the Federal Reserve applies the term to financial firms that do not qualify in any other institutional corporate charter class, such as bank or credit union.

There are some very large financial institutions in the finance company grouping, including the affiliates and partners of the automobile manufacturers already mentioned. Other very large finance companies include the General Electric Capital Corporation, Citifinancial Corporation, and CIT Financial Corporation, among others.

Some of these finance companies illustrate another aspect of the definitional ambiguities mentioned above. Namely, some of them, such as Citifinancial, are subsidiaries of parent companies whose main subsidiary is a banking company that directs the overall corporate strategy. Citifinancial, for example, is a subsidiary of Citigroup, the large bank holding company that owns huge banks such as Citibank NA and Citibank (South Dakota) NA. Nonetheless, consumer credit of the nonbank subsidiary is still counted as finance company credit, according to the corporate charter of the subsidiary rather than the main business line of the entire company or the operating method of the bulk of the organization. As mentioned, funding of the large finance companies is much like the monoline credit card banks whose credit is counted as bank credit. Both raise most of the funds they invest in consumer credit through large securities issues of various kinds in Wall Street and in other key financial markets worldwide.

There are also hundreds of smaller finance companies operating in one or more segments of the consumer credit marketplace. Some specialize in small, unsecured, direct consumer loans; others specialize in indirect financing through a network of automobile, appliance, furniture, mobile home, or other dealers; others specialize in mortgage credit. Some also issue credit cards or engage in all of these activities. One thing for sure is that there is great diversity in size, products, and individualized operating methods in the finance company industry.

At this point, it seems reasonable to mention briefly two additional kinds of nonbank lending companies: mortgage banks and mortgage brokers. They are not generally considered within the traditional definition of finance company consumer lenders, even though they are nonbank lenders that make loans to consumers. Mortgage *banks* are not actually chartered banking institutions as discussed above but rather companies that make mortgage loans using their own or borrowed funds but that typically do not become the actual lenders by holding the loans in their own asset portfolios. Instead, they sell the loans they make to other investors, the largest purchasers being the huge "government sponsored entities" (GSEs) in the mortgage area, Fannie Mae and Freddie Mac.

Mortgage *brokers* are not financial institutions at all but rather are matchmakers that bring together mortgage borrowers and mortgage lenders. Mortgage brokers typically deal with several mortgage lenders and shop from among these lenders to find a mortgage for a borrower. The broker takes the application, performs a financial and credit investigation, produces documents, and closes the loan. The broker may also conduct financial counseling with the borrower, if necessary. The actual lender in a broker-originated transaction underwrites (evaluates the risk), funds (supplies the money), and may service the loan (taking the payments and doing the accounting, even if the loan is sold to another entity such as one of the GSEs).

In bringing potential loan accounts to mortgage banks and other lenders, a division of labor takes place. The mortgage banks and brokers specialize in the mechanics and process of lending and have the necessary personnel and office locations to do so as needed. This allows those who provide the funds to focus on funds sources and the economics of investing in mortgage loans without needing the lending and processing personnel themselves. As with any division of labor, this arrangement can promote lending efficiency in the best of circumstances, but it also raises many issues about management and control of lending risk. In the worst of circumstances, when the risk control needs are not fully understood or controls are mismanaged, there can be substantial risk of losses. Both of these problems were part of the causes of the financial crisis in 2008–2009.[13]

There are two reasons for not calling these nonbanking companies finance companies in describing providers of consumer credit. First, they are active primarily in the mortgage area of lending to consumers, outside the definition of consumer credit adopted by the Federal Reserve and used here. Second, they do not, for the most part, actually hold in their own portfolios the loans they make or process. When mortgage banks sell the loans, the purchaser is the ultimate lender

---

13. For further discussion of the functions of mortgage brokers and related agency issues, see Kleiner and Todd (2009).

that provides the funds and owns the loan, not the mortgage bank. Brokers do not even make the loans themselves, let alone hold them as the source of funds.

Pools of Securitized Assets

But sale of loans made also commonly takes place in the consumer lending that is the focus here, and Federal Reserve statistics on consumer credit take this fact into account when providing figures on volumes of consumer credit. These loan sales give rise to another category of lenders in the official consumer credit statistics, the category of the "pools of securitized assets." The mechanics of securitization are discussed in more detail in chapter 5, but it is appropriate to outline the basic concept here, since securitization and the resulting asset pools have been important for supplying the underlying funds for consumer lending.

For undertaking securitization, banks, finance companies, and other lenders form legally separate asset holding corporations, usually referred to as special purpose entities (SPEs) or sometimes as conduits, to own portfolios of pooled consumer credit contracts. The SPEs legally own the underlying consumer credit assets after the originating institution sells the assets to them. The originating bank or finance company retains servicing responsibilities (receiving monthly payments and handling accounting), and sometimes much of the risk, under a contractual arrangement with the SPE.

The SPEs then fund the pools of accounts they purchase from loan originators by issuing their own securities, collateralized by the pools of underlying consumer credit assets, in worldwide financial markets. The process is known as securitization, and the resulting securities issued to acquire the funding are known as asset backed securities, or ABS. Prior to March 2010, lenders routinely removed from their balances sheets the assets that were sold and securitized in this manner. This process was the genesis of the category of consumer lender categorized in the official Federal Reserve statistics on consumer credit as pools of securitized assets. Following commercial banks, the securitized pools became for a time the second largest source of consumer credit in the official statistics (second panel of table 1.3).

In response to losses on mortgage-backed securitizations during the financial crisis, in June 2009, the Financial Accounting Standards Board (FASB) issued the Statement of Financial Accounting Standard No. 167 (SFAS 167), Amendments to FASB Interpretation No. 46(R). SFAS 167 revised the criteria for determining whether securitized assets are removed from lenders' balance sheets. This revision caused by far most securitized consumer credit to be reconsolidated onto lenders' balance sheets in 2010.[14] Since much of the consumer credit owed to these pools was originally generated by automobile finance companies and monoline credit

---

14. The revisions replaced a calculation reflecting the probability that a securitizing entity would absorb most of a security's losses with consideration of the possibility that the entity would absorb a significant loss. For discussion, see Dodwell (2010).

card banks in the first place, adding it back into the official consumer credit statistics beginning in 2010 increased the share of these entities and presents a better picture of their importance. The consumer credit statistics for 2010 and 2012 in table 1.3 reflect this change.

It is also worth mentioning again that during 2008–2009, some SPEs holding mortgage credit assets with "subprime" credit risk characteristics and originated primarily by mortgage banks and mortgage brokers produced large losses to some entities sponsoring the SPEs. Although full discussion of the causes of the subprime mortgage fiasco in these years is beyond the scope of the discussion here, problems of the SPEs were an important component of the subprime mortgage financial upheaval during those years.[15] The massive losses on mortgage-related assets did not extend to consumer credit SPEs making up the consumer credit "asset pools," although availability of more funding through securitization became highly constrained in the second half of 2008 when securitization markets froze up.

Credit Unions

After banks and finance companies, credit unions are next in importance among private sources originating consumer credit. Credit unions are consumer cooperative institutions chartered to accept the savings of and make loans only to members. From small beginnings early in the twentieth century, growth of credit unions (often referred to as the credit union movement by participants) has tended to be controversial at every step among owners and managers of the other institutions.

By act of Congress, membership of every credit union must have some commonality of interest, a "common bond," in order for the individual institution to be a real consumer cooperative.[16] As consumer self-help organizations, credit unions are exempt from federal income taxes, a never-ending irritation to their profit-oriented (and, when profitable, taxpaying) competitors. The irritation seemed manageable as long as credit unions were small cooperatives, but in the latter part of the twentieth century, some of them, such as Navy Federal Credit Union, Pentagon Federal Credit Union, and United Airlines Employees Federal Credit Union, have become large, sophisticated financial institutions. As some individuals and institutions in the credit union movement began to push the limits of the required common bond to include all citizens of an area or all employees of a *group* of employers, competitors cried foul, and the common-bond issue

---

15. For discussion by newspaper reporters of some of the events, companies, and personalities surrounding the subprime mortgage episode, see Muolo and Padilla (2008).

16. Over the years, Congress has slowly expanded the common-bond concept until today it is a fairly complicated collection of rules dealing with single-common-bond credit unions, multiple-common-bond credit unions, and community credit unions (see section 1759 of the Federal Credit Union Act, 12 *USC*, chapter 14).

degenerated into recriminations and lawsuits, mostly between banking trade associations and credit union groups and regulators. Many credit unions contend that switching to a community-based approach has been necessary as factories close or move and jobs of members change but they still want to belong to their credit unions.

Credit unions are active in all areas of consumer credit, but direct, closed-end loans are the most important. Many credit unions are not large enough to be able to afford the sophisticated computer systems needed for administering large-scale revolving credit operations such as credit card portfolios by themselves, but some large credit unions issue their own credit cards with the MasterCard and Visa brand names, and others have entered into agent relationships with other institutions to issue credit cards with these brands. In general, credit unions have been able competitors in the areas where they are active, aided undoubtedly by their tax exemption and in some cases by reduced personnel and office space costs as a result of subsidies by cooperating common-bond employers.

Other Institutions

Until mid-2012, the official consumer credit statistics also separately broke out "savings institutions," but, as discussed above, savings institutions are now combined with commercial banks in the "depository institutions" category. Savings institutions include savings and loan associations and federal and state chartered savings banks. Before the 1980s, these institutions were largely restricted to mortgage credit, and consumer credit was only a minor product at a minority of institutions. More recently, legislative changes in the 1970s and 1980s have permitted savings and loan associations and savings banks to become more active in granting consumer credit, but overall financial difficulties of these industries in the 1980s caused them to decline in overall importance in financial markets generally, including consumer credit. This is the reasoning behind including them with commercial banks after the 2012 statistical revisions.

The remaining consumer creditors listed in the official statistics are nonfinancial institutions, the federal government, and nonprofit, state, and educational institutions. "Nonfinancial business" refers to consumer creditors such as retail stores and automobile dealerships that are not primarily financial institutions by assets or operations. In the nineteenth and early twentieth centuries, retail establishments were the most important consumer creditors, but today their place has largely been taken by the financial institutions. Nonetheless, some department and specialty stores are still important consumer creditors, in terms of number of consumer credit accounts and credit cards on their books. In the past decade or so, some of these companies have acquired or opened their own special-purpose monoline banking subsidiaries to issue the cards for the parent retail companies, and others have sold their credit portfolios to financial institutions and disbanded their in-house credit operations. The relative, and now absolute, decline in importance of retail store credit sources is clearly visible in table 1.3.

Finally, for years, commercial banks and other financial institutions have made loans to students and their families for payment of expenses associated with higher education, sometimes with loan guarantees by the federal government under the (now discontinued) Federal Family Education Loan Program (FFEL). Because these loans were made by private lending institutions, the amounts of credit outstanding normally was included in the routine estimates of consumer credit outstanding at these institutions compiled and released monthly by the Federal Reserve Board.

In 1993, the federal government, through a new program called the Federal Direct Student Loan Program (FDSLP), also began to make student loans directly. At the time, these loans were not routinely included in estimates of consumer credit outstanding, because they were made by the federal government and not by private lending institutions, although they were essentially equivalent to the loans made by private institutions. Likewise, loans held by the federal government's sponsored enterprise chartered to purchase outstanding student loans (Sallie Mae) also were not included in consumer credit for the same reason.

But growth of these federal loans eventually led the Federal Reserve in October 2003 to begin to publish a new estimate of consumer credit from these federal sources and to include it in the monthly estimates of total consumer credit outstanding (see Dynan, Johnson, and Pence 2003). When the Federal Reserve Board began to release the figures for student credit outstanding from the federal sources separately, it also provided retroactive estimates of amounts outstanding in earlier years, so as to maintain continuity in the statistical series over time without an upward jump in the initial month of the new estimates. The Board also provided for a retroactive phase-in of Sallie Mae's student loan credit into the finance company category reflecting privatization of the former GSE (see Dynan, Johnson, and Pence 2003, 420). The Sallie Mae statistical phase in was accomplished by August 2004.

The volume of federal direct student loans increased sharply beginning in 2007, as credit market disruptions from the financial crisis reduced the ability of many private lenders to originate guaranteed student loans. The crisis stimulated Congress to enact a temporary program (Ensuring Continued Access to Student Loans, or ECASLA) that authorized the Department of Education to purchase guaranteed student loans originated by private lenders under the FFEL program. Subsequently, Congress passed legislation in 2010 eliminating the FFEL program that provided federal guarantees for new student loans originated by private lenders after July 1, 2010. Following that date, new student loans dramatically increased the amount of consumer credit generated and held by the federal government (for historical discussion of the federal programs, see New America Foundation 2011).

In August 2013, the Federal Reserve added a statistical category for student loans still held by nonprofit, state, and educational institutions. Like many of the private student loans discussed above, student loans originated in this sector were guaranteed under the FFEL program. New data from the Department of Education in 2013 enabled the Federal Reserve scorekeepers to add the nonprofit, state, and educational institutions sector to consumer credit back to 2006.

CONSUMER CREDIT AND PUBLIC POLICY

Despite the obvious importance of consumer credit for both consumers and the growth of certain industries, increases in consumers' indebtedness over time continue to raise policy issues for each generation of government officials, including some issues that actually are as old as recorded human history.[17] Among the foremost is the basic one: whether widespread credit use is a good thing or not and, consequently, whether further credit use by consumers should be encouraged or discouraged. In American policy circles, the answer has been a resounding "both encouraged and discouraged." There are government programs and policies in place both to encourage more credit availability (for example, the federal Equal Credit Opportunity Act, the Community Reinvestment Act, and the student loan programs) and simultaneously to discourage or bring under greater control the spread of credit products (for example, Truth in Lending and its many amendments to show its true costs). An opposing set of goals for policy actually should not be too surprising, given both the diversity of financial conditions and needs among consumers and the great disparities in their individual understanding of how the credit system works. This gives rise to the fundamental policy question of whether credit should be available to everyone, including lower-income and younger credit users (chapter 8).

Policy concerns sometimes lead to laws and regulation, and it turns out that few areas of the American economy are as closely regulated as consumer credit (chapters 9, 10, and 11). The states have regulated most aspects of consumer credit transactions in one way or another over the years, but probably the most important state regulations have been in the areas of interest rate ceilings and entry into the marketplace. While both of these issues are still important today, they are much less so now than in less competitive, earlier decades.

The federal government entered the field of consumer credit regulation in the 1940s with limitations on credit use instituted for macroeconomic stabilization purposes during World War II. These controls, known as Regulation W, were reinstituted in the late 1940s and during the Korean War, although passage of sufficient time means this episode is largely forgotten today by most observers (for discussion, see Shay 1953). Much better known today is federal consumer protection legislation in the consumer credit area, which began with passage of the Truth in Lending Act (Title I of the Consumer Credit Protection Act of 1968). Since that time, Congress has initiated a variety of other protections in the credit area, including the Fair Credit Reporting Act (1970), the Equal Credit Opportunity Act (1974 and 1976), and the Fair Debt Collection Practices Act (1977).

Congress has also amended each of these acts from time to time as it has perceived that market conditions warranted a legislative update.[18] In some cases,

---

17. For a very long-term perspective on policy issues in consumer credit, see Rasor (1993), Homer and Sylla (1996), and Gelpi and Julien-Labruyere (2000).

18. Each of the mentioned acts regulates more than just consumer credit as defined here to exclude credit secured by real estate. Truth in Lending, for example, covers residential real estate

individual states have enacted similar laws either before or after the federal initiative, but these federal laws are fundamentally different from the main historical thrust of state regulation. The states have primarily been interested in regulating the price of the lending and the types of creditors that may offer consumer credit (chapter 11), while the main emphasis at the federal level historically has been on the content and quality of the service itself. Especially important at the federal level have been the requirements that creditors treat all consumers fairly on the basis of their personal characteristics (for example, the Equal Credit Opportunity Act; chapter 9) and that they make certain kinds of information readily available to consumers (for example, the Truth in Lending Act; chapter 10).

In 2010, Congress passed legislation establishing for the first time a federal consumer financial protection bureau. Formally called the Bureau of Consumer Financial Protection but somewhat anomalously generally referred to by the initials CFPB, it was established under Title X of the Dodd-Frank Wall Street Reform and Consumer Protection Act that year, usually simply called the Dodd-Frank Act. This agency has extensive regulatory powers over consumer credit in many areas previously the province of the states. By 2013, the bureau had engaged mostly in organizing itself and in taking over responsibility for federal rules and rule making previously the responsibilities of other agencies, especially the Federal Reserve System, but it surely will become more active on its own initiative in future years.

Within the totality of the consumer credit system, there also are some related products that are not themselves credit but are either complements or substitutes. One complement is credit insurance and other kinds of debt protection products that repay the indebtedness or cancel or delay payments in case of death or disability of the debtor. Some advocates have contended over the years that this kind of insurance is too expensive for the protection it provides, but since the 1920s, credit insurance has covered millions of consumer credit transactions without a great deal of product change, suggesting that many borrowers find it useful (chapter 12).

---

lending in addition to consumer credit. All lending, including business lending, falls under the Equal Credit Opportunity Act.

In addition to the consumer protections mentioned, Congress has also enacted consumer protections geared solely to mortgage credit. These statutes include the Real Estate Settlement Procedures Act (1974), typically known as RESPA, and the Home Mortgage Disclosure Act (1975), widely known as HMDA. Sometimes amendments to federal consumer protection statutes become almost as well known as the original acts. Such enactments include an amendment to Truth in Lending concerning credit card billing called the Fair Credit Billing Act (1974) and another Truth in Lending amendment for high-cost mortgage loans called the Home Ownership and Equity Protection Act (1994), typically referred to as HOEPA. Another is an amendment to the Fair Credit Reporting Act in 2003 called the Fair and Accurate Credit Transactions (FACT) Act. The latter is the act that required, among other things, that credit reporting agencies (credit bureaus) provide free copies of credit reports annually to consumers at the consumers' request, which is now so widely advertised.

Another related product is automobile leasing. Consumer auto leasing is an interesting substitute for automobile credit that comes and goes in relative importance in the marketplace depending on the needs and uses of creditors and consumers. Automobile leasing gained in popularity through the 1980s and 1990s before peaking late in the 1990s. After that time, it waned a bit in popularity for about a decade, although it by no means disappeared, especially for higher-priced automobiles. Around the middle of the last decade, auto and truck leasing began to increase again. Regulations concerning required leasing disclosures changed in the late 1990s, making auto leasing less controversial than it sometimes had been before that time.

Finally, there is the question of what happens when something in the consumer credit marketplace goes badly awry for a consumer to the point of the consumer being unable to repay the credit on time or at all. Answering this question highlights the usefulness of looking at the credit counseling and bankruptcy systems (chapter 13). In recent years, counseling in advance of a problem has become a popular approach to trying to prevent consumer overextension and possible default on credit obligations. When all else fails, there remains the possibility of consumer bankruptcy. Although bankruptcy has become very legalistic and sometimes difficult for consumers, millions of consumers in recent years have availed themselves of this approach to debt management problems.

2

Consumer Credit in the Postwar Era

As briefly touched upon in chapter 1, it seems that few goods or services in widespread daily use in the early twenty-first century have histories as long and developed (or, it appears, bring along with them as much mythology and baggage) as the use of credit by consumers. Credit for individuals is at least as old as recorded human history and probably much older, but some users, in addition to some casual observers and government officials, still seem uncomfortable with this now ubiquitous product. This has been especially true if the credit use is for anything other than those often preferred by policy makers such as home purchases, and even housing credit has recently had highly visible difficulties leading to criticism.[1]

---

1. As outlined in chapter 1, sometimes the term *consumer credit* might be employed generically to refer to all credit for consumers, but in this book, the term excludes credit extended on the security of real estate, which is *mortgage credit*, and credit extended using for security financial assets such as stocks, bonds, or insurance policies. Consumer credit covers short- and intermediate-term credit extended to individuals that is not secured by these assets. As discussed more fully in chapter 1, it includes noninstallment credit (not important today and actually now subsumed within installment credit for statistical purposes), nonrevolving installment credit (such as secured and unsecured installment credit for automobiles, mobile homes, boats, other durable goods, education, vacations, and other purposes), and revolving installment credit (credit card credit and balances outstanding on unsecured revolving lines of credit such as overdraft checking accounts). Thus, consumer credit excludes mortgage loans for home purchase, home equity loans, and home equity lines of credit. When used here, the term *consumer credit* conforms to the Federal Reserve definition, which excludes real estate secured credit.

Sometimes the view is expressed that conventions employed in defining consumer credit and some simplifications made in collecting data on its use cause the published total to be either understated or overstated. Factors that might lead to an overstatement include measuring as consumer credit outstanding those balances on credit cards with a revolving feature that arise not so much as credit but as a convenience to consumers in the payments process but which will be repaid in full upon receipt of the monthly statement. Although such credit is counted as revolving consumer credit, since it is extended on cards with a revolving feature, it cannot, in this view, be regarded as truly a behavioral component of revolving credit. Rather it is essentially a historical artifact of the time when cards were a convenience to shoppers mainly issued by retail stores and payment was expected within a short time of receipt of the monthly bill. These amounts are often referred to today simply as "convenience credit" on credit cards that

This has meant that consumer credit has been a constant topic of policy discussions over the years, but it also sometimes seems that there has been more talk than serious analysis of many aspects of consumer credit, including its long-term growth. This view is hardly new. Among a few others, economist Michael Prell, who would become director of the Federal Reserve Board's Division of Research and Statistics, pointed out this anomaly decades ago:[2]

> Surprisingly, very little attention and even less serious study have been devoted to the long run expansion of installment credit. While many statements of alarm have been heard from observers who associated that expansion of indebtedness with moral decay and impending financial collapse, thoughtful investigations of installment credit growth or the relationship between installment credit and economic activity have been relatively rare. (Prell 1973, 3)

should not, under this view, really be counted as credit since it merely facilitates the payments process and is not intended to be repaid in installments over time. By some estimates it could be 10 to 25 percent of revolving consumer credit outstanding. Retaining these amounts within consumer credit, however, actually is consistent with past (and present) practice of including balances on charge cards within consumer credit, even though charge account balances are also largely a payment convenience and are outstanding only briefly, unlike true credit use.

Alternatively, factors that might cause an understatement of consumer credit outstanding encompass placing home equity credit for consumer purchases within mortgage credit rather than within consumer credit and excluding consumer automobile leasing totals from consumer credit.

There actually are many conceptual and practical issues involved in defining credit by type and collecting statistical information about them that go beyond the scope of this chapter (for discussion of the conceptual problems, see chapter 1, and for some of the statistical data collection difficulties, see Luckett 1994 and Dynan, Johnson, and Pence 2003). It seems that these understatements and overstatements probably offset each other to a large enough degree that they do not greatly compromise the basic underlying consumer credit trends reviewed here. For very precise analyses of credit growth trends, such as the impact of credit use on consumer spending over a short time period, study of these issues might benefit from a closer look.

2. Prell and others who discussed growth of consumer credit in the past typically based their discussions on trends in consumer installment credit, the largest component of total consumer credit. Historically, total consumer credit has always also included noninstallment credit made up of charge accounts, service credit (credit extended by professionals such as doctors and lawyers), and some single-payment loans by financial institutions to consumers (see discussion in chapter 1). The Federal Reserve no longer compiles separate figures for installment and noninstallment credit, however, and so separate discussion of consumer installment credit is no longer possible. Indeed, as discussed more fully in chapter 1, the growth of credit card credit appears to have eliminated much of noninstallment consumer credit anyway. Because new statistical information is available only for total consumer credit without subdivisions into installment and noninstallment credit, newer discussions of consumer credit trends are always in terms of the total. In the past, when both installment and total consumer credit series were available separately, growth trends for installment credit and the total were very similar, particularly in later years, when revolving credit on credit cards had largely supplanted the charge accounts at retail stores that were common earlier.

The passage of four decades since Prell wrote this paragraph does not appear to have altered greatly the ratio of alarm to thoughtfulness about consumer credit growth in more recent decades, but hope has risen on the horizon. More recently, Anthony Santomero, then president of the Federal Reserve Bank of Philadelphia, predicted in a speech to a conference on related matters that interest in studying consumer credit, while mostly absent in the more distant past, seemed to be growing and likely to continue to grow, a view borne out since then:

> Generally, economic forums have tended to ignore the broader issues in consumer credit....When the consumer is discussed, it is typically consumer consumption and savings decisions that are studied and analyzed. This neglect of consumer credit seems remarkable, given that debt owed by households represents over 25 percent of total credit market debt outstanding....
>
> Only recently has this begun to change. With the emergence of the asset–based securities markets, financial theorists and empiricists have begun to examine the behavior of financial assets that have resulted from the aggregation of consumer debt. This is most obvious in the mortgage market. (Santomero 2001, 1)

As these statements suggest, competent studies of consumer credit growth have not been especially common over the years; but this does not mean that they have been nonexistent, and interest in this and other aspects of consumer credit does seem to have picked up recently. There actually were some thoughtful analyses of consumer credit growth even in the more distant past, as Prell went on to discuss in the rest of his article, to go along with the journalistic excesses that this subject has seemed to generate over the decades.

This chapter provides a look at the growth of consumer credit within the context of the consumer sector's general financial condition. In particular, it examines the growth of consumer credit use in the post–World War II period, within the broader perspective of the overall development of consumers' finances. Following basic review of consumer credit growth trends, the chapter then looks more closely at a group of studies of consumer credit growth that analysts have conducted during the postwar period. It closes with some further discussion of what we have learned from consumer surveys about the distribution of credit use across the population.

THE CREDIT GROWTH CONTEXT

Media pronouncements about consumer credit growth have generally been dismal (see Durkin and Jonasson 2002, discussed further below). It is difficult to estimate how influential such statements have been, if at all, but even the casual empiricism of asking one's neighbors for their views of the domestic credit picture reveals the widespread notion that credit for consumers simply has grown too fast for too long. This claim is hardly new. As an example of such journalistic nuggets from more than a decade ago, the July 5, 2000, issue of the *Wall Street Journal* contained the following in a prominent location:

> In a nation that once saved all it could and resisted taking on debt, Americans no longer just borrow money to buy houses. They load up on debt to buy stock. To go on vacation. To pay the electric bill. To buy groceries. Even to pay federal income taxes.
>
> Americans have gone on an unprecedented borrowing binge in recent years.... The numbers are startling. (Sherer 2000, C1)

The point of citing the quotation here is not to establish a straw man for attack, although attacking this statement would be easy on a number of levels, but rather merely to illustrate the kind of pronouncement so often encountered. Certainly, this sort of "analysis" is nothing new. For example, a generation earlier, when consumer credit outstanding for nonhousing purposes was less than one-fifth its current level, *Business Week* reported in a cover story in October that year: "The soaring consumer debt load plainly heightens the risk for government economic policy.... Consumers' debt may already be so huge that Washington—having encouraged the boom in consumer debt through easy money and a stimulative fiscal policy—may have to keep pumping up the economy to enable consumers to pay the bills." (Business Week 1978, 88)

Two generations ago, the story was the same. According to *Fortune* for March 1956, when consumer credit was about *one-fiftieth* its current level:

> Consumer short term debt, perhaps the most controversial force in the booming US economy, is approaching a historical turning point. Having risen at an abnormally fast rate for ten years, it must soon adjust itself to the nation's capacity for going into hock, which is not limitless. Whether the rate of growth in consumer debt will slow down is no longer the question, as this article will document; it *must* slow down. (Burck and Parker 1956, 99; emphasis in original)

These passages make it abundantly clear that much of the concern over consumer credit use and growth over the years arises because of concerns that "too much" credit growth or credit outstanding will somehow lead to some sort of economic dislocation, usually not well defined. Going on fifty years ago, economics professor Warren Smith wrote that these worries even then were "not entirely new":

> Although the sources of anxiety about the growth of private debt have not always been made entirely clear by commentators who have addressed themselves to the subject, it is possible to distinguish several different strands in discussion:
>
> 1. There is a view that the pace of debt growth in recent years has been so rapid that it cannot possibly continue indefinitely....

2. There is a fear that the burden of debt repayments would considerably accentuate the effect of a decline in income if such a decline should occur for any reason.

3. A third concern has to do with the so called quality of credit reflected in an increased frequency of defaults, foreclosures, repossessions of collateral, and so on....

4. There is a further question.... Do our financial institutions and financial markets possess sufficient flexibility to enable them to adjust readily to major shifts in the composition of credit demand if such shifts should occur? (W. Smith 1967, 73)

Sound familiar? It certainly is not difficult to find such passages about consumer credit either in the historical record or in recent pronouncements. Even more than a century ago, the press seemed to regard consumer credit as potentially more damaging than beneficial to consumers. Writing about press reports of 1893–1894 in his excellent cultural history of consumer credit, historian Lendol Calder noted the tone of the journalists:[3]

Everywhere the elements of the problem were the same: working class people with emergency needs for cash were being victimized by the high rates, bullying tactics, and legal deceptions of unscrupulous lenders. But while publicity gave to the victims a measure of public sympathy, it offered no solutions. High rate lending was not going to be shamed out of existence. (Calder 1999, 120)

Within recent memory, there was, of course, a financial dislocation in 2008–2009 with roots at least partly in the consumer financial area. The crisis did not originate in consumers' use of nonmortgage consumer credit as so long predicted, however, but rather in the overextension of mortgage credit at a time when there was an unsustainable upward bubble in housing prices. When the bubble burst, it threw the housing credit market into turmoil and dramatically weakened the lending institutions and the financial system, precipitating government intervention. But the question for further examination here is how well the facts about *consumer credit*, not mortgage credit, in recent decades fit the fears of recent and earlier worriers.[4] It turns out that the answer is "a lot less than expected."

3. Calder also discusses at some length how every generation seems to believe that profligate spending because of credit use arose only recently, unlike in earlier, simpler times when people were more devoted to saving first and spending later. But, as he reports, even in the eighteenth century, Benjamin Franklin's Poor Richard had observed that staying out of debt was not always practiced: "the People heard it and approved the Doctrine, and immediately practiced the contrary" (quoted in Calder 1999, 87).

4. Worries over consumer credit in the past have not been limited to journalists but also include much more authoritative sources. For example, federal restrictions on consumer credit for macroeconomic control (Regulation W) were in place under congressional and Federal Reserve

DEBT BURDEN AND SPENDING

In fact, economic studies employing sophisticated theoretical and statistical approaches have failed to produce hard evidence from past experience that consumer credit growth has led to the biggest expressed concern: that such growth leads to decreases in future spending and causes or dramatically accentuates macroeconomic downturns (recessions). If anything, evidence is available to the contrary. For example, a bit more than a decade ago, Federal Reserve economist Dean Maki summarized a number of past studies that investigated the relationship between the "burden" of consumer credit arising from repayments and subsequent consumer spending before reporting his new work in the area. According to Maki (2002, 43), "In stark contrast to the view of growth of consumer credit as a negative force in the economy, a consensus seems to be emerging from recent research that consumer credit growth is *positively* related to consumption in future periods" (emphasis added). A few years later, Johnson and Li (2007) discussed the issue further and carefully reviewed more studies, with the same general result. Interestingly, among the policy responses in 2009 to the unfolding financial crisis at that time were attempts by the federal government to promote *more* consumer credit growth, not less.[5]

Burden Trends

Maki began his review by echoing the earlier views of Prell and Santomero that the effects of consumer credit growth on the economy remained underresearched. He then described a new measure of debt burden that he had developed for the Federal Reserve Board based on the relationship of estimated debt service payments to income rather than the relationship of debt itself to income.

He argued that conceptually, the ratio of payments to income is a better measure of consumer credit burden than some others often employed. In particular, he contended that it is better than the ratio of the *amount* of consumer credit outstanding to income, because the payment ratio directly represents the relationship between outgoing resources necessary to avoid debt default and incoming

direction from September 1, 1941, until after the end of World War II, again from September 1948 until June 1949 and from September 1950 until May 1952, and again in the first half of 1980, the latter at the behest of President Carter (not called Regulation W then). Sometimes concern has been more ambivalent. For example, following the end of Regulation W in 1952, the Federal Reserve Bank of New York noted: "Comments on the liberalization of credit terms following the suspension of Regulation W last May, and the subsequent rise in the amount of credit in use, have varied from alarm and apprehension to complacency to approval" (Federal Reserve Bank of New York 1953, 54).

5. Consumer credit outstanding declined every month in 2009, which was unprecedented in the post–World War II period. It seems, however, that this episode arose from concerns and pessimism over a failing banking system, a sharply declining stock market, and a ballooning federal budget deficit rather than from the prior level of consumer credit per se.

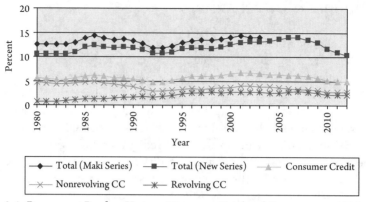

Figure 2.1 Repayment Burden, Various Measures: Total and Components, 1980–2012.

resources available to meet the obligations. Over the years, other analysts had also constructed repayment measures with a variety of approaches (see Paquette 1986), but Maki's new method updated earlier methods in light of newly available data. After discussing some practical difficulties of developing a satisfactory measure of repayment burden, he offered some graphs and then some new econometric analyses of his measures for total repayment burden and its components (mortgage credit and nonmortgage consumer credit repayments relative to income) over the prior two decades.

Figure 2.1 shows Maki's estimates of total repayment burden over two decades through 2003, the final year of construction of this data series by the Federal Reserve (top line in the figure). The figure also illustrates a further refinement to the repayment burden concept prepared by other Federal Reserve Board staff economists who worked with Maki and introduced their own further adjustments in 2003. These analysts then extended their revised measure backward and also continued it for later periods (second line of figure 2.1). Their work involved additional changes to the estimating method, along with newly including student loans made by the federal government and its formerly affiliated enterprise, student loan lender Sallie Mae (see Dynan, Johnson, and Pence 2003).

Despite this new inclusion in the student loan area, the revised debt service burden measure was actually below the old (Maki) measure for years when both were calculated (top lines). The important point, however, is that while both of these statistical series show a fluctuating pattern of repayment burden over the course of these decades, the trends are hardly sharply upward. In the course of the most recent business cycle, they do not show a great deal of difference from experience of a generation ago.

Whether by themselves these trends are significant, or worrisome, is to some degree in the eye of the beholder. To be sure, the new measure of total debt burden has risen (figure 2.1), even if only by a few percentage points over decades. But there is also no reason that debt measures should stay the same as time passes and income rises. Credit, or at least the purchase of things such as housing, large durable goods including vehicles and appliances, home repairs and modernization, college education, large hobby items, and other things often associated with credit use, are by and large economic "luxury" goods that show a positive income effect. As such, they are precisely the kinds of purchases that might be expected to increase as incomes rise. These purchases would then also cause credit use to rise slowly as income rises.[6]

Most important for the discussion here, figure 2.1 shows that the rise in the burden measures in recent decades has been caused primarily by mortgage credit, not consumer credit as defined here. Part of the rise in the burden of mortgage credit was a result of growth of subprime credit during the housing price boom, as became well known in 2008. But the payment burden for consumer credit actually has fallen continuously over the past decade and fluctuated only in a narrow range in the decade before that.[7]

Statistical Studies

More important than the trends illustrated by the basic graph are the correlations Maki found in his econometric work using his measure of consumer credit burden.

6. This is not to say that no consumers have debt difficulties. During recessions, and especially at the year-end holiday season, the news media are filled with feature stories about debt burdens and other difficulties of the unemployed, but as sad as these cases are, they do not represent anything close to the majority of credit users. For discussion by observers who find the debt rise worrisome, see, for example, Belsky and Essene (2007) and references there.

7. In 2008–2009, previous overextension of mortgage credit to subprime borrowers, along with decline in housing prices that affected borrowers who made small down payments or otherwise had little equity in their property, provoked a worldwide financial crisis and recession. The situation was exacerbated by difficulties of lenders fearing for their own solvency that then drastically restricted new lending.

Although the crisis clearly was associated with past lending and associated debt levels, it is misleading to maintain that the cause was debt burden by itself, especially among mainstream borrowers or in the consumer credit area as defined here. There were many causes, visible best in hindsight, which included easy mortgage credit to subprime borrowers, US government housing policies that encouraged such borrowing, easy past monetary policy that encouraged a rapid rise in housing prices, an abrupt slowdown in housing price growth, insufficient risk management by Wall Street packagers and purchasers of debt securities based on mortgages, failure of debt rating agencies to understand new securities sufficiently, compensation policies of some lenders that encouraged poor mortgage loan underwriting, and so on. Analysis of each and all of the issues causing the crisis during those years is beyond the scope of this book, but it is safe to say that debt burden resulting from consumer credit as defined here was not the dominant concern. As shown by figure 2.1, the statistical record does not even indicate much of an increase in debt burden resulting from consumer credit in recent years.

For further discussion of this episode, see generally Berger, Molyneux, and Wilson (2010). Long-term recovery is another issue. Some observers from the legal profession have even contended that growth of inconsistent federal and state regulation after the crisis has become so onerous in some jurisdictions as to "cast doubt on the rule of law in some jurisdictions, undermining the legal pillars of mortgage credit" (Lampe, Miller, and Harrell 2009, 468). This development is certainly of long-term concern for restoring stability in mortgage lending, and it also affects consumer credit.

He noted that within business cycles, higher consumer credit debt service burden appeared to be a leading indicator of higher delinquencies among individuals but not by itself a predictor of a forthcoming slowdown in overall consumer spending. He attributed this apparent anomaly to a variety of factors, including the obvious one that most consumers do not become delinquent. As a consequence, the budgetary problems of the few are far outweighed by the absence of any delinquency problems among the majority that might cause a spending slowdown for them or overall. He also pointed out that consumer survey studies demonstrate how the lion's share of debt service payments resides with the small fraction of high-net-worth individuals in the economy. For them, the payment burden is small relative to their individual net worth, and consequently, their spending is less constrained by debt.

Instead of a negative impact, Maki found that high debt growth is statistically associated *positively* with future growth rates of consumer spending. He attributed this finding to the likelihood that credit growth really is a proxy for a favorable economic outlook: people are more willing to spend and to take on credit obligations when they expect good things in the future. At these times, lenders are also more willing to make credit available. Maki noted the apparent robustness of his finding:

> Of course, the results in this section rely on a fairly simple model of consumption [note omitted], but they are consistent with the evidence compiled from other studies. They suggest that strong consumer credit growth should not necessarily be seen as an ominous sign that the economy is set to slow because consumers are being forced to take on debt; instead it may indicate that households are optimistic about future income growth, and are borrowing in anticipation of this growth in income. From this point of view, strong growth in consumer credit is worrisome only to the extent that it reflects unrealistic expectations on the part of households. (Maki 2002, 53)

If it is difficult, as Maki suggested, to point to specific studies that demonstrate that higher consumer credit leads to spending slowdowns or other macroeconomic dislocations, then why the apparently recurring state of alarm that seems to prevail in the popular media when consumer credit rises? It is natural and reasonable to assume that higher aggregate debt levels might be associated with greater prevalence of individuals in debt difficulties, but even this is by no means automatic. As discussed below, higher aggregate debt may also be associated with large numbers of individuals each using a little more, but not worrisome amounts of, debt.

To be sure, there has been research on the importance of spending constraints at the individual level. One significant body of work has involved the implications of underlying illiquidity on consumers' ability to follow a preferred spending pattern over their life cycle.[8] There also have been statistical studies focusing on the

---

8. On this point, see, for example, Hall and Mishkin (1982), Zeldes (1989), Runkle (1991), and Garcia, Lusardi, and Ng (1997). See also chapter 3 for theoretical discussion of the role of credit use.

impact of individual debt burdens on spending of the individuals in question. These latter studies are somewhat less common, but findings are consistent with what one might expect, namely, that higher debt burdens can limit the spending of liquidity-constrained individuals (see Johnson and Li 2007 and 2008).

But at the macroeconomic level that is the focus here, the reason for increasing alarm as debt levels rise appears to lie in the obvious and important fact that consumer spending accounts for approximately two-thirds of US gross domestic product, and so any risks to continuation of spending at a high level are important. Ultimately, it seems that much ongoing concern arises from the possibility that even if consumer credit levels have not caused the dislocations so often predicted in the past, maybe "this time," the growth and level of debt will finally catch up with us. As Calder (1999) recalled in his cultural history of consumer credit when he reviewed some journalistic views of trends in debt growth, even the boy who cried wolf eventually saw a real wolf. Maki followed the paragraph quoted above with a limited acknowledgment of the potential for there to be a consumer credit wolf out there. Economists refer to careful delineations of limits to their statements as caveats:

> While rapid growth in consumer credit seems to be associated with rapid future growth in spending, this relationship does not rule out the possibility that high debt-service burdens might eventually cause future spending to fall in response to a drop in income by more than it otherwise would. The results so far simply indicate that there is no direct and consistent short term impact of debt-service burdens (or other measures of credit quality) on spending that is discernible using simple regression models. (Maki 2002, 53)

Thus, Maki carefully acknowledged the obvious possibility that the future could still be different, a truism concerning almost any trend or relationship. He noted that more complex theoretical specifications and modeling of consumer behavior and financial markets might conceivably produce an alternative estimate in the future concerning the relationship of debt burden and future spending. He added that this might especially be true in the modern economic environment after 1980. In the 1980s, many sorts of credit constraints were loosened, and this might cause the macroeconomy eventually to respond differently to trends in debt burdens. Thus, if individual debt burdens rise in the future, the economy might conceivably respond differently. Possibly, the economy might be more vulnerable to economic shocks when aggregate debt burdens are high in the future, even if an effect of this sort has so far not been visible frequently:

> This does not mean debt service burdens do not affect future consumption, however. Some theoretical models suggest that high household debt service burdens may make household spending more sensitive to changes in expectations of future income. In short, consumer credit growth is high when households are optimistic about their future income prospects; it is only when households conclude that their

expectations were too optimistic that the debt begins to look too high. From this point of view, high debt burdens are not a negative force in and of themselves; they should only be viewed as a problem to the extent that the expectations of future income on which the borrowing was based are too high. (Maki 2002, 59)

It seems that this unusual combination happened in early 2009, an unprecedented time it is hoped will not be repeated.

Determinants of the relationships among interest rates, debt use, and spending at the individual level are discussed further in chapter 3, but for the purposes here of examining long-term macroeconomic trends, it is important to note that Maki did not find evidence in the economic literature at the time, or in his own econometric work, that consumer credit growth by itself has adversely affected aggregate consumer spending in normal times. He did not categorically dismiss the idea that such an effect might sometime be possible, however, even if he seemed to realize that this acknowledgment has elements of the story of the boy who cried wolf. At least for that boy and his listeners, the arrival of a wolf was a well-defined problem with easily understandable potential results; the specific difficulty with consumer credit in normal times is much less clear. In the absence of any evidence of rapidly rising consumer credit debt burden over time or compelling evidence of specific macroeconomic difficulties brought on by consumer credit alone, or any convincing evidence of likely future dislocations, the basic fear of consumer credit will remain a lot less clear. This, of course, does not rule out or make less problematic the unfortunate financial circumstances of individuals who find themselves in debt difficulties either as a result of their own irresponsibility or because of conditions beyond their control, such as job loss.

Apart from the obvious fact of specific woes of individuals who find themselves in debt troubles, what, then, *is* the economic difficulty associated with consumer credit? Is the level of aggregate consumer credit itself somehow inherently problematic in some undefined way, outside of its undemonstrated possible impact on future spending? Is there some specific component or feature of debt that will somehow lead to economic dislocations? Is it the growth rate of debt rather than its level that is worrisome? All of the above? Something else? Certainly, focusing on debt growth only during the part of a business cycle where it is rising, as so often seems to be the case with the media, has the potential to confuse and mislead. Consequently, the first aspect of further examining concerns over consumer credit use involves providing more detail about the consumer debt picture, especially over longer time periods than one phase of a single business cycle. As with the weather, everyone has an opinion on consumer credit, and the view seems widespread that such credit has recently grown without bound. But is this really true? Maybe it is time to look more closely at the data.[9]

---

9. The statistics on consumer credit outstanding, credit growth rates, and so on, used subsequently in this chapter are on the revised basis (Dynan, Johnson, and Pence 2003), except where referring specifically to the findings of earlier researchers who used earlier measures.

GROWTH OF CONSUMER CREDIT

Certainly, consumer credit has grown in the postwar era. From a total of $6.8 billion at the end of 1945, consumer credit outstanding grew to more than $2.5 trillion at the end of 2012 (see table 1.1). This is clearly a significant amount, which, of course, is not necessarily the same as being a meaningful worry. Many other economic magnitudes have also risen sharply in the years since World War II, including employment, income, assets, and wealth. Comparisons of consumer credit to other economic magnitudes, rather than absolute amounts of credit, should help put the changes in better perspective.

Growth Rates

One way to compare credit is to itself or, more specifically, to compare the increase in credit during a period of time, such as a year, with the amount of credit outstanding at the beginning of the period. Doing this for a succession of years produces a time series of the growth rate.

Figure 2.2 shows annual percentage growth rates for mortgage and consumer credit since 1946. It is immediately apparent that credit growth has not been steady in the postwar period; annual growth rates for mortgage and consumer credit both have fluctuated over the postwar business cycles. Possibly more interesting is how the cyclical episodes have been relatively similar over time. Nonmortgage consumer credit annual growth peaked in each cyclical upswing after 1955 at a growth rate of roughly 15 to 17 percent, with the all-time highs in the earliest postwar period, when it was responding to the end of wartime

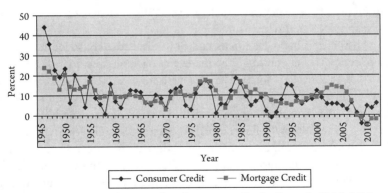

Figure 2.2 Consumer Credit Growth and Mortgage Credit Growth, 1946–2012.

Undoubtedly, research economists will over time subject the new figures to the same sorts of rigorous testing that Maki and others did for his and older statistical measures, but based on the patterns observed in the new data, it seems unlikely that the revisions and additional tests will produce dramatically new econometric conclusions caused solely by the changeover to the new data series.

controls during the 1940s. The yearly growth rate of mortgage credit has generally been somewhat less sharp in its cyclical fluctuations, reaching a peak growth rate of 16 to 17 percent in the early 1950s and again in the 1970s. Notably, there has not been a long-term sharp uptrend in growth rates in either series. Although the relative consistency of pattern does not provide a forecast, it is at least an indication that the recent growth pattern of consumer credit is not anomalous or startling in percentage terms. Consumer and mortgage credit grew rapidly in recent cyclical upswings, but they always have done so in upswings before falling off in downswings. Possibly the most noticeable change has been the sharp decline in mortgage credit growth after 2004 to negative territory beginning in 2008. Although the negative growth numbers are new, a multiyear decline in growth rate is not.

Consumer Credit Stocks and Flows

There are further comparisons that can help to put credit growth in perspective and a variety of approaches to reporting the statistical comparisons. Fortunately, the various methods lead to the same general conclusion.

Debt at any instant is a certain amount outstanding. Quantities that are fixed at a point in time are known in economics as *stock* items. Common examples include the money stock (the amount of currency and deposits or other definition of money that the public holds at a given time), the amount of pension assets in individuals' IRA and 401(k) accounts at the end of a year, the amount of bank assets subject to reserve requirements, the total public debt of the United States, and so on. In contrast, the variation in a stock from one time to another is a change measure, an amount per period of time, and is known as a *flow*. Income, for example, is a flow measure, consisting of the change in a person's or the economy's financial condition (wealth) over a period such as a year. The change in credit outstanding over a year is another flow measure.

This distinction between stocks and flows immediately suggests four basic kinds of comparisons that might be made among economic quantities: stock to stock, stock to flow, flow to stock, and flow to flow. Maki focused on a particular flow-to-flow comparison, the ratio of consumer credit repayments to income. When journalists compare consumer debt outstanding to something else, they often use a certain stock-to-flow ratio, debt outstanding relative to income. Both of these comparisons can be interesting, but they are not the only ones available, and others also are illustrative. Candidates for further comparisons include both stock and flow ratios of consumer credit to other important consumer balance sheet and income statement quantities: to specific assets, total assets, wealth, and the change in wealth (income). All four potential types of ratios for comparing aggregate consumer financial statistics (stock to stock, stock to flow, flow to stock, flow to flow) produce essentially the same conclusion concerning experience with consumer credit in recent years: recent trends are quite similar to experience in earlier decades.

COMPARISON OF CONSUMER CREDIT TO ASSETS AND NET WORTH

It seems that viewing stock-to-stock ratios of consumer credit to other consumer balance sheet totals (such as debt outstanding relative to assets or wealth) is much less common among analysts than looking at ratios of stock to flow (such as debt outstanding relative to income). Nonetheless, the stock ratios are useful for developing a complete picture of consumers' aggregate financial situation. After all, debts can be repaid not only from income but also in whole or in part by liquidating assets.

Figure 2.3 provides three such comparative stock-to-stock ratios: the ratios of consumer credit to financial assets (CC/FA), consumer credit to total consumer assets (CC/TA), and consumer credit to total consumer net worth or wealth (CC/NW). All three of these ratios demonstrate the same general shape: there was a rise in consumer credit outstanding relative to consumer assets and wealth in the immediate postwar period until a peak in 1974, followed by a flattening of the long-term rise for more than thirty-five years. There actually is very little trend in any of the ratios since the mid-1960s. Certainly, there is little that appears startling in the long-term consumer credit pattern in these charts. The uptrend from 2000 to 2002 occurred in large part because of the dramatic decline in those years in the stock market (lowering the denominator of the ratio relatively), an event that turned around again in 2003 and brought the ratios back into their ranges of the previous three decades. The rise in 2008 came about as stock market and housing prices declined that year and turned around again as the asset price trends recovered.

Although the third of these ratios, debt relative to net worth, is mathematically dependent on the first (because assets minus debts determines net worth), it is especially interesting precisely because it is a composite. Perhaps surprisingly, the ratio of consumer credit to total net worth shows no trend whatsoever since the 1960s. This is despite the widespread general view that consumers have become worse off financially in recent years because of consumer credit use, especially credit cards. In fact, the ratio underlying the chart rounds to 3 or 4 percent every year from 1963 to 2012. By itself, the credit-to-wealth ratios hardly indicate development of anomalous consumer credit conditions in the recent past.

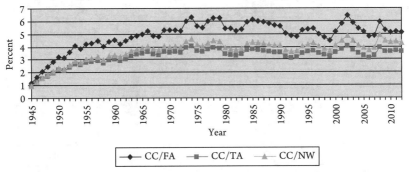

Figure 2.3 Consumer Credit Outstanding Relative to Consumers' Financial Assets, Total Assets, and Net Worth, 1945–2012.

COMPARISON OF CONSUMER CREDIT TO INCOME FLOWS

As noted, the most common way that observers illustrate consumer credit trends has been to draw a picture of the ratio of credit outstanding to income over some time period. The rising phase of this particular stock-to-flow ratio early in a business cycle upswing sometimes appears to underlie much of the visible public concern over trends in consumers' debt use. This ratio is easy to calculate from readily available statistics, and so the calculation is often made; it serves as the most common definition of debt "burden." The logic behind this usage is simple, in that debt outstanding is an obligation, and income represents the typical resource to satisfy the obligation, although this overlooks how assets can also be used to satisfy debts and overlooks the time span over which the debt may be repaid.

Figure 2.4 shows consumer credit over time relative to disposable personal income (that is, consumer spendable income, including transfer payments such as social security payments from the government, but after taxes). The underlying data show that consumer credit growth (illustrated previously in figure 2.2) is more variable than consumer income after taxes. Consequently, when debt is rising sharply, it is also rising relative to income. This seems to be a large part of what sets off the alarm bells with many observers of credit trends. When this ratio rises, the fear seems to be that it is headed for the stratosphere. There appears to be much less public notice of the phase of the business cycle when debt is declining relative to income.

Figure 2.4 also illustrates the subdivision of total consumer credit outstanding relative to income into its components, open-end or revolving credit and closed-end installment credit, each also compared with income. Revolving credit (mostly credit card credit) has generally been rising relative to income since first recorded separately in 1968. Closed-end installment credit relative to income mostly fell from 1968 to 1992 before rebounding somewhat since then. These trends show how open-end credit appears to have replaced a part of closed-end credit over time, as also shown by consumer surveys discussed in chapter 1 (see table 1.2).

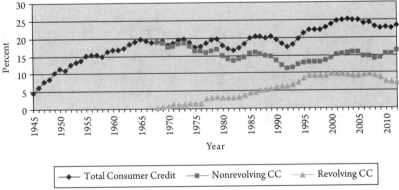

Figure 2.4 Consumer Credit and Components Relative to Disposable Personal Income, 1945–2012.

In the most recent cyclical upswing, the ratio of total consumer credit outstanding relative to income reached a record level (2001–2005), by about five percentage points, after being almost flat overall in the three decades from 1965 to 1995. To be sure, this latest episode caused concerns in some quarters, but more debt outstanding is also not really very surprising in a growing and wealthier economy, and the trend has declined again in recent years. Because of widespread interest in the debt-to-income ratio, however, a number of economists have examined the trends in the debt-to-incomeratio more closely, notably Enthoven (1957), Hunter (1966), and Luckett and August (1985), among many others. Some of their analyses and findings are discussed in more detail later in this chapter.

COMPARISON OF CONSUMER CREDIT CHANGES TO FINANCIAL AND LIQUID ASSETS

Moving on with the list of potential comparisons, another method for comparing consumer credit trends involves relating flow measures such as the change in credit (rather than the amount outstanding) to various asset and wealth stocks. Ratios of this sort are not commonly constructed for consumer credit flows, but looking at credit this way again leads to the observation that recent consumer credit experience does not deviate much from experience in past decades.

Figure 2.5 compares yearly change in consumer credit outstanding to year-end consumer deposits (upper curve) and year-end net worth (lower curve). Both ratios are sharply cyclical, but the pattern in both ratios is very similar from one business cycle to the next. Looking at the former, the change in consumer credit relative to consumer deposits has fluctuated within a narrow range of about five percentage points for decades; during the years of peak consumer credit growth in each business cycle upswing, the yearly increase in consumer credit reaches about 3 to 4 percent of consumers' deposits, and it then retreats to about 0 to 1 percent or a little lower toward the business cycle trough periods. The trend in the ratio of credit change to net worth is very similar, although the percentages are much smaller on account of a much larger denominator. The increase in consumer credit relative to net worth has never risen even by one percentage point in a single year in the period from 1946 to 2012 (the largest measure was 0.67 percent

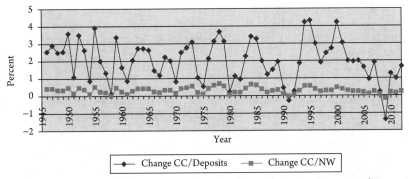

Figure 2.5 Change in Consumer Credit Outstanding Relative to Consumers' Deposits and Net Worth, 1946–2012.

in 1978); it also declines as often as it increases. Even though wealth is concentrated and an aggregate net worth ratio does not say anything about underlying individual cases, the stability of aggregate consumer credit change relative to net worth certainly does not by itself support the frequently expressed notion that consumer credit simply has grown too rapidly for too long.

Nonetheless, the similarities in the recurring pattern of the ratios of debt change to deposits and net worth is noteworthy, because both appear generally to lead the business cycle. A comparison of their patterns with business cycle turning points shows that they tend to turn downward before the cycle peaks and the slowdown or recession begins.[10] As with other leading indicators, their record as forecasting tools is less than perfect; a turndown in 1986, for example, did not predict a slowdown termed a recession in 1987, although the economy did slow somewhat in the latter year. The same was true following the credit growth slowdown in 1966 and some other years (business cycle specialists have long considered 1967 as very close to a recession year). In the other direction, these credit ratios continued to fall during the business cycle expansion after 2002 and did not demonstrate the familiar rise during that experience of a cyclically rising economy. A rising trend is again visible in the early stages of the business cycle rise after 2009.

COMPARISON OF CONSUMER CREDIT CHANGES TO INCOME FLOWS

Finally, it is also possible to relate credit flow measures to other economic flows. Maki did this with repayment flows to income, but figure 2.6 exhibits another comparison, the ratio of the yearly change in consumer credit to yearly disposable

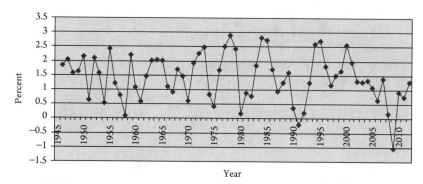

Figure 2.6 Change in Consumer Credit Outstanding Relative to Disposable Personal Income, 1946–2012.

10. The National Bureau of Economic Research (NBER), the scorekeeper in this area, dates business cycle peaks and troughs in the period after World War II as follows (see http://www.NBER.org/cycles.html).

Peaks: November 1948, July 1953, August 1957, April 1960, December 1969, November 1973, January 1980, July 1981, July 1990, March 2001, and December 2007.

Troughs: October 1949, May 1954, April 1958, February 1961, November 1970, March 1975, July 1980, November 1982, March 1991, November 2001, and June 2009.

income. This chart shows a pattern much like the flow-to-stock ratio measures in figure 2.5. The flow-to-flow comparison in figure 2.6 fluctuates cyclically within a narrow range and, like the other ratios, does not exhibit any recent anomalous upsurge. If anything, the trend over the decade or so beginning in 2001 has been downward. This measure also tends to lead the business cycle, peaking before the onset of a general economic slowdown or downturn. Thus, the flow-to-flow comparison does not produce a fundamentally different picture from the other ratios. In sum, none of the methods of comparing consumer credit outstanding or changes in consumer credit outstanding produces a conclusion that recent experience is startling or obviously problematic.

STUDIES OF LONG-TERM TRENDS

Although the studies of long-term growth of consumer credit have not been especially numerous, there have been some serious studies in this area that go beyond just outlining the basic statistical trends. This section of the chapter reviews some studies, beginning with the three that are arguably the most important for understanding consumer credit growth: Luckett and August (1985), Enthoven (1957), and Hunter (1966). While each of these studies is rooted in the questions and issues of the times when it was written, each explores the underlying conceptual questions in a way still relevant for understanding these matters today. After lengthier discussion of these three papers, there follows a group of shorter reviews of other relevant studies of consumer credit growth organized by decade. The message from this lengthier list is that serious analysts have reached similar conclusions concerning long-term growth of consumer credit, regardless of the time period covered by their individual efforts.

Luckett and August

Even though it was written some time ago, a paper by Federal Reserve Board economists Charles A. Luckett and James D. August (1985) is still in many ways among the most interesting and useful, because it discusses many underlying reasons that consumer credit might grow cyclically. For this reason alone, their paper is still well worth rereading today, more than twenty-five years after publication. Luckett and August also looked at issues arising from the rapid growth of consumer credit during 1983 to 1984 and concluded that the specific experiences causing alarm during those years had been quite consistent with past relationships. They also briefly examined cross-section consumer survey evidence concerning the distribution of consumer credit outstanding and newly available at the time of their writing. They reported that much of the increase in consumer debt during those years was acquired by upper-income individuals, which produced a different perception of consumer credit growth than if all the increase at the time were owed by lower-income consumers exclusively. They focused particularly on explaining trends in the ratio of consumer credit to income, the stock-to-flow comparison that appeared to generate the most discussion in its cyclically rising phase.

They argued that the concern over debt burden was twofold: (1) concern that a rising share of consumer income would necessarily be devoted to debt service causing diminution in the willingness to spend and (2) worry that there would be an accompanying deleterious indirect effect through reduced willingness of lenders to lend when debt is already high relative to income. They contended that these worries about consumer debt trends apparently arise from two sorts of ready observations: the slow long-term rise of the debt-to-income ratio in the postwar period and its apparent cyclicality, which produces episodes of rapid rise. Both of these trends are visible in figure 2.4, discussed above. To examine these issues, Luckett and August broke down the postwar period before 1982 into four subperiods and reviewed trends and potential reasons for the experiences within each: rapid credit growth from the end of the war to the mid-1950s, deceleration of debt growth from the 1950s to the 1970s, resurgence in 1977 and 1978, and slower growth again through 1982. They then studied the rapid growth in 1983 and 1984 in more detail.[11]

Concerning long-term growth, Luckett and August first reexamined the simple structural model of credit growth proposed by Alain Enthoven (1957) and noted that more recent data through 1984 still seemed to fit this model (also true after 1984), even though the Enthoven model was purely algebraic and did not attempt to model consumer behavior explicitly (this model is discussed further below). Luckett and August added that at the date of their writing, the ratio of consumer credit to income still had not exceeded the potential upper bound derived by Enthoven in the 1950s, but even if it had done so or would do so in the future, there was nothing in the Enthoven prediction that suggested that an upward breach would necessarily be significant. They next discussed some reasons that changing market factors in later years, such as lengthening maturities on consumer credit, more of the debt being owed by upper-income households, and so on, might alter the asymptote that Enthoven had derived for the debt-to-income ratio twenty-five years earlier.

Luckett and August then analyzed some reasons for cyclicality in the ratio of consumer credit to income that are rooted in the short-term nature of consumer credit, focusing especially on the experience in the early 1980s. One reason for

---

11. As mentioned briefly in an earlier footnote, Luckett and August (and also other analysts at that time) based their calculations, tables, and charts on amounts and growth of consumer installment credit, rather than total consumer credit as here. Consumer installment credit is by far the largest component of total consumer credit (which also includes noninstallment credit such as charge accounts and single-payment loans), but it is no longer calculated and released by the Federal Reserve separately, and so tables and charts strictly comparable to those in the Luckett and August paper can no longer be prepared. Differences in growth rates and ratios between the two concepts of consumer credit are very small, but careful comparison of Luckett and August's growth rates and ratios with those employed elsewhere in this chapter that are based on total consumer credit outstanding will show some small differences that are not important for the discussion.

the cyclical growth pattern is the observation, obvious upon brief reflection but overlooked by most observers, that changes in the growth rate of consumer credit do not arise solely from variations in credit extensions. Rather, they represent the net effect of extensions and repayments, which may follow different paths. Thus, statements arguing how an increase in credit growth means that consumers are borrowing a lot more are not necessarily more than partly correct. It may also mean that repayments are growing only slowly or not at all, either because of slow extensions in a prior period or because of longer maturities.

Consider a period in which consumer credit extensions are taking place at a positive pace while extensions exceed repayments so that the net change (growth) is positive. Suppose that in the next period, new consumer credit extensions increase less rapidly or decline, maybe because of higher interest rates or reduced consumer optimism. Because the falloff occurs only in extensions but not in repayments, since the latter depend on credit extended at a high rate in the prior period, there is an exaggerated falloff in growth, which is the net of extensions and repayments. In effect, cyclicality that arises in the rate of credit extensions has an exaggerated impact on net change because of the impact of past extensions on current repayments. Building on this hypothesis (also mentioned by Tapscott 1985), Luckett and August developed a simple growth model based on prior relationships and found that it fit well the consumer credit growth pattern in 1984.

Unavailability of information on the pattern of actual extensions and repayments after this time has prevented ready replication of the Luckett and August growth model with newer data, but careful theoretical economic modeling today employing reasonable assumptions might well still produce an interesting mathematical representation. Most important for their purposes at the time, Luckett and August did not find anything anomalous or sinister in the pattern of rapid growth in consumer credit during 1983 and 1984, given that it followed a period of slower growth (and lower future repayments) from 1980 to 1982. A similar effort today for subsequent years likely would produce interesting and possibly informative results.

Luckett and August closed their article with a brief review, almost without comment, of a whole list of factors that might cause a long-run upward trend in the ratio of consumer credit outstanding relative to income without necessarily being cause for concern:

(1) Expanded use of credit cards solely for purpose of payments (typically referred to as convenience use of credit cards, as discussed earlier) is counted within consumer credit even though it is not credit for more than a few days to a month or so. Luckett and August suggest that as much as 40 percent of credit card credit at that time might consist of convenience credit. Subsequent, unpublished estimates by them and others are somewhat lower, more on the order of 10 to 15 percent of revolving consumer credit outstanding. An adjustment of consumer credit, even of this magnitude, however, would substantially change the general pattern of growth in addition to reducing the aggregate ratio of outstanding consumer credit to income.

(2) Lengthening maturities of credit over time, which means that there is more credit outstanding for any given burden of payments.

(3) Demographic changes arising arose from the bulge of the baby boom generation within the heavy debt-using years (an impact not judged to be large by Luckett and August in the 1980s and probably now passing).

(4) Adjustable-rate credit and new technologies such as improved methods of credit screening that make creditors willing to lend to a wider risk spectrum of clientele (sometimes referred to today as the "democratization of credit").

(5) Secondary markets have developed for lender assets based on credit to consumers;

(6) The growth of student loans finance higher education and a more productive work force.

(7) Use of consumer credit, especially credit cards, support the financial needs of small businesses.

The Enthoven Model

As mentioned, more than a quarter-century before publication of the Luckett and August article, RAND Corporation and later Stanford University economist Alain Enthoven (1957) had published a useful paper about consumer credit growth that still has relevance today. Enthoven was not attempting to model consumer credit use behavior explicitly. Instead, his purpose was to design an algebraic model based on available cross-section evidence of consumers' credit use to explain the rapid growth of consumer credit and the rise of the debt-to-income ratio after World War II that was causing so much concern in the mid-1950s. The paper concludes that the pattern of credit growth and the increase in the credit-to-income ratio experienced after the war fit well within a set of reasonable expectations; it appears that subsequent growth in credit and the credit-to-income ratio still fit broadly within the scope of Enthoven's projection.

Enthoven argued that there were two areas of concern being expressed over consumer credit growth, the cyclical issue and the long-term issue, and he noted that his paper was devoted to the long-term question. At the very outset, he postulated that the public concern in this area was misguided:

> This paper is concerned with the long run problem. It is my intention to show that alarm over the postwar experience is based upon a misleading view of the burden of installment debt and an incorrect extrapolation of its growth. Consideration of the distribution of the debt and its economic significance should lead us to a new concept of its effects on consumer expenditure. My method of analysis will be to assume that income grows steadily, to extrapolate the growth of installment debt since the war by the use of a model based upon the distribution of debt, and to show that the

continued growth of installment debt, when correctly extrapolated, is not inconsistent with the assumed pattern of growth. (Enthoven 1957, 915)

He assumed that the economy in the future would be characterized by increasing aggregate income caused by both increasing population and rising income per family. If consumer credit use were chiefly among younger families as the cross-section evidence suggested, then credit outstanding would increase as the population increases. He then postulated an algebraic growth model to demonstrate the implications of these basic assumptions.

Specifically, the solution to his equations showed that under his model's assumptions, the debt-to-income ratio would approach from below a long-run asymptotic stable limit dependent on (1) the ratio of the growth of consumer credit relative to income and (2) the growth rate of income itself. For the purpose of illustrating how credit conditions at the time were understandable and not in any sense anomalous, Enthoven did not need to model debt-using behavior explicitly, especially the causes of its cyclicality. Instead, he could merely use available statistics on debt and income from recent experience to illustrate current trends and make his point about expected long-term growth of the ratio of consumer debt to income:

> We shall now see that...the growth rate of debt in terms of itself will exceed that of an economy with a low initial debt level, and that the two rates will approach each other asymptotically. In the limit the ratio of debt to income will be constant and stable. These aspects of the theory can be expressed algebraically in a simple model which will provide us with a basis for the extrapolation of the postwar experience and a means for its quantitative assessment. (Enthoven 1957, 923)

Using the debt and income growth experience of 1945 to 1956 as the basis of the model's parameters, Enthoven derived the conclusion that the long-term expectation for the ratio of consumer installment credit to income was about 19 percent. Since this asymptotic ratio was higher than the aggregate ratio of installment credit to income at the time (between 9 and 10 percent in 1955–1956), he concluded that the ratio could continue to rise for some time:

> If we extrapolate the postwar growth in installment credit on the basis of this model, we may conclude that although debt will continue to grow more rapidly than income for some time, it will, in the limit, approach about 19 percent of income. According to this reasoning, there is no reason to think that debt will swamp income or that the overall postwar growth of debt, when extrapolated correctly, is inconsistent with the continued growth of income. (Enthoven 1957, 926)

In this view, the rapid rises of consumer credit in the 1950s merely represented response to disequilibrium conditions arising from the war, including rationing and general unavailability of durable goods, along with regulatory restrictions on consumer credit that prevailed during the war and immediately afterward. Thus, those observers who projected then-recent experience with debt growth far into the future were simply making an analytical mistake. It was merely a response to a disequilibrium condition after the war that would right itself in the future, and the debt-to-income ratio would approach a limiting value.

The years since Enthoven published his paper show that despite the simplicity of his growth model, he seems to have been on to something. At a minimum, it is clear that his prediction has been quite consistent with experience. Although consumer credit growth has been intensely cyclical over the past five decades, and his simple model does not really allow for this fact, the aggregate ratio of consumer credit to income (the only consumer credit measurement available today) does appear to have approached an asymptotic limit of 20 to 25 percent from below (figure 2.7), only a bit above Enthoven's original projection in 1957, which was based only on installment credit and not total consumer credit anyway. Total consumer credit outstanding has never really exceeded the prediction of his model by very much, and it still does not.

It is possible to reestimate Enthoven's projection using his original model but with updated parameters for income growth and credit use based on later historical data. Figure 2.7 illustrates such a reconstruction, using moving averages of the preceding ten years for each of the necessary parameters. This approach derives a new asymptote for the debt-to-income ratio yearly, based on the (rolling) experience of the preceding decade.

The patterns of the actual yearly ratio of consumer credit to income and its limiting value predicted by the Enthoven approach (and illustrated in figure 2.7) show the overall consistency of Enthoven's approach with subsequent experience. The ratio of consumer credit outstanding to income converged with the path of the level predicted by the rolling Enthoven model by the early 1970s, and the two ratios have tracked each other remarkably closely since that time. Again, as with other illustrations of consumer credit trends above, it does not appear that there is anything in the Enthoven way of looking at consumer credit trends that suggests that recent credit experience is in any way anomalous.

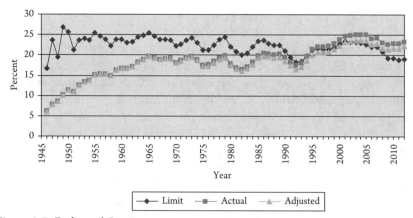

Figure 2.7 Enthoven's Limit.

The Hunter Model

About a decade after Enthoven's article and almost two decades before Luckett and August's paper, Helen Manning Hunter (1966) set out to build a behavioral model of the long-term growth of consumer credit based on her understanding of relationships revealed in consumer surveys of credit use. The goal in her paper was to find an explanation of the high growth of consumer credit relative to income over the years from 1910 to 1962. In effect, this is the same issue explored by Enthoven, although he focused on the postwar period only and did not try to develop or to estimate statistically the parameters of a behavioral equation.

Based on the findings of earlier cross-section studies by Lansing, Maynes, and Kreinin (1957) and Miner (1960), Hunter hypothesized that liquid asset holdings, income, change in income, and life cycle stage of individual consumers were the most important relevant variables. After reviewing some theoretical and empirical considerations, she estimated an equation in which various measures of consumer credit outstanding or extended are a function of population, average incomes, and a measure of liquid assets.

Although her parameter estimates are probably no longer useful, since they depended so much on the depression years of the 1930s and the immediate postwar years from 1946 through the 1950s (she did exclude the war years 1917–1919 and 1942–1945 as probably abnormal), her discussion of the relevant underlying variables still is important. Credit use does seem related to population and income growth and possibly to liquid asset changes, even if income elasticity of growth does not appear as high now that the effects of the depression of the 1930s and the wartime credit restrictions of the 1940s and early 1950s have faded farther into the past. In a recent paper, Durkin, Ord, and Walker (2010) show this with a series of Hunter-type equations and modern econometric techniques that also demonstrate the consistency of Enthoven's 1957 predictions with subsequent experience over a very long time interval.

The 1970s

Although the Luckett and August, Enthoven, and Hunter papers are clearly among the three most useful sources for outlining the conceptual issues associated with analyzing long-term growth of consumer credit statistically, they are not the only papers that examine the matter. In fact, each business cycle upswing produces discussion of the consumer debt picture at the time.

In the early 1970s, for example, Michael Prell (1973), in the article mentioned above, wrote about consumer installment credit when it totaled $111 billion at the end of the twenty-five-year postwar period of 1946 to 1971, but its growth had "outpaced by generous margins the increases in most other important economic aggregates" (Prell 1973, 3). His main purpose, however, was not so much to analyze consumer credit growth as to examine its slowing toward the latter part of the period, especially in the late 1960s.

Prell's article discussed how rising income over time implies both a greater capacity for debt and increased consumption expenditure, and both may influence (and be influenced by) credit use. Nonetheless, he noted how over time, the growth rate of installment credit had tended to fall into line with growth rates of personal income and expenditure. He extensively discussed how Enthoven had been one of the analysts in the 1950s who reached this conclusion, despite the concerns of the time that the trend of consumer credit growth was incompatible with continued prosperity. He also discussed how Hunter was another analyst who realized that consumer credit was not simply out of control.

Prell then expanded on the discussion by Enthoven and Hunter by examining many of the economic phenomena that might affect the consumer credit growth path over shorter periods and influence its cyclicality, beyond their impact on its long-term growth path. Most of these influences are only listed in this brief synopsis of Prell's paper, since the discussion here does not much concern cyclicality per se. It seems, however, that each of these factors would need to be taken into account in some manner in constructing a complete model of consumer credit growth in the postwar period: (1) consumer expenditures trends; (2) composition of expenditures, such as durable expenditures and big-ticket expenditures, which rose more rapidly from 1945 to 1956 than later; (3) dependence of future spending trends on tastes, innovations, and relative prices; (4) variable intensity of credit use for durables expenditures, because of such factors as changed attitudes toward credit and acceptable uses of credit, population changes, and increased proportion of the population using credit; (5) supply side changes such as legal reforms, changing views toward consumer credit by lenders, and changes in market competitiveness; (6) lengthening maturities; and (7) special factors in the late 1960s, including credit crunches, inflation, and special demand factors, such as a slower rise in liquid assets.

In concluding, Prell noted that a full explanation of the postwar consumer credit pattern probably required an integrated interaction among a variety of factors, but he certainly did not express the view that credit growth during these years was out of the ordinary:

> In a more eclectic approach, three proximate sources of CICO [consumer installment credit outstanding] growth were discussed, i.e., growth and changing composition of consumer expenditure, increased use of credit, and lengthening of installment contracts. It was concluded that each of these factors contributed to the growth of CICO and did so in such a way that the deceleration of CICO growth seemed largely explained. The major elements in that deceleration seem to have been the early postwar surge in durables purchases, which constituted a catch up with demands unsatisfied during the wartime years, the decontrol of installment credit, the widening acceptance of credit use, and the expansion of the consumer lending business. By the mid 1950s, most of those factors had spent themselves, and the impulse of CICO growth in excess of personal income growth came largely from a further moderate lengthening of average loan maturities and a continued widening of the range of acceptable uses for installment credit.

The conclusion offered here is that these latter two forces will also decline in quantitative significance in the years ahead and, as a result, the rate of CICO growth may not exceed by much that of personal income during the 1970s. (Prell 1973, 13)

Expressed this way as a rhetorically hedged forecast made in the early 1970s, Prell's prediction nonetheless proved remarkably accurate. In fact, the ratio of consumer credit outstanding to disposable personal income peaked in 1973 and was almost exactly the same in the business cycle peak year of 1979 as it had been in the earlier peak year of 1969 (figure 2.4, above). Furthermore, we now know from hindsight that his prediction still would have been reasonable even if he had extended it for three more decades: the ratio of consumer credit to disposable personal income was only a handful of percentage points higher between 1994 and 2012 than it had been in 1969 and 1979.

Other analysts in the 1970s and 1980s mentioned many of the same factors as contributing to the pattern of consumer credit growth during these years, and they sometimes added to the list. In a paper in the later 1970s, Federal Reserve Bank of New York economists Maury Harris and Karen Bradley (1977) also indicated some changing conditions at the time as probably contributing to the ability to repay debts: a trend toward smaller families, more working women and teenagers, and relatively more household heads at the time in the age groupings during which income gains had traditionally been highest (notably the movement at the time of the so called baby boomers into the higher earning years). They noted that traditional measures of debt burden (the ratios of installment debt to income and installment debt repayments to income) were moving upward at the time, but they were still below previous peaks, and there was no specific evidence of an overburdened consumer sector, despite growing concerns among some observers. Without specifically mentioning Enthoven, in effect, they revisited the Enthoven issue by noting that the debt-to-income ratio was still rising, although slowly, as Enthoven had predicted two decades earlier: "There is some concern that debt relative to income is getting too high because the ratio is nearing its previous peak. However, the particular level that might signal a slowdown in consumption is difficult to determine since in postwar business cycles the debt-income ratio has peaked at successively higher levels" (Harris and Bradley, 1977, 23).

After reviewing the debt picture at what turned out to be about two-thirds of the way through the lengthy economic upswing in the 1970s, Harris and Bradley concluded that the consumer debt situation did not appear out of line. As Maki would do a generation later, they included the obligatory caveat that it still could so develop:

Household debt can undoubtedly become too large, thereby curbing consumption and raising delinquency rates. However, analysis of various measures of consumer debt burdens—notwithstanding their imperfections—indicates that they are generally not out of line. Nevertheless, the whole consumer debt situation warrants continued close attention. (Harris and Bradley 1977, 26)

Toward the end of the same business cycle upswing, an article by Carl Palash (1979), a New York Federal Reserve Bank economist, expressed the same general views. After discussing how consumer indebtedness had risen especially rapidly during the preceding two years, he listed some reasons that increasing indebtedness might be less worrisome than its recent trend was suggesting: delinquency rates well less than during the preceding recession, continued growth of income and employment, the existence of inflation at the time that lowered the burden of fixed repayments over time, deductibility of interest payments for income tax calculation, and availability of substantial amounts of liquid assets and unrealized capital gains on other assets within consumers' portfolios. Significantly, he also pointed out that debt appeared at the time to be more widely distributed across the population than in earlier years, and there was also growing convenience use of credit cards: "The wider distribution of debt and other demographic developments explain part of the increase in the debt and repayments ratios. Other factors point to a somewhat lighter burden than that implied by the aggregate ratios. Among these are the role of credit cards and the tax system" (Palash 1979, 11).

As with the other analysts, putting all of these factors together, Palash concluded that the consumer debt picture was no more worrisome than experienced at earlier times. In offering his conclusion, he seemed compelled, however, to deliver the warning familiar to those looking out either for wolves or for the feared downturn in consumer spending to be brought about by past debt use:

> The burden of repaying debt is considerably less onerous than the standard ratios indicate. Adjusting the repayment-to-income ratio for the percentage of households with debt, "on time" credit card payments, and the other factors discussed here, the adjusted ratio in 1978 is within the range experienced in the 1960s and early 1970s. This suggests that the financial position of households is less precarious than suggested by the conventional indebtedness measures. Nevertheless, in the event of an economic downturn the burden of indebtedness is likely to worsen as income and the value of assets decline. Indeed, in such circumstances, the incidences of loan delinquencies and personal bankruptcies are likely to increase. As a consequence, the financial condition of households should continue to receive close attention. (Palash 1979, 12)

Palash prepared and published his article coincident with the cyclical peak in consumer credit growth and the various ratios illustrated in the charts, 1978 and 1979. The following three years witnessed two sharp economic recessions and a brief period of federal control actions on consumer credit in 1980 as part of President Carter's anti-inflation efforts of that year. The rate of growth of consumer credit dropped precipitously during these years (figure 2.2, above), and the standard debt burden measures also declined (figures 2.3 and 2.4), muting some of the criticism of consumer debt growth during this time.

The 1980s

Trends can reverse, though, and so can levels of concern about them. Rising consumer credit use following the double recession episode brought the burden questions back into the spotlight after 1983. This was the period analyzed extensively by Luckett and August (1985), discussed above. Similarly to Prell and the other analysts in the 1970s, Luckett and August concluded that the debt picture at this time was not out of the ordinary. Likewise, the findings of other analysts at the time were very consistent and need only be mentioned briefly.

In a preliminary paper, David B. Eastwood and Cynthia A. Sencindiver (1984) also dusted off the Enthoven model and, as with the Luckett and August paper a year later, found Enthoven's discussion still relevant for the postwar years up to that point. They provided an update on the Enthoven equations and proposed a listing of some factors that could be taken into account in a formal restatement and updating of the Enthoven approach. Not surprisingly, their listing of factors that might be considered and their conclusions about consumer credit conditions at the time appeared very similar to the views of the other economic analysts:

> Consumers over an extended period of time appear to have been quite consistent in their use of credit. Actual debt-to-income ratios seem to be growing in a fashion which is approximated by a long term asymptotic pattern. Rapid credit expansion over a short period of time does not have to be a cause for alarm. Changes in income growth and demographic composition can be sources of installment debt growth. As the postwar baby boom enters the life cycle stage in which borrowing is most likely to occur, it will lead to credit growth; and as this segment of the population enters subsequent stages, continued adjustment towards the long term debt-to-income ratio should occur. (Eastwood and Secindiver 1984, 12)

Toward the middle of the decade, Douglas Pearce (1985), an economist with the North Carolina State University and the Federal Reserve Bank of Kansas City, also turned his attention to reviewing consumer debt trends. Not surprisingly, since he was looking at the same set of facts, his paper reached conclusions similar to those of the other analysts. Specifically, despite some more years of consumer credit growth that had "rekindled concerns that households have become financially overextended" (Pearce 1985, 3, citing some articles in the popular press), he listed a variety of other explanations of consumer and mortgage credit growth that led to much less worrisome conclusions. They included changing demographic patterns among the population producing a bulge in the heavy credit-using years of ages 25 to 44, low real after-tax interest rates (especially for fixed-rate mortgage loans), high expected (and generally not immediately taxable) capital gains on housing and other assets, absence of any severe economic downturns in the post–World War II years, changes in financial markets that improved the efficiency of funds flows, increasing maturities on consumer credit instruments, and rising convenience use of credit cards. The final paragraph in Pearce's conclusion sounds very familiar:

> Even with the increase in debt, households do not appear to be in a weak financial condition. Ratios of debt to total assets and financial assets have not risen significantly, and households have substantial liquid assets. Although the ratio of debt to income is high, evidence suggests that this ratio overstates the debt burden of households. And while the mortgage delinquency rate has risen somewhat, the consumer loan delinquency rate is at a relatively low level. Therefore, assuming there is no general economic downturn, the overall financial condition of households should not be an impediment to future consumer spending. (Pearce 1985, 17)

During this cyclical upswing, US Department of Commerce analyst Tracy Tapscott (1985) echoed some of the same conclusions as Luckett and August. She also specifically added some legal changes that took place during these years to the list of factors considered by other analysts that likely affected consumer credit growth during the 1970s and 1980s and that help make continued growth at the time understandable:

> Several long term developments affected consumer installment credit in the 1980s. Two of these—consumers' increased awareness and understanding of credit instruments [due to the federal Truth in Lending Act], and financial deregulation [due to the Depository Institutions Deregulation and Monetary Control Act]—interactively led to the expansion of credit and greater competition in consumer credit markets. (Tapscott 1985, 14)

Toward the end of this decade, a paper by William C. Dunkelberg (1989), then dean of the School of Business at Temple University and chief economist for the National Federation of Independent Business, also indicated that a variety of economic factors were continuing to cause consumer credit growth without indicating development of any fundamental economic dislocations. Dunkelberg's paper mentioned that rapidly increasing employment during these years would cause an increase in both supply and demand for credit. Within this context, he also focused on some statistical reasons that debt could appear to be rising more rapidly than was actually the case: growing convenience credit on credit cards within the statistical totals for debt outstanding and some market changes that affected the numerator of the debt-to-income ratio more than the denominator without implying an increase in debt difficulties. Among the most prominent of the latter sort of changes were growing democratization of credit as a result of interest rate deregulation, increasing use of credit by higher-income families, and high returns on financial assets that made consumers less willing to sell them in lieu of using credit. He then provided tables and further discussion to illustrate each of his main points.

The 1990s and Beyond

Like the 1980s, the early months of the following decade witnessed the onset of an economic downturn accompanied by a downward movement in the common measures of consumer credit debt burden. This presented the opportunity for a brief hiatus in the worry over debt burden, but observers did not have to wait too long for renewed discussion of the issue.

Early in the decade, Federal Reserve Bank of Chicago analyst Francesca Eugeni (1993) examined the question of whether changing financial markets might mean that the commonly employed measures of debt burden had become less useful as measures of the consumer sector's financial condition. Specifically, she was concerned about whether greater use of mortgage credit and automobile leasing as substitutes for common installment credit might mean that consumer credit ratios were understated relative to past norms. Eugeni's paper noted that convenience and flexibility of the plans for consumers, tax deductibility of the interest payments, and generally lower interest rates on this type of credit had made home equity plans attractive substitutes for other forms of consumer credit by the early 1990s. This raised the question of whether the traditional debt burden ratios were not actually understated relative to their past relationships to consumers' assets and income.

To examine this issue, Eugeni employed various assumptions to construct a succession of estimates of the amount of home equity credit outstanding at the time that might actually represent a substitution for ordinary, nonmortgage, consumer credit. These estimates were then added to consumer credit outstanding to construct revised debt burden ratios. Thus, the approach was to add to reported consumer installment credit outstanding various estimates of home equity credit. The additions were used to construct revised ratios of debt to income.

Without commenting here on the methodology she used in estimating the amounts of home equity related credit that should be added to consumer credit, Eugeni's proposed changes to the consumer credit definition merely halt the slide of the ratio of consumer credit to income otherwise observed from 1990 to 1992. None of her three proposed definitional substitutions produced a rising debt burden trend over the period (see Eugeni 1993, 8, tab. 2). The four-year estimates presented certainly do not indicate that the ratio of adjusted total consumer credit to income had risen anomalously at the time or in any sense had spun out of control. Significantly, it seems that if adjustments are to be made to the definition of consumer credit to account for changing availability of types of credit products in the marketplace, then it is also necessary to undertake subtractions along with additions. Many analysts mentioned previously have noted that convenience use of credit cards properly should be subtracted from consumer credit outstanding in order to make comparisons over time as markets and products have changed.

The same year, economist Sangkyun Park (1993) of the research department of the Federal Reserve Bank of St. Louis examined and compared the growth of consumer credit relative to measures of consumption, especially of durable goods. He showed that consumer spending growth does not explain credit growth during these years, and so it is important also to consider other economic variables. He looked at both the apparent long-term absence of a real growth trend in the relation of consumer credit to measures of consumption of durable goods in the 1980s and early 1990s and its sharp cyclicality.

Park explored relationships between consumer credit growth and other economic variables, including demographic trends, interest rates and spreads, measures of consumer confidence in the economy, debt burden of households, availability of substitute credit products, and willingness of lenders to lend. As so many other analysts had done, he concluded that fluctuations in common measures of debt burden were not especially influential in explaining future debt growth:

> A careful comparison of the debt/income ratio with the total credit ratio, however, does not convincingly support the economic relationship between the two variables. Since 1970, the debt/income ratio generally lagged behind the credit ratio, indicating that changes in the debt/income ratio may have been a result rather than a cause of movements in the credit ratio. Thus, Figure 5 [in the article] shows more of an accounting relationship than economic causality; the debt burden increased as a result of heavy borrowing in previous periods.... The debt service burden shows a similar pattern of movements. (Park 1993, 34–35)

A bit later in the same decade, Federal Reserve Bank of Kansas City economist C. Alan Garner (1996) became the latest to examine the old issue of the rising ratio of consumer credit to income in an economic upswing. His article reviewed a variety of measures of debt burden in common use and concluded that none conclusively indicated anomalous consumer credit conditions at the time. Using charts, he showed that common debt burden measures do not necessarily predict a slowdown in spending, and then he employed statistical techniques to demonstrate this fact more formally. The statistical tests provided little support for the contention that common debt burden measures were useful predictors of future spending on durable goods or growth patterns of aggregate spending.

Garner then asked the rhetorical question that so many economists have asked on this point over the years: "Why do so many economic observers believe, then, that the consumer debt burden and real variables [i.e., spending measures] are closely associated?" (Garner 1996, 70). In speculating about this question, he went on to discuss briefly the opposite possibility, outlined in more detail by Maki a few years later (and discussed above), that the relationship actually is the reverse. With some more statistical tests, he examined more closely the reverse possibility that advances in the real economy may help predict future movements in debt burden, as consumers boost spending to reflect improved income prospects. He closed by discussing some structural changes in consumer credit markets such as growth in credit card use for transactions purposes and concluded with a paragraph that could have been written by any of the economic analysts of consumer credit markets over the previous three decades, offering, of course, the by now obligatory warning that things still could get bad:

Most measures of the consumer debt burden have not risen recently, with alternative measures giving somewhat different impressions about the current situation. Such measures have not been reliable in predicting the growth of consumer durables purchases or real GDP in the past. Moreover, structural changes in the financial system have increased the uncertainty about how to interpret the rise in measures of the consumer debt burden. Nevertheless, analysts should continue to monitor consumer debt measures in case recent structural changes, such as aggressive promotion of credit cards and greater access to credit by lower income households, have strengthened the relationship between debt and real economic variables. (Garner 1996, 74)

Later in the 1990s, Alan Murray (1997), a senior official and analyst with Fuji Bank, again raised the same general issues. Sounding a bit frustrated with the whole idea of debt burden being worrisome, Murray laid down the challenge in his opening sentences:

The often repeated statement that the U.S. consumer is overburdened with debt conveys the notion that the average household's financial condition differs only in degree from that of those well publicized few who are unable to meet their debt service obligations. We contend that such a generalization is unwarranted and leads to the erroneous conclusion that rising ratios of consumer debt to income provide a leading indicator of weakness in consumer spending. (Murray 1997, 41)

He then reviewed familiar ground, such as how the ratio of repayments to income was not at the time out of its historical range and how the familiar ratio of consumer credit to income did not take into account assets that are also available to repay debts. Following this discussion, he reviewed some reasons that the debt-to-income ratio might rise more than various debt-to-assets ratios. Suggestions included declining interest rates in the 1990s, along with tax-planning reasons, such as the availability of tax-deferred vehicles such as 401(k) investments, which frequently make taking on some debt more attractive than selling assets. He also mentioned convenience use of credit cards and extension of credit to small businesses on credit cards, which may not be adequately deducted from consumer credit statistics. The point here is not so much that he said anything dramatically new but rather that he continues into the later 1990s a decades-long tradition among economic analysts: after peering into the darkness of consumer credit growth, they all appear to conclude that they have not seen the wolf out there.

In early 2004, Federal Reserve Board chairman Alan Greenspan (2004) summarized trends in consumer debt burden measurements in a speech shortly after the Board had introduced a new way of calculating some ratios of household debt repayments to income that it uses in its own internal analyses (see Dynan, Johnson, and Pence 2003 and figure 2.1, above). Although Greenspan concentrated his discussion on trends in the 1990s and especially the period of 2001 to

2004, he acknowledged that he was also interested in the longer-term picture. He clearly indicated his basic agreement with the views of many economists over the decades who examined the consumer sector's economic health associated with its use of credit:

> In evaluating household debt burdens, one must remember that debt-to-income ratios have been rising for at least half a century. With household assets rising as well, the ratio of net worth to income is currently somewhat higher than its long run average. So long as financial intermediation continues to expand, both household debt and assets are likely to rise faster than income. Without an examination of what is happening to both assets and liabilities, it is difficult to ascertain the true burden of debt service. Overall, the household sector seems to be in good shape, and much of the apparent increase in the household sector's debt ratios over the past decade reflects factors that do not suggest increasing household financial stress. And, in fact, during the past two years, debt service ratios have been stable. (Greenspan 2004, 4)

A bit more than a year later, Federal Reserve Board economist Kathleen Johnson (2005) usefully pointed out that when reviewing the story told by time series statistics, it is always necessary to examine how conditions underlying the statistical series may themselves have changed too, making the time series message less obvious than if viewed in isolation. In particular, she looked at growth in the ratio of repayments to income for open-end credit from 1989 to 2005. Her analysis of (in her terminology) "counterfactual" conditions explored how the ratio might have been different if conditions underlying the statistical series had not changed.

She found that a greater convenience use of credit cards, a decline in credit card interest rates, and a spread of credit card availability to wider segments of the population during these years together accounted for all of the increase in revolving credit debt service burden. In other words, if these underlying conditions had remained the same over the period, there would not have been any increase in the revolving credit ratio, the most controversial segment of consumer credit. Although it is possible to argue whether an increase in credit use caused by lower interest rates and wider dispersion among population segments is worrisome, she contended that the portion arising from greater convenience use of credit cards certainly was not. She concluded that it is necessary to look for changes of this sort before single-mindedly concluding that conditions have worsened markedly:

> All told, an important implication of the analysis here is that researchers should exercise caution when comparing levels of the financial obligations ratio [FOR] over long periods. Specifically, the factors behind an increase in the FOR should be identified and evaluated before one concludes that the increase implies greater financial fragility for the U.S. household sector or for the macroeconomy more broadly. (Johnson 2005, 484)

In mid-2007, Federal Reserve official Karen Dynan and then Board vice chairman Donald L. Kohn (2007) weighed in on the causes and consequences of consumer debt, this time focusing not only on consumer credit but also on the combination of consumer and mortgage credit. In some ways, their paper echoed elements of the Luckett and August (1985) effort of two decades earlier, because both papers interestingly outline and explore a litany of possible reasons that consumer debt may have risen in the longer term. Dynan and Kohn specifically discuss implications for consumers' credit use of changes in both supply and demand factors.

Because Dynan and Kohn explore the combination of consumer and mortgage credit, their discussion is somewhat different from that in the other papers described here, in that it finds special importance for the growth of housing prices as an explanatory factor in the recent rise in debt use. In 2008 and 2009, financial markets found out how important the growth of housing prices had become to mortgage credit growth, with devastating consequences for many financial institutions. Their paper is similar to the others, however, in that it does not note any especially worrisome new trends specifically in the consumer credit area.

In 2010, Durkin, Ord, and Walker (2010) examined the long-term income elasticity of consumer and mortgage credit growth since World War II. They found econometrically that over this period, credit growth had not changed as dramatically as was frequently supposed. Using a vector autoregressive error correction (VAREC) model, they found that growth experience had been very close to that projected by Enthoven more than fifty years before.

DISTRIBUTION OF CONSUMER CREDIT USE

From the discussion so far, it is not obvious that consumer credit growth in the post–World War II years warrants the gloomy assessments sometimes associated with it, whether expressed in dollars or in typical analytic form as an aggregate ratio of credit outstanding to income. Neither the trends in the ratio itself nor the conclusions of the serious analysts of consumer credit give clear reasons for the expressions of concern so often articulated in other quarters. There still are distributional questions worth exploring, however, because by themselves, the aggregates do not indicate how the debt and income may be spread among an economically diverse population. A potentially disturbing possibility is that income growth may not accrue to the same consumers who increase their credit use. Credit use may only be among lower-income consumers, for example, while only higher-income individuals receive pay raises and become better off financially, maybe never needing to use credit. Or the relationships among credit users and income earners may change over time (for better or worse). Because of such questions, it is useful also to look at cross-section evidence that arrays the holdings of debts and the reception of income. Consequently, this section introduces this so far missing element in the discussions of rising debt burdens: the distribution of debts and burdens across the population.

Basically, there are at least two possibilities for the slowly increasing aggregate ratio of debt to income over time (there also may be some combination of the two): (1) more people have taken on some debts (wider dispersion of credit use and, therefore, greater total debt), given income; or (2) at least some previous debtors have taken on more debt relative to income (increased intensity of use). The former is possibly more sanguine than the latter, but how much of which is happening? If debt is simply becoming more widespread across the population (maybe because of a changing population age distribution or changed cultural attitudes toward debt), then spending patterns may be less affected by increasing indebtedness than if some population segments are using debt much more intensely and becoming overloaded. Of course, wider debt dispersion might also indicate that less creditworthy consumers are now receiving some credit. What is more or less sanguine is to a degree in the eye of the beholder.

As discussed in chapter 1, the only way to examine such distributional matters is through surveys of the actual holders of assets and debts, and for this reason, the Federal Reserve has sponsored or cosponsored the series known as the Surveys of Consumer Finances, beginning in 1946. The latest available data are for 2010. (Results of the 2013 survey will become available in 2015.)

Incidence of Credit Use

Prevalence of credit use and dollar amounts of credit outstanding are two areas in the Surveys of Consumer Finances in which there is enough consistency of questioning over time to permit constructing a time series of cross-section results. The resulting evidence over six decades shows how the slow long-term rise in the debt-to-income ratio is caused by both greater debt dispersion (debt widening) and greater credit use by the kinds of consumers already in debt (increased intensity, or debt deepening). The finding of a combination is not especially surprising, but it is also worth keeping in mind that the aggregate ratio of consumer credit to income has risen only moderately for nonmortgage consumer credit over these years, especially after the mid-1960s, despite some debt widening and deepening.

The surveys illustrate how the widening dispersion of debt use across the population that is sometimes referred to today as the democratization of credit is actually not new; debt widening has been going on for decades. Comparison of survey results show that in 1956, about 45 percent of American households were consumer installment credit users, a credit definition that included in those days only closed-end installment credit. The proportion of consumers using closed-end consumer installment credit rose only slightly to 50 percent by 1963 and has remained roughly within this range, at about 41 to 49 percent, since then (first line of table 2.1).[12]

12. Rather than using any data tables from other sources, the tables here were recalculated from the original source data in order to ensure, as far as possible, comparability of conception and definition of variables over time. For this reason, the data tables here may show some small differences from otherwise apparently comparable tables in other analyses using the same survey data. For example, the tables here always define credit for mobile homes as consumer credit and not mortgage credit

Table 2.1 Proportions of Households Using Credit, 1951–2010, in Percent

Type of Credit	1951	1956	1963	1970	1977	1983	1989	1995	2001	2004	2007	2010
Closed-end installment Credit	32	45	50	49	49	41	44	45	44	46	46	46
Note:												
Have auto credit (part of closed-end installment credit)	26	21	26	29	34	28	33	31	34	35	34	30
Credit card with revolving balance[a]				22	34	37	40	47	44	46	46	39
Notes:												
Have any credit card[a]				51	63	65	70	74	76	75	73	68
Have bank-type credit card				16	38	43	56	66	73	71	70	65
Have revolving balance on bank-type credit card				6	16	22	29	37	39	40	41	34
Consumer credit[b]	46	53	59	54	61	61	62	64	63	64	66	61
Mortgage credit[c]	20	24	32	35	40	39	38	39	42	45	46	44
Consumer credit or mortgage credit	53	62	67	64	70	69	70	72	73	75	75	73

[a]In 1995–2004, includes a few respondents with open-end retail revolving credit accounts not necessarily evidenced by a plastic credit card.

[b]Closed-end installment credit, open-end installment credit (including credit card accounts and unsecured lines of credit), and noninstallment credit (excluding credit for business or investment purposes).

[c]Includes home equity credit and home equity lines of credit with balance outstanding.

SOURCE: Data from the Surveys of Consumer Finances.

Beginning in 1970, however, survey changes made it possible to provide more detail on use of credit cards. Most credit cards in 1970 were issued by retail stores and gasoline companies for use only at their own outlets. Many of these issuers originally provided only charge cards, where payment of the bill in full was due shortly after receipt, and the amounts of credit outstanding were counted within noninstallment credit. But attaching a revolving credit feature to these cards was rapidly becoming more popular by 1970.

Even more important for consumer credit markets in the long run, three-party cards such as MasterCard and Visa (then known as Master Charge and BankAmericard) began to become widely available from banks in the late 1960s. Originally issued only by commercial banking organizations, these cards are often still called bank-type credit cards, although other financial institutions, including savings institutions, credit unions, and others, now also issue them. Bank-type cards were in the pockets and purses of only 16 percent of households in 1970, but the proportion grew to 73 percent in 2001, before falling off slightly to 70 percent in 2007 and 65 percent in 2010 following the sharp recession that ended the previous year (fifth line of table 2.1). Over these decades, as discussed further in chapter 1, credit cards have taken over much of the work of routine extension of consumer credit for many household purposes. Including those consumers with outstanding balances on charge accounts and later revolving credit card accounts within the definition of consumer credit users raises the total proportion of consumer credit using households from 46 percent in 1951 and 53 percent in 1956 to more than 60 percent since 1977 (line 7 of the table).

Mortgage credit use has also increased in the postwar period. The surveys reveal that only about one-fifth of households had mortgage credit outstanding in 1951, but this proportion rose rapidly from 1951 to 1963; it then continued to rise more slowly for another decade and a half until the 1977 survey (line 8 of the table). For about two decades, the proportion of households measured by the surveys with mortgage credit outstanding fluctuated in a narrow range right around two-fifths, before rising a bit in the new century to a peak of 46 percent in 2007. Combining all the sorts of credit frequently used by consumers, the proportion of households using at least some kind of consumer-oriented credit (installment credit, revolving credit card balance, or mortgage credit) reached three-quarters in the 2004 survey and remained in the same range, at 73 in 2010 (last line of the table).

Distribution of Consumer Credit within Population Segments

The surveys also permit examination of trends in debt use within population segments. Sometimes the view is expressed that use of consumer credit is a

(since mobile homes are not real property, and credit to purchase them is consumer credit in the Federal Reserve Board's statistical series). But such credit may not always be considered consumer credit instead of mortgage credit by other analysts (since it is housing related), and other analysts may prefer to keep mobile home credit with the rest of housing related debt. There also may be other definitional differences between these and tables in other sources. The definitions of consumer credit employed here follow Federal Reserve usage, as discussed above.

low-income or lower-middle-income phenomenon and that any credit expansion might well promote more woe than benefit. Actually, the surveys show that low- and middle-income consumers have always been users of consumer credit, but it is more nearly correct to say that consumer credit use is a middle- to upper-income phenomenon.

To look at the use of consumer credit by income level, respondents to each of the Surveys of Consumer Finances illustrated in table 2.1 were arrayed according to income and then placed in one of five groups of equal size (quintiles) from lowest to highest income. Looking at income quintiles this way frees the discussion from the issue of how the definition of "low income" or "high income" might change over time because of either inflation or economic growth. In each year, the lowest-income quintile, for example, includes the fifth of the surveyed population with the lowest incomes, and the highest-income quintile consists of the upper one-fifth of the population grouped by income.

Table 2.2 shows the proportion of each income quintile with some kind of consumer credit outstanding at the time of the survey (including closed- or open-end installment credit and noninstallment credit) for each of the survey years illustrated in the preceding table. The second panel of the table provides a similar look at the proportions with *any* sort of consumer-oriented credit outstanding (installment credit, noninstallment credit, or mortgage credit) for the same income groupings over the same span of years. Table 2.3 then measures the proportion of households with these kinds of credit outstanding among population age groups arrayed from the youngest respondents to the oldest.

These tables reveal that there has been growth in consumer credit use in all income and age segments from 1951 to 2010. Among income groups, the greatest relative growth in frequency of credit use occurred in the lowest income quintiles from 1951 to 1963, but since then, growth in the credit-using population has been slight in the three lower income groups and only moderate in the upper groups (upper panel of table 2.2).[13] Each of the three highest income groupings registered half or more of their members as consumer credit users as long ago as 1951 (lines 3, 4, and 5 of the upper panel of table 2.2), and the proportion in the third and fourth quintiles reached two-thirds by 1963 and has remained at or above this level since then (lines 3 and 4).

The patterns are similar for the "any credit" part of the table, although at a higher level. As with consumer credit alone, the growth in the proportion using any credit (including either consumer or mortgage credit) was greatest among the lowest income quintile over the whole period of 1951 to 2010, but only about half of this group were users in 2010 (line 1, lower panel of table 2.2). Credit use among the highest two income quintiles reached about four-fifths by 1970 and has remained above that high level over the following decades (lines 4 and 5).

13. There is a drop in credit use among the lowest income segment recorded by the 1970 survey. This may reflect that 1970 was the only recession year among the survey years in the table. The 2010 survey followed the end of a sharp recession by about six months. It also shows a general drop in credit use.

Table 2.2 Proportions of Households Using Consumer-Related Credit by Income Group, 1951–2010, in Percent

	1951	1956	1963	1970	1977	1983	1989	1995	2001	2004	2007	2010
Consumer credit[a]												
Income quintile												
Lowest	24	37	45	26	38	38	43	44	44	45	45	46
Second lowest	41	57	58	49	57	53	52	60	62	60	59	55
Middle	56	59	67	65	68	69	69	70	71	72	76	67
Second highest	55	61	69	70	73	75	78	78	73	74	80	74
Highest	52	52	59	57	71	72	68	70	62	69	68	65
All	46	53	59	54	61	61	62	64	63	64	66	61
Any credit (consumer credit or mortgage credit)												
Income quintile												
Lowest	29	40	46	30	44	42	45	47	47	51	50	51
Second lowest	46	61	64	56	62	58	58	66	68	67	66	64
Middle	63	67	74	75	76	76	76	77	81	83	83	80
Second highest	64	70	78	81	84	84	85	86	84	85	90	86
Highest	63	71	75	79	85	87	86	86	86	88	87	84
All	53	62	67	64	70	69	70	72	73	75	75	73

[a]Closed-end installment credit, open-end installment credit (including credit card accounts), and noninstallment credit (excluding credit for business or financial investment purposes).

SOURCE: Data from the Surveys of Consumer Finances.

Table 2.3 Proportions of Households Using Consumer-Related Credit by Age Group of Family Head, 1951–2010, in Percent

	1951	1956	1963	1970	1977	1983	1989	1995	2001	2004	2007	2010
Consumer credit[a]												
Age group												
Younger than 35	54	71	76	70	77	74	74	78	76	72	76	71
35–44	61	60	72	67	78	78	78	78	74	76	72	73
45–54	45	54	62	60	69	70	71	72	68	72	72	68
55–64	34	42	45	42	54	55	53	59	58	62	66	60
65–74[b]	16	19	26	16	26	29	38	41	42	44	51	48
75 and older				9	13	13	17	22	23	30	23	27
All	46	53	59	54	61	61	62	64	63	64	66	61
Any credit (consumer credit or mortgage credit)												
Age group												
Younger than 35	59	76	81	76	82	79	78	82	81	78	82	76
35–44	69	74	82	83	90	87	88	85	87	87	85	84
45–54	54	63	72	74	82	81	83	83	83	88	85	82
55–64	42	52	53	51	65	66	65	73	73	74	80	75
65–74[b]	23	25	33	27	34	36	47	51	54	57	63	64
75 and older				14	13	17	20	26	28	40	30	35
All	53	62	67	64	70	69	70	72	73	75	75	73

[a]Closed-end installment credit, open-end installment credit (including credit card accounts), and noninstallment credit (excluding credit for business or investment purposes).

[b]In 1951, 1956, and 1963, 65 and older.

SOURCE: Data from the Surveys of Consumer Finances.

Within age groups, consumer credit use has always been most prevalent among younger consumers. It has long been understood that use of credit is strongly influenced by stage of life cycle. Households headed by younger individuals, for example, are more likely below their long-term average lifetime income level. They also are bearing the costs of acquiring housing and household durable goods, rearing and educating children, and so on, and so they are willing to use credit knowing that their ability to repay debts that finance these activities likely will be rising. Consequently, it is not especially surprising that more than three-fifths of households with heads younger than forty-five were consumer credit users in the mid-1950s, and this proportion rose to three-quarters in 1977 and has remained around that level since then (lines 1 and 2 of the upper panel of table 2.3).

In contrast, households near or past retirement may not have as many such needs, and they may also have accumulated more liquid savings and not need to use credit as often. This life cycle effect is also visible in table 2.3, although the greatest growth of credit in percentage terms occurred among older consumers. The proportion of those using consumer credit in the fifty-five to sixty-four age bracket rose substantially over these years, to about three-fifths by 1995 (line 4 of the upper panel). Furthermore, only about one-fifth of households with heads older than sixty-five were consumer credit users in the 1950s, but this proportion rose sharply until 1989 and has continued to rise since then (lines 5 and 6). Thus, along with population growth, it seems that an aging population, combined with a higher proportion of older consumers who still use consumer credit, accounts for at least some of the increase in consumer credit outstanding in recent decades.

Enlarging the credit use concept to include also mortgage credit produces a use pattern across age groups that is similar over time to the pattern for consumer credit use but naturally at a higher level (lower panel of table 2.3). Older consumers again were the least likely to be debtors, but the percentage increase over the decades in the older age groups using some form of credit likewise has been the sharpest.

Shares of Credit Outstanding

Cross-section surveys also permit calculation of the share of total debt held by various groups of consumers. The next two tables contain calculated shares of selected kinds of debt outstanding owed by consumers segmented first by income (table 2.4) and then by age (table 2.5). Results of this effort turn out to be revealing, and maybe a bit surprising, in light of ongoing discussions in recent years about the overall democratization of credit.

The central message from the distribution of debt shares measured by the cross-section surveys is stability over time rather than dramatic change; there have been debt increases in all income and age groups, leaving the shares quite similar over time. Focusing on consumer credit, the third panel of table 2.4 shows that the upper two income quintiles owed 58 percent of consumer credit outstanding in 1951, exactly the same proportion as in 2010. It must be kept in mind, of course, that some of this pattern is produced by keeping the sizes of the income

Table 2.4 SHARES OF KINDS OF CONSUMER-RELATED DEBT OUTSTANDING BY INCOME GROUPS, 1951–2010, IN PERCENT

	1951	1956	1963	1970	1977	1983	1989	1995	2001	2004	2007	2010
Closed-end consumer installment credit												
Income quintile												
Lowest	7	6	6	3	5	4	4	7	8	9	8	12
Second lowest	14	12	15	16	13	12	9	13	15	14	12	11
Middle	22	23	25	24	23	19	22	22	21	19	22	20
Second highest	27	30	26	31	27	27	34	28	28	30	30	25
Highest	31	29	27	27	31	37	31	30	29	29	29	32
All	100	100	100	100	100	100	100	100	100	100	100	100
Revolving balances on any credit card												
Income quintile												
Lowest				2	4	4	2	7	7	7	6	6
Second lowest				10	12	10	9	15	13	14	9	11
Middle				24	19	20	21	20	22	23	18	18
Second highest				35	35	30	30	24	26	26	32	27
Highest				30	31	36	38	34	32	30	34	38
All				100	100	100	100	100	100	100	100	100

(*Continued*)

Table 2.4 (Continued)

	1951	1956	1963	1970	1977	1983	1989	1995	2001	2004	2007	2010
Consumer credit[a]												
Income quintile												
Lowest	6	10	8	3	5	7	5	7	8	8	9	12
Second lowest	14	14	14	15	13	12	10	13	15	14	11	11
Middle	23	22	25	24	22	18	22	21	21	20	20	19
Second highest	27	25	25	31	28	25	32	27	27	29	30	25
Highest	31	29	28	27	32	38	31	31	29	29	29	33
All	100	100	100	100	100	100	100	100	100	100	100	100
Mortgage credit												
Income quintile												
Lowest	3	2	2	2	3	3	1	2	2	3	3	4
Second lowest	8	5	7	7	7	6	5	7	5	6	5	7
Middle	17	16	15	17	17	12	12	12	14	15	15	14
Second highest	28	26	31	31	28	25	26	26	24	24	26	25
Highest	44	51	45	43	44	54	56	53	54	53	51	51
All	100	100	100	100	100	100	100	100	100	100	100	100

Any credit (consumer or mortgage)

Income quintile											
Lowest	4	4	3	2	4	4	2	3	3	4	5
Second lowest	9	7	8	8	8	7	6	8	8	6	7
Middle	18	17	17	18	18	13	14	14	16	15	15
Second highest	28	26	30	31	28	25	27	26	24	27	26
Highest	42	46	42	40	42	51	51	49	49	48	48
All	100	100	100	100	100	100	100	100	100	100	100

[a]Closed-end installment credit, open-end installment credit (including credit card accounts), and noninstallment credit (excluding credit for business or investment purposes).

Columns may not add to totals because of rounding.

SOURCE: Data from the Surveys of Consumer Finances.

Table 2.5 SHARES OF KINDS OF CONSUMER-RELATED DEBT OUTSTANDING BY AGE GROUPS OF FAMILY HEADS, 1951–2010, IN PERCENT

	1951	1956	1963	1970	1977	1983	1989	1995	2001	2004	2007	2010
Closed-end consumer installment credit												
Age group												
Younger than 35	33	42	38	46	41	37	31	35	32	27	35	30
35–44	33	31	28	21	23	27	31	28	32	26	22	25
45–54	21	18	22	22	20	21	22	24	21	21	23	23
55–64	9	8	9	10	13	12	10	8	10	14	14	14
65–74[a]	4	2	5	1	2	3	4	3	3	4	5	5
75 and older				0	1	0	1	1	1	8	1	3
All	100	100	100	100	100	100	100	100	100	100	100	100
Revolving balances on any credit card												
Age group												
Younger than 35				44	35	29	32	27	25	16	16	12
35–44				25	23	30	29	29	28	27	23	25
45–54				21	27	20	21	26	24	29	27	31
55–64				9	11	16	11	11	12	15	22	19
65–74[a]				1	3	4	6	5	9	8	10	8
75 and older				0	0	1	1	1	2	5	2	4
All				100	100	100	100	100	100	100	100	100

Consumer credit[b]

Age group

Younger than 35	34	36	37	45	40	35	32	33	30	25	30	26
35–44	32	28	27	21	24	26	31	28	31	26	22	25
45–54	21	20	22	22	20	20	21	25	22	23	24	24
55–64	10	10	9	10	12	14	10	9	11	14	17	16
65–74[a]	3	5	5	1	2	3	4	4	5	5	6	6
75 and older				0	1	1	2	1	1	7	1	3
All	100	100	100	100	100	100	100	100	100	100	100	100

Mortgage credit

Age group

Younger than 35	30	31	27	29	38	29	29	20	18	18	19	15
35–44	33	39	36	36	30	34	38	34	32	29	27	26
45–54	23	18	25	24	20	20	19	29	30	31	28	30
55–64	10	8	8	7	9	12	11	12	13	16	18	19
65–74[a]	3	3	3	3	2	3	3	4	6	4	7	8
75 and older				0	0	0	1	1	1	2	1	3
All	100	100	100	100	100	100	100	100	100	100	100	100

(Continued)

Table 2.5 (CONTINUED)

	1951	1956	1963	1970	1977	1983	1989	1995	2001	2004	2007	2010
Any credit (consumer or mortgage)												
Age group												
Younger than 35	31	33	29	32	38	30	30	23	20	19	21	16
35–44	33	37	35	34	29	33	36	33	32	28	26	26
45–54	23	19	25	23	20	20	19	28	29	30	27	29
55–64	10	8	8	8	10	13	11	12	12	15	18	18
65–74[a]	3	4	3	3	2	3	3	4	6	4	7	8
75 and older				0	0	0	1	1	1	3	1	3
All	100	100	100	100	100	100	100	100	100	100	100	100

[a] In 1956 and 1963, 65 and older.

[b] Closed-end installment credit, open-end installment credit (including credit card accounts), and noninstallment credit (excluding credit for business or investment purposes).

Columns may not add to totals because of rounding.

SOURCE: Data from the Surveys of Consumer Finances.

groups the same (quintiles). If the group sizes were allowed to change over time, say, groups representing "low income" versus "middle class" or "comfortable," the amount of debt owed by the latter would undoubtedly rise as the group becomes larger because of increasing income and wealth among the population as a whole over time.

The similarity over the long period is also evident in the mortgage debt shares held among income groups, especially if 1956 is used as the base year. In that year, the upper two income groups held 77 percent of the mortgage debt; in 2010, it was 76 percent (lines 4 and 5, fourth panel of the table). Not surprisingly, the total debt portion of the table reflects the similarity of the components.

By age, where the size of the groupings is not static, the story is a bit different. Younger families have always been larger users of credit, but there has been a gradual shift of the share owed toward older users over the decades. Households classified as headed by individuals younger than forty-five have been and remain the largest users of consumer credit, but these households have lost share since 1951 (lines 1 and 2 of the third panel of table 2.5). Households with heads older than forty-five have increased their shares of installment credit owed, presumably in part because the population has aged.

Balances owed on credit cards definitely show an aging effect (second panel of the table). In 1970, when credit cards with a revolving credit feature were relatively new, the youngest households owed 44 percent of the card debt (line 1). This probably represents the ages-old phenomenon of the young being more willing to try new things. By 2010, when the older cohort surveyed that year had literally grown up using credit cards, the share of card debt owed by households in the youngest age grouping had fallen by more than two-thirds to 12 percent. The bulk of the offsetting increases in share were among households with heads older than forty-five.

Mortgage credit and total credit also show a shifting toward a greater portion of the debt owed by older consumers over time (panels 4 and 5 of the table). In 1956, households headed by individuals younger than forty-five owed about 70 percent of mortgage credit and total credit to consumers (last two panels of the table). By 2010, these proportions were less than half, with households with heads older than fifty-four picking up much of the difference. In 2010, households headed by individuals older than fifty-four owed 30 percent of mortgage credit and 29 percent of total credit owed by consumers, up from 11 to 12 percent in 1956.

Previous Studies Using Cross-Section Data

Over the years, researchers have used the Surveys of Consumer Finances both to examine current conditions and to test hypotheses about a variety of aspects of consumers' financial behavior, especially concerning spending and saving. In describing the surveys, Katona et al. (1960–1970 [1961], xix) pointed out many years ago that the surveys had two main purposes: "to obtain a variety of statistics which were previously not available, and to promote the understanding of consumer behavior." In the credit area, the data permit analyses of the distribution of debts, such as the tables in the previous section of this chapter. Although it is always possible to find some woeful individual cases in any survey, the frequency of severe credit difficulties has not been the main focus of the survey efforts. Rather, the main thrust of these cross-section studies has been to review the over-all debt picture, not to examine only a limited number of unfortunate cases.

The basic data from the Surveys of Consumer Finances in the 1940s and 1950s are found in a large group of articles in the *Federal Reserve Bulletin*.[14] Data from the surveys in the 1960s are in a series of monographs, one for each year, issued by the Institute for Social Research of the University of Michigan (Katona et al. 1961–1970); and tables for 1977 are in Durkin and Elliehausen (1978). After 1977, data highlights are again found in a series of articles in the *Federal Reserve Bulletin*.[15] Over the years, many analysts have used the data in a long list of articles and monographs that explore a variety of questions associated with use of consumer credit. The following are a few noteworthy examples.

One of the economists mentioned above as coauthoring a paper on long-term trends in consumer credit growth also analyzed some surveys. In a paper presented to a convention of business economics analysts during the 1990 recession, Federal Reserve Board economist Charles A. Luckett again referred to the experience that rising consumer debt relative to income "periodically provokes questions about whether consumer debt is 'too high'" (Luckett 1990, 1). He reminded readers that to evaluate this question, one ideally would like to have data on the joint distribution of debt and income in the population, which is only available from surveys and not obtainable from broad statistics such as the aggregate debt-to-income ratio. With survey data, analysts can explore such questions as the extent to which the debt in the aggregate ratios is held or not by those with the resources to repay it comfortably.

Luckett investigated this and related questions using the 1983 Survey of Consumer Finances. He found that there clearly are some people with debt difficulties, but on the whole, he suggested that the cross-section picture is more reassuring than disturbing. After exploring such questions as the distribution of consumer debt by income and asset levels, he provided some interesting conclusions in a summary that he used to open the paper:

> Analysis of the survey data revealed installment debt to be heavily concentrated within the higher income segment of the population (the lowest income quintile holding 7 percent of the debt and highest income

---

14. Fifty-five articles in the *Federal Reserve Bulletin* from 1946 to 1959 are listed in a bibliography in chapter 17 of Katona et al. (1960–1970 [1961]), along with a variety of other articles and books using the survey data.

15. See Avery, Elliehausen, Canner, and Gustafson (1984); Kennickell and Shack-Marquez (1992); Kennickell and Starr-McCluer (1994); Kennickell, Starr-McCluer, and Sunden (1997); Kennickell, Starr-McCluer, and Surette (2000); Aizcorbe, Kennickell, and Moore (2003); Bucks, Kennickell, and Moore (2006), Bucks, Kennickell, Mach, and Moore (2009), and Bricker, Kennickell, Moore, and Sabelhaus (2012).

quintile holding 43 percent). In addition, debtors in the two highest income groups held substantially more financial assets than they owed on consumer debt. Both these facts suggest that the bulk of consumer debt is owed by households with the resources to manage their debts....

In all, relatively few debtor households (58 out of 2168) were characterized by having both low income and large debts. Examination of individual cases found that many of them in fact held sizable amounts of assets, and that many of the remainder were much younger and better educated than the norm, i.e., were at a stage of their earnings cycle with a favorable outlook for future income and asset growth.

On balance, study of consumer debt on a disaggregated basis tended to alleviate rather than aggravate concern over the capacity of consumers to handle their debt loads. (Luckett 1990, 2)

A few years later, he and two other Federal Reserve economists compared results of three successive Surveys of Consumer Finances and reached largely similar conclusions (Canner, Kennickell, and Luckett 1995). Examining these three particular surveys permitted study of credit conditions in a year well before the mild recession of 1990 (namely, 1983), just before the recession (1989), and shortly after (1992). The authors compared such measures as incidence of debt use, amounts of debt outstanding, debt-to-income ratios, and shares of total debt held by various population subgroups classified by demographic and financial characteristics such as income, age, and assets. They found that household survey information is easily consistent with the pattern of slower credit growth revealed by the aggregate statistics during these years (figures 2.2 through 2.6, above). According to their summary:

Data collected from individual households in 1983, 1989, and 1992 generally confirm the observations drawn from the aggregate statistics. At the all household level, the surveys show a pattern of rise and subsequent decline over 1983–1992 in ratios of debt-service payments to income and indicate that the incidence of late payments on loans was lower in 1992 than in the other survey years. (Canner, Kennickell, and Luckett 1995, 336)

Two other economists associated with the Federal Reserve examined debt burden measures using the 1989, 1992, and 1995 Surveys of Consumer Finances. Edelberg and Fisher (1997) compared aggregate debt burden measured as total household debt service payments to income, a flow-to-flow ratio, with a similar measure constructed from the consumer surveys, both for all consumers and within income groupings. Their conclusion, much like that of many others, was that the available information does not suggest significant overburdening in the consumer sector:

We have presented new evidence on the household burden from the Survey of Consumer Finances. Our analysis suggests that, perhaps contrary to evidence based on macro data, the household debt burden has not changed very much over the period covered by the survey and does not represent a substantial increase in macroeconomic sensitivity to interest rate changes. In addition, we have found that households have tended to use more secured debt over the period covered by the survey and that increases in credit card debt service of lower income households have been offset to a large extent by reductions in the servicing of installment debt. (Edelberg and Fisher 1997, 3)

Thus, the distributions of debt and debt payments among households grouped by various economic and demographic characteristics add further perspective on household sector finances. Although the picture is not unambiguously positive, and there certainly are individuals who experience debt difficulties, the overall thrust of the evidence from the disaggregated data is that much of the sector's debt is owed by households that have ample resources to service it. Households with high income and substantial net worth account for the bulk of the debt.

CONSUMER CREDIT AND THE NEWS MEDIA

If neither long-term consumer credit growth patterns nor distribution of consumer credit across the population as a whole seems to suggest unambiguously worrisome trends, the question remains of why consumer credit growth seems to generate alarm, as Prell put it, regardless of time considered. Availability of consumer credit has obvious benefits early in an economic recovery. As the economy begins to improve after a recession, consumer credit expansion can bolster retail sales, industrial production, and the pickup in economic growth. These things happen in every upswing, but even casual perusal of old newspaper files on consumer credit suggests that credit growth also typically generates a variety of concerns.

Apparently, increasing credit use in economic advances, and the inevitable buildup of consumer debt levels that results, has a tendency to lead observers, including reporters, to have misgivings about longer-term economic prospects. Examining aggregate statistics, such as the nominal level of consumer credit outstanding, its recent growth rate, and the ratio of total consumer debt to income, they fear that increasing consumer credit promises future economic problems. Press attention then demonstrates concerns for both the economic health of the individual (microeconomics) and the well-being of the whole economy (macroeconomics). For example, articles often contend that the debt burden creates possibilities of both overextensions and bankruptcies among consumers, often illustrated with sorrowful individual examples. On the macroeconomic side, there may be discussions of overall slowdowns in consumer spending arising from the overhang of debt. The worry with the latter is that the sheer size of the consumer sector of the economy almost dictates that any spending hiatus will cause an overall economic recession.

When reporters articulate gloomy views, the question naturally arises of whether this is good reporting of the consumer credit aspect of the business cycle. At least two important issues are involved here. First, do reporters, as is being implied, in fact tend to concentrate on the negative aspects of consumer credit? It may be that bad news is just more noticeable or more easily remembered but that the actual reporting of consumer credit trends is more balanced or even mostly favorable. Second, if news attention toward credit matters does focus especially on negative aspects of experience, are such views well founded? If, for example, experience demonstrates that reporters gloomily forecast outcomes that actually happen, then it seems that the reporting is appropriate. If, in contrast, the reporting pattern frequently presents worrisome outlooks but actual economic experience is much better on average, then its value is more questionable.

A paper by Durkin and Jonasson (2002) quantified the content of reporters' commentary in a particular important news source (the *New York Times*) on the economics of consumer credit and debt burden over a long period of time and to compare the commentary with actual economic developments. They developed and tested specific hypotheses about news reporting in the area of consumer credit compared with actual credit growth and business cycle patterns both over individual business cycles and among cycles over time.

The authors offered a number of hypotheses: (1) news reports on consumer credit emphasize negative views and analysis, (2) reporting on consumer credit shows cyclicality correlating with the business cycle, (3) negative reporting about consumer credit concentrates around the time of the business cycle downswing, and (4) reporting on consumer credit exhibits a similar content pattern from one cycle to another. To explore these hypotheses, they undertook an extended content analysis of all the articles on consumer credit in the *New York Times* over a forty-five-year period from 1950 to 1995. In effect, content analysis as they engaged in it is analogous to performing a questionnaire study on inanimate subjects (in this case, words in the newspaper). To do this, they carefully designed rules and procedures that involved reading every article in the newspaper index for consumer credit over the years in question, separated the articles they determined under their rules were "topical" and "significant" in their analysis, as opposed to mere mention of new government statistical reports without analysis, and established rules for classifying and weighting articles and sections of articles in a variety of ways, including by subject matter, size, placement, prominence, "voices" of speakers, speaker methodology, and overall tone. In all, the procedures tabulated thirty-one variables for each "significant" article in six groupings (see Durkin and Jonasson 2002, table III).

Overall, they found agreement with all of their hypotheses about the news reporting on developments in consumer credit. Probably not surprisingly, they found that on balance, news reports were predominantly negative. Probably more interesting, they also found that the negativity increased over the time horizon of the study. Negativity further increased when the universe of opinions was limited to the reporters themselves (the reporters' "voice") rather than the views of others they interviewed.

The evidence from the data also supported their other hypotheses. Reporting about the economics of consumer credit appears to be intensely cyclical, correlating well with the pattern of the business cycle itself. In addition, positive reporting on consumer credit appears to take place most often around the middle of the cyclical upswing, with negative reporting concentrating early and late in the upswing and in the downturn. Furthermore, this pattern seems quite similar from one cycle to another.

Their evidence clearly shows the cyclicality of consumer credit reporting, but they found in their review of the articles on consumer credit that the pattern of reporting on consumer credit over the business cycle actually "contradicts the content of the articles themselves" (Durkin and Jonasson 2002, 24). They found that reporting on the negative aspects of consumer credit growth is actually greatest in the parts of the business cycle when growth is slow and most benign when growth is more rapid, despite the contentions that the rapid growth causes economic problems. In their view:

> This pattern would seem to indicate that consumer credit growth is not an agenda-setting item for reporters [reference omitted]; it appears that reporters do not set their own agenda concerning reporting of credit growth. Rather, they follow developments, but the developments they follow when reporting about credit conditions are more closely associated with other economic indicators than with credit changes, despite the content of the articles. The pattern (timing) of articles may be determined by a different set of considerations than what is reported. (Durkin and Jonasson 2002, 25)

In further statistical work, they found that trends in inflation actually forecast trends in reporting about consumer credit growth better than the consumer credit growth trends themselves. This finding did not encourage them concerning the likelihood that consumers would learn much about the significance of consumer credit trends by reading the newspaper, although they noted that the findings were from only one newspaper, albeit an important one. They suggested the usefulness of also studying other news sources, including other newspapers, magazines, and electronic sources. As of this writing, such analysis has not been done.

CONCLUSIONS

In sum, consumer credit use has grown sharply in the post–World War II era but not very much relative to income or assets since the early 1960s. Historical patterns in these ratios have been intensely cyclical, however, which likely at least partially explains why there are expressions of concern when they rise, despite lack of firm evidence that rising debt ratios have led to economic calamity. Debt growth has occurred in all income and age groups, but the bulk of consumer credit outstanding currently is owed by the younger and higher-income population segments, much as in the past. The share of consumer credit outstanding owed by the upper income fifth of the income distribution was 33 percent in 2010, not much different from 1951, despite interim fluctuations. The proportion of mortgage debt owed by the upper income fifth rose a bit by 2010 compared with 1951 but not at all since 1956, again despite some interim fluctuations. By age, younger consumers still owe more of consumer and mortgage credit than consumers older than fifty-four, but more older consumers owe on mortgages and consumer credit recently than in the immediate postwar years, and the share owed by older consumers has increased.

3

The Demand for Consumer Credit

The previous chapters have noted how individuals have taken on debt obligations since antiquity, but economists largely ignored consumer credit until early in the twentieth century.[1] In the late eighteenth century, classical economist Adam Smith (1723–1790), generally considered the patriarch of modern economics, mostly dismissed the question of credit use for consumer purposes because of his belief that such credit could never be popular, since it was contrary to individuals' self-interest and innate thriftiness. In the nineteenth century, British economist and philosopher John Stuart Mill (1806–1873) viewed credit for consumers as a diversion of resources from productive uses, a view very close to the popular perception of the time. According to Mill, "Credit given by dealers to unproductive consumers is never an addition, but always a detriment to the sources of public wealth. It makes over in temporary use, not the capital of unproductive classes to the productive, but that of the productive to the unproductive" (Mill 1909, 513).

By the early years of the twentieth century, however, consumer credit use had become somewhat common, and entrepreneurs had established or were building much of the modern institutional framework to support it. These changes practically begged analysts to reevaluate the growing consumer credit phenomenon with the tools of modern economic analysis. In the 1920s, this led to the first major effort to examine consumers' credit decisions based on the theory of rational economic choice. Subsequently, economists have extended the basic economic choice model, considered additional psychological influences, and examined the effects of institutional change over time on consumers' credit-using behavior.

This chapter explores factors associated with consumers' choices to use credit, including psychological influences and institutional changes that affect their demand for credit. The next chapter expands on the psychological discussion. Taken together, the chapters review the development of thought in this area and examine the reasons so many consumers enter into credit obligations. It is notable that many controversial issues addressed by early analysts remain today in the forefront of policy discussions about consumer credit use and are at least partly

1. For a long view of the use of credit by individuals, from ancient civilizations to the present, see Homer and Sylla (1996) and Gelpi and Julien-Labruyere (2000).

unresolved in the minds of some observers of modern credit markets. Some critics still question the rationality of consumer credit use based on the very same objections raised long ago. These views have persisted into the twenty-first century despite years of subsequent research into credit-using motivation and behavior that have produced favorable conclusions about much of consumer credit demand and wide public acceptance of its usefulness.

EMERGENCE OF MODERN CONSUMER CREDIT

Ultimately, consumer credit and the modern consumer credit industry in the United States emerged with growth of the middle class and the increasing availability and affordability of consumer durable goods in the second half of the nineteenth and the first decades of the twentieth centuries. Industrialization not only enlarged the numbers and incomes of middle-class consumers in the period following the Civil War, but it also reduced the cost of producing many goods and brought about the production of new consumer goods. Employment of electricity and the internal-combustion engine stimulated the growth of whole new industries of consumer-oriented durable products in the six decades following the end of the Civil War.

At the same time, many consumers began to generate monetary surpluses in their monthly budgets after meeting basic needs for food and shelter. For the first time in history, consumers experienced this phenomenon on a broad basis. The cash cost of many of the new consumer durable goods still generally exceeded the monthly surplus in most consumers' budgets, though, highlighting the problem of lumpy expenditure outflows compared with more constant wage and salary inflows noted in chapter 1. Consumers could, of course, accumulate monthly surpluses until they could afford to purchase large-ticket durable goods for cash, but for reasons that constitute the core of this chapter, this often was not the preferred time pattern if alternatives were available. They soon became available.

Specifically, many merchants began to facilitate purchases of large-ticket durable goods in the later years of the nineteenth century by providing for installment sales to consumers on credit, a development that became even more pronounced after World War I. Installment credit entailed weekly or monthly periodic payments better attuned to the resources available in consumers' budgets during these short time intervals. Furniture, sewing machines, pianos and parlor organs, coal furnace stokers, and later automobiles and electric appliances were commonly financed using installment credit. Installment credit for specific purchases allowed consumers to pay for items as they used them. Not only was the timing change preferable to many consumers, but it saved the costs of doing without or using alternatives in the meantime, for example, inconvenient public transportation, expensive work of tailors and seamstresses rather than using home sewing machines, and frequently visiting the market instead of refrigerating food at home.[2]

2. Calder (1999) extensively examines the cultural implications of the increasing use of consumer credit in his lively history of the phenomenon.

At the same time, loans of *cash* also became more widely available to households, although this kind of lending had to overcome a legal barrier that installment purchases of *goods* did not. In the developing urban areas, many families facing difficulties or financial emergencies often were newly displaced from their extended families, still on ancestral farms or in Europe and elsewhere, on whom they could have relied for help in times past. Statutory interest rate ceilings (known as usury laws or ceilings) initially limited the development of cash lending to help meet such needs, because the small amounts of legal interest did not cover the relatively large costs of making these loans and bearing the associated risk. This made small loans generally unprofitable and, for this reason, unattractive to potential lenders.[3]

But demand for cash loans encouraged such lending, and it developed nonetheless, first illegally and then legally following adjustment in usury and other lending laws. Before these legal changes, most small cash loans made by nonfamily sources were extended by those willing to break the law, not likely the most savory of businesses (often called loan sharks, then and now). Charitable organizations could not keep up with needs, and so beginning about 1910, many states enacted legislation creating special rate ceilings for personal lending, thus making small loans more attractive to legitimate lending enterprises.

Sale of goods on installment plans, as opposed to loans of cash, had been able to develop more quickly because of the "time price doctrine," a legal principle permitting a seller to establish two prices, a cash price for payment now and a different (higher) credit or "time price" for installment payment over some future period. Courts generally did not consider the difference between the cash price and the time price of goods as interest, enabling merchants (but not cash lenders) to avoid the restrictive usury ceilings that applied to cash loans. By the advent of World War I, both sales credit and legal cash credit on an installment repayment basis were widely available.[4]

Nonetheless, consumer credit generated controversy in the late nineteenth and early twentieth centuries, and it has never fully escaped from it. At that time, many people distinguished between "productive" credit, say for investment in a business or housing, both of which were good, and "consumptive" credit, which, in this view, was not so good. Productive credit, people believed, created wealth and therefore was acceptable. Consumptive credit included credit for furniture, household goods, clothing, and most other purposes, and many people believed that credit for such purposes merely facilitated living beyond one's means. In this view, obligating oneself to make future payments for the sake of immediate consumption was neither appropriate nor wise, an outlook still held by some people today. Low monthly payments on installment debt, many people contended,

---

3. See chapter 5 for discussion of lending costs and chapter 11 for discussion of state rate ceilings.

4. For more detailed history of the development of consumer credit and the institutions that grant it, see Michelman (1966), Rogers (1974), Olney (1991), Calder (1999), and Gelpi and Julien-Labruyere (2000). For historical development of the law, see Curran (1965).

merely enticed consumers to use too much debt, another position often articulated today. In this view, the burden of such debt resulted in hardship, and it exacerbated fluctuations in the business cycle by causing debt-strapped consumers to reduce spending sharply during recessions.[5]

DEVELOPMENT OF THE ECONOMICS OF CONSUMER CREDIT DEMAND

Concern over such views prompted the General Motors Company, which obviously had an interest in this debate, to seek in 1925 a reputable and independent researcher to study and write about the economics of consumer credit. The company approached Edwin Robert Anderson Seligman (1861–1939) of Columbia University, who was a leading authority on public finance, a founder of the American Economic Association, and one of the most respected academic economists in the country.[6] Before taking on this task, Seligman requested and was granted unrestricted access to General Motors' records on automobile financing and complete freedom to form his own conclusions and publish them. He released the resulting two-volume study, *The Economics of Installment Selling*, two years later (Seligman 1927).

Development of the Investment-Consumption Model

Seligman conducted a comprehensive study of consumer credit, containing descriptive, analytical, and empirical review. A major contribution of the study was Seligman's application to consumer credit of the theory of intertemporal investment-consumption choices, under development at that time by Yale economist Irving Fisher (1867–1947; see Fisher 1907 and 1930). Fisher's approach to investment analysis has become a part of standard microeconomics and today is the foundation of the branch of modern economic theory known as finance.

In his analysis of consumer lending, Seligman questioned some of the then-popular views about consumer credit. As noted, one component was a preference for production over consumption, which underlay the distinction between productive and consumptive credit popular at the time. Seligman reminded the reader that the ultimate goal of any production is consumption.

5. Extended discussion of the development, maintenance, and ultimate (incomplete) dissolution of the widely held view that creditworthiness is good but taking on consumer debt nonetheless is bad is a core element of Calder's (1999) cultural history of the development of consumer credit and its institutions.

6. Seligman was born April 25, 1861, just two weeks after the Civil War began on April 12 with Confederate bombardment of Fort Sumter, South Carolina. Apparently, his parents believed that Major Robert Anderson, the Union commander at Fort Sumter that day, was a hero.

Economists have always maintained this point, even if they have not always emphasized it, but it has not always been fully understood by lay observers. According to Adam Smith in 1776, for example, "Consumption is the sole end and purpose of all production;. . . the maxim is so perfectly self-evident, that it would be absurd to attempt to prove it" (Smith 1994, 715). Alfred Marshall (1842–1924), the noted Cambridge University neoclassical economist of the late nineteenth and early twentieth centuries, expressed this view similarly: "For consumption is the end of production; and all wholesome consumption is productive of benefits" (Marshall 1920, 56).

The underlying economic process is that production creates goods and services; the output can either be purchased and used by consumers (consumption) or otherwise retained and used to create more goods and services for the future (savings/investment). The latter component of current production provides for further production and consumption later. It is intuitive that savings/investment adds to wealth and makes consumers better off only if it produces future consumption that is more highly valued than the current consumption forgone to undertake the investment. Investment that does not satisfy this criterion does not create wealth and is not preferable to current consumption. In other words, investment must produce value through enhanced future consumption, or it will not be undertaken. But what is "value" in this context?

The old example of the fish net provides a useful, though simplified, illustration of this economic process. Suppose an individual works all day at fishing and spears enough fish (production) to provide for the daily food requirement of self and family with no leftovers (full consumption of all income and no saving). The next day, the family spear fisher labors again with the same result and never seems to "get ahead." Maybe the spear fisher eventually gets a little better at the task and sometimes produces a small daily surplus over the basic survival need to share with someone else or to enlarge the family, but there is never enough to get much beyond the need for the daily, dreary fishing task.

Now, suppose that technological change leads to invention of the fish net, expanding production (and consumption) possibilities measurably. If only the spear fisher could purchase such a net, the family could rapidly become much better off, eating better and trading surplus for other things.

But suppose also, for the purposes of this limited example, that the spear fisher is never able to store enough surplus out of the daily catch (without refrigeration) to be able to pay for a net through trading (that is, savings for investment is impossible). Therefore, even with technological change and the possibility of greater production, there is no change in the family's economic condition.

Enter the capitalist and financial markets. If a producer with a fish net and a surplus is willing one day to lend enough fish to the beleaguered laborer to permit trading for his or her own fish net, then there is a chance for an overall increase in both production and consumption by the struggling spear fisher. The question is under what circumstances would this lending/borrowing outcome reasonably be expected?

Fisher's investment-consumption theory provides the formal answer, but the fundamentals are also intuitive: the individual will borrow to purchase the fish net if doing so has a favorable impact on consumption possibilities *after* repaying the loan with any necessary interest. This is merely an informal rendering of Fisher's formal theoretical conclusion: borrowing to undertake the investment is rational if there is a positive *net present value* from the investment (in this example, from investing in the fish net). Under the condition of a positive net present value from borrowing and investing, the family of the (former) spear fisher clearly is better off. If, in contrast, borrowing to purchase the fish net does not produce a positive net return, then the rational choice is not to undertake the investment. The following subsection of this chapter elaborates on each of these ideas.

Seligman addressed at considerable length the view that consumer credit financed only immediate consumption rather than investment that leads to improved total consumption possibilities. Many goods purchased by consumers, he noted, provide utility (through consumption) over a period of time. Durable goods such as automobiles, sewing machines, furniture, and even suits of clothes are all examples. They are not used up (consumed) immediately after purchase but rather provide consumption services over a period of time. Acquisition of consumer goods that bring not only present but also future utility is not fundamentally different from business investment. Indeed, acquisition of such goods can be thought of as "consumer investment."[7]

Irving Fisher's intertemporal investment-consumption economic model provides the analytical framework for such decisions. His investment-consumption framework relates investment opportunities, time preference, the possibility of lending and borrowing, and the market interest rate to solve the problem of maximizing and allocating consumption over time. The solution provides an individual's optimal time pattern of consumption. It also shows formally when borrowing is a rational economic decision for consumers (and also for investors in commercial and industrial enterprises). Since there are many common circumstances when credit use by consumers is rational, this leads immediately to the theoretical inference that there will be widespread rational economic demand for consumer credit. After examining in the next subsection of this chapter the core of the Fisher-Seligman theory of why consumers use credit, it is then possible to isolate more precisely what critics believe is lacking from the theory.

The Fisher-Seligman Framework

The simplest version of the Fisher-Seligman approach considers a perfect market in which the costs and returns of alternative investment opportunities are known with certainty. The model assumes that the individual can borrow or lend at a given market interest rate and that the interest rate is unaffected by the amount

---

7. At about the same time, Plummer (1927) made a similar observation that many of the items commonly purchased using consumer credit produce savings in effort over a period of time. He noted that "the dividing line between these labor saving devices [sewing machines, washing machines, vacuum cleaners] and the machines in factories is not very distinct" (Plummer 1927, 23).

a single individual borrows or lends. It is possible to relax each of these assumptions, as later analysts have done, but first is the simplest version. A full analysis covering multiple periods would require mathematical treatment, but the basic ideas are clear enough in a two-period graphical presentation.[8] In some ways, the discussion that follows may seem a bit more technical than other discussion here, in that it includes some symbols, graphs, and basic equations. They are included so the discussion may be read at more than one level, but the fundamental ideas are also in the words.

INVESTMENT OPPORTUNITIES

Figure 3.1 illustrates the basic framework for determining the optimal time pattern of consumption for an individual over two periods. The horizontal axis represents the possible amounts of income and consumption in the present period 0, and the vertical axis represents the amounts of income and consumption in the future period 1.

The curves U_0 through U_2 are normal indifference curves representing the individual's preferences for consumption in periods 0 and 1. Each curve denotes constant satisfaction ("utility") along the curve, with various combinations of consumption in periods 0 and 1. Movement along any of the curves shows the trade-off between present and future consumption at a fixed satisfaction (utility) level; that is, moving along the curve, the consumer values the additional consumption gained in one period exactly equal to the value of consumption forgone in the other period, a result that leaves the consumer with neither an increase nor a decrease in satisfaction. Thus, any point along this curve defines a rate of preferred trade-off between future and current consumption. This rate is the "marginal rate of time preference," and it equals the slope of the curve at that point.

More *total* income is always better than less, of course, since it allows more total consumption. The possibility of either higher income in both periods (along the diagonal QX, for example) or higher income in at least one period without lower income in the other (along QA or QB) would produce a rightward movement to a higher satisfaction-indifference curve: movement from U_0 to U_1 and U_2. Such movement is always better, because it allows more possible consumption in one or both periods.

Now, assume that an individual's income endowment for the two periods is represented by point Q in figure 3.1. Period 0 income is Y_0, and period 1 income is Y_1. Without any opportunities to lend, borrow, or invest, consumption in each period would equal income $(C_0 = Y_0 \text{ and } C_1 = Y_1)$, and satisfaction level would be U_0. This is the condition of the fish spearer in the example. This person is able to produce only enough to satisfy his or her current needs in each period.

Next, assume, though, that this individual has opportunities for productive investments, such as a new technological fish net. In this case, shown in figure 3.2, the individual's investment possibilities are given by curve QSV, unsurprisingly

8. The graphical representation arises from the work of Fisher and later analysts; Seligman expressed the same ideas but in words.

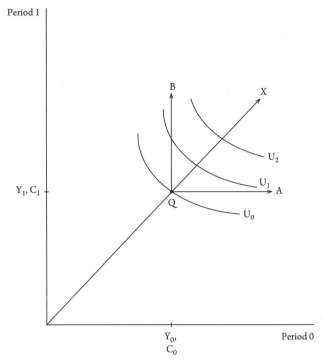

Figure 3.1 Preferences for Consumption over Time.

called in economics an "investment opportunity curve." Again, Q is the individual's income endowment. By moving from Q upward to the left along this curve, that is, by forgoing some consumption in period 0 (saving) and investing that period 0 income along QSV, the individual can transform period 0 income into period 1 consumption. This shows how by giving up some consumption today (saving some amount $Y_0 - C_0^S$) and investing this amount, the individual can produce period 1 consumption greater than that sacrificed in period 0.[9]

The rate of return on this investment undertaking, that is, the gain (or loss) in period 1 consumption from investment of period 0 income relative to the amount of income saved and invested in period 0, is given by the slope at each point of the investment opportunity curve QSV. The curve flattens out with movement upward to the left, which indicates that the rate of return is reduced with each successive investment undertaken; in other words, the best (highest return) investments are made first.

Seligman concentrated on the implications of this theory for consumers. For an individual, not consuming some period 0 income and instead using the income

---

9. This is what the spear fisher could have done if he or she had been able to save some fish and trade them directly for a net, an assumed impossibility in that example because of inability to refrigerate surplus. An absolute impossibility of saving and investing would not normally be the case in a money, or even a barter, economy, but the example made this assumption to illustrate most plainly and simply how borrowing could sometimes be advantageous.

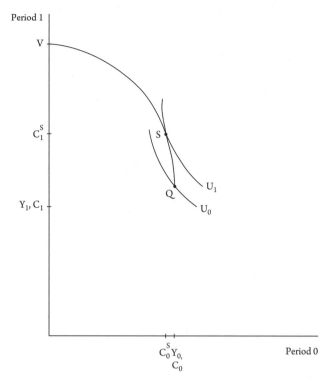

Figure 3.2 Intertemporal Consumption with Investment Opportunities.

to purchase durable goods that provide consumption benefits over time would provide additional consumption and utility in period 1. The individual would invest period 0 income as long as the utility of the current consumption forgone is less than consumption utility gained in period 1. This condition is true up to tangency at point S of the investment opportunity curve QSV and the indifference curve U_1 in figure 3.2. Optimal consumption becomes C_0^S in period 0 and C_1^S in period 1, point S in the diagram. The amount of saving and investment (sacrifice in current consumption in period 0) is $C_0 - C_0^S$ $(= Y_0 - C_0^S)$, which yields an additional amount of consumption equal to $C_1^S - C_1$ $(= C_1^S - Y_1)$ in the next period. The consumer prefers this combination because it produces satisfaction level U_1, higher than U_0.

In sum, in this example, purchasing durable goods in period 0 provides benefits over time by permitting enough later consumption to make the consumer better off even if the individual gives up a bit of current consumption. The gain in period 1 consumption outweighs the modest sacrifice of consumption in period 0. In this simplified scenario, where there is only investment and no market opportunities for lending or borrowing, the optimal investment-consumption decision is given by point S, where the investment opportunity curve is tangent to indifference curve U_1, the highest possible satisfaction level given income and the possibilities for productive investment. At this point, the rate of return on the marginal investment again just equals the marginal rate of time preference (that is, the rate of substitution between present and future consumption), although at a higher satisfaction level, U_1. But the scenario also is not very realistic so far, because it does not yet permit the existence of lending or borrowing opportunities to go with saving and investing.

LENDING AND BORROWING

The Fisher-Seligman investment-consumption model also allows for lending and borrowing, in addition to saving and investment. Lending permits exchange of current income and consumption for future income and consumption by application of the rate of interest available in the marketplace. Figure 3.3 illustrates graphically the lending/borrowing process. Line $Q''QQ'$ passing through income endowment Q shows the possibility for shifting income between periods 0 and 1. An amount of current income y_0^*, for example, might be lent at market interest rate i, to produce interest income of iy_0^*, which is added to the return of the loan principal in the next period.

In a bit more detail, the income and consumption given up in period 0 for lending in the financial market is y_0^*. Graphically, it is movement to the left along the horizontal axis in figure 3.3 in amount y_0^*. It produces additional income and consumption in period 1 equal to $y_1^* = y_0^*(1 + i)$, which is an amount upward on the vertical axis. The additional amount available in period 1 equals the amount given up in period 0 and now returned (the loan principal) plus the interest. Thus, additional income in period 1, y_1^*, is given by the following equation (in equation

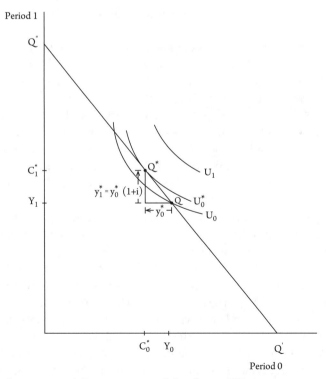

Figure 3.3 Intertemporal Consumption with Lending and Borrowing.

form, the return in period 1 is an *inflow* and so opposite in sign to the *outflow* in period 0):

$$y_1{}^* = -y_0{}^* + i(-y_0{}^*) = -(1 + i)(y_0{}^*) \quad \text{(Equation 3.1)}$$

Conversely, in a perfect capital market where lending and borrowing interest rates are the same, the same market for lending and borrowing also permits exchange of any amount of future income $Y_1{}^*$ into current period income by borrowing (moving to the right along line segment QQ′). With the same interest rate i, this transformation is illustrated by rearranging the same equation:

$$y_0{}^* = \frac{y_1{}^*}{-(1 + i)} \qquad \text{(Equation 3.2)}$$

This is how financial markets work. Lending today (forgoing consumption today) leads to more income and consumption in the future; and conversely, borrowing today (increasing immediately available resources for consumption or investment) leads to payback of interest and principal in the future. Lending or borrowing permits a change in the timing of consumption but, as will be shown, also provides the opportunity for increasing consumption currently and in the future.

These two simple equations (actually just rearrangements of each other) are extremely important, because they represent the essence of financial markets. The first equation shows that lending today in financial markets leads to a return of the loan plus interest tomorrow.

In contrast, rearrangement of the same equation shows what happens when future inflows are used as a basis for borrowing. More available resources today leads to a reduction later by application of the rate of interest, a process sometimes referred to as discounting. Extending these simple processes to the full range of possibilities where there are imperfect capital markets such that lending and borrowing rates are not the same and the rates are affected by uncertainty and risk and can extend for multiple periods or even indefinitely is what constitutes the branch of microeconomics called finance. This field is inherently fascinating, but it can also be highly technical and seemingly complicated, though ultimately based on an extremely simple idea.

For purposes here, the relationship in equation 3.1 and shown in figure 3.3, $y_1{}^* = -(1 + i)y_0{}^*$, represents the terms for exchanging income in one period for income in the other. This exchange relationship, the "market opportunity," can be drawn graphically as a line through any income endowment (for example, $Q = Y_0, Y_1$) to show the market opportunities for borrowing or lending associated with that income endowment. The line Q′Q″ in figure 3.3 is such a line. For the assumed perfect capital market where lending and borrowing takes place at the same rate of interest, this "market opportunity line" has a constant slope equal everywhere to $-(1 + i)$.

Let us look at this market opportunity a bit more by bringing over the income combination Q from the earlier figure 3.1. As mentioned, figure 3.3 then illustrates the possibility of such exchanges for the income endowment represented by point Q from figure 3.1. An individual with income (and consumption) possibilities initially at point Q (or, for that matter, at any other initial point) could exchange period 0 income and consumption for period 1 income and consumption by lending at interest rate i along segment Q"Q of market opportunity line Q"QQ' (or a parallel line for any other initial point). This exchange allows greater consumption in period 1. Conversely, the individual could exchange period 1 income and consumption for period 0 income and consumption by borrowing at interest rate i along segment QQ'. By borrowing, the individual obtains greater consumption now but less consumption later, another possible timing change.

Since the market opportunities are constant along this line in the example, it is a straight line with a constant slope, and this slope reflects the rate of interest. Each incremental reduction $(-y_0)$ in period 0 resources that is lent (moving upward along the line to the left) returns $-(1 + i)$ times that amount in period 1. And conversely, each incremental amount of resources from borrowing in period 0 changes period 1 income and consumption by $y_0 = y_1/-(1 + i)$. The negative sign in the equation indicates how the change is in the opposite direction. Thus, the market opportunity line shows the transformation between present and future income through lending or borrowing at interest rate i.[10]

Significantly, it is also possible to see in the diagram that the *present value* of any income stream, then, is given by hypothetically exchanging along this market opportunity line *all* potential income into the present through financial markets. This is shown by the intersection of the market opportunity line with the horizontal axis, point Q' in figure 3.3. It is also possible to show this present value algebraically using equation 3.2:

$$PV(Y_0, Y_1) = \frac{Y_0 + Y_1}{(1 + i)} \qquad \text{(Equation 3.3)}$$

Equation 3.3 shows, as does figure 3.3, that the present value equals period 0 income plus the discounted value (from equation 3.2) of period 1 income.

Figure 3.3 also shows the future value of the income endowment stream. It is given by intersection of the market opportunity line with the y axis (future year). The diagram shows that with interest rate i and income endowment Q, then Q" is the maximum future value. Using equation 3.1 to determine the value of period 0 income in period 1, future value of the income stream (Y_0, Y_1) is obtained:

$$FV(Y_0, Y_1) = Y_0(1 + i) + Y_1 \qquad \text{(Equation 3.4)}$$

10. If the interest rate were 0, indicating that current consumption could be lent only for the same amount of future consumption, it would be a 45-degree line with slope exactly equal to -1 (assuming the same increments on the axes). But since in this figure the interest rate is positive rate i, the line slopes upward a bit more steeply to the left at $-(1 + i)$

In the example here, the individual with income endowment at point Q in figure 3.3 whose time preferences are represented by U_0 and U_1 would obtain a higher satisfaction level moving to the left from Q (lending) along the market opportunity line Q''QQ' to point Q^*, where the (higher) indifference curve U_0^* is tangent to Q''QQ'. To achieve this outcome, the individual would lend y_0^*, consuming C_0^* in period 0. In period 1, the individual would receive y_1^*, which equals principal and interest from the loan $y_0(1 + i)$, in addition to other period 1 income. This would allow consumption of C_1^*.

With different time preferences, other outcomes would result. An individual whose highest indifference curve is tangent to the market opportunity line Q''QQ' to the right of point Q would borrow (not shown in the figure). And an individual whose highest indifference curve is tangent to Q''QQ' exactly at point Q would neither lend nor borrow.

INVESTMENT OPPORTUNITIES WITH LENDING AND BORROWING

Next, the developing graphical representation also permits exploration of saving, investing, and the optimal consumption time pattern when lending and borrowing are also possible. This is the case of the spear fisher operating in a capitalist society. Graphically, putting saving and investing together with lending and borrowing means combining figure 3.2 with figure 3.3.

So far, discussion of productive investment opportunities, illustrated by investment opportunity curve QSV in figure 3.2, has suggested that the best plan is to engage in investment in productive assets (and give up current consumption in favor of future income) until the investment opportunity curve through endowment income touches the highest possible satisfaction indifference curve, point S in figure 3.2. At that point, the marginal rate of investment return just equals the marginal rate of time preference (rate of substitution between present and future consumption); any further investment (moving farther along QSV) would produce a return lower than time preference and lead to lower satisfaction.

But the discussion of this first example did not yet take into account the existence of financial markets. In the second example, with financial markets but not investing in productive assets, the individual would lend or borrow along Q''QQ'until the rate of interest just equals the marginal rate of time preference, point Q^* in figure 3.3. Now, with the possibility of borrowing and lending *together* with saving and productive investment, the individual with income endowment Q has available more opportunities. Important because of the possibility of lending and borrowing, the individual has available *any* potential combination of present and future consumption along Q''QQ'in figure 3.4 (the same line as in figure 3.3).

This individual is also able to transform present income into future income by investing in productive assets, illustrated by moving along investment possibilities curve QSV in figure 3.4 (the same concept as in figure 3.2). Unlike the individual in figure 3.2, who was unable to lend and borrow, however, the one in figure 3.4 can engage in both investment and financial transactions. And so at point S, where the investment opportunity curve is tangent to indifference curve U_1, the individual's borrowing and lending opportunities are given by market opportunity curve S''SS', parallel to Q''QQ' and reflecting the same financial choices and

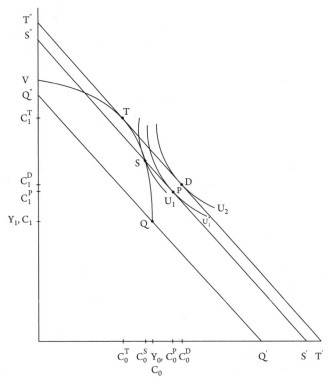

Figure 3.4 Intertemporal Consumption and Investment Opportunities with Lending and Borrowing.

interest rate. In this situation, points to the left of S on S"SS' involve both investment and lending. But these points are below indifference curve U_1 and therefore represent less preferred outcomes than those on U_1. Points to the right involve investment and borrowing and are preferred to S because they lie above U_1.

And so, in the example illustrated in figure 3.4, the best possible outcome for an investment of $Y_0 - C_0^S$ at point S is achieved by borrowing $C_0^P - C_0^S$ to point P along the market opportunity line. This choice permits consumption of C_0^P in period 0 and C_1^P in period 1. At this point, the highest possible indifference curve U_1^* is tangent to the market opportunity line. Note that in this example, consumption is higher in both periods at point P (with investment and borrowing) than at the initial endowment at point Q.[11]

It is possible to see in the diagram, however, that the outcome at point P is not optimal, however. The marginal return on investment, given by the slope of the investment opportunity curve at S, is greater than the rate of interest (and the marginal rate of time preference). Additional investment would produce more period 1 consumption than the cost of borrowing additional funds to finance the

11. Of course, other outcomes are possible with different investment opportunities or time preferences for consumption.

investment at the market interest rate i. The optimal solution, then, is to invest to the point where the marginal return on investment is equal to the market interest rate, which occurs at point T on QSV. The individual then borrows along the market opportunity curve to point D, where the marginal rate of time preference, market interest rate, and the return on investment are equal. This outcome achieves the individual's highest possible indifference curve, given the initial income endowment, investment opportunities, time preferences, and market interest rate.

The emerging diagram in figure 3.4 shows that the optimal investment at T maximizes the individual's *present value* of current and future consumption (point T' on the *x* axis). It is easy enough to see in the diagram that from point T, any change in investment in favor of investing more or less in real assets to produce future income produces a lower present value, given the interest rate and investment opportunities.

But this diagram also shows why point T is not the optimal position. Point T is not the only combination of current and future consumption that is consistent with maximum present value of household investment. Actually, *any* point along T"TT' has this characteristic, and they are all attainable by lending or borrowing in financial markets. Thus, an individual faced by the investment and market opportunities of figure 3.4 would first invest along curve QSV to T, in order to maximize present value and then lend or borrow along market opportunities line T"TT' to the preferred combination of present and future consumption. Because any point along T"TT' represents a combination of possible consumption in period 0 and period 1 that is consistent with maximum present value and is attainable by lending or borrowing, actual consumption choice along it depends only on preferences.

Thus, *whether* the individual lends or borrows depends on the shape of the time preference function, the indifference curves whose slope indicates the rate of time preference, together with market opportunities for lending and borrowing designated by the rate of interest i. With the preferences represented by the indifference curves in figure 3.4 (the same as in figures 3.2 and 3.3), the lending/borrowing decision involves borrowing to reach point D on U_2. This choice represents the preferred time pattern of consumption and is consistent with an investment decision that maximizes the present value of current and future consumption. At this point, the marginal rate of time preference equals the market rate of interest, which also equals the marginal rate of return on investments. Later theoretical work shows that this conclusion also extends to multiple periods (see technical discussion in Fama and Miller 1972).

To summarize, the individual with income endowment Q, investment opportunities QSV, interest rate i, and preferences represented by indifference curves U_0, U_1, and U_2 would undertake investment $y_0 - C_0^T$ in durable goods to maximize wealth (net present value of the income stream. This individual also would borrow so that the saving/investing process would not have to be paid fully in period 0 by reduced consumption in that period; borrowing would make it possible to reach the preferred consumption time pattern. In figure 3.4, this would mean borrowing in amount $C_0^D - C_0^T$ in period 0 and repaying in amount $C_1^T - C_1^D$ in period

1, producing consumption combination D (higher than Q in both years) and satisfaction level U_2 (also higher). For this individual, both investment in durable goods and associated borrowing to adjust the timing of consumption flows are rational behaviors.

Seligman's analysis undermined the then-popular views on inappropriateness of credit use by consumers, because it demonstrated there were many occasions when borrowing made sense for individuals. In the new view, credit demand depended on investment opportunities, consumption time preferences, and the rate of interest. Credit facilitates acquisition of consumer durable goods, which can increase wealth (that is, increase the present value of the income stream), while permitting the consumption stream to follow a preferred pattern. Seligman's application of investment-consumption theory to consumer credit demonstrated that the optimal decision with borrowing opportunities can involve greater investment in consumer durable goods that produce their return over time, together with a more highly valued intertemporal pattern of consumption than the optimal decision without borrowing opportunities.[12]

These results are important, and they are clear enough from the theory, but is investment financing how consumers use credit? As discussed in chapter 1, it is difficult to ascertain with certainty the underlying motivations for taking on a particular credit obligation, but there is no question that much consumer credit is used for the purpose of fitting the expenditures for durable, investment-type goods and services, including automobiles and trucks, appliances, furniture, home repairs and modernization, large hobby items, and education expenses, into family budgets. Surveys of consumers in the post–World War II period, discussed in chapter 1, have provided a look at how consumers have used consumer credit during these years (see especially table 1.2 and discussion about it). There is no question that most of consumer credit use is closely associated with the purchase of durable, investment-type goods and services.

This is not to say that the Fisher-Seligman approach has been a sufficient explanation of consumer credit demand and consumers' credit-using behavior to convince all observers at all times of the efficacy of consumer credit use. In fact, critics began to complain almost immediately, and they remain active today.

Danielian's Institutional and Psychological Critique of Seligman's Approach

In the years immediately following publication of Seligman's two volumes, some economists questioned the applicability of the Fisher investment-consumption model to the credit decisions of many consumers. They pointed to institutional and psychological conditions that they believed limited applicability of the theory,

---

12. Seligman's view that consumers use durable goods to produce a flow of future utilities also presages later developments in consumer theory concerning household production through "human capital" (see Becker 1965, Juster 1966, and Lancaster 1966).

in some ways foreshadowing critics in the late twentieth and early twenty-first centuries.

Shortly after publication of *The Economics of Installment Selling*, N. R. Danielian (1929) expressed reservations about Seligman's analysis. Danielian acknowledged that Seligman's model might apply to the decisions of some consumers and that consumer credit might benefit consumers under ideal conditions. He argued, however, that circumstances surrounding consumer credit transactions generally can be far from ideal. The circumstances he questioned included both institutional and psychological considerations that could vitiate models of rational choice and limit the benefits derived from credit use. Among the institutional conditions he noted were consumers' difficulties in determining the interest rate and the lack of a competitive market structure for consumer credit. The psychological circumstances included a pressing need for credit, because of most consumers' lack of available cash, and an asymmetry in consumers' valuation of future utilities and disutilities. With these criticisms, Danielian presaged both the later support of economists for the Truth in Lending Act (passed in 1968) and the later application of a new branch of economic analysis called behavioral economics to consumer credit in the closing decades of the century and the early years of the following one (discussed here below and in the next chapter).

Concerning first his institutional criticism, Danielian pointed to the different methods of quoting interest rates or interest charges on consumer credit at that time. In large part arising from historical and legal factors, these methods varied according to the type of institution offering the credit. Only one of the methods reflected a theoretically correct interest rate, but that method was not the usual pricing method for most credit transactions.

At that time, creditors commonly used one of three methods for calculating finance charges on consumer credit, depending on their institutional type, and they generally quoted percentage rates to consumers based on their method of calculation for the finance charge. In many cases, the calculation methods they used had become enshrined in state laws setting pricing ceilings for each institution class: retailers and sales finance companies generally employed and quoted so-called add-on rates that arose ultimately from the two-price method of selling goods for cash versus sales on credit; banks preferred discount rates that permitted them to calculate and charge interest in advance; and credit unions, remedial (charitable) loan societies, and small loan companies used and quoted monthly percentage rates, because they thought they were less confusing for consumers. Although the National Commission on Consumer Finance (NCCF) noted in 1972 that practices of the times sometimes had permitted valid comparisons among institutions of the same class (among retail stores, banks, credit unions, finance companies, etc.), "shopping for credit across industry lines was almost impossible," and this "helped create a climate favorable for legislation requiring uniform quoting of rates of charge" (National Commission on Consumer Finance 1972, 170).[13]

---

13. For further discussion of conditions before the federal Truth in Lending Act became effective in 1969 and for fuller description of these calculating methods, see Mors (1965). Disclosure

Danielian contended that most consumers did not understand these methods, nor were they aware of actual interest rates charged by creditors. Subsequent empirical investigations supported this contention (see Due 1955 and Mors 1965). This lack of knowledge of interest rates could prevent consumers from properly assessing the cost of using credit and, therefore, the rationality and usefulness of consumer credit.

Consumers' problems in assessing the cost of credit were made worse, in Danielian's view, by psychological considerations. Danielian focused particularly on an asymmetry in consumers' valuations of future utilities and disutilities that caused consumers to overestimate the desirability of purchasing a durable good in a credit transaction. Underlying this part of his analysis was his belief that consumers tend to discount future disutilities more than satisfactions. He contended that in a cash transaction, this tendency is less problematic: the consumer compares the present value of utility from durable goods to the present sacrifice of other goods that must be given up to make the purchase. Both the benefits and costs are immediately perceived and consistently valued. In his view, consumers would be better able to make rational (wealth- and utility-maximizing) choices under these circumstances.

In contrast, Danielian argued, the possibility of valuation asymmetry can lead consumers to overestimate benefits and underestimate costs in a credit transaction. As before, the future utilities from the durable good are reflected in present value of current satisfactions from increased total consumption and its new time path. Payment in a credit transaction is largely deferred, however, leading to relatively little current sacrifice in alternative consumption to satisfy any down payment requirement. The sacrifices in future consumption to satisfy future monthly payments may be only vaguely foreseen at the time of the transaction. Thus, in this view, consumers are apt to discount future disutilities from sacrifices in future consumption more than future utilities from the durable good. This tendency causes consumers to overestimate the net present value of durable purchases when credit is involved. As a result, consumers can overinvest in consumer durables and at the margin acquire durables that decrease their wealth.[14]

In his 1929 article, Danielian also suggested further difficulties he perceived in the functioning of consumer credit markets. For example, in the institutional area, he noted a high degree of market concentration in finance companies, which along with retail outlets were the primary sources of consumer credit at

requirements following implementation of Truth in Lending are discussed further here in chapter 9. See also the companion book to this one, Durkin and Elliehausen (2011).

14. Assigning different discount rates to different sources of utility (such as utilities from a durable good and utilities from alternative consumption) violates the single constant discount assumption of Samuelson's (1937) discounted utility model, a generalization of Fisher's model. Such deviation represents an interesting theoretical contention, the details of which are the subject of ongoing current modeling efforts by contemporary behavioral economists. Unfortunately, its extreme modern adherents in policy arenas have proposed prescriptions concerning consumer credit that go way beyond the contentions of the theory. More will be said about these matters later, especially in the next chapter.

the time, which he believed could inhibit competition and lead to higher prices.[15] Moreover, consumers' lack of knowledge of interest rates hampered shopping for lower interest rates, and most consumers' lack of savings limited alternatives to using credit. Danielian also pointed to other psychological considerations that may further weaken consumers' bargaining position. For example, he contended that a lack of resistance to high-pressure salesmanship could make the consumer unwilling to consider deferring the purchase and, therefore, enhance the likelihood that consumers would become dependent on credit.

In effect, Danielian simply argued against the assumptions underlying Seligman's theory, although he offered no real supporting evidence one way or the other, and his view by itself does not invalidate Seligman's or any other theory. In effect, he contended that circumstances prevent consumers from fully understanding either costs or benefits of consumer credit use, and this could lead to overinvestment in durable goods and too much credit use. His criticism still resonates with some observers of consumer credit today, despite decades of growing familiarity with costs and benefits of credit use among consumers and substantial institutional changes since the time of Danielian's article. One especially important institutional change was the implementation on July 1, 1969, of the federal Truth in Lending Act of 1968 to provide credit cost disclosures to consumers in a consistent manner.

Development of the Monthly Payments Model

Based, at least in part, on these criticisms, an early alternative approach to the theory of consumer credit demand emerged, especially in the years during and just after World War II. But this alternative economic model depended intellectually not so much on another foundational microeconomic analysis of optimal individual behavior as on macroeconomic statistical analyses of aggregate consumption across all consumers.[16] The efforts of the macroeconomists produced an empirically based theory of consumer credit, which can be characterized as the "monthly payments model." This alternative theory posited a critical role for the size of monthly payments as a determinant of consumer behavior, and proponents found the size of monthly credit payments to be significantly related statistically to purchase of various types of goods. Later theoretical work by Juster and Shay (1964), discussed in the following subsection of this chapter, reconciled the apparently contradictory investment-consumption and monthly payments models and demonstrated where the predictions of each approach apply.

The empirical foundation of the macroeconomic approach during these years is the simple observation that disposable income, durable goods purchases, and

---

15. Among possible reasons for uncompetitive markets were asymmetric information and fragmented and restrictive regulation of creditors. See chapter 11 for discussion of these issues.

16. Durkin and Staten (2002) provide some discussion of the long-term trends in consumer credit research in their introduction to a group of papers on policy issues.

consumer indebtedness tend to rise during a business expansion and fall during a contraction. The macroeconomists were interested in explaining both the causes and the business cycle effects of this phenomenon. Prominent among the researchers were Haberler (1942) and Kisselgoff (1952), but there also were others.

Developers of the monthly payments model shared Danielian's view that consumers are impatient and lack the willpower to defer consumption and accumulate savings to acquire durable goods whose price exceeds monthly budget surpluses. So far, this is not inconsistent with the Fisher-Seligman microeconomic investment-consumption model, which concludes that they will use credit to purchase durable goods and change the timing of consumption when the return from use exceeds the interest rate on the credit. In the Fisher-Seligman analytic case, there is positive net present value from purchasing more durable goods on credit. But the macroeconomists' assessments of consumers' impatience were quite similar to Danielian's, in that they posited that consumers are not always able to make rational choices. According to Haberler:

> Many persons simply lack the will power to renounce a series of daily enjoyments in order to pile up a cash balance for the purchase of a high priced commodity; others cannot resist the temptation to buy an expensive article if it is offered on credit, but would resist it if they had to pay the price in advance. Both types of behavior illustrate the famous principle of underestimation of future needs or enjoyments as compared with present ones. (Haberler 1942, 42)

Kisselgoff later expressed a similar view: "For the consumer anxious to obtain possession of a desired commodity, the addition of a few more monthly installments, coming as they do in the not too immediate future, or a small increase in the amount of each installment, is probably of no great significance" (Kisselgoff 1952, 17).

This view of consumer psychology led these macroeconomists to the assumption that only monthly payment size matters to consumers. Since most consumers must rely on installment credit to purchase durable goods, they reasoned, then their ability to afford such debt depends critically on the size of the monthly payments required to service such debt. Rising income during an economic expansion increases consumers' ability to repay installment debt and interest, and improvements in consumer confidence that accompany an expansion increase consumers' willingness to incur debt. In contrast, consumers' uncertainty during economic contractions causes them to postpone purchases of durables and reduce their use of debt.

According to this model's proponents, assessing the cost of credit involves considering the term to maturity and down payment requirement in addition to the interest rate, because these terms affect the demand for credit through their effect on the size of monthly payments. An increase in the interest rate, other things being equal, increases monthly payment size and reduces amount demanded. Proponents of the monthly payments model argued, however, that the effect of interest rates on consumer credit demand was nearly negligible. They argued that over the business cycle, consumers would normally see differences in interest rates of only a few percentage points, and such differences, or even larger ones, would have only a very small effect on the size of monthly payments. The impact of differences in interest rates, they concluded, would hardly be noticed in the budgets of most consumers and therefore would not affect their credit decisions. According to Haberler, "It is not likely that many consumers calculate so closely that such small changes in their monthly budgets will induce them to change their plans" (Haberler 1942, 101).

In contrast, they believed that the term to maturity and the down payment had much larger effects on consumers' credit decisions than the interest rate, because changes in these quantities could have direct and measurable effects on monthly payments. Of the two credit terms, the macroeconomists regarded the term to maturity as the more important. In their view, an increase in the term to maturity reduces monthly payment size and increases amount demanded. Calculations showed that differences in terms to maturity of the size consumers might encounter in the market at that time could have a large effect on the size of monthly payments (see discussion in Haberler 1942, 102). Statistical evidence employing macroeconomic data and indicating that the increases in terms to maturity produced significant and proportionately greater increases in credit supported such conclusions (see Kisselgoff 1952 and Suits 1958).

Proponents of the monthly payments model thought that the down payment requirement, unlike the term to maturity, was important in some cases but not in others. For many first-time purchasers of automobiles, they argued, the down payment requirement was large enough to have a significant effect on credit demand, because many first-time purchasers would have to supplement surpluses in their monthly budgets with accumulated cash savings to satisfy down payment requirements. Because a large percentage of consumers had limited cash, especially younger consumers who were more likely than older consumers to be first-time purchasers, the down payment requirement would be important in some cases. But in this view, the down payment requirement would not be very important either for replacement purchases of automobiles or for purchases of most other durables. On replacement purchases of automobiles, the trade-in would often satisfy the down payment requirement, and down payment requirements for other durables were generally a small dollar amount because of the relatively smaller size of the transaction.

Thus, the monthly payment size, which is largely dependent on the term to maturity and, to a lesser extent, on the down payment requirement and the interest rate, represents the price of installment credit in this approach to consumer credit demand. The surplus in the consumer's monthly budget after meeting the costs of necessities serves as a budget constraint in the model. Statistical analyses using macroeconomic data that found a positive relationship between income and consumer debt and a negative relationship between size of monthly payments and consumer debt were consistent with the model's predictions.

Although it was highly influential in its time, in hindsight the monthly payments model of consumer credit use has become less significant. The macroeconomists produced little empirical evidence on the effects of the interest rate and the down payment requirement on demand for consumer debt, even though today Annual Percentage Rates appear to be for many consumers among the most significant differentiating characteristics among credit plans, and rates are widely advertised today. Furthermore, although some predictions of the model may seem reasonable, the model also has some implausible implications. At the individual consumer level, the monthly payments model implies that consumers would be indifferent to different interest rates if the term to maturity were adjusted to keep the monthly payment the same. This might be true in some cases but certainly not always. The model also implies that all consumers would choose the longest term to maturity, since the longest available term to maturity would give them the lowest monthly payment and hence the lowest price. Such behavior also seems unlikely in all cases, and even casual discussions with neighbors and acquaintances show that it is not nearly universally true.

Juster and Shay's Extension of the Investment-Consumption Model

In a monograph that was part of the National Bureau of Economic Research's multiyear consumer credit research program in the early 1960s, F. Thomas Juster and Robert P. Shay (1964) reevaluated and extended Seligman's intertemporal investment-consumption model of consumer credit decisions, and in the process, they prompted a reconciliation of the investment-consumption model with the empirical observation that some consumers are highly sensitive to size of monthly payments. Their extensions also included and adapted some then-new developments in finance theory addressing market imperfections (see Hirshleifer 1958). These new theoretical developments allowed Juster and Shay to consider how certain institutional features of consumer credit markets affected consumer choices. The extended model enabled them to formulate hypotheses about consumers' sensitivity to interest rates and provided for tests of the investment-consumption versus monthly payments models and produced conclusions concerning the applicability of each.[17]

Like Seligman before them, Juster and Shay focused on consumer credit arising from the purchase of household durable goods. But they suggested that the valuation of benefits from durable goods need not be made in terms of utilities, and by implication, they argued that these valuations were not as difficult to undertake as posited by Danielian. Rather, they contended, consumers can often at least intuitively measure the economic value of the stream of services from durable goods by comparison with the cost of purchasing those services or alternatives in the marketplace. For example, the value of the services of a washing machine can be measured by the alternative cost of obtaining the services over time in a laundromat, or the services of an automobile can be measured by the cost of using public transportation. Even the services of durable goods such as televisions or home entertainment centers can be valued in this way. The value of

---

17. Juster and Shay's extended model is in their Appendix A.

services of a television, for example, can be measured, at least intuitively, by the cost of going to the movies, concerts, sports events, or other entertainment activities that would be attended if television were not available.

DIFFERENT BORROWING AND LENDING INTEREST RATES

In addition to their other advances, Juster and Shay extended Hirshleifer's (1958) investment-consumption model of an imperfect capital market, in which the interest rate for consumer borrowing i is greater than the interest rate for consumer lending r. Figure 3.5 illustrates Hirshleifer's investment-consumption model graphically. For imperfect capital markets, the single market opportunity line for borrowing and lending from point Q in the previous figures is replaced in figure 3.5 by two line segments, QQ' for borrowing opportunities and Q"Q for lending opportunities associated with the income stream represented by point Q. The steeper line segment QQ', with slope −(1 + i) denoting a higher interest rate i, is the market opportunity line for borrowing at interest rate i. The flatter line segment Q"Q, with slope −(1 + r), is the market opportunity line for lending at interest rate r. Thus, maximum consumption possibilities are given by the kinked line Q"QQ'. Individuals whose highest indifference curve is tangent to segment Q"Q would lend some period 0 income, consuming less in period 0 and more in period 1. Individuals whose highest indifference curve is tangent to segment QQ' would borrow, consuming more in period 0 and reducing consumption in period 1 to repay principal and interest. And if the highest indifference curve passes through point Q, the individual neither lends nor borrows.

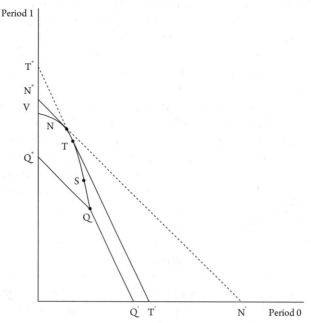

Figure 3.5 Intertemporal Consumption and Investment Opportunities with Different Lending and Borrowing Rates.

As in figure 3.4, investment opportunities are given by the curve labeled QSV. Again, the market opportunity line for *borrowing* is determined by the tangency to the investment opportunity line of a line T'''TT' with slope –(1 + i). This occurs at point T. The individual can borrow along the solid segment TT' to the right of point T. The dashed segment T'''T' is not feasible, because the model assumption is that the lending rate is less than the borrowing rate.

Conversely, the market opportunity line for *lending* is derived from the tangency to QSV of a line N''N' with a slope of –(1 + r). This occurs at point N. The individual can lend along the solid segment N''N of the line N''N'. Lending along the dashed segment NN' is also by model assumption not feasible.

Between points T and N, neither borrowing nor lending is wealth increasing. In this region, borrowing would produce a lower present value of consumption, because the marginal return on additional investment (slope of the investment opportunity curve) would be less than the cost of the additional funding (slope of TT'). Similarly, lending would produce a lower present value of consumption, because the marginal return on the additional investment would be greater than the interest that would be obtained if the funds were lent (slope of N''N) instead of invested. Thus, investment and market opportunities are given by the curve N''NTT'.

Unlike the perfect market case, the optimal investment decision in the imperfect market case where borrowing and lending rates differ depends on individuals' time preferences for consumption. Specifically, first, individuals with preferences for high levels of future consumption, whose highest indifference curve is tangent to the N''N segment of the investment and market opportunities curve, would invest at N and lend along N''N. Next, individuals with stronger preferences for current consumption and whose highest indifference curve is tangent to the NT segment would invest at the point of tangency and neither lend nor borrow. Finally, individuals whose highest indifference curve is tangent to the TT' segment would invest at T and borrow along TT'.

These solutions imply that different interest rates are required to calculate the present value of investment decisions. In the first case, the lending rate is the appropriate interest rate. In the next case, the appropriate rate is the marginal rate of time preference at the tangency of the indifference curve and segment NT. This rate is greater than the slope of the investment possibility curve at N and less than the slope at point T. In the final case, the borrowing rate is the appropriate rate.

Before turning to Juster and Shay's extensions to Hirshleifer's model, it should be noted that the investment opportunity curves in the figures have very steep slopes initially and through much of their range. This characteristic implies that the individual has many high-return investment opportunities. Young individuals with growing families might have such investment opportunity curves. Other individuals, such as ones with established households and grown children, might have relatively few high return investment opportunities. Their investment opportunity curves might start with a more moderate slope and flatten out quickly (see figure 3.6), and the lending segment of the market and investment opportunities curve for these individuals might be relatively larger than the lending segment shown in figure 3.5.

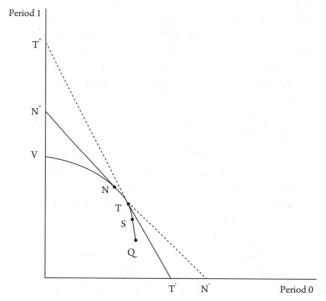

Figure 3.6 Lending and Borrowing with Relatively Few High Return Investment Opportunities.

These possibilities explain why some people borrow and some do not. Individuals can have different preferences for consumption timing. Some are more oriented toward present spending than others, and some are more oriented toward the future. Importantly, household investment opportunities have a strong influence on borrowing. Some individuals, likely often those in younger age categories, have strong future prospects for economic advancement but have few durable goods in hand or are planning for higher education. They may well be in the category of those with a high rate of return for investment in durable goods or education but also with a preference for not dramatically restricting current consumption when they make the investment. They well may be candidates for borrowing.

Conversely, individuals who are somewhat older and less in need of further durable goods or education may be faced with a lower available return on additional investment and also a reduced preference for additional current consumption relative to future consumption. They may become candidates for lending budget surpluses, possibly through financial intermediaries that hold their reserves in the form of deposits and retirement assets. Third are the intermediate cases with intermediate return on additional durable goods and intermediate preference for more current consumption. They neither borrow nor lend.

This three-way categorization of consumers argues for the possibility of a life cycle approach to credit use. Younger individuals more likely are borrowers and older ones more likely lenders. While surveys of consumers have shown that there is not a perfect dichotomy along age lines or that those who borrow do not lend at all or vice versa, the life cycle view of credit use has become obvious to analysts who have examined these survey results (see chapter 2, especially tables 2.3 and 2.5).

LIQUIDITY CONSTRAINTS

As indicated, Juster and Shay also extended the work of Fisher, Seligman, and Hirshleifer to address certain institutional characteristics of consumer credit supply. These market factors have been designated as credit rationing or liquidity constraints in subsequent economic literature, and they are important when considering the contentions of the behavioral economists of later decades. Juster and Shay's work is especially important in examining the more extreme positions of the "behavioral law and economics" specialists advanced in the policy area in the early twenty-first century and discussed elsewhere (see Durkin, Elliehausen, and Zywicki 2014).

Notably, Juster and Shay's extensions of the neoclassical Fisher-Seligman model of consumer credit demand address situations in which credit demand is particularly high for certain individuals. These situations include even potential Danielian outcomes where psychological considerations might predispose consumers to borrow at high rates and even to borrow irrationally (beyond the levels suggested by theories postulating economic rationality as discussed by Fisher and Seligman).

Juster and Shay's extended theory pointed out that in these instances, there are also other important credit market forces at work to limit credit use. These mechanisms include (1) absolute limits on the amount of credit available and (2) situations in which larger amounts of borrowing have a higher marginal borrowing rate. These extensions to theory can account both for many aspects of creditors' unwillingness to finance the entire cost of consumer durable goods and for the existence of specialized lenders offering unsecured credit at high interest rates. The specialty lenders are discussed further in chapter 8, but let us look now briefly at these further extensions to the basic economic model. Taken together, the theoretical extensions concern equity requirements and other liquidity constraints.[18]

The extensions to the economic model of rational borrowing that show how borrowing is limited by market forces, even where borrowing demand might be irrational, arise because of the inherent riskiness of lending, particularly to consumers. Because this risk is always going to exist, mainstream creditors may reduce their risk exposure by requiring debtors to repay the credit relatively rapidly, in many cases before the end of the service life of the durable good purchased. A requirement of this kind forces debtors to build equity in the durable goods

18. Juster and Shay discussed at some length other extensions involving (3) limits on credit with a discontinuous investment opportunity curve for durable goods that are not divisible and (4) availability of liquid assets that could be used to purchase durable goods. These extensions add complexity and address circumstances that actually exist in markets, but they are not reviewed further here because they do not vitiate the fundamental conclusions of the simpler analyses that borrowing can facilitate greater productive household investment leading to more highly valued patterns of consumption and, as discussed below, that limiting credit can result in less than optimal household investment and consumption.

being financed, consequently reducing default risk for the creditors by making default costly to the borrower. Creditors may also retain a security interest in the durables purchased while the associated debt is outstanding. Many consumer durable goods used for collateral have little market value as used items. They nevertheless may serve as collateral if they have value to the borrower (such as providing a stream of services); loss of the goods would thus be costly to borrowers, and so they are willing to make payments on their debts and build the equity as required.[19]

Equity building requirements that are part of many consumer credit arrangements raise the cost of financing the durable products for buyers, because building equity forces borrowers to forgo current consumption. If the cost of forgoing current consumption is sufficiently high, borrowers sometimes may obtain additional credit by using unsecured personal credit, but this credit is riskier still for creditors and, therefore, more costly to extend than other forms of credit. For many consumers, additional unsecured personal credit is available only from specialized high-risk lenders at a substantially higher cost. And at some point, a consumer may not be able to borrow additional amounts at all.[20]

Even though these considerations clearly are important in many decisions to use credit, it seems nonetheless that equity requirements are less constraining today than when Juster and Shay wrote in 1964. Many household durables, especially those having relatively low market values ("low-ticket" items), are now financed by prearranged revolving credit that does not tie the financing and equity building to a specific durable purchase in the way that nonrevolving credit does. Down payments are still common for purchases using nonrevolving credit, although down payment requirements have generally eased and proceeds from trade-ins are often used for down payments (which was also the case earlier). Terms to maturity also have lengthened considerably since Juster and Shay's time. Six-year terms are widely available on auto loans, for example. While the longer-term loans reduce the rate at which borrowers build equity, they often do so at the cost of a higher rate of interest, however.

And it is important that despite the many changes in consumer credit markets since Juster and Shay's time, consumers continue to face absolute limits on the amount of credit they can obtain from any lender and higher interest rates when they seek additional credit beyond these limits from secondary lenders. Consequently, examining Juster and Shay's extended analysis continues to be relevant, although it is more technical than the rest of the discussion in this chapter. The point of the somewhat technical discussion that follows is that there are market forces that limit credit demand, even in cases where the demand by itself reaches or even surpasses the threshold of irrationality. The more technical discussion in the next two chapter subsections demonstrates how this happens for absolute limits on further credit and further credit only at higher interest rates.

---

19. See Barro (1976) and Benjamin (1978). See also chapter 5 for further discussion.

20. See Bizer and DeMarzo (1992) for a model of markets with sequential credit decisions.

Absolute Limits on the Amount of Credit

Absolute limits on the amount of credit can readily be visualized in the graphical model developed here. Consider from previous figures the initial income endowment at point Q in figure 3.7A. The borrowing segment of the market opportunity line through point Q again is QQ'.

Let the maximum credit amount involve moving along segment QQ* on QQ' in figure 3.7A. The maximum amount of credit feasible in period 0 is designated $Y_{Max0} = L_0 - Y_0$. In other words, points beyond Q* and, therefore, amounts of credit beyond $L_0 - Y_0$ exceed the limit and are therefore not feasible.

Figure 3.8 adapts Figure 3.5 to show the effect of absolute limits on borrowing opportunities when investment is possible. As before, the market opportunity line for borrowing is tangent to the investment opportunity curve at T where the rate of interest is equal to the marginal rate of return on investment (the slope of the investment opportunity curve). But now, the maximum credit amount is reached at point T* (corresponding to Q* in figure 3.7A). This permits

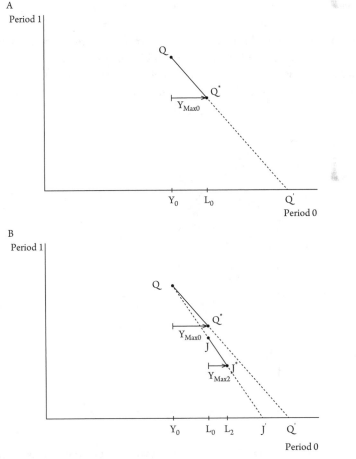

Figure 3.7 Absolute Limits to Borrowing and a Higher Rate for Supplemental Credit.

a maximum amount of consumption in period 0 reflecting this constraint; let us call it C_0^T (not shown in figure).

Individuals wishing to consume more in the current period than C_0^T must reduce investment and borrow along a market opportunity line extending from points on QST corresponding to the lower investment levels. For example, an individual investing to point S could borrow along SS* (parallel to TT*) and consume C_0^S, or the individual investing to point R could borrow along RR* (also parallel to TT*) and consume C_0^R. Consequently, market opportunities involving (feasible) borrowing extend from T* along the envelope curve T*S*R*Q*, which connects the end points of all such market opportunity lines associated with investment levels less than T.

Note that borrowing along the T*S*R*Q* segment of the market opportunity curve would not be optimal for the consumer, because the interest rate is less than the rate of return on investment, but the consumer cannot borrow more at this interest rate to achieve optimal investment and consumption.

Under these circumstances, two types of outcomes are possible: (1) an equilibrium outcome along the TT* segment of the market opportunity curve and (2) a rationing outcome along T*S*R*Q*. An equilibrium outcome occurs at the tangency of an individual's indifference curve with the market opportunities curve corresponding to an optimal investment, such as the tangency of U_1 and TT* in figure 3.8 at point D. At equilibrium outcomes, the marginal rate of return on investment, borrowing rate, and marginal rate of time preference are equal.

Rationing outcomes occur at the tangency of the T*S*R*Q* segment of the borrowing opportunities envelope and the individual's highest indifference curve

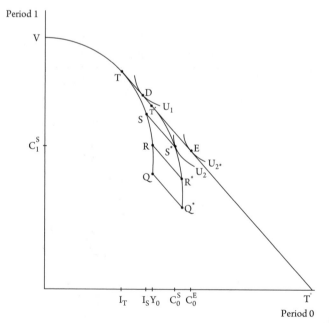

Figure 3.8 Intertemporal Consumption and Investment Opportunities with an Absolute Limit to Borrowing.

(U_2 at point S^*, for example). At such points, the marginal rate of return on investment and the marginal rate of time preference are equal. However, as mentioned, such points are not optimal, because the interest rate is less than the rate of return on investment, and in the absence of rationing, more investment would be preferable.

If more credit were available, the individual could invest more and achieve a higher indifference curve (that is, one with more highly valued levels of period 0 and period 1 consumption). This conclusion can be illustrated by extending the market opportunities line TT^* to the right, which is shown by the dashed line segment T^*T'. Indifference curve U_2^*, which represents higher valued period 0 and period 1 consumption than U_2, is tangent to the dashed line at point E. To achieve this result, the individual moves along the investment opportunity curve to point T, investing $Y_0 - I_T$. From T, the individual moves to the right along the market opportunity line TT^* to point E, borrowing $C_0^E - I_T$. For the additional investment of $I_T - I_S$, the individual is able to consume $C_0^E - C_0^S$ more in period 0, while period 1 consumption C_1^S is the same.[21]

Additional Credit at a Higher Interest Rate

Juster and Shay further extended the consumption/investment model to allow additional borrowing from secondary lenders at a higher interest rate. Figure 3.7B includes the same absolute limit to borrowing Y_{Max0} at the same interest rate as the previous example but provides the possibility of additional borrowing at a higher interest rate. This second borrowing opportunity also has an absolute limit to the amount of credit that the individual can obtain at the lower rate, but the individual can obtain additional credit up to Y_{Max2} at the higher rate. The second borrowing opportunity starts at point J along line segment QJ' in figure 3.7B, where the individual has exhausted borrowing opportunities at the lower interest rate. The individual borrows along JJ' until the loan equals $Y_{Max2} = L_2 - L_0$ at point J^*. Points beyond J^* would be greater than Y_{Max2} and would therefore be infeasible.

Figure 3.9 adds to figure 3.8 the possibility of additional borrowing from secondary lenders at higher interest rates. As before, line segment TT^* represents borrowing opportunities at some initial market interest rate. Again, it is tangent to the investment opportunity curve at T. Also as in figure 3.8, the maximum amount that can be borrowed at this rate (Y_{Max0}) is given by T^*. Beyond T^*, the individual can borrow up to Y_{Max2} at a higher rate along line segment FF^*.

Similarly, additional borrowing opportunities at the higher rate are also available for investment levels given by points S, R, and Q. At point R, for example, borrowing amounts greater than Y_{Max0} are given by line segment HH^*; and at point S, additional borrowing opportunities are given by GG^*. In each case, the amount of borrowing at the higher rate is limited to Y_{Max2}.

---

21. Relaxation of the absolute limit to borrowing leads to an optimal solution in this example. In other circumstances, relaxation of the absolute limit to borrowing could lead to another rationing outcome but one that is better than the initial outcome.

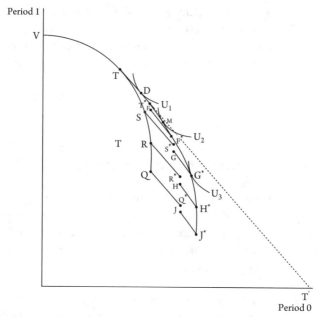

Figure 3.9 Intertemporal Consumption and Investment Opportunities with Absolute Limits to Borrowing and a Higher Rate for Supplemental Credit.

Market opportunities are given first by the segment TT^* tangent to point T, then the envelope of end points (maximum credit amount) of borrowing opportunities at the lower rate between T^* and F^*, and finally the envelope of end points of borrowing opportunities at the higher interest rate between F^* and J^*. Thus, the entire market opportunity curve for borrowing is given by $TT^*F^*G^*H^*J^*$.

As in previous examples, market outcomes involving borrowing are determine by tangency of the market opportunity curve and an indifference curve. Three types of outcomes are possible: (1) equilibrium outcomes, (2) rationing outcomes at the lower interest rate, and (3) rationing outcomes at the higher interest rate. Again, from figure 3.8, point D, the point where indifference curve U_1 is tangent to TT^*, illustrates an equilibrium outcome. At D, the marginal rate of return on investment, the lower borrowing rate, and the rate of time preference are equal.

One rationing outcome involves rationing at the lower interest rate. Point M in figure 3.9, where indifference curve U_2 is tangent to segment T^*F^* on the envelope of borrowing opportunities, is a rationing outcome at the lower interest rate. The individual borrows the maximum amount of credit available at the lower interest rate. The rate of return on investment is equal to the rate of time preference. The individual has a smaller level of investment than that at T. A line passing through M and parallel to TT^* intersects the investment opportunity curve (not shown in figure 3.9). At that point, the rate of return on investment is greater than the lower interest rate but not greater than the higher one. Hence, the individual would not borrow additional funds at the higher rate. Relaxing the limit to include borrowing at the higher interest rate provides additional borrowing opportunities along the dashed line running from T* to T'. Borrowing additional funds enables an individual to invest more current income and increase consumption in both periods.

A second type of rationing outcome occurs at the higher interest rate i_2 along the F*G*H*J* segment of the market opportunity curve. Indifference curve U_3, which is tangent to F*G*H*J* at point G*, illustrates such an outcome. The individual's investment decision in this case is given by point S. The highest valued consumption pattern at G* is achieved by first exhausting available credit at the lower interest rate and then borrowing the maximum credit available at the higher interest rate. In this case, the rate of investment return is equal to the marginal rate of time preference and higher than both interest rates, and so relaxing the limits to the amount of credit at either rate would permit greater productive investment. A sufficiently large increase in the credit limit along the dashed line T*T', for example, would make an optimal investment at point T feasible and allow attainment of a higher indifference curve with greater levels of consumption in both periods 0 and 1. Increases in loan limits for borrowing at the lower rate (such as an extension of SS* toward the x axis) or for borrowing at the higher rate (such as an extension of FF* toward the x axis) would also provide additional borrowing opportunities to allow greater productive investment and more highly valued patterns of intertemporal consumption. But the maximum amount that can be borrowed at both rates is limited: borrowing at the lower rate is limited to the value of the x-ordinate of T*, S*, or R* minus period 0 income Y_0 (not labeled in Figure 3.9); and borrowing at the higher rate is limited to the value of the x-ordinate of F*, G*, and H* minus the value of the x-ordinate of T*, S*, or R*.

Rationed and Unrationed Borrowers

Juster and Shay identified characteristics that likely distinguish "rationed" from "unrationed" borrowers. They called rationed borrowers those who have high marginal rates of time preference and are constrained by equity requirements that limit amounts that can be borrowed. Rationed borrowers typically are in early family life cycle stages. They have relatively few durable goods and frequently have growing families. Consequently, rates of return on household investment tend also to be high.[22]

Rationed borrowers also often might have relatively low or moderate current incomes compared with expected future incomes, making the sacrifices in current consumption necessary to satisfy creditors' equity requirements costly. And because of their moderate incomes and young age, rationed borrowers generally have not accumulated large amounts of liquid assets. At this stage in the life cycle, precautionary motives loom large in consumers' saving decisions. Thus, their liquid asset holdings have a high "subjective yield." Subjective yield refers to the full psychological benefit to the asset holder, including precautionary motives for

---

22. A few researchers have estimated rates of return for household durables using methods suggested by Juster and Shay. Calculations by Poapst and Waters (1964) and Dunkelberg and Stephenson (1975) provide support for the view that rates of return on investment in household durables can be high. Elliehausen and Lawrence (2001) adopted a similar approach to explore the when the use of "payday" loans might increase wealth.

holding liquid assets, such as fear of running out of liquidity at the worst possible moment. The high subjective yield to the asset holder exceeds the marketplace yield, usually referred to as the nominal yield, and makes it personally costly to liquidate assets to acquire durable goods. High marginal rates of time preference and high subjective yields on liquid assets cause equity requirements to be expensive for rationed borrowers, making them willing to pay higher interest rates to obtain more credit, at least compared with those in other financial circumstances.

Many consumers employ liquid assets for purchases only grudgingly, especially when events occur that impair their earning potential or require large expenditures. Their reluctance to use liquid assets stems from a belief that the worse the current situation, the greater is the need to maintain reserves for future emergencies, which puts a premium value on the liquid assets (see Katona 1975 and chapter 4 of this book). As a consequence, subjective yields on liquid assets can often be substantially greater than nominal yields.

This characteristic of consumers' financial behavior can explain many consumers' simultaneous holding of consumer debt and relatively large amounts of liquid assets. The weighted average annual percentage rate on the outstanding consumer credit is greater than the nominal market yield but less than the subjective yield on the liquid assets. Therefore, the cost of the consumer credit use is less than the subjective opportunity cost of giving up the liquid assets. Since some consumers who have personal loans from finance companies or credit card debts at high annual percentage rates also hold liquid assets, it seems that the subjective yield on liquid assets is likely to be quite high for some consumers.

In contrast, unrationed borrowers typically are in later family life cycle stages or have relatively high incomes. Unrationed borrowers in later life cycle stages and in better economic circumstances may have relatively fewer high-return household investment opportunities. And relatively high income may provide discretionary income that allows unrationed borrowers to satisfy equity requirements on new purchases without costly reductions in current consumption. Moreover, their age and income may allow unrationed borrowers to accumulate relatively high levels of savings and liquid assets. Consequently, subjective yields on liquid assets are often substantially lower for unrationed borrowers than for rationed borrowers. Availability of low-cost discretionary income and liquid assets for acquisition of durable goods makes unrationed borrowers unwilling to pay high interest rates for additional credit. They may, or may not, exhibit substantial credit demand depending on interest rates and their needs and desires. They may, for example, demonstrate demand for lower-cost debt such as prime mortgage loans at the same time that they are investing substantial sums in financial assets including stocks and bonds or mutual fund shares.

TESTS OF THE JUSTER-SHAY MODEL
Juster and Shay's model suggests several empirically testable hypotheses about rationed and unrationed borrowers' demand for credit. Their model predicts that:

(1) Unrationed borrowers' demand for credit would be more sensitive to interest rates than rationed borrowers' demand.

(2) Rationed borrowers' (but not unrationed borrowers') response to a change in the interest rate would be caused entirely by the effect of the change in the amount of the monthly payment.

(3) A simultaneous increase in the interest rate and term to maturity that reduces the amount of monthly payments would increase borrowing by rationed borrowers and decrease borrowing by unrationed borrowers.

(4) Demand for credit by unrationed borrowers would be unaffected by a lengthening of term to maturity that lowers payment size, with the interest rate being held constant.

(5) Rationed borrowers would respond more strongly than unrationed borrowers to differences in monthly payments.

Juster and Shay tested these hypotheses in an experimental study in which a panel of consumers was asked to express preferences for different hypothetical sets of credit terms. Consumers were classified into rationed and unrationed groups based on their income and family life cycle stage, and responses were used to compute elasticities of credit demand for rationed and unrationed groups.

Evidence from the experimental data was generally consistent with the predictions of Juster and Shay's theoretical model. The evidence strongly supported hypotheses that unrationed borrowers' demand was more sensitive to interest rates than rationed borrowers' demand (hypothesis 1) and that a simultaneous increase in the interest rate and term to maturity that reduces the amount of monthly payments increased rationed borrowers' demand and decreased unrationed borrowers' demand (hypothesis 3). Juster and Shay also found that rationed borrowers responded more strongly than unrationed borrowers to changes in monthly payments (hypothesis 5). However, the evidence did not suggest that unrationed borrowers were completely unresponsive to the amount of monthly payments when the interest rate remains the same (hypothesis 4) or that rationed borrowers were completely unresponsive to interest rates when the amount of monthly payments remains the same (hypothesis 2).

It is notable that Juster and Shay's evidence contradicts predictions of the simple form of the monthly payments model. According to the monthly payments model, both rationed and unrationed borrowers would have a similar response to a simultaneous increase in interest rate and term to maturity that reduces the amount of monthly payments. Since the amount of monthly payments is the price in this model, both rationed and unrationed borrowers would be expected to increase demand for credit.

Significantly, Juster and Shay's analysis reconciled the apparent inconsistency between consumers' lack of sensitivity to interest rates and the predictions of neoclassical economic theory as handed down from Fisher and Seligman. Rationed consumers, whose demand for debt exceeded the amount available at going interest rates and who, therefore, were not sensitive to these interest rates, likely made up a large majority of the population at that time. Thus, aggregate data from then and earlier largely reflected the behavior of these rationed borrowers. The aggregate data obscured the behavior of the smaller group of unrationed borrowers, who were sensitive to interest rates.

The hypothesized large proportion of rationed consumers at that time also provides insight into consumers' lack of knowledge of interest rates at the time. Rationed consumers do not need to know the interest rate to minimize credit costs. Rationed consumers find the longest available maturity and shop for the lowest monthly payment (payment size is perfectly correlated with interest rate for a given loan size and maturity). Juster and Shay found that knowledge of interest rates actually paid on recent credit transactions was concentrated mainly among the unrationed consumers, who need to know the interest rate to make rational credit decisions. Nevertheless, at that time, before Truth in Lending, many of the unrationed borrowers also underestimated or did not recall the rate paid. Later studies have shown that lack of knowledge has changed in the years since Truth in Lending went into effect in 1969 (see chapter 10).

Juster and Shay believed that the proportion of unrationed consumers (and, therefore, consumers' overall sensitivity to interest rates) would increase gradually over time. They pointed to secular growth in consumer income and a trend toward longer terms to maturity as factors that would shift consumers from rationed to unrationed groups. In addition to the factors identified by Juster and Shay, advances in creditors' ability to assess and price risk have likely reduced the proportion of rationed consumers in the population in recent years.

Some subsequent empirical tests of Juster and Shay's theory also are available. Walker and Sauter (1974) presented to a random sample of consumers pairwise comparisons of five alternative sets of financing terms for a household appliance. The sets of financing terms varied in terms of interest rate, product price, monthly payment size, and amount of down payment. For each of ten possible pairs of alternatives, consumers chose in each case the one that they preferred. Comparing the responses of lower-income and higher-income consumers, Walker and Sauter found that greater proportions of lower-income consumers than higher-income consumers preferred alternatives with lower monthly payments regardless of interest rate over sets with higher monthly payments or positive down payment. They interpreted these results as consistent with Juster and Shay's hypotheses.

Walker and Sauter's analysis has several technical flaws that diminish its contribution to understanding consumers' credit preferences, however (see Burstein 1978). For instance, they did not take into account that the size of monthly payment is not independent of price, down payment, interest rate, and term to maturity. Some of the alternatives were clearly preferable to others, and the choice between a higher product price or a higher interest rate is a matter of indifference for all consumers when the monthly payment and the down payment are the same. Several pairs of alternatives did involve trade-offs that theory predicts would cause rationed or unrationed borrowers to choose one or the other of the alternatives, but Walker and Sauter's classification of consumers as rationed or unrationed solely on the basis of income is inadequate.[23] Walker and Sauter reported statistically significant differences by education, occupation, marital status, and

23. For example, a household in retirement may have low income but would not normally be rationed, because demand for credit would often be low.

sex. However, they did not discuss how such differences might be related to Juster and Shay's or any other hypotheses about consumers' behavior.

More recently, Attanasio, Goldberg, and Kyriazidou (2000) used automobile purchase data from the Consumer Expenditure Surveys of 1987 to 1995 to estimate interest rate and maturity elasticities for households hypothesized to be more or less likely to be rationed.[24] Both their modeling and their statistical work are somewhat technical, but they provided evidence based on actual consumer behavior that credit choices of households likely to be rationed are sensitive to loan term (hence, other factors being equal, to the size of monthly payments). In contrast, they found that credit choices of households likely to be unrationed were sensitive to the interest rate but not to the loan term. Classifying consumers as rationed or unrationed on the basis of age or income alone is not precise, since rationing involves both high demand for debt and limited resources for servicing the debt.[25] Nevertheless, these findings provide additional support for Juster and Shay's theoretical model of consumer credit use.

CONCLUSIONS

In sum, neoclassical economic theory based on the work of Fisher, Seligman, Hirshleifer, and Juster and Shay suggests many conditions under which consumers will employ consumer credit that are both wealth increasing and rational. This argues that many consumers will employ this kind of credit over their economic life cycles, which is entirely consistent with even casual observation. Theory suggests that consumers will borrow when the marginal rate of return on further investment actions exceeds the borrowing rate facing them and that they will borrow to equate the marginal rate of return on investments with the borrowing rate and the marginal rate of time preference. These actions can often result in a pattern of credit use that raises real wealth and corresponding consumption over time. Such credit use often involves purchase of goods and services such as automobiles, appliances, home repairs, and education that provide their services over time, also consistent with even casual observation. This is not to say that some consumers may sometimes miscalculate and behave irrationally, but even in these cases, there are market mechanisms that limit credit use, including equity costs and liquidity constraints up to and including rationing. The next chapter looks in more depth at the psychological aspects of credit use and the one after that examines supply constraints in more detail.

24. Attanasio, Goldberg, and Kyriazidou extended Attanasio's (1994) earlier analyses of Juster and Shay's hypotheses.

25. Attanasio, Goldberg, and Kyriazidou also estimated their model for age groups (younger than thirty-five or thirty-five and older) interacted with education (high school diploma or less and some college or college degree). Partial derivatives were not statistically significant except for the group of households headed by persons younger than thirty-five with a high school diploma or less education. For that group, the partial derivative with respect to maturity is statistically significant and positive. As lower levels of education are associated with lower income, this group is likely to have both high demand and limited resources.

Behavioral Analysis and the Demand for Consumer Credit

During the post–World War II period, and certainly since at least the 1960s when Juster and Shay (1964) were formally analyzing the rationality conditions behind consumers' credit use, the view that consumer credit use is a normal development in a modern economy seems to have gained traction with the public at large. No longer is consumer credit broadly viewed as unproductive or somewhat disreputable, as it was in the 1920s and 1930s and earlier periods. In large part, this new view is likely a result of decades of experience with consumer credit that has demonstrated its usefulness. There are risks with consumer credit, to be sure, but most middle-class consumers do not have serious credit troubles, and they apparently view credit availability reasonably favorably. Reversing the old saying that familiarity breeds contempt, familiarity with consumer credit apparently seems to breed understanding and permissibility, even if not quite joy or love.

Widespread acceptance of consumer credit is observable from public opinion surveys. Surveys also show that consumers appear well able to differentiate in their minds among acceptable purposes for borrowing; some purposes are more acceptable than others and have been so for a long time (see table 4.1).

In general, these opinion surveys show that many more consumers view using credit for making household investments favorably compared with spending for luxuries or even smoothing consumption when income is cut (table 4.1). These views suggest a degree of thoughtfulness and deliberation in credit decisions, but this kind of differentiation also suggests that consumers' analyses of their credit decisions may not be entirely consistent with a strict interpretation of economists' axioms of rational choice.

The economic model of chapter 3 addresses borrowing in terms of enhanced utility, regardless of the specific items in the associated purchases. Evidence that consumers view credit use as appropriate for some purposes but less so for others suggests, however, that when making credit decisions, consumers may use heuristics ("rules of thumb") that simplify decision making or employ some kind of mental accounting or sorting for making distinctions. Such behavior may be purposive, intelligent, and utility enhancing but still fall something short of the extensive weighing of alternatives underlying the economic model of utility

Table 4.1 Consumers' Attitudes toward Installment Credit: Appropriate Reasons for Borrowing
(Percent of Respondents)

Reason Given	1959	1967	1977	1983	1989	1992	1995	1998	2001	2004	2007	2010
(1) Cover expenses caused by illness	86	80	85	83	*	*	*	*	*	*	*	*
(2) Finance educational expenses	70	77	80	80	82	82	82	81	79	83	83	81
(3) Finance purchase of car	67	65	84	82	80	78	81	79	79	81	80	77
(4) Consolidate bills	44	43	47	49	*	*	*	*	*	*	*	*
(5) Cover living expenses when income is cut	26	40	49	47	44	42	46	43	48	47	52	49
(6) Finance boats, snowmobiles, and other hobby items	*	*	23	19	*	*	*	*	*	*	*	*
(7) Cover expenses of vacation	5	9	17	13	12	13	16	14	15	14	14	14
(8) Finance purchase of fur coat or jewelry	2	4	6	5	5	5	7	6	6	6	5	5

* Question not asked in this year.

SOURCE: Surveys of Consumer Finances, various years.

maximization. This fact alone encourages further consideration of the underlying psychological conditions for consumers' choices.

Also, as frequently indicated earlier in chapter 3, consumer credit has never been without its problems and its critics. Reservations expressed by Danielian (1929), Haberler (1942), Kisselgoff (1952), and others based on psychological considerations have not disappeared but have foreshadowed newer analyses of psychological considerations influencing consumers' credit use.

This chapter examines some of the modern psychology-based extensions of the theory of credit demand and some of the recent controversies. Development of psychological aspects of the theory of consumer credit demand falls into two broad categories: (1) analyses based on psychologists' models of the cognitive process and (2) economic hypothesizing about credit use based on assumptions about consumers' cognitive biases. Analyses in the first category are largely empirical and provide insights into the processes that lead to economic decisions. They are outlined in the following section. Analyses in the second category have generated many recent theoretical discussions, mostly about credit card use, but to date have produced relatively few empirical generalizations about consumers' credit or credit card use behavior. Nonetheless, they form a new genre of consumer credit analyses in recent years and are discussed in the second section of the chapter. A prominent subset of theories in the second category appears to be mostly concerned with implications of cognitive biases for legal and policy prescriptions, rather than development of either theory or empirical evidence per se. This work is sometimes described as the "behavioral law and economics (BLE) of credit cards. We do not discuss this genre here at any length but have done so elsewhere (see Durkin, Elliehausen, and Zywicki 2014).

COGNITIVE MODELS OF CONSUMERS' CREDIT DECISIONS

Behavioral economists and psychologists have studied consumers' credit decisions for decades, especially using consumer survey techniques. Their studies are empirical, and many are concerned with the extent to which consumers' behavior is rational. Behavioral economists' concept of rationality is broader than that of economic theorists, however. Economic theory is concerned with specific goals such as utility maximization, evaluation of all available alternatives, choice of the alternative that best achieves the goal, and consistency in choice. In contrast, behavioral economists expand this concept of rationality. They view rational behavior as purposive and deliberative but not necessarily strictly optimal. They note that consumers often simplify, taking shortcuts and using heuristics. Consumers are often satisfied to take small steps toward goals (adaptive and satisficing behavior) rather than making the effort to achieve the optimum. Culture, group membership, attitudes, past experience, and even biases may influence the decision process.

There are many examples of how such factors may be influential, such as experience from a previous decision that may predispose a consumer to limit the length or scope of search on a subsequent purchase. Or differences in the way a problem or an option is perceived may produce different decisions. While such influences may result in decisions that are not strictly optimal in terms of economic theory, they do not necessarily preclude the conclusion that consumers' decisions are purposive, intelligent, and, therefore, rational in this broader conception.[1]

Much of the early empirical analysis of the effects of psychology on consumers' economic behavior in the United States was produced by George Katona and his colleagues John B. Lansing, James N. Morgan, Eva Mueller, F. Thomas Juster, Richard T. Curtin, and others at the University of Michigan's Survey Research Center, founded by Katona in 1946. For consumer credit, passage of the Truth in Lending Act in 1968 further stimulated research using psychology-based models to study the role of information in the credit decision process (see Day and Brandt 1973 and 1974 and Day 1976). A bit later, the work by Kahneman and Tversky on decision making under uncertainty has further reawakened the interest of economists in psychological influences on consumer behavior, including credit use behavior (see Tversky and Kahneman 1974 and 1981, for example, for some of their important work). Daniel Kahneman won the Nobel Prize in economic science in 2002 for his contributions to the psychology of judgment, decision making, and behavioral economics.

Early Behavioral Studies at the Survey Research Center

During the 1950s and 1960s, Katona and his colleagues at the Survey Research Center studied extensively the process of consumer spending, especially spending on consumer durable goods. They included consideration of the role of credit in household investment and the influence on consumer behavior of expectations about both personal finances and macroeconomic conditions. Katona (1975) summarized much of a quarter-century of survey research on consumers' financial behavior at the Survey Research Center in his classic *Psychological Economics*.

The survey research on the process of spending in large part supports the theoretical analyses that treat consumer credit as a part of consumers' investment-consumption decisions. As introduced earlier in chapters 1 and 3, the surveys found that the bulk of consumer credit arises in the process of purchasing household durable goods and services that do not fit conveniently into monthly budgets. Consistent with the theories of the economists, surveys find that credit use is greatest in early family life cycle stages, particularly in families with young children. As discussed previously in chapter 3, such families typically start with relatively low stocks of durables and can often obtain high rates of return on additional household investments.

Consumers generate comparatively little new consumer credit for current consumption of nondurable goods and services or for dealing with the financial

---

1. For extended discussion of the concept of rationality in economics and psychology, see Katona (1975) or Simon (1986).

consequences of hardship or distress, such as medical expenses, paying recurring bills, or shifting the burden of already existing debts. Indeed, this research found that concern over personal financial situation or future macroeconomic conditions is associated with less, not more, use of credit by consumers.[2]

A major focus of the survey research was to investigate the extent to which consumers' durable goods purchasing and financing decisions were deliberative and rational. The research indicated that few purchases include all of the elements of rational decision making, namely, planning for purchases, extensive search for information, formulation of evaluation criteria, and careful consideration of alternatives before making decisions.[3] As indicated, consumers often simplify, taking shortcuts and using rules of thumb (heuristics). Consumers may focus on one or a few product characteristics or rely on the experience of friends, for example. Nevertheless, evidence suggests that most consumers use one or more elements of deliberative behavior in decisions about consumer durables and credit.

The research identified several circumstances that lead to more or less deliberation in durable goods purchases. Situations in which consumers tend to follow more closely the economists' model of rational decision making include purchase of an item that is considered expensive or particularly important, purchase of a new or unfamiliar product, dissatisfaction with a previous purchase, and a strong new stimulus that causes uncertainty about previous attitudes or experience. In these situations, consumers are more likely to gather additional information, formulate or revise evaluative criteria, and deliberate more about alternatives, although they may still take shortcuts, simplify, or use heuristics. Few consumers collect all available information, carefully consider all possible choices, or use compensatory decision rules that weight all product characteristics, however. The economic model of rational choice suggests that they may not want to collect all available information because the collection and decision process is costly. Learning about all product characteristics, identifying sellers, collecting information about prices and characteristics of specific product choices, and evaluating alternatives are time-consuming and may include explicit expenses. Consumers will collect additional information only as long as the cost of the search is less than its benefits (see Stigler 1961 and Durkin and Elliehausen 2011 chapter 3).

In contrast, consumers tend to limit deliberative behavior in situations where they perceive a special opportunity that would not be available in the future, have an urgent need, or are satisfied with a previous purchase of the item. Such decisions still may include important elements of rational decision making, however. For example, consumers gathering information about products and sellers may perceive a special opportunity and decide without much further information gathering or careful evaluation of alternatives. Or consumers who are satisfied

2. See, for example, Maki (2002) and comments on his paper by Richard T. Curtin, director of the Surveys of Consumers program at the Survey Research Center. Maki's paper is discussed in chapter 2.

3. Katona and Mueller (1954) provide an especially comprehensive analysis of deliberation in consumers' durable goods purchase decisions.

with a recent previous purchase may feel they have sufficient information to make a decision without much search or consideration of alternatives. Even consumers who perceive an urgent need, such as a need to replace an important household durable good or an automobile, may recognize the problem in advance and take steps to prepare for the eventual purchase.

Another area of survey research examined the extent of consumers' knowledge of the cost of credit. As discussed in chapter 3, empirical evidence indicated that most consumers were not fully aware of the cost of installment credit in the period before Truth in Lending. Surveys conducted by the Survey Research Center in the 1960s contributed part of this evidence. When asked what would be the interest rate on a two-year automobile loan (a much more common term to maturity then than today), many consumers said that they did not know, and a substantial proportion reported rates that were unreasonably low. At that time, between 20 and 30 percent of consumers reported interest rates that could be considered accurate. Katona (1975) argued that the reason few consumers were aware was that the interest rate had little effect on their credit decisions. Most consumers, he explained, were concerned with the size of monthly payments, because the amount that they would have to pay each month affected their decision to buy or not, an explanation reminiscent of the once-popular monthly payments model. As discussed in chapter 3, Katona's explanation is not necessarily inconsistent with informed behavior, however. Juster and Shay's theoretical analysis provided an explanation for the role of monthly payments in some consumers' decisions. Their empirical analysis supported their theoretical explanation.

Survey work by Katona and others also provided evidence that monthly payments had an additional role in budgeting. This role, called "precommitment" in some studies (Strotz 1955–1956, for example) and, more recently, "mental accounting" in others (Thaler 1980 and 1985, for example), involves use of installment credit contracts by consumers to force themselves to set aside money each month for specific purposes. The survey efforts found that a considerable percentage of consumers used installment credit to purchase durable goods despite having sufficient liquid assets to pay cash. One explanation for this behavior is that consumers doubt their ability to save, believing that they do not have the discipline to replenish the liquid assets if they deplete them. Installment credit contracts force consumers to budget their money, saving via the debt repayment rather than frittering away future income on the numerous goods and services that are available in the marketplace (Katona 1975, 277–278).

The practice of precommitment is costly, but evidence suggests that many consumers are willing to pay to protect themselves against their own bad habits.[4] While, strictly speaking, such behavior does not represent definitional economic rationality, it does not imply irrationality, either, if that term means uncontrolled credit use outside the general boundaries posed by the economic theory devised

---

4. Consumers have also used other types of contractual arrangements, or precommitments, to force themselves to budget money. Whole life insurance, layaway plans, and Christmas Club or Holiday Club accounts are other examples of precommitments. See Strotz (1955–1956) for theoretical analysis of precommitment.

by Fisher, Seligman, and Juster and Shay. Rather, it implies a high perceived return on held liquid assets, as discussed previously.[5]

Information and Search in the Decision Process

The passage of the Truth in Lending Act in 1968 stimulated further research on the role of credit in consumers' decision process. Much of the motivation was an interest in evaluating the effects of Truth in Lending disclosures on consumers' use of credit. The decision to use credit is often itself part of a series of interrelated decisions involving choices for the type of product, the amount to spend, the time and effort to gather information, and sources for the product and credit. To evaluate the effects of the new law, researchers drew on contemporary advances in modeling consumers' purchase decisions that produced a comprehensive theory of the purchase decision, which has come to be known as the "buyer behavior model" or "consumer decision process model" (see Nicosia 1966; Engel, Kollat, and Blackwell 1968; Howard and Sheth 1969; and Bettman 1979).

The buyer behavior model formally links psychological and social influences into the stages of a rational decision process. The details of buyer behavior models differ, but the basic outline is similar across models. The decision process consists of several stages: (1) identification of a problem, (2) acquisition of pertinent information, (3) development of possible solutions, (4) evaluation of alternatives using relevant decision criteria, (5) choice of an alternative, and (6) assessment of the decision. Each stage of the decision process is affected by many individual, psychological, and social influences that cause the length and intensity of the decision process to vary from consumer to consumer and from decision to decision. Individual or psychological influences include consumer resources, motivation and involvement, knowledge, attitudes, personality, values, and lifestyle. Social influences include culture, social class, personal influences, family, and the situation.[6]

Day and Brandt's (1973) study of durable goods and credit purchase decisions undertaken for the National Commission on Consumer Finance is perhaps the most comprehensive of the consumer credit studies based on the buyer behavior model. Their findings suggest that most consumers were purposive and deliberate

---

5. Precautionary motives may underlie high subjective returns on liquid assets. For example, interruptions in receipt of income caused by illness or unemployment may make raising funds through borrowing difficult at that time, and the relatively high cost of small, short-term loans may make borrowing for unexpected emergencies expensive. See Katona (1975, 233).

6. For further discussion, see Blackwell, Miniard, and Engel (2006). Studies using this model as a framework for examining aspects of consumers' credit decisions include Day and Brandt (1973), Deutscher (1973), Durkin and Elliehausen (1978), Shay and Brandt (1981), Lawrence and Elliehausen (2008), Elliehausen (2005, 2006, and 2009), and Canner and Elliehausen (2013). Durkin and Elliehausen (2011) review studies of consumer credit in the buyer behavior framework at some length in their chapters 3 and 7.

in their purchase decisions.[7] By far, most consumers planned for major purchases for several weeks or more. The lengthy planning periods after a need is recognized suggest that few purchases were truly urgent, a condition that Katona and others had found to limit deliberative behavior. Day and Brandt noted that planning periods for purchases of replacements for items that were no longer usable tended to be longer than those for other purchases. Apparently, many consumers in this situation recognized the condition of the present item and took steps to prepare for the eventual breakdown. Well more than half shopped for a period of at least a few days, during which they obtained information about the item and sometimes also credit before making a decision. Nearly three-fourths of consumers considered more than one brand or store. Most did not shop extensively, but many consumers' knowledge from previous experience may have limited shopping, since well more than half of the items purchased were additions or replacements of items already owned.

As mentioned, satisfaction with previous purchases was another condition that Katona and others had found to be associated with limited search. Day and Brandt also considered the effect of previous product and store experience on search behavior. Previous experience was associated with significantly less search in some of their regressions predicting the number of brands considered, stores visited, and information sources consulted.

Day and Brandt found that consumers were less deliberative in their credit decisions than in their product decisions. A little more than a quarter of consumers using credit searched for information about credit sources, and only one in five considered alternative types of creditors. Many consumers apparently simplified the decision process and relied on the retail dealer for credit, either by using a retail credit plan or by allowing the retailer to arrange a loan at a financial institution. Today this approach has been replaced in many nonautomotive purchases by use of an existing bank-type credit card account (Discover, MasterCard, Visa, and American Express revolving credit card brands).[8]

Credit availability did not appear to have much effect on shopping or choice of retailer. Credit purchasers' product and credit shopping behavior was similar regardless of whether they could have paid in cash had they wanted to do so. While almost half admitted that they gave some consideration to credit availability in their selection of a retailer, only a little more than one in ten credit purchasers said that they would have purchased elsewhere if credit had not been available. A likely explanation for the lack of effect is that credit availability was not a critical issue for most consumers. When questioned about it, relatively few survey respondents believed that credit was extremely or very difficult for them to obtain from any source.

7. For their empirical work, Day and Brandt surveyed a representative sample of 650 California households and a separate sample of 150 black families. The oversample of black families was obtained to allow separate analysis of any particular credit problems of minorities at that time.

8. Recall that the percentage of consumers using credit for nonauto durables declined as the percentage of consumers using revolving credit increased since the 1950s (see table 1.2, in chapter 1, above).

The survey evidence provided by Day and Brandt suggests that consumers often chose to simplify the decision process by limiting credit shopping and allocating time and effort to the product decision. When asked about the difficulty of different choices in the decision process, most consumers mentioned as most difficult the choices on amount to spend or product characteristics. Credit choices were rarely considered among the most difficult and often considered among the least difficult choices to be made when purchasing durable goods. That the cost of credit is usually only a small part of the total purchase outlay makes credit a likely area for simplification. Consumers also relied on past experience. Many consumers purchased from retailers from which they had previously made purchases, often using credit. Consumers were much more likely to have relied on past experience for purchases of household durable goods than for cars. The difference here may be explained by the smaller outlay required for most other durable goods.

A major motivation for Day and Brandt's study was an interest in assessing early effects of the Truth in Lending Act. Awareness of credit costs was one criterion for evaluating the act. While awareness does not imply that cost information was used in making credit decisions, a lack of awareness suggests that the information probably was not used. Consumers are less likely to have retained information that they did not use.

Day and Brandt observed an increase in the level of awareness in annual percentage rates over levels before the law, but still fewer than half of credit purchasers at the time of their survey reported reasonably accurate annual percentage rates fifteen months after Truth in Lending. Awareness of annual percentage rates was positively related to income, education, and previous experience. Most consumers were generally aware of interest rate differences among different types of creditors at that time, however, a distinction sometimes called "institutional knowledge." Large percentages of consumers said that finance company loans, retail credit, and bank credit card credit were more expensive than bank installment loans and that credit union loans were less expensive than bank installment loans. By far, most consumers reported believing that differences in credit costs across lenders justified shopping around, but, as mentioned, only a small percentage of them actually shopped for credit.

Of the more than half of credit shoppers who noticed Truth in Lending information on credit costs, fewer than one in ten said that the information caused them to compare rates or would cause them to compare rates or postpone purchases in the future. Awareness of annual percentage rates was positively related to credit shopping, but only a little more than a quarter of credit purchasers actually shopped for credit.[9] Awareness of annual percentage rates was not significantly related to the decision to use cash or credit, probably because the greater percentage of these consumers did not have sufficient savings to purchase the item without credit. Thus, Truth in Lending appears to have had only a small effect on consumers' behavior at that time.

---

9. The survey responses did not indicate whether shopping caused awareness or awareness caused shopping.

Later surveys show large increases in awareness of annual percentage rates since Day and Brandt's study. Using the same definition of awareness, Durkin and Elliehausen (1978) found that more than half of borrowers using closed-end credit reported reasonably accurate annual percentage rates in 1977, which was about a twofold increase in the level of awareness since 1970. Durkin (2000) reported that nearly all holders of bank credit cards in 2000 provided reasonably accurate annual percentage rates for bank cards, compared with a little more than six in ten bank credit card holders in 1970. Changes in behavior have been much smaller than changes in awareness, however. The proportion of borrowers using closed-end credit who shopped for credit terms increased from a little more than a quarter in 1970 to a third in 1997 (Durkin and Elliehausen 2011 chapter 7). That credit shopping has not changed much despite large increases in awareness suggests that consumers today continue to simplify and focus more on the product decision. More recent greater awareness of credit costs permits further simplification of the shopping process in this area. Indeed, the widespread availability of prearranged credit through bank cards may make the credit decision a less important part of many consumers' overall decision processes than it was in the 1970s.

New Behavioral Models: Heuristics and Cognitive Biases and Intertemporal Choice

Work by Kahneman and Tversky on decision making under risk and uncertainty, which they summarized in influential articles in *Science* (Tversky and Kahneman 1974 and 1981), further enhanced economists' interest in psychological influences on economic choices, including credit use. Much of this work involves an experimental approach rather than surveys and does not involve specifics of credit use per se, although it has been influential in developing hypotheses in this area.

Based on the results of experiments, Kahnemen and Tversky in a group of articles described various cognitive biases that result from individuals' use of heuristics (simplified decision rules). They also described a tendency for individuals to prefer avoiding losses much more strongly than for acquiring gains. This tendency can produce inconsistent choices depending on whether an outcome is defined as a loss or a gain (that is, depending on its "framing"). From these considerations, Kahneman and Tversky (1979) proposed a model of choice under risk, which they called "prospect theory." Prospect theory, they argued, provides more realistic behavioral assumptions and predicts individual choices better than the traditional economic model of decision making under uncertainty.[10] Their work is discussed in the following subsection.

---

10. The traditional economic theory of decision making under uncertainty defines the expected utility of a risky prospect U as the sum of the utility of each possible outcome x_i multiplied by the probability of the outcome p_i. That is, $U = p_1 u(x_1) + \cdots + p_n u(x_n)$. For further discussion, see Schoemaker (1982).

Additional behavioral theories addressed other empirical observations of deviations from the standard expected utility model.[11] For instance, experimental and other evidence suggest that individuals discount proximate outcomes more than distant ones. But if discount rates vary by time horizon, then the choice between two options might differ depending on when the choice is made. Such behavior might lead individuals to deviate from optimal intertemporal allocations depending on the time period in question. This possibility immediately raises questions about such things as shortsightedness and self-control. New behavioral theories of this kind challenge assumptions about rationality in economic decision making, including decisions about consumer credit use. These issues are also discussed below.

Heuristics and Cognitive Biases

As indicated, heuristics are decision rules that reduce the complex tasks of assessing values to simpler judgmental operations. They allow individuals to make decisions quickly using limited information. Heuristics may be specific to certain tasks or be more general, but notably, heuristics are not optimizing techniques. They are methods that take account of computational limitations to achieve satisfactory outcomes with moderate amounts of computation (Simon 1990). The term *satisficing* has been coined to designate such behavior.

Common heuristics include the "availability" and "representativeness" heuristics (Tversky and Kahneman 1974) and the "recognition" heuristic (Goldstein and Gigerenzer 1999). The availability heuristic assesses the likelihood of an event by how easily an example can be brought to mind. For example, an observer might assess the likelihood of a price rise for a particular stock based on information recalled from a newspaper article just seen reporting yesterday's changes in the Dow Jones Industrial stock market index. The representativeness heuristic judges the likelihood of an event by its similarity to a known event. Using this heuristic, one might expect, for example, the next quarter's stock price change to be similar to changes in recent past quarters. The recognition heuristic infers that a recognized object has a higher value on some criterion than an object that is not recognized. Thus, one might expect the performance of the stock of a known company to exceed that of an unknown company.

Heuristics work well under many circumstances. Limited theoretical evidence suggests that a satisficing heuristic (choose an action again if it previously satisfied aspirations; search otherwise) produces optimal long-run outcomes in some situations and higher-valued, though not optimal, outcomes in others (see Bendor, Kumar, and Siegel 2009).[12] Indeed, evidence from some studies suggests that

---

11. For discussion of the origin of this standard model, see Samuelson (1937).

12. Satisficing does not work well in situations in which all alternatives sometimes fail. Because satisficing is failure-driven (that is, search if the outcome does not satisfy aspirations), it sometimes causes individuals to switch from a better to a worse alternative. Satisficing also has problems in situations of environment change where what works today does not work tomorrow. However, even in these situations in which satisficing is ill suited to producing optimal long-run outcomes, it may still lead to higher-valued outcomes than previous outcomes (Bendor, Kumar, and Sigel 2009, 24–25).

simple heuristics often perform as well as an optimization or full information/ weighting of alternatives approach.[13] For consumers' credit decisions, Juster and Shay's analysis examined here in chapter 3 suggests that the heuristic of choosing the lowest monthly payment from among consumer credit contracts with the longest available term to maturity may be equivalent to optimizing behavior for rationed borrowers.[14]

Evidence suggests that individuals make by far most decisions quickly using heuristics rather than extended decision processes, as might often be the case for durable goods. But when they use heuristics, certain cognitive processes or biases can produce outcomes that violate principles of strictly rational choice. For example, considerations that influence one's ability to imagine an event (such as a recent coverage of an airline accident, even though such accidents are relatively rare) or misperceptions about statistical influences (such as ignoring the effect of a small sample size when assessing observed sequences or frequencies) may bias estimates produced by the availability or representativeness heuristics.

Numerous studies investigating possible cognitive biases exist. Collectively, these studies have been referred to as the "heuristics and biases program." A comprehensive discussion of these studies is beyond the scope of this chapter, but the nature of the problem and the research issues are similar across studies. The following discussion examines broadly some of the observed biases, psychological hypotheses about them, and evidence associated with them. The important question here is whether identified causes of possible cognitive biases have an important impact on rationality of consumer credit use. Most of the studies investigate individuals' ability to solve logical or statistical problems and do not involve credit decisions. For the few studies that propose hypotheses about biases in credit decisions, evidence is largely from experiments using hypotheticals. Evidence that cognitive biases influence actual credit decisions of consumers is very limited.[15]

13. For example, Borges, Goldstein, Ortmann, and Gigerenzer (1999) found that stock portfolios chosen on the basis of firm name recognition (an availability heuristic) performed better than portfolios run by fund managers (and random portfolios); and DeMiguel, Garlappi, and Uppal (2009) found that portfolios divided equally among available assets (the 1/N portfolio allocation rule) performed better than mean-variance portfolios. See also Oaksford and Chater (1996), Gigerenzer and Goldstein (1999), and Griffiths and Tenenbaum (2006) for analyses and evidence suggesting that heuristics provide accurate predictions in many other areas. See Gigerenzer and Brighton (2009) for a review and assessment of the evidence on the use of heuristics in decision making. See also Gigerenzer and Goldstein (2011) and Gigerenzer and Sturm (2012).

14. Indeed, for the case where the decision to use credit is already made and under reasonable assumptions concerning identical choice of product across retail sources and identical down payment, this heuristic can also produce the best choice in the unrationed case. There is further discussion of this issue in Durkin and Elliehausen (2011 chapter 5) as part of the Truth in Lending "outlay issue."

15. A few studies based on market experiments have appeared recently. Navarro-Martinez et al. (2011) provide evidence suggesting that the amount of the minimum payment information on credit card statements may lead some consumers to anchor on that small amount and thus make smaller repayments. Bertrand and Morse (2011) tested several payday loan disclosures intended

Example of Experimental Evidence for Cognitive Biases

Tversky and Kahneman's (1983) "Linda Problem," one of the best-known experimental tests of cognitive bias, illustrates some of the issues. For the test, participants were presented with the following problem:

Linda is thirty-one years old, single, outspoken, and very bright. She majored in philosophy. As a student, she was deeply concerned with issues of discrimination and social justice and also participated in antinuclear demonstrations.

Which is more probable?

(1) Linda is a bank teller, or

(2) Linda is a bank teller and is active in the feminist movement.

The correct answer to this statistical problem is (1). The probability of any one of two events is always equal to or greater than the probability of the two events occurring together. That is, the probability that Linda is a bank teller has to be at least as great as the probability that she is a bank teller *and* a feminist.

Kahneman and Tversky presented this problem to three groups: (1) a naive group consisting of undergraduate students who had no background in probability and statistics; (2) an informed group consisting of first-year graduate students in education and medicine, who had taken one or more courses in statistics; and (3) a sophisticated group consisting of doctoral students in decision sciences, who had taken several advanced courses in probability and statistics.

Eighty-nine percent of participants in the naive group said that the correct answer was (2), that Linda being a bank teller and active in the feminist movement was more probable than Linda being a bank teller. Surprisingly, about the same percentages of the informed and sophisticated groups (90 and 85 percent, respectively) also said that the correct answer was (2). Apparently, the representativeness heuristic caused study participants to view Linda as more typical of someone who is active in the feminist movement rather than someone who is a bank teller. This view led participants to provide an incorrect response to the statistical problem, even when they should have known better.

Framing, Loss Aversion, and Mental Accounts

Kahneman and Tversky proposed that framing and loss aversion produced other cognitive biases, some of which may be important for economic behavior. Framing is the manner in which an option is presented. Loss aversion is the preference for avoiding losses more strongly than acquiring gains. This preference is postulated to cause individuals to avoid risky choices when individuals evaluate

---

to mitigate possible cognitive biases. One disclosure, which was motivated to address overconfidence in ability to repay, had a small but statistically significant effect on payday loan use. Mann (2013) also investigated overconfidence in payday lending and found that most payday loan borrowers accurately predicted their ability to repay, which suggests that this was not an issue for these borrowers. Mann's finding does not preclude that some borrowers' behavior was influenced by an overconfidence bias.

a possible gain, since they prefer avoiding losses to making gains. However, in some situations, individuals may prefer a riskier prospect, if the riskier prospect provides the possibility of mitigating a loss.[16]

Tversky and Kahneman (1981) presented experimental evidence that individuals' risky choices may differ depending on whether the option is framed as a gain or a loss. Participants were asked to choose a public program to prevent the deaths of six hundred persons from a disease. One problem was presented in terms of gains, the other in terms of losses; otherwise, the problems were identical:

Potential Public Health Programs

Problem 1
Program A: 200 lives will be saved.
Program B: one-third probability of saving 600 lives, and two-thirds probability of saving no lives.

Problem 2
Program C: 400 people will die.
Program D: one-third probability that no one will die; two-thirds probability that 600 people will die.

Participants who were presented with problem 1 were more likely to choose program A than program B: certain saving of two hundred lives over one-third chance that no one would die. In contrast, participants who were presented with problem 2 were more likely to choose program D than program C: a one-third chance that no one would die over a certain loss of four hundred. In problem 1, where outcomes were framed in terms of gains, participants' choices were risk averse, but in problem 2, where outcomes were framed in terms of losses, participants' choices were risk seeking.

Kahneman and Tversky also pointed to inconsistencies in preferences for options when contingencies are involved, such as a two-stage process where an uncertain outcome in the first stage determines movement to an uncertain second stage. In one experiment, a group of participants was presented with a choice between (A), a certain win of $30, or (B), an 80 percent chance to win $45, with both outcomes contingent on being selected with a probability of 25 percent in a first stage. Participants in this experiment were asked to state their preferred option

---

16. Loss aversion may also influence choices in situations that do not involve any risk. For instance, loss aversion may wrongly induce individuals to consider sunk costs (costs that cannot be recovered once incurred) in decisions involving future actions. For instance, managers considering future funding of an unprofitable project might be tempted to continue funding the losing project anyway, in the misplaced hope of avoiding a certain loss that has already taken place, when only the future possibilities actually are relevant to the decision. Likewise, individuals may stick with a loser stock market investment in the hope they eventually "can get their money back," even when only future outcomes for the company in question versus other companies are relevant. Current and past losses have already taken place. Only prospective revenues and costs are relevant to the decision of whether to continue funding or holding. Loss aversion may also explain some individuals' willingness to reject a credit card surcharge (a loss) but not an equivalent cash discount (a gain), even when the outcome for them is the same.

before the beginning of the first stage. Their choices were similar to choices of a second group that was presented with options (A) and (B) without any first-stage contingency. Of the two groups, 74 and 78 percent chose option (A), respectively.[17]

A third group was offered a choice with the same expected values as the choice offered the first group, (C), a 25 percent chance to win $30, and (D), a 20 percent chance to win $45; but in this case, no contingency was involved. Only 42 percent of this group chose option (C), which was equivalent to option (A) for the first group. Kahneman and Tversky concluded from these findings that participants tended to overlook the 25 percent chance of moving to the second stage, focusing only on the outcomes of the second stage in making their choice. For participants in the first group, option (A) appeared more attractive because it had the appearance of being certain. Thus, whether or not prospects are framed as contingencies may affect individuals' choices.

Kahneman and Tversky developed "prospect theory" to address such deviations from expected utility theory. One psychological assumption of prospect theory is that individuals commonly perceive outcomes relative to a reference point rather than as an absolute value. That is, individuals perceive outcomes in terms of gains and losses.[18] Prospects are first edited and then evaluated. In the editing phase, individuals organize and reformulate options to simplify subsequent evaluation and choice. This feature of prospect theory is consistent with earlier behavioral research indicating that individuals tend to simplify decisions. Kahneman and Tversky identified several possibilities for simplification:

- Sometimes prospects can be simplified by combining probabilities of identical outcomes. For example, two $200 outcomes having probabilities of 0.25 and 0.33 can be combined into a single outcome having a probability of 0.58.
- Sometimes prospects can be segregated into risky and riskless prospects. A prospect paying $100 with probability of 0.67 and $300 with probability of 0.33 could be segregated into certain receipt of $100 and a risky prospect paying $200 with probability of 0.33.
- For two prospects having a common component, the common component can be discarded. For example, in the two-stage process described above, in which participants were presented with a choice between (A), a certain win of $30, and (B), an 80 percent chance to win $45 in the second stage, the first stage might be ignored because it was common to both choices.[19]

17. Expected values are, for the first group, (A) $7.50 = 0.25 × 1.00 × $30 and (B) $9.00 = 0.25 × 0.80 × $45 and, for the second group, (C) $30 = 1.00 × $30 and (D) $36 = 0.80 × $45.

18. In the cash discount/credit card surcharge example, for instance, the outcome is the deviation from the posted price, not the final price, that matters. Whether the outcome is framed as a gain or a loss may influence whether an individual pays with a credit card.

19. The prospects (1), $200 with probability 0.20, $100 with probability 0.50, and –$50 with probability 0.30, or (2), $200 with probability 0.20, $150 with probability 0.50, and –$100 with

- Prospects can also be simplified by rounding outcomes or probabilities ($101 to $100 or 0.49 to 0.50) and discarding extremely unlikely outcomes. In addition, clearly inferior prospects can be rejected without further consideration.

Kahneman and Tversky suggested that many anomalies and inconsistencies in preferences result from the editing phase. The experiment involving the contingent two-stage prospect is an example where ignoring information in the editing phase (the 25 percent probability of being eligible for the second-stage lottery) may have changed preferences.

Edited prospects are then evaluated, and the highest-valued prospect is chosen. The value of a prospect is a weighted sum of the utility of outcomes associated with the prospect. The utility of each outcome is an individual's evaluation of a monetary value of an edited gain or loss (a "value function"). The weight for each outcome (decision weight) reflects the likelihood of the outcome but is not a probability.[20]

Based on experimental data on hypothetical choices between risky alternatives, Kahneman and Tversky argued that individuals overweight very small probabilities. Hence, individuals are willing to buy insurance (incur a certain small loss [insurance premium] in order to avoid a smaller expected loss [a very small probability of incurring a large loss]) and to purchase a lottery tickets for a higher price than the expected payout (a large payout received with a very small probability).[21] Over the entire range of probabilities, they argued, individuals are not especially sensitive to variations in probabilities, and decision weights need not and typically do not add up to unity.

Thaler (1980 and 1985) adapted elements of prospect theory to develop the concept of mental accounting, a set of cognitive operations to organize, evaluate, and manage budgets. He focused his attention on the value function $v(x_i)$. He maintained the assumptions that individuals define utility derived from outcomes in terms of gains or losses relative to a reference point.

Considering Kahneman and Tversky's evidence on loss aversion, Thaler hypothesized that individuals edit prospects according to the following rules:

- Evaluate gains separately (because utility increases less than proportionately with the amount of gain).

---

probability 0.30, provide another example of a possibility for discarding a common component. Eliminating the common component $200 with probability 0.20 reduces prospects (3) and (4) to a choice between (1a) $100 with probability 0.50 and $50 with probability 0.30 and (2a) $150 with probability 0.50 and –$100 with probability 0.30.

20. The value of a prospect is $V(x,p) = \Sigma \pi(p_i)v(x_i)$, where x_i is the monetary value of the outcome i, $v(x_i)$ is the utility of x_i, p_i is the probability of outcome i, and $\pi(p_i)$ is weight-associated with p_i. The value of a two-outcome prospect of $600 with probability of 0.33 and $200 with probability of 0.67, for example, would be $V(x,p) = \pi(0.33)v(\$600) + \pi(0.67)v(\$200)$. This valuation differs from standard economic theory (expected utility theory), where the $v(x_i)$ are weighted by probabilities p_i, not the $\pi(p_i)$.

21. Overweighting is not the same as overestimating the probability of an event.

- Combine losses (because disutility of two smaller losses is greater in absolute value than that of the sum of the two losses).
- Integrate smaller losses with larger gains (to offset disutility arising from loss aversion).
- Segregate small gains from larger losses (because the utility of a small gain may be greater than the utility from a small reduction in the amount of a loss).

These editing rules, he argued, would optimize utility from a set of prospects. He cited evidence from a small experiment in which most participants judged events (assessed prospects) consistent with these rules more favorably than events not edited according to these rules.[22]

Individuals then evaluate edited prospects. Thaler posited that individuals consider two types of utility in evaluating prospects: (1) "acquisition utility," which depends on the value of the prospect relative to the outlay required to obtain the prospect, and (2) "transaction utility," which reflects the outlay relative to a reference price. Thaler defined the reference price as a "fair" price. This evaluation process might explain why an individual would pay a higher price for an item in one context but not in another. For example, an individual might be willing to pay a considerably higher price for a bottle of water at an expensive hotel than at a supermarket. The hotel price would be considered unreasonably expensive at a supermarket.

Thaler further argued that prospects are grouped in categories of expenditure. The purchase decision takes place within the context of a category and is subject to a local temporal budget constraint. The budget constraint is more likely to be based on current income flows (perhaps augmented by access to credit that the income can service) than the more general concept of present value of lifetime wealth suggested by the neoclassical economic models.

Thus, in effect, Thaler contended that the mental accounting system consists of a set of expenditure categories or mental accounts with a portion of monthly income allocated to each category. The individual would normally restrict monthly expenditures in each category to the income allocated to the category. This simple heuristic likely works well in most circumstances but can be nonoptimal. It prevents an individual from shifting income from one category to another to equalize marginal consumption across categories.

But mental accounting is a heuristic that simplifies decision making and may facilitate self-control. Mental accounting may help explain the often cited observations that many consumers focus on monthly payments in making credit decisions (simplifies decision making) and that many consumers simultaneously have substantial liquid assets and owe credit card debt (prevents depletion of funds saved for emergencies). Researchers have also suggested that mental accounting may help explain consumers' unwillingness to use credit to smooth income

---

22. In a later experimental study, Thaler and Johnson (1990) found support for three of these four rules. Most study participants did not prefer to combine losses.

over time, as opposed to smoothing expenditures on durable goods. The mental accounting explanation for this behavior is developed more fully in a mental accounting model proposed by Prelec and Loewenstein (1998).

Prelec and Loewenstein argued that when individuals make purchases, the pain of paying may undermine the pleasure derived from consumption. To evaluate the interactions between the pleasure of consumption and the pain of paying, they proposed a "double-entry" mental accounting model in which an individual evaluates both the net utility from consumption after subtracting the disutility of associated payment and the net disutility of payments after subtracting the utility of associated consumption.[23] When net payments or costs occur over a period of time, they are discounted, not necessarily at a constant rate.

Three assumptions underlie their model. First, they assume that past events are largely written off (prospective accounting). This assumption implies, for example, that when a vacation is paid for in advance, the cost is essentially zero, and the vacation feels as if it were free. In contrast, much of the utility of a vacation financed by credit would be forgotten, and the pain of future debt repayments would be paramount in the mind. The second assumption is that individuals allocate future payments to consumption or allocate consumption over future payments, prorating over multiple events. In other words, individuals try to match consumption to payments. Third, individuals do not necessarily fully link payments and consumption, however, referred to as "decoupling." The extent to which payments and income are coupled, they suggested, varies according to the situation, payment method, and individual.

Prelec and Loewenstein argued that prepayment enhances consumption. The prospect of future consumption diminishes the pain of prepayment, while the prospective accounting assumption implies that past payments are largely written off at the point of consumption. In contrast, debt financing tends to diminish the utility of consumption. Future payments are discounted for current consumption, but past consumption is written off when future payments are made.[24] Thus, consumers would tend to have an aversion to debt.

These considerations do not imply that prepayment would always be preferred and credit purchases avoided. According to this view, as mentioned, an individual may well prefer prepaying for a vacation, because the payments would be a memory when consuming the vacation (with no thought of future debt payments diminishing the pleasure). However, an installment purchase of a durable good may be attractive if the durable good provides a series of surpluses of consumption over the periodic payments. The durable good may even provide continuing services after the loan is paid in full. Indeed, chapter 3 suggests that these outcomes can often be the case for installment purchases of durable goods or services (automobiles and education, for example).

---

23. These categories are analogous to Thaler's (1980 and 1985) acquisition and transaction utilities.

24. These propositions bring to mind Danielian's (1929) psychological critique of consumer credit, which is discussed in chapter 3.

Prelec and Loewenstein suggested that debt aversion resulting from mental accounting may help explain why individuals with temporarily low incomes fail to borrow sufficiently against future income to maintain a constant consumption profile over their lifetimes. Thoughts of future debt repayments diminish the utility of the additional present consumption, while in the future, no benefits diminish the disutility of the debt repayments.

They also suggested that mental accounting might prevent consumers from paying off credit card debts. The pain of repaying a credit card debt immediately would be relatively large and possibly greater than the discounted disutility of making relatively small minimum payments in the future to repay the debt.[25] And if expenditures financed by credit cards provide little or no stream of *future* consumption, any benefits experienced in the past would tend not to be recalled and therefore available to offset the pain of current full repayment. Prelec and Loewenstein speculated further that credit cards may actually enhance consumption paid by credit card if payment is associated with the monthly credit card payment rather than signing the credit card slip. This possibility arises because mental accounting enables the consumer to decouple the consumption from thoughts about paying.

Prelec and Loewenstein's mental accounting theory might account for several observations about consumers and credit. These observations include how some consumers view credit as appropriate for some purposes (for instance, automobiles and other household durable goods) but not for others (vacations or living expenses), spend more freely using credit cards than they would had they been required to pay cash, or often make only minimum payments on their credit card accounts. Empirical evidence (discussed next) is mostly from experimental studies, which are unable to rule out other possible explanations for the observations or may be an artifact of the experimental methods.

Prelec and Loewenstein provided evidence from several small-scale experiments involving hypothetical choices to support the theoretical predictions of their mental accounting model. Experiments included rankings of schedules for taking vacation and payment, preferences for fixed or variable fees for different services, pleasure associated with a windfall used to pay various types of bills or purchases, and preferences for saving or borrowing to pay for a party or miscellaneous expenses. Other researchers have considered Prelec and Loewenstein's double-entry mental accounting model to investigate in experimental settings how differences in the timing or form of payment affect choices (Soman 2001, Soman and Gourville 2001, and Soman 2003, for example). Experimental results in these studies appear to be consistent with predictions of the mental accounting model, but it is difficult to ensure in such studies that participant responses are affected by the substance of the matter and not by some transaction cost, incentive, or other environmental factor embedded in the experimental approach. In

---

25. Prelec and Loewenstein suggested that this hypothesis might account for Ausubel's (1991) conjecture that certain credit card borrowers do not intend to borrow but end up doing so repeatedly. See discussion of Ausubel (1991) later in this chapter.

general, the experimental methodology is a significant issue for these studies (see, for example, Einhorn and Hogarth 1981).

Robustness of Experimental Evidence of Cognitive Biases

Replications of results of experimental studies strongly support the existence of certain cognitive biases, although the extent to which cognitive biases affect actual behavior, including economic and financial behavior, is not clear. As it turns out, the experimental tests are sensitive to the format of the problem and the experimental procedures. Changing the format of questions or implementing different procedures can make cognitive biases disappear. There is no generally accepted theory explaining why cognitive biases occur or what causes them to disappear, although researchers have suggested some hypotheses. Thus, the extent to which cognitive biases affect actual behavior, including purchasing behavior, remains unresolved.

For instance, researchers in the field of evolutionary psychology have proposed hypotheses to explain why cognitive biases are observed in some situations and not in others. Evolutionary psychologists approach the problem on the basis of a theory that humans have many specialized cognitive processes that underlie their reasoning, and these responses are adaptations to humans' natural environment.[26]

One of the hypotheses of evolutionary psychologists is that human cognition of statistical processes occurs naturally through observation of series of events. Thus, human cognitive processes have adapted to process frequency information rather than statistical probabilities. Based on this theory, these researchers have in turn hypothesized that presenting statistical problems in terms of frequencies should produce fewer violations of statistical principles than presenting problems in terms of probabilities.

In one test of this hypothesis, Fiedler (1988) replicated Kahneman and Tversky's experiment using the original formulation of the Linda problem. Again, 91 percent of participants responded that the feminist bank teller option was more probable than the bank teller option. He also conducted a second experiment in which, instead of asking which is more probable, he substituted a frequency format: "There are 100 people who fit the description above. How many of them are (1) ...bank tellers? (2) ...bank tellers and active in the feminist movement?" In this experiment, only 22 percent of participants responded that the feminist bank teller option was more probable than the bank teller option. Similarly, Hertwig and Gigerenzer (1993; reported in Gigerenzer 1994) found that 88 percent of participants made errors for the probability format, but only 20 percent made errors for the frequency format.

The frequency format also reduced cognitive biases in other experimental problems. Gigerenzer and Hoffrage (1995) and Cosmides and Tooby (1996) conducted experiments comparing responses to probability and frequency formats in medical diagnosis problems. In both studies, participants were considerably

26. For a brief description of evolutionary psychology, see Samuels, Stich, and Faucher (2004).

more likely to provide correct responses to frequency formats than to probability formats. Such results support the hypothesis that frequency formats facilitate statistical inference under at least some circumstances. They do not suggest that cognitive biases do not exist, but they do refute the notion that all statistical reasoning is biased.

The context of the problem may also influence how individuals respond. In a later study, Hertwig and Gigerenzer (1999) investigated this possibility further, again using Tversky and Kahneman's (1983) Linda problem. Recall that participants were asked whether it was more probable that (1) Linda is a bank teller or that (2) Linda is a bank teller and active in the feminist movement. Hertwig and Gigerenzer pointed out that the opening statements in the problem (that Linda is thirty-one years old, single, outspoken, and very bright; that she majored in philosophy; and that as a student, she was deeply concerned with issues of discrimination and social justice and also participated in antinuclear demonstrations) are not needed to answer the statistical problem. They hypothesized that these statements can be interpreted as asking for a typicality judgment. In that case, a representativeness heuristic might well be an efficient process for producing an appropriate judgment.

Hertwig and Gigerenzer's empirical analyses supported this possibility. In a small-scale experiment, they found that by far most participants chose response (2) as the correct answer when they were presented with a frequency rather than a probability format. Further, when asked about their understanding of "probable," most provided responses suggesting a nonstatistical understanding.

In a second experiment, Hertwig and Gigerenzer presented the problem in the original format to half of the participants and in a modified format asking for both typical and statistical judgments to the other half. Participants responding to the modified, two-part format provided correct answers to the statistical problem much more frequently than participants responding to the original format.

Hertwig and Gigerenzer conducted a similar analysis of participants' understanding of the question in a frequency format. When participants were asked about their understanding of "frequently," only one of 55 responses was nonstatistical. Thus, it seems that findings of considerably lower error rates for the frequency format than the probability format are not surprising.

Krynski and Tenenbaum (2003) suggested another potential source for observed cognitive biases in experimental studies. They argued that human reasoning under uncertainty naturally operates through causal mental models, rather than through purely statistical representations. Typically, individuals make correct statistical inferences only when the data can be incorporated into a causal explanatory model consistent with individuals' theories of the environment.

For empirical analysis, they considered the problem of predicting the incidence of cancer in the population, given the existence of false positive test results. The possible cognitive bias for this problem arises from failure to consider the overall (low) base rate of cancer in the population. (Kahneman and Tversky 1982 called this bias "base rate neglect.")

Krynski and Tenenbaum hypothesized that individuals lacking an explanation for high false positive test results apparently will tend to believe the test is tantamount to a doctor's diagnosis of cancer and focus only on the information from the test. Alternatively, when provided with an explanation for existence of false positive results (for instance, a benign tumor looks like a cancerous tumor on an X-ray), individuals will consider information that cancer is uncommon in predicting its incidence.

They conducted two experiments. In the first experiment, they tested whether describing false positive test results as uncertain would lead participants to believe the false positive rate could be in error and incorporate that information into their estimates. In the second test, they compared responses to a statistical question with those to a question that attributed the existence of false positive results to benign cysts. In both experiments, they found that providing a way for participants to make sense of false positive results improved estimates. The number of participants who failed to consider the low base rate (and high false positive rate) was lower for the causal format, and the number of correct or nearly correct estimates was higher. They interpreted these findings as evidence that human probabilistic reasoning operates over causal mental models. These findings suggest that failing to consider or misunderstanding causal structure may be an important source of error in experimental studies of problem solving involving uncertainty. In order to construct such causal models, theories of cognitive processes for specific environments are needed.

Gigerenzer, Hell, and Blank (1988) provide another example that suggests that specific heuristics are highly specialized, operating in some environments but not others. In this example, participants in a small-scale experimental study were provided with six personality descriptions selected from a group of thirty engineers and seventy lawyers (or seventy engineers and thirty lawyers). For each personality description, participants were asked to indicate the probability that the person described was an engineer. In one case, participants were told that the descriptions were randomly selected. In the other case, participants chose descriptions from urns. Participants actually received the same descriptions as in the first case, but participants in the second case were led to believe that they actually were observing a random selection process.

The first case replicated results of an earlier study by Kahneman and Tversky (1973). In that case, the average predicted probability was closer to 50 percent than to 30 percent (or 70 percent), when the latter would be expected based on the percentage of engineers in the group. In their study, Kahneman and Tversky concluded that participants ignored the base rate of engineers in the group. Kahneman and Tversky suggested that this was the result of applying a representativeness heuristic, in which participants evaluated descriptions on the basis of their stereotype of an engineer.

In the second case, where participants observed the selection process, the average predicted probability that the person described was an engineer was much closer to the base rate for engineers (30 or 70 percent) than the average predicted probability for the first case (in which base rates appeared to be neglected). In other words, participants' evaluations in the second case reflected differences in the actual base rate for engineers.

When participants were asked about their evaluation strategies, those who visually observed selection were more likely to have employed strategies that used base rate information than participants who were told that descriptions were randomly selected. In contrast, participants who were told that descriptions were randomly selected were more likely to have used the representativeness heuristic.[27]

Gigerenzer, Hell, and Blank concluded that the difference in the presentation of information, namely, verbal presentation or visual observation, influenced participants' internal representation of the problem. They noted that the degree to which base rate neglect was observed in several other studies examining the engineer/lawyer problem was also sensitive to the presentation of the problem. They proposed that base rate neglect is not a general property of the human mind and that the representativeness heuristic is not a general-purpose cognitive process. Their hypothesis suggests that the questionnaire and other methods of displaying the problem are not neutral but are of essential theoretical relevance to participants' internal representation of the problem and thus the cognitive process used.

Even without accepting the theories of evolutionary psychologists, the sensitivity of experimental results to the format, context, and content of the problem suggests that some skepticism about the extent and impact of cognitive biases is warranted. Economists also have questioned the significance of experimental evidence of cognitive biases. Plott and Zeiler (2005) investigated differences in preferences attributed to an "endowment effect," which is hypothesized to cause individuals' willingness to pay for an item ("willingness to pay") to differ from their willingness to accept payment to do without the item ("willingness to accept"). The endowment effect is attributed to loss aversion: individuals value an item that they own much more than an identical item that they do not own. Hence, they demand much more to do without the item than they would pay to obtain it.

Plott and Zeiler examined in detail previous experimental studies of the endowment effect. They noted that the different studies had employed various procedures to avoid participant misunderstanding of the nature of the problem. The procedures included approaches that

- Explained the nature of the experiment and optimal response.
- Provided an opportunity to practice and experience the consequences of decisions.
- Offered incentives to provide true valuations rather than respond strategically.
- Elicited valuations in a market environment with incentives for optimal responses.
- Measured differences based on actual trades rather than willingness to pay and willingness to accept responses.

27. The most commonly reported strategy (a little more than 40 percent of participants in each case) was a lexicographic representativeness strategy in which participants first evaluated the similarity of the description to their mental images of engineers and lawyers, and if this evaluation was inconclusive, they then considered the base rates. This strategy does not seem irrational considering the small sample, consisting of only six descriptions.

But previous studies did not agree on the nature of misunderstanding, and no study included all of these procedures identified to avoid participant misunderstanding. Therefore, participant misunderstanding still may have influenced the results of any of these experiments. It is also notable that the evidence is not robust across studies, despite some beliefs to the contrary.[28] Twelve of thirty-nine experiments examined by Plott and Zeiler reported no significant difference in willingness to pay and willingness to accept. Thus, evidence of an endowment effect is not conclusive.

In the absence of a complete theory of how perceptions might influence experimental results, Plott and Zeiler developed an experimental design to avoid *all* possible sources of misunderstanding identified in previous studies. They initially chose the experimental design reported in Kahneman, Knetsch, and Thaler (1990) and replicated Kahneman, Knetsch, and Thaler's results that median willingness to pay was significantly less than willingness to accept. Plott and Zeiler then modified the survey procedures to avoid possible participant misunderstandings identified in the literature. To elicit valuations, they used a market mechanism that provides incentives for participants to provide "true" valuations. They explained to participants how providing true valuations maximizes earnings and provided practice rounds for both selling (willingness to accept) and buying (willingness to pay) valuations. Participants kept any earnings from the practice rounds. Participants were told that strategic behavior was not optimal, and practice rounds allowed participants to learn that such behavior reduced earnings. Plott and Zeiler also ensured that decisions and payments were anonymous so that participants would not be tempted to consider how others (experimenters or other participants) would view their valuations.

Results of the modified experiment indicated that participants' willingness to accept was not significantly different from willingness to pay. Based on their findings, Plott and Zeiler concluded that the observed differences in willingness to accept and willingness to pay do not reflect a fundamental feature of preferences and do not support the endowment effect hypothesis:

> The fact that the gap [between willingness to pay and willingness to accept] can be turned on and off demonstrates that interpreting gaps as support for endowment effect theory is problematic. The mere observation of the phenomenon does not support loss aversion—a very special form of preferences in which gains are valued less than losses. That the phenomenon can be turned on and off while holding the good constant supports a strong rejection of the claim that WTP-WTA [willingness to pay–willingness to accept] gaps support a particular theory of preferences posited by prospect theory. (Plott and Zeiler 2005, 542)

---

28. See Kahneman, Knetsch, and Thaler (1991, 205), for example: "After more than a decade of research on this topic we have become convinced that the endowment effect, status quo bias, and the aversion to losses are both robust and important."

Plott and Zeiler did not advance a theory explaining participants' perceptions but did speculate about possible explanations for their findings. One is that the valuations reflect some motivation to announce a value other than the true value. Plott and Zeiler's experimental procedures sought to eliminate motivations based on strategic considerations or concern about how others might judge their valuations, but other motivations might still exist. Another possibility is that a gap between willingness to pay and willingness to accept might reflect a learning process of some kind, but Plott and Zeiler's experimental results provided no evidence of this explanation.[29]

Heuristics and Market Performance

As mentioned earlier in this chapter, limited theoretical evidence indicates that a satisficing heuristic produces long-run optimal outcomes in some circumstances. Empirical evidence from experimental economics, a branch of economics that applies experimental methods to study how markets and other exchange systems work, supports this theoretical conclusion. The studies consistently indicate that individual decisions based on limited information in experimental markets produce prices and allocations that converge quickly to the neighborhood of optimal equilibrium values (see Smith 1991 for references and a summary of the findings from many studies). This result occurs even though participants do not engage in extensive weighing of alternatives.

These findings suggest that the behavior of participants using various heuristics with limited information can produce efficient market outcomes. Experimental studies have also found that market environments reduce the incidence of preference reversals for risky prospects and losses from failure to recognize sunk costs and opportunity costs.[30] Smith contended that the findings of these studies argue that markets reinforce or even induce individual rationality, even though the manner in which markets promote rationality is not well understood (Smith 1991, 881).

In a later paper, Smith (2005) speculated on how markets promote rationality. In his view, market prices provide stimuli that cause individuals to take actions that better their situations. These actions move prices and allocations toward competitive equilibrium, reinforcing the individual actions. Thus, focusing on

---

29. See Plott (1996) and Loomes, Starmer, and Sugden (2003) for further discussion and evidence of learning in repeated markets.

30. Evidence from equity markets supports the findings of studies in experimental economics. Reviewing studies of stock return anomalies attributed to behavioral biases, Malkiel (2003) noted that although statistically significant, the anomalies are generally quite small and sometimes persist for short periods but usually disappear quickly. Malkiel argued that while market participants clearly do make mistakes and the actions of some market participants are demonstrably less than rational, the preponderance of evidence suggests that the market is remarkably efficient. Whatever evidence of anomalies in pricing of equities has been found, he concluded, they do not persist and provide few opportunities for investors to obtain extraordinary returns. For a similar assessment of the evidence on behavioral anomalies in stock market returns, see Fama (1998).

whether or not individual decisions are optimal misses the point: operation of markets to move outcomes toward optimal ones (Smith 2005, 146).

Conclusions: Cognitive Biases and Rational Behavior

Discussions in previous subsections illustrate the sensitivity of experimental studies of cognitive biases to the format, context, and content of the problems presented to participants. They suggest that considerable care is required to design meaningful experimental questions and to produce appropriate conclusions. Some of the problems presented to participants in experimental studies likely do not reflect the problems actually experienced by most individuals in making decisions under uncertainty, and participants in experimental studies may not use the same decision processes that they use in making actual decisions. In an experimental study, as opposed to in the "real world," there is little cost to making an error and not much reward for efforts to provide a correct response. Results of the experimental studies should be interpreted with considerable caution and cannot be applied to specific problems without an understanding of the decision process and the environment.

Nonetheless, it seems reasonable to conclude that individuals sometimes do make cognitive mistakes. We cannot directly conclude that all, most, or even many human decisions are influenced by cognitive biases, however. Both the heuristics and biases program and evolutionary psychologists would probably agree with these conclusions, although the heuristics and biases program may be reluctant to admit it freely (see Samuels, Stich, and Bishop 2002).

Assessing actual decisions requires understanding the cognitive process and the environment in which the decisions are made, as the marketers have pointed out with the buyer behavior model. Research in evolutionary psychology has contributed to this understanding and deserves to be taken seriously. Precise and falsifiable (testable) models that predict the circumstances that elicit various heuristics are needed. Specific statistical, logical, or other rational models of decision making may not necessarily be the norm for evaluating decisions (see Gigerenzer 1996; Samuels, Stich and Faucher 2004; and Gigerenzer and Gaissmaier 2011).

As indicated, another definition of rationality is behavior aimed to achieve one's goals or objectives. Katona's (1975) view of rationality presented earlier in this chapter conforms to this definition. Limited available evidence suggests that simple heuristics often perform as well as rules based on rational decision making in various situations. Oaksford and Chater (1996), Gigerenzer and Goldstein (1999), Griffiths and Tenenbaum (2006), and DeMiguel, Garlappi, and Uppal (2009) all present analyses and evidence suggesting that heuristics provide accurate predictions in many areas but require less information to implement. Such heuristics may efficiently facilitate achievement of goals in an environment of limited and costly information. To date, the applications of theories have generally been to relatively simple problems.[31] Theories on use of specific heuristics

---

31. For an overview of findings on well-studied heuristics, see Gigerenzer and Brighton (2009).

in consumer credit decisions or cognitive biases arising from such use have not specifically been tested.

EXPECTED UTILITY AND TIME PREFERENCES

Psychology played a major role in economists' discussions of intertemporal choice until Samuelson's (1937) paper "A Note on Measurement of Utility."[32] In this paper, Samuelson developed a discounted utility model as a generalization of Fisher's model of intertemporal choice (discussed here in chapter 3) over multiple time periods.

Samuelson proposed that an individual behaves so as to maximize the sum of all future utilities and that the future utilities are reduced to comparable magnitude with current utilities by discounting. For simplicity, Samuelson assumed that individuals discount by a single constant discount rate, which is the same for all types of consumption and across all time periods. Assuming the same discount rate across all types of consumption precludes different discount rates for different items, such as gains being discounted more heavily than losses (that is, "loss aversion" as discussed earlier in this chapter). Assuming the same rate across all time periods precludes discounting items closer in time more than more distant items. (A declining rate of time preference is often termed "hyperbolic discounting," because in this case, a hyperbolic mathematical function provides a better fit to experimental data than a constant, exponential function.) Samuelson did not claim that individuals actually discounted using a single constant rate. Instead, he maintained that a single constant rate was a hypothesis, subject to refutation by observable facts.

Many researchers have since observed behavior consistent with hyperbolic or other nonconstant rate of time discounting (see Frederick, Loewenstein, and O'Donoghue 2002 for a list). Thaler (1981) undertook one such study, in which participants were asked to imagine that they had won a small lottery. They could receive an amount of money immediately or could receive a larger amount if they waited. Participants were asked how much money they would need to receive if they waited for different time intervals. For one set of options involving receipt of $15, for example, the median amount for participants required to wait three months was $30, which implied a discount rate of 277 percent. A one-year wait required $60, or 139 percent, and a three-year wait required $100, or 63 percent. For another set of options also involving receipt of $15, the median amount for participants required to wait one month was $20, or 345 percent per annum. The median amount for three months was $30, or 277 percent; for one year, $50, or

---

32. Fisher (1930), for example, extensively discussed personal characteristics that either (1) contribute to or (2) lessen impatience. These characteristics include shortsightedness (foresight), weak will (self-control), habit of spending freely (thrift), emphasis on shortness and uncertainty of life (expectation of a long life), selfishness (concern for welfare of family after death), and slavish following of whims of fashion (independence to maintain a balance between income and expenditures). For a brief discussion of economists' views on intertemporal choice before development of the discounted utility model, see Becker and Mulligan (1997) or Frederick, Loewenstein, and O'Donoghue (2002).

120 percent; and for 10 years, $100, or 19 percent. Other researchers, also using experimental data, have found similar patterns. Such findings suggest that individuals are more impatient when delays are shorter than when they are longer. Hyperbolic discounting is not the only plausible explanation for such responses. Rubinstein (2003) proposes a heuristic based on similarity relations for prospect attributes that is consistent with experimental evidence. Consider the choice between two prospects that differ in payout and delay. An individual first considers whether one prospect dominates (is unambiguously superior) than the other. If no alternative is superior, the individual considers whether the payout or the delay is similar for the two prospects. If they are similar on one dimension, the individual chooses the prospect with the higher value of the other dimension. Finally, the individual considers another criterion if the first two rules are not decisive. Rubinstein's experimental findings indicated time-inconsistent choices, which were consistent with this heuristic, but not hyperbolic discounting. Like many of the experimental findings presented in support of hyperbolic discounting, Rubinstein's findings involved hypothetical choices by university students.

Available evidence from many different studies suggests that discount rates decline sharply during the short run and then level off and become practically constant. Frederick, Loewenstein, and O'Donoghue (2002) plotted estimated mean or median discount factors—that is, $1/(1 + \text{discount rate})$—from different studies against the average time horizon associated with each discount factor. They found that the discount factor was positively related to the length of the time horizon, which means the discount rate declines as the time horizon increases, since the discount factor and discount rate are inversely related. The lowest discount factors (highest discount rates) were for time horizons of one year or less. Discount factors increased with the length of the time horizon. After a year, the discount factor was nearly constant, on average about 0.80, which implies a discount rate of about 25 percent. Estimates from the individual studies varied quite substantially.

Constant (exponential) discounting ensures that decisions are time consistent (Strotz 1955–1956). Time consistency means that if receiving Y tomorrow is preferred to receiving X today, then receiving Y in 101 days will also be preferred to receiving X in 100 days. With hyperbolic discounting, the discount rate for evaluating options received tomorrow is greater than the discount rate for evaluating options received between the 100th day and the 101st day. Consequently, an individual could well prefer receiving X today while preferring to receive Y in 101 days to receiving X in 100 days. In other words, the individual's preference over options X and Y reverses as the decision gets closer. Such preferences are called time inconsistent.

Besides a constant discount rate, the standard discounted utility model includes several other assumptions:

- Integration of new alternatives with existing plans: Individuals evaluate a new prospect by considering how accepting the prospect will affect consumption in all future periods. This assumption is a consequence of the effect that accepting the prospect alters the budget constraint. Such integration requires that individuals have well-formed plans for future consumption and reallocate future consumption every time a decision is made.

- Utility independence: Utility is the discounted sum of each period's utility. Aside from discounting, the distribution across time does not matter. This assumption rules out preferences for a flat or improving utility profile over a highly uneven utility profile.
- Consumption independence: Utility of consumption in any period is unaffected by consumption in any other period. Consumption independence rules out, for example, that an individual's preference between lobster and steak for dinner tonight is related to having steak last evening or expecting to have steak tomorrow evening.
- Stationary instantaneous utility: An individual's well-being from an outcome in any time period is constant regardless of the time at which utility is evaluated. This assumption precludes changes in preferences over time.

Empirical evidence indicates that individuals do not behave entirely in accordance with these assumptions, either (see Frederick, Loewenstein, and O'Donoghue 2002).

Unlike the cognitive biases studied by Kahneman and Tversky and others, most departures from assumptions of the discounted utility model largely do not appear to be problematic. That individuals may prefer to spread consumption over time, for instance, or allow variety to influence their choices for dinner today and in the future does not suggest irrational behavior. Failure to integrate new prospects in existing plans and hyperbolic discounting are more problematic, however.

New prospects alter the intertemporal budget constraint. To evaluate a new prospect, an individual must consider both the existing consumption plan and the optimal consumption plan if the prospect is accepted. This decision is difficult, but failure to integrate new prospects may preclude reallocations that equalize marginal consumption over time, resulting in suboptimal intertemporal allocation of consumption. It seems more plausible that individuals consider many new prospects independently of existing consumption plans. Mental accounting may play a role in simplifying such evaluations.

Hyperbolic Discounting

Hyperbolic discounting has raised the most concern. As discussed above, hyperbolic discounting causes individuals to value proximate utilities more than more distant ones.[33] Higher valuation of present utilities may lead individuals to deviate

---

33. Such behavior may have a biological basis. Hyperbolic discounting also predicts animals' behavior in foraging and predation. Animals often choose a smaller reward if it is available sooner over a larger reward later, even though waiting for the larger reward would maximize their rate of energy intake. Some biologists have hypothesized that such discounting of the value of future rewards may be an adaptive response to the risks associated with waiting for delayed rewards. See Real and Caraco (1986) and Green and Myerson (1996). That said, evidence from experiments with animals seems unsatisfactory as explanation for human choices over time and under uncertainty.

from prior optimal intertemporal allocations in future time periods. For example, individuals may postpone or abandon earlier plans for setting aside money in savings. To enforce previous decisions, individuals sometimes precommit to future actions, such as having automatic contributions from pay to tax-deferred savings accounts or using consumer installment credit to purchase relatively expensive household durables (see Strotz 1955–1956 or Laibson 1997, for example).

Whether or not hyperbolic discounting is irrational is perhaps less clear. Hyperbolic discounting can be linked to behavior that can be or is harmful, such as procrastination, (O'Donoghue and Rabin 1999) or addiction (O'Donoghue and Rabin 2000). But individuals make numerous intertemporal choices, in most cases apparently without suffering great harm. In some cases, choosing a more proximate reward may be sensible. Examples include when more distant prospects are risky or uncertain, when future resources or preferences are uncertain or unknown, and when the proximate prospect ensures survival. Individuals can exercise self-control to prevent impatience from jeopardizing long-term plans. Individuals can also enter into contractual agreements that obligate them to carry out long-term plans (precommitting).

Self-control is achieved through cognitive control structures that enable individuals to coordinate thought and action to achieve internal goals. Activation of cognitive control structures can inhibit automatic processes that are susceptible to impulsive behavior.[34] Benhabib and Bisin (2005) model such a structure for a consumption/saving decision. The structure trades off impulsive immediate consumption with a saving rule requiring self-control for its implementation. Self-control requires actively maintaining attention to the saving rule. An individual facing temptation might yield to a temptation if it does not perturb the saving plan too much and does not have large permanent effects on the prescribed wealth accumulation pattern. To be effective, the saving rule requires that the internal inhibitions become stronger as the awareness of the cost of impulsive consumption increases. Such a structure might also regulate consumption/borrowing decisions.

As suggested by Strotz (1955–1956) and others, individuals also may choose to precommit. Consumer installment credit, Christmas or Holiday Club accounts, whole life insurance, and layaway plans are examples of financial contracts that consumers sometimes choose to constrain future behavior (Juster and Shay 1964).

Ariely and Wertenbach (2002) provide experimental evidence that in circumstances where time-inconsistent behavior is costly, many individuals self-impose binding constraints to overcome perceived self-control problems. Their evidence arises from two studies. One involved course requirements for student-written papers, with students in one class being allowed to choose their own deadlines for each of three written papers and students in the other being assigned three evenly spaced deadlines. A grade penalty was imposed for missing a deadline. When

---

34. See Miller and Cohen (2001) for a neurobiological description of cognitive control structures. See also Camerer, Loewenstein, and Prelec (2005) or Politser (2008).

given a choice, most students chose deadlines before the end of the course: Only twelve of fifty-one students chose to submit all three papers on the last day of class.

Comparing the performance of students in the two classes, Ariely and Wertenbach found that students in the no choice class performed better than students in the free choice class.[35] However, the performance of students in the free choice class who chose approximately evenly spaced deadlines was not statistically significantly different from the performance of students in the no choice class. Together these findings suggested that some individuals (those who did not choose approximately evenly spaced deadlines) did not set self-imposed deadlines optimally. Ariely and Wertenbach did not report the number of free choice students choosing various deadlines, but the chart of the frequency distribution of declared deadlines by week shows that declared deadlines clustered around evenly spaced intervals.

The second study involved a paid proofreading task. Participants were randomly assigned to three experimental groups: (1) self-imposed deadlines, (2) mandatory evenly spaced deadlines, and (3) an end of study period deadline. Payment was $0.10 per correctly identified error, with a $1.00 penalty for missing a deadline.

Results of the experiment indicated that the number of errors correctly detected, timely submissions, and payment amounts were greatest for the mandatory evenly spaced group and lowest for the end of study period deadline. Again, Ariely and Wertenbach found that performance for self-imposed evenly spaced deadlines were not statistically significantly different from mandatory evenly spaced deadlines. Thus, they concluded that individuals self-impose costly deadlines to overcome procrastination, that self-imposed deadlines improve performance, and that self-imposed deadlines are not always optimal.

In sum, overall, the evidence from a variety of studies suggests that individuals tend to discount proximate prospects more highly than more distant ones; but for long-run time horizons (that is, greater than a year), discount rates appear to be approximately constant, the latter consistent with the standard expected utility model and economists' notion of rationality. The tendency to discount proximate amounts more highly can cause harm. Sometimes the harm is great, as in the case of addiction, for example. However, as discussed, individuals make numerous intertemporal decisions, and in most cases, they do not suffer any apparent harm. Individuals have cognitive control structures that enable most of them to resist temptation for impulsive immediate gratification and undertake actions to achieve goals. Individuals can also choose various external precommitment mechanisms to control impulsive behavior. External controls may not always produce optimal outcomes, but they represent purposeful actions to achieve desired goals. Thus, concluding that hyperbolic discounting is in itself always irrational or that individuals generally do not make purposive and deliberate intertemporal choices is not justified at this time.

Regarding consumer credit, evidence is limited, but empirical evidence on credit card behavior, discussed in the next section, suggests that consumers

---

35. All students submitted papers on time.

generally behave as economic theory predicts and that when consumers make mistakes, the mistakes are small or are usually corrected when large. Consequently, it is not at all clear that behavioral research undermines neoclassical economic theory of credit use as much as it enriches and enhances it. Instead, the behavioral analyses suggest the details of the elements of rational economic choice and where the theory should accommodate differences. More on this point will become known in the future as economists model consumer credit behavior more fully, employing more fully the insights from behavioral sciences and testing the enlarging body of theory with specific empirical data.

RATIONALITY OF CREDIT CARD DEBT

Today, general-purpose credit cards with a revolving feature and carrying the American Express, Discover, MasterCard, and Visa brand names have become ubiquitous in the United States and in many other countries. Individuals use them for everything from fast food to college tuition and automobile down payments. Surveys of consumers found that more than two-thirds of American families held and used general-purpose credit card accounts in 2010, up significantly from 38 percent in 1970 (see table 7.3 in chapter 7, below). Ultimately, growth of these credit products reflects consumer acceptance, along with rapid technological progress and falling costs in data processing and communications. The technological advances have permitted users to access prearranged credit accounts on demand instantaneously and simultaneously at millions of retail outlets and automated teller machines (ATMs) around the globe.[36]

It is important that when individuals use these accounts to generate consumer credit, they directly access open-end credit available at the user's discretion whenever desired. Once a card-issuing financial institution opens an account for a consumer, it authorizes the account holder to use any amount of credit up to a preauthorized limit without seeking the creditor's further approval. To prevent frauds, the creditor may verify that the account is valid, the transaction is legitimate, and the credit limit is not exceeded, but card use is rarely denied, even if repayment of existing balances is moderately delinquent.

Unlike most traditional closed-end consumer credit accounts such as an automobile credit contract, there usually is no direct link between establishing a general-purpose credit card account and purchase of any particular durable asset usable as collateral, nor is the account subject to discipline imposed by the creditor for repayment before the end of the service life of a particular asset. With open-end credit, the consumer is much more on his or her own. This feature of open-end accounts generally, and especially credit card credit, has reopened economic and political interest in the issue of consumers' ability to use consumer

---

36. See chapters 1 and 7 for further discussion of these cards and their uses. For extended discussion of credit card technology and credit card operating systems, see Evans and Schmalensee (2005).

credit independently and rationally. This debate extends back at least as far as the article by Danielian (1929) questioning the rationality of consumer credit use in the early decades of the twentieth century, if not to much earlier times, even to prehistory.

The development and acceptance of general- purpose credit cards has have caused some observers to propose more than new experimental attempts to understand this economic behavior more fully. Based on hypotheses arising from experimental studies, a series of articles in the economics and legal litera-ture focusing on credit cards has energized the rationality issue. In general, these papers take either of two tacks: (1) an economic focus debating the contentions of Lawrence Ausubel that much credit card use is irrational or (2) a legal and policy focus extending the irrationality hypothesis to prescriptive policy recommenda-tions. The latter grouping of discussions has come to be classified as a legalistic offshoot from behavioral economics; therefore, it can be characterized as behav-ioral law and economics (BLE) of credit cards. The remainder of this chapter reviews the first of these tacks at some length because of contemporary interest, beginning with the Ausubel hypothesis of the early 1990s. We discuss the BLE of credit cards elsewhere (Durkin, Elliehausen, and Zywicki 2014).

The Ausubel Hypothesis

In a controversial article published some years ago, economist Lawrence M. Ausubel (1991) proposed that consumer irrationality in credit card use was a reason for what he saw as an apparent failure of competition in the market for general-purpose credit cards in the 1980s. In his view, the manifestation of the fail-ure of competition was stickiness of interest rates on general-purpose, bank-type credit cards. The Federal Reserve's reported average of the most common interest rates on issuers' general-purpose credit card plans varied within a range of about one percentage point in width during most of 1980s, but Ausubel's estimate of the cost of funds to card issuers varied within a range of about four percentage points. Based on a regression analysis indicating that movements in the cost of funds explained only a very small, albeit statistically significant, proportion of move-ment in general-purpose credit card interest rates, Ausubel argued that credit card rates were stable and largely unresponsive to the cost of funds, showing, in his view, a lack of competition.

Stickiness of rates was obvious at the time, but Ausubel's suggestion of the cause was more controversial. Ausubel argued that stickiness of interest rates on credit cards arose from consumer irrationality that renders a large class of bor-rowers insensitive to these rates. To reach this conclusion, he proposed a model of the credit card market with high- and low-risk credit card borrowers. In positing this dichotomous view of credit card users, Ausubel ignored a third type of bank card customers, "convenience" customers, who use bank cards only as a transac-tion medium; these latter card holders pay balances in full at the end of the month to avoid finance charges. Because they do not incur finance charges, they would not likely be sensitive to interest rates. But the existence of a group of convenience customers in itself does not explain why credit card issuers would not change interest rates for others who use the cards for longer-term credit.

Ausubel argued that the low-risk borrowers do not intend to borrow but find themselves repeatedly doing so anyway. Since these borrowers do not intend to borrow, they do not seek out or respond to offers of lower interest rates. That these borrowers do not learn from their past mistakes and continue to borrow at high rates is arguably irrational behavior. In contrast, he contended, the high-risk borrowers fully intend to borrow. High-risk borrowers are willing to pay high bank card interest rates because they are high risk and have few alternatives. But since they expect to pay interest, they are responsive to lower interest rates if available, and, therefore, they are more likely to respond to a lower interest rate than low-risk card holders. Given these two types of borrowers, creditors competing on the basis of interest rates would attract mostly the less profitable higher-risk borrowers if they lowered their interest rate. As a result of this "adverse selection," bank card issuers would be reluctant to reduce interest rates to attract new customers, who would be disproportionately higher risk.

Ausubel acknowledged that search and switching costs could also cause interest rates to be sticky. Search and switching costs include the costs of finding and identifying (other) cards with low interest rates, the time and effort in applying for a new card, the possibility of rejection, uncertainty about the size of the new credit limit, and the waiting time between application and receipt of the card. Certainly, some search and switching costs characterized the credit card market of the 1980s that was Ausubel's subject, but he doubted that the search and switching costs provided a full explanation for sticky credit card rates. He argued that the premiums paid on sales of portfolios of credit card accounts by one card company to another in the 1980s by far exceeded the costs that credit card companies would have had to pay to induce consumers to switch to their cards. Therefore, he contended, the sales premium on the portfolios sold must reflect the expectation of supranormal profits from interest-insensitive customers.

Ausubel's adverse selection model relies crucially on the assumption that a large group of consumers do not intend to use the cards for long-term credit, and so they are insensitive to interest rates, but they repeatedly use the cards for credit anyway. Otherwise, if the large majority of card holders were actually interest-sensitive, new firms entering the card business and aggressive competitors already in the industry would compete for their business by offering lower rates.

In his analysis, Ausubel based his assumption on several observations. First, he suggested that borrowing at the prevailing credit card interest rates was in itself irrational: "The proclivity of consumers to borrow at these high rates suggests a substantial breakdown in optimizing behavior among credit card holders" (Ausubel 1991, 71–72). He contended that rational behavior would cause many of these lower-risk consumers to shop for lower-priced credit cards, use lower-priced types of credit, or abstain from further credit use. They did not do so, and in his view, this showed that there was irrational inertia among consumers, leading to insufficient competition for their business.

Second, Ausubel noted apparent inconsistencies in behavior among card holders. About half of credit card holders responding to Federal Reserve

Board–sponsored consumer surveys at the time reported that they always or nearly always paid their bank or retail credit card balances in full (see Canner and Fergus 1987). In contrast, he reported that a survey of large bank card issuers indicated that on average, only about one-quarter of active card holders pay in full, and three-quarters owe finance charges at a given time. Ausubel argued that this discrepancy between the actual account behavior from credit card issuers and reported behavior from consumer surveys, with a smaller percentage actually paying in full than saying they do so, suggests that many consumers repeatedly borrow despite the intention to pay in full.[37]

Third, Ausubel also noted evidence from credit card marketers that consumers' responses to changes in annual fees on card plans at that time were much greater than responses to commensurate changes in interest rates. This observation, he suggested, is difficult to reconcile with the frequency of consumers' owing interest on their credit card accounts. It seemed to him that if interest accrued every month, it should be more important to consumers than annual fees that applied only once in twelve months. Again, Ausubel regarded the observation as evidence supporting his assumption that many consumers do not intend to use their cards for credit but find themselves doing so anyway.

Finally, he cited other examples of credit-using behavior that he considered inconsistent with rational choice. The examples involved conscious choices of credit that was not the lowest-cost credit available and precommitments of income to various areas by some consumers in order to avoid impulsive purchases using credit cards. Two of the three examples that Ausubel provided were anecdotal, however, rather than from systematic gathering of evidence. The only statistical evidence was from a study two decades earlier by White and Munger (1971), who found that a considerable percentage of consumers choosing a high-cost source for automobile loans would have qualified for a loan from a lower-cost source and were aware of nearby lenders offering lower-cost credit. While interesting, that study did not involve credit card use.

Ausubel's general, mostly theoretical conclusions of widespread consumer irrationality leading to lack of competition among credit card issuers generated some controversy at the time. They also caused some other economists to suggest competing explanations for the phenomenon of sticky interest rates on credit cards that was his motivating observation. But Ausubel also extended his views with a second paper using data on consumers' card-using behavior.

In the later empirical study, Ausubel (1999) explored consumers' responses to preapproved credit card solicitations from a large credit card issuer and contended that the findings supported the hypothesis of irrational consumer use of card credit. The data were from three randomized experiments undertaken by the

---

37. Apparently, Ausubel's data turn out to have been not good enough for him to draw strongly the conclusions he reported in this area. It is true that a large proportion of card holders revolve their accounts, but it appears that they are not always the same consumers. The proportion who revolve continuously is actually much lower, more in line with the survey proportions. See chapter 7, below, for later data and discussion of consumer payment performance. Using the 1989 Survey of Consumer Finances, Cargill and Wendel (1996) raise essentially the same point.

credit card issuer for its own marketing research but made available to him for analysis. The experiments involved varying within solicitations mailed to consumers the level and duration of reduced introductory interest rates and the level of postintroduction interest rates and then looking at the results of the experiment. The data are unusual in that they involve actual consumer choices among a variety of related offerings, not merely responses to hypothetical alternatives. As pointed out earlier in this chapter, most experimental data in economics arise from hypothetical choices and are subject to the criticism that consumers may not behave as they say they will do when making actual decisions.

Much of Ausubel's second study concerns evidence on the impact of adverse selection on credit supply rather than on the demand side considered in this chapter. He observed that those responding to an offer had, on average, riskier characteristics and subsequently performed worse than the whole pool of consumers receiving the particular offer, based on the underlying credit reports of both groups. This fact could make creditors wary of lending to them and affect credit supply.[38]

But Ausubel's second study also investigated elements of consumer demand permitted by the experimental design format. They included such issues as sensitivity of consumers to variations in both introductory interest rates and postintroductory rates, together with related duration of introductory rates.

To examine these matters, Ausubel derived "implied demand curves" for variations in the offered interest rates. Figure 4.1 shows implied demand curves for two experiments, one with five different six-month introductory rates and the same 16 percent postintroductory rate and the other with the same 5.9 percent introductory rate and four different postintroductory rates. (These are Ausubel's market experiments I and III, respectively.) The horizontal axis in the chart measures the acceptance rate of each offer (accepting respondents per 100,000 solicitations associated with a given rate offer). The vertical axis measures the average saving in the dollar amount of finance charges that borrowers would have incurred in the first twenty-one months after account opening if they had chosen a particular offer relative to the highest-rate offer. The points on each curve represent different offers.

Savings associated with each offer were estimated in the following manner. For the 4.9 percent introductory rate offer, for example, Ausubel calculated that borrowers accepting the 4.9 percent offer would have paid an additional $13.07 in finance charges based on the actual amounts they borrowed during the first twenty-one months had they chosen the 5.9 percent offer. Borrowers choosing the 5.9 percent introductory rate would have saved on average $10.21 if they had

38. Also using data on randomized trials of credit card solicitations at a large financial institution, Agarwal, Chomsisengphet, and Liu (2010) found that consumers accepting credit card offers had higher risk characteristics than consumers who did not accept offers and that consumers who accepted inferior offers had higher risk characteristics than consumers accepting superior offers. Furthermore, consumers accepting inferior performed worse ex post than consumers accepting superior offers. These results, which are similar to those of Ausubel, provide further evidence suggesting adverse selection in the credit card market.

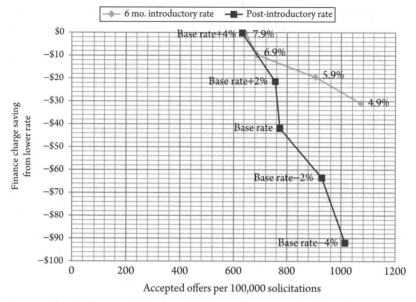

Figure 4.1 Implied Demand Curves of Credit Card Experiments Offering Different Introductory and Post Introductory Rates.

chosen the 4.9 percent offer based on their borrowing over twenty-one months. The average of these two values—that is, $(10.21 + 13.07)/2$, or $11.64—is the vertical distance between the 5.9 and 4.9 percent offers. Similarly, Ausubel calculated differences in finance charges for the 5.9 and 6.9 percent offers ($9.92) and the 6.9 and 7.9 percent offers ($9.48). Thus, the savings in finance charges for the 4.9 percent offer relative to the 7.9 percent offer ($30.04) is the sum of $11.64, $9.92, and $9.48.[39]

A notable characteristic of the implied demand curves is that both are downward sloping. That is, larger savings in finance charges are associated with greater acceptance rates. This characteristic is consistent with economic theory. That better deals are more likely to be accepted suggests a degree of rationality in consumers' behavior.

Ausubel first compared the implied demand curve for four different introductory interest rates with the one for five different postintroductory rates (this is the comparison in figure 4.1). That the implied demand curve for introductory rates was flatter than the implied demand curve for postintroductory rates suggests that borrowers were more responsive to differences in introductory rates than dollar equivalent postintroductory rates.

39. An assumption behind this calculation is that amounts borrowed would be the same for both interest rates. This assumption probably produces an overestimate of the dollar impact, since quantity demanded is normally inversely related to price. Amounts borrowed at the higher interest rate would be lower than amounts borrowed at the lower interest rate, making the difference in finance charges smaller than his measurement (see further discussion by Gross and Souleles 2002, reviewed below).

Using the same procedure as in the first exercise, he also estimated implied demand curves (not shown) for different introductory rates (4.9 to 7.9 percent for six months) and for different introductory rates for longer periods of time (6.9 percent for nine months versus 7.9 percent for twelve months). The curve for differences in the introductory rate for the short period was flatter than either of the two curves involving extensions of the duration at either of the higher rates. This finding suggests that consumers were more responsive to the level of introductory rates than to dollar equivalent extensions of duration.

Finally, he compared options involving low introductory rates for a short period of time (for example, 4.9 percent for six months) to options involving higher introductory rates for a longer period of time (for example, 5.9 percent for nine months). The offer with the lowest introductory rate (4.9 percent for six months) had the highest acceptance rate, but based on actual balances for the first thirteen months of new accounts, this account had a higher effective interest rate than two offers that involved higher introductory interest rates for a longer period of time (that is, the 5.9 percent for nine months offer and the 7.9 percent for twelve months offer).[40] He found that borrowers choosing a lower interest rate for a shorter period would have paid on average less if they had chosen an offer with a higher introductory interest rate for a longer period of time. This outcome was because of the more rapid jump to the full rate for the shorter-term offer. But because the lower introductory rate offers were accepted more frequently than those higher introductory rate offers, Ausubel argued that this finding provides substantial support for his hypothesis that consumers are prone to underestimate their future use of credit and therefore make suboptimal choices of credit cards. The evidence is perhaps not as strong as Ausubel suggested, however. As measured, the difference in response rates between the lowest and highest introductory rate was quite small, just 0.00129 (0.129 percentage points). And his calculations also indicated that many borrowers chose the right offer relative to their future outcome. These borrowers presumably did not underestimate their future borrowing.

In sum, Ausubel's second study suggested that borrowers may be more sensitive to variations in introductory rates than to either dollar equivalent postintroductory rates changes or to the duration of introductory rates. He interpreted both of these results as inconsistent with rational behavior and as evidence supporting his earlier hypothesis that consumers systematically underestimate future credit card borrowing. Nonetheless, strictly in terms of the traditional economic model of rational choice, much of what Ausubel reported is consistent with traditional economic rationality; namely, he found that more consumers responded to lower-priced offers than to higher-priced offers, hardly a surprising outcome.

Moreover, comparing his implied demand curves for variations in introductory rates with those for variations in the other terms suggests that the difference in finance charges between the alternatives are generally relatively small and

40. His effective interest rate is an average of introductory and postintroductory rates weighted by the amount of borrowing over the thirteen months.

perhaps small enough that they do not concern many consumers, even if in some sense this is "irrational." For example, based on amounts subsequently borrowed, the finance charges for an account with an introductory rate less than 5.9 percent were at most sixty to seventy dollars higher than finance charges for an account with the lowest postintroductory rate over a period of twenty-one months, about three dollars per month. And in the comparisons involving trade-offs between lower introductory rates for a shorter period of time and higher introductory rates for a longer period of time, borrowers choosing the shorter introductory rates would have saved less than fifteen dollars over thirteen months. Differences of these magnitudes over a year or more likely are not seen as a major concern by many people, even if not paying attention is, in some sense, "irrational."[41] Indeed, at the time Ausubel was preparing his second paper, *Don't Sweat the Small Stuff* was even the title of a series of best-selling books (still available from online booksellers).

Finally, the implied demand curves are based on assumptions that consumers could have chosen any one of the experimental options and, as mentioned, would have borrowed the same amounts if they had chosen the next higher or the next lower price option. Many consumers likely were not presented with all such choices at the time they chose the account, however; and most consumers probably are not completely insensitive to price when they borrow (see the discussion of Gross and Souleles 2002 in the next section of this chapter). Thus, support for the underestimation hypothesis is probably not as strong as it appears at first glance.

To be sure, Ausubel's analyses do suggest that consumer decisions may involve factors other than slavish consumer calculations regarding the lowest cost. This also is not especially surprising; behavioral economists have studied consumer decisions for many years, including psychological antecedents to economic behavior such as attitudes, expectations, and motives, and they have long since concluded that complete consistency with the assumptions of economic theory likely is lacking in many consumer decisions. In reaching this view, they also have considered a concept of rationality that is conceptually broader than its meaning in traditional economics, and this view has become the basis of the field of behavioral economics, as discussed earlier. Now it is worthwhile to examine a few studies by some other economists who have also considered the role of credit cards in consumers' credit decisions but have concluded that consumers' use of credit cards does not reflect irrationality.

Consumer Sensitivity to Credit Card Interest Rates

Since Ausubel's conjecture that credit card borrowers are insensitive to interest rates, Gross and Souleles (2002) obtained data that enabled them to examine sensitivity of bank card debt over the period of a year to changes in credit limits and interest rates. The data consisted of monthly panel data of several thousand

---

41. See Cargill and Wendel (1996, 381) for similar discussion.

individual bank card accounts from several different lenders in 1995. The data included information from monthly statements, credit bureau reports, and credit applications. Some of the largest bank card issuers in the United States were among the lenders.

The first dependent variable that they examined was the change in debt from one month to the next. The explanatory variables were either increases in credit limits or changes in interest rates in preceding months and monthly time dummies to account for seasonality, business cycle, trends in debt, and aggregate interest rates.

Results of estimation indicated that increases in credit limits produce immediate increases in debt. The response was strongest for accounts starting near their limit, but statistically significant increases were also observed for accounts starting well below their credit limit. The increases in debt for accounts starting near their limit can be explained by binding liquidity constraints (rationing). The increases in debt for accounts starting well below their limit cannot be explained this way, however.

Gross and Souleles found a plausible explanation for increases in debt for accounts starting well below their limit by looking at utilization rates (proportion of credit line in use). Using utilization for the dependent variable instead of debt, they found that after an initial drop in utilization caused by an increase in the credit limit, consumers quickly increase borrowing, returning to their original utilization within a relatively short period of time. This behavior was true both for accounts starting near their limit and for accounts starting well below their limits. This finding suggests that consumers may have target utilization rates, which may arise from behavioral rules of thumb about appropriate amounts of borrowing or from precautionary motives for maintaining a reserve of available credit.[42]

Gross and Souleles also studied changes in interest rates. Results of regressions in this area indicated that borrowing was quite sensitive to interest rates. Estimates of the interest rate elasticity were about −0.8 in the short term and about −1.3 in the long term. In other words, an increase in the interest rate produces a nearly proportionate decline in borrowing within a short period of time and eventually a greater than proportionate decline in borrowing. These estimated interest rate elasticities are larger than estimates in other studies.

Next, Gross and Souleles examined responses to introductory rates and to balance transfer offers, which had become a ubiquitous part of competition in the bank-type card market since the 1990s. They found that large decreases in interest rates, such as those typically occurring when an introductory rate is taken, have stronger effects than small decreases. They also found that large decreases in rates had greater effects than large increases, which follow the expiration of

---

42. Analyzing data from the Survey of Consumer Finance, Castronova and Hagstrom (2004) found that consumers hold a certain fraction of their credit limits as debt and that this fraction does not vary systematically in the population. Consumers' demand for credit limits was responsive to income, the interest rate on the card with the highest balances, and demographic characteristics. They interpreted these results as consistent with Gross and Souleles's (2002) hypothesis that consumers have a precautionary motive for unused credit card limits.

introductory rates. Thus, introductory rates would produce a rise in debt, a result that helps explain card issuers' widespread use of introductory rates.

Finally, using changes in balances on other credit cards (from credit bureau reports) as the dependent variable, Gross and Souleles also were able to investigate the extent to which increases in interest rates cause consumers to shift balances to other accounts. They found that balances on other accounts rise when the interest rate on an account rises, but the rise in balances on other accounts is less than half the decline in the balance on the first account. Thus, while some balances are shifted to other accounts, an increase in the interest rate still causes a large decrease in debt overall.

Gross and Souleles's evidence is quite consistent with the predictions of economic models and does not support Ausubel's (1991) contention that credit card borrowers are irrational. Both Ausubel's (1999) own experimental results showing that more consumers responded to lower-price bank card offers than higher-price offers and Gross and Souleles's (2002) findings that an increase in the interest rate reduced balances in an account and caused a shift in balances to other accounts are consistent with downward sloping demand curves and rational behavior. Consumers do not always act in a fully optimal manner, however. As mentioned, Ausubel (1999) found that consumers may be more responsive to introductory rates than to equivalent reductions in post introductory rates or the duration of the introductory rate, and Gross and Souleles found that introductory rates produce temporary increases in debt. These results certainly suggest that consumers do not calculate precisely and may respond differently when price changes are framed in different ways. That increases in debt induced by the introductory rate were temporary suggests that consumers' actions do not tend to be contrary to their intentions, however, contrary to Ausubel's hypothesis. Instead, consumer responses to introductory rates appear to be short-term increases in debt in response to short-term reductions in price. As such, these responses may be utility increasing, even if not utility maximizing.[43]

Further Evidence on the Rationality of Consumers' Credit Card Behavior

Results of a large-scale experiment undertaken by a bank produce further supporting evidence that consumers are sensitive to credit card interest rates and that, based on subsequent behavior, their choices involving trade-offs between interest

---

43. Analyzing consumer panel data on deposit and credit account activity from a market research firm, Stango and Zinman (2011) found considerable variation in distributions of annual percentage rates on accounts for individual consumers with multiple accounts. Consumers were generally effective in allocating balances to their lowest-rate cards. Their calculations suggested that by far most borrowers would benefit little if at all from a reallocation of balances to lower-rate cards. They found that search behavior helped explain some of the variation in distributions of APRs of individual borrowers and noted that use of rewards cards, which they did not include in their analyses, might also explain the holding of higher-APR cards.

rates and annual fees on new accounts are usually cost minimizing. Agarwal, Chomsisengphet, Liu, and Souleles (2005) analyzed results of a program by "a large bank" that offered consumers a choice between credit card contracts, one with a fee but a low fixed interest rate and another with no fee but a higher fixed rate. The offer included the option to switch contracts after the initial choice.

These authors found that the majority of consumers made the "right" choice based on their subsequent card use behavior, suggesting that the majority understood the likelihood of their future use of the card to add debt and chose the lowest-cost card under the circumstances. Consumers who chose to pay an annual fee in order to obtain a lower interest rate (perhaps because they planned to use the card for debt purposes) more frequently revolved balances and borrowed greater amounts than consumers who chose a higher interest rate and no fee.

In more detail, they found that 60.0 percent of the consumers who remained with their initial choice had made an optimal choice.[44] The likelihood of making an optimal choice was much greater for consumers who did not pay a fee (79.0 percent) than for consumers who paid a fee (44.5 percent). That the frequency of errors was much higher for those who paid an annual fee can be explained by the magnitude of the potential cost of the mistake. For consumers who paid the fee, the potential cost is limited to the amount of the fee (in the study, the range was ten to twenty-four dollars). In contrast, the potential cost for those who did not pay a fee depends on the amount of borrowing and can become quite large with frequent or large amounts of debt.

Significantly, consumers who initially chose not to pay an annual fee were more likely to switch as the net savings from paying the fee increased, and consumers who initially chose to pay the fee were less likely to switch as net savings increased. Of the small percentage (3.4 percent) of consumers who eventually switched accounts, nearly all had made a suboptimal choice initially and corrected their mistake by switching.

In sum, Agarwal, Chomsisengphet, Liu, and Souleles concluded that most consumers made cost-minimizing choices of credit card contracts. Further, they reported that the probability of making the wrong choice declined with the size of the potential error, and "those who made a larger error in their initial contract choice were more likely to subsequently switch to the optimal contract" (Agarwal, Chomsisengphet, Liu, and Souleles 2005, 5). It is hard to reconcile these results with the hypothesis of consumer insensitivity toward rates. These authors do note, however, that a "small minority of consumers persisted in holding substantially suboptimal contracts without switching" (Agarwal, Chomsisengphet, Liu, and Souleles 2005, 5).

In another study, Agarwal, Driscoll, Gabaix, and Laibson (2008) provided evidence that credit card holders' behavior is sensitive to late, over limit, and cash advance fees. In their data obtained from a large bank, they observed that when

---

44. A choice that turns out to be a mistake ex post may not be a mistake ex ante. Consumers may experience unexpected expenses or shortfalls in income that cause them to borrow when they initially had not intended to borrow.

consumers incurred these fees, they did so most commonly soon after opening an account. Subsequently, the incidence of these fees declined, falling by 75 percent during the first four years of account life. To explain this behavior, Agarwal, Driscoll, Gabaix, and Laibson suggested that consumers often learn about fees by incurring them, but having incurred a fee, they are then more careful in managing their accounts. Consumers learn from their mistakes and take steps in the future to avoid making a mistake again. In the case of late payments, they found that incurring a late payment fee reduced the probability of a late payment in the next month by 44 percent. They also found that a recent fee payment had a larger effect than more distant fee payments.

The findings of Agarwal, Driscoll, Gabaix, and Laibson suggest that consumers may not consider all available information in opening accounts or may not always manage their accounts carefully. That alone does not indicate that consumers' behavior is irrational, however. That consumers learn from experience and correct their behavior after mistakes is consistent with rationality, where rationality is viewed as taking actions to achieve objectives.

A Transaction Cost Model of Credit Card Borrowing

Ausubel's (1991) skepticism about search and transactions costs as an explanation for credit card borrowing was not universally accepted. In particular, Brito and Hartley (1995) reexamined the rationality of "high interest" credit card debt using an approach to cash management developed by Baumol (1952) and Tobin (1956) to analyze consumers' transactions demand for cash. Models of this sort analyze trade-offs between transaction costs of switching into and out of cash and other payment media and opportunity costs that arise from holding idle an inventory of cash to pay for consumption expenditures rather than investing the cash to earn a return.

In Brito and Hartley's approach, consumers use cash or credit cards to make expenditures during a period of time. Credit cards allow consumers to borrow within their credit limit at any time without any transaction cost but at the cost of interest charges. Alternatively, it is possible to hold cash for expenditures either by forgoing financial investments that earn a return or by arranging for closed-end loans at the beginning of the period. Therefore, the cost of using cash to finance expenditures is the forgone return on investments not made or the interest cost of a closed-end loan taken out at the beginning of the period.

In the case where consumers would obtain cash simply by forgoing a portion of possible investments, Brito and Hartley's representation suggests that consumers are able to hold lower cash balances (and consequently more interest-bearing assets) with credit cards than without them. Consumers finance some of their consumption with cash, but they also finance a fraction using credit cards. The fraction of expenditure financed using credit cards depends on the ratio of the interest rate on investments to the credit card interest rate. Thus, for example, with an interest rate of 4.6 percent per annum on investments and a credit card interest rate of 19.6 percent per annum, Brito and Hartley's model indicates 23 percent of consumption could be financed using credit cards during some period of time before it would be more expensive to use the card rather than spend the cash.

In the case of arranging a closed-end loan to obtain cash at the beginning of the period, Brito and Hartley assumed a fixed transaction cost associated with arranging the loan. The fixed transaction cost might include the time and effort to find a lender, inquire about terms and availability, apply for the loan, and wait for a decision. The alternative interest rate in this case is the interest rate for the closed-end loan.

Using this model, Brito and Hartley investigated the effect of transaction costs on the sensitivity of consumers to interest rates for different types of credit. The model indicates that even moderate amounts of transaction costs can make substantial amounts of credit card debt less costly than closed-end debt. For example, with transaction costs of $100, total borrowing would have to exceed $2,434 for a closed-end loan at a 7 percent interest rate to be less costly than credit card debt at a 15 percent interest rate over the period of a year.

Finally, Brito and Hartley also used this model to investigate the sensitivity of consumers to differences in credit card interest rates in the presence of switching costs. In this case, the model suggests that even small switching costs, such as personal time and effort costs associated with such application, would deter consumers from changing to a credit card with a lower interest rate. If a consumer is currently using a credit card with an 18 percent interest rate to finance expenditures of $1,000 over one year, for example, switching costs of just $5.62 would deter him or her from switching to a credit card with an interest rate of 17 percent, and $16.76 would deter switching to a credit card with an interest rate of 15 percent. The differences are almost trivial to consumers who value their time at all highly.

Thus, Brito and Hartley provide a very different explanation for the rise in credit card debt from Ausubel's. Ausubel suggested that credit card use was evidence of consumer irrationality. In contrast, in Brito and Hartley's analysis, credit cards are a desirable substitute for closed-end consumer credit under circumstances that likely prevail in the marketplace. Consumers may use credit cards to finance acquisition of appliances or household goods that were often financed by closed-end retail credit in the past. Consumers may also substitute credit cards for unsecured personal loans, which rationed consumers historically used to raise additional credit in the Juster and Shay (1964) analysis (see chapter 3). Statistics on purpose of credit use in chapter 1 are consistent with such substitution. From 1977 to 2004–2007, the proportion of households using credit cards for debt increased by more than a third before falling off in the recession during 2008–2009, probably a temporary phenomenon (upper panel of table 1.2). During the same period, the proportion of households using closed-end consumer credit for nonauto durable goods, home improvements, and "other" declined sharply.

Evidence on Adverse Selection and Switching Costs

Ausubel's hypothesis also directly stimulated further empirical analyses of the other specific issues he raised. Calem and Mester (1995) examined data from the

1989 Survey of Consumer Finances for evidence that credit card issuers would face an adverse selection problem if they were to reduce interest rates. Calem and Mester looked for evidence of consumer search costs, tendency to underestimate future borrowing, and switching costs that might bring about an adverse selection result.

To investigate the possibility that search costs or underestimations of future borrowing cause an adverse selection problem, they estimated a model in which a household's general-purpose credit card revolving balance is a function of the household's propensity to shop for credit, its attitudes toward debt, and various economic and demographic characteristics.[45] They measured the propensity to shop by the response to a question asking the consumers to describe their propensity to shop for the best terms when making decisions about borrowing or saving on a scale, where zero represented almost no shopping and ten represented a great deal of shopping. Calem and Mester defined shoppers as consumers who described their shopping propensity as seven or higher.

They found a statistically significant, inverse relationship between bank card balances and shopping for financial services. That is, they found that shoppers were more likely to be lower-balance customers than higher-balance customers. Shoppers presumably have low search costs and would be more likely to find and therefore respond to low price offers. Since Calem and Mester assumed that lower-balance accounts are less profitable than higher-balance accounts and they found that shoppers are more likely to have lower credit card balances, they concluded that credit card issuers face adverse selection if they attempt to compete by lowering interest rates. Calem and Mester also contended that high-balance customers' lack of shopping is consistent with their underestimation of future borrowing, causing them to fail to shop for lower rates.

Calem and Mester contended that switching costs may induce adverse selection upon rate reduction, if higher-balance households have more difficulty switching cards even if they are more profitable when on the books. To investigate the role of switching costs, Calem and Mester looked for ways to identify consumers who are likely to have problems transferring credit card balances to lower-rate credit cards. They modeled credit denial and delinquency as a function of the household's bank card balance, its propensity to shop, and various economic, attitude, and demographic characteristics. In each equation, the coefficient for credit card balance was statistically significant and positively related to the delinquency or denial measure. Consequently, Calem and Mester argued that households having large bank card debt were more likely to be credit constrained than low-balance households, and they would have greater difficulty transferring balances to lower-rate offers. They argued that from the standpoint of creditors, the positive relationship between delinquency and the level of credit card debt makes it rational for the lenders to view high credit card debt as a signal of credit risk and limit the amount of credit offered to high-balance borrowers.

45. As indicated in chapter 1, the Survey of Consumer Finances excludes balances arising from transaction (or convenience) use of bank-type credit cards by asking respondents to report the balance remaining after the last payment made.

Crook (2002) reexamined Calem and Mester's hypotheses for a later time period. He generally used the same variables and models Calem and Mester used, but there still were some differences between the studies. For one, the data for Crook's study were from the 1998 Survey of Consumer Finances, whereas Calem and Mester used the 1989 Survey. A notable difference from the earlier Survey of Consumer Finances is that the 1998 survey asked separate questions for credit and financial asset shopping, rather than a single question combining both sides of the consumer balance sheet. Respondents were asked to describe their propensity to shop in each area on a five-point scale, with five the highest propensity. Crook defined credit shoppers as consumers who described their shopping propensity for credit as greater than three.

Unlike Calem and Mester, Crook found no significant relationship between bank card balances and credit shopping as defined in his study. This result is not consistent with either of the hypotheses that high-balance consumers do not shop because they believe that their borrowing will be short-lived or because they have high search costs. Crook did find similarities to Calem and Mester's analysis for switching costs. Credit denial and delinquency were positively related to bank card balances, which hypothetically could lead to elements of adverse selection.

To explore this further, Crook developed a model of search behavior that allowed him to address the adverse selection issue from a somewhat different perspective. His theoretical model predicts that search and credit demand should be positively related, because greater demand increases the benefit from further shopping for a lower interest rate. This is the opposite of the predictions of Calem and Mester, who contended that switching costs would cause those with high demand to search less or not at all.

To test the predictions of his model, Crook used the five-response variable for credit shopping as the dependent variable in an ordered logistic regression. Results of estimation indicated that households that are better educated, pay on time, are relatively young, and generally repay bank card balances in full without incurring finance charges shopped more than other households. Regarding the adverse selection hypotheses, neither a poor repayment history nor higher bank card balances were significantly related to the amount of search. This finding does not suggest that bank card issuers offering lower interest rates would attract disproportionate shares of high-risk borrowers or less profitable, low-balance borrowers, contrary to the adverse selection hypothesis.

Crook suggested that the difference in the shopping question or an increase in competition in credit card markets between the times of the two studies may have caused his results on shopping to differ from those of Calem and Mester. The shopping variable used by Calem and Mester reflected shopping for credit and financial assets, while the shopping variable used by Crook reflected only credit shopping.[46] Differences in questions may indeed influence responses. Of the two shopping questions, the 1998 question used by Crook is more specific, although even then, credit is a broad category. It is not clear that in either survey a reported high propensity to

---

46. It is possible that the behavior of high-income consumers who shopped for financial assets but did not revolve bank card balances influenced Calem and Mester's results. Crook's results would not be affected by such confounding of credit and financial asset shopping.

shop indicated a high propensity to shop for low-interest credit cards. Competition in the bank card market does appear to have increased between 1989 and 1998, potentially increasing the gains from search (see Zywicki 2000a).[47]

A study by Calem, Gordy, and Mester (2005) revisited the question of whether high credit card debt is viewed as a signal of risk that hinders high-balance borrowers from switching to lower-rate credit cards. Using an expansion of Calem and Mester's (1995) model and data from the 1989, 1998, and 2001 Surveys of Consumer Finances, they found a significant positive relationship between the credit card balance and experiencing a turndown in each of the three survey years. They observed similar results for three subgroups hypothesized to have greater financial resources and therefore to be less likely than all households to have been subject to liquidity shocks that caused them to resort to credit cards after experiencing a loan turndown. Thus, the results suggest that high credit card balances may be a signal of risk that leads to turndowns and acts to inhibit switching.

Calem, Gordy, and Mester also found evidence that the relationship between delinquency and the level of credit card debt became weaker in 1998 and again in 2001 compared with 1989. This result suggests that improvements in credit information and lenders' ability to evaluate risk reduced the importance of credit card balances as a signal of risk. Calem, Gordy, and Mester also looked at the relationship between credit card interest rates and credit card balance, propensity to shop, and credit risk score in 1998 and 2001.[48] Among households that revolve credit card balances, they found that credit card balances were inversely related to credit card interest rates for those with a propensity to shop and with high credit scores in both years. Thus, high-balance households with these characteristics were able to find credit cards with lower interest rates. In contrast, credit card balances were not significantly related to credit card interest rates for households with low credit risk scores regardless of whether they shopped or not. In other words, high-balance households with low credit risk scores were not able to find lower interest rate cards.

In sum, evidence suggests that adverse selection concerns may have played a role in the credit card market. Ausubel's (1999) evidence that consumers responding to an offer of bank card credit are on average higher credit risks than those not responding clearly is consistent with the presence of adverse selection. Evidence that search costs prevent high-balance borrowers from obtaining lower interest rates is mixed, but calculations based on a theoretical model focusing on the transaction costs suggest that such costs need not be large to deter borrowers from moving balances to accounts with lower interest rates. Switching costs arising from high credit card balances being viewed as a signal of risk may have prevented some high-balance borrowers from obtaining accounts with lower interest rates. Better credit information and advances in credit evaluation appear to have reduced the importance of credit card balances as a signal of risk, however.

---

47. See chapter 11 for further discussion of competition in consumer credit markets.

48. The credit card interest rate for households that revolve credit card balances is the rate for the account with the largest outstanding balance.

Evidence suggests that high-balance borrowers with high credit risk scores and a propensity to shop had credit card accounts with lower interest rates than other high-balance borrowers.

CONCLUSIONS

Behavioral research indicates that consumers do not always make the cognitive efforts required for an extensive decision process. Individuals often take short-cuts, simplify, and use heuristics. Cognitive effort tends to be reserved for situations where commitments in money and duration are great, past experience and information are insufficient or obsolete, and outcomes of previous decisions are regarded as unsatisfactory. In situations where consumers have previous experience and are satisfied with past decisions, consumers often make choices with little further deliberation. That cognitive biases and time-inconsistent discounting exist is well established in the behavioral literature. Some research suggests that these psychological considerations influence consumers' credit behavior. The extent to which cognitive biases and time-inconsistent discounting affect actual credit decisions is not known at this time.

The experimental evidence supporting cognitive biases and time-inconsistent discounting is sensitive to the format, content, and context of the problems presented to study participants, however. When problems are framed differently, the results sometimes contradict previous findings. Experimental problems often appear more similar to test questions than choices that consumers actually face in the markets. Hypothetical situations are likely perceived as such by study participants. And it seems unlikely that participants in experimental studies view the consequences of their choices as very important, even when they are paid or their course grades may be affected. Individuals may be predisposed to impulsive behavior, but they also have the capacity to exert self-control to implement forward-looking plans. Self-control requires actively maintaining attention to the plan. An individual facing an impulse might yield to the impulse if it does not perturb the plan too much. To be effective, self-control requires that the internal inhibitions become stronger as awareness of the cost of impulsive behavior increases. It is not clear that participants exert the same cognitive efforts in experimental situations that they exert in actual situations where commitments in money and duration are great, past experience and information are insufficient or obsolete, and outcomes of previous decisions are regarded as unsatisfactory.

Empirical evidence indicates that consumers generally use credit to finance purchases of relatively expensive consumer durable goods, not to smooth consumption. In doing so, behavioral concepts such as precommitment and mental accounts may be used to manage behavior. Such concepts may not be optimal in the sense of global utility maximization, but they may be sensible when future prospects, preferences, and resources are uncertain.

Evidence from analyses of actual credit card behavior indicates that consumers are sensitive to price, consistent with the predictions of economic theory. When a credit card company increases the interest rates on an account, consumers reduce new charges, reduce existing balances, and shift charges to other credit card accounts, and over the course of a year, they reduce total credit card balances from the level before the price increase. Based on subsequent account use, consumers generally make cost-minimizing choices, trading off interest rates and annual fees when choosing new credit card accounts. When they make mistakes, the mistakes are usually relatively small. If mistakes are large, consumers generally correct the mistakes. Although some consumers do not correct large mistakes, persistent large mistakes are not the rule. Analyses of credit card behavior based on survey data also suggest that consumers are sensitive to costs and do not incur costly mistakes. And by far most consumers believe that credit cards provide a useful service and are satisfied with their dealings with credit card companies. Thus, neither behavioral nor conventional evidence provides much support for the conclusion that market failure is pervasive.

5

The Supply of Consumer Credit

The second side of any market is supply, and the supply of any kind of new goods or services entails some sort of production process. Production can be defined as the creation of utility, and utility is, of course, the ability of a good or service to satisfy a human want (see Ferguson 1969). As described in earlier chapters, consumer credit satisfies the want of shifting the time pattern of consumption, and it often involves financing household investment in durable goods or services such as automobiles, appliances, home repairs, large recreational or hobby items, and education. Production of consumer credit involves the transfer of funds from savers who have them to borrowers who have need of them, along with the subsequent collection of loan repayments from the borrowers and return to the savers. For consumer credit, the transfer from savers to borrowers and back is usually effected not directly from one to the other but rather by financial firms through a production process called financial intermediation.

This chapter discusses financial intermediation for consumer credit, its costs and its risks, and how it benefits both savers and borrowers. After initial review of the role of and basic economic services provided by financial intermediaries in effecting transfers and reducing risk, discussion turns to the costs of intermediation. Although both economic theory and common sense suggest that financial intermediaries reduce risk-adjusted costs of resource transfers, it is not possible to reduce these costs to zero. Consequently, the first two sections of the chapter discuss the expenses of producing consumer credit and how risk costs can lead to credit rationing. Next, the chapter turns to review of how intermediaries have tried to reduce operating and risk costs through technology such as statistical credit scoring. Finally, discussion turns more specifically to the sources of funds for consumer credit, with a brief review of the role of capital markets in providing funds to the intermediaries that pass them on to consumers.

Throughout this discussion, it is worth keeping in mind that the intermediation process must benefit market participants if it is to exist as a method of transferring funds. Intermediation must satisfy both sides of the transfer process by providing both higher risk-adjusted returns on savings and reduced costs for borrowers, or the transfer process would take place through other means. Although it seems that for centuries, policy leaders (emperors, kings, churches, presidents, and politicians) and many individual citizens have not always appreciated the role of financial intermediaries in the economic system, it is hard to deny objectively their economic significance and importance, either in the past or now.

FINANCIAL INTERMEDIATION

Most consumers do not borrow directly from other consumers who have surplus funds, nor do consumers with surplus funds generally lend directly to borrowers. Instead, borrowing and lending by consumers usually occurs through firms called financial intermediaries. Financial intermediaries raise the funds they lend either directly from consumers and businesses, in the form of deposits, insurance reserves, pension reserves, and other savings, or indirectly in capital markets, by issuing corporate securities such as stocks and various kinds of bonds or money market liability instruments that are purchased (funded) by other intermediaries. Thousands of intermediaries in the United States obtain their funds directly from consumers/savers, and further thousands of intermediaries obtain their funds indirectly by raising them from more intermediaries that acquire them directly from savers. Ultimate funds sources always are savers. They typically are consumers, but they sometimes also are businesses and governments, both domestic and foreign.[1]

The lending intermediaries then provide the funds, obtained directly or indirectly, to borrowers in the form and amount that the borrowers desire. Banks and credit unions are examples of financial intermediaries that provide financial services to both savers and borrowers. They obtain their funds directly from consumers, businesses, and governments and then turn around and directly lend the funds to the same or other consumers. Commercial banks also lend directly to businesses and governments; credit unions lend mostly to consumers.

In contrast, finance companies are examples of intermediaries that commonly raise their funds indirectly in capital markets in large amounts rather than directly from consumers. They then lend the funds in smaller amounts to consumers and businesses. The capital market funds they obtain are provided mostly by other intermediaries, such as pension funds and insurance companies, that raise them directly from savers.

Financial intermediaries perform several functions that facilitate the transfer of funds from savers to borrowers, none of which individuals likely want to, or are able to, provide for themselves: (1) information processing, (2) risk intermediation, (3) monitoring, (4) temporal intermediation, and (5) size intermediation. In performing these functions, financial intermediaries produce distinct financial products for market participants—borrowers, savers, or both.

As indicated, banks and credit unions produce products for both borrowers (loans) and savers (deposits). Finance companies primarily produce products for

---

1. Detailed statistical information on sources and uses of financial flows in the United States is available in *Flow of Funds Accounts of the United States*, Federal Reserve Statistical Release Z1, available quarterly.

borrowers (loans). Mutual funds are examples of financial intermediaries that produce primarily a savings product, raising funds from many savers to purchase a diversified portfolio of securities. Through economies of scale and specialization, financial intermediaries are able to perform these functions in financial markets at a lower cost than individuals could do on their own (see Benston and Smith 1976).[2]

What distinguishes financial intermediaries from brokers is that intermediaries internalize the funds they obtain, either directly from savers or indirectly in financial markets, and then employ them as inputs to their own distinct products for borrowers. In contrast, brokers match sellers of a product with buyers, buyers and sellers of a house, for example, or borrowers and lenders for loans. Financial intermediaries do not match borrowers and savers but rather obtain funds from one source and then use them in their own products for others, typically in much different form. The remainder of this section describes how the information processing, risk intermediation, monitoring, temporal intermediation, and size intermediation functions of financial intermediaries produce financial products.

Information Processing

As discussed in the previous chapters, consumer (or any) credit involves the present transfer of resources for use of a borrower, in exchange for the promise to repay principal and interest in the future. The performance of this promise is uncertain, however, because the borrower may be unable or unwilling to repay as promised. The uncertainty arises from both external sources (inability to perform as agreed) and the possibility of opportunistic behavior by the borrower (unwillingness to perform as agreed).

External sources of uncertainty include possible loss of employment because of business conditions, unexpected sickness of the borrower or a family member, or a natural disaster such as fire, hurricane, or earthquake. Any of these external events could bring timely repayment of a credit obligation into question. A borrower also may behave opportunistically before consummation of a loan by withholding or concealing information about creditworthiness. A borrower may also take actions that compromise the ability to repay after credit is granted, such as subsequently incurring additional debts or failing to maintain the value of assets pledged as collateral. Consumer-oriented financial intermediaries obtain and process information on these contingencies and experiences as part of their intermediation business.

The uncertain performance of a prospective borrower requires the lender to collect and evaluate information that provides a prediction of the likelihood

---

2. The discussion that follows focuses on intermediation functions from the perspective of consumer lending. These functions also apply to business lending and saving. See Arshadi and Karels (1997) for discussion of the role of intermediation in business lending and saving. For early discussion of the theory of financial intermediation, see Gurley and Shaw (1960).

that the borrower will repay. The information may include evidence of the borrower's ability to repay, such as the adequacy and stability of current and future income, assets, and other debts. The information may also include evidence of the borrower's performance on previous loans from the same or other lenders. By collecting and evaluating information from many past experiences, financial intermediaries are able to develop expertise and even statistical systems for predicting prospective borrowers' likely behavior, a process generally referred to as credit underwriting. There is no doubt that financial intermediaries know much more about how to lend than typical individual consumers who have resources available. Most consumers would rather place their available cash or retirement reserves in a financial institution (intermediary) than lend them directly to others.

Risk Intermediation

Very few, if any, borrowers are able to borrow without exposing a lender to some risk of default. Regardless of income, wealth, or assets pledged as collateral, any consumer borrower may have difficulty repaying debt as a result of a loss or reduction in income, sickness, divorce, a legal judgment, or some other hardship. But if the risks arising from such hardships are not highly correlated across individual consumers, a lender can reduce risk by lending to many consumers.[3]

For instance, some risks, such as those arising from sickness or divorce, are not highly correlated across individuals. Some individuals in a given lending area experience these difficulties, while others do not. In other words, on average, positive outcomes from other borrowers offset the negative outcomes of some borrowers. By making many similar loans, an intermediary can expect an average level for a pool of individual risks, and loan pricing can then cover this average risk. An individual making a single direct loan cannot do this; loan performance could range from very good to very bad, and an individual might not be willing to take this risk, especially without lending expertise. Thus, by pooling the loans of different consumers, a financial institution is able to reduce overall risk. In this way, pooling also can facilitate lending to consumers who exhibit individually higher risk characteristics. They might be unacceptably high credit risks on an undiversified basis but not as a whole after pooling.

Some risks, however, such as those arising from unemployment, may be highly correlated, especially in some geographic areas that rely heavily on a particular industry for employment. For these risks, if one borrower has difficulty making payments, other borrowers may have similar difficulties, and they do not cancel out; losses in the portfolio as a whole rise. Lenders often undertake geographic

3. Markowitz (1952) showed that for any given expected return, diversification can reduce risk in a portfolio of securities if returns are not perfectly correlated. With others, he received the Nobel Prize in Economic Science for his insights in this area. This general concept is now discussed in any textbook on financial markets.

diversification to attempt to mitigate this kind of risk, but they cannot entirely eliminate it.[4]

Monitoring

Once a loan is made, a lender must monitor the borrower's performance in order to manage risk. The payment process provides the primary means for monitoring. Consumer loans typically require periodic payments of interest and principal. In closed-end loans, the payments are usually regular amounts for a fixed period of time that fully amortize the loan. In open-end loans, the payments may be largely at the borrower's discretion, with only a minimum amount being required each month. In either case, timely payments provide evidence of the borrower's continued ability and willingness to repay. Late payments are an indicator that a problem may have arisen; specific charges imposed for late payments are an attempt to discourage such behavior. Lenders attempt to contact borrowers who are late to seek resumption of payments and assess likelihood of future repayment problems. If the problems are serious, a lender may arrange for workout or a resolution. When a resolution is not feasible, a lender may liquidate or foreclose on collateral, if available.

A lender may also obtain credit reports from a credit reporting agency, popularly known as a credit bureau, to monitor the borrower's behavior. Information that may be obtained from credit reports includes incurrence of new loans, performance repaying loans from other lenders, and legal judgments against the borrower. Information in credit reports may detect possible problems before late payments occur. Sometimes the information may influence changes in contracts, particularly open-end contracts. For example, credit card issuers may consider information on credit reports in processing automatic credit line increases or offering account upgrades. In the past, some credit card issuers also changed annual percentage rates based on credit bureau reports of negative payment performance on any account (see Furletti 2003b). Negative publicity about the latter practice curtailed its use in more recent years (see Government Accountability Office 2006). In late 2008, Federal Reserve Board regulations made raising rates more time-consuming and difficult, with effective date in mid-2010. Federal legislation in 2009 further curtailed this practice, also effective in 2010.

Temporal Intermediation

Individual borrowers and savers often prefer different terms to maturity. Borrowers financing the purchase of expensive consumer durable goods may

---

4. Diversifiable and nondiversifiable risks are also called systematic and nonsystematic or unsystematic risks. The difference was shown clearly in the subprime mortgage crisis in 2008. Attempts by lenders to mitigate risk by geographic diversification were overwhelmed by economic downturn in many places simultaneously (correlated, systematic risk), which raised losses dramatically.

prefer a relatively long term to maturity, which produces smaller monthly payments. On automobile loans, for example, this consideration leads some borrowers to choose terms to maturity of four or five years or even longer.

Many savers prefer a shorter term to maturity for their savings than what borrowers prefer, or they may even want immediate access to their savings. Both firms and consumers want a place to keep temporary surpluses until they are needed for payments or until sufficient funds are accumulated for investment. Individual savers do not normally withdraw all savings simultaneously, nor do they all add to their savings at the same time, however. Pooling the savings of many savers enables financial intermediaries to maintain sufficient funds to lend on a longer-term basis while satisfying the needs of individual savers to withdraw savings on short notice.[5] Financial intermediaries normally are able to anticipate the need for funds to cover withdrawals, and they may raise additional funds to meet needs in wholesale money markets.[6]

Size Intermediation

As mentioned earlier, financial intermediaries may raise funds in small or large amounts but then lend them in the opposite size extreme, a function called size intermediation. Commonly, banks acquire small amounts of funds from savings or checking accounts, for example, and then lend them as larger automobile, mortgage, and business loans. Some financial institutions may also raise large amounts of funds at one time in capital markets to make small loans, such as finance companies that raise large amounts in international commercial paper and bond markets to fund smaller loans to consumers and businesses.

5. Recognition of this concept led to the beginning of deposit banking in England in the seventeenth century. At that time, people deposited gold at London goldsmiths for safekeeping. Goldsmiths soon came to realize that they did not need to hold the entire amount of deposited gold to redeem deposits and began to lend part of the deposited gold. Thus, goldsmiths became financial intermediaries. Furthermore, goldsmiths functioned essentially as banks when goldsmiths' receipts became accepted as a means of payment because the receipts were more convenient to exchange than the deposited gold. For discussion, see Newlyn (1962).

6. Occasionally, financial intermediaries experience sudden unexpected large withdrawals because of concerns about an intermediary's own solvency, concerns about other similar intermediaries' solvency, or changes in macroeconomic conditions that quickly shift savers' preferences among savings instruments. Financial intermediaries that raise large shares of funds from short-term savings instruments, especially accounts such as checking accounts that can be withdrawn on demand, are potentially vulnerable to such events. Concerns about the solvency of a particular bank, or the banking system as a whole, have caused bank runs in the past, a large part of the reasoning behind establishing federal deposit insurance.

Increases in the level of market interest rates have also sometimes caused savers to withdraw funds from banks and savings institutions more gradually and shift them to direct US Treasury securities, a process called disintermediation. Such disintermediation occurred from time to time during the period from 1936 to 1986, after which removal of interest rate ceilings on consumer deposit accounts dramatically reduced the incidence of disintermediation.

COSTS OF CONSUMER LENDING

As indicated, a credit transaction involves an advance of resources to a borrower by a lender. In exchange, the lender receives from the borrower a promise to repay in the future the amount advanced plus a finance charge (interest). The amount of the finance charge must cover the lender's operating and nonoperating expenses. Operating expenses include costs of originating the loan, processing payments, and collection and bad debt expenses. Nonoperating expenses include taxes, interest expense for the share of funds advanced to the borrower that are obtained from borrowing by the intermediary, and a return on the owners' equity share of the advance to the borrower. Although economic theory, along with experience, suggests that intermediation *lowers* the overall cost of the transfer of resources from ultimate savers to borrowers, it is still true that the prices charged for loans must fully cover operating and nonoperating costs of the transfer process if the intermediary is to remain in business.

Operating Costs

Operating costs arise from a lengthy list of activities the intermediaries must undertake to grant credit and collect payments. All types of credit share the same basic activities, although the extent of specifics depends on whether the credit is open-end or closed-end, the amount of credit and term to maturity, whether or not collateral is taken, and the credit quality of the customers. Regardless of the type of credit, activities and resulting operating costs can be assigned to one of three general categories: (1) credit origination, (2) processing, and (3) collection and bad debt expense.

ORIGINATION

To originate a loan, a lender must solicit customers, take applications, evaluate information in applications to determine whether to grant credit and how much credit to grant, prepare documents, and disperse the funds. All these things must be done in compliance with a variety of sometimes complicated and costly legal requirements.

A lender must first establish the types of credit it is willing to offer and the credit risk it is willing to accept. The lender develops marketing efforts and programs to attract customers by such means as media advertising, over-the-counter or "take one" brochures, mailings, and acquisition of lists of potential customers from a variety of sources. Many intermediaries in the closed-end credit market acquire customers by purchasing credit contracts from a network of originating retail stores or durable goods dealers, including automobile and boat dealers, a lending method known as indirect credit (see discussion in chapter 1). Credit card companies often prescreen potential customers, typically by providing credit bureaus with criteria for selecting consumers from credit bureau files to receive the lender's solicitations. Credit bureaus charge the credit card companies for this service.

Consumers may apply for consumer loans by visiting an office of a lender, mailing an application to the lender, calling the lender, filling out an application on the Internet, or purchasing a product from a store or dealer in an indirect credit arrangement. In many cases, an employee will be involved in taking the application, and capable employees can be expensive. The employee may answer an applicant's questions, provide applications, copy documents, and enter information on a paper or electronic medium. The application might be quite short, as in the case of a credit card solicitation, which most often is made on the basis of information on consumers' past credit payment performance from credit bureau reports. Other applications can be quite lengthy, especially for credit involving relatively large amounts, long terms to maturity, collateral such as home or automobile loans, or a guarantor. Except for an Internet application, an employee probably performs at least some of these activities.

An important characteristic of these activities is that they occur because an application is made, and, other things being equal, they do not normally vary much by the amount of credit requested. As a consequence of this characteristic, a significant component of origination costs does not rise proportionately with loan size. The cost of taking an application for a $500 personal loan, for example, may not be much different from that for a $2,000 personal loan or a $30,000 automobile loan. This characteristic is also present in many of the other activities, such as record keeping, that give rise to operating costs. As a result, the portion of the finance charge to cover operating expenses on a small loan is going to be much larger relative to the loan amount than on a larger loan. This means the annual percentage rate (APR) of charge to cover the operating expenses is also going to have to be higher on a small loan, other things being equal.

Many other aspects of the lending process also produce operating costs. After an application is taken, for instance, a lender must evaluate the applicant's loan request. The lender must verify the applicant's identity and legal capacity to borrow. Lenders typically request information on an applicant's name, address, date of birth, and social security number. The information may be verified by inspecting or obtaining copies of a driver's license, a passport, or other documents such as tax returns, bank statements, or recent bills. Applications request information on changes in name or address, and changes may be verified to prevent identity theft.

Clearly, the lender also considers in some manner the applicant's ability to repay, the likelihood that the applicant will behave opportunistically in repaying the debt, and the adequacy of any asset taken as collateral. The ability to repay debt typically depends on the amount of monthly income left over after necessities and payments on other debts. The lender may require the applicant to provide documentation on income or assets, verify information on employment and income by contacting the applicant's employer, and obtain information on other debts by purchasing a credit bureau report. Lenders often use target debt-payment-to-income or debt-to-income ratios in evaluating credit requests. It is notable that credit bureau risk scores do not consider income (credit bureaus' files do not contain income) and, therefore, do not directly evaluate ability to repay, although applicants' previous performance obviously indirectly reflects their ability to repay. Ability to repay may be evaluated manually by an employee or included as a variable in a lender's proprietary application credit scoring system that evaluates application information systematically. On preapproved applications, such as credit card solicitations, ability to pay is typically considered in determining the amount of the credit limit.

Assessing the likelihood that an applicant will behave opportunistically is typically based on past payment behavior on debts or other financial obligations. The lender may obtain a credit bureau report for this assessment or review performance on previous loans that the applicant has obtained from the lender. If the applicant has little or no credit history, a lender may consider payment performance on other financial obligations such as rent or utility bills. Again, the information may be evaluated manually by an employee or included as a variable in a lender's proprietary application credit scoring system. A lender also may obtain a risk score from a credit bureau. Much of the evaluation relies heavily on information on the applicant's past payment performance from credit bureau reports to predict future performance. Preapproved solicitations usually screen potential applicants largely on the basis of credit bureau information on previous payment performance. This sort of screening is done by computer as a way of trying to contain operating expenses.

Lenders perform additional activities when assets are taken as collateral for a loan. These activities include assessing the value of the collateral and satisfying legal requirements for taking a security interest in the asset. Assessing the value of collateral may be fairly straightforward for new, standardized assets. Price lists for new automobiles, for example, are readily assessed using published and Internet lists of prices and dealer costs. Many financial assets are regularly traded in markets, where current prices provide good assessments of their current value. The value of used assets or specialized assets, however, may be quite difficult to determine. The value of a used automobile depends on its how its owner used and maintained it, which may require an examination by a mechanic. Works of art are unique, and many types of jewelry or antiques have distinct styles that make one item an imperfect substitute for another. Similar items may be a guide to value, but such items are often traded infrequently in markets that do not have very many potential buyers. Thus, the value of the item as collateral may be subject to considerable uncertainty.

The lender takes collateral in an asset through a security agreement. The security agreement indicates that the lender has given value (that is, has agreed to lend), identifies the loan and the asset taken as collateral, and affirms that the borrower owns the asset. The security agreement is enforceable upon final agreement of the arrangements between the lender and the borrower (referred to as execution of the security agreement). The lender may take additional legal actions to "perfect" the agreement, which makes the agreement effective against a third party or retain its effectiveness if the borrower goes into bankruptcy. For many secured consumer loans, lenders perfect security interest by registering the security interest in a public registry system. In some cases, however, lenders may perfect the loan by taking possession of the asset pledged as collateral (pawnbroker loans and loans using securities such as stocks or bonds as collateral) or just the ownership title to the asset (typical automobile loans, for instance). Actually possessing the asset requires a lender to take additional measures to ensure safekeeping of the collateral. Pawnbrokers typically store jewelry, guns, musical instruments, and other valuables in vaults and have extensive security systems to prevent theft. Possessing securities or the title to an asset requires a secure location to hold the collateral and a system of keeping track of assets. All of these activities concerning collateral agreements increase operating costs.

PROCESSING

After origination, there are further operating costs associated with consumer lending. Closed-end credit is typically paid in regular installments, which involve the processing of a series of payments over the term of the loan and entail record keeping. In some cases, payments are made electronically, either through a pre-authorized debit to the consumer's deposit account or by the customer through the Internet, but many payments continue to be made by check, which involves specialized equipment and employees. Internet systems require the necessary computers, software, and operators.

Open-end credit involves multiple extensions of credit and repayments. As most open-end accounts involve frequent, relatively small extensions, processing is highly automated. Nevertheless, employees perform several processing activities, and the necessarily extensive processing and communications systems are costly on an ongoing basis. Lenders typically have systems to authorize and process credit extensions automatically, although sometimes an employee may authorize an extension that exceeds a borrower's credit limit or an increase in the credit limit. Lenders monitor open-end extensions for fraud using automated systems, but fraudulent extensions are often detected by the borrowers when they receive their periodic statements. In these cases, employees in call centers record, evaluate, investigate, and act on the information as needed, but the call centers are expensive to operate.[7] Payments may be processed electronically, but many payments on open-end accounts are made by check, and even automated equipment must be supervised by employees. Employees also process account status and billing questions; replacements for lost, stolen, or damaged cards; name and address changes; and requests for account closings and responsibility changes resulting from divorce or death.

COLLECTION AND BAD DEBT EXPENSE

Further, some borrowers do not always make timely payments. A lender must monitor loans for late or delinquent payments. While identification of delinquent accounts and initial contact with the borrower may be automated, an employee may eventually have to contact a delinquent borrower to seek payment. Depending on circumstances, the employee may remind the borrower of an overdue payment, make repeated contacts to receive payment, negotiate a new schedule for repayment, or decide to turn a delinquent account over for more

---

7. A notation in the *American Banker* daily banking newspaper for February 26, 2008, reported that the credit card call center of a single company, JPMorgan Chase, by itself receives 80 million calls a year and that "reducing that number by even 1 percent would save millions of dollars in annual costs and improve customer service.".

serious collection efforts such as a lawsuit. Employees must document promises to pay, payment plans, and account holder actions or circumstances relating to the delinquency. Employees may decide to pursue legal remedies such as wage garnishment or to recover assets taken as collateral. While some accounts with late payments and delinquencies may eventually be paid in full, processing such accounts can be quite costly. Other accounts are eventually charged off. For many lenders, losses resulting from charge-offs are a significant cost of lending.

Nonoperating Costs

Clearly, the above listing of operating expenses for consumer lending is lengthy, but there also are nonoperating expenses. Nonoperating costs consist of cost of borrowed funds, income taxes, and return to equity funds. Much of the funding for consumer lending consists of borrowed funds. Sources of borrowed funds vary by the type of lender. Banks, except for the specialized monoline credit card banks, obtain by far most of their borrowed funds from customer deposits. Because of deposit insurance, most deposits are risk-free for the depositors and consequently are a low-cost source of funds. Most banks also borrow relatively small amounts of funds at market rates in capital markets.

Finance companies obtain borrowed funds from banks, the commercial paper market, and the capital market. The capital market is the largest source of borrowed funds for finance companies.

The residual after paying interest on borrowed funds and income taxes is the return to equity, which may be distributed as dividends to owners or retained in the firm. The return to equity compensates suppliers of equity capital for the funds they invest in the firm and the risk to which these funds are exposed. Like nonfinancial firms, banks and finance companies that do not provide a sufficient return on equity to satisfy the requirements of the market for equity capital ultimately will shrink and eventually disappear.[8]

Credit unions depend on members' share deposits for nearly all their funding. Credit union share deposits, like bank deposits, are a low-cost source of funds. Unlike most other types of lenders, credit unions are cooperative, not-for-profit organizations. As such, their income is not subject to income taxes.

EMPIRICAL EVIDENCE ON COSTS OF CONSUMER LENDING

In providing intermediation services, financial institutions must cover their costs, and so study of the specifics of cost-causing activities is important for

---

8. Realization that lenders must provide a competitive rate of return to attract equity capital sufficient to satisfy consumer demand for small loans informed policy decisions about setting rate ceilings for licensed (finance company) small loan lenders early in the twentieth century. This development led to the emergence of the consumer finance industry at that time. See chapter 11 for discussion.

understanding the intermediation process. Unfortunately, detailed empirical data on the costs of consumer lending have been available to researchers only infrequently and for limited time periods or for subsets of lenders, but some illustrative information has become available from time to time.

Only a few data sources have involved a regular data collection program on the costs of consumer lending, including, notably, the Federal Reserve System's Functional Cost Analysis program, which examined banking costs over a period of decades. This data collection effort assembled information on costs of producing several different financial products for a group of small and medium-sized commercial banks between 1957 and 1998. The purpose of this program was to help individual banks understand and control their costs by being able to compare them with the costs of others (see Ors 2004). For licensed consumer finance companies, some state regulatory agencies collected and reported cost and other data in the past (see Durkin and McAlister 1977 for description), and the American Financial Services Association's annual collection of operating and financial data for consumer finance companies between 1960 and 1989 provided further systematic information on this industry (see Benston 1975 and Durkin and Elliehausen 1998).

Some special one-time surveys have also provided data on consumer lending costs in a few other areas. Examples include the Visa USA functional cost study of the bank credit card industry in 1995 and the earlier New York State Council of Retail Merchants study of retail revolving credit costs in 1973 (see Shay and Dunkelberg 1975). Most recently, the Federal Deposit Insurance Corporation studied office level data on costs and revenues for two large monoline payday loan companies from 2002 to 2004 (Flannery and Samolyk 2005).

The various studies of consumer credit costs using these data sources have had to address many methodological issues, including differences in accounting methods among companies and across institutional classes of companies, allocation of overhead costs among different products, problems with estimating missing data arising from gaps and inconsistencies in approach among companies in available accounting records, samples of companies that may not be representative of the industry, and changes in company participation from year to year. Examination of specific lending functions, such as automobile loans versus boat loans, has seldom been possible, and current data are not available. Despite these difficulties, an examination of some existing past studies of the cost of consumer lending remains worthwhile for generating a basic empirical feel for the costs of consumer lending. Some information on lending costs for both closed-end and open-end consumer credit is available.

Closed-End Consumer Credit

Although now dated, information on costs of producing closed-end consumer credit has been available from consumer finance companies and commercial banks during the post-automation era, and it may be compared with much older information. Historically, these types of lenders have served different risk segments of consumers, with consumer finance companies lending to riskier customers and banks preferring the better risks.[9] Table 5.1 presents cost information for the most recent years available for each kind of lender and for some earlier years in which data from both finance companies and banks were collected at the same time.

CONSUMER FINANCE COMPANIES

The single-product nature of the consumer finance company industry has made this industry especially useful for studying the cost of consumer lending. As discussed earlier, consumer finance companies are financial intermediaries and have a source and use of funds. But, unlike the depository and insurance types of intermediaries whose sources of funds (deposits, policies, pension plans) are products in themselves, the consumer finance companies' funds sources (bonds and commercial paper issued locally and in national and international capital markets) are not a product directly for savers. This means they provide their financial service largely to one side of the market, the lending side, and obtaining funds is largely incidental to the lending function, at least in terms of operating costs.[10] Therefore, arbitrary cost allocations among multiple kinds of products (savings and lending products) are unnecessary for analyzing costs of this specialized industry (discussion in this subsection draws on Durkin and Elliehausen 1998).

The most recent data for consumer finance companies are from the American Financial Services Association (AFSA) data collection program, now discontinued. Eighty companies provided complete data for 1989, the last year in which data were collected. Companies ranged from very small (one-third were single-office companies) to the largest companies in the industry. Together, their gross consumer loans receivable accounted for about three-quarters of the Federal Reserve's estimate of total consumer credit at finance companies at that time.

Relatively small consumer loans accounted for nearly all of the loans of the companies not mostly engaged in automobile lending. Eighty-eight percent of the domestic accounts of these consumer lenders were consumer accounts in 1989, and most of the rest were business loans. The average amount outstanding was $5,420 for retail consumer accounts and $30,150 for business accounts. Revenue of the finance companies studied consisted primarily of finance charges but also small amounts of insurance income and other fees. Gross revenue was $23.73 per $100 of average loans outstanding in 1989 (upper panel of table 5.1).

9. See chapter 11 for discussion of risk segmentation of consumer credit markets.

10. Large finance companies that lend to consumers typically have only a relatively few employees in their headquarters location whose responsibility is to obtain the funds, compared with their much more extensive staff involved in lending and record keeping on the consumer borrower side. Those who manage the funds sources function (by borrowing in capital markets) are typically referred to as the financial or treasury personnel. Even in smaller consumer-oriented finance companies, owner-managers spend a disproportionate amount of their time on the lending side relative to the funds-obtaining side.

Table 5.1 INCOME AND EXPENSES FOR CLOSED-END CONSUMER CREDIT AT FINANCE COMPANIES AND COMMERCIAL BANKS, SELECTED YEARS

	Finance Companies			Commercial Banks			
	1989	1964	1959	1989	1998	1964	1959
Income and expenses per $100 of average outstanding loans (dollars)							
Total gross domestic revenue	23.7	21.4	23.9	9.5	12.2	8.8	9.4
Salaries and wages	5.5	5.6	6.4	1.5	1.4	1.6	2.3
Advertising and publicity expense	0.4	0.7	0.9	NA	0.1	0.2	0.3
Losses and additions to loss reserves	2.0	2.3	2.0	0.6	0.5	0.4	0.3
Administrative expenses	NA	NA	NA	0.8	NA	0.5	NA
Other operating expenses	4.8	3.1	4.9	1.5	1.1	1.2	1.2
Total operating expenses	12.7	12.7	14.2	4.3	3.1	3.9	4.2
Cost of borrowed funds	8.0	4.2	4.0	3.3	7.0	2.4	1.5
Net income before taxes	3.0	4.5	5.6	1.9	2.1	2.6	3.8
Percent of total gross domestic revenue							
Total gross domestic income	100.0	100.0	100.0	100.0	100.0	100.0	100.0
Salaries and wages	23.2	26.2	27.0	15.5	11.7	17.9	24.7
Advertising and publicity expense	1.6	3.3	3.7	NA	0.7	2.8	3.6
Losses and additions to loss reserves	8.6	10.6	8.3	5.9	3.9	4.0	3.0
Administrative expenses	NA	NA	NA	8.0	NA	5.8	NA

Other operating expenses	20.2	14.7	20.7	16.1	9.3	13.8	13.0
Total operating expenses	53.6	59.5	59.7	45.4	25.6	44.2	44.3
Cost of borrowed funds	33.8	19.5	16.6	34.7	57.0	26.9	15.9
Net income before taxes	12.6	21.0	23.7	20.0	17.4	28.9	39.8
Percent of total operating expense							
Total operating expense	100.0	100.0	100.0	100.0	100.0	100.0	100.0
Salaries and wages	43.3	44.0	45.3	34.3	45.5	40.4	55.9
Advertising and publicity expense	2.9	5.6	6.2	NA	2.9	6.4	8.2
Losses and additions to loss reserves	16.1	17.8	13.9	13.0	15.3	9.0	6.7
Administrative expenses	NA	NA	NA	17.6	NA	13.0	NA
Other operating expenses	37.7	24.7	34.6	35.4	36.3	31.2	29.3

Finance company income and expenses include revenue and cost of insurance in 1989.
NA: not available.

SOURCES: Finance companies—1959 Smith (1964); 1964 P. Smith (1967); 1989 American Financial Services Association, calculations by the authors. Commercial banks: 1959 Smith (1964); other years Federal Reserve System Functional Cost Program.

As discussed earlier, operating expenses are the costs of originating, servicing, and collecting loans. Since cost-causing activities begin to take place as soon as an application is taken or a loan is made and because loan amounts in this kind of credit are relatively small, operating expenses are a large part of the total cost of finance company consumer lending. From the survey in 1989, operating expenses were $12.72 per $100 of average loans outstanding the same year. This was more than half (53.6 percent) of gross revenue (second panel of table 5.1). Nonoperating expenses, which consisted mainly of funding costs, were a minority of expenses. The cost of borrowed funds, $8.02 per $100 of average loan receivables, was 33.8 percent of gross revenue. Net income before taxes was $2.99 per $100 of average receivables, or 12.6 percent of gross revenue.

These cost data support the contention that this kind of consumer lending was labor-intensive. Salary and wages ($5.51 per $100 of total receivables outstanding) were the largest component of operating expenses, accounting for 43 percent of total operating expenses (third panel of table 5.1). Advertising expenses were relatively small, just 2.9 percent of total operating expenses in 1989. Losses and additions to loss reserves were 16.1 percent of total operating expenses in 1989. Other operating expenses, including occupancy costs, data processing, telephone, printing, postage, taxes and license fees, legal and accounting fees, insurance, and depreciation, could not be presented separately because of different categorization methods employed by the accounting records of the various companies. Taking them together, they amounted to about 38 percent of total operating expenses.

Although technological and regulatory changes have in many ways transformed the consumer finance industry since 1989, the historical data suggest that changes and automation that took place up to that time had not fundamentally altered the cost structure of this industry from earlier decades, at least relative to its sources of revenue. Salary and wages at 23 percent share of gross revenue in 1989 were just three or four percentage points less than their share of 26 to 27 percent decades earlier (middle panel of the table). Total operating expenses as a share of total revenue fell by about six percentage points over the decades, from their three-fifths share of total revenue in the late 1950s and early 1960s.[11] Technology may have reduced companies' costs of evaluating and managing risk, and regulatory changes promoting competition may have forced companies to become more efficient. Nevertheless, these changes did not reduce very much the sizable share of expenses for salary and wages at consumer finance companies.[12]

11. Data for 1959 and 1964 are from nine large consumer finance companies. See Paul F. Smith (1964, 1967) for a description of the data.

12. See discussion on technological advances through development of statistical credit evaluation models later in this chapter and through access to credit history databases at credit bureaus in the following chapter. chapter 11 discusses regulatory changes and their effects on competition.

COMMERCIAL BANKS

As indicated, the most recent data on costs of producing closed-end consumer lending by commercial banks are from the Federal Reserve System's Functional Cost Analysis (FCA) program, which was discontinued in 1999. That data collection effort involved assembling cost accounting information for different financial products primarily from commercial banks but also from savings institutions and credit unions.[13] Participation in the cost analysis program was voluntary. Evidence indicates that participating banks were not representative of the population of US banks, although the economic significance of the cost differences between Functional Cost Analysis participants and the population of commercial banks may have been small (see Ors 2004).

Regardless of year, the FCA data indicate that installment loans at commercial banks were in some respects quite different from installment loans at consumer finance companies. Gross lending revenue relative to credit amount outstanding was about half or less than that of consumer finance companies (top panel of table 5.1). This finding reflects differences in the risk profiles of credit customers at finance companies and banks. Commercial banks also had much lower losses than consumer finance companies. In 1989, for example, commercial banks' losses and additions to loss reserves were just $0.48 per $100 of average outstanding loans, compared with $2.05 at consumer finance companies.

Operating expenses at FCA commercial banks were about three or four dollars per $100 of credit outstanding in each year recorded in table 5.1. This was less than the majority of gross revenue but still a large part. In three of the four years in the table, operating costs were about 44 to 45 percent of gross revenue, the exception being 1989, a year of relatively high market interest rates. (Higher interest rates that year caused the relatively constant operating expenses to become a smaller proportion of the higher gross revenue from loan interest that year. The higher loan revenues that year were matched by higher costs of obtaining loanable funds that year).[14] Operating expense experience in 1998 was quite similar to expenses in 1964 and 1959; all three were years in which market interest rates were considerably lower than in 1989.

Salaries and wages at commercial banks accounted for a little more than a third of operating expenses in 1998. This share is noticeably less than the share in 1989 and earlier years. The decline may have been caused by increases in labor productivity from advances in information technology during the 1990s, although in the absence of specific studies of the issue, this explanation remains only speculative. Again, regardless of the effect of technology or lending costs, the most recent data

---

13. The commercial bank product categories in 1999 were demand deposits, time deposits, investments, real estate loans, home equity loans, consumer installment loans, credit cards, commercial and other loans, trust services, other customer services, data services, automated teller machines, funds transfer, and automated clearinghouse services.

14. Operating cost at consumer finance companies was also a smaller percentage of gross revenue (about six percentage points less), and the cost of borrowed funds was a greater percentage of gross revenue (fourteen percentage points or more) in 1989 than in 1964 or 1959.

for commercial banks suggest that activities performed by employees remained a significant part of the loan production process.

Open-End Credit

As in the case of closed-end credit but even more severely, only limited cost data have been available to researchers on open-end credit plans, notably bank credit card plans. Only an old study is available for retail store credit card plans, today a relatively uncommon kind of credit anyway, at least in comparison with bank card credit.[15]

BANK CREDIT CARDS

Visa USA periodically has commissioned a functional cost study to provide benchmark data to its members on costs of providing credit card services to card holders and merchants. The study develops a methodology for measuring costs of a standardized set of activities (such as credit processing, card holder billing, payment processing, collections) and expense categories (such as salaries and wages, information services, postage, occupancy, credit reports). The 1995 study included twelve issuers and reflected expenses incurred in 1994 (see Visa USA 1995).

Total revenue of bank card issuers in 1994 was $16.05 per $100 of average outstanding credit (see table 5.2). Operating expenses were $7.15 per $100 of average outstanding credit, which was 44.6 percent of total revenue. Both gross revenue and operating expenses for bank card credit relative to the amount of credit outstanding are notably greater for bank credit card credit than for closed-end bank consumer credit (compare table 5.2 with table 5.1).

Net credit charge-offs were the largest component of operating expenses for bank credit cards, at nearly half of total operating expenses. Bank card charge-offs were many times greater than charge-offs for closed-end installment credit at FCA reporting commercial banks (compare tables). Charge-off experience for bank card credit appears more comparable to experience at consumer finance companies. This is not especially surprising, since both bank credit card credit and most direct consumer loans at consumer finance companies are forms of unsecured credit.[16]

The second largest expense category for bank card credit was salary and wages. Salary and wages were $0.99 per $100 of average outstanding credit, or 13.9 percent of total operating expenses. It is notable that despite considerable reliance on information services to originate and maintain accounts and to process transactions, information services expense ($0.38 per $100 of average outstanding credit) was less than half that of salary and wages. (The information services category

15. Other uncommon kinds of open-end consumer credit include check credit and charge card credit. Check credit is a line of credit associated with a checking account. Charge card credit must be paid in full at the end of the billing cycle.

16. See discussion later in this chapter on the effects of collateral on credit risk.

includes salary and wage expenses for development and operation of information systems.) The evidence supports the conclusions from the qualitative discussion above of the cost-causing activities that many of the actions performed in originating, processing, and collecting credit are undertaken by employees.

Retail Credit Cards

There are no publicly available recent studies on two-party retail store credit cards, but an older study gives some information about the orders of magnitude and distribution of such costs. More recently, there are few remaining relatively sizable credit operations among retail store companies anyway, most of which have outsourced their credit operations to others or which now only accept bank credit cards.

In 1973, the New York State Council of Retail Merchants commissioned a study of retail revolving credit costs (Shay and Dunkelberg 1975). The study collected data on revolving credit costs for thirteen local department stores and the New York stores of four national retailers. They developed a cost accounting framework to identify the incremental costs of providing credit during the twelve-month period from February 1972 to January 1973.

Total revenue was $11.33 per $100 of average outstanding credit (see table 5.3). Operating expenses were $7.28 per $100 of average outstanding credit, which was 64.3 percent of total revenue, a much higher proportion than the later Visa study of bank cards (compare tables 5.2 and 5.3).[17] The largest operating expenses for retail revolving credit were salary and wages (39 percent of total operating expenses) and net credit charge-offs (29 percent of total operating expenses). The finding that salary and wages were a substantial component of lending costs for retail revolving credit is similar to findings for the other kinds of consumer credit. That charge-offs were also substantial suggests that the provision of retail revolving credit was risky. Charge-offs per $100 of average outstanding credit for retail revolving credit were comparable to those for closed-end credit at finance companies, which historically have served the high-risk segment of the consumer credit market, and considerably greater than the relatively low levels of charge-offs for closed-end credit at commercial banks.

Shay and Dunkelberg discussed the various tasks performed for various credit activities at some length (new account acquisition, customer servicing, account collection, and so forth) and provided more detailed statistics on the salary and wage costs for each activity. Today most of this discussion is only of historical interest, but some summary information is provided in table 5.3.

The Special Case of High-Price Closed-End Credit Products

Studies of production costs of any kind of consumer lending are uncommon enough, but studies of costs outside the mainstream of consumer credit are

---

17. Revenue per $100 average outstanding credit from retail credit cards in New York was about the same level as that for closed-end credit at commercial banks in earlier times (table 5.1).

Table 5.2 INCOME AND EXPENSES OF BANK CARD ISSUERS, 1995

	Dollars per $100 of Average Outstanding Credit	Percentage of Total Revenue	Percentage of Operating Expense
Total revenue	16.1	100.0	
Salaries and wages	1.0	6.17	13.9
Information services	0.4	2.4	5.4
Postage	0.5	3.2	7.3
Telecommunications	0.2	1.2	2.6
Occupancy, furniture, equipment	0.2	1.2	2.8
Stationery and supplies	0.3	1.9	4.2
Credit reports	0.2	1.0	2.3
Outside vendors	0.8	4.7	10.5
Other direct expenses	0.1	0.9	2.0
Credit investigation	0.1	1.2	1.9
Net credit charge-offs	3.5	21.9	49.1
Total operating expenses	7.2	44.6	100.0
Funding cost	5.0	31.1	
Net income before taxes	3.9	24.4	

SOURCE: Visa USA (1995).

even less common, although much of the recent public controversy over consumer credit arises from the latter products. These controversial products involve small loan amounts, typically at short terms to maturity, that have high, often triple-digit, annual percentage rates. They include pawnshop loans, payday loans, auto title loans, and tax refund anticipation loans (these products are discussed in more detail in chapter 8). Some state laws also permit high rate ceilings on very small short-term loans made on an installment basis by licensed consumer finance companies. Cost data have only been available for two types of high-price credit: an old study of very small short-term finance company installment loans and a more recent look at payday loans.

VERY SMALL SHORT-TERM CONSUMER FINANCE COMPANY LOANS

Durkin (1975) analyzed 1968–1970 income and expense data of so-called Article 3.16 lenders reporting to the Texas Consumer Credit Commissioner. (These loans are described at somewhat greater length in chapter 8. Today they are called Chapter 301-F loans in Texas.) The 1975 analysis included all companies operating

Table 5.3 INCOME AND EXPENSES FOR RETAIL REVOLVING CREDIT IN
NEW YORK, 1972

	Percentage of Average Outstanding Credit	Percentage of Total Revenue	Percentage of Operating Expense
All stores			
Total revenue	11.3	100.0	
Salaries and wages	2.8	25.2	39.1
Information services	0.5	4.5	6.9
Postage	0.6	4.9	7.6
Telecommunications	0.2	1.3	2.0
Occupancy, furniture, equipment	0.2	1.8	2.8
Credit investigation	0.1	1.2	1.9
Collection agency fees	0.3	2.3	3.5
Supplies and other	0.6	4.9	7.6
Net credit charge-offs	2.1	18.4	28.6
Total operating cost	7.3	64.3	100.0
In-state stores (not national chains)			
Total revenue	10.9	100.0	
Salaries and wages	2.0	18.4	29.1
Information services	0.6	5.1	8.1
Postage	0.5	4.5	7.2
Telecommunications	0.1	0.5	0.7
Occupancy, furniture, equipment	0.2	1.5	2.4
Credit investigation	0.1	1.0	1.6
Collection agency fees	0.3	2.8	4.4
Supplies and other	0.6	5.8	9.1
Net credit charge-offs	2.6	23.5	37.2
Total operating cost	6.9	63.1	100.0

SOURCE: Shay and Dunkelberg (1975).

continuously during the three-year period, 338 companies operating 521 offices in 1968.[18] These companies were quite small. Most employed just two or three persons.

18. The number of companies varied slightly in each year, because a few companies reorganized into different entities or because some reports were being amended at the time of the study.

Ratios for operating expense items were several times greater at Article 3.16 lenders than at Article 3.15 lenders, which made larger loans. Salaries and wages, for example, were $40.77 per $100 for Article 3.16 lenders, which is more than seven times greater than salary and wages for Article 3.15 lenders around the same time ($5.60 per $100; see Durkin and McAlister 1977). The higher expense ratios for Article 3.16 lenders were partly the consequence of smaller loan size, since lending costs are spread over fewer loan dollars. Average loan size was $65.09 for Article 3.16 loans in 1968, compared with $508.00 for Article 3.15 loans at that time. (In 2013 dollars, average loan size was $435.93 at Article 3.16 lenders and $3402.32 at Article 3.15 lenders.)

Article 3.16 loans were also riskier than Article 3.15 loans. Loan losses were $8.99 per $100 of average outstanding loans at Article 3.16 lenders, more than three times higher than loan losses at Article 3.15 lenders ($2.83 per $100). The greater risk of very small loans at Article 3.16 lenders can affect other operating expenses. Salaries and wages may be affected, for example, as employees may spend more time monitoring loans and trying to collect delinquent accounts. The cost of borrowed funds was a relatively unimportant component of costs at Article 3.16 lenders, because most of the lending capital was from owners' resources.

Payday Loans

A payday loan is a small, short-term, single-payment consumer loan (discussed further in chapter 8). For this type of credit, the customer writes a personal check for the sum of the loan amount and finance charge and leaves it with the lender at the time of receiving the cash. The payday loan company agrees in writing to defer presenting the check until the customer's next payday, which is often ten to thirty days later. At the next payday, the customer may redeem the check by paying the loan amount and the finance charge, or the payday loan company may cash the check. In some cases, a customer may extend a payday loan by paying only the finance charge and writing a new check. A customer seeking to extend payday borrowing may instead repay the existing loan and engage a new payday loan (some states prohibit or limit such extensions of payday loans).

Researchers at the Federal Deposit Insurance Corporation obtained office-level cost, revenue, and operating data for 2002 to 2004 for a sample of 300 offices of two large, monoline payday loan companies (Flannery and Samolyk 2005).[19] Although the companies were large, the offices were quite small. Offices had on average 2.4 full-time equivalent employees. They made 6,370 loans per year, incurring direct operating costs of $166,957. The two companies had a relatively large proportion of new offices. Nearly one-fifth of the payday loan offices were open less than a year, and a third were one to four years old.

---

19. Monoline companies are companies that provide only payday loans, and therefore, their costs reflect only the costs of payday lending, without any need to allocate overhead among different products. Some companies provide payday loans and other services such as check cashing, pawnbroker loans, and wire transfers.

Gross revenue of payday lending was $407.16 per $100 of average receivables outstanding in this study (see table 5.4). Operating expenses were $393.08 per $100 of average receivables outstanding, which was 96.5 percent of gross revenue. Salaries and wages were 24.6 percent of operating expenses. Administrative expense was about a third of operating expenses. The high expense ratios are partly explained by small loan size; the average loan size at these offices was just $246.58.

The large proportion of new offices at these companies contributed to high expense ratios. Expense ratios were generally larger for new offices than for established offices, because the fixed expenses of the offices were spread across lower loan volumes at new offices (numbers not in table). The income and expense ratios reflect the relatively high cost of payday lending.

Losses at payday loan companies were 13.7 percent of revenue, 57 percent higher than losses at the Article 3.16 consumer finance companies (8.7 percent of revenue). Payday loan companies' relatively higher losses may be attributed to the nature of the product and their more limited underwriting process. Article 3.16 companies lend on an installment basis and attempt to arrange a loan with a low monthly payment, which the borrower can afford to pay with ease. In contrast, payday loan companies lend on a single-payment basis up to a specified percentage of the customer's take-home pay without consideration of other obligations the customer may owe.[20] Thus, payday customers may be less constrained than Article 3.16 customers in the amount that they can borrow and require more discipline to pay down the loan over time if they are unable to liquidate the entire loan on the due date.

Cost of borrowed funds for payday loan companies was $6.29 per $100 borrowed. As with Article 3.16 lenders, payday loan companies' cost of borrowed funds was very small relative to total revenue, amounting to only 1.5 percent of total revenue. The low percentages of total revenue for cost of funds and high percentages for operating expenses for payday loan companies and Article 3.16 lenders are consistent with the contention that much of the cost of consumer lending arises because an application is taken or a loan is made.

Economies of Scale and Loan Size Cost Elasticity

Beyond overall averages of the costs of consumer lending illustrated in the tables above, econometric modeling procedures known as statistical cost analysis reveal a bit more about cost relationships. In particular, this kind of technical work permits exploration of the relationship of costs to size of lending company (economies of scale) and to size of loan (loan size cost elasticity). Concerning economies of scale, ascertaining the proportion to which cost rises with increases in company size has been an important goal of these studies. If cost rises less than proportionately with the level of output (that is, economies of scale exist), then

---

20. See chapter 8 for further discussion of the underwriting process used by these lenders.

Table 5.4 INCOME AND EXPENSES FOR SELECTED HIGH-PRICE CREDIT PRODUCTS

| | Payday Loans | Finance Company Installment Loans | |
| | | Very Small | Larger |
	2002–2004[a]	1968[b]	1968[c]
Income and expenses per $100 of average outstanding loans			
Total loan revenue	407.2	102.8	24.1
Salaries and wages	96.6	40.8	5.6
Advertising and publicity expense	15.3	NA	NA
Losses and additions to loss reserves	55.7	9.0	2.8
Administrative expenses	133.9	NA	NA
Other operating expenses	91.6	31.9	6.2
Total operating expenses	393.1	81.6	14.6
Cost of borrowed funds	6.3	3.4	5.6
Net income before taxes	7.8	17.7	3.9
Percent of total domestic revenue			
Total loan revenue	100.0	100.0	100.0
Salaries and wages	23.7	39.7	23.3
Advertising and publicity expense	3.8	NA	NA
Losses and additions to loss reserves	13.7	8.7	11.8
Administrative expenses	32.9	NA	NA
Other operating expenses	22.5	31.0	25.6
Total operating expenses	96.5	79.4	60.6
Cost of borrowed funds	1.5	3.3	23.2
Net income before taxes	1.9	17.3	16.1
Percent of total operating expenses			
Total operating expenses	100.0	100.0	100.0
Salaries and wages	24.6	50.0	38.4
Advertising and publicity expense	3.9	NA	NA
Losses and additions to loss reserves	14.2	11.0	19.4
Administrative expenses	34.1	NA	NA
Other operating expenses	23.3	39.0	42.2
Average loan size, current dollars	227.5	65.1	508
Average loan size, 2005 dollars	243.0	360.8	2618.2

[a]source: Flannery and Samolyk (2005).
[b]Loans made under Article 3.16 of the Texas Consumer Credit Code. Source: Durkin (1975).
[c]Loans made under Article 3.15 of the Texas Consumer Credit Code. Source: Durkin and McAlister (1975).
NA: Not Available.

unit cost (cost per loan) is lower for larger companies, giving them a competitive advantage. Likewise, cost elasticity of loan size is important in estimating the willingness of lenders to make loans of various sizes. If cost rises less than proportionately with loan size, then larger loans are more attractive to lenders for a given interest rate, and this has implications for legal ceilings on rates of charge and credit rationing. Unfortunately, statistical cost analyses of consumer lenders are not common, because of paucity of data, but some studies have been done, and they reveal interesting findings and relationships.

Technically, statistical cost analyses involve estimating the parameters of cost functions of the following general form:

$$C = C(q, p_1, p_2, \ldots p_n)$$

where C represents the smallest expenditure that enables a firm to produce output q at input prices p_1, p_2, ... p_n. Cost functions for financial services are commonly estimated using data from cross sections of firms in an industry, such as the data collections described earlier in this chapter.[21]

21. Early studies of costs of financial firms specified a Cobb-Douglas functional form for econometric estimating purposes (see Bell and Murphy 1968, Benston 1972). This function is conveniently linear in logarithms but poses the restriction that its shape is linear regardless of whether it slopes upward or downward as output is higher. More recent studies have used a transcendental logarithmic (translog) functional form, which can be interpreted as a second-order approximation of an unknown functional form (see Durkin and Elliehausen 1998 and further references there). The translog functional form has the advantage that it makes less restrictive assumptions about the shape of the cost function than the Cobb-Douglas functional form. In particular, the translog function allows estimates of economies of scale to vary with the level of output, whereas the Cobb-Douglas function restricts economies of scale to the same value across all levels of output (see Durkin and Elliehausen 1998 for further discussion).

Using cross-section information from a number of firms for cost analysis of this kind makes the assumption that the cross-section observations trace out the cost curve for a typical firm, although no one firm is actually followed over the whole range of output. Bell and Murphy (1968), Benston (1972), and, more recently, Durkin and Elliehausen (1998), have argued that this assumption is reasonable, because the level of output arises from outside, that is, it is largely exogenous to each individual firm. Supporting this view, these authors have noted that firms in the financial industry have no access to secret technology or processes that might provide them with an inherent production advantage over their rivals. As a result, loan demand is not cost determined, but rather loan demand determines individual scale. Although technological changes in credit granting and marketing functions might appear to suggest that some firms could have a cost advantage, the technology of statistical lending evaluation, such as credit scoring techniques (both application-based credit scoring and generic credit bureau scores), is well known to all firms in the industry and widely available from a variety of vendors. In effect, companies compete in a succession of local markets with basic technology that is known to all. Under these circumstances, local demands for loans determine the level of output. Thus, the level of output is exogenous, and the cost function can be estimated by a single equation using cross-section data on costs and output. Output is never completely exogenous, of course. Lenders may influence demand through advertising or promotions, and so these studies typically leave promotion costs out of the cost functions estimated.

The consumer finance company industry is especially useful for investigating consumer lending economies of scale. As indicated earlier, although these companies are financial intermediaries, they produce most of their output for only one side of the marketplace, the lending side. This precludes any need for tricky cost allocations to produce usable data for the estimating equation for lending costs alone. Funds sources (deposits, policies, pension plans) are products in themselves for some other intermediaries, but the funds sources for consumer finance companies (bonds and commercial paper issued locally and in worldwide financial markets) are largely incidental to the lending function, at least in terms of costs. This makes arbitrary cost allocations between products unnecessary. Similarly, if consumer finance companies produce only one product, there can be no output-cost joint relationships known as cost complementarities between or among products. Called scope economies, such complementary relationships among products produced together may obscure visibility of the scale effects for each product by itself, but this is not an issue for consumer finance companies.

ECONOMIES OF SCALE IN CONSUMER LENDING

As indicated, whether or not economies of scale exist is an important issue because of the impact on size distribution and the number of firms in the marketplace. If scale economies exist, the market would consist only of larger firms, because larger firms would be able to produce loans at a lower cost per loan than smaller firms. Large economies of scale could discourage entry of new firms into the marketplace and cause the market to be dominated by a few entrenched large firms. This, in turn, could have adverse effects on the extent of competition. In contrast, if economies of scale do not exist or are small, unit costs for small and large firms would be similar. Small and large firms would then be able to coexist in the market, and market entrants would not face a cost disadvantage. Thus, absence of significant economies of scale would tend to favor development of a competitive marketplace.

In this context, economies of scale are defined as the percentage change in cost resulting from a small percentage change in output, that is, the cost "elasticity" with respect to output. In testing for the presence of scale economies at lending institutions, the economic research literature distinguishes between two types of scale economies, each involving different assumptions about the number of production facilities (in this case, lending offices). The first measure, called simple scale economies, is the cost elasticity when the number of lending offices does not change as output varies. In contrast, augmented scale economies allow

---

Kwast, Starr-McCluer, and Wolken (1997, table 3) found that in 1992, most consumers using various types of credit obtained that credit from a local financial institution. For some products, three-fourths or more consumers obtained the product from a local institution.

Location has become less important over time, but local institutions still originate a very large share of loans to households. Amel, Kennickell, and Moore (2008) found that in 2004, a little more than half of all loans to households were obtained from local institutions, where local was defined as thirty miles or less from the home or a household member's place of work, and nearly half of closed-end consumer loans were from local institutions.

the number of offices to vary along with output (for discussion, see Benston, Hanweck, and Humphrey, 1982).

In effect, simple scale economies reflect a short-run relationship. It is the relationship of cost to output for existing offices of a company in a period short enough that the number of production offices does not vary. By comparison, augmented scale economies reflect longer-term cost relationships where everything is variable, including the number of locations. Large augmented scale economies may cause a lender to open additional offices in new locations, especially in the absence of simple scale economies encouraging larger offices. Because lending generally does not require specialized assets or especially large investments to open new offices, providing additional lending offices is a relatively simple matter for many lenders.[22] But large augmented diseconomies may cause a lender to close offices, especially if simple economies are present, although the size of the geographic market and resulting customer remoteness may limit a lender's ability to consolidate offices.

Durkin and Elliehausen (1998) estimated cost functions for consumer finance companies in 1987, 1988, and 1989, using a functional form that allows estimates of scale economies to vary at different levels of output. Costs were estimated as a function of number of loans serviced, factor prices (labor and office space prices), average loan amount, and number of offices. They used the data on consumer finance companies from the American Financial Services Association discussed earlier in this chapter.[23]

To illustrate how costs vary by loan volume, they estimated simple and augmented scale economies for firms in different quintiles of average annual loan volumes. Their estimates of the simple scale economies measure suggest that there are economies of scale at the office level in the operating costs of consumer finance companies, although these simple scale economies diminish as output increases (Durkin and Elliehausen 1998, table 3). For the smallest output quintile, estimates indicate that a 10 percent increase in output raises costs about 4.38 percent at an annual loan volume of 6,000 loans. Scale economies gradually fell from the second to the fourth output quintiles: a 10 percent increase in output raised costs about 5 to 7 percent in the second quintile and about 7 to 8 percent in the fourth quintile. In the highest-output quintile, simple economies of scale appear to be

22. Some types of lenders might have larger costs of opening new offices than others. For example, pawnshops require additional costs to secure storage areas for safekeeping of assets pledged as collateral, and bank offices typically require vaults and other security measures for cash, because retail bank offices typically offer cash and deposit services in addition to loans.

23. Technically, to calculate simple scale economies, they followed the usual practice of holding constant in a regression equation factor prices, average loan size, and number of offices at the mean for medium-sized firms, which are defined as firms in the third quintile of firms arrayed by annual number of loans serviced. (Medium-sized firms operated an average of forty-seven offices each.) Output levels for each quintile reflected the typical range of values for firms in each quintile. Calculated simple scale economies with values of less than one indicate the presence of scale economies, values equal to one indicate constant costs, and values of more than one indicate diseconomies of scale.

exhausted. The finding of significant scale economies at the office level up to the largest offices generally holds regardless of the number of offices of a company.

The assumption that firms keep the number of offices constant may be appropriate in the short run, but it probably is unrealistic over longer periods of time. As mentioned, firms might look for economies of scale by opening additional offices. Augmented scale economies measures reflect these longer-term relationships between cost and output.

To investigate augmented scale economies, Durkin and Elliehausen used the same output levels that they used for estimates of the simple scale economies measure. But instead of a constant number of offices across all output levels, they varied the number of offices, using the appropriate mean number of offices for each output quintile.[24]

The augmented scale economies estimates suggest that firms adjust the number of offices to exploit all scale economies or, in other words, that when all things are variable, there are no further economies of scale for consumer finance companies. According to the statistical estimates, even relatively small firms are able to operate at approximately constant cost elasticity. None of the estimates of the augmented scale economies measure is significantly greater than one, which suggests that firms also can adjust the number of offices to avoid diseconomies of scale (Durkin and Elliehausen 1998, table 4). For example, a firm in the first output quintile having 3,400 loans and two offices would have average office size of 1,700 loans and operating expenses of $0.06 per dollar of loans or $220 per loan. A substantially larger fourth-quintile firm with 528,700 loans could have the same average office size and about the same operating expense ratios with 311 offices.

By consolidating loans in half the number of offices, the second firm might reduce operating expenses to $0.05 per dollar of loans or $163 per loan. Such reductions in operating costs may not always be feasible in small markets, however. Because small loan markets are still largely local, limits on the size of local markets could prevent the firm from servicing the 2,800 to 3,400 thousand loans per office needed to attain that level of operating costs. Thus, large firms operating in small local markets would not enjoy a cost advantage over smaller firms.

COST ELASTICITY OF AVERAGE LOAN SIZE

Durkin and Elliehausen also estimated cost elasticities of average loan size. This measure shows the relationship between operating costs and the average size of loans in creditors' portfolios. An elasticity of less than one suggests that firms producing smaller loans have higher costs per dollar of credit than firms producing larger loans. Such might be the case if some expenses of consumer lending are not

---

24. Factor prices and average loan size again were held constant in a regression equation, using means of the third output quintile for factor prices and average loan size to maintain comparability with estimates of the simple scale economies measure. Again, values of less than one indicate the presence of scale economies, values equal to one indicate constant costs, and values of more than one indicate diseconomies of scale.

related to the size of the loan. Costs for recording and booking loans or payments are likely relatively constant, regardless of loan size, for example.

Like the scale economy elasticities, the cost elasticity of average loan size depends on the values for number of loans outstanding, factor prices, and number of offices and also average loan size. Durkin and Elliehausen assumed average values of number of loans serviced, factor prices, and number of offices for medium-sized firms. Values chosen for average loan size lie between the tenth and ninetieth percentiles of the sample distribution of average loan size.

They found that elasticity of costs with respect to loan size are significantly less than one for most loan sizes (Durkin and Elliehausen 1998, tables 5 and 6). This indicates that production costs increase less than proportionately with loan size and suggests that smaller loans are indeed more expensive to produce per loan dollar than larger loans. At an average loan size of $980 (the tenth percentile), for instance, a 10 percent increase in loan size would increase costs just 2.11 percent.

Average loan size economies are smaller at higher average loan amounts but still quite large. At $2,210 (the median value of average loan size for these companies), a 10 percent increase in average loan size would increase costs 3.00 percent; and at an average loan size of $8,620 (the ninetieth percentile for consumer finance companies in 1989), estimated values of SCA indicate that a 10 percent increase in average loan size would increase costs 4.49 percent. The decline in average loan size economies as average loan size increases likely occurs at least in part because firms incur greater costs for credit evaluation, obtaining collateral, monitoring, and collection on larger loans than on smaller loans.

The effect of average loan size on operating costs can also be expressed in terms of average cost per dollar of loans. For the typical medium-sized firm (46,000 loans at forty-seven offices), average cost per dollar of loan fell from $0.18 per dollar of loans for an average loan size of $980 to $0.10 per dollar of loans for an average loan size of $2,210 and to $0.04 per dollar of loans for an average loan size of $8,620.[25]

These findings are now dated, but they again raise the question of whether lenders are going to be willing to make loans of all sizes. Past findings that lending costs were higher per loan dollar for small loans led the federal consumer lending study commission, the National Commission on Consumer Finance (NCCF), to conclude in 1972 that lenders were unlikely to make many small loans under the interest rate ceilings (commonly known as usury laws) then prevailing (see National Commission on Consumer Finance 1972, chapter 7). For a variety of reasons, interest rate ceilings on consumer loans were either eliminated or significantly relaxed over the next decade after publication of the commission's report, but they are still a public policy issue. Interest rate ceilings are discussed further in a later section of this chapter and in chapter 11.

---

25. Size of firm does not confer a cost advantage in processing loans of a particular size. The average cost per dollar of loans at each level of average loan size at small or large firms is nearly the same as that at medium-sized firms (number not in table).

THE LOAN OFFER CURVE, DEFAULT RISK, AND CREDIT RATIONING

Production costs govern the willingness to produce and supply commodities and services, and credit is no different from other goods and services on this basis. But credit is different from other products in that it involves an intertemporal transaction, and this also gives rise to uncertainty and risk, which are naturally also going to have an impact on credit supply. Because all credit shares the common feature of being an intertemporal transaction in which the lender advances funds to a borrower for repayment later, the lender will not lend unless there is an expectation that future cash flows will be sufficient to replenish the funds and provide satisfactory return on capital. For consumer lending, as with all lending, this means proper management of the possibility of default risk. Discussion earlier indicated that risk costs of consumer lending are substantial and potentially dangerous to the lender, even with the care that goes into managing such risks. Experience with subprime mortgage lending in 2008 and 2009 demonstrated this beyond any doubt.

The Default Risk Model of Credit Supply

Economists originally developed formal economic models of credit supply to explain the economic reasons behind credit rationing, which they believed was an important channel for transmission of monetary policy. Credit rationing occurs when the price of credit is less than the equilibrium price based on supply and demand and lenders restrict supply. In such situations, the amount of credit offered is less than the amount demanded.

Normally, an excess of demand over supply in a market leads to a price increase, but credit is different, in that a supply restriction may result instead. Economists believed that a formal theory of credit supply was needed to explain why lenders would limit credit rather than raise its price as monetary policy tightened. The models they developed investigated the effects of default risk on lenders' willingness to offer credit.

The basic theoretical economic model of the supply of credit to an individual borrower starts with the quite reasonable assumption that wealth of borrowers (including wealth arising from future wages), and thus their ability to repay, is limited and not known with certainty by the lender. Under these conditions, increasing the amount of credit extended to borrowers increases the probability of default as the likelihood that wealth will be sufficient to repay larger loan amounts falls. Indeed, beyond a certain amount of credit, default may be virtually certain, so that no offer to pay a higher interest rate would induce a lender to supply additional credit. As a consequence, the supply curve for an individual borrower becomes completely inelastic or even backward bending at some rate of interest (see figure 5.1).

Economists developed several variants of this basic idea. Among them, perhaps the best known is the model of Jaffee and Modigliani (1969); other variants include those by Hodgman (1960), Miller (1962), and Freimer and Gordon

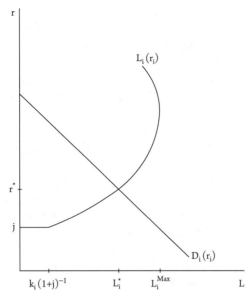

Figure 5.1 Loan Offer Curve with Loan Demand.

(1965). Economists originally developed these default risk models for commercial loans, but the critical feature of the models, the assumption that the borrower's ability to repay the loan is finite, clearly applies also to consumer loans. Because of the importance of the Jaffee-Modigliani model, there is extended discussion of it in an appendix to this chapter.

Jaffee and Modigliani considered a lender's loan offer amount and associated interest rate decision when the borrower's wealth, and hence ability to repay, is not certain but rather is a random variable. They demonstrated mathematically that an optimal loan is one that equates the probability of default to the discounted difference between the offered loan interest rate and the "opportunity rate," the rate available on some alternative loan. This result gives the loan supply curve for an individual borrower its specific shape.

Normally, market supply curves have a positive slope as higher prices elicit larger quantities offered. In contrast, the loan supply curve for an individual loan has several distinct components. First, for very small loan amounts, where repayment is virtually a certainty, the loan supply curve is horizontal. That is, larger loan amounts do not entail higher interest rates in this size range.

Beyond some loan amount, default risk becomes a consideration, however. Greater loan amounts entail greater default risk and hence higher interest rates. This means the supply curve has a positive slope in this range. The maximum loan amount is limited, though, because the borrower's wealth is finite. As a consequence, a borrower's promise to pay larger and larger amounts of interest is not credible to the lender. Borrowers cannot possibly pay very large loan amounts, even under the best of circumstances. Indeed, beyond the maximum loan amount, higher interest rates entail smaller loan amounts offered. Consequently, the loan offer bends backward.

The existence of a maximum loan amount is not, by itself, credit rationing, however. Credit rationing requires consideration of not just supply but also demand and the determinants of the interest rate in the marketplace. Jaffee and Modigliani argued that credit rationing occurs because legal restrictions, along with considerations of goodwill and social mores, prevent charging different market rates to different customers. Therefore, some borrowers end up facing market rates below the rate at which they would be in equilibrium, but they are unable to obtain more credit; they are rationed.

Why would lenders ration borrowers instead of charging each customer a rate appropriate to risk? Jaffee and Modigliani noted that one possible explanation was the existence of legal interest rate ceilings, which prohibited lenders from charging more than a specified maximum rate. Legal restrictions were an important consideration at the time Jaffee and Modigliani wrote their paper. All borrowers whose equilibrium rate exceeds the legal limit will be rationed.[26]

Aside from interest rate ceilings, Jaffee and Modigliani also argued that there were some special features of the functioning of loan markets that also caused rationing. According to them (Jaffee and Modigliani 1969, 860), "the pressure of legal restrictions and considerations of good will and social mores make it inadvisable if not impossible... to charge different rates to different customers." They suggested that lenders "would tend to limit the spread between the rates and justify the remaining differences in terms of a few objective and verifiable criteria." This could easily mean that some potential borrowers could face rationing if their equilibrium rates were above the general rate the lenders felt compelled to offer, even if not above legal rate ceilings for that loan type. (See chapter appendix.)

In part, Jaffee and Modigliani's argument for assigning borrowers to different broad classes was based on a view that such an arrangement facilitates collusion among lenders in an oligopolistic market. They suggested that "to make the whole arrangement manageable, the number of different rate classes would have to be reasonably small" and that "the structure of class rates could be facilitated by tying these rates through fairly rigid differentials, to a prime rate set through price leadership" (Jaffee and Modigliani 1969, 860). They believed that the rate for each class would tend to be set near the lowest individual rate for the class. Together with rate ceilings, Jaffee and Modigliani concluded, this arrangement results in widespread rationing, especially in higher-risk classes.[27]

In sum, Jaffee and Modigliani's theoretical analysis established, first, that lenders would not extend credit to a borrower beyond a certain amount because the borrower's resources for repaying debt are limited. This result can explain why a borrower may not be able to obtain additional credit by offering to pay higher

---

26. In the past, interest rate ceilings could easily affect different classes of borrowers differently, because interest rate ceilings typically were graduated by size of loan and often were different among institutional classes of lenders (see chapter 11 for further discussion and National Commission on Consumer Finance 1972, chapter 7).

27. See the appendix to this chapter and Jaffee and Modigliani (1969, 859–861) for further discussion.

interest rates. This result is not rationing per se, however. Jaffee and Modigliani also correctly pointed out that rationing involves consideration of both supply and demand and the interaction of the two in the market. To obtain a rationing outcome, Jaffee and Modigliani resorted to outside (exogenous) considerations such as law, lender mores, and price leadership. Their suggestions of exogenous causes of rationing were plausible, but apart from legal interest rate ceilings at the time, they ultimately had little directly observable empirical support.

The lack of an internal (endogenous) explanation for credit rationing stimulated further examination of the issue and led to extensions of the default risk model. Economists looked at possible effects of (1) equity and collateral on loan supply and (2) adverse selection caused by information asymmetry between borrowers and lenders as possible endogenous factors governing loan supply.

Extensions of the Default Risk Model I: Equity and Collateral

As introduced in chapter 3 and earlier in this chapter, the lender requirement that borrowers build ownership share in financed assets (known as equity requirements) and their frequent insistence on collateral to back loans are common institutional features of consumer and commercial lending. In a technical comment on Jaffee and Modigliani's paper a few years later, Vernon Smith (1972) proposed an extension of the default risk model to take into account formally the reasons for and the potential effect of equity requirements on borrowers' and lenders' decisions.

In Smith's model, borrowers allocate their wealth between risk-free assets and equity in assets being financed with debt. They naturally choose loan amounts and equity so as to maximize expected utility (see chapter 3). Lenders, in turn, allocate their wealth between risk-free assets and risky loans, choosing loan amounts that maximize their own expected utility.[28] Both borrowers and lenders take risk-free and risky rates of return as market-determined parameters. The notable feature of Smith's model is that a lender's utility depends on the borrower's equity choice. This occurs because greater amounts of borrower's equity, such as through down payments, allow the loan to be repaid at lower realized levels of income and hence reduce the likelihood of default.

Thus, the lender's loan supply function must contain the borrower's equity decision as a parameter. (Smith assumed that the borrower's other asset holdings are protected from the lender in the event that income is insufficient to repay the loan, so that only the borrower's equity in the risky investment is available to repay the loan.) In contrast, the borrower's loan demand function depends only

28. Smith further considered the case in which the size of the investment is allowed to be variable. Jaffee (1972) noted that the loan supply curve for a variable-size investment has the same distinctive characteristics as the loan supply curve for a fixed-size investment, namely, that the loan supply curve is horizontal when default risk is zero, slopes upward with increasing default risk, and becomes vertical and then bends backward when default becomes a virtual certainty. These properties hold as long as investment exhibits decreasing returns to scale.

on market rates of return and the borrower's own wealth and is independent of the lender's utility. This disparity implies that the borrower's equity acts as an external economy to the lender.

Theoretical work in other areas has shown that when external economies (or diseconomies) are present in a market outcome, a competitive equilibrium is not generally optimal or efficient. When left to itself, the market provides too little (or too much) of a good as the market price is greater (or less) than the marginal social benefit (or cost). This idea has been explored extensively with respect to public goods such as clean air and water or a well-functioning financial system, all of which provide market benefits beyond those accruing solely to those party to the specific transaction. Because the borrower's equity is an external economy, the lender would be willing to pay to see it increased. But such a payment would change the borrower's decision, which in turn would affect the lender's decision. In the end, Smith's model does not produce a mutually acceptable competitive equilibrium.

Instead, Smith proposed that a rationing system involving quotas might produce an efficient outcome for loans. Lenders could set a minimum equity quota for borrowers, and borrowers could set a minimum loan amount quota for lenders. The lender chooses a loan amount subject to the borrower's loan amount quota, and the borrower chooses an amount of equity subject to the lender's equity quota. This loan amount might be less than the amount the borrower prefers at the interest rate offered, however, which would result in a rationing outcome.[29]

That a lender would not consider the effect of a borrower's equity in its lending decision seems unlikely, however. Since the time of Smith's paper, other theoretical researchers have argued that the determination of interest rate and loan amount must include endogenous consideration of ownership equity. At the same time, they also have expanded the discussion further to include collateral.

Collateral is similar to equity in that collateral increases resources available to repay a loan and thereby reduces the likelihood of default (see Azzi and Cox 1976, Baltensperger 1976, Barro 1976, and Benjamin 1978). These theoretical researchers treated loans as a heterogeneous product, in which equity and collateral are product characteristics affecting the quality of the loan. This approach allowed development of theory in which the market sets prices that reflect the cost of producing loans with different amounts of collateral and equity.

---

29. Smith's full analysis actually is more complex than described here. He contended that an optimal outcome could be achieved if the borrower's quota constraint on equity has a shadow price (that is, the change in borrower utility from a small relaxation in the equity constraint) that reflects the lender's marginal utility of equity and the lender's constraint on loan amount has a shadow price that reflects the borrower's marginal utility of debt.

But Smith did not offer an explanation of how borrowers and lenders set optimal quotas in the market. To be consistent with efficiency, the borrower's quota must reflect the lender's marginal utility of equity, and the lender's quota must reflect the borrower's marginal utility on debt finance. Thus, he essentially begged the question of how equity requirements function in reconciling supply and demand, and full theoretical explanation awaited further review. For further discussion, see Smith (1972).

While the details of the models of this kind differ to some extent and are generally quite complex, these theoretical analyses essentially describe a competitive equilibrium for a product defined in two dimensions, quantity (loan amount) and quality (amount of equity or collateral). Each loan product is defined by different values of quantity and quality. Borrowers and lenders choose loan products that maximize utility (for borrowers) or profit (for lenders). These choices are guided by a market-determined price function relating the interest rate to the value of loan amount and quality. In equilibrium, the price function matches borrowers and lenders such that borrowers' marginal valuations of each specific loan product are equated with lenders' marginal costs of producing that loan product (see Rosen 1974).

Using this framework, Azzi and Cox (1976) examined effects of equity and collateral on loan amount. They first considered the case of the perfect capital market, in which the lender has investment opportunities that have the same distribution of returns as the borrower. They demonstrated that a borrower must provide a positive amount of equity or collateral to elicit a loan from a lender, because the provision of equity or collateral provides a return to the lender in cases where the borrower's rate of return is insufficient to repay the loan. They then demonstrated that a borrower can increase the size of the loan by offering more equity or collateral. Furthermore, the finding that a borrower can elicit a larger loan amount by offering more equity or collateral was valid under a variety of different technical assumptions about returns on alternative investments, lender risk aversion, and collateral value. Even when they considered the possibility of a stochastic debt repayment amount on a pure consumption loan, Azzi and Cox found that the borrower can increase loan size by offering greater collateral.

Based on their theoretical analysis, Azzi and Cox argued that in general, the market process would produce an equilibrium in which borrower demands for credit are satisfied at different equity, collateral, and interest rate combinations, a theoretical outcome that seems very sensible in common experience. Furthermore, they noted, if exogenous constraints prevent lenders from adjusting the interest rate, the amounts of credit supplied and demanded may still be equated when sufficient amounts of equity or collateral are provided.[30] The idea that the amount of equity or collateral influences the level of the interest rate quickly leads to the concept of risk-based pricing: those willing or able to offer only smaller amounts of equity or collateral can obtain larger loan amounts only by paying higher interest rates, up to some limit.

Barro (1976) extended further the thrust of the model for heterogeneous loans (loans with multiple characteristics). He investigated the role of collateral in the lending decisions under the simplifying assumption that the borrower defaults when repayment of interest and principal is greater than the value of collateral (a serious practical concern during the subprime mortgage collateral crisis of

---

30. In a later paper, Jaffee and Modigliani (1976) argued that such outcomes might still be regarded as rationing, since many borrowers have very limited assets available to pledge as collateral and can provide equity only at sharply rising costs.

2008–2009). His analysis indicated that the maximum loan amount is limited by the expected present value of the collateral, which declines with any increases in the risk-free rate of interest or the transaction cost to the lender of liquidating collateral. Therefore, the explicit interest cost to the borrower increases with the loan-to-collateral-value ratio, the risk-free rate of interest, and the transaction cost to the lender of liquidating collateral. Again, this theoretical outcome seems eminently reasonable in practice.

Using a similar model to that of Barro, Benjamin (1978) replicated Barro's theoretical results mathematically and extended the analysis of collateral to include cases in which the asset pledged as collateral has no market value to the lender. Benjamin demonstrated that an asset that has value to the borrower but no market value can still function as collateral if its loss is costly to the borrower.

Ultimately, the heterogeneous loan models of Azzi and Cox, Barro, and Benjamin do not involve credit rationing per se, where the loan amount supplied by the lender is less than the amount demanded at the explicit loan interest rate. Barro argued this point forcefully:

> "[P]rices" in this market cannot be fully represented by the explicit loan rate r, but must also include a specification of collateral characteristics.... It is unfortunate that much of the previous literature on loan markets has viewed the unwillingness of lenders to provide unlimited funds to a borrower (with a fixed amount and type of collateral) at the "going" interest rate as a "disequilibrium" or "credit rationing" phenomenon. In fact, this unwillingness reflects simply the upward slope of the loan supply curve graphed versus the appropriate price that includes consideration of collateral. (Barro 1976, 448)

Baltensperger (1976) went further and explicitly derived mathematically the marginal conditions for efficient lending decisions in a competitive market for heterogeneous loan products, but acceptance of his process seemed deterred at the time by the empirical observation that lenders then did not generally fine-tune interest rates to the conditions of each loan. When much of this theoretical literature on credit rationing was written, lenders generally did not offer schedules of different interest rates for different sets of loan terms. As discussed by Jaffee and Modigliani (1969), lenders at the time typically offered a set of loan terms to all borrowers who qualified and rejected or limited credit to borrowers who did not. To be sure, different classes of lenders offered different sets of loan terms, based on their decision about which part of the market to enter and the costs of providing their preferred kinds of loans, as discussed earlier in this chapter.

Juster and Shay (1964) had noted that some lenders at the time (in particular, consumer finance companies, as discussed here in chapter 3) specialized in unsecured personal loans at relatively high interest rates to borrowers who wished to use more debt than primary market lenders, such as banks, were willing to lend. Nothing in the theoretical economic literature on markets for heterogeneous credit products developed during these years suggests, however, that any individual producer, such as a bank, would individually offer all varieties of a credit product. Differences in underlying costs and production technologies for different kinds and risks of credit may well provide different lenders with a comparative advantage in producing different types of loans and cause them to limit the breadth of the loan services they individually offer. The cost data discussed earlier in this chapter suggest that such differences in cost structures for different types of credit did and do exist. These differences can offer lending institutions an incentive to focus on one credit type or another. And so credit rationing may not occur to the same degree or in the same way at all lenders.

Historically, state regulatory limits on interest rates, loan size, and term to maturity created another incentive for product differentiation, segmenting loan markets by type of credit and type of lender in ways that still appear to have an influence (see chapter 11). A market in which lenders specialize in producing different loan products could produce an outcome that is reasonably competitive, especially if borrowers are able to combine loan products to produce desired amounts of leverage.

Developments in credit markets since publication of much of this theoretical economic literature on credit rationing have increased the plausibility of reasonably competitive markets for consumer credit and general movement toward reduced rationing. Development of credit bureau statistical risk scores has greatly facilitated risk-based pricing by lenders, and there is greater availability of information about payment performance through automated credit bureaus (see discussion later in this chapter and in chapter 6). Further, new forms of unsecured revolving consumer credit through credit cards (chapter 7) and high-price closed-end credit have become available (chapter 8). Regulatory restraints on interest rates have also generally relaxed. In this environment, schedules of different interest rates for different loans with different credit risk have become common, especially for automobile loans, mortgages, and credit cards. Subprime lenders, for example, have schedules of different rates for different levels of the loan-to-value ratio, and auto lenders charge different rates for different terms to maturity (different paces of equity accumulation).

Extensions of the Default Risk Model II: Asymmetric Information and Adverse Selection

Another line of theoretical research on willingness to lend concerns the impact of unavailability of perfect information to lenders. Abstracting from concerns of equity and collateral, it certainly is no secret that different potential borrowers exhibit different probabilities of default. As discussed earlier in this chapter, to reduce associated lending costs, lenders collect information about credit applicants and attempt to distinguish applicants who have relatively low probabilities of default ("good" borrowers) from applicants who have high probabilities of default ("bad" borrowers). In recent decades, they have brought sophisticated technology to bear on this issue, such as statistical credit scoring, discussed further below. In spite of all efforts, however, lenders are unlikely to distinguish perfectly between good and bad borrowers, if only because the determining events take place in the unpredictable future. Lenders may offer credit to some bad borrowers and refuse some good borrowers. This is another way of saying that even after lenders' evaluations of potential borrowers, information remains imperfect. Not surprisingly, unavailability of perfect information is an important influence on willingness of lenders to supply credit.

In fact, potential borrowers may have better information on their probabilities of default than lenders, a condition known as asymmetric information. Such information asymmetries raise the possibility of opportunistic behavior by bad borrowers who are offered credit despite relatively high probability of default. These borrowers, perceiving their own high probability of not repaying, may be more willing to borrow at high interest rates than good borrowers. If so, it is easy enough to surmise that as the interest rate rises, the overall average default risk of borrowers in the borrower pool increases, and expected profit decreases. This possibility is called adverse selection, and it also may cause the loan offer curve to bend backward.

The basic default risk model of Jaffee and Modigliani does not consider the possibilities that lenders' information about borrowers may be imperfect or that the terms of a loan may affect borrowers' choices regarding risk or performance, but there are numerous other models of credit markets with asymmetric information and adverse selection. The models of Jaffee and Russell (1976) and Stiglitz and Weiss (1981) are among the best known and most influential.

Jaffee and Russell (1976) focused on changes in the risk distribution of borrowers arising from asymmetric information on their potential default costs. For borrowers, default costs include loss of access to future credit, loss of reputation, forfeiture of collateral, and legal costs. Jaffee and Russell measured the cost of default as a fixed penalty Z that is potentially deducted from the borrower's income in the period the default takes place. There is a distribution of these default costs. Individuals with the highest personal default cost Z_{max} never default, but borrowers with lower levels of personal default cost do so whenever default is less costly for them than loan repayment, $Z < Loan(1 + r)$. Lenders do not directly observe these defaults costs, however. They cannot distinguish between borrowers who will never default and those who will.

Under this condition, the loan supply curve relates the loan interest rate to the opportunity rate for the lender and the proportion of borrowers who do not default. This credit supply curve has the features already noted: it is horizontal when the loan amount plus interest is less than the lowest default cost, but thereafter, the loan supply function rises, because larger loan amounts require higher interest rates to compensate for possible defaults. Eventually, the curve may become backward bending as the size of the repayment makes default a virtual certainty. Then higher interest rates necessarily entail lower loan amounts. A no-rationing equilibrium occurs at the intersection of borrower demand and the loan supply curve, as in any market (point S in figure 5.2).

Jaffee and Russell also show that a rationing contract could exist along the loan supply curve at loan amounts less than supply and demand equilibrium. This result is possible because at a smaller loan size, fewer borrowers are going to default than at a larger loan size. Jaffee and Russell suggest that at the market

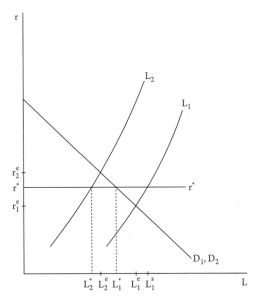

Figure 5.2 Credit Rationing.

borrowers with high personal default costs (low-risk borrowers) are willing to accept a smaller loan size, because lenders offer the smaller contract, involving fewer defaults, at a lower interest rate. This benefit to lenders of lower default cost is passed on to borrowers in a competitive market as a lower rate.[31]

But other, higher-risk, borrowers prefer to remain with the original contract, because their lower personal default costs prompt them to remain with the greater credit amount, which they know with some probability that they will not repay. But the process of lower-risk borrowers self-selecting out of the pool leads dynamically to disappearance of the original contract from the marketplace. After the better-risk customers take the smaller contract, the original contract will disappear from the market, because it is unprofitable for lenders without the low-risk borrowers still there. The process leads to a pattern of market entry and exit in which lenders enter the market possibly making short-run profits but are forced to exit in the long run, or to a rationing contract so severe that no one defaults. That neither of these outcomes characterizes actual credit markets caused Jaffee and Russell to speculate that institutional constraints leading to monopolistic behavior or use of equity and collateral requirements by lenders stabilized credit

31. Jaffee and Russell derive indifference curves for consumption with respect to loan size and interest rate. Because of the axes of the graph, they do not look like standard indifference curves, but the concept is the same. At all the points on each curve, the combination of interest rate and loan amount leaves the borrower's satisfaction the same. These indifference curves have zero slope where they intersect the demand curve and are rising below the demand curve and falling above the demand curve. They increase in utility from right to left, indicating, as expected, higher utility for the same loan at a lower interest rate or a larger loan at the same interest rate. For discussion, see Jaffee and Russell (1976).

markets. This conclusion then leads back to the previously discussed studies of nonprice loan terms, which then look for an endogenously determined explanation for limits on the amount of credit that a borrower can obtain.

In a related model, Stiglitz and Weiss (1981) derived credit rationing outcomes arising from asymmetric information about the riskiness of borrowers' income.[32] They posited that lenders observe borrowers' expected income but not the risk associated with the expected income.[33] In contrast, borrowers know both the expected income value and the risk. Thus, an individual borrowing loan amount L_i at interest rate r_i realizes net income $X - (1 + r_i)L_i$ in the subsequent period. Default occurs whenever $C + X < (1 + r_i)L_i$, where C is the amount of any assets pledged as collateral.

The borrower's income, then, is the greater of income minus repayment of principal and interest (in cases where there is no default) or income minus forfeited assets (when default occurs). This function is asymmetric, because the borrower keeps any excess above the amount of loan repayment but cannot lose more than the amount of assets pledged as collateral.

Stiglitz and Weiss's definition of risk allowed the possibility that lower-risk individuals would be less likely to benefit from the limitation in downside risk or to receive large surpluses than higher-risk individuals.[34] Thus, rises in the interest rate would cause fewer lower-risk individuals to apply for loans. This worsening of the risk distribution of applicants caused by rising interest rates is called adverse selection, as noted earlier.

The lender's return is the lesser of $(1 + r_i)L_i$ (principal plus interest) or $X + C$ (any income realized plus forfeited assets). This amount is also asymmetric, because the lender cannot receive any more than the actual repayment amount of interest and principal but may lose up to the repayment amount minus the value of any assets pledged as collateral. Greater risk would increase the likelihood of receiving less than the contracted amount of principal and interest and, other things being equal, reduce the lender's profit per loan. Consequently, raising the interest rate would increase the lender's profit per loan for a while, but eventually, a higher interest rate causes lower-risk borrowers to drop out of the market and worsens credit risk through adverse selection. This reduces profit overall. In other words, the lender's profit does not always rise with increases in the interest rate; it

32. Theoretical analysis of credit rationing has seemed to attract future winners of the Nobel Prize in Economic Science. Among the authors of theoretical works discussed here, Franco Modigliani, Merton Miller, and Joseph Stiglitz all later won Nobel Prizes for various accomplishments.

33. Stiglitz and Weiss expressed the model in terms of an investment project yielding an uncertain return from which the proceeds of the loan would be repaid, but income could be any flow of funds from human or other capital that can be used to repay a loan. Individuals' income may be risky because they cannot work as many hours as desired or because household investments do not generate anticipated flows of services or money.

34. Stiglitz and Weiss define risk in terms of mean-preserving spreads, which might occur if a riskier income had greater probabilities in the tails (that is, the lowest and highest parts) of the probability distribution than a less risky income (see Rothschild and Stiglitz 1970).

may fall at some point, because at a higher interest rate, lower-risk borrowers do not apply for credit.

Credit rationing may occur then, because lenders' supply of funds depends on lenders' profit, but borrowers' demand depends on the loan interest rate. Lenders will not increase interest rates to equilibrate supply and demand if doing so reduces their profits. As described above, this outcome may occur when higher interest rates cause lower-risk borrowers to accept smaller loans or leave the market. Lenders choose the supply of funds and interest rate that maximize their profit and ration credit if demand exceeds the supply of funds at the chosen interest rate.

The interest rate may also affect lenders' expected profit by changing borrowers' behavior. This result, which is called moral hazard, occurs because borrowers' and lenders' incentives differ. A borrower may prefer the riskier of two income choices having the same expected value when the interest rate is high. The borrower's expected return from the riskier choice may be greater because the borrower's downside risk is limited. The lender, in contrast, prefers the less risky income choice, because the less risky choice has lower default losses (and hence higher profit) than the riskier choice. The lender does not benefit from the nondefault, higher-income outcomes of the riskier choice.

Jaffee and Russell's and especially Stiglitz and Weiss's models have frequently been cited in the literature to support hypotheses of credit rationing caused by adverse selection or moral hazard. Such papers as those by Calem and Mester (1995) and Ausubel (1999) discussed in chapter 4 are of this kind. Ausubel's experimental data on credit cards provide convincing evidence of adverse selection in a credit market. In addition, models of adverse selection have influenced studies addressing the utility of specific loan contract provisions. For example, Brueckner (2000) and Steinbuks (2008) relied on credit rationing through adverse selection arguments to explain prepayment penalties in mortgage contracts. Barth et al. (1983) and Barth, Cordes, and Yezer (1986), both discussed later in chapter 11, analyzed effects of restrictions on creditor remedies (legal arrangements that facilitate collection of loans that are in default) in markets with asymmetric information.

Expansion of credit bureau credit histories and the development of credit bureau risk scores have undoubtedly reduced but probably not eliminated adverse selection problems arising from asymmetric information. Ausubel's (1999) evidence clearly suggests that adverse selection continued to exist in the credit card market at the end of the twentieth century.

Whether because of imperfect information, legal or moral considerations that limit risk-based pricing, or borrowers' inability to provide equity or collateral to satisfy lenders' noninterest requirements, it seems reasonable to believe that some consumers experience binding limitations on the amount of credit they can obtain; in other words, they experienced credit rationing. The next section of this chapter reviews some evidence on the extent of credit constraints facing households in the United States. This discussion is expanded further in chapter 11.

Further Evidence on the Extent of Credit Rationing

Evidence from the Federal Reserve Board's 2010 Survey of Consumer Finances, indicates that at that time, about 21 percent of US households were turned down or received less credit than initially requested in the last five years, and 18 percent of households did not apply for credit on at least one occasion because they perceived that they might be turned down. These percentages are not much different from percentages in recent previous years and suggest that credit constraints remain a problem for a considerable share of households.

Several studies have investigated the significance of responses to survey questions of this kind. They have considered whether responses to survey questions are consistent with the predictions of economic theory on the characteristics of households that are likely to be rationed and, if so, how much credit constraints reduce households' debt holdings.

Using data from the earlier 1983 Survey of Consumer Finances, Cox and Jappelli (1993) estimated a statistical probit model to predict whether households were unconstrained, where unconstrained households were defined as households that answered negatively to both actual and perceived turndown questions. They found that the probability of being unconstrained was directly related to age, permanent earnings, and net worth and negatively related to family size. These results are entirely consistent with predictions of economic theory that borrowers in a later life cycle stage with greater income and wealth are less likely to be rationed, or conversely, borrowers in an early life cycle stage with limited income and wealth are more likely to be rationed.

Cox and Jappelli then estimated a model to predict the desired level of mortgage and consumer debt. To account for unobserved influences from lender decisions to limit credit and household decisions not to hold debt, they included in the model selection variables derived from the probit model predicting whether households were unconstrained and a similar probit model predicting zero debt holding.[35] The selection variable for whether households were unconstrained was statistically significant and negative in the debt prediction model. The negative coefficient in the prediction equation suggests that there are some unobserved variables that increase the probability that a household is not constrained but decrease the level of debt (opportunities for household investment, attitude toward debt, or risk aversion, for example).

Other estimation results for this equation suggest that the desired level of debt increases with wealth. The level of debt was positively related to permanent income and net worth and negatively related to current income. The level of debt

---

35. Ordinary least squares estimation of models with censored dependent variables, which have a cluster of observations at zero, and excess demand caused by credit constraints produce biased and inefficient estimates of parameters. Cox and Jappelli used a model suggested by Heckman (1979), which treats censored observations as missing values. Heckman's model includes a selection variable (the inverse Mills ratio) indicating the likelihood that an observation is censored. The selection variable is derived from a probit model predicting whether an observation is included in the sample. For further discussion of the statistical issues, see Maddala (1983).

also exhibited a pronounced life cycle effect increasing until age thirty-four and then declining.

Using their estimated model for the level of debt to predict desired debt levels of constrained households, Cox and Jappelli calculated that aggregate household debt would increase by 9 percent if credit constraints were removed. The effect of removing credit constraints would be large for some individual households, however. Debt would rise 44 percent for households headed by persons younger than twenty-five and 24 percent for households headed by persons between twenty-five and thirty-four if credit constraints were removed.

Crook (2001) reexamined the question of credit constraints using data from the 1995 Survey of Consumer Finances. He noted that since the 1983 survey used by Cox and Jappelli, changes in credit markets may have reduced the influence of credit constraints.[36] The changes over time included the widespread adoption of statistical credit evaluation (credit scoring) and relaxation of regulatory restraints (especially interest rate ceilings). The development of credit bureau scores in the mid-1980s had facilitated the widespread adoption of statistical credit evaluation and stimulated credit bureaus to collect comprehensive information on credit histories. This development probably reduced information asymmetry between borrowers and lenders and promoted competition among lenders.[37] The development of credit bureau scores also likely facilitated lenders' ability to price credit according to risk, thereby reducing Jaffee and Modigliani's concern about legal and moral restraints on price differentiation.

Crook's model was similar to that of Cox and Jappelli, but some variables differed. For example, Crook, but not Cox and Jappelli, included type of occupation, years on job, home ownership, and number of credit cards. Crook did not include permanent income, but Jappelli and Cox did. Nevertheless, Crook's results for the more recent survey are broadly consistent with Cox and Jappelli. For his probit equation estimating whether the household was unconstrained, Crook found that household heads ages fifty-five to sixty-four and sixty-five or older to be more likely than younger household heads to be unconstrained. Larger households were less likely to be unconstrained. Higher income and higher net worth were more likely to be unconstrained.

For the model estimating desired debt, the selection variable reflecting the likelihood of being unconstrained was statistically significant and negative. Again, the negative coefficient suggests that there are unobserved variables that increase the probability that a household is not constrained but decrease the level of debt. Crook also found significantly lower debt levels for ages fifty-five to sixty-four and sixty-five or older and greater debt levels for higher-income households and for larger households. Greater net worth was associated with lower debt; but home

36. In an earlier paper, Crook (1996) discussed these changes and investigated statistically the types of households that were credit constrained using the 1989 Survey of Consumer Finances.

37. However, competition does not necessarily preclude credit rationing in markets with asymmetric information. See Jaffee and Russell (1976).

ownership, a large component of most households' wealth, was positively related to debt levels.

Crook did not estimate the effects of credit constraints on aggregate household debt. Nevertheless, Crook's results provide evidence that credit constraints continued to influence household debt holdings in 1995.[38]

RISK EVALUATION AND CREDIT SCORING

The importance of operating costs associated with loan origination, together with the high costs of losses on consumer lending, has kept the goal of reducing expenses constantly in the sight of the managers of consumer lending intermediaries. It is, of course, possible to reduce both operating costs and losses to zero or close to zero by not making any loans or making very few. Not surprisingly, managers have not found this approach very useful, because it naturally also relegates profits to zero or very close to zero. More useful over the years have been attempts to lessen operating costs and losses while keeping lending volume the same or increasing it. Managers have instituted a variety of approaches with this in mind, including the whole area of technological change associated with development of revolving credit to replace much of closed-end installment credit. Today, many consumers can use the credit cards they obtain from a single application and underwriting process rather than a costly succession of applications and processing each time they make a new purchase using credit.

For both closed-end and open-end credit, creditors have attempted to reduce costs by using technology. In particular, the high volumes and repetitive nature of modern consumer credit generation permit application of office automation and improved employee quality and training to substitute for more employees. Improvements have been especially important for evaluating risk of customers using sophisticated automated statistical approaches, a development generally referred to as credit scoring. This, in turn, has led to an expansion of automation in information systems known as credit reporting agencies, more popularly as credit bureaus. Credit scoring is discussed in more detail below, and credit reporting agencies are examined in chapter 6.

Judgmental versus Statistical Risk Evaluation

Through most of the twentieth century in American consumer finance, lenders trying to assess a borrower's creditworthiness were guided by an industry maxim known as the five Cs of lending: character, capacity, capital, collateral,

---

38. Duca and Rosenthal (1993) and Gropp, Scholz, and White (1997) have also considered the effects of credit constraints on debt levels and found results similar to those reported here. Fissel and Jappelli (1990) found evidence that credit constraints vary over the business cycle. Carroll (2001) discussed the role of credit constraints on aggregate consumption, and Crook (2003) reviewed evidence from the United States and Italy.

and conditions. An evaluation of character was really an assessment of the borrower's willingness to repay, typically gauged by the borrower's past credit history, as discussed previously. Capacity referred to the size, source, and stability of the borrower's income stream relative to existing (and proposed) debt obligations. Capital referred to the borrower's assets, liquid or otherwise, which could be tapped if income proved insufficient to meet the required payments. The value of collateral and the possibility that it might be repossessed by the lender came into play on secured loans, such as automobile loans or home mortgages, both as an incentive to the borrower to continue making payments and as an assurance to the lender that some portion of the loan principal could always be recovered through sale of the repossessed asset. Lastly, an assessment of economic conditions was prudent, because the possibility of unemployment or reduced income might affect the borrower's capacity to repay.

Until the mid-1960s, consumer lending decisions were made individually by thousands of loan officers who exercised their individual judgment on each application. Loan officers gathered information from and about the applicant in each of the five critical areas and applied lessons from their own and the firm's lending experience to decide whether an application should be approved. Loan officers' individual analysis applied to each account the lending policies of their various employers.

A number of factors combined to push the consumer credit industry away from this "judgmental" model of underwriting, however. For one, the post–World War II boom in consumer lending generated increasing pressure on lending institutions, especially retail stores and consumer finance companies, which were the largest consumer lenders, to process a rising tide of loan applications efficiently at a time when a human-based judgmental approach to consumer loan underwriting was slow and labor-intensive. Not surprisingly, one early academic study of credit scoring effectiveness noted that lenders were intrigued by the prospect of numerical tools for screening applications: "The resulting increase in demand has taxed credit departments of many larger companies beyond their capacities to train and maintain an adequate staff of experienced credit evaluators, and thus increasing amounts of retail credit are being granted by younger and less experienced individuals" (Myers and Forgy 1963, 799).

In addition, the inconsistency across credit evaluators inherent in a judgmental approach rendered establishing a company-wide underwriting policy nearly impossible. In the view of one observer:

> Management had no way of expressing a corporate policy such as: "Accept only those applications whose risk is 13 to 1 or better." As a result, each individual credit evaluator decided for himself or herself what level of risk the applicant represented and what level of risk the enterprise as a whole should tolerate. In a nationwide loan company with, perhaps, one thousand offices, there might be as many as two to three thousand people defining overall corporate policy. (Lewis 1992, 2–3)

The advent of statistical credit scoring dramatically changed consumer loan underwriting. The five Cs of lending were no less important for conceptualizing the factors that determined loan risk, but credit scoring gave lenders a powerful tool for rapidly and consistently evaluating risk and for summarizing it via a numerical score. Between 1970 and 2000, judgmental credit decision systems in consumer and mortgage lending were gradually replaced with empirically derived, demonstrably and statistically sound scoring systems. This dramatic change in risk evaluation technology largely automated the underwriting process and greatly reduced the subjective nature of the lending decision.

The underlying rationale for statistical credit scoring is essentially the same as for judgmental lending. Patterns observed in the past are expected to recur in the future. Borrower and loan attributes observed to have been associated with loan defaults in the past become the basis for expecting default on similar loans in the future. Using multivariate statistical methods and data on tens of thousands of loans made in the past, statisticians built credit scoring models to identify predictive relationships between loan performance and a wide variety of variables. More precisely, credit scoring models use a numerical formula from some form of statistical regression analysis to assign points (regression coefficient weights) to specific pieces of information in order to predict an outcome.

The first credit scoring models were built to guide the loan application process, and application scoring remains an important use of scoring technology. The primary concern in granting a new loan (although not the only concern) is whether the borrower will repay the loan as agreed. Consequently, most new account application models focus on predicting the likelihood that a loan will default within a given time period, usually twelve to twenty-four months. In the models, the statisticians can define default in a variety of ways, but it often refers to a loan that achieves a level of serious delinquency, for example, ninety days or more past due, or generates a repossession or charge-off loss for the lender. From the outset of scoring and through decades of evolution in commercially available models, discriminant analysis and multivariate regression techniques have been the most common statistical tools used to model loan defaults. These models calculate credit scores for each application in such a way as to rank applications according to their relative risk of a loan default. Typically, scoring systems are scaled so that a lower score signals higher risk. That is, applications that receive lower scores are more likely to default within a specified time period than are applications with higher scores.

Although a credit scoring system will assign a given loan application a specific score within a continuous distribution of scores, it is important to remember that for most application scoring systems, there are only two distinct outcomes: pay as agreed or default. The continuous distribution of credit scores reflects the model's probabilistic assessment of the likelihood of default. Obviously, though, some applicants with low credit scores will actually pay as agreed, and some applicants with high credit scores will default. This fact underscores the probabilistic nature of risk assessment: at the time of the loan application, the lender never knows with certainty who will repay and who will not. What the lender wants is a scoring system that achieves significant separation in the score distributions of good accounts and bad (defaulted) accounts. More separation is better. This gives the lender more confidence that the event of a high-scoring applicant defaulting on a loan will be an anomaly. So the key to building a good (predictive) application scoring model is to find readily observable borrower and loan characteristics that consistently distinguish consumers who will pay as agreed from those who will not.[39]

As credit scoring evolved from 1970 to 2000, statisticians employed increasingly sophisticated statistical modeling (for example, logistic regression) to enable scoring models to generate specific predictions regarding probability of default (see Mays 2004, 8). These models allowed estimation of potential portfolio losses and appropriate pricing of loans based on the level of measured risk. Calculations of probability enabled lenders to set "cutoff" scores, above which an application would be accepted and below which it would be rejected, which would translate into expected loss rates on the loan portfolio. A credit card lender using a scoring model and cutoff score set to generate an expected 3 percent charge-off rate on receivables, for example, still will not know which customers are going to default, but it will be possible to plan on a 3 percent loss rate. Setting a lower cutoff score for approval will boost the number of loans accepted but will also raise the loss rate on the resulting portfolio. Scoring gives creditors a valuable planning tool and a consistent decision tool that can be implemented across hundreds or thousands of loan officers with predictable results.

An important point to keep in mind regarding application credit scoring systems is that they are designed to predict default statistically and are not constructed based on specific hypotheses regarding causal influences of default. Credit scoring development sifts through hundreds of variables to identify a small subset of items that minimize prediction errors. As one statistician put it, "Credit scoring has always been based on a pragmatic approach to the credit granting problem. If it works, use it! The object is to predict who will default, not to give explanations for why they default or answer hypotheses on the relationship between default and other economic or social variables" (Thomas 2000, 152). Over the years, this characteristic of credit scoring has given fuel to critics who distrust automated risk evaluation and argue that scoring models may be discriminatory to some individuals, such as minorities, because of the weights placed on some borrower characteristics that may be statistically associated with default but have not been causally linked to default.[40]

Evolution of Credit Scoring

Published studies of numerical credit scoring systems began to appear in the academic literature as far back as the 1940s. With the sponsorship of the National

---

39. For a more detailed overview of development of a typical scoring model, see Mays (2004, 63–130).

40. See Capon (1982). Other observers contend that statistical systems are fairer, because computers and statistics are unaware of demographic identifications and, therefore, free of preferences or potential irrational prejudices.

Bureau of Economic Research, David Durand (1941) conducted an exploratory study using discriminant analysis to analyze "good" versus "bad" account performance for hundreds of personal loan account files from a variety of consumer lenders. Over the next two decades, some lenders, especially retail stores and personal finance companies, experimented with the development of scoring systems and allowed results to be reported. Wolbers (1949), Myers and Cordner (1957), and Myers and Forgy (1963) reported results of scoring studies conducted on accounts of a national retail department store chain, a Los Angeles personal loan chain, and a West Coast mobile home finance company, respectively. These published studies all found that numerical scoring models generated some degree of improvement in the risk evaluation process relative to judgmental risk evaluation.

In 1956, engineer William Fair and mathematician Earl Isaac, both affiliated with the Stanford Research Institute, saw enough promise in the power of statistical analysis of account level data to found a new company, Fair Isaac. It eventually became the world's leading provider of credit scoring systems and was the source of what had become by the late 1990s the most recognized and widely used personal credit score, the FICO score. Looking back to conditions at the time of the company's founding, it is clear that Fair and Isaac were visionaries. It was not obvious in the late 1950s that numerical scoring systems would unseat judgmental lending in consumer finance. Myers and Forgy (1963) noted that in the early 1960s, numerical scoring was not widely used by creditors, despite its demonstrated success in a few experimental studies. They attributed the slow uptake to natural reluctance on the part of lenders to abandon judgmental evaluation methods that had worked for decades and the lack of empirical proof that statistical scoring systems could predict accurately enough to generate substantial savings in the overall credit operation. At the time, there were sizable difficulties in creating a workable business model for implementing complicated scoring technology into large, nationwide credit operations. Indeed, the Fair Isaac Company reported that in 1958, its founders sent letters to the fifty largest American credit grantors at the time, asking for the opportunity to explain a new concept: credit scoring. Only one company accepted, and Fair Isaac developed and delivered its first scoring model to American Investment and Finance Company in 1958.

A close look at the early published studies of scoring reveals the major source of gains for lenders willing to adopt credit scoring, gains that eventually persuaded virtually the entire consumer credit industry to adopt scoring. Statistical scoring of loan applications, even in its infancy, was showing that it could do a better job of separating good risks from bad risks than the prevailing judgmental processes. Lenders did not want just a method of reducing bad loans; they could do that by reducing overall lending. What they wanted was a way of separating good and bad so that they could also maximize good loans. For a given pool of loan applicants, the profit-maximizing creditor wants a risk evaluation tool that will generate the highest acceptance rate possible given a target default rate. Or, phrased another way, for a given applicant pool and loan acceptance rate, the creditor wants a risk evaluation tool that generates the lowest possible default rate.

By the early 1960s, the published studies of scoring were reporting significant reductions in loan losses with little or no sacrifice of loan volume. Wolbers (1949) had found that a scoring model reduced credit losses by 7 percent with only a negligible loss of volume of good business. Myers and Cordner (1957) found that 24 percent of losses at one retail lender could be eliminated via a scoring model at the cost of only 3 percent of loan volume. Myers and Forgy (1963) developed a model that eliminated 13 percent of bad accounts at a cost of only 1 percent of good accounts. Later studies confirmed the potential for gains of this magnitude and larger.[41] Experimental studies of credit scoring were demonstrating its power to reduce processing costs *and* expand a lender's portfolio without raising loss rates.

During the 1970s and 1980s, many lenders, including most of the large national lenders, invested in the development of proprietary custom application scoring models using information from their own companies' experience (see Mays 2004). A custom application scoring model is built for a specific loan product, using a single lender's account data and experience with that product. A general-purpose credit card issuer might build its own model, for instance. Custom models typically incorporate both credit bureau data and data from the lender's file of credit applications. There are very few published studies of these models, perhaps not surprisingly, since an accurate scoring model can confer a distinct competitive advantage on a lender and is expensive to develop. As scoring advanced during this period, new ideas were plentiful, lots of variables were explored, and public discussion of successful model components could quickly dissipate the value of the intellectual capital generated by a company developing a scoring model.

During these formative years, the Federal Reserve Board also recognized the increasing use of application scoring systems when it developed its Regulation B, which implemented the Equal Credit Opportunity Act of 1974 (ECOA) and the ECOA amendments of 1976. Both pieces of legislation were intended to prohibit unacceptable forms of social discrimination in lending by prohibiting the use of information on the borrower's sex, marital status, race, nationality, age, and certain other attributes from consideration in the underwriting process. Regulation B established criteria that scoring systems must satisfy to be considered methodologically and statistically sound.[42]

At the same time, academic exploration of scoring techniques continued. A few examples illustrate the range of scoring problems considered and the flavor of the analyses. Altman (1968) used discriminant analysis to develop a scoring system for predicting commercial bankruptcy, groundbreaking work that took

---

41. See Rosenberg and Gleit (1994) for an interesting review of early published scoring studies and a catalog of the variety of statistical techniques that had been applied to the consumer loan scoring problem as of the early 1990s.

42. Interestingly, Regulation B made the case for using credit scoring to standardize risk evaluation even more compelling than did the economic efficiencies alone. The ECOA created liability for a lender if it could be shown that loan acceptance policies were based on prohibited attributes. Credit scoring gave lenders an easily monitored tool for demonstrating that their loan acceptance decisions were consistently based on economic factors associated with the borrower and the loan that could be shown to have an impact on loan risk.

credit scoring in an entirely new direction. Apilado, Warner, and Dauten (1974) found that streamlining application models by reducing the number of variables need not reduce a model's predictive power, as most of the predictive power was in a small subset of variables. Long and McConnell (1977) confirmed this finding in developing an application scoring model for second mortgages. They found that of the 117 variables considered, the maximum predictive power was obtained using only 9 variables: length of time at current address, largest previous amount of credit, employment classification, if the applicant has a telephone, monthly income minus committed payments, and four credit payment experience variables.

Eisenbeis (1978) provided an excellent early discussion of methodological and statistical shortcomings of the first three decades of scoring models described in published articles. Many of the statistical issues he raised, such as those associated with functional equation form (for example, questions of linear versus quadratic versus exponential) and those involving sampling concerns (for example, use of development samples of approved loans with no consideration of loans rejected or borrowers who do not apply) have been addressed over the years since then (see Hand and Henley 1997 and Thomas 2000).

One methodological problem that Eisenbeis noted is worth further discussion here, however, because it persists in most of today's scoring models. He pointed out that, with few exceptions, the models in the published scoring literature took the whole life of the loan into account at once, not how experience within the period might differ. In his view:

> [Scores] are essentially directed toward only one dimension of the credit granting function, albeit a critical one, and that is the assessment of the likelihood that loans will default, go "bad," or experience difficulty over their life. In this sense they are all single period models with that period being the life of the loan. No attempt is made to determine at what specific intervals over the life of a loan it is more or less likely to default or become slow paying. (Eisenbeis 1978, 12–13)

But timing of delinquency or default is important to profitability. If default is sufficiently delayed on an installment loan, the lender may still receive a positive net revenue stream. Perhaps more important, a profit-maximizing lender considering a new loan application should also take into account the prospect of continuous dealings with a borrower, either contemporaneously, through other types of loans and products, or in successive loans. The potential for multiple revenue streams affects the net present value of the new application. Nevertheless, most application scoring models, then and now, are built on the assumption of a single period model and the likelihood of a single event within that period. We will return to this point later in this chapter in discussing new frontiers for scoring in the twenty-first century.

By the mid-1980s, a clear divergence in processing procedures had emerged across loan products. Larger loan transactions (mortgage and automobile loans) still warranted loan officer scrutiny of paper application forms, credit reports, and supporting documents. In contrast, the application process for smaller, high-volume credit products, such as credit card accounts of the time, had become increasingly automated. Increased automation for credit cards was in large part a result of improved quality of credit report data and the demonstrated success of statistical scoring models in rapidly and accurately determining applicant risk.

The drive to lower processing costs favored more automation for large-volume products. This further pushed the credit card industry toward risk assessment based mostly on credit bureau data rather than on applications. Information from a loan or credit card application was time-consuming to code into machine-readable form that could be used by the scoring models. Moreover, application data were costly to verify, which meant that they were subject to exaggeration and outright fraud by applicants. And verification delays an approval decision, a clear negative for a retail store considering a new account application at the point of sale. For all these reasons, the retail store industry migrated early to the use of statistical scoring of credit origination decisions, first for its credit cards, and based the analyses more on credit bureau data than on applications. Eventually, automobile loans and virtually every other type of consumer loan followed by the early 1990s. Last to accept scoring was the mortgage industry. By the mid-1990s, however, credit scoring was endorsed as a valid tool for evaluating mortgage applications by the Federal Reserve (see Avery et al. 1996) and by the government-sponsored enterprises Freddie Mac and Fannie Mae. By the end of the decade, automated underwriting of mortgage risks using credit scoring had become the industry standard (see Straka 2000).

Components of Scoring Models

What types of information enter into the scoring models? This, of course, depends on the outcome to be predicted and the information available. As indicated, credit scoring began as a tool for evaluating new loan applications, and in the early days of credit scoring, model builders sought data that would approximate the various factors represented in the five Cs of lending. Models were initially designed to incorporate information that was commonly collected on loan application forms along with information from credit reports. Eventually, loan application forms were redesigned to reflect the information found to be most useful to scoring models.

Credit card application data in the 1980s included attributes such as the applicant's age, time at current and previous residence, time at current and previous job, housing status, occupation group, income, number of dependents, presence of telephone at residence, banking relationships, outstanding debts, and open credit accounts. In addition, the models would also typically utilize credit bureau variables, including the number, type, and recentness of any delinquencies; balances on open accounts and lines of credit; and the number and type of creditor inquiries to the credit bureau concerning this consumer, an indicator of credit shopping and new account activity (see Chandler and Parker 1989, 47–48).

Eventually, Chandler and Parker (1989) demonstrated that US credit bureau data outperformed application data in predicting risk on bank and retail credit card applications, in addition to its easier availability. Using models built to score bank card applicants and data from a period during which credit card issuers still collected detailed application information, the authors found that application data without the credit bureau data yielded the lowest predictive power and fared poorly when compared with predictions based on any level of credit bureau data. The predictive power increased substantially when the models incorporated higher levels of credit bureau detail, with the most detailed model exhibiting predictive power 52 percent greater than the simplest credit bureau treatment. In fact, a model incorporating the detailed credit bureau data plus application data actually performed worse than a model based on the detailed credit bureau data alone. Perhaps this is not surprising, given that most application data on bank card products is not verified because of the cost and consequent delay in the accept/reject decision. The authors noted that for most applicants (those with an established credit history), a detailed examination of credit bureau data alone provided the most accurate assessment of new account risk.[43]

Generic Scoring Models and the FICO Score

In response to the advantages of using credit bureau data alone in scoring models, Fair Isaac and other scoring system developers, including the major credit bureaus themselves, created and introduced "generic" credit bureau scoring models. Generic models employ only credit bureau information as inputs. In addition to the other cost advantages of using solely credit bureau information, generic models have the further advantage that they can be used by multiple creditors, creating further savings.

---

43. Lay observers of the credit card industry, sometimes including members of Congress, often misinterpret the credit card industry's lack of explicit consideration of income in the application process. Income has much intuitive appeal as an important predictor of repayment risk, but credit bureau data allow a creditor to infer repayment capacity from the degree to which past and existing lines of credit have been utilized and whether payments were made on time or late. In short, risk assessment based on credit bureau data rewards those consumers who find a way to make their payments, not those with high application income. This is why credit bureau data can be more predictive than credit card application data that are unverified. The empirical evidence of the predictive superiority of credit bureau data over application data might change if application data were verified, but verification is costly. In the mortgage arena, where the stakes are larger (loan size, potential interest income, and loss in the event of foreclosure), it pays to measure risk attributes more precisely. The gains are larger and help to offset the higher costs of verification. But for smaller loans such as credit card loans, the number of accounts is much larger (driving up total risk evaluation costs), and the size of the loan is typically much smaller (reducing the potential loss). Also, objective credit bureau data are readily available. Once the predictive power of credit bureau data was demonstrated (and it also improved over time as bureau data quality improved), it was not surprising that credit scoring gained widespread adoption, first in the credit card industry and later in auto lending and mortgage lending.

Generic scoring models opened up credit scoring to the entire consumer credit industry, including smaller creditors.[44] The first generic scoring model was brought to market by Fair Isaac in 1986. Called PreScore, the product evaluated new applicant risk on credit card solicitations mailed to consumers. In 1987, Management Decision Systems (MDS) rolled out the first generic scoring models that used credit bureau data to predict bankruptcy, as opposed to simple loan default. In 1989, in partnership with Equifax, one of the three major US credit reporting agencies, Fair Isaac introduced the first general-purpose credit scoring model employing its FICO score methodology, a product that fifteen years later would become so ubiquitous that *FICO score* was a household term. By 1991, Fair Isaac had also developed similar models for the other two major US credit bureaus, Experian and Trans Union, using their credit report databases. This meant that all three credit bureaus were selling their equivalent of the FICO score product under each bureau's marketing brand name. Growth in the following decade was very rapid.

The precise composition of commercially available generic scoring models is proprietary.[45] According to the Fair Isaac website (www.myfico.com), however, the key determinants of a consumer's FICO score can be divided into the five general categories described below. At any one time, a consumer's score may vary across the three credit bureaus, because the FICO score obtained from each bureau is built on the information in that bureau's database, which may vary somewhat across the three bureaus. The website hints at the direction of influence of specific attributes and provides, in percentage terms, the approximate influence on the overall FICO score:

1. Payment history: accounts paid as agreed, late payments, delinquencies, bankruptcies (35 percent). Fair Isaac advises individuals who seek to improve their FICO score always to pay their accounts before the due date. Simply put, the fewer late payments, the better the score. In the event of a late payment, the more serious the degree of delinquency, the greater the negative impact on the score. In addition, more recent late payment experience tends to be more indicative of future default than older experience.

2. Outstanding debt (30 percent). Fair Isaac advises consumers who seek to improve their credit scores to keep balances low, especially credit card

---

44. The following discussion draws on an article by Gary Chandler (2004), one of the pioneers of generic credit bureau model development and another visionary in the credit scoring field.

45. For a variety of reasons, commercial generic scoring models such as the FICO score are typically constrained to the twelve to twenty most predictive variables from the credit report. Also, generic bureau scorecards marketed to date have generally been customer-based rather than loan-based models. That is, the observation unit for the generic bureau scorecard is a customer, not a loan, and the dependent variable describes whether a customer with a given credit profile at the start of the observation period becomes seriously delinquent (more than ninety days) by the end of the period (eighteen to twenty-four months) on at least one account.

balances. People who have used a large portion of the credit available to them tend to be higher risks than those who use credit conservatively.

3. Length of credit history (15 percent). Fair Isaac advises that the longer someone has had credit established, the better is his or her credit score. For example, a borrower who has had credit for less than two years represents a relatively higher risk than someone who has had credit for five years or more.

4. New applications for credit or inquiries (10 percent). Fair Isaac advises individuals to apply for new credit sparingly if they seek a better credit score. In particular, they suggest that borrowers not open lots of new accounts in a short period of time, as multiple new account acquisition can be a sign of financial distress and higher risk.

5. Types of credit in use (10 percent). The model considers how many types of credit accounts (credit cards, mortgages, auto loans, other installment loans) a consumer has and how much credit use falls into one category versus others. The website notes that a good score doesn't require accounts in all categories and that opening accounts just to broaden the mix probably won't boost the score.

Generic credit bureau scores such as FICO scores are now used to evaluate individual credit risk in virtually every sector of the consumer and mortgage credit industry.[46] The nearly instantaneous availability of rich and comprehensive credit bureau information on a borrower, coupled with the proven predictive power of scoring models, has made instant credit at the point of sale commonplace. Credit bureaus sell literally billions of credit reports annually to creditors and other providers of credit-related services. The credit card industry alone accounted for 6 billion credit report and/or credit score sales in 2005 to support its prescreened credit card solicitations sent to consumers through direct mail (see Synovate 2006). The industry-wide shift from manual to automated underwriting between 1970 and 2000 provided enormous cost savings to lenders and greatly increased the optimal scale of lending operations in segments such as the bank credit card industry. Most important, it transformed the competitive landscape by bringing a broader range of product offerings, wider credit availability, and lower prices to consumers.

Credit Scoring to Support Other Credit Decisions

Risk scoring, and especially generic bureau scores, provided the catalyst for widespread adoption of risk-based pricing for credit accounts. Until the late 1980s, the consumer loan decision typically focused on application approval or denial: the

---

46. Chandler (2004) cataloged 70 different generic credit scoring systems containing more than 100 different scoring models or scorecards that were available in the market at that time to assist in a wide range of credit decisions.

price of the loan was fixed as part of the loan package for which the borrower applied. But the greater precision in estimating borrower risk made possible through credit scoring has facilitated a decoupling of the loan acceptance and loan pricing decisions. Since the late 1980s, consumer lenders have relied on statistical credit scoring models to set loan interest rates appropriate for a borrower's risk. This practice, known as risk-based pricing, attempts to tailor the price of a loan to a borrower's estimated likelihood of repayment. Borrowers who are less likely to become delinquent on a loan pay lower interest rates.

It is no coincidence that the expansion of credit to consumers in the United States over the last two decades occurred simultaneously with the widespread adoption of risk-based pricing, first by bank credit card issuers (beginning around 1989) and automobile lenders (by 1990) and eventually by mortgage lenders (since the mid-1990s). The practice has expanded credit availability to higher-risk borrowers, lowered prices for low-risk borrowers, and led to a broader array of loan products available to all risk and income groups (see Edelberg 2006). In addition, banking regulatory agencies have encouraged lenders to adopt risk-based pricing to protect the safety and soundness of financial institutions as they broaden credit availability to include higher-risk borrowers.[47]

Further, the use of credit scoring today is not confined solely to new account acquisition and pricing. Although the new account application decision was the first target for credit scoring, by the 1970s, lenders had begun experimenting with other uses for statistical scoring and have continued ever since. These other uses for credit scoring have come to be known as "behavioral scoring," a term that includes modeling accounts for a variety of things, including overall account profitability (for discussion of the variety of uses for behavioral scoring, see Thomas, Edelman, and Crook 2002). Even such decisions as how much time, how much effort, and the form (and expense) of various kinds of collection efforts, ranging from reminders to repossessions and foreclosures, now depend on statistical modeling of behaviors and outcomes.

An existing account relationship provides the lender with additional data on account activity and payment behavior. Behavioral scoring can incorporate the extra data together with the original account information and past and current credit report data. Behavioral credit scoring is now used to determine when and by how much to increase the credit limit on credit card accounts, approve authorizations of new credit card purchases at the point of sale, monitor credit card account transactions for possible fraudulent activity (including identity theft), predict account attrition so that lenders can take steps to recruit and keep loyal customers, initiate collection strategies on delinquent accounts, set their tone and predict dollar recoveries, select potential new customers for receipt of

47. The Credit Card Accountability, Responsibility, and Disclosure (CARD) Act of 2009 restricted risk-based penalty repricing for credit cards, however. The act limited interest rate increases and required credit card companies to provide forty-five days' notice before increasing rates on accounts of users whose account use behavior suggests greater default risk. These restrictions have tended to increase underlying rates and reduce credit limits on accounts deemed to have high risk of default.

preapproved invitations to apply for credit, and identify existing customers who may respond favorably to the cross-selling of other products.[48]

Another very important area of ongoing statistical scoring development activity stems from a reorientation of scoring model objectives. As mentioned, application scoring models typically were originally constructed to predict a specific event: default. They were estimated as models of single period loans that may or may not default. But what the profit-maximizing lender is arguably really after when evaluating a new loan application is an estimate of the full expected stream of net revenues associated with the new account opening over its associated lifetime, that is, its long-run profitability. Profitability is a function of interest and fees paid on the account over time and costs associated with the account, including costs of servicing the account (such as collection costs and expected losses) and expected future dealings with the account holder (see Wells 1999, Groenfeldt 2000, Ratcliff 2000, and Thomas 2000). The requirements for data capture and warehousing for this kind of analysis are substantial, but many large financial institutions are now incorporating the broader view into their decision systems.

The most significant improvements in the power of credit scoring models in recent years have come from the collection and use of alternative payment history data for consumers with little or no past credit history of the kind captured in traditional credit reports. A study in 2006 showed that an estimated 35 million to 54 million American adults had limited or nonexistent credit files (Turner et al. 2006). Most of these consumers in what the industry calls the "thin-file/unscorable population" are new to or completely outside of the credit-granting system, either because they are young or are recent immigrants or they have simply operated on a cash basis or through nontraditional sources of credit. Their lack of traditional credit history makes them appear to lenders, especially to those that rely heavily on automated underwriting systems, as high-risk when they often are not.

Creditors and credit reporting agencies have recognized the market potential in this large population and are increasingly looking to collect and utilize information on the recurring payments made by these consumers that are not captured in standard credit score calculations.[49] Examples of such data include payments for rent, utilities, private mortgages, nonprime auto loans, insurance premiums, payday advances, and rental furniture. Utility and telecommunications sources

---

48. An additional but important application beyond the scope of this book is credit scoring for small business loans. Because many small business start-ups are financed with personal loans taken by their founders, consumer credit report data has proven to be very predictive of small business loan defaults. Small business credit scoring has been shown to generate many of the same benefits to small business credit markets as consumer risk scoring has conferred on consumer loan markets, including broader credit access (see Berger and Udell 2002 and Berger, Frame, and Miller 2005).

49. The use of alternative payment data to build creditworthiness and foster asset acquisition has become a priority for efforts to spur community development and reduce the number of unbanked consumers (Afshar 2005; Dole and Levy 2012)

of data show the most promise, as studies estimate that 90 percent or more of the thin-file/unscorable population have one or more such accounts.

In a 2012 study, Turner et al. found dramatic increases in credit scores of consumers in the thin-file population as a consequence of including utility and telephone payment data in their credit files. Twenty-five percent of thin-file consumers experienced an upward score migration (moving from a higher-risk tier to a lower-risk tier), while only 6 percent of the thin-file population experienced a downward score migration. Consumers receiving the largest benefit from including alternative payment data were low-income consumers (21 percent increase in acceptance rates for consumers earning less than $20,000 annually; 14 percent increase for those earning between $20,000 and $30,000 annually), minorities (14 increase in acceptance rate for African Americans), and renters (17 percent increase, versus just 7 percent for home owners).

Other sources of data, including public records, show promise as predictive indicators of good payment behavior on more traditional loans. Examples of such public record data include derogatory history about consumers' economic behavior (bankruptcy, liens, judgments), important positive life events (professional and occupational licensure, real property deeds, aircraft and watercraft registrations), and evidence of life stresses (address instability, utility disconnects, felony convictions, evictions, foreclosures, etc.).[50] Continued success in expanding the flow of alternative payment data to creditors, either through credit bureaus or through alternative data providers, should further expand credit availability and open up a large segment of the consumer market to competition from major national lenders.

In sum, the shift from manual and judgmental systems for evaluating credit decisions to automated underwriting using statistical scoring has transformed production of consumer and mortgage credit. The quantity of available credit has expanded as scoring facilitated better sorting of the pool of potential borrowers according to likelihood of default. Credit decisions now are made much faster and at far lower cost than under the traditional manual system. Scoring brings consistency to credit decisions company-wide, supports better estimates of portfolio losses, allows for rapid implementation of company-wide changes in lending policies, and provides assurance that lending decisions will be in compliance with regulatory rules regarding fair lending practices.

FUNDING AND SECURITIZATION

As outlined in chapter 1, most of the consumer credit generated by financial institutions is financed by issuing their own liabilities, notably by deposits at

---

50. For example, a 2012 report from Lexis Nexis described its development of a credit scoring product (RiskView) based entirely on public record data assembled for approximately 37 million no-file consumers and 35 million thin-file consumers. The report stated that sufficient behavioral data was available to create a RiskView score for 24 million of the no-file consumers and 17 million of the thin-file consumers. See Lexis-Nexis (2012).

depository institutions and by commercial paper, bonds, and other credit market debt instruments at finance companies and monoline credit card banks. Nevertheless, financial markets also play an important role in funding consumer loans through a process known as securitization. By the end of 2009, asset-backed securities (ABS) that arise in the securitization process had funded $572.5 billion of consumer credit outstanding, which was almost a quarter of total consumer credit outstanding at that time. (The order of magnitude is visible in table 1.3, although not specifically for 2009.)

In the first quarter of 2010, new accounting rules (Financial Accounting Standards, or FAS, 166/167) changed financial institutions' accounting for securitizations and special purpose entities.[51] Previously, financial institutions included on their balance sheets only the value of the interest that they retained in securitizations. FAS 166/167 required most financial institutions to carry the entire value of the securitized assets on the asset side of their balance sheets and include the securitized debt as a liability.

Securitization had become especially important for some types of consumer credit; for instance, 48.2 percent of outstanding credit card debt was securitized at the end of 2009. The change in accounting rules in 2010 diminished the attractiveness of securitization, but securitization remains a significant source of financing. At the end of 2012, for example, a much smaller proportion was securitized.[52] ABSs are also an important source of financing of automobile loans. The importance of the securitization process and resulting ABSs in recent decades suggest the usefulness of outlining in some detail how the securitization process works.

Asset-backed securities are bonds or notes collateralized by cash flows from a specified pool of assets. The asset pools typically are consumer loans or receivables, but they may also be various nonconsumer assets that generate cash flows, such as equipment leases or loans, trade accounts receivable, dealer floor plan arrangements, and even flows of royalties from a variety of other specialized sources, such as entertainers. The ABS market emerged in 1985 for financing automobile loans and equipment leases (see Johnson 2002). Credit card asset-backed securities were introduced in 1987 (see Furletti 2002). In the consumer area, ABSs are also used to finance home equity loans, mobile home loans, student loans, and closed-end residential mortgages.

Securitization has been attractive to consumer lenders because it transfers the funding and sometimes some of the risk of consumer lending from the intermediaries that make the loans to entities that participate in financial markets. For these reasons, securitization normally provides the consumer lenders with greater liquidity and a less costly source of funding than direct issuance of their

---

51. FAS 166 governs whether securitizations are treated as sales or financings. FAS 167 provides accounting rules for determining when assets may be securitized and moved off the balance sheet.

52. In bringing securitizations on book, banks also faced higher capital requirements than previously.

own liabilities into financial markets and holding the loans in their own asset portfolios (called portfolio lending).

Securitization is also attractive to intermediaries that purchase the ABSs, because it provides these investors with a wider choice of fixed-income investment options to fit their needs. ABSs typically have had higher credit ratings than the lender originating the loans.[53] These benefits are created by the structure of the ABS, although outcomes sometimes can go wrong, as they did for some securitizations undertaken before the financial crisis in 2008–2009.

Structure of Asset-Backed Securities

The issuance of ABSs is structurally more complicated than direct issuance of a lending institution's own credit market debt. The lender originating the underlying loans to be securitized (or another institution arranging the securitization for the lender) first sells the loans to a bankruptcy-remote trust called a special-purpose entity (SPE). The trust then issues bonds backed by the loans.

The trust structure protects the underlying loans backing the ABSs from the creditors of the lender in the event that the lender enters bankruptcy or insolvency. This feature can permit the ABS to receive a higher credit rating than the lender. The trust employs a servicer to process payments from consumers, provide various customer services such as information call centers, collect delinquent accounts, and, for secured loans such as home loans or automobile loans, supervise property foreclosures, repossessions, and dispositions. Typically, the originator of the loans is the servicer, at least for consumer credit. The servicer receives a fee from the trust for providing these services.

Before the trust issues the bonds, a credit rating agency rates them. A rating reflects the rating agency's assessment of the risk of default or the expected loss from default, which are expressed in the same series of letter grades that they use for corporate bond ratings.[54] In determining a rating, the credit rating agency first considers the lenders' underwriting standards for the loans and subjects the loan pool to a variety of what-if scenarios, or "stress tests," which simulate the performance of the loans under a variety of different economic conditions.

---

53. The economic literature identifies several motivations to explain the use of securitization: exploiting private information to mitigate regulatory capital requirements or to specialize in areas of comparative advantage (origination and monitoring, for example), avoiding underinvestment or asset substitution arising from conflicts of interest between bondholders (or other creditors) and shareholders, and reducing agency costs of asymmetric information in asset funding. For a brief discussion of this reasoning, with references, see Jobst (2005).

54. The three major credit rating agencies differ somewhat in their assessments. Standard and Poor's evaluates the probability of default, whereas Moody's evaluates expected loss. Fitch appears to be somewhere in between. See Ashcroft and Schuermann (2008). In early 2013, the federal government sued Standard and Poor's for alleged inappropriate methodologies associated with some of its ratings at the time of the 2008–2009 financial crisis, but it did not sue the other rating agencies.

The ABS process has its own features and terminology. For instance, "excess spread" is the gross portfolio yield of the underlying loans minus the amounts that go to the investors (investor coupon), servicing expense, and expected charge-offs. The excess spread is analogous to a profit margin for the lender selling the underlying loans to the trust. It is the first line of protection for investors, because it absorbs unexpected fluctuations in payments and charge-offs. Should the excess spread drop below a specified level, the existing excess spread may be trapped into a reserve fund, which can be drawn on by the investors to cover possible future return shortfalls. If excess spread is above the "trapping level," it is retained by the lender.

The cash flows from the securitized loans typically consist of interest and principal and can be structured in either of two ways. First, the cash flows can be directly passed through to investors after subtracting servicing expenses. Securities having this feature are called pass-through securities; many mortgage-backed ABS securities are pass-throughs. For investors, pass-through securities have the disadvantage that possible prepayment of the underlying loans makes cash flows more difficult to predict.[55]

Alternatively, cash flows may be specified by rules that allocate interest and principal to different classes of the ABSs, known as tranches. Such ABSs are called structured securities. A common rule is to allocate all principal payments on a basis known as subordination: payments go first to the first tranche until it is fully paid off, then to the second class until it is paid off, and so forth. These are known as planned amortization class tranches. This structure can provide investors with different terms to maturity, since the tranches do not have to have the same terms.

Another common rule is to create a fixed principal payment schedule for one or several tranches (called targeted amortization class tranches) and allocate cash flow variations that arise from faster or slower prepayments to a support tranche. The support tranche receives a higher yield in exchange for greater uncertainty in cash flows. There may be fifty different tranches in a complicated securitization.

As indicated, structured securities typically have subordinated components where different tranches have different priority in payments. Higher-priority tranches are paid before lower-priority tranches. This gives the different tranches different risk characteristics. In the event of a cash flow shortfall, the lower-priority tranches absorb losses before higher-priority tranches. Thus, bonds in a higher-priority tranche of an ABS may have higher credit quality than the underlying loans backing the ABS. In this way, subordination may allow investors restricted to highly rated "investment grade" securities to fund higher-risk loans.

The lowest tranche may be privately placed with investors that have a taste for higher returns and higher risk rather than sold in the marketplace. Or it may be held by the lender or originator of the loans, in which case the originator retains much of the underlying loan risk. In either case, it serves as another protection for higher-level investors in the subordination outline. This tranche absorbs losses

---

55. See Saunders (2000, chapter 28) for discussion of prepayment risk in ABS.

before the publicly traded tranches if the excess spread should fall to zero. The tranche is itself protected by a limited spread account that is not available to other investors and available excess spread. If this tranche absorbs losses during some time period, it can be reimbursed from future excess spread, if any.[56]

Credit Enhancements

Credit enhancements are sources of funds that can be drawn on to cover shortfalls in interest, principal, or servicing expense, and they serve to protect the interests of the investors in the ABS. Excess spread and subordination are credit enhancements. Additional credit enhancements include overcollateralization, reserve accounts, cash collateral accounts, third-party insurance, and letters of credit. They further insulate investors from variations in payments and charge-offs and allow ABSs to obtain investment-grade ratings. The amount and type of enhancement depends on the historical loss experience of similar loans and the ABS rating sought by the lender. The following paragraphs briefly discuss each of these kinds of enhancements.

Overcollateralization is the provision of more collateral than the value of the security that the collateral backs. For example, a mortgage-backed security might have a principal amount of $100 million, while the principal value of the mortgages underlying the issue might be $120 million.

A reserve account may be created to pay investors if loan losses are higher than expected. Reserve accounts are typically funded by an initial deposit from the originator, and they can trap excess spread up to a target level. A reserve account is often used to obtain higher investment grade ratings for subordinated tranches.

A cash collateral account is a segregated trust funded at the time the security is issued. The account is funded by a loan from a third-party bank. The cash is invested in highly rated short-term securities that mature on or before the next distribution date. Any drawdowns of the cash collateral account may be reimbursed from future excess spread.

Third-party insurance includes surety bonds and other outside guarantees. A surety bond is an insurance policy that reimburses the ABS for any losses. ABSs with a surety bond have the same rating as the surety bond's issuer. In other cases, known as wrapped securities, a third party guarantees to absorb any losses up to a specified amount. Third-party guarantees are typically provided by AAA rated financial guarantors or monoline insurance companies, but sometimes the parent company of the issuer provides a guarantee. Problems developed in the 2008–2009 financial crisis because of unforeseen weakness among some monoline insurers.

A letter of credit is a commitment by a bank to provide cash payments to the ABS trustee up to some specified amount in the event that there is a shortfall in cash needed to pay interest, principal, or servicing expenses. Letters of credit have

56. This tranche is called a collateral invested account in credit card ABS.

fallen out of favor and have largely been replaced by cash collateral accounts. The downgrading of debt of several letter of credit issuing banks and the subsequent downgrading of the ABS that they enhanced in the past stimulated this change.

Characteristics of Asset-Backed Securities

Most ABSs amortize, that is, they pay back principal gradually over the term of the security, rather than as a lump sum at maturity. Fully amortizing ABSs are generally backed by fully amortizing loans such as automobile loans or mortgages. Prepayment risk is a concern for fully amortizing ABSs. If the underlying loans prepay, for instance, if interest rates fall and consumers refinance their mortgages, then the ABSs prepay, and the investors do not receive the expected yield for as long as they planned.

Credit card ABSs also may amortize, even though the underlying assets do not. After a predetermined revolving period during which only interest is paid on the ABS, credit card ABS can return principal in a series of defined periodic payments. In these cases, principal typically is amortized in twelve equal payments over twelve months, a process called controlled amortization. Any principal collected in excess of the predetermined amount is reinvested. Interest is paid only on the amount of securities outstanding at the beginning of the monthly period.

Severe asset deterioration, problems with the lender or servicer, or certain legal concerns may trigger early amortization. Such problems include insufficient payments from borrowers, insufficient excess spread, defaults in excess of a predetermined amount, shortfalls in credit enhancements, bankruptcy of the lender or the servicer, and false representations or warranties that are not remedied. Early amortization helps protect investors from long exposure to a deteriorating transaction.

ABSs can be issued with either fixed or floating rate coupons. Fixed-rate ABSs set coupon rates at the time of issuance. They subject the investors to interest rate risk like all fixed-income securities. When interest rates rise, their prices fall, and vice versa.

Floating rate ABSs adjust the coupon rate periodically according to an index rate. Index rates may be a US Treasury rate or more typically a London Interbank Offered Rate (LIBOR). The floating rate is the index rate plus a fixed margin, which depends on the risk associated with the tranche.

Types of Consumer Asset-Backed Securities

Automobile, credit card, and home equity loans are the most common types of consumer loans that are securitized. Luther (1999) provides a summary of the basic characteristics of ABSs for these types of loans.

AUTOMOBILE LOANS
Common automobile loans to consumers generally are closed-end loans, have six or fewer years to maturity, are fully amortizing, and are secured by the automobile.

Automobile loans typically finance 80 percent to 90 percent of the value of the automobile being purchased. Prepayments result from trade-in or defaults. New automobile loans generally are not refinanced, since a refinancing would be a used car loan, which is much more costly for the consumer than a new car loan.

Most automobile ABSs are pass-through securities, but structured securities have become more common in recent years to attract investors who prefer short repayment periods and highly predictable cash flows. Structured automobile ABSs typically have a senior/subordinated structure. The senior tranches may be planned or targeted amortization class tranches, with subordinated support tranches.

Automobile loan loss rates historically have been low, and automobile ABS credit quality has been quite high. Prime automobile loans are secured by new cars, have terms to maturity of less than five years, are characterized by relatively conservative underwriting standards, and are originated by lenders with records of low delinquency and loan losses. Subprime automobile ABSs also exist, and additional credit enhancements are needed for pools of automobile loans that deviate from prime pool characteristics. Average excess spread for automobile ABSs has been about four percentage points (400 basis points). Other common credit enhancements for automobile ABSs are reserve accounts and surety bonds.

CREDIT CARDS

Receivables from a pool of credit card accounts establish the collateral for credit card ABSs. To establish the basis for the ABSs, a credit card company sells both the current balances and future cash flows that arise from the receivables to the trust.

There are two basic types of credit card ABSs: investor securities and issuer securities. As the names suggest, investor securities are issued to outside investors by the trust, and issuer securities go to the credit card company that originates the card loans. The issuer securities amount to an equity interest in the trust that the originator of the card loans is required to retain. The issuer's equity represented by the issuer securities absorbs seasonal fluctuations in the credit card balances and any balance cancellations caused by such things as product returns or fraud. The issuer's equity also provides an incentive for the credit card company to maintain the quality of the pool, since the issuer owns part of it. The size of the issuer's share must remain above a specified percentage of the trust's receivables, usually 7 percent. The issuer must add accounts to the pool if its share falls below the minimum.[57]

Credit card ABSs use a subordinated structure for the investor securities, with portions subordinate to the remaining portions. Common credit enhancements found in credit card ABSs include cash collateral accounts that amount to privately placed tranches subordinate to publicly placed investor tranches.

---

57. Failure to maintain the minimum share is an event that triggers early amortization. See Fitch IBCA (1998) for further discussion.

Credit card ABSs may have a fixed or floating interest rate. As mentioned, credit card ABSs have an initial revolving period in which principal is not repaid. Investors receive interest during this period, and principal payments are reinvested in the pool. At the end of the revolving period, principal is repaid either as a lump sum (a "bullet" payment) or through a controlled amortization.

The primary factors affecting the performance of underlying credit card receivables are card issuer underwriting standards, servicer quality, seasoning (time since account opening), geographic concentration, and economic conditions. These factors are especially important for credit cards, because credit cards are unsecured credit. There is no collateral providing an incentive for the borrower to repay or revenue to the seller from the sale of the collateral. High underwriting standards and aggressive servicing of delinquent accounts reduce the likelihood of default. Seasoned accounts tend to have more stable performance than unseasoned accounts. Credit card performance is vulnerable to regional economic difficulties and deterioration in overall economic conditions.

HOME EQUITY LOANS

The home equity ABS category is a catch-all category that includes ABSs for several distinct types of mortgage loans other than prime grade purchase-money loans secured by the equity in borrowers' homes. Thus, home equity ABSs involve subprime mortgages, high loan-to-value mortgages, traditional second mortgages, and home equity lines of credit (see Davidson et al. 2003 and Adelson 2004). It was the subprime mortgage component of these markets, including the associated ABSs, that touched off the financial crisis of 2008–2009. Discussion here focuses on traditional second mortgages and home equity lines of credit, because consumers often use these products as substitutes for consumer credit products (see Canner, Durkin, and Luckett 1998).[58]

Traditional second mortgages have a fixed term to maturity, usually ten to twenty years. The interest rate may be fixed or adjustable. Traditional second mortgages are usually fully amortized. ABSs for traditional second mortgages generally use closed-end amortizing structures. These securities may have a single class pass-through structure or more commonly a multiple tranche structure. Principal payments may be distributed to tranches sequentially over time or in some other order, depending on the terms of the individual transaction. The issuer usually retains a residual interest in the trust.

Home equity lines of credit are a form of revolving credit. Though not consumer credit, home equity lines of credit are often used in place of consumer credit products. These lines have a credit limit, and borrowers can borrow or repay principal largely at their discretion. Home equity lines usually remain open for ten to fifteen years. Interest rates are adjustable.

---

58. As discussed in chapter 1, the Federal Reserve Board, which produces statistics for various types of credit in the United States, distinguishes between mortgage credit and consumer credit. Mortgage credit is any credit that is secured by real estate. Consumer credit is credit used by individuals or households that is not secured by real estate.

ABSs secured by home equity lines of credit use a revolving trust structure similar to that of credit card ABSs. The receivables and future cash flows of a pool of home equity lines of credit are sold to the trust. The trust issues both issuer securities that are retained by the lender and investor securities, which can consist of multiple tranches with varying terms to maturity. During a revolving period, principal payments are used to purchase new receivables generated by the lines or a portion of the lender's equity share. The minimum size of the lender's equity share is commonly 2 percent of the trust's receivables (see Roever, McElravey, and Schultz 2000).

Home equity ABSs typically have subordinated structures. Most are completely or partially credit enhanced by a surety bond. Overcollateralization, reserve accounts, and cash collateral accounts are other types of credit enhancements that are commonly used for home equity ABSs.

Defaults on traditional second mortgages and home equity lines of credit are sensitive to home values, loan-to-value ratios, and unemployment rates, but they are riskier than prime quality first mortgages. Because of their second lien status, both experience higher losses when defaults occur; hence they tend to have higher levels of credit enhancements than first mortgages. After the early 2000s, a variety of market changes, notably increases in prevalence of purchase-money second mortgages ("piggyback seconds"), higher levels of combined loan-to-value ratios, and an increase in second-mortgage borrowers' willingness to default when they did not have equity, resulted in significant losses on second-mortgage ABSs, including on higher, investment-grade rated tranches (see Adelson 2008).

Asset-Backed Securities and the 2008–2009 Credit Crisis

ABS rate spreads over other securities started rising in late 2007 with the onset of the financial crisis. After the breakdown of financial markets following the failure of Lehman Brothers in October 2008, ABS spreads exploded. Spreads over swaps on AAA rated auto-backed securities rose from a pre-crisis level of only a few basis points to nearly 600 basis points in late 2008. Issuance of new auto-backed securities plummeted. Credit card and student loan securitizations also plummeted (see Agarwal et al. 2010).

Concerned with the lack of liquidity in the ABS market, the Federal Reserve Board introduced the Term Asset Backed Securities Facility (TALF) in November 2008. The TALF, which began operations in March 2009, provided loans to investors purchasing newly issued AAA rated ABSs for loans collateralized by consumer and small business loans.[59] TALF loans were nonrecourse loans and were collateralized by the securities being purchased. To protect the government from loss, loan amounts were less than the value of the collateral. Spreads on TALF loans were well below market spreads in late 2008 but considerably higher than

---

59. The Board subsequently expanded the list of securities eligible for TALF financing to include business and commercial mortgage loans.

the spreads that prevailed before the crisis. Thus, as market conditions improved and spreads returned to more normal levels, investors would have an incentive to repay their TALF loans.

AAA spreads for auto and credit card securities fell by more than 200 basis points shortly after the announcement of the TALF. ABS issuance backed by TALF was heaviest in the first three quarters of 2009. Spreads continued to fall through 2009, and non-TALF ABS issuance resumed. The TALF ultimately extended about $70 billion in loans. The last TALF loan was made in March 2010, and the facility closed in April 2010.

Since 2010, spreads over swaps for AAA rated auto ABSs have returned to pre-crisis levels. Spreads for lower-rated auto ABSs remain slightly higher than pre-crisis levels. Issuance of auto ABSs has returned to pre-crisis levels.

Spreads over swaps for credit card ABS are at about pre-crisis levels for AAA rated securities and slightly elevated for lower-rated securities. Credit card ABS issuance has not returned to pre-crisis levels, however. After large decreases in 2009 and 2010, growth in revolving credit has been weak. And FAS 166/167 has made securitization less attractive for financing credit card receivables.

APPENDIX: THE JAFFEE-MODIGLIANI MODEL OF THE LOAN OFFER CURVE

Jaffee and Modigliani posited that a lender's beliefs about a borrower's ability to repay can be represented by a probability distribution $f_i(x)$ for the borrower's final wealth x. They assumed a certain minimum wealth k_i and a maximum possible wealth K_i. Letting L_i be the amount of the loan, r_i be the loan interest rate, and j be the opportunity rate, the lender's expected profit is

$$P_i = (1+r_i)L_i \cdot \pi_i\left[(1+r_i)L_i < x \le K_i\right] + E\left[x \mid k_i \le x \le (1+r_i)L_i\right] - (1+j)L_i$$

$$(1)$$

The first term is the payment of interest and principal, $(1 + r_i)L_i$, if the borrower's wealth is sufficient to repay the debt, which occurs when final wealth is between $(1 + r_i)L_i$ and K_i with probability π_i. If the borrower's wealth is less than $(1 + r_i)L_i$, the borrower makes a partial repayment equal to the borrower's wealth. The second term, then, is the expected value of wealth when the borrower's final wealth is less that the amount of the interest and principal. The third term is the cost of the loan.[60]

An optimal loan to a borrower is the loan size that maximizes the lender's expected profit for a given loan interest rate. The supply function for the individual borrower is the schedule of optimal loan sizes corresponding to alternative

---

60. This formulation subsumes any fixed lending costs in the opportunity rate j.

possible loan interest rates. Jaffe and Modigliani showed that this supply function can be written:

$$1 - \pi_i\left[(1 + r_i)L_i < x \le K_i\right] = \frac{(r_i - j)}{(1 + r_i)} \tag{2}$$

In words, an optimal loan is one that equates the probability of default $1 - \pi\left[(1 + r_i)L_i < X \le K_i\right]$ to the discounted difference between the loan interest rate and the opportunity rate. This supply function for an individual borrower is commonly called the loan offer function.

The loan offer function has several distinctive features that give it its shape. First, because final wealth will be at least k_i, there is a loan amount below which the probability of default is zero. If the probability of default is zero, the appropriate loan interest rate r_i is equal to the lender's opportunity rate j. Thus, the maximum risk-free loan size is $k_i/(1 + j)$, which is the present value of the borrower's minimum future wealth. This feature implies that the loan offer curve is horizontal up to $k_i/(1 + j)$; see figure 5.1.

Beyond $k_i(1 + j)^{-1}$, the probability of default increases as L_i increases. The loan interest rate r_i must therefore be greater than j and increase as L_i increases. This feature gives the supply curve a positive slope for loans amounts greater than $k_i/(1 + j)$.

L_i and r_i do not increase without limit, however. The borrower cannot repay more than his or her maximum possible final wealth K_i. When the loan amount increases to the point where repayment of principal and interest $(1 + r_i)L_i$ is equal to K_i, the borrower cannot credibly promise to pay more. This point (L_i^{max} in figure 4.1) defines the maximum loan amount. Further increases in the loan interest rate necessarily require smaller loan amounts. Thus, the loan offer curve bends backward beyond the maximum loan amount.

Equilibrium is at the intersection of the loan offer curve $L_i(r_i)$ and the borrower's loan demand curve $D_i(r_i)$, where the loan amount is L_i^* and the loan interest rate is r_i^{**}. Rationing will occur whenever the lender charges an interest rate less than r_i^e, since at that rate, loan demand is less than the loan offer. This is the standard prediction of price theory.

Jaffee and Modigliani went on to consider cases in which a lender would charge less than the equilibrium loan interest rate. These cases can arise when the lender must charge a single price to borrowers with different equilibrium loan rates. To illustrate this situation, consider two borrowers having identical demand curves but different loan offer curves (figure 5.2). Equilibrium rates are r_1^e and r_2^e, where $r_1^e < r_2^e$. The single rate r* is between r_1^e and r_2^e.[61] At r*, borrower 1 demands L_1^*, which is less than the amount the lender offers L_1^s. Thus, borrower 1 would not be

61. Jaffee and Modigliani demonstrated that the common rate must be between the optimal rates that a discriminating monopolist would charge each borrower, shown as r_1^* and r_2^* in figure 5.2, if expected profit is a concave function of the interest rate in the neighborhood of r_1^* and r_2^* (see Jaffee and Modigliani 1969, 856–857).

rationed, although borrower 1 would borrow less and pay a higher interest rate than he or she would in equilibrium. In contrast, borrower 2 demands L_2^* at rate r^*. As this amount is less than the amount the lender is willing to lend L_2^s which is determined by the intersection of R^* and $L_2(r_i)$, the borrower is rationed. The amount of borrower 2's excess demand is $L_2^* - L_2^s$.

Jaffee and Modigliani suggested that lenders classified borrowers in one of a small number of classes, within each of which a single rate is charged even though risk differs within the class. For any class, the common rate would be between the lowest and the highest individual rates within the class.[62] Customers whose individual rate is less than the common class rate will not be rationed. Customers whose individual rate is greater than the class rate will be rationed whenever their r_i^e is greater than the class rate.

---

62. Individual rates are the r_i^* charged each borrower by a discriminating monopolist.

6
Credit Reporting

The previous three chapters began discussion of the importance of information for credit decisions. chapters 3 and 4 examined the importance of pricing information for consumers making borrowing decisions, and chapter 5 then looked at the importance of information about consumers for creditors making lending decisions as part of the financial intermediation process. Uncertain repayment performance of a prospective borrower requires the lender to collect and evaluate information that provides evidence on the likelihood that potential borrowers will repay as agreed. After reviewing the costs of this and other aspects of the intermediation function, a sizable portion of chapter 5 was then given to the credit rationing implication of incomplete information and review of how consumer-oriented lending intermediaries have attempted to reduce costs by automating their information procedures through statistical credit scoring. This latter part of chapter 5 also introduced the source of the information used in credit score development work, namely, the databases of information that reside in repositories known as credit reporting agencies. The importance of these credit reporting agencies is the subject of this chapter.

Credit reporting agencies, colloquially known as credit bureaus, stand as direct testimony to the magnitude of the information difficulty that characterizes nearly all lending transactions. Lenders will invest in tools and procedures to reduce the uncertainty surrounding a new borrower in order to assess the risk better. Borrowers may hinder or help those efforts, as they have an incentive to disguise their relative risk (if it is high) or to signal it (if it is low). The resulting efforts to quantify borrower risk generate substantial transaction costs for the lender, and the credit bureau is an institution that has evolved to reduce those costs.

This chapter begins by examining the conceptual rationale for the emergence of information sharing across lenders, the foundation for a credit reporting industry. Next, the discussion focuses on the particular variety of credit reporting that evolved in the United States through the twentieth century, along with review of the federal regulation of the credit reporting industry that began in 1971. The uniquely American style of credit reporting that developed has harnessed competitive pressures and voluntary reporting to produce the most detailed and comprehensive consumer credit histories of any system in the world. Availability of the information files, in turn, has led directly to producing the wide array of innovative data-based decision tools and scoring products now available to assist

lenders. The chapter then examines the resulting benefits to consumers, creditors, and the macroeconomy. The system is not without flaws, however, and the
chapter also reviews currently available evidence on the accuracy and quality of
credit reports.

CONCEPTUAL FOUNDATION FOR THE EMERGENCE OF CREDIT REPORTING

The twin threats of adverse selection and moral hazard nag every loan officer examining a new loan application (chapter 5). An old maxim from the early twentieth
century that "a banker will only make a loan to a customer who doesn't need it"
suggests the long-standing institutional wariness toward customers who say they
need loans. Akerlof (1970) was perhaps the first economist to recognize formally
that adverse selection posed significant barriers to new entry into credit markets.
New entrants have no experience with local borrowers to draw upon and are likely
to attract applications disproportionately from higher-risk borrowers who have
been rejected by incumbent lenders. Credit card issuers likely discovered this
decades ago, but the first academic study to document the adverse selection effect
using loan application data was Ausubel (1999), finding that responders to credit
card solicitations were higher risk than nonresponders.

As discussed more fully in chapter 5, Stiglitz and Weiss (1981) used the adverse
selection problem to explain credit rationing, which occurs when the price of
credit is less than the equilibrium price based on supply and demand but lenders restrict supply. When lenders cannot distinguish low-risk borrowers from
high-risk borrowers, lenders do not let loan price rise to clear the market, because
only higher-risk borrowers would be willing to pay higher rates. In this environment, low-risk borrowers drop out, thereby shrinking the quantity of lending,
lowering the quality of the applicant pool, and further raising the average rate
that must be charged to remaining borrowers. Equilibrium in a market plagued
by adverse selection comes about when borrowers who receive loans are charged
an average loan price that reflects their pooled experience, and factors other than
price are used to determine which borrowers receive loans. Some borrowers who
would have been willing to pay the posted interest rate are denied credit.

Of course, clever lenders will develop alternative ways to sort borrowers by
risk when information is limited. As discussed in chapter 5, Jaffee and Russell
(1976) offered a model in which lenders use collateral requirements as a signal
of borrower risk. Lenders may also encourage borrower self-selection in order to
reduce the cost of sorting borrowers according to risk. Staten, Umbeck, and Gilley
(1990) provided such an example in modeling the commonly observed practice
of indirect lending. In the past, banks often simultaneously utilized separate and
distinct lending channels (for example, direct automobile loans made through
the bank for better credit risks and indirect auto loans made through the auto
dealer acting as an agent of the bank for somewhat higher- risk borrowers). There
were different qualification standards so as to encourage borrowers to self-select
based on their private information about likelihood of repayment (see discussion

of direct and indirect lending in chapter 1). These and other examples of lending practices involve methods of attempting to manage adverse selection. Lender sharing of information about a borrower's past credit experience is an alternative to advance the same result.

Moral hazard presents lenders with a different problem. Once a loan is obtained, borrowers have a greater incentive to default when the expected future consequences of default are low. But a reputation for past default that is readily communicated to potential lenders can raise those costs of default, thereby reducing the moral hazard by boosting the incentive to repay now. Credit bureaus also serve this purpose as well.[1]

In one of the earliest attempts to model how credit bureaus evolved to curb moral hazard, Klein (1992) aptly noted that the discipline imposed by the prospect of continuous dealings was recognized by Adam Smith in a 1763 lecture on "The Influence of Commerce on Manners." Klein quotes Smith as follows:

> Of all nations in Europe, the Dutch, *the most commercial*, are the most faithful to their word. The English are more so than the Scotch, but much inferior to the Dutch....
>
> This is not at all to be imputed to national character, as some pretend; there is no natural reason why an Englishman or a Scotchman should not be as punctual in performing agreements as a Dutchman. It is far more reducible to self-interest,...[which] is as deeply implanted in an Englishman as a Dutchman. A dealer is afraid of losing his character, and is scrupulous in observing every engagement. When a person makes perhaps twenty contracts a day, he cannot gain so much by endeavoring to impose on his neighbors, as the very appearance of a cheat would make him lose. When people seldom deal with one another, we find that they are somewhat disposed to cheat, because they gain more by a smart trick than they can lose by the injury which it does their character. (Klein 1992, 17)

Klein's thesis is that in addition to whatever benefits may accrue to lenders from managing the adverse selection problem, the credit bureau has the distinction of being a method of changing behavior. It promotes good behavior because it is "the most standardized and most extensive reputational system humankind has ever known" (Klein 1992, 121). To the extent that an interest in preserving reputations encourages consumers to alter their behavior, then through the market's evolution of the credit bureau, "commerce promotes morality as though it were guided by an invisible hand" (Klein 1992, 134).

---

1. Another variation on the moral hazard problem is when a borrower obtains credit from multiple sources. Each additional loan adds to total debt (relative to a given income) and so raises the probability of default, not only on the new loan but for all other existing loans. If lenders are unaware of the multiple exposure and do not take countermeasures, borrowers have an incentive to overextend (see Bizer and DeMarzo, 1992). Exchange of information about existing loans to a borrower helps lenders to curb this problem.

Academic study of the evolution of credit reporting is a relatively recent development. Pagano and Jappelli (1993) demonstrated that voluntary exchange of information among lenders improves the quality of the borrower pool (reduced default rates) and may increase the volume of lending. Their theoretical model showed that lender incentive to share information about borrowers (regarding payment experience, current obligations, and exposure) rises with the mobility and heterogeneity of borrowers, the size of the credit market, and advances in information technology. The intuition here is straightforward. Mobility and heterogeneity in the borrower pool reduce the likelihood that a lender's own experience will be sufficient to gauge the risk of a new applicant.[2] In addition, they showed that the need for information to supplement a lender's own experience also rises with the number of competitors, because new loan applicants may have multiple relationships across financial institutions, and a single lender's relationship may underestimate the extent of a borrower's exposure.

A credit bureau institutionalizes the sharing of information that is relevant to the assessment of borrower risk. Padilla and Pagano (1997) modeled the emergence of the credit bureau as an integral third-party participant in credit markets. In their model, cooperation increases the size of the lending pie. Lenders collectively benefit if they commit to exchanging information about borrower types, even at the expense of restricting their individual abilities to extract informational rents from the experience they amass on their existing customers, and they create an enforcement mechanism that ensures accuracy of the information exchanged. The third-party credit bureau fills the role of both clearinghouse and enforcer. On average, both interest rates and default rates are lower, and interest rates decrease over the course of the relationship between the client and the client's bank.

The exchange and retention of increasingly detailed information about borrowers are not necessarily completely better, however. Vercammen (1995) and Padilla and Pagano (2000) offered separate but related models of the optimal amount of information to be shared based on its impact on borrower incentives to repay loans. Vercammen set forth a conceptual model for limiting the amount of time that negative information (for example, delinquencies, defaults, or bankruptcy) should remain a part of the borrower's reported credit history. Negative information that never rolls off discourages borrowers from performing well on loans. In contrast, the prospect of "cleaning the slate" reinvigorates the borrower's incentive to handle a new loan well, so as to rebuild a record of positive performance. The flip side of this argument is that truly low-risk borrowers reveal themselves over time as such. The presence of a long record of good payment history convinces lenders that the borrower is low-risk and consequently reduces the borrower's incentive to perform well on the next loan. Vercammen concluded that limiting the length of the reported credit history (i.e., mandatory deletion of older information) would keep both types of borrowers honest, because it raises the

---

2. They offer supporting evidence: countries with greater residential mobility (for example, Canada, Japan, Australia, and the United States) have more extensive private credit reporting activity, as measured by number of credit reports per capita, than some other countries.

reputational stakes associated with the performance of their next loan. Similarly, Padilla and Pagano (2000) concluded that fine-tuning the amount of information shared to some level below "perfect" can maximize the disciplinary effect resulting from credit reporting.[3]

Around the globe, the pooling of borrower credit histories has become commonplace, although much of the reporting infrastructure has been established in just the past four decades or so (see Miller 2003, 34–37). Credit information sharing may take place on a voluntary basis through private credit bureaus that are set up either through lender consortiums or by third parties. In many countries, the information sharing and pooling may be mandatory through public credit registries (PCRs) set up and run by the country's central bank.[4] In some countries, both types of credit bureaus serve the market.

Jappelli and Pagano (2006) synthesized the results of two detailed cross-country surveys conducted to determine the extent of credit reporting and when it originated. One survey covered forty-nine countries (Jappelli and Pagano 2002); the other survey was commissioned by the World Bank and surveyed seventy-seven countries (Miller 2003). Together, the surveys revealed that before 1950, fewer than 20 percent of surveyed countries had a private credit bureau, and fewer than 5 percent had a PCR. By 2000, 60 percent of countries surveyed had a private bureau, and 50 percent of countries had a PCR.

Private credit bureaus are usually structured around reciprocal agreements, in which furnishers of data (creditors) voluntarily agree to contribute accurate data (usually in prescribed formats) in exchange for access to consolidated reports on potential customers. The level of detail in the report varies widely across countries. The threat that a data furnisher will be denied future access to reports if the furnisher fails to report, or knowingly contributes inaccurate data, helps to reduce the "free rider" problem inherent in sharing. Reported data can range from a simple statement of current or past delinquencies (negative information) to more detailed statements that itemize account balances, credit limits, and account age, by type of account (positive information). In some countries, credit reports also include information on borrower assets and employment.

Because sharing with a PCR is compulsory, all lenders are covered, but PCR reporting is typically required only for loans that meet or exceed a certain loan

---

3. Jappelli and Pagano (2006) point out that a stronger case can be made for more punitive retention and sharing of negative information in many developing countries, where credit reporting serves to offset weak judicial enforcement of credit contracts. Weak creditor collection remedies elevate the importance of reputation in the lending decision, and the reporting of prior delinquency and default boosts the borrower's incentive to pay as agreed. For example, in Brazil a well-developed network for sharing information on bad checks has so effectively reinforced consumer incentives to avoid being blacklisted for writing bad checks that the exchange and acceptance of postdated checks by merchants have become one of the most widely used forms of consumer financing.

4. Jappelli and Pagano (2002 and 2006) discuss the factors that encourage the establishment of a PCR versus a private credit bureau. PCRs are more likely to evolve in countries where private arrangements have not yet arisen and where creditors' rights are poorly protected.

size threshold.[5] Credit accounts with balances below the threshold are not reported or might only be reported if delinquent. Frequently, only the borrower's aggregate balances are reported to lenders making inquiries, not the itemized listing of accounts and creditors. Because there is typically credit activity below the PCR threshold, private credit bureaus may still operate in countries with PCRs by focusing on the market segment below the PCR threshold. Generally speaking, private credit bureaus are less complete in coverage of a borrower's liabilities but offer more detailed information on individual accounts and may merge credit information with other types of data.

A more detailed discussion of global differences in credit reporting and the reasons for the evolution of different species of credit bureaus in different countries is beyond the scope of this chapter, the remainder of which will focus on credit reporting in the United States. Before turning to the US credit reporting system, however, it is worth considering Jappelli and Pagano's summary of the major implications of theoretical modeling of credit reporting and its influence on the functioning of credit markets. According to them, the sharing of information among lenders via credit reporting does the following:

1. Facilitates more accurate prediction of repayment probabilities (reducing adverse selection problems).
2. Enhances competition (and reduces informational rents that lenders could otherwise extract from borrowers), because risk assessment poses a barrier to entry.
3. Encourages repayment (reduces moral hazard).
4. Prevents overextension by borrowers as lenders gain a more comprehensive view of borrower credit obligations. (see Jappelli and Pagano 2006, 347)

The following sections discuss the structure and regulation of credit reporting in the United States and its impact on US consumer lending markets in light of these implications.

THE CREDIT REPORTING SYSTEM AND ITS REGULATION IN THE UNITED STATES

The United States does not have a public credit registry or any legislative requirement that mandates that financial institutions participate in credit reporting; instead, data are furnished voluntarily by creditors. Credit reports are produced as a result of competition among credit reporting firms in the market to supply creditors and other end users with the information needed to conduct

---

5. For example, Miller (2003) reported the smallest loan size required to be reported to the PCR in the following countries (as of 1999, in US dollars): France, $81,558; Spain, $6,450; Mexico, $21,424; Brazil, $25,905.

credit-related transactions. The credit reporting industry is currently dominated by three separate credit reporting agencies (Equifax, Experian, and TransUnion), each of which maintains computerized, automated credit reporting systems that store and instantaneously retrieve many years of payment history for more than 200 million adult residents.

Since 1971, the Fair Credit Reporting Act (FCRA) has regulated the US credit reporting industry at the federal level. Competition among credit bureaus and flexible regulations that largely avoid restrictions on credit report content have combined to give US lenders the most detailed credit histories for a larger segment of the population than in any other country in the world. Ready access to such personal credit histories has fueled an explosion in consumer credit products since the mid-1970s. This section briefly recaps the evolution of credit reporting in the United States, the FCRA's legislative history, and the trade-offs that shaped the resulting rules that govern credit reporting.

Emergence and Early Growth

Credit reporting evolved in the United States as a market-driven response to commercial needs. Because retail stores were the primary source of consumer credit in the United States in the late nineteenth and early twentieth centuries, the first credit bureaus in the United States were cooperatives established by local retailers to pool credit histories of their customers and to assist in debt collection.[6] In addition to merchants, the local finance companies also organized pools of credit histories, as did local chambers of commerce. As a result, hundreds of small credit bureaus emerged, each focused on a particular business line in a particular geographic area.[7] The number of bureaus increased from fewer than 100 in 1916 to 800 in 1927 and to 1,600 by 1955 (see Hunt 2006, 308).

Through the twentieth century, legal and economic changes increased the demand for credit, expanded the number and variety of creditors, and created a need for credit reports for a variety of new purposes. Demand for consumer credit escalated in the aftermath of World War II as the population expanded rapidly and became more mobile. The market for credit also became more national in scope. Many local merchants merged or went out of business, giving way to regional and national department store chains, and the chains moved their credit operations from local stores to their headquarters.[8] At the same time, finance companies and

6. Retail stores provided 80 percent of consumer credit in 1919, and in 1929, credit financed one-third of all retail sales. For a history of the early days of credit reporting in the United States, see Hunt (2006).

7. In 1906, the National Federation of Retail Credit Agencies was formed to facilitate the nationwide sharing of consumer credit information across industries. It subsequently changed its name to Associated Credit Bureaus of America, then to Associated Credit Bureaus, Inc., and by the end of the 1990s, to the Consumer Data Industry Association (Hunt 2006, 308).

8. Such chains accounted for less than 15 percent of department stores sales in 1929 but nearly 80 percent of sales by 1972 (see Hunt 2006, 9).

banks greatly expanded their share of consumer lending, at the expense of retailer credit. The share of consumer credit held by retailers fell by half between 1941 and 1965 (Hunt 2006, 309). By the 1970s, credit card lending was rapidly expanding, but the card-issuing banks were marketing on a regional and eventually national scale. With these developments, no single locally oriented credit bureau could satisfy a card issuer's need for credit report data.

At the same time, new technologies were making it possible to collect and store more data at less cost and to share that information faster and more efficiently through automated, computer-driven systems.[9] In 1960, reporting was still characterized by filing cabinets of paper-based credit history data, and "reports" were transmitted through the mail or over the telephone. A decade later, a number of credit bureaus in larger cities had begun to automate data retrieval, making it possible to link the databases of multiple local bureaus into an automated credit reporting system to satisfy the demand from regional and national lenders. By the late 1980s, three major automated credit reporting systems had emerged as the main competitors in the industry, each claiming to have universal coverage of the US adult population of credit users. Remarkably, this all occurred within a voluntary "sharing" framework in which data furnishers provided information to the credit bureaus under reciprocal agreements that ensured the furnisher access to data from the consolidated credit report for a given borrower.

Credit Report Content before 1970

Significantly, there was virtually no legal regulation of credit reporting during much of its evolution in the United States.[10] Until 1970, there was no federal statute covering credit reporting, and only one state (Oklahoma) had a law that constrained the compilation or use of reports. Common law remedies to consumers harmed by credit reporting were unavailable, in large part because every state (except for Georgia and Idaho) recognized a common law privilege that protected credit bureaus from defamation actions unless the plaintiff could prove that the bureau intended to cause harm.[11]

As the reporting system evolved in the United States, credit reports contained information primarily from two sources: creditors and investigators who worked for the credit bureaus. Information from creditors typically included data about credit transactions with their customers (for example, type of account and payment history). Information supplied by investigators was more diverse and ultimately proved far more controversial. This information addressed subjects including "personal character, habits and reputation... obtained primarily from conversations with one's neighbors, employer, landlord, and fellow workers"

---

9. This paragraph draws heavily from Hunt (2006, 307–313).

10. The authors thank Fred Cate for assembling the legal background material for this section.

11. See Protecting the Subjects of Credit Reports (1971, 1050–1051) and sources cited therein.

(Protecting the Subjects of Credit Reports 1971, 1036, n. 6). A 1962 credit report on a form supplied by the Associated Credit Bureaus of America, for example, asked these questions: "Is applicant well regarded as to character, habits, and morals?" "Did you learn of any domestic difficulties?" "Does he have a reputation of living within his income?" (see Karst 1966, 342, 372). According to evidence presented to Congress in 1968 and 1969, investigators were paid on a piecework basis for this type of information and completed their work on a file in an average of thirty minutes (see US House of Representatives 1968, 68, 88; and *Congressional Record* 1969, 2410, 2413).

Not only did this type of information have the potential to intrude significantly on personal privacy, but it was also highly subjective and, therefore, prone to considerable inconsistency and inaccuracy. Credit bureaus typically did not undertake any further independent investigation of information obtained from either creditors or investigators. Neither did most users of credit reports. Moreover, reports were often provided orally over the telephone, which further increased the chance for error and decreased the ability of anyone to go back later and discern what was included in the original report or whether it was accurate.

Most credit bureaus supplied reports to anyone who asked and was willing to pay for them, except for individuals who sought access to records about themselves. Credit bureaus flatly refused such requests (mostly because they contended that this would help consumers trying to "game" the system), and they included nondisclosure language in their contracts with regular commercial subscribers to prevent disclosure of credit report information to consumers. As a result, not only did consumers not have the chance to dispute the accuracy of information in their own credit reports, but many did not even know of their existence.

The Fair Credit Reporting Act of 1970

Congress first became interested in the regulation of credit files in the mid-1960s, after a series of study commissions examining proposals for a federal data bank about citizens discovered and raised issues about similar files maintained by private firms in the credit reporting industry. Legislative hearings began in 1968 and focused congressional attention for the first time on the existence of comprehensive credit reports and the lack of government regulation or oversight (see McNamara 1973, 67, 72–76). The hearings and a spate of articles that followed in major national publications brought forward hundreds of anecdotes about consumers being denied credit because of inaccurate information in credit reports or otherwise being treated unfairly by creditors and credit bureaus.

The most emotion-laden aspects of the hearings involved the segment of the consumer reporting industry that produced investigative reports. Investigative methods were invasive, and because the resulting information was inherently subjective, its accuracy was suspect, but even credit information in credit reports received its share of criticism. The hearings cited accuracy problems related to creditors' reporting inaccurate information, bureaus' inadvertent merging of one person's data with another person's file, incomplete or missing information, and basic data entry errors.[12] Testimony focused on the absence of legal incentives for accuracy and on the significant impediments to consumers learning what was on their credit reports. Ultimately, three broad themes came to dominate the legislative debate: fairness, accuracy, and privacy. Congress responded by adopting the Fair Credit Reporting Act (FCRA), which it passed in amended form on October 26, 1970, and which took effect in April 1971.[13]

Under the circumstances, the FCRA was a notably moderate attempt to enhance fairness, accuracy, and privacy, while not undermining the competitive, voluntary credit reporting system that produced such detailed credit reports. In its "findings" in the preamble to the Act, Congress highlighted the delicate balance it was trying to craft:

> The banking system is dependent upon fair and accurate credit reporting. Inaccurate credit reports directly impair the efficiency of the banking system, and unfair credit reporting methods undermine the public confidence which is essential to the continued functioning of the banking system.... There is a need to ensure that consumer reporting agencies exercise their grave responsibilities with fairness, impartiality, and a respect for the consumer's privacy.
>
> It is the purpose of this title to require that consumer reporting agencies adopt reasonable procedures for meeting the needs of commerce for consumer credit, personnel, insurance and other information in a manner which is fair and equitable to the consumer, with regard to the confidentiality, accuracy, relevancy, and proper utilization of such information in accordance with the requirements of this title. (15 USC 1681)

The law permits credit bureaus to assemble credit reports freely, without constraints on content. However, the FCRA also introduced the concept of an "investigative consumer report," which it defined to mean any portion of a consumer report in which information on a consumer's "character, general reputation, personal characteristics, or mode of living is obtained through personal interviews with neighbors, friends, or 'associates of the consumer' or others, other than factual information obtained directly from a creditor or from a credit report if the bureau obtained the information directly from a creditor." Because the FCRA treats investigative consumer reports differently from regular consumer reports,

---

12. Senator William Proxmire, who introduced the bill that later became the Fair Credit Reporting Act, gave the following justification for the bill on the Senate floor in 1969: "First, the problem of inaccurate or misleading information; second, the problem of irrelevant information; and, third, the problem of confidentiality." He identified the most serious problem as inaccurate or misleading information. Conceding that "it is unrealistic to expect 100 percent accuracy," he concluded that the prevailing level of inaccuracy was intolerable (see *Congressional Record* 1969, January 31).

13. Fair Credit Reporting Act of 1970, Public Law 91-508, 15 USC 1681–1681t.

investigative reports evolved thereafter as a separate product, distinct from what is commonly known as a credit report today.

Under the FCRA, market forces eventually dictated that credit reports in the United States contain four categories of data in credit files:

(1) Personal identification information (for example, name, address, social security number).

(2) Open and closed "trade lines" (credit accounts such as credit card accounts, auto loans and leases, first and second mortgage accounts, personal loans, student loans, etc.) with data such as outstanding balance, credit limit, date account opened, date of last activity, and payment history.

(3) Public record items related to the use of credit, including bankruptcies, accounts referred to collection agencies, legal collection judgments, and liens.

(4) Inquiries on the credit file, including data and identity of inquirer, for at least the previous two years.

To balance the consumer's value of privacy against the business need for information and its inevitable storage for reuse, the FCRA mandates that credit reports can only be released for permissible purposes. In the original FCRA, permissible purposes were defined as those in conjunction with a variety of voluntary, consumer-initiated transactions. These included credit and credit-related transactions (for example, loan or credit card, apartment leases, telephone service contracts, etc.), insurance, and employment applications, along with a vague category defined as "legitimate business need." Since the consumer must initiate the transaction, nobody would be in a position to learn the consumer's credit report contents unless it was relevant to a transaction the consumer was trying to arrange.

The FCRA limits the disclosure of certain information deemed by the statute as "obsolete." For example, most negative information on the credit file (including delinquencies, charged-off accounts, and legal collection judgments) is permitted to reside on the file no longer than seven years. Originally, bankruptcy information could remain on the file for fourteen years, later reduced to ten years. This provision was perceived at the time as an important component for achieving the stated goal of "fairness" in credit reporting, even though it also clearly affected the accuracy of the credit profile. Theoretical discussion in the previous section suggested that forced obsolescence of negative information can reinforce important incentives for borrowers, but the optimal roll-off of information is not known.

The FCRA also encourages the production of accurate credit reports by adopting a uniquely simple and flexible regulatory approach.[14] In effect, the FCRA requires credit bureaus to follow "reasonable procedures to assure maximum possible accuracy" of the information in their credit reports and then offers

14. For further discussion of how the FCRA promotes accuracy, see Staten and Cate (2005, 241–244).

consumers the equivalent of a "warranty" on the final product. If the consumer disputes an item, the bureau is compelled to reinvestigate the matter and fix it whenever an error is confirmed.

The "warranty" works as follows. First, and most important, consumers received the right to view their files. Upon request, the credit bureaus needed to provide consumers with a copy of their reports, including a list of recipients of those reports during the past six months.[15] Further, users of credit reports that took "adverse action" toward a consumer (for example, denied credit, insurance, or employment or imposed a higher charge) because of information contained in a credit report were required to inform the consumer of this fact and supply the consumer with the name and address of the credit bureau that supplied the report. The consumer was then entitled to a free credit report if he or she contacted the credit bureau within thirty days of receiving the "adverse action" notice. This feature alerted a consumer that there might be a problem with the credit report and provided the opportunity to inspect it for inaccuracies. The FCRA also required the bureau to implement a dispute resolution process to investigate and correct errors alleged.[16]

Staten and Cate (2005) argued that it is not the case that the FCRA's remedial approach leaves the credit bureau with no incentive to *prevent* errors:

> Although there is no explicit dollar fine imposed when a consumer detects an error, the mandatory re-verification process is costly for both bureaus and creditors. Like the automaker who must reimburse dealers for warranty work to repair defective vehicles, both creditors and the bureaus would like to reduce the costs they will be required to incur if a consumer finds an error. They will invest in reporting and updating procedures that eliminate most errors. Bureaus [in the competitive US market] have an additional, powerful incentive to invest in procedures that eliminate problems in matching new information to files: the creditors are their customers and they pay for accuracy. A bureau with a reputation for file errors will suffer lost sales in a competitive market for credit reports as creditors shift their

15. Note that this prompted a major change in reporting industry practice, because before the FCRA, bureaus had refused to share credit file contents with consumers and essentially had no consumer relations function at all. Under the original FCRA, bureaus were permitted to impose a "reasonable charge" for access in most cases, although later amendments capped the charge and eventually required that the bureaus offer consumers one free credit report per year. The disclosure of a credit report to consumers must include names of recipients of files for the past two years, which helps consumers to enforce the permissible purpose provision.

16. In the original FCRA, bureaus were to delete any disputed data that they could not verify within a "reasonable period of time." In later amendments, "reasonable time" was defined as forty-five and, eventually, thirty days. If the bureau determines that the information is accurate but the consumer disagrees, the law requires the bureau to include a statement from the consumer of not more than one hundred words with future credit reports that contain the disputed data.

business to vendors that establish a reputation for greater reliability. (Staten and Cate 2005, 243–244)

The economic rationale for the "warranty" part of the regulation is that at some achieved degree of accuracy, it becomes cheaper to correct the error the consumer finds than it is to adopt procedures that would scrutinize every item in every file in an attempt to detect potential errors before release. By assigning consumers the legal role of quality inspector, the FCRA reinforces the financial incentive for bureaus to invest in accurate reporting and prevent those errors for which it has a comparative advantage. But a requirement that bureaus eliminate errors entirely in advance of release would make the system substantially more expensive to maintain and operate, with negative implications for the price and availability of credit and related products. The FCRA explicitly places responsibility for monitoring file accuracy on the party who can determine accuracy at the lowest cost: the consumer.[17]

1996 FCRA Amendments

The FCRA took effect in 1971 and for the next twenty-five years regulated credit reporting with no major amendment, although the FCRA had the benefit of frequent rule writing and clarification by the Federal Trade Commission. Given the preexisting competitive reporting market, the original FCRA created a flexible and largely self-enforcing regulation that proved remarkably robust despite dramatic changes in technologies, markets, and uses for credit report information.

By the late 1980s, however, the growth and national scope of credit marketing, coupled with new uses for credit reports and greater consumer awareness of the importance of credit reports, raised new concerns about credit reporting. In particular, four issues triggered an ongoing policy debate: (1) the privacy implications of using credit reports for "prescreening" consumers to determine which were eligible and likely to respond to an offer of credit, for example, credit card, mortgage, home equity line of credit, or other credit related offers; (2) the extent to which information from credit reports could be shared among corporate affiliates without direct consumer consent; (3) the accuracy of credit reports; and (4) allegations of lack of responsiveness by the credit bureaus to consumer requests and concerns. In addition, by the mid-1990s, credit bureaus and credit grantors worried that a growing number of state-level credit reporting and privacy laws enacted in the absence of federal legislation to address the ongoing issues were beginning to threaten the efficiency and cost-effectiveness of the national credit reporting system.

---

17. It is clear from decades of commentary on the FCRA that the Federal Trade Commission recognized the important role and responsibility that consumers played in facilitating the system's production of accurate credit reports. For example, see the testimony of Jeanne Noonan (1991, 40).

Congress began considering the first substantial set of amendments to the FCRA in March 1990, but it took more than six years before it finally adopted the Consumer Credit Reporting Reform Act as part of a bank regulatory relief package in September 1996.[18] The 1996 Act addressed each of the four areas of concern. It expressly authorized "prescreening" of credit report information for the purpose of marketing credit or insurance opportunities to consumers but on the condition that credit bureaus establish and publish a toll-free telephone number that consumers can call to have their names removed from lists provided for such direct marketing purposes. The law also authorized the sharing of consumer report information among affiliated companies, provided that the consumer is given an opportunity to "opt out" of that sharing. These and other changes reflected an effort to balance privacy concerns with new uses of credit reports, by conditioning authorization of those uses on the creation of new opportunities for consumers to restrict them.

The Act also gave consumers greater power to challenge and correct erroneous information in their credit reports. It required credit reporting agencies to delete any disputed data that could not be verified within thirty days and to comply with a variety of new procedural requirements intended to ensure that inaccurate data are deleted or corrected and that inaccuracies do not reoccur in future credit reports. The law also capped the fee that credit bureaus could charge individuals to access their own credit reports, in those situations in which the bureau was permitted to charge a fee. At time of passage in 1996, the fee cap was eight dollars, but the Federal Trade Commission could adjust the cap upward as necessary to keep pace with the Consumer Price Index.

The 1996 Act authorized individual states to enforce the FCRA, but recognizing the inherently national nature of credit markets and credit reporting, Congress preempted the states from enacting laws or regulations dealing with a number of specific issues. Preemption of state laws was viewed by supporters of this provision as necessary to prevent disparate or conflicting state rules from triggering a decline in voluntary reporting and the resulting erosion in credit file content and quality. Specifically, the 1996 amendments prohibited state laws dealing with:

(1) Information sharing among affiliates.
(2) Prescreening.
(3) Notices to be included with prescreened solicitations.
(4) Summary of consumer rights to be provided to individuals.
(5) Responsibilities of persons who take adverse action based on a credit report.
(6) Time to complete reinvestigations.

---

18. Consumer Credit Reporting Reform Act of 1996, Public Law 104-208 (September 30, 1996), 15 USC 1681–1681t. The legislative history of the 1996 amendments is documented in Seidel (1998).

(7) Information furnisher responsibilities.

(8) Time periods for determining the obsolescence of information in
     consumer credit reports.[19]

Given the dramatic changes that were continuing to reshape technologies and
the uses of credit reports, Congress built into the statute an opportunity to revisit
the law's performance by providing that these preemption provisions would
expire on January 1, 2004.

2003   FCRA Amendments

Looming expiration of the 1996 preemption of state and local regulation of credit
reporting provided impetus in 2003 for a new congressional look at the Fair
Credit Reporting Act. The result was the Fair and Accurate Credit Transactions
(FACT) Act, passed by Congress on November 22, 2003 (Public Law 108-159).
The FACT Act actually went well beyond consideration of the preemptions,
which the law made permanent. Consumer groups and some state attorneys
general had lobbied Congress to drop federal preemption and let state and local
jurisdictions adopt tougher consumer protection standards. Industry and academic experts argued that a balkanized credit reporting system would ultimately
cost consumers more in terms of lost opportunities and higher prices caused by
higher compliance costs than would be gained from the opportunity to experiment with tougher consumer protections. Although the FACT Act contained
a variety of new consumer protection provisions, the industry and academic
experts provided ample evidence to convince Congress of a need for continuing
the preemptions.

Hunt (2006) has provided an overview of the expanded consumer protections. New rules established a system of fraud alerts that gave additional protection and rights to victims of identity theft. Consumers also became entitled to
one free copy of their credit report annually from each of the three major national
bureaus. Further, affiliated companies were required to begin offering consumers an opportunity to opt out of having their personal financial information, not
just credit report information, shared across corporate affiliates for marketing
purposes. The Act also expanded the definition of adverse action based on information in a consumer's credit report to incorporate situations beyond just denial
of credit. In particular, the FACT Act specified that adverse action, which triggers a required notice from the creditor to the consumer, occurs if a consumer is
offered credit "on terms materially less favorable than those the creditor grants to
many of its customers." Finally, the FACT Act mandated a number of studies to
be conducted by agencies such as the Federal Trade Commission and the Federal

---

19. The law permitted continuation of several state-level exceptions to the preemption that
existed before passage of the preemption provisions. Further action was prohibited in these
states.

Reserve Board, including a ten-year review of credit report accuracy. In 2010, the Federal Trade Commission provided congressional testimony that summarized and outlined its completion of almost all of the "almost 30 rules, guidelines compliance forms, notices, educational campaigns, studies and reports" required under the FACT Act with references (see Federal Trade Commission 2010). At that time, the ten-year accuracy review required under section 319 of the Act was still ongoing. The FTC released the study in late 2012 (Federal Trade Commission 2012, discussed further below).

COMPREHENSIVE CREDIT REPORTING AND CREDITOR DECISION MAKING

As indicated, the credit reporting environment varies widely around the world, and the difficulty and cost of risk evaluation rise and fall accordingly. Some countries, such as the United States, Canada, and the United Kingdom, have credit reporting systems characterized by comprehensive, full-file reporting that yields a credit report for each consumer containing both positive and negative information about the borrower's experience across all types of credit products. At the other end of the reporting spectrum are credit reporting systems that produce consumer credit files containing only negative information (delinquencies, charge-offs, bankruptcies, etc.). Essentially, consumers in a negative-only reporting country would have either derogatory information in their credit report or no information at all.

The problems for a lender trying to assess the applicant's risk in a negative-only reporting environment are readily apparent. Such credit reports give a lender little or no information for lower-risk borrowers who use credit responsibly. The lender cannot discern the length and breadth of the consumer's past credit experience, nor can the lender determine the consumer's current credit obligations. The consumer gets no benefit from handling credit responsibly in the past, and the lender cannot tell the extent to which the consumer is burdened with other credit obligations at the time of the application. Only when the file contains some negative information does it help the lender at all. Otherwise, the applicant remains shrouded in a fog of uncertainty.

In between the full-file comprehensive reporting systems and the negative-only systems are a host of intermediate reporting environments that contain some positive information but not a complete history of a consumer's credit experience. Common examples are reporting systems that evolved from lender consortiums within a particular segment of the industry. For example, banks may have historically participated in the exchange of information within the banking community about their consumer loan experience but did not share that information with nonbank creditors. Retail stores or finance companies may have developed their own sharing arrangements within their segment of the credit market. Even with positive data present, however, a credit report produced by any one consortium would be incomplete, because it would contain the information from lenders in only one segment of the industry.

Across all reporting environments, comprehensive, full-file reporting provides the greatest benefit to risk evaluation. Barron and Staten (2003) demonstrated this with a comparative assessment of benefits from reporting environments as part of a World Bank project to explore the role of credit reporting infrastructure in developing economies. Their report offered a set of simulations that demonstrated the benefits of increasingly comprehensive information about a borrower's credit profile. With these simulations, they showed the effects of differences in credit reporting.

By using a comparatively large set of credit report data elements from credit reports available in the United States to build a predictive scoring model and then removing particular data fields that in other countries are either banned by regulation or unavailable because of credit reporting limitations, they identified the reduction in predictive power attributable to the restriction. This technique quantified in two ways the cost imposed on lenders and consumers by the missing data. First, it revealed the increase in predicted delinquency rates for a group of accepted loans, relative to what lenders could achieve when more information is available about credit experience. It also identified the increase in the number of loans that can be approved for a given pool of consumer applicants, while maintaining a target delinquency rates.

In particular, Barron and Staten built credit scoring models that compared a lender's ability to measure borrower risk first under the US Fair Credit Reporting Act and second under the more restrictive Australian rules adopted with the passage of Australia's Commonwealth Privacy Amendment Act of 1990. This law was essentially a "negative-only" law. The simulations compared the accuracy of risk scoring models for a large group of consumers under each set of rules and determined the impact on the predicted default rate and on the percentage of customers who would receive loans under each regime.

A third simulation examined an intermediate reporting scenario that would allow the reporting of a limited amount of positive credit information, specifically the existence (and type) of accounts that are in good standing or have been paid in full, but not current revolving credit account balances or credit limits. In this scenario, borrowers are recognized for having established a successful history of handling credit but without revealing details about the level of current indebtedness or their maximum credit available. Table 6.1 displays the set of predictive variables available for use in the three simulations and also provides a sense of the types of credit report variables typically available to the credit risk scorecard builder in the United States.[20]

20. The list represents only a small subset of the standard credit report characteristics maintained by the three major US credit reporting agencies. A complete list would include several hundred variables. Because the precise components of commercial scoring models are proprietary, the scoring models in the simulations used are only approximations of a commercially developed scoring system, although the authors utilized the same sets of variables that commercial model builder Fair Isaac (FICO) has indicated on its website are important determinants of a borrower's creditworthiness.

The risk scoring models were built using US credit report data provided by one of the three major US credit bureaus using anonymous credit files with personal identifying information removed. The simulations were conducted with samples drawn from a database containing a

Table 6.1 VARIABLES USED IN THE DIFFERENT SCORING MODELS

	Full US Model: Positive and Negative	Australia Intermediate: Positive but No Balances or Minor Negative	Australia Current: Only Major Negative
Type of Variable: Outstanding Debt, Types of Debt, and Debt Usage			
Total number of open, paid, or closed accounts	*	*	
No open, paid, or closed accounts	*	*	
Number of accounts open with a balance ≥ zero	*		
No accounts open with a balance ≥ zero	*		
Number of accounts opened in last 6 months	*	*	
No accounts opened in last 6 months	*	*	
Number of accounts opened in last 12 months	*	*	
No accounts opened in last 12 months	*	*	
Proportion of open accounts that is revolving	*	*	
Proportion of open accounts that is finance installment	*	*	
Proportion of open accounts that is real estate/property	*	*	
Zero balance on open accounts	*		
Number of open bank card accounts with amount ≥ $5000	*		
Average balance across all open accounts	*		
Average balance across open revolving accounts	*		
Proportion of debt that is revolving	*		
Proportion of debt that is finance installment	*		
Proportion of debt that is real estate/property	*		

(Continued)

Table 6.1 (Continued)

	Full US Model: Positive and Negative	Australia Intermediate: Positive but No Balances or Minor Negative	Australia Current: Only Major Negative
Total of available credit (credit limit minus balance on all open bank card accounts)	*		
Bank card balance/limit ratio on all open accounts reported in last 6 months	*		
Bank card balance/limit ratio on all open accounts opened in last 12 months	*		
Number of open revolving accounts with balance/limit ratio ≥ 50	*		
Number of open revolving accounts with balance/limit ratio ≥ 75	*		
Number of open revolving accounts with balance/limit ratio ≥ 90	*		
Type of Variable: Length of Credit History			
Age, in months, of oldest account	*	*	
Age, in months, of most recently opened account	*	*	
Type of Variable: Applications for Credit (Inquiries)			
Average age, in months, of all accounts	*	*	
Ratio of number of open accounts reported, last 12 months, to age of oldest account	*	*	
Total number of inquiries made for credit purposes	*	*	
No inquires made for credit purposes	*	*	
Total number of bank card inquiries made for credit purposes	*	*	
No bank card inquires made for credit purposes	*	*	

(Continued)

Table 6.1 (CONTINUED)

	Full US Model: Positive and Negative	Australia Intermediate: Positive but No Balances or Minor Negative	Australia Current: Only Major Negative
Months since most recent inquiry for credit purposes was made	*	*	
Months since most recent bank card inquiry for credit purposes was made	*	*	
Total number of inquiries for credit purposes made, last 6 months	*	*	
Proportion of inquires to open accounts, last 6 months	*	*	
Total number of inquiries for credit purposes made, last 12 months	*	*	
Proportion of inquiries to open accounts, last 12 months	*	*	
Type of Variable: Delinquencies and Derogatory Public Records			
Proportion of all accounts that have never been delinquent, last 6 months	*		
Proportion of all accounts that have never been delinquent, last 12 months	*		
Positive number of accounts ever 30 or more days delinquent or derogatory	*		
Total number of accounts 30 or more days delinquent or derogatory, last 12 months	*		
Proportion of accounts ever 30 or more days delinquent or derogatory	*		
Positive number of accounts ever 60+ days delinquent or derogatory	*		
Number of accounts ever 60+ days delinquent or derogatory	*		
Proportion of accounts ever 60+ days delinquent or derogatory	*		

(*Continued*)

Table 6.1 (CONTINUED)

	Full US Model: Positive and Negative	Australia Intermediate: Positive but No Balances or Minor Negative	Australia Current: Only Major Negative
Positive number of accounts ever 90+ days delinquent or derogatory	*	*	*
Number of accounts ever 90+ days delinquent or derogatory	*	*	*
Proportion of accounts ever 90+ days delinquent or derogatory	*	*	
Positive number of accounts 30+ days delinquent or derogatory, last 12 months	*		
Number of accounts 30+ days delinquent or derogatory, last 12 months	*		
Proportion of accounts 30+ days delinquent or derogatory, last 12 months	*		
Positive number of accounts 90+ days delinquent or derogatory, last 12 months	*	*	*
Number of accounts 90+ days delinquent or derogatory, last 12 months	*	*	*
Proportion of accounts 90+ days delinquent or derogatory, last 12 months	*	*	
Positive number of open accounts, payment behavior last 6 months worse than preceding 6 months	*		
Number of open accounts, payment behavior last 6 months worse than preceding 6 months	*		
Proportion of open accounts, payment behavior last 6 Months worse than preceding 6 months	*		
Positive number of accounts ever derogatory, including collection, charge-off, etc.	*	*	*

(Continued)

Table 6.1 (CONTINUED)

	Full US Model: Positive and Negative	Australia Intermediate: Positive but No Balances or Minor Negative	Australia Current: Only Major Negative
Number of accounts ever derogatory	*	*	*
Proportion of accounts ever derogatory	*	*	
Positive number of derogatory public records	*	*	*
Number of derogatory public records	*	*	*
Proportion of derogatory public records	*	*	
Positive number of bankruptcy account lines ever	*	*	*
Total number of bankruptcy account lines ever	*	*	*
Proportion of accounts ever bankruptcy account lines	*	*	
Months since most recent account line bankruptcy	*	*	*
Positive number of bankruptcy public record filings, last 10 years	*	*	*
Positive number of bankruptcy public record discharges, last 10 years	*	*	*
Months since most recent bankruptcy public record event	*	*	*
Worst status ever (including current) on an account	*		
Worst status ever on accounts reported, last 12 months	*		
Worst present status on an open account	*		
Worst status ever (including current) on a bank card account	*		
Worst status ever on bank card accounts reported, last 12 months	*		

(Continued)

Table 6.1 (CONTINUED)

	Full US Model: Positive and Negative	Australia Intermediate: Positive but No Balances or Minor Negative	Australia Current: Only Major Negative
Worst present status on an open bank card account	*		
Months since most recent 30–180 day delinquency on any account	*		
Not ever delinquent or derogatory on any account	*		
Months since most recent 90+ delinquency or derogatory, any account	*	*	*
Not ever 90+ days delinquency or derogatory item on any account	*	*	*

Table 6.2 shows the change in predictive power associated with incremental expansion in the information available to the scoring models. Under each of the scenarios depicted in the table, the estimated models were used to calculate individual credit scores for each borrower in a holdout sample. Individual borrowers were ranked according to their credit scores. The authors then picked various "approval rates" (for example, 40 percent or 60 percent) and displayed the corresponding percent of borrowers who would become seriously delinquent (i.e., ninety or more days past due) on their newly opened accounts within two years.

To illustrate, at a targeted approval rate of 60 percent, the model built on Australian rules and practices (only negative information available and no delinquencies of less than ninety days reported) produced a 3.92 percent rate of serious delinquency among accepted applicants.[21] This compares with a 1.89 percent rate

random sample of 10 million individual credit files on US consumers. For each simulation, the authors estimated credit scoring models using a random sample of 312,000 US borrowers who opened new credit accounts (all types) during May 1997. The scoring models were built to rank order borrowers according to the probability that a new account opened in May 1997 would become ninety or more days delinquent within twenty-four months, that is, by the end of April 1999. The models were then tested against a similarly sized holdout sample to gauge their predictive power. Details on the methodology and discussion of the limitations are in Barron and Staten (2003, 291–296).

21. This result is somewhat higher than reported by Barron and Staten (2003), which was 3.35 percent given a 60 percent approval rate. The difference arises because the 2003 study incorrectly assumed that both major delinquencies (more than ninety days) and minor delinquencies (sixty days and less) were being reported under Australian rules, when in the reestimations, only

Table 6.2 EFFECT ON DEFAULT RATE FOR VARIOUS APPROVAL RATES
(PERCENTAGES)

Target Approval Rate	Current Australia Default Rate	Full US Model Default Rate	Default Reduction US from Australia	Australian Intermediate Model	Default Reduction US from Australia Intermediate	Predictivity: Australian Intermediate versus US
40	3.47	1.01	70.9	1.60	53.9	76
60	3.92	1.89	51.8	2.46	37.2	71
75	4.65	3.31	28.8	3.71	20.2	70
100	10.10	10.10	0.0	10.10	0.0	—

SOURCE: Reestimation of equations in Barron and Staten (2003).

of serious delinquency utilizing a full credit reporting scenario that mirrors the US reporting environment, a 52 percent reduction in delinquency for the same number of new accounts opened (fourth column in the table). The Australian intermediate model that utilized a limited amount of positive credit information (account type but no balances or limits) cut the rate of serious delinquency to 2.46 percent, a decline of 37 percent. The intermediate model provided some 71 percent of the reduction in delinquency achievable under the full US scenario.

Table 6.3 presents an alternative view of the gain in predictive power associated with expanding the information available to the scoring model. Suppose the economics of a lender's operation dictate an optimal default rate of 4 percent. The model simulating current Australian rules and practices could approve 50.9 percent of applicants and not exceed the target default rate. Under full US credit reporting, 80 percent of applicant customers could be approved, an increase of 57 percent for the same percentage of accounts in default. Moving to the intermediate model utilizing a limited amount of positive credit information boosted the approval rate to 77 percent, an increase in credit availability of 51 percent relative to the Australian rules. Put another way, the simulation showed that while maintaining a delinquency rate of 4 percent, similar to those experienced in many US consumer credit markets, a limited amount of positive credit data made available to Australian creditors would have allowed them to extend credit to about 26,000 more consumers per 100,000 applicants than with the restricted reporting rules.

How can this be? The reason for the improvement in the models' performance is intuitive: when risk assessment tools have less information available to them, creditors have greater difficulty piercing the "fog of uncertainty" that surrounds new borrowers. Consequently, creditor efforts are less effective at matching loans

---

major delinquencies were reported. In fact, the corrected analysis reported here is intuitively appealing. The model is less predictive when delinquencies of lesser magnitude are omitted. Even mild delinquency is predictive of serious problems in the future. The comparative amounts in table 6.2 also were reestimated.

Table 6.3 SIMULATED EFFECT ON CREDIT AVAILABILITY OF ADDITIONAL
INFORMATION FOR VARIOUS DEFAULT RATES (PERCENTAGES)

Target Default	Able to Obtain Loan		Availability Increase, US versus Australia	Australia Interme- diate	Availability Increase, Australia Intermediate vs. Australia	Australia Interme- diate versus US
	Australia	US				
3%	NA	72.5	–	67.3	–	–
4%	50.9	80.0	57	77.0	51	96
5%	65.2	85.8	32	84.5	30	98
6%	86.6	90.3	4	89.8	4	99
7%	91.8	93.5	2	93.5	2	100
8%	95.3	96.0	1	96.0	1	100
9%	97.8	98.3	1	98.0	0	100
10.1%	100.0	100.0	0	100.0	0	100

SOURCE: Reestimation of equations in Barron and Staten (2003).

to borrowers who will repay as agreed. More loans go to borrowers who will default. More borrowers are rejected who would have repaid. The negative impact on worthy borrowers is greatest for those who are young, have short time on the job or at their residence, have lower incomes, and are generally more financially vulnerable. These are precisely the borrowers for whom the ability to see *successful* handling of credit on the credit report is most important, to offset attributes that otherwise make them appear to be higher-risk.[22]

A corollary to these findings, and one that can be addressed statistically through simulations such as the ones described above, is that in any reporting system, the more lenders that report, the better. The intuition follows directly from the simulations on types of data reported. Lenders who drop out of the voluntary system or report only negative information and omit accounts in good standing, impose a predictive drag on the rest of the data. Credit reporting is a good example of an action that produces externalities. A nonreporting creditor, especially a large one, imposes an "external" cost on all other creditors, because omission of its data impairs the value of the remaining credit bureau information for everyone. The predictive power of models built with the reported data is diminished,

---

22. Barron and Staten (2003) also reported simulations of credit reporting fragmented by the type of lender originating the loan, the kind of reporting that occurs frequently around the world in countries where the evolution of credit data repositories was driven by industry affiliation. In several Latin American countries (Brazil, Mexico, Argentina) and in Japan, banks historically shared information about their customer loan experience and created databases that captured only bank loan experience. Nonbank creditors often were not allowed to draw information from the repository, so they pooled their own loan experience to form a separate database. Simulations demonstrated that fragmented reporting also results in deterioration of a scoring model's predictive power.

and the fog of uncertainty surrounding a given borrower is a little bit thicker when lenders know that the consumer may have an account (of unknown size and payment status) with a nonreporting creditor.

Other researchers have also applied the simulation approach. A study by Turner (2003) used commercially available scoring models and US data to show the impact of a negative-only reporting environment in which only serious delinquencies (ninety days past due or worse) are reported. Powell et al. (2004) used credit report data from Brazil and Argentina and found dramatic increases in loan acceptance rates resulting from full-file information. Another study, by Turner and Varghese (2007), used Colombian credit files and a commercial scoring model to show the predictive boost from the availability of full-file information. Although the magnitude of the gain from full-file reporting varies across these studies because of differences in the depth and quality of the information in the respective credit reports across countries, all the studies showed a significant gain-to-risk assessment when full-file information is used rather than negative-only information.[23]

To summarize, statistical simulations show that a regulatory environment that expands a lender's ability to recognize borrowers for successful use of credit can produce significant increases in *both* the availability of credit and the likelihood that loans are repaid. The results highlight the distinct trade-off between limits (regulatory or otherwise) on the collection and use of personal credit histories and making credit available to consumers at reasonable prices.

BENEFITS FROM COMPREHENSIVE FULL-FILE REPORTING SYSTEMS

As discussed in chapter 5, US creditors routinely apply statistical scoring models to estimate an individual's repayment risk on all types of consumer loan transactions, including home mortgages. Creditors use scoring to set and adjust virtually every dimension of the loan relationship. They include, besides the initial acceptance decision, pricing, collateral requirements on secured loans, size of credit line on unsecured credit cards, authorization of purchases at the point of sale, decisions to cross-sell other financial products, and the appropriate steps to collect the debt if the account becomes delinquent or even looks as if it might become delinquent (see Demery 1998, Adler 2002, and Lucas 2002). With access to the deepest, most comprehensive consumer payment histories in the world, lenders routinely tap credit bureau information to build the underlying scoring models and aid these decisions.

The United States has been unique in achieving a remarkable combination of (a) widespread access to credit across the age and income spectrum, (b) relatively low interest rates on secured loans (for example, home mortgages and

---

23. Direct cross-country studies have corroborated the simulation results linking broader credit availability to the degree of credit information sharing. Jappelli and Pagano (2002) found that the volume of consumer and mortgage lending in a country rises as a direct result of greater information sharing within a country's credit reporting system.

automobiles), (c) exceptionally broad access to open-end, unsecured lines of credit (for example, bank-type credit cards), and (d) relatively low default rates across all types of consumer loans. The previous section of this chapter showed how full-file credit reporting has been instrumental in bringing about the growth of credit availability. This section expands on the benefits of credit reporting to the credit marketplace and its participants and even touches upon broader macroeconomic benefits linked to the availability of detailed information sharing arising from a voluntary but competitive reporting industry.

Preventing Delinquencies and Defaults

By improving the quality of lending decisions, full-file credit reporting including positive information allows lenders to be proactive, not only at the application stage but also for existing account holders requesting more credit, in preventing potential debt problems and delinquencies that benefit no one.

Credit reporting that takes into account the full breadth of a borrower's obligations (and past payment history) allows creditors to detect overextension. Because the comprehensive credit reports available in the United States give lenders a broad picture of a borrower's changing financial circumstances, credit scoring is used by many US lenders to determine appropriate intervention for borrowers headed for financial trouble, including possible recommendations for credit counseling assistance.[24]

If the comprehensive credit reports available in the United States are so useful for predicting risk and overextension, why, then, did the global credit crisis of 2008–2009 begin with soaring default rates in the US subprime mortgage market? The short answer is that while credit reports provide critical input to a risk manager's decision process, they aren't the only tool in the manager's toolbox. Mortgage lenders in the United States had multiple tools but used them badly.

The credit risk posed by a given loan depends on a variety of factors other than the borrower's skill in handling credit and current level of debt (both of which a full-file credit report helps to measure). Other key factors in determining mortgage loan risk include the size, source, and stability of a borrower's income stream; the value of the borrower's assets that could be tapped if income proves insufficient to maintain payments; and the value of the loan collateral (for mortgage credit, the house and property backing the mortgage loan) as an assurance to the lender that all or most of the loan principal could be recovered if foreclosure becomes necessary. Clearly, an assessment of economic conditions that could affect all of the above is also important. The art and science of risk management rests on gathering and using information on all of these factors to make accurate estimates about the probability of repayment.

---

24. A project sponsored by the Inter-American Development Bank (Pagano 2001) offers some international insights into how retail credit markets in six Latin American countries have also evolved institutions, including unique forms of information sharing, to curb excessive default rates that have hampered consumer and small business lending.

Most observers agree that between 2002 and 2007, many mortgage lenders in the United States willingly accepted borrowers for whom credit reports and scores indicated higher risk. And, during most of that five-year period, lenders put these borrowers into increasingly risky loan products with terms that made economic sense only if the underlying collateral continued to rise in value. By 2006, the underlying home prices had stopped rising, and in 2007, they began a steady downward slide, triggering massive defaults across lender portfolios. While a thorough analysis of how this translated into a global credit crisis is beyond the intended scope of this chapter, it is safe to say that virtually no observers have identified credit reporting as the source of the problem. It would be closer to the truth to say that lenders chose to ignore the information they had on borrower risk (for a variety of reasons) and bet that continued home price appreciation would insulate them from losses caused by borrower payment problems.

That bet looked smart in 2003 and 2004, while home prices (and lender profits) were soaring, but it ultimately turned out to be a bad one as market prices collapsed and bank capital evaporated as lenders covered the resulting losses. The question of why regulators failed to take earlier and more aggressive action is interesting but also beyond the scope of this chapter. It was not for lack of information on borrower credit profiles or signs of the growing risk of a home price bubble, however. Indeed, much of the debate over how to prevent a similar credit crisis in the future focuses on how much the government should become involved in limiting the risk-taking behavior that borrowers and lenders are otherwise willing to accept.[25]

Enhanced Competition

Because it dramatically reduces the cost of assessing the risk of new borrowers, credit report information encourages marketplace entry by new lenders and greater competition. A significant obstacle to new entry into an established loan market is the prospect that the only customers interested in the new lender's product are the ones who have been rejected by other lenders because of their higher risk. This problem of adverse selection can sharply limit the number of competitors in a market, especially if information on borrowers' past credit experience is costly to obtain (see Dell'Ariccia, Friedman, and Marquez, 1999). Credit report information lowers those costs. Other things being equal, the more detailed the credit history available to new entrants, the more competitive will be the market for new loans.

The massive new entry into the US bank credit card market beginning in the late 1980s provides a compelling example of how credit report data facilitate rapid entry into new geographic markets. Through the late 1970s, most credit card holders acquired their cards through their local financial institutions, often by

---

25. For an extended discussion of the subprime mortgage meltdowns and resulting financial crisis, see Sowell (2009) and Zandi (2009).

applying at a branch. Customers in smaller towns had fewer choices than residents of large cities, because few banks issued credit cards to customers outside their charter state. Because local institutions faced little threat of entry, there was little variance in either credit card prices or product features (see Knittel and Stango 2003).

All of this began to change by the mid- to late 1980s. A key Supreme Court decision in 1978 gave national banks the ability to launch national credit card marketing programs without being constrained by cross-state differences in the legal limits on pricing.[26] The nationwide availability of detailed credit histories for potential card holder prospects made it possible for companies to enter new geographic markets. Established, full-service banks with credit card programs (for example, Citibank, Bank of America, and First Chicago National Bank) began national marketing campaigns. Over the course of the next decade, the opportunity to market credit cards nationally through the mail, without a network of brick-and-mortar branches, spawned the entry of branchless, "monoline" credit card specialists such as MBNA, Providian, First USA, and Capital One.

Beginning in 1985 and continuing through the early 1990s, retail stores and manufacturers including Sears, General Motors, Ford, AT&T, and General Electric also began introducing their own "co-branded" bank credit cards as unique alternatives to the traditional Visa and MasterCard products offered by established banks. These entrants combined data about existing customers of their corporate affiliates with information from credit reports and other external sources to identify and reach likely prospects. Entry often occurred with astounding speed.[27] The use of credit report data to prescreen borrowers and target desirable prospects provided the jet fuel for an acceleration in card offerings and competition.[28]

Entry initially generated aggressive nonprice competition. Many of these new products came without the annual fees prevalent at the time and gave consumers an opportunity to earn cash rebates or free products and services depending on their charge volume. As a result, cards offering frequent-traveler miles, rebates, and other consumer benefits became commonplace.

26. *Marquette National Bank of Minneapolis v. First of Omaha Service Corp.*, 439 US 299, 310 (1978).

27. Following its introduction in 1992, the General Motors MasterCard product established 2 million accounts and more than $500 million of balances in its first sixty days on the market. This made it the most successful credit card launch in US history (see Dickson 1992, 26).

28. The number of direct mail credit card solicitations soared from 1.0 billion in 1989 to 2.4 billion in 1994 (see Stango 2000). Staten and Cate (2003) provided a case study of MBNA Corporation, the large monoline credit card issuer that was among the top three bank credit card issuers in the United States until its acquisition by Bank of America in 2005. The study offered a detailed description of how a large national credit card issuer utilized credit report data, externally acquired demographic information, and data about the existing customers of its corporate affiliates to successfully target millions of profitable customers throughout the United States via direct mail and telephone solicitations.

The wave of new entrants to the credit card market put increasing downward pressure on the finance charge rate and annual fees charged by existing issuers. Incumbent credit card issuers saw attrition escalate, particularly among their lower-risk customers.[29] Competitors knew no geographic boundaries, and their offers reached consumer mailboxes from thousands of miles away. Knittel and Stango (2003) found that the flood of new entrants eventually broke what had been a pattern of tacit price collusion among incumbent banks for more than a decade. All of this was possible because credit bureau data provided a low-cost means of assessing the risk of potential new customers, negating some of the advantages of the incumbent issuers.

Increased Mobility of Labor and Capital

Economic studies have found that the proliferation of computer and information technology during the 1990s was associated with the productivity surge in the United States. However, what was remarkable about this development was that the same factors were available worldwide, but for the most part, there was not similar productivity growth elsewhere. Economists who study productivity growth pointed to the US institutions that promote efficiency in labor and capital markets as the basis for the flexibility and resiliency of the US economy at that time.[30] These institutions allow both capital and labor to reallocate to their highest-valued uses.

Credit bureaus in the United States are good examples of such institutions. Portable credit "reputations" promote greater mobility for consumers. There is less risk associated with severing old relationships and starting new ones, because objective information is available that helps US residents to establish and build financial trust in new locations more quickly. From a labor market perspective, structural shifts within the economy can cause temporary disruptions without crippling longer-term effects.

In contrast, more restrictive credit reporting laws in Europe prevent consumers in the European Union from taking full advantage of their complete credit histories. The fact that credit information is not mobile can restrict the mobility of consumers themselves, especially across borders, because of the resulting difficulty of obtaining credit from new institutions. Consumer lending in Europe tends to be concentrated among a few major banks in each country, each of which has its own large customer databases.

A well-developed credit reporting system also makes capital more mobile. Securitization of consumer loans has been a prime example (discussed in chapter 5). Comprehensive credit reporting allows investors in securities backed by credit card, automobile, and mortgage receivables to cut through the "fog of

---

29. For a description of the attrition pressures that eventually led to steep rate cuts by incumbent issuers, see Hilder and Pae (1991), Spiro (1991), Pae (1992), and various issues of *Credit Card News* in 1992.

30. For example, see Gust and Marquez (2004).

uncertainty" to evaluate the underlying accounts better. Borrower credit risk scores and account performance data are used by analysts to rate the quality of the securitized receivables, which facilitates appropriate pricing of the asset-backed securities. The transparency of risk in individual loans enables creditors to document and pool loans of similar risk and sell them to investors (see chapter 5). As a result, the securitization process brings loanable funds into consumer and mortgage credit markets, making credit cheaper and more readily available.

To be sure, unexpected losses in securitized mortgage loan receivables were at the heart of the financial contagion that caused global credit markets to freeze in the third quarter of 2008. The procedures and contracts used to package mortgage-backed securities for sale in secondary markets appear to have been a prime suspect in creating uncertainty about who was responsible for underlying losses at the time and about the size of those losses. More direct oversight of the securitization market is in store but precisely because the securitization process has been so valuable in making huge quantities of investor funds available to loan markets.[31]

Another area in which credit reporting has facilitated the influx of new capital in the United States is the financing of small business start-ups. Here again, the ready availability and comprehensive nature of US credit reports has given American small business formation a unique advantage. According to the National Federation of Independent Businesses, seven out of ten small business owners start their businesses with less than $20,000.[32] By the early 1990s, credit analysts had determined that personal credit reports for small business owners and partners were highly predictive of the success of the business, and commercial credit scoring for evaluating small business loans were introduced to the market in 1995.[33] Subsequent research found that the adoption of small business credit scoring expanded the volume of loans and caused a net increase in lending to relatively risky marginal borrowers that would not otherwise receive credit (Berger, Frame and Miller, 2005). This result mirrors findings discussed

31. Commercial rating agencies that evaluate the quality of asset-backed securities also appear responsible for accepting large fees from issuers of securities in exchange for high ratings, without the necessary degree of careful scrutiny of the underlying assets using information (such as credit scores and property valuation data) that was readily available. For more on this last point, see US House of Representatives, Committee on Oversight and Government Reform, hearing on "Credit Rating Agencies and the Financial Crisis," October 22, 2008. In early 2013, the federal government sued rating agency Standard and Poor's over these issues arising in the earlier mortgage meltdown.

32. National Federation of Independent Businesses (www.nfib.com). From this source, small businesses represent more than 99 percent of all employers in the United States, create about two-thirds of all net new jobs, and account for about half of privately generated gross domestic product.

33. Fair Isaac introduced its Small Business Scoring System in 1995 in a joint effort with Philadelphia-based Risk Management Association (formerly Robert Morris Associates, or RMA), a trade association of lenders. See Mester (1997, 7).

previously regarding the positive benefits of credit scoring for credit availability in consumer markets.

Credit Availability and Economic Resiliency

As discussed in chapter 3, consumer credit allows households to change the timing of consumption. This is particularly important for families early in their life cycle (ranging in age of adults from the early twenties through their forties), when the demand for housing, durable goods, and education is relatively high, and income is relatively low but expected to rise over time. But credit can also be important for households weathering temporary income disruptions or unexpected expense shocks.

The availability of consumer credit to bridge income disruptions has important macroeconomic implications. Cross-country studies have found that credit availability and consumption fluctuations are linked. Consumer spending is more sensitive to changes in income in countries with less developed consumer credit markets, especially during periods of tighter credit constraints (Bacchetta and Gerlach, 1997). Credit markets that make loans accessible to large segments of the population can provide a cushion that neutralizes the macroeconomic drag associated with temporary declines in income, lowering the risk of outright recession and reducing the magnitude of downturns when they do occur (Krueger and Perri, 2002).

These studies imply that the United States and other countries with comprehensive credit reporting systems enjoy a macroeconomic growth advantage as a consequence of well-developed consumer credit markets. In a study of forty-three countries, Jappelli and Pagano (1989) found that total bank lending to the private sector (scaled by country GNP) is larger in countries where information sharing through credit reporting is more solidly established and intense, even after controlling for factors such as country size, growth rates, and the legal environment. In addition, the volume of consumer and mortgage lending in a country rises as a direct result of greater information sharing within a country's credit reporting system (Jappelli and Pagano, 2002).

The intuition for both results is straightforward. Detailed personal credit history data give lenders confidence in assessing the risk associated with new borrowers. Such data also allow lenders to design and price products to meet the credit needs of previously underserved populations. Because of the underlying credit reporting network, US consumers can get credit, insurance, and a host of other financial services based on their individual credit records, not their family name or how long they have known their banker. In addition, they can rent apartments, purchase cell phones and cable television service, and rent automobiles without either large deposits or an established relationship with the service provider, all because their reputation for paying as agreed is documented through their credit reports.

A benefit not to be overlooked is the remarkable speed at which these credit-related decisions can take place. The depth of information in US credit reports enhances the speed of credit, insurance, and other financial service decisions. Even very significant decisions about financing college tuition or a new home are often made in a matter of minutes, instead of days or weeks, as is the case in many other countries, because credit history data are readily accessible.[34]

DATA QUALITY ISSUES AND IMPLICATIONS FOR CREDIT SCORING

Chapter 5 discussed how lenders and other providers of credit services have become increasingly reliant on credit bureau risk scores, such as the FICO score and its competitors, to make a wide range of credit-related decisions. The relatively low-cost availability of credit report data, coupled with the predictive power of scoring models based on it, makes the credit bureau risk score almost irresistible to lenders who need to make large numbers of rapid and consistent decisions. Nonetheless, ubiquitous use of bureau-based scoring models has raised some concerns.

For example, credit bureau risk scores are built only with credit report data, and this means they are subject to omitted variable bias (see Avery et al. 2000). No other information that might be predictive is utilized, including borrower income, employment, demographic data, assets, or local economic conditions.[35] Moreover, the credit history data on which the entire scoring model is based could be incomplete in a voluntary credit reporting environment, but a model based on credit bureau scoring has no other information on which to make an assessment.

Further, in a country in which use of credit and other financial services is known to vary considerably across population subgroups, a model based solely on credit report data may have been estimated over a different population or product than that for which it will be used to predict future performance. If the experience of certain populations, such as young consumers, is underrepresented in the sample used to develop the model, then it is possible that the scoring model may not correctly represent the risk associated with members of those groups.

Such difficulties may impair the effectiveness of the scoring model to match creditworthy borrowers to loans. As problems of this kind increase, lenders might find that they have taken on greater risk than anticipated (if the resulting credit

34. A bit more than a decade ago, a survey of auto lenders in the United States revealed that 84 percent of automobile loan applicants in 2001 received a decision within an hour; 23 percent of applicants received a decision in less than ten minutes (Consumer Bankers Association 2002).

35. Bureau scores are usually developed without incorporating local or regional economic data, but Avery et al. (2000) and Fellowes (2006) found that median credit scores vary significantly with local economic conditions. It also would be important for a creditor to know individual economic circumstances. Without such data, the model would treat someone who performs poorly while unemployed the same as someone who compiled a similar credit profile (and credit score) while employed. This would likely mean that despite identical credit scores, the two borrowers have very different likelihoods of payment difficulty in the future.

bureau scoring model underestimates the risk), or worthy borrowers might be denied credit opportunities (if the model overestimates the risk).

Chapter 5 briefly discussed the incorporation of local economic conditions as proxies for individual characteristics that are otherwise excluded from bureau-based scoring models, but there is much more to the question of insufficient information than is reviewed there. The remainder of this section of the chapter examines evidence on the quality of credit report data that are the foundation for the ubiquitous bureau-based credit score in the United States. The issue of whether widespread reliance on bureau-based scoring models results in unfair treatment of some groups is discussed further in chapter 9.

Credit Report Quality

Since implementation of the FCRA in 1971, accuracy in credit reporting has been a perennial issue. During the congressional hearings leading up to passage of the FACT Act, consumer advocacy groups argued that the changing market for credit products called for renewed scrutiny of credit file content. They correctly pointed out that not only can an inaccurate depiction of a consumer's credit history trigger a rejection of a loan application, but the advent of risk-based pricing can also lead to overpricing loans for which the borrower is approved. One advocacy group asserted that inaccuracies in credit reports could cause at least 8 million Americans to be miscategorized as subprime risks and pay tens of thousands of dollars in excess interest payments over the term of a thirty-year mortgage loan (see Brobeck 2003).

At the request of Congress, the US General Accounting Office (GAO, later Government Accountability Office) undertook a review during 2003 of available studies and databases to determine the frequency, type, and cause of credit report errors (see General Accounting Office 2003). It concluded that "the lack of comprehensive information regarding the accuracy of consumer credit reports inhibits any meaningful discussion of what more could or should be done to improve credit report accuracy. Available studies suggest that accuracy could be a problem, but no study has been performed that is representative of the universe of credit reports" (see statement of Richard J. Hillman, in General Accounting Office 2003, 17).

Accuracy is a stated goal of the reporting system, but exactly what does that mean? The FCRA itself is not clear on this point. It states that consumer reporting agencies must "follow reasonable procedures to assure maximum possible accuracy."[36] Accuracy is not defined, however, nor is it clear what should be expected about the quality of credit files once the upper limits of reasonable procedures are reached.

Files can contain certain factual errors, such as misspelled name, outdated address, misspelled current street, and so on, but still be accurate representations of a consumer's credit history. Also, files often contain stale or outdated

36. 15 USC 1681e(b).

information, such as outstanding balances that are thirty to sixty days old, and so on. Most stale information was accurate at the time it was submitted, but with continued activity on an account (charge activity, payments, etc.), the information can become outdated very quickly.

Conversely, files can be factually correct but provide an incomplete representation of a consumer's credit history because of missing accounts. Currently, for the vast majority of consumers in the United States, conventional credit files are missing entire categories of relevant information, such as a history of rent or utility payments.[37] For most of these consumers, their credit files are sufficiently rich in other elements of conventional credit history to predict future risk accurately, even without the rent and utility payment history. But for an estimated 35 million to 54 million Americans with "thin" or nonexistent files, the conventional credit history fields are not sufficient for predicting future payment risk, and the data on rental and utility payments can provide a more accurate representation of credit-related behavior (see Lee et al. 2006, 2).

As discussed earlier, there may be good reasons that perfect accuracy in all historical details is not desirable. The FCRA specifically limits the reporting of old derogatory information as part of a consumer's credit profile. Delinquencies, charge-offs, repossessions, and collection activity cannot be reported after seven years, personal bankruptcy after ten years. So some degree of inaccuracy is mandatory under the FCRA in the interest of giving consumers a fresh start.[38]

Further reflection suggests that the importance of "accuracy" of a credit file is dependent on the purpose to which the information will be put. The relevant question is not how accurate the file is but rather whether credit report files contain

---

37. Utility account information does appear in US credit reports, but Lee et al. (2006) report that less than 5 percent of all credit files have payment information on one or more utility or telecommunication accounts. Such "alternative" credit history data make up less than 1 percent of all trade lines in one major credit bureau's database.

38. Proponents of accelerated deletion argue that old information is "stale" and therefore may no longer be relevant to determining an individual's creditworthiness, but the point at which "old" information becomes "stale" and unpredictive is not at all clear. Empirical work conducted in 1990 by Fair Isaac on behalf of a credit reporting industry trade association demonstrated that "the presence of derogatory information continues to distinguish levels of credit risk in the studied populations even as the information ages" (Fair Isaac Companies 1990, 3).

A separate study also conducted and published in 1990 by a competing scorecard developer found that "significantly more people who declare bankruptcy have older public record derogatory information but none in recent years, than do all people. As a result, if creditors are not allowed to know of public record derogatory information that is four years old or older, they may lose an important predictor of future bankruptcy" (Lyons and Allen 1990, 6).

More recently, a startling study by Musto (2004) found that the mandatory removal of a bankruptcy indicator from individual credit reports (after ten years, as required by the FCRA) led to an artificial boost in credit scores, excessive acquisition of new debt in the short run, and eventual scores that had fallen back below their level just preceding the mandatory roll-off. In short, even after ten years on the file, the bankruptcy flag was still a predictive indicator of higher risk for the debtor. Musto concluded that "this is concrete evidence that the flag removal has real economic effects" (Musto 2004, 747).

sufficient information to allow creditors and other authorized users to assess the eligibility of consumers for the services they seek. Credit file *quality* may be a better term than *accuracy* for assessing how well the credit reporting system performs in facilitating opportunities for consumers, where quality refers to the predictive value of information contained in the file.

File quality is affected both by information that is present but potentially misleading and by information that is missing but could be useful. At the risk of oversimplifying, consider two categories of file inaccuracies or "errors." *Errors of commission* consist of items that find their way into a consumer's file that were never correct at any time, such as accounts and public record items that do not belong to the consumer or delinquencies that never occurred. For most consumers, "errors in credit reports" probably connotes an image of errors of commission. This is especially true for victims of identity theft. In contrast, *errors of omission* are items or updates that do not appear in the file, such as missing balances or credit limits, outdated information on account status or last reported balance, missing records of prior payment history on accounts (both positive and negative), and existing but unreported accounts. Both types of errors reduce file accuracy and may or may not reduce a file's quality in terms of its value for assessing risk.

As the General Accounting Office (2003) noted, statistically representative information on the accuracy of file content is sparse. The few statistically representative studies of credit file accuracy conducted to date have necessarily focused on file inconsistencies within a given file. Such studies pose fewer obstacles for researchers, because they do not require the consumer's participation in the review of credit reports. Without consumer participation, however, researchers are constrained to identifying information in a single credit file that is either missing or inconsistent with other information in the file or inconsistent with a credit file on the same consumer from another bureau. It is worth reviewing two significant studies.

Federal Reserve Board Study of Credit File Quality

In 2003, research staff at the Federal Reserve Board examined a large, nationally representative random sample of 248,000 consumer credit reports as of June 1999 (Avery et al. 2003). The sample was supplied by one of the three major credit bureaus. Each record contained approximately 350 variables that described credit use and payment performance. In total, the sample contained information on 2.58 million credit accounts, from more than 23,000 furnishers of information.

The authors found that the degree of reporting by those data furnishers who chose to report was quite comprehensive.[39] Only about one-half of one percent of all accounts were reported by creditors that report only negative information (i.e.,

---

39. Some small retail, mortgage, and finance companies and some government agencies did not report to the credit reporting agencies. In addition, loans extended by individuals, employers, insurance companies, and foreign entities typically were not reported.

do not report accounts in good standing). This is remarkably low by international standards.[40]

The authors noted, however, that "although credit reporting company data are extensive, they are not complete.... Complete information is not always provided for each account reported. Sometimes creditors do not report or update information on the credit accounts of borrowers who consistently make their required payments as scheduled. Credit limits established on revolving accounts are sometimes not reported" (Avery et al. 2003, 50). They also noted that credit report information is perishable. Some pieces of information, such as outstanding balance on revolving credit card accounts, can become outdated the day after the information is sent to the credit bureau. All of these issues make credit files merely an approximation of the borrower's credit profile. Data fields that the authors singled out as particularly troublesome included the following:

(1) Missing credit limits. About one-third of the open revolving accounts in the sample were missing information on the account's credit limit; about 70 percent of all consumers in the sample had a missing credit limit on one or more of their revolving accounts. Missing credit limits are a concern, because the credit limit on a revolving account is used to calculate revolving account utilization (how much of an available credit line the consumer has utilized), which is an important factor in determining a borrower's credit bureau risk scores. A higher utilization rate correlates with higher risk. On accounts missing the credit limit, creditors typically substitute the highest previous balance (if available) in place of the actual account limit. This typically will overstate utilization and, therefore, overstate risk.

Further analysis showed that the missing limits were mostly attributable to a relatively small group of creditors that apparently were routine nonreporters of limits and reported limits on fewer than 5 percent of their accounts. The authors found that 12 percent of creditors accounted for 74 percent of all missing limits. They also found that, for the most part, the nonreporting of limits affected prime and subprime consumers equally. There was no strong evidence of discriminatory underreporting on subprime accounts (as might be the case if a lender was trying to shield such accounts from competitive offers). There was a small group of subprime lending specialists, however, about 5 percent of all creditors in the analysis, that reported credit limits selectively, reporting 77 percent of limits for prime customers versus 40 percent for subprime customers.[41]

40. As discussed previously in this chapter, negative-only reporting poses two problems: (1) because some consumer accounts and balances are not reported, overindebtedness problems are masked, leading to erroneously positive risk assessment for some borrowers, and (2) some consumers miss out on the positive effects of well-handled accounts, because their accounts in good standing are not reported.

41. The authors noted that their findings on missing credit limits were especially sensitive to the period in which the sample was selected (1999). In the late 1990s, several large credit card issuers had stopped reporting account limits for competitive reasons (see Fickenscher 1999 and Timmons 2000). Pressure from credit bureaus and the banking regulators substantially reduced such nonreporting, so that by 2003, the authors found in a new representative sample that credit limits were missing on only about 14 percent of accounts (see Avery, Calem, and Canner 2004, 306).

(2) Balance information significantly out of date. One of the useful dimensions of a comprehensive credit report is that it allows calculation of a borrower's total outstanding debt, but a meaningful calculation requires accurate and up-to-date information on outstanding balances. Avery, Calem, and Canner (2004) found that 92 percent of accounts in the sample had reported information that would allow a creditor to determine the balance without ambiguity. The remaining 8 percent of accounts showed positive balances but no recent reporting of activity (that is, the last report was more than two months before the sample date). These balances accounted for more than 25 percent of total balance dollars (many of them involved mortgage loans). In addition, nearly 60 percent of all accounts that indicated a major derogatory item at last reporting were among these 8 percent of accounts for which the actual balance was questionable. Accounts with both an outstanding balance and a major derogatory item listed as the last reported status can have a significant negative impact on consumers applying for credit.[42]

(3) Nonreporting of minor delinquency. About 11 percent of all accounts were reported by creditors who did not report delinquencies of less than one hundred twenty days. An additional 12 percent of all accounts were reported by creditors that did not report delinquencies of less than sixty days. In other words, there is a significant amount of underreporting of minor delinquency in the system, even though data on payment problems have been shown to be the most predictive factor in scoring models. As a consequence, the credit scores of many borrowers are higher (better) than they would otherwise be, indicating that scoring models are underestimating the risk of some consumers.

(4) Inconsistent reporting of public records, collection agency accounts, and inquiries. For consumers with derogatory public record information or collection agency activity in their files, about 40 percent have more than one such record. The study authors found that for many of these consumers, the multiple listings were associated with the same episode, for example, one record posted when collection action initiated and another record posted when account paid. To the extent that the creditors' risk assessment tools count these flags as separate incidents when they actually are not, double counting could penalize consumers. The study found that the data lacked sufficiently detailed codes to allow a creditor to distinguish multiple events associated with the same incident from multiple incidents. The same was generally true of multiple inquiries in a credit file. Data furnishers failed to provide the appropriate code for their inquiry in 98 percent of the inquiry records. Consequently, a creditor examining multiple inquiries in a credit file would not be able to determine if multiple inquiries reflected shopping around for the best loan to finance a single purchase or applications for multiple loans. The first interpretation would have much less impact on risk assessment than the second.

---

42. The report indicated that many of the nonderogatory accounts (especially mortgages and installment loans) in this group were likely closed or sold to other companies but were not reported as such. For their part, the three major credit reporting agencies claim to have recognized this problem and developed stale-account rules that reset balances to zero and mark an account closed under certain conditions.

The problems identified by the Avery, et al. (2003) study involved credit file information that was missing, clearly outdated, or ambiguous, but the report did not tackle the important question of how much the reduction in file quality affected credit options for consumers, as determined by impact on the credit score. Systematic correction of the data shortcomings in each of these categories (if it were feasible) would unambiguously improve the performance of risk models to some degree by providing a more accurate picture of each borrower's credit profile. The study noted, however, that the resulting improvement in clarity would not unambiguously help consumers seeking more credit; it would help some consumers and harm others. For example, some consumers with unreported accounts in good standing are harmed by not being acknowledged for building a good credit record. Other consumers are helped because creditors do not see the full extent of their indebtedness. Similarly, more complete reporting of revolving account limits helps those whose balances are well below limits and harms those with balances at or near the limits. In each of these cases, of course, the impact of missing or ambiguous data is very much dependent on the other information present in the consumer's file.

To address the relationship between file accuracy and access to credit, the authors conducted an innovative follow-up study with another nationally representative sample of credit reports taken in June 2003 from the same major bureau (see Avery, Calem, and Canner 2004). Because the credit bureau provided credit scores along with the full set of underlying credit report data, the authors attempted to reverse-engineer a commercially viable scoring model. This exercise approximated the actual weights that a bureau-based scoring model might assign to credit report elements without actually obtaining the commercial weights.[43] Next, the authors identified fifteen types of anomalies, ambiguities, and instances of missing information in individual credit reports whose "correction" they could simulate. Finally, the authors used their scoring model to determine the impact of the hypothetical corrections on the borrower's credit score.

An example illustrates the analysis. The authors found that one-third of all borrowers had one or more revolving accounts with a missing credit limit. In this example, they found that a simulated correction of this problem would increase the simulated credit score by ten points or more for only 4 percent of borrowers. Overall, the authors concluded that "the effect of each type of problem on the credit history scores of affected individuals was modest" (Avery, Calem, and Canner 2004, 321). They offered two reasons to explain this result. First, most individuals have plenty of other account information in their credit reports, so deficiencies and anomalies of the type studied have relatively little impact. Second, the authors noted that risk scorecard builders are already modifying

43. Actual weights in these models are closely guarded, proprietary information, as they result from multi-million-dollar development efforts and are a potential source of competitive advantage in the marketplace.

their procedures in acknowledgment of some of these problems.[44] However, there is a disproportionate impact of some of these problem areas, especially accounts referred for collection activity, on some groups of borrowers, most notably on those individuals with relatively short or thin credit histories such that negative information is not offset by lots of positive experience.

Most of these problems stem from nonreporting in a voluntary reporting system or from the failure of data furnishers to clarify adequately the information being reported. Avery et al. (2003) suggested that creditors and the credit reporting agencies could jointly develop better codes and reporting protocols for public records and inquiries and encourage their use. The repositories could also expand and refine their stale-account rules and flag the accounts from creditors that are no longer reporting information. These steps would clean up some of the ambiguities in the data.

Consumer Federation of America Comparison of Reports across Bureaus

Another illuminating study was sponsored by the Consumer Federation of America and jointly conducted with the National Credit Reporting Association (Consumer Federation of America and National Credit Reporting Association 2002, the "CFA report"). The CFA report resembles the Federal Reserve Board staff's study in that it identified and tabulated discrepancies and inconsistencies in credit reports, but it added a new dimension by comparing reports for each consumer across all three major credit reporting agencies. The study focused on the magnitude of differences in consumer credit scores across the three major credit bureaus. Differences in credit report content across furnishers of credit reports have always existed to some degree but have declined in recent years. Nevertheless, critics of automated underwriting in mortgage lending worry that the acceleration in the turnaround time for a mortgage decision made possible by credit scoring may be causing some lenders to give short shrift to investigation of differences in credit scores for an applicant, especially in regard to the pricing of the loan.

To determine the frequency with which file discrepancies across the repositories generated relatively large differences in credit scores, the CFA report undertook a manual review of a sample of 1,704 combined credit files for consumers who had applied for mortgages during June 2002. The combined files consolidating separate credit reports from each of the three major bureaus along with calculated FICO risk scores from each bureau had been requested by mortgage lenders in conjunction with mortgage applications. As was the case with the

44. For example, mortgage lenders commonly require a consolidated credit report on borrowers that merges information from all three of the major credit reporting agencies. This reduces the risk posed by data missing from a single repository's file. Regarding ambiguous creditor inquiries, Fair Isaac has indicated that it modified its FICO risk scoring algorithm to recognize multiple inquiries from the same type of lender within a short time period as related to a single transaction, as often occurs with multiple inquiries from auto dealers or auto finance companies (see Fishelson-Holstine 2005, 193–194).

Federal Reserve staff study, the CFA approach could not identify whether information in each file was correct or incorrect; it could only identify inconsistencies and missing data. The CFA sample was not a representative national sample of all consumers, but it did provide intriguing information on the differences in file content across the major repositories for selected mortgage borrowers as of 2002. The results included the following:

(1) Score differences. Twenty-nine percent of consumers had a range of fifty points or more between their highest and lowest FICO scores across the bureaus. Five percent of consumers had a range in excess of one hundred points.

(2) Types and frequency of inconsistencies. The in-depth review of fifty-one combined files quantified the inconsistencies that undoubtedly led to the variance in FICO scores:

One-third of combined files had a mortgage reported by one repository but not all.

Two-thirds of files had an installment loan reported by one repository but not all.

Seventy-eight percent of combined files had a revolving account reported by one repository but not all.

Twelve percent of combined files had a revolving account with late payments reported by one repository but not all.

Eight percent had a revolving account with a charge-off reported by one repository but not all. Twenty percent of files had a medical account collection reported by one depository but not all.

Forty-three percent of combined files had conflicting information across repositories about the number of times an account was thirty days or more late. The report does not indicate, however, how many of these could be differences of only one instance, which could result from different reporting/loading timelines across the three bureaus.[45]

Eighty-two percent of combined files had inconsistencies on account balances, and 96 percent of files had inconsistencies on reported limits.

The results of CFA's comparison of credit file content for the same consumer across the three major repositories serve as a reminder of the voluntary nature of the credit reporting system in the United States. They also highlight how credit reports for most adults today, certainly anyone older than fifty or so who has been active in credit markets, still reflect the regional roots of the reporting industry. All credit bureaus evolved from local operations. End users of credit reports

---

45. Fair Isaac responded to the CFA report by noting that it recognizes the potential for ambiguity in interpreting differences in the number of reported delinquencies on the same account, so it does not include this in its FICO score models. It does include the number of different accounts on which the consumer has been delinquent (see St. John 2003).

widely recognized that the three major repositories still had regional strengths and weaknesses as recently as the mid-1990s. At that time, many medium-sized banks, retail stores and dealers, mortgage companies, and other creditors were still dealing with one, but not all, of the repositories.[46] Some of that reporting heritage remains in the credit files of older adults. These differences will likely fade over time as younger consumers obtain credit in an increasingly national market, from creditors that report to all three bureaus, and the three major repositories devote resources to capturing public record items in all localities and more rapid posting of account updates from furnishers.

Political and Economic Research Council Study

In 2011, the Political and Economic Research Council (PERC) released a new study of the accuracy of credit bureau reports (Turner, Varghese, and Walker 2011). With the help and participation of the three nationwide CRAs, the project enabled selected consumers to review and identify their own credit reports, to file complaints of inaccuracies in the reports through the consumer dispute resolution process governed by the Fair Credit Reporting Act, and to report on the outcomes and their satisfaction. This was the first published study with direct participation of a large sample of consumers in checking their own credit reports for errors. It also allowed for verification of consumer allegations of errors.[47]

The Turner, Varghese, and Walker study involved recruiting consumers to obtain, examine, and comment on by survey their credit reports at one or more of the three large CRAs. Those indicating that they had found errors were urged to file a dispute with the CRA under provisions of the Fair Credit Reporting Act. The CRAs then responded to the dispute filing and recalculated the consumer's credit score after making any relevant corrections. This approach allowed the authors not only to examine the allegations of errors but also to focus on the willingness of those alleging errors to file disputes, which may reveal a great deal about the seriousness of the alleged errors in the consumers' minds, and to see the outcome and significance of the disputes actually filed.[48]

46. Knowing that the depth of credit files differed across the repositories, depending on the geographic location of the consumer, creditors historically adjusted their decisions regarding the company from which to purchase credit reports. Of course, these potential differences in file content are the primary reason mortgage underwriting typically requires a consolidated report based on reports from all three repositories.

47. In 2004, the National Association of State Public Interest Research Groups published results of a consumer survey of possible errors in credit reports. This was a small-scale project, however, and did not well define what was an error with consequence as compared with an inconsistency of some sort. For brief discussion, see Turner, Varghese, and Walker (2011, 16).

48. The methodology for a study of this kind is necessarily quite complex and involves the potential for statistical biases to creep in at multiple stages (see the flow chart of the methodology on page 21 of the Turner, Varghese, and Walker study and discussion there). For this reason, there

Results indicated that participants identified potential errors in about 19 percent of their credit reports. About two-thirds of the individuals in this situation indicated that they had contacted a CRA to file a dispute, and approximately another 15 percent said they still planned to do so. The most common reason given by the others was that the potential errors were too minor to dispute. Among those with potential errors, only about a quarter said they had more than two potential disputes. According to the authors, "The frequency of credit reports having 'many' potential disputes was low, with around 2 percent of all credit reports containing five or more potential disputes" (Turner, Varghese, and Walker 2011, 34).

The authors noted the obvious fact that potential disputes can vary tremendously in importance. In this context, the authors found that about 10 percent of credit reports contained potential disputes over items that might have a material effect, although the true proportion could not actually be known from consumers at the outset of the process. (It could only be known by correcting true errors and then rescoring the account.) The authors were able to examine this distinction by following the dispute resolution process pursued by the disputing consumers and then examining the resulting impact on rescored credit records.

The authors determined that the whole process resulted in an increased credit score of as much as twenty-five points for slightly less than 1 percent of the credit reports originally examined by the panel of subjects. Only one-half of one percent of participants had credit score increases sufficient to migrate to a better "credit risk tier," as the authors discuss and define it on pages 44–45 of the study report. The authors also noted that about 95 percent of disputing participants indicated satisfaction with the outcomes of their disputes, suggesting to the authors "widespread satisfaction among participants with the FCRA dispute resolution process" (Turner, Varghese, and Walker 2011, 8).

Federal Trade Commission Study

As indicated earlier, section 319 of the Fair and Accurate Credit Transactions (FACT) Act of 2003 required the Federal Trade Commission (FTC) to study the accuracy and completeness of information in consumers' credit reports and to consider methods for improving the reporting of such information. Of particular interest to the FTC was information on the factual accuracy of information contained in consumers' files (for example, an erroneously attributed late payment, inquiry for new credit, or public record such as a bankruptcy), as opposed to the errors of omission that were well documented in the Federal Reserve Board studies. The FTC commissioned two pilot studies between 2005 and 2008 to develop

has been some critical discussion of the methodology that has caused the authors to issue some further discussion of their own (see Political and Economic Research Council 2011). Review of the original report and the discussion of the criticisms suggests that the authors recognized the potential for biases and took steps to minimize them and correct for them as far as they could.

a research methodology that could be employed in a comprehensive nationwide study of credit report accuracy.

Based on findings from these feasibility pilot studies, the FTC commissioned a full national study in 2010 that (1) involved engagement of consumers in detailed reviews of their credit reports, (2) educated the consumers as necessary on the contents, (3) identified alleged inaccuracies found in the credit reports, (4) assisted consumers in preparing dispute letters that properly addressed the issues, (5) followed up to determine the results of disputes (as indicated by rein-spection of credit reports sixty days later), and (6) recalculated credit scores to measure the impact of changes to the record. A representative sample of one thou-sand consumers was recruited to review their credit reports from the three major US credit bureaus, with guidance from the researchers. Fair Isaac collaborated with the research team to provide consumers with credit reports and FICO credit scores.

The results of this careful study revealed error frequencies similar to, if some-what higher than, those in the Turner, Varghese, and Walker (2011) study. In the FTC study, 26 percent of study participants claimed to find at least one poten-tially material error *and* filed formal disputes with the relevant credit bureau(s). For 20 percent of participants overall (78 percent of the 263 consumers who filed disputes), at least one bureau altered the credit report accordingly. Thirty-three percent of disputants (8.7 percent of all participants) experienced a resulting increase of ten or more points in one or more of their FICO scores. Twenty-one percent of disputants (5.5 percent of study participants) had one or more scores cross a threshold that would typically result in more favorable terms of credit.

What are we to make of the results from these varied studies regarding credit file accuracy? Compared with unscientific studies over the past decade that reported error rates as high as 60 to 70 percent, both the PERC and the FTC study findings are something of a relief. Both studies were methodologically superior to previous studies for judging the accuracy of information actually contained in a credit report, because they used representative random sampling, involved consumers in a review of their own reports, utilized the FCRA's dispute resolu-tion process to validate alleged errors, and judged the severity of actual errors in terms of impact on the consumer's credit score. Coupled with previous studies that focused more directly on errors of omission, the evidence suggests that credit bureau data are sufficiently accurate to facilitate efficient lending and creditors' management of accounts, but individual consumers need to be vigilant to protect themselves against potentially costly errors in their files. For nearly 95 percent of consumers, any problems in their credit reports are minor and do not appear to have much impact on their credit-related opportunities. But 5.5 percent of the FTC sample represents more than 10 million individuals economy-wide for whom errors would likely impose a significant cost in the form of denial of service or a significantly higher interest rate.

There is, of course, one important but underutilized remedy for this "accu-racy" problem already in place. As noted earlier, since the Fair Credit Reporting Act (FCRA) of 1971, consumers have had the right to check their credit reports and to dispute apparent errors with the bureau. Since 2003, they have been able to do so once a year for each bureau, free of charge. The FCRA was designed to serve as a warranty that defects discovered by the consumer would be investigated and rectified promptly, with minimal cost to the consumer. Assigning the consumer the role of quality inspector with the authority to demand reinvestigation and correction of errors was a brilliant stroke on the part of the authors of the original law.

It appears, however, that only a minority of consumers participate in this important role. A 2012 survey sponsored by the National Foundation for Credit Counseling found that only 38 percent of consumers *said* they had requested a copy of their credit reports within the past twelve months (see National Foundation for Credit Counseling 2012). A Consumer Financial Protection Bureau report in December 2012 used credit bureau data to conclude that only 20 percent of consumers had actually followed through and viewed a credit report in the past twelve months (Consumer Financial Protection Bureau 2012).

Summary

Despite some element of inaccuracy that appears inevitable in a credit reporting system involving millions of diverse and mobile consumers, evidence to date does not suggest a huge element of significant and avoidable error in the system. There is ample evidence that, detailed as they are, credit files in the United States do not represent an exhaustive listing of all past credit experience for many borrowers. Yet, despite missing some elements of borrower's past credit history, the credit files produced by the voluntary reporting system in the United States are the most comprehensive of any reporting system in the world. More important, US credit files support risk assessment tools, such as scoring models, that are able to rank borrowers according to likelihood of repayment with remarkable precision. The 2003 Federal Reserve Board staff study concluded that "research and creditor experience has consistently indicated that credit reporting company information, despite any limitations that it may have, generally provides an effective measure of the relative credit risk posed by prospective borrowers."[49] The authors further observed: "Available evidence indicates that these data and the credit scoring models derived from them have substantially improved the overall quality of credit decisions and have reduced the costs of such decision making" (Avery et al. 2003, 70). Almost certainly, consumers would receive less credit and the price of the credit they received would be higher, if not for the information provided by credit reporting companies.

That said, it is also clear that there is room for improvement in making consumer credit reports more complete representations of each consumer's past and current credit experience. The problem, of course, is that steps to further reduce credit report errors or inconsistencies impose costs on the credit reporting system and the consumers and businesses that rely on them. Depending on where the

---

49. Avery et al. (2003, 51). See also Avery at al. (1996).

regulatory burden is placed, these steps could lead to dropout by data furnishers, thus reducing the completeness and predictive value of credit reports.[50]

Commenting on the incentives for accuracy under the FCRA, Staten and Cate contended:

> Ultimately the consumer pays. How much accuracy are we willing to buy? Prescriptions involving more regulatory requirements on furnishers and bureaus are offered up easily by industry critics, but every one of them involves a tradeoff—imposes a cost—that is rarely articulated. The FCRA is all about balancing these tradeoffs ... [that are] inherent in any reporting system, especially the US system which owes so much of its effectiveness to reliance on voluntary reporting and competitive incentives to innovate new products and risk management services. (Staten and Cate 2005, 262–263)

50. Turner (2003), using credit bureau files, simulated a variety of furnisher dropout scenarios and also restrictions that would eliminate the reporting of minor delinquencies and the impact on the predictive power of credit bureau scoring models.

Consumer Credit and the
Payments System

Evolution of the Credit Card

Rapid growth in the availability and use of credit cards is certainly high on the list of significant changes in consumer financial services in the United States over the past few decades. Little more than a curiosity fifty years ago, credit cards today are the most ubiquitous consumer financial product except for deposit accounts.[1] Credit cards have ensured their place in the modern economy by becoming a ready means of making ordinary payments but also because they are the most convenient and commonest means of accessing consumer credit. Data collected by the Federal Reserve Board show that (nonmortgage) total consumer credit outstanding in the United States increased from $119 billion at year end 1968 to $3 trillion at the end of 2013 (in current dollars, not seasonally adjusted). Of this total, the revolving credit component, consisting of both credit card and other unsecured revolving credit but mostly card credit, grew from $2 billion to about $862 billion over the same period. During the past three and a half decades, credit cards have become easier to obtain, although since the financial crisis in 2008–2009 more difficult for subprime risks than earlier. By the beginning of the new century, many adult Americans had multiple credit cards in their pockets and purses.

Credit cards are, of course, much more than credit devices. Small pieces of plastic, specifically credit cards but also debit cards that directly access deposit accounts and do not originate credit balances, have become an important modern means for making routine payments. There are many reasons cards have gained importance for payments.

Payment cards enable consumers to minimize cash, thereby limiting the chances for loss or theft associated with carrying and handling cash. Further, payment cards provide easier usability than checks and, therefore, greater convenience for consumers when the merchant does not know the consumer. They

---

1. For lively historical accounts of the formation of the credit card industry, see Mandell (1990) and Nocera (1994).

minimize bad debt risk for merchants. Credit cards also permit consumers to economize on checking account balances for much of the month. For these and other reasons, payment cards have become much more widely accepted by merchants over time and today are usable for many purposes worldwide. In some areas of commerce, such as car rental and purchase of airline tickets, plastic cards with numbers on the front and strips of magnetic tape on the back or an internal chip have become virtually the only means of payment. Even at domestic grocery stores and doctors' offices, payment by card has become acceptable and often preferred. Some taxis now accept plastic cards for fare payment, and it is possible to use cards to pay for subway and bus public transportation. Many colleges accept them for tuition payments, and auto dealers often accept cards for down payments and sometimes for payment in full. The extensive and growing catalog and Internet retailing industry probably could not function as we know it today without availability of the electronic accounts evidenced by plastic payments cards. With the spread of electronic vending machines and sales terminals, it is difficult to imagine any area of legal payments in the future where plastic access devices will be entirely absent. A major societal change has taken place in only a few decades.[2]

Dramatic improvements in data processing and electronic communications in recent decades have made it feasible to use cards for myriad payments but also, in the case of credit cards, for instantaneous access to more convenient revolving credit. Credit cards as credit access devices represent significant technological change. They allow more convenient and less costly credit origination and have substituted for older kinds of retail installment credit, as discussed in chapters 1 and 5. Declining interest rates on card credit since the early 1990s have also encouraged substitution of card credit for other kinds of consumer credit.

Thus, the amount of card credit outstanding is the sum of the true credit amount and the amount generated in the process of making routine payments. This sort of "convenience credit" is a result of a cultural tradition in the United States that has long permitted creditworthy individuals to defer payment for many retail purchases without cost until presented a bill at the end of the month. As discussed in chapter 1, historically many retail establishments offered customers charge accounts that allowed customers to defer and accumulate payments for purchases for up to thirty days. (These accounts were not always accessed by using a card.) Today convenience credit arises because credit card bills are not received instantaneously upon card use, but there is no charge if the bills are paid in full by the due date, usually about three weeks after the bill arrives. Convenience credit is counted as credit outstanding in the statistics gathering process, but to the typical consumer, it is just a delay in money outflow, much like

2. For extended discussion of consumers' choice of payments medium, see Zywicki (2000a) and Evans and Schmalensee (2005). For a more technical discussion, see Brito and Hartley (1995), also discussed here in chapter 4.

"float" on a check before the recipient deposits or cashes it, rather than true credit use in the consumer's view.

It is the consumer credit aspect of plastic payment cards that makes them controversial, however, as discussed earlier, especially in chapter 4. Because of their convenience, their prevalence, and the rapid growth pattern mentioned above, and because consumer delinquencies, defaults, and bankruptcies have also grown in recent decades, the view has arisen in some quarters that maybe consumer credit growth has been excessive and problematic, especially growth with credit cards. Discussion in chapter 2 suggested that consumer credit has not risen as much or as rapidly as commonly supposed, at least in comparison with other important economic magnitudes, but concern continues. Chapter 4 reported how some observers contend that much credit card use is irrational, but neither their theoretical arguments nor empirical evidence warrants this conclusion without substantial additional discussion. Nonetheless, the view persists in some quarters that credit cards are mostly troublesome. Chapter 13 examines more closely the suggestion that credit cards are the cause of higher consumer bankruptcies in recent decades.

Today the credit card is a relatively mature product that has settled into and filled a niche in the marketplace, serving both as a payment device and as access to consumer credit. Consumers seem to like the convenience provided by cards both for making payments and for accessing consumer credit, but attitude studies suggest that they maintain a wary eye toward them. This is not especially surprising, since consumers always have been a bit suspicious of credit and creditors, especially when they contemplate how others may be using credit and their credit cards. Because of this suspicion that sometimes generates complaints, regulators and congressional committees also maintain a watchful eye on developments in the credit card area.

This chapter examines the modern credit card phenomenon in more detail than heretofore in this book, extending to credit cards the various themes developed in earlier chapters. The first section describes the kinds of credit cards found readily in the marketplace today, the size of the domestic market, and who holds and uses credit cards. The following section describes consumers' attitudes toward credit cards. It shows that consumers find credit cards to be useful for their credit demand and financial affairs generally but also are wary of them, maybe responding to negative impressions they have of the experience that other consumers may have had with credit cards. The next section explores how consumers actually use their cards, with some information on how often they pay off their card accounts or not. This section continues discussion from chapter 4 about whether consumers are irrational in their use of credit cards and examines card account use for insight into some potential problems with effectiveness of a new disclosure regulation affecting credit card account statements. The section also looks at some other regulatory changes during the years 2008 to 2010 affecting pricing practices in the card industry. The last section of the chapter discusses trends in the profitability of the credit card industry. Good profitability for the most part, together with indications of demand for the product, demonstrates why credit cards have become the ubiquitous product they are.

THE CARD CONTEXT

Before examining trends in card holding and use or consumers' attitudes toward credit cards, it is appropriate first to describe briefly the kinds of credit cards available in the marketplace today. Given the widespread issuance, availability, and use of credit cards in recent years, it should not be surprising that there is more than one way to classify them. The distinctions are probably not highly important to individual consumers, but some differences among cards and card plans do affect how consumers use their credit cards.

Kinds of Credit Cards

From the consumer's standpoint, one important distinction among credit cards is according to the outlets where individual cards are acceptable for purchases. Under this classification scheme, "two-party cards" are those issued to a consumer that are usable only at the retail locations of the issuer. Department and specialty store cards are the best example, such as Macy's, Target's, or Talbot's cards, but there are also gasoline cards such as Chevron cards and others usable only at one brand's outlets. In contrast, "three-party cards" are offered to consumers by an issuer for use at a variety of unrelated outlets (third parties). American Express, Discover, MasterCard, and Visa are widely known and used three-party card brands.[3]

A second classification approach is by the required pace of repayment specified in the card account contract. Cards that require payment of the outstanding balance in full shortly after presentation of the monthly bill more properly are called charge cards rather than credit cards. They facilitate purchasing and payments without using cash or checks, but they generate consumer credit only in an accounting sense while the issuer sends the bill and awaits arrival of the full payment due in a short time. This is an example of the "convenience credit" noted above. Charge cards do not provide extended consumer credit, although amounts owed at month end are counted statistically in consumer credit outstanding, largely because of the difficulty of separating convenience credit from other credit.

Cards that do not require payment in full shortly after presentation of the bill are far more common today than charge cards. These cards leave decisions on both use and repayment pace to the customer, within contractual account limits; such cards often are referred to as "revolving" credit cards. Account agreements

---

3. In 2005, Citigroup, the owner of the Diners Club brand and system, the original three-party card, began to shift its Diners Club portfolio to Diners Club MasterCards. In 2008, Citigroup agreed to sell the international portion of the brand to Discover Financial Services, issuer of the Discover Card; in late 2009, it sold the North American part of the franchise to the Bank of Montreal. In the past, other widely held three-party card brands also existed, including Carte Blanche, Choice, Uni-card, and others now discontinued or merged into the remaining brands.

for these cards typically set an upper usage limit or "credit line" for each account, and they require a minimum monthly repayment amount or percentage of the outstanding balance. Each monthly payment renews the available credit line by the amount of the balance repaid. Contractual right to repay only part of the balance is the reason these cards are known as revolving credit cards: consumers can "revolve" the balance by not paying it in full. The card issuer typically assesses a finance charge on the unpaid balance, and the consumer has the choice the following month of paying the new balance in full or revolving a portion of it again. Unsecured credit lines, whereby a consumer can access consumer credit by using special checks not attached to the credit card account, also generate revolving consumer credit, but credit cards produce the bulk of revolving consumer credit outstanding.[4]

---

4. There also is a revolving form of mortgage credit (not consumer credit as defined here), usually referred to as a home equity line of credit (HELC or HELOC). A home equity line of credit is a line of credit using equity in a consumer's home as security or collateral on the credit line, in contrast to most credit card and other revolving credit accounts that are unsecured credit. The Federal Reserve does not classify home equity credit lines as consumer credit, however, leaving the amounts outstanding instead within mortgage credit. Revolving mortgage credit and revolving consumer credit are both more flexible and more modern than other types of credit for consumers. They had to await the development of cost-effective computer and communication systems before they could become truly feasible products.

Revolving consumer credit is sometimes interchangeably also called open-end consumer credit, as done here when describing kinds of consumer credit in chapter 1, but strictly speaking, these terms are not completely synonymous. The term *open-end credit* is actually broader than *revolving consumer credit*, because open-end credit also includes charge account credit that does not revolve. The term *open-end credit* also describes revolving mortgage credit, which is not consumer credit as defined here.

The term *open-end credit* (mortgage or consumer) arises from the Truth in Lending Act and its implementing regulation, Federal Reserve Regulation Z (12 CFR, Part 226), now transferred to the new Consumer Financial Protection Bureau. The law and regulation contain their own sets of definitions. This regulatory area requires careful definitions because it mandates different disclosures for different kinds of credit. The law and regulation carefully define open-end credit and accompany the definition with a listing of required disclosures for mortgage-secured open-end credit and for unsecured open-end credit. The regulation then lists a different set of disclosures for "other than open-end credit," typically called "closed-end credit" in common usage. The latter includes familiar mortgage loans other than home equity credit lines and the more traditional sorts of consumer credit, such as automobile credit and personal loans. Both of these kinds of "other than open-end credit" (i.e., closed-end credit) involve a fixed amount of credit for a specific term.

Open-end credit is defined in full in section 226.2(a)(10) of the regulation as consumer credit extended under a plan in which

    (i) the creditor reasonably contemplates repeat transactions;

    (ii) the creditor may impose a finance charge from time to time on an outstanding unpaid balance;

    (iii) the amount of credit that may be extended to the consumer during the term of the plan (up to any limit set by the creditor) is generally made available to the extent that the outstanding balance is repaid.

In sum, these two basic methods of classifying credit cards designate four sorts of cards: two- or three-party cards with or without a revolving credit feature. Of these card types, three kinds are widespread today, but the two-party card without a revolving feature is less common. Three-party cards with a revolving feature are the most common and they attract the most attention and commentary.

As indicated, one of these four types of cards has become increasingly rare in recent years: two-party cards with no revolving feature, properly known as charge cards. Charge cards usable at only one outlet (two-party charge cards) are an older device, often issued in the past by department stores but now mostly obsolete. Their main purpose was to encourage customers to visit the retail locations of the issuer and to make purchasing there more convenient and therefore more likely. Such cards once were familiar features of the department store industry, but by comparison, today they amount to a mere footnote for consumers. There is still relatively limited issuance today by such vendors as country clubs, business supply houses offering credit to local small businesses (not consumer credit), and a few smaller retail establishments. But most consumers, even those with many credit cards, probably do not have even one of these cards anymore.

The second card type, the two-party card *with* a revolving feature, has largely replaced the old nonrevolving cards among those department stores and other retail outlets that still issue their own credit cards. These newer revolving cards are still somewhat common with department store companies such as Macy's and Target but are not as prevalent as in the past, supplanted today by three-party cards, especially American Express, Discover, MasterCard, and Visa. Even then, most of the stores that still desire to provide cards in their own name for use only at their own outlets now contract with third-party vendors to issue the cards and service the card accounts (send bills, process payments, and keep the records). Often referred to as private label cards, these cards typically carry the logo of the retail store or chain, and the bills arrive under its name (and possibly with its advertising and statement stuffers), but the cards actually are issued on behalf of the retailer by some other independent financial entity such as General Electric Capital Services or the card division of the worldwide HSBC bank. Consequently, even among cards that appear to be two-party cards with a revolving feature, strict two-party arrangements have become scarcer.

The best-known cards today are the three-party cards, here again both with and without a revolving credit feature. American Express Green Cards, Carte Blanche cards, and Diners Club cards have long been well-known three-party nonrevolving cards, the latter two charge cards largely of only historical interest today. They have sometimes been referred to as three-party charge cards but

---

Closed-end credit is then defined by the regulation as "other than" open-end credit (Regulation Z 226.2[a][20]). It is easy enough to see in this definitional scheme that both charge cards and home equity credit lines are included within open-end credit, along with revolving credit card and other unsecured revolving credit. Closed-end mortgage credit is encompassed within the general definition of closed-end credit by default as included in "other than open-end credit." The rules then specify additional disclosures for closed-end mortgage credit beyond those required generally for closed-end consumer credit.

more often in the past as "travel and entertainment cards," which indicates their origin and most common use, frequently for business purposes (not consumer credit). The card agreement with the consumer or business generally requires repayment of any outstanding balances on these cards in full within a short time after receipt of the monthly bill. These cards usually entail payment of an annual membership fee by the customer. They also typically have high (or no) credit limits. The high limits are possible because large amounts of credit typically are not outstanding long enough to involve the same sorts of default risk that might arise on revolving account cards where repayment terms can be lengthier. During the relatively short time that balances are outstanding, few card holders are likely to suffer unexpected reverses such as divorce, job loss, or business failure that can complicate repayment plans over a longer time.

The fourth kind of card is by far the best-known type of credit card today: the three-party card with a revolving credit feature attached. Issued at the outset only by banking institutions, these cards are also sometimes known as "bank-type" cards, although today savings and thrift institutions, credit unions, and others also issue them. Discover Card and American Express issue such cards using their own brand names, and many depository institutions issue them under the MasterCard and Visa brands. The latter two names originally were the property of joint venture companies founded by the card issuing banks. From 2006 to 2008, the financial institutions that owned the joint venture companies spun them off as freestanding companies whose shares today are publicly traded.

Credit Card Networks

Although probably not of much interest to consumers, credit card industry personnel and close observers of the industry also like to classify credit cards according to the type of card "network" through which credit card systems operate. A card's network consists of the operating, communications, and computer systems and linkages necessary to make the card a device for making payments rather than merely an inert piece of plastic, together with the necessary ownership and operating contracts and agreements that give the hardware system life. Looking at the industry this way, there are two basic kinds of networks: "closed loop" and "open loop."[5]

Closed-loop networks are those owned and operated by a single entity that both issues the cards and captures the sales information upon use. Credit cards issued by or for individual merchants (such as Macy's or Target) involve closed-loop networks, but so do American Express, Discover, and formerly Diners Club and Carte Blanche cards. In each case, a single entity issues the cards

5. These are the descriptive terms chosen by Evans and Schmalensee (2005), who have written a whole (very interesting) book on the components of payment and credit card networks and the economic incentives necessary to make them work. For further discussion of networks and some of the regulatory and policy questions involved, see Prager et al. (2009).

and receives transaction information from outlets where consumers use the card to buy something or obtain cash at ATMs. This single entity then converts the information into billing notices to its card-using customers. It is obvious that both communications and underlying contractual relationships are simpler in a closed-loop system. The single firm (although possibly through its subsidiaries or agents) manages all the communication necessary to undertake and account for the transaction, and it contracts with consumers over terms of card use and payment and with merchants over operating rules of the system and conditions for accepting the card for transactions.

In contrast, transactions on cards with the MasterCard and Visa brands often involve more than one network entity, because the consumer's card may well be issued by a financial institution other than the one that signs up merchants where the cards are usable. Cards may be issued to consumers by their own neighborhood banks, for example, or by monoline credit card banks somewhere else in the country, but merchants where the cards are accepted for payments often are signed up by a different entity that receives the transaction information. The latter institution may be the merchant's own bank or a large bank with special interest and heightened level of activity on the merchant side of the card industry, called merchant acquirers. Cooperation among financial institutions nationwide (and worldwide) in signing up geographically diverse merchants to accept cards with the same limited number of brand names undoubtedly has made cards with the MasterCard and Visa brands more useful to consumers than otherwise, but such joint efforts also contain seeds of complexity and accompanying operating and legal problems.

As an example of how the system works, imagine a traveling consumer with a card issued by a bank in Wilmington, Delaware, but desiring to make a purchase from a merchant using a local bank in Phoenix, Arizona. The transaction would set off a train of electronic messages. The merchant in Phoenix would need access to the network through its local bank or processor so that the card issuer in Wilmington could verify the existence in good standing of the card account and approve the transaction. The merchant would then receive payment for the sale credited quickly to its account in Phoenix (minus a fee distributed within the network), a process known as settlement. The debit would be to the holder's card account at the Wilmington bank which would eventually bill the customer.

It is easy enough to see the complexities of allocating the costs and revenues of such a network so as to retain the participation of all parties. Because communications are more complicated in an open-loop network, so also are the decisions concerning allocations of costs and fees (the latter known as interchange fees). The allocations must be made in a way that maintains economic incentives for all participants for all of the sorts of transmissions that take place over the network. The decision-making process itself and the governance of the network are also more complicated than in a closed-loop system. The underlying incentives and decision making also must pass muster within a legal system that is constantly on the lookout for potential or actual violations of antitrust laws. Complexity in the latter area was highlighted in 2002–2003, when the joint ventures operating the

MasterCard and Visa networks either lost or settled out of court at great expense some antitrust complaints filed by some of their own merchant base.[6]

Size of the Credit Card Market

The widespread acceptance in only a few decades of pieces of plastic for payments and generating credit is among the most rapid changes in the history of consumer financial behavior. By comparison, it took millennia for individuals to accept money as a replacement for barter in exchanges of goods and services, and it took additional centuries for deposit banking and drafts on accounts (checks) to replace coin money for routine transactions. Today plastic cards and fully electronic transfers have not completely replaced cash and checks in modern economies, but they certainly have become common, and the three-party plastic cards now dominate payments in many areas of domestic commerce in the United States.

Research by the Federal Reserve System (2008, 2011, and 2013) shows that the number of electronic payments, including credit card, debit card, automated clearinghouse (ACH), and government electronic benefits transfers (EBT), exceeded the number of payments by check in the American economy by more than five to one by 2012 (table 7.1). This represents a sharp change from twelve years earlier, when electronic payments were less common than check payments. In 2012, the Federal Reserve estimated that there were more than 26 billion payments by credit card in the United States, with an average size of $95.

One well-known industry source estimates that there were more than 1.2 billion credit cards of all types in circulation in the United States at year end 2007 (table 7.2).[7] Of this total, 494.4 million, or a bit less than half, were two-party cards, or cards that resemble two-party cards but are actually issued by a financial firm under contract. The total of three-party cards outstanding passed the number of two-party cards for the first time in 1999 and undoubtedly will stay in the lead. Among three-party cards, the surge in growth has been among the bank-type cards with the American Express, Discover, MasterCard, and Visa brands. Only a relatively small fraction are "travel and entertainment" charge cards such as American Express Green Cards.

---

6. In the card industry, this case became known as the Wal-Mart case, although many companies were involved. The case is reviewed extensively in Evans and Schmalensee (2005, chapter 11). More recently, retail merchant organizations have attempted to persuade Congress to legislate changes in the allocations of fees in the system (see Zywicki 2010b). In 2010, as part of the huge financial reform package passed that year, Congress mandated that the Federal Reserve System undertake price regulation in the area of debit card, but not credit card, interchange fees. This episode, widely known as the swipe fee regulation, quickly became very controversial. For discussion of the swipe fee rule, see Evans, Litan, and Schmalensee (2011).

7. Source for statistics in the table and used in this and the following paragraph: SourceMedia (2008), tables on pages 16–18. After 2008, SourceMedia no longer compiled this information.

Table 7.1 Means of Domestic Noncash Payments in the United States, Selected Years 2000–2012

	2000			2006		
	Number (billions)	Value (trillions of dollars)	Average Size (dollars)	Number (billions)	Value (trillions of dollars)	Average Size (dollars)
Total noncash payments	72.5	60.0	827	93.3	75.8	813
Checks	41.9	39.8	950	30.6	41.7	1366
Electronic	30.6	20.2	660	62.7	34.1	544
Memo: included within electronic payments						
ACH[a]	6.2	18.6	2,989	14.6	31.0	2,122
Debit card	8.3	0.3	42	25.3	1.0	39
Credit card	15.6	1.3	82	21.7	2.1	98
Prepaid card[b]	NA	NA	NA	3.3	0.08	23
	2009			2012		
	Number (billions)	Value (trillions of dollars)	Average (dollars)	Number (billions)	Value (trillions of dollars)	Average Size (dollars)
Total noncash payments	109.0	72.2	662	122.8	79.0	643
Checks	24.5	31.6	1,292	18.3	26.0	1421
Electronic	84.5	40.6	480	104.4	52.9	507
Memo: included within electronic payments						
ACH[a]	19.1	37.2	1,946	22.1	48.4	2190
Debit card	37.9	1.4	38	47.0	1.8	38
Credit card	21.6	1.9	89	26.2	2.5	95
Prepaid card[b]	6.0	0.14	24	9.2	0.2	22

[a]ACH refers to payments such as direct payroll deposits and other electronic payments through automated clearinghouses (ACHs).
[b]Includes electronic benefits transfers to consumers under various government programs.
Averages may not exactly equal results of divisions because of rounding in all columns.

source: Federal Reserve System (2008, 2011, 2013), various pages. There are further breakdowns and compound annual growth rates in the original sources.

Table 7.2 Numbers of Credit Cards, Charges on Credit Cards, and
Amounts of Credit Card Credit Outstanding in the United States,
1991–2007

	Number of Credit Cards, by Type (millions)				Bank-Type Card Credit (billions of dollars)	
	All[a]	Bank Type[b]	Retail Store	American Express	Charges[c]	Credit Outstanding[d]
1991	660.6	266.8	368.0	25.8	282.0	181.2
1992	686.8	285.3	377.2	24.3	318.8	194.8
1993	729.7	318.4	386.6	24.7	385.1	224.6
1994	821.0	370.4	425.3	25.3	480.3	279.3
1995	879.7	406.4	446.6	26.7	585.7	350.4
1996	928.7	430.6	468.9	29.2	667.1	399.5
1997	988.9	447.8	511.5	29.6	736.5	437.2
1998	1,057.7	472.4	557.5	27.8	808.4	426.3
1999	1,205.5	596.1	579.5	29.9	909.3	468.2
2000	1,257.3	642.0	582.0	33.3	1,028.7	524.9
2001	1,328.0	708.4	585.0	34.6	1,144.8	573.0
2002	1,191.9	571.8	585.0	35.1	1,192.3	603.5
2003	1,171.9	579.7	555.8	36.4	1,059.3	622.5
2004	1,162.6	622.5	500.2	39.9	1,147.0	644.0
2005	1,146.9	628.7	475.2	43.0	1,263.8	659.2
2006	1,151.7	619.0	484.7	48.0	1,376.5	672.9
2007	1,188.8	642.1	494.4	52.3	1,445.3	760.9

[a]Includes general-purpose cards with a revolving feature issued with the Discover, MasterCard, and Visa brands; travel and entertainment cards with the American Express brand; and cards issued in the name of retail outlets. For 1999–2001, includes MasterCard and Visa offline debit cards.

[b]Includes general-purpose cards with a revolving feature issued with the Discover, MasterCard, and Visa brands. For 1999–2001, includes MasterCard and Visa offline debit cards.

[c]Includes general-purpose cards with a revolving feature issued with the Discover, MasterCard, and Visa brands. Before 2003, includes MasterCard and Visa cash disbursements.

[d]Includes general-purpose cards with a revolving feature issued with the Discover, MasterCard, and Visa brands. Amount outstanding at year end.

SOURCE: Calculated from SourceMedia (2008, tables on pages 16–18).

As indicated, the cards that typically attract the most attention are the three-party, general-purpose, bank-type cards that can be used at many locations and that have a revolving credit feature attached to them. Estimates suggest that there were more than 640 million of these cards outstanding in the United States alone at the end of 2007 (table 7.2).[8] Charge volume on cards with the Discover, MasterCard, and Visa brands exceeded $1.4 trillion in the United States in 2007. More than 6 million merchant locations in the United States accepted at least one of these three card brands, usually all three.

The federal statistical sources do not give a precise estimate of the dollar volume of credit outstanding on credit cards. The Federal Reserve Board, which processes and issues statistics on consumer credit outstanding in its monthly statistical release G19, makes a basic distinction between nonrevolving and revolving consumer credit, but it provides further details only on class of institutional source. As discussed earlier, the Board estimates that the revolving credit portion of consumer credit outstanding grew from about $2 billion at year end 1968 to about $862 billion at the end of 2013; most of this volume outstanding involves credit cards. An estimate from the private sector is that 84 percent of revolving consumer credit outstanding at the end of 2007 involved general-purpose credit cards.[9]

Credit Card Growth

Chapter 2 discussed more fully how the growth of consumer credit can be put in perspective by comparing it with the growth of consumers' income and assets. The same can be done for the revolving or open-end fraction of that credit, largely originated by means of credit cards. Figure 2.4 in chapter 2 shows that total (non-mortgage) consumer credit outstanding increased only about five percentage points at its high point relative to disposable personal income over the past generation, although with noticeable cyclicality. That figure also shows how within total consumer credit outstanding, the revolving component has increased relative to income over most of the past three decades, but the nonrevolving component has on balance decreased relative to income. This kind of growth pattern is, of course, first of all a natural statistical outcome of a component of something

---

8. What appears to be a decline in 2002 in the number of reported bank-type cards outstanding in 2002 (second column of table 7.2) really just reflects removal of so-called offline MasterCard and Visa debit cards from the estimate of credit cards outstanding. These cards function like credit cards, in that they require a signature for normal use and are cleared through the credit card authorization and clearing system but actually directly debit a consumer's deposit account rather than create or add to a balance on a credit account. They could not be eliminated from totals in the table for 1999–2001 but were removed again in 2002–2005. SourceMedia (2008) eliminated the footnote about this from the relevant table continued from earlier editions of its annual compilation of credit card information, but the numbers in the earlier years did not change in the 2008 statistical compilation.

9. Calculated from SourceMedia (2008, 17).

(anything) that grows from a zero base (in this case, a component of consumer credit). It must seize market share from some other component if it exhibits any growth at all.

But the increasing share of revolving credit relative to nonrevolving has gone on for long enough now, however, that it is today much more than merely a new product securing a niche. In the past two decades, an increase simultaneously in both revolving and nonrevolving consumer credit compared with income has also caused total consumer credit to increase relative to income, although not in the most recent years (figure 2.4).

The decades-long general rise in the share of revolving consumer credit outstanding apparently reflects both consumer preference and technological change. Many consumers seem to like the convenience associated with prearranged lines of credit, and technological developments, especially declining unit costs of data processing and telecommunications, have made it much easier for creditors to offer access to this data-intensive product simultaneously at millions of locations worldwide. It appears that a substantial portion of the newer revolving credit product has merely replaced credit generated by the installment purchase plans that were common at appliance, furniture, and other durable goods stores in the past. It is also worth noting again that some of revolving credit outstanding is really convenience credit on credit cards that is more akin to float than to true consumer credit. This convenience component is "credit" on credit cards that consumers will pay in full upon receipt of the statement at the end of the monthly billing cycle. It is included within consumer credit in an accounting sense, because the convenience component is difficult to remove from the statistics. By comparison, closed-end loans or installment purchase plans have no convenience component included within its total.

Credit Card Holding by Consumers

Dollar amounts of credit card credit outstanding and related growth rates can be estimated from issuers' data, but only surveys of consumers can provide information about the users and uses of credit cards. For this reason, each Survey of Consumer Finances since 1970 has contained a section on holding and use of credit cards (the 1967 and 1968 surveys also included a few questions on credit cards).[10]

The surveys show that in 2001, more than three-fourths of American households had one or more credit cards, up from about one-half of a smaller population in 1970 (table 7.3). This proportion fell off a bit after that date but still remains

---

10. This section draws upon Durkin (2000), Canner and Elliehausen (2013), and the references below. As discussed more fully in chapter 1, the Survey of Consumer Finances series is sponsored by the Federal Reserve Board, sometimes jointly with other agencies. For a general description of results from recent surveys, see Kennickell, Starr-McCluer, and Surette (2000); Aizcorbe, Kennickell, and Moore (2003); Bucks, Kennickell, and Moore (2006); Bucks et al. (2009); and Bricker et al. (2012).

Table 7.3 Prevalence of Credit Cards among Households, Selected Years, 1970–2010, in Percent

Item	1970	1977	1983	1989	1995	2001	2004	2007	2010
Have a card									
Any card[a]	51	63	65	70	74	76	75	73	68
Retail store card[b]	45	54	58	61	58	45	44	41	38
Bank-type card[c]	16	38	43	56	66	73	71	70	65
Have a card with a balance after the most recent payment									
Any card[a]	22	34	37	40	47	44	46	46	39
Retail store card[b]	15	25	29	28	29	21	20	19	17
Bank-type card[c]	6	16	22	29	37	39	40	41	34
Memo:									
Households having any card with an outstanding balance after the most recent payment as a proportion of all households having cards	44	56	57	57	61	56	59	61	55

Households having a bank-type card with an outstanding balance after the most recent payment as a proportion of all households having bank-type cards	37	44	51	52	56	54	56	58	52
Proportion of households having a bank-type card who "hardly ever" pay revolving balance in full		22	26	27	29	26	24	25	25

[a]Includes cards issued by banks, gasoline companies, retail stores and chains, travel and entertainment card companies (e.g., American Express and Diners Club), and miscellaneous issuers (e.g., car rental and airline companies).

[b]The 1970 figure is for 1971.

[c]A bank-type card is a general-purpose credit card with a revolving feature; includes BankAmericard, Choice, Discover, MasterCard, Master Charge, Optima, and Visa, depending on year. In 1970, respondents were asked about *using* credit cards; in all other years, they were asked about *having* cards. In 1995–2004, retail card holders include some respondents with open-end retail revolving credit accounts not necessarily evidenced by a plastic card.

SOURCE: Surveys of Consumer Finances.

above two-thirds. Among credit cards, the three-party or general-purpose cards that have a revolving feature, the bank-type credit cards, show the most notable increase over the period. In the early 1970s, two-party cards issued by retail firms and usable only in the firm's stores were the most commonly held type of credit card; bank-type cards were much less common.

Bank-type credit cards issued under the MasterCard and Visa brands are so widely held and used today that it is difficult to recall that they were not especially common only four and a half decades ago. Known then as Master Charge and BankAmericard, they were a new product in the mid-1960s, and by 1970, together they (and some limited regional brands at that time) reached only about one-sixth of households. By 1995, however, holding of bank-type cards had become more common than holding of retail store cards. In 2010, bank-type cards (including newer Discover and American Express Optima brands), but not "travel and entertainment" cards that do not have a revolving feature, were themselves in the hands of almost two-thirds of households.

As discussed earlier, consumers use credit cards for two main purposes: as a substitute for cash and checks when making purchases and as a source of revolving credit. In 1970, just more than one-fifth of all households owed a balance on a credit card after making their most recent card payment. By 1989, the fraction reached two-fifths, and it has stayed near or above this proportion since. Most of the increase was caused by the growing popularity of bank-type cards as devices for generating revolving credit, which overshadows a relative decline in the importance of revolving credit on store cards. In 1970, only 6 percent of households had a bank-type card with an outstanding balance after their most recent payment. The proportion rose steadily until 1995 and then grew more slowly to 39 to 41 percent from 2001 to 2007 before falling off to 34 percent in 2010, following the end of the recession about six months before the survey. In contrast, the proportion of households reporting an outstanding balance on a retail store card peaked in 1983, at 29 percent, and in 2010, at 17 percent, it was the lowest it has been since the 1970 survey.

The Surveys of Consumer Finances show that the holding of general-purpose credit cards with a revolving feature has become more widespread among households at all income levels. For households in the lowest income group, about 2 percent had a bank-type credit card in 1970, compared with a third or more of households beginning with the 2001 survey (table 7.4). For those in the highest income group, the holding of bank-type cards almost tripled between 1970 and 1995.

For each income group, the percentage of card holders carrying a balance on bank-type cards also increased over four decades, as did the mean and median revolving credit balances (in constant dollars). Despite some shifts within the period, the shares of total revolving balances on these cards accounted for by each income group have not changed dramatically over the decades, perhaps contrary to popular impressions. For example, despite a sharp increase in card holding by the lowest income group, the group's share of total revolving debt on bank-type cards rose only to 6 percent in 2010, up from 2 percent in 1970 but still not a large proportion of the total. The highest income group accounted for about 30 percent

Item	1970	1977	1983	1989	1995	2001	2004	2007	2010
Lowest quintile									
Have a card	2	11	11	17	28	38	37	38	33
Carrying a balance	27	40	40	43	57	61	61	58	56
Mean balance (2010 dollars)	1,194	974	1,529	1,045	3,181	2,389	3,382	4,040	4,032
Median balance (2010 dollars)	447	717	1,091	788	1,326	1,128	1265	982	1,100
Share of total revolving balance	2	4	3	2	7	6	7	6	6
Second-lowest quintile									
Have a card	9	23	27	37	55	65	61	57	50
Carrying a balance	39	44	49	46	57	59	60	57	54
Mean balance (2010 dollars)	878	1,407	1,208	2,280	3,495	3,173	4,476	4,051	4,210
Median balance (2010 dollars)	672	806	873	1,752	2,140	1,349	2,071	1,866	1,500
Share of total revolving balance	9	14	9	8	14	13	14	9	10
Middle quintile									
Have a card	14	37	41	62	71	79	76	75	67
Carrying a balance	47	45	58	56	58	61	64	65	56
Mean balance (2010 dollars)	1,093	1,177	1,547	2,877	3,934	4,134	5,453	5,441	5,923
Median balance (2010 dollars)	979	896	981	1,682	2,140	2,454	2,301	2,650	2,300
Share of total revolving balance	23	19	20	21	21	22	23	18	19
Second-highest quintile									
Have a card	23	51	57	76	83	87	87	88	82
Carrying a balance	39	52	55	62	60	55	57	65	59

(*Continued*)

Table 7.4 (CONTINUED)

Item	1970	1977	1983	1989	1995	2001	2004	2007	2010
Mean balance (2010 dollars)	1,346	1,127	1,678	2,947	3,582	4,956	5,982	7,982	6,599
Median balance (2010 dollars)	1,119	1,004	1,091	1,577	2,140	2,454	3,451	3,927	3,000
Share of total revolving balance	35	31	28	30	23	25	26	31	27
Highest quintile									
Have a card	33	69	79	89	95	95	96	94	94
Carrying a balance	30	39	47	46	50	40	45	47	42
Mean balance (2010 dollars)	1,015	1,198	2,042	4,552	5,945	8,273	8,284	11,303	11,690
Median balance (2010 dollars)	840	896	1,222	3,504	2,994	3,681	3,451	5,988	6,000
Share of total revolving balance	30	32	40	39	36	34	30	35	39
All income groups									
Have a card	16	38	43	56	66	73	71	70	65
Carrying a balance	37	44	51	52	56	54	56	58	52
Mean balance (2010 dollars)	1,118	1,185	1,709	3,203	4,213	4,744	5,772	7,057	6,969
Median balance (2010 dollars)	840	896	1,091	1,752	2,140	2,209	2,416	2,945	2,900
Share of total revolving balance	100	100	100	100	100	100	100	100	100

In 1970, respondents were asked about *using* cards; in all other years, they were asked about *having* cards. Proportions that "have a card" are percentages of all households; proportions "carrying a balance" are percentages of holders of bank-type cards with an outstanding balance after the most recent payment. Mean and median balances are for card holders with outstanding balances after the most recent payment and are in 2010 dollars, adjusted using the Consumer Price Index for All Urban Consumers, all items. Shares may not add to 100 percent because of rounding.

SOURCE: Surveys of Consumer Finances.

of revolving debt on bank-type cards in 1970. This proportion rose to 40 percent in 1983 and has fluctuated within this range since then.

Some Studies of Credit Card Holding

Widespread interest in growth of credit cards includes interest among economists, and they have offered a number of studies of the phenomenon. Because card credit outstanding continues to grow, there probably will be more studies of this sort in the future.

In a pair of studies using data from the Surveys of Consumer Finances, economist Peter S. Yoo (1997, 1998) of the Federal Reserve Bank of St. Louis examined the economic factors contributing to the growth of credit card debt from 1992 to1995. Specifically, he studied whether growth in card-related debt was the result of more households with cards or of more debt outstanding per card account. A reasonable expectation is that both are responsible, but the real question is the degree.

Yoo found that relatively little of the increase in credit card debt from 1992 to 1995 came about because of an increase in the number of card holding households. From his calculations, 17 percent of the debt increase was a result of increasing numbers of card holders. Most of the rest was a result of higher balances (a little was also a result of the interaction of the two effects, higher average balances also among those newly with cards). According to Yoo:

> Changes in average balances accounted for the vast majority of the increase in total card debt between 1992 and 1995. Average credit card debt of all households grew at a 9.6 percent annual rate during those three years, considerably faster than the increase in prices, 2.8 percent annual rate, and household income, 4.9 percent annual rate. In sum, the increase in average credit card balances accounted for 77 percent of the increase in household credit card debt between 1992 and 1995. (Yoo 1998, 26)

Yoo also found that lower-income households (those in the bottom half of the income distribution) increased their holding of credit cards and the balances outstanding on their cards somewhat faster than the population as a whole during these years, but upper-income households were responsible for most of the rise in total credit card debt.

The view that growth in card use would eventually come from more intensive use rather than from more widespread use is, not surprisingly, not a new one. In fact, as card holding gradually has become almost universal over the years, it becomes virtually a truism that growth must come from greater intensity of use; card use cannot spread further when all those who want to use cards and can qualify for cards have and are using them. At some saturation point, any further growth at all must come from more intensive use among those who have cards.

The authors of a study more than two decades ago, although one limited in geographic coverage, noted that evidence they presented was "consistent with the behavior expected in a market approaching saturation" (Lindley, Rudolph, and Selby 1989, 139). Notably, they found that card use for big-ticket items such as furniture and household durable goods purchases appeared to be increasing along with clothing. An increase in use for household durable goods is consistent with the view that credit card use is substituting, at least in part, for old-style, closed-end consumer installment credit for these products, as figure 2.4 and previous discussion have suggested.

New York Federal Reserve Bank economists Sandra E. Black and Donald P. Morgan examined the increase from 56 to 66 percent in the proportion of households with bank-type cards from 1989 to 1995. They wrote that it appeared to them that the upsurge in card holding at that time probably meant that card issuers were taking on riskier customers:

> [W]e find that cardholders in 1995 were more apt to be single, more likely to rent, and had less job security than cardholders in 1989. The new borrowers were also more willing to borrow, and to borrow for seemingly riskier purposes, such as vacation…. Much more important is the higher debt burden among cardholders: the new borrowers owe substantially more relative to their income, so even small drops in income can cause financial distress. (Black and Morgan 1999, 1–2)

Again, this would not be especially surprising if card credit had substituted for other sorts of consumer credit that long have been available to these same sorts of riskier customers.

In a careful technical paper originally prepared for a conference on consumer transactions and credit at the Federal Reserve Bank of Philadelphia, economists David Gross and Nicholas Souleles (2002) looked at the impact on debt outstanding on bank-type credit cards of (1) changes made by the bank in the credit limit on the card and (2) changes in the bank's finance rate imposed (known as the annual percentage rate, or APR). For their empirical analysis, they used data from a large sample of individual card accounts "from several different credit card issuers," which they believed "should be generally representative of credit cards in the U.S. in 1995" (Gross and Souleles 2002, 157). They discussed how these data have a number of advantages over other data, including consumers' self-reported balance sheets explored through surveys. Notably, they pointed out that account data eliminated measurement error and, because the data included both credit lines and outstanding amounts, they allowed the authors to distinguish better between credit demand and credit supply.

Using methodology similar to an event study, Gross and Souleles found that an upward change in the credit limit was associated with "immediate and significant rise" in debt. They found that the impact was greatest on people near their credit limit, but there was a response also from people below their limit. Likewise, they found that a downward alteration of the finance rate produced a rapid increase in debt with elasticity –1.3, which is large relative to estimates made elsewhere. The authors then discussed implications of their findings for consumption theory and the channels of monetary policy.

They pointed out that their work did not explain all of consumers' credit decisions and, in particular, did not account for all the determinants of credit demand. Their finding that card credit is sensitive to finance rates is consistent with the long-run substitution of card credit for other forms of consumer credit, however, in that rates on card credit have generally been declining for two decades, especially over the decade before their study. They pointed out that their findings did not explain why consumers with (still expensive) card debt outstanding often also maintain a stock of low-return liquid assets. While this phenomenon might generally be explainable in terms of cautionary motivations and high perceived usefulness of liquid assets by consumers, they did not attempt to provide a full economic model of this effect. Importance of the Gross and Souleles paper for understanding credit card demand is discussed further above in chapter 4.

CONSUMERS' ATTITUDES TOWARD AND UNDERSTANDING OF CREDIT CARDS

Products used as widely as credit cards commonly generate strong opinions among users and observers, both favorable and less so. Television, for example, is so ubiquitous that virtually every household has one or more such devices in its kitchen or den (often both), but not everyone is happy with this cultural development. For some individuals, television is their main source of relaxation and entertainment, while others call it the idiot tube or worse and maintain that it has led to the downfall of everything from genteel conversation to family cohesiveness and commonality of interests. Some people hold both views at different times (for instance, summer versus football season). Likewise, virtually everyone patronizes fast-food restaurants, at least occasionally. Sometimes they are viewed as a salvation for a frequently on-the-go public and overly programmed and highly stressed suburban culture. Simultaneously, other people, or even the same individuals in a different mood, blame these omnipresent establishments for everything from visual blight on the highways to chronic obesity.

Potentially more important than the existence of attitudes is how they may affect behavior, including buyer behavior. It seems reasonable that individuals with a positive attitude about a product may be more favorably inclined to purchase it, which certainly is important to its producers and sellers. It also is reasonable to expect that there might be a recursive relationship: those individuals who have a successful experience with a product or brand likely have a favorable attitude and, therefore, are more likely to purchase it again.

Because of the possibility of multiple channels of influence between the psyche and behavior, business-oriented social scientists have long concerned themselves with forming general theories of purchase behavior that include consumer attitudes in addition to other factors (see Nicosia 1966; Engel, Kollat, and Blackwell 1968; Howard and Sheth 1969; and further discussion above in chapter 4).

Formulating, testing, refining, and retesting theories that broadly might be characterized as buyer behavior theories have consumed much energy in the social
science of marketing, in effect a branch of applied psychology, over the past two
generations. Strong viewpoints may also influence other aspects of behavior, such
as political behavior. Because there is diversity of opinion in many areas and about
many products, the depth and breadth of such viewpoints become both interesting
and researchable.

In the marketing area, if attitudes toward any product are overwhelmingly
one-sided, it seems the product will either thrive or quickly change or disappear. For
politicians, if the public's view is one-sided about an individual, that office seeker
will likely win or lose (depending on the view), but what if feelings across the population are mixed or changing? Many controversial products, including television
and fast-food restaurants, have succeeded in enough ways that they have become
commonplace, even though they remain contentious. So indeed are credit cards,
which are used by the majority of Americans but are controversial nonetheless. The
public's attitudes toward credit cards, now moving into their second half-century of
widespread availability, remain an interesting question not only for buyer behavior
but also potentially in other areas. Not only are marketers interested in these issues,
but so are other social scientists, cultural observers, and even government officials,
who sometimes must sort and filter both the praise and the blame directed at products and institutions.

Marketing departments of financial institutions have undertaken many scientific
explorations of consumers' use of and attitudes toward their products, including
credit cards, and they have examined the results along highly sophisticated metrics.
The monoline credit card banks that specialize in card products and other large card
issuers spend large amounts of time and money trying to understand consumers'
views about financial products and their receptivity to marketing pitches for credit
cards. The whole business approach of the monoline institutions is based on such
"data mining." Results of their studies are only available to officials and sponsoring
departments of the institutions that commission them, of course, but there are a few
recent explorations of attitudes toward credit cards that are publicly available, and
this section reports some of the findings.

General Attitudes toward Credit Cards

One publicly available source is questioning undertaken by the Survey Research
Center of the University of Michigan. In the past, the center has from time to time
included questions about attitudes toward credit cards in surveys undertaken as
part of its ongoing monthly Surveys of Consumers program.[11]

In a first line of questioning, both those consumers who hold and use credit
cards and those who do not have been asked about their broad feelings concerning

---

11. This and the following three subsections of the chapter draw on Durkin (2000 and 2002) and
Canner and Elliehausen (2013).

this financial product. So that attitude changes could be tracked over time, the question wording has been identical: "People have different opinions about credit cards. Overall, would you say that using credit cards is a good thing or a bad thing?" This is certainly a blunt first line of questioning to begin exploring consumers' general viewpoints on this product.

Because of the large differences in economic and cultural conditions that can occur over a long number of years, it does not seem reasonable to make too much of small measurement differences in responses to questions, but there certainly appear to have been some important overall changes in attitudes toward credit cards over the years. Survey findings show that overall, public opinions about credit cards were more negative and polarized in 2000 and 2012 than they were a generation earlier, especially among holders of bank-type cards (table 7.5). Opinions among all families that credit card use is "good" registered a bit higher in later years than in 1970, although if those who also said "good" but with some qualification are included, there has been falloff since 1970. The view that card use is "bad" was stronger in 2000 and especially in 2012 than in either of the earlier years, however. It is possible to have higher proportions answering both "good" and "bad" in more recent years, because opinions were more polarized: fewer respondents were in the middle in 2000 or 2012 than in earlier years.

In all four surveys, views among those holding one or more bank-type credit cards were more favorable than those among the population generally. Nonetheless, unfavorable views even among card holders have increased over the decades. Negative attitudes among card holders were much more prevalent in 2012 (51 percent) than they had been in 1970 or 1977. In 2000 and 2012, holders of bank-type cards were about equally divided in their opinions that credit card use is good or bad, much different from 1970 or 1977, when a considerably larger proportion had a favorable opinion.[12]

Consumers' opinions about credit cards also vary depending on their use of and experience with cards. Less enthusiastic viewpoints apparently are somewhat more common among those who use credit cards as credit devices rather than primarily as substitutes for cash or checks. This possibly reflects an underlying concern with their overall financial condition that necessitates credit use. Specifically, the surveys have shown that cards are viewed less positively among those who have three or more cards, have an outstanding balance of more than $1,500, have transferred a balance between cards, hardly ever pay their outstanding balance in

---

12. The 2012 survey took place shortly after a lot of negative publicity and discussion about banking conditions and practices during and after the financial crisis of 2008–2009. In this period, Congress passed the Credit Card Accountability Responsibility and Disclosure Act (the CARD Act) in 2009 and the Dodd-Frank Wall Street Reform and Consumer Protection Act (the Dodd-Frank Act) in 2010.

Interestingly, contrary opinions about consumer credit generally, even from the same person, apparently have been around much longer than these surveys. Referring to the paradox of dichotomous views as the "Victorian money management ethic," cultural historian Lendol Calder (1999) has pointed out that the simultaneous belief that credit is good but debt is bad is actually at least as old as American history.

Table 7.5 Consumers' Opinions about Using Credit Cards, Selected Years 1970–2012, in Percent

Opinion	1970		1977		2000	
	All Families	Bank-Type Card Users	All Families	Bank-Type Card Holders	All Families	Bank-Type Card Holders
Good	28	45	39	54	33	42
Good, with qualification	13	17	19	20	10	9
Both good and bad	12	14	11	8	6	5
Bad, with qualification	4	4	4	3	1	1
Bad	43	20	27	14	51	42
Total	100	100	100	100	100	100
	2012					
Good	40	46				
Good, with qualification	2	2				
Both good and bad	2	2				
Bad, with qualification	*	*_				
Bad	56	51				
Total	100	100				

* Less than 0.5 percent.
Components may not add to 100 because of rounding.

SOURCE: For 1970 and 1977, Surveys of Consumer Finances; for 2000 and 2012, Thomson Reuters/University of Michigan Surveys of Consumers. The table is from Canner and Elliehausen (2012, 31).

full, hardly ever pay more than the monthly minimum, or have received a collection call (table 7.6).

Conversely, those who have fewer cards, have no balance or a low balance outstanding, generally pay more than the minimum, or have not received a collection call have more favorable views (not shown in the table). Demographic measures also appear to be related to attitudes toward credit cards, but the relationship is not as strong as that associated with the variables related to the use of cards.

Table 7.6 PREVALENCE OF BELIEF THAT USING CREDIT CARDS IS "BAD" AMONG
HOLDERS OF BANK-TYPE CREDIT CARDS, 2000 AND 2012

Card Holder Group	Percent 2000	Percent 2012
All holders of bank-type cards	42	51
Have a new card account in the past year	47	44
Have three or more cards	49	52
Have an outstanding balance after the last payment greater than $1,500	57	61
Have transferred a balance to another account in the past year[a]	60	70
"Hardly ever" pay outstanding balance in full	59	71
"Hardly ever" pay more than the minimum[a]	63	73
Have paid a late fee in the past year	47	65
Have received a collection call in the past year[a]	62	72
Family's annual income is $40,000–$74,999	49	57
Respondent has high school diploma or some college but not a degree	46	55
Respondent is 35 to 54 years old	48	60

[a]Weighted sample size less than 50.

SOURCE: Thomson Reuters/University of Michigan Surveys of Consumers. The table is from Durkin (2000, 628) and updated from the 2012 source data.

More Specific Views about Credit Cards

To examine why card users might have the general attitudes they do about credit cards, surveys in 2000 and 2012 also asked questions about specific features of credit cards and about card issuers and users. The questions took the form of statements with which respondents could agree or disagree. Although data from earlier years are not available for comparison, responses to these questions reveal an interesting divergence of views that might help explain why overall attitudes deteriorated over time. The responses suggest that the negativity may have arisen in part from an individual's perceptions of *other* consumers' difficulties rather than from the individual's own experiences. Without data from earlier periods and questions designed specifically to address this hypothesis, one cannot be certain, but from the survey results, it seems likely that as card use has become more common, negative opinions about card use may have increased as a result of perceptions about "the other guy." Views about personal experiences with credit cards, in contrast, have been more positive.

Consumers in both surveys seemed to be concerned about specific practices of credit card issuers. Most holders of bank-type credit cards (more than 80 percent) believed that the annual percentage rates charged on outstanding balances were too high (table 7.7). This is not exactly a surprising finding; consumers may think

Table 7.7 ATTITUDES OF HOLDERS OF BANK-TYPE CREDIT CARDS TOWARD CREDIT CARDS AND CARD ISSUERS, 2000 AND 2012, IN PERCENT

Attitude	Strongly Agree		Agree Somewhat		Disagree Somewhat		Strongly Disagree	
	2000	2012	2000	2012	2000	2012	2000	2012
Specific practices of card issuers								
The interest rates charged on credit cards are reasonable	3	6	16	13	26	25	55	55
Credit card companies show enough concern for protecting consumers' privacy	17	na	30	na	21	na	31	Na
Credit card billing statements are accurate	54	58	39	34	5	6	2	2
Card issuers and consumers in general								
Credit card companies make too much credit available to most people	68	61	20	28	9	7	4	3
Sending solicitations that offer low rates but only for a short time probably misleads a lot of people	79	75	14	20	4	4	3	2
Credit card companies make it hard for people to get out of debt	55	61	27	27	10	7	9	5
Credit card companies should not be allowed to issue credit cards to college students	30	33	25	21	23	31	22	16

Table 7.7 (Continued)

Attitude	Strongly Agree		Agree Somewhat		Disagree Somewhat		Strongly Disagree	
	2000	2012	2000	2012	2000	2012	2000	2012
Overspending is the fault of consumers, not the credit card companies	63	57	27	30	6	9	4	4
Card issuers and me								
I am generally satisfied in my dealings with my credit card companies	51	51	40	44	6	4	4	1
My credit card companies treat me fairly	54	46	36	47	6	5	4	3
It is easy to get a credit card from another company if I am not treated well	63	56	23	34	10	6	4	4
I trust that my credit card companies will keep my personal spending information confidential	31	na	38	na	16	na	15	na
General satisfaction/dissatisfaction								
Credit card companies provide a useful service to consumers	44	47	48	46	6	5	2	2
Most people are satisfied in their dealings with credit card companies	15	9	54	41	20	28	11	21

(Continued)

Table 7.7 (Continued)

Attitude	Strongly Agree		Agree Somewhat		Disagree Somewhat		Strongly Disagree	
	2000	2012	2000	2012	2000	2012	2000	2012
Consumers would be better off if there were no credit cards	15	14	26	25	30	35	29	26
Information availability								
Information on the statement about how long it would take to pay off the balance if I make only the minimum payment would be very helpful to me	65	51	24	27	7	10	4	12
Mailings and other ads that offer a low rate at first followed by a higher rate are confusing to me	36	35	25	19	15	17	24	29
Memo: General satisfaction/dissatisfaction with closed-end creditors and lenders in 1977								
They provide a useful service to consumers	42		51		6		1	
Most people are satisfied in their dealings with them	17		60		18		5	
It would be a good thing for consumers if they were not around	6		21		36		38	

NOTE: Components may not sum to 100 because of rounding.
na: question not asked in year.

SOURCE: Thomson Reuters/University of Michigan Surveys of Consumers; memo items, 1977 Survey of Consumer Finances. The table is from Durkin (2000, 629) and Canner and Elliehausen (2013, 32).

all prices are too high. In 2000 they also expressed concern over privacy practices. In contrast, relatively few expressed concern about billing accuracy.

Feelings about consumers' experiences with credit cards in general were even more negative than their feelings about specific practices, although this may again reflect views about the experiences of others.[13] Holders of bank-type credit cards believed that too much credit was available, that consumers were confused about some practices, and that credit users had difficulty getting out of debt. More than half said that issuers should not be allowed to market cards to college students. However, they appeared to believe that the consumers bring on themselves many of the problems associated with credit cards: About 90 percent agreed to some extent that overspending is the fault of consumers, not of card issuers.

Survey evidence does not suggest that increasingly negative views of credit cards have arisen from adverse personal experiences, however. Rather, consumers' opinions about *their own* relationships with their current card issuers were much more favorable than their opinions of the relationships of consumers in general. Approximately nine in ten holders of bank-type credit cards questioned said that they were satisfied with their dealings with card companies, that their card companies treated them fairly, and that it was easy to get another card if they were not treated fairly. In 2000 almost seven in ten trusted that their own card companies would keep their personal information confidential, substantially more than the proportion believing that card companies in general show enough concern about protecting privacy (a bit fewer than five in ten that year). Card holders' opinions about their own experiences were almost the reverse of their views about consumers' experiences in general, suggesting considerable concern over the behavior of others and possibly a belief that they can handle credit cards but other people cannot.

Despite expressed concerns about some practices and experiences, consumers appeared to be satisfied with the credit card market in general. Approximately nine in ten holders of bank-type credit cards said that credit cards provide a useful service to consumers, and about seven in ten in 2000 said that most people are satisfied in their dealings with card companies, a proportion that fell to about half in 2012. About six in ten disagreed that consumers would be better off without cards. These results are similar to those from a 1977 survey of users of nonrevolving credit (memo items in table 7.7). It seems that credit and creditors are rarely viewed completely favorably, even by users of the service, but that most users are favorably inclined.

Many holders of bank-type cards in 2000 said that it would be helpful to include on their billing statement information about the length of time it would take to pay off the balance if only the minimum payment were made each month. Exactness, and presumably the usefulness, in such a calculation assumes, of course, that the consumer does not use the card during the repayment period and that the balance declines on schedule. If the balance were to fluctuate, the calculation would be difficult or impossible and most likely meaningless as the

13. Survey interviewers did not offer the statements in the order given in table 7.7; the table groups topically-similar questions for analytical purposes.

actual time to pay off fluctuates. Survey respondents probably did not consider the implications and complexity of the calculations but were simply acknowledging a desire for a practical measure of the burden they are incurring. In 2012 a somewhat smaller proportion indicated that the information actually is helpful, following revisions to Truth in Lending between the two survey dates requiring this disclosure. Many respondents also reported that "teaser rates" are confusing. They could, of course, avoid teaser rates altogether by ignoring the mailings that promote them; consequently, this survey finding may reflect concerns among consumers that card issuers have complicated their promotional materials sufficiently that it is difficult to understand and accept advantageous offers when card issuers offer them. The proportion answering affirmatively fell by about seven percentage points in the second survey; perhaps this reflects the less prevalent use of this marketing device in recent years.

What emerges from these responses to opinion questioning, in sum, is a multifaceted set of attitudes about credit cards. Multifaceted opinions are not especially surprising, given that consumers overall seem to think that credit cards are both good and bad. They believe that finance percentage rates on outstanding balances are too high, are suspicious of how personal information is used, and have relatively little confidence in other individuals who use credit cards. When they imagine "the other guy" in contact with card issuers whose behavior is already suspect, they imagine possibly negative consequences, such as excessive credit use.

When the focus shifts to more personal experience, however, they view the outcome much more favorably, suggesting that actual problems with credit cards are not nearly as widespread as consumers imagine them when they think about the population of largely unknown "others." On balance, holders of bank-type credit cards appear to believe that credit cards are useful and that consumers are better off with them than without them, despite concerns over the inability of "other (unknown) consumers" to exercise self-discipline and avoid overuse. These opinions seem to mirror earlier views about closed-end installment credit. Finally, consumers believe that additional, less confusing information about payments and rates would be useful.

Perceptions of Information Availability

A survey of consumers with one or more bank-type credit cards the next year (2001) asked about their perceptions of information availability for card accounts in a way that permitted comparisons with earlier questioning about other kinds of consumer credit. It also permitted further examination of the possibility of the "other guy" effect among holders of bank-type credit cards. The first question asked about degree of difficulty in obtaining useful information about credit terms. Following up on the surveys in 2000, this and some following questions made a distinction between respondents' views of their own experiences with information and their conception of the experiences of others, specifically because of the finding in the earlier survey that reports about their own experiences might well differ from views of the experiences of unknown others.

Almost two-thirds of holders of bank-type card accounts in the 2001 survey reported that they believed that getting useful information on credit terms was either "very easy" or "somewhat easy" for themselves (first panel of table 7.8). Only 6 percent of the card holders believed that obtaining this information was "very difficult." This finding was comparable to results of the same question asked about perceived difficulties in obtaining information on closed-end credit accounts in earlier years, but it differed substantially from current respondents' views of the experiences of others with credit card accounts. Fewer than half of holders of bank-type cards believed it was easy for others to acquire useful information on credit terms. Repeat of this question in 2012 indicates substantial worsening of views at this time that followed the financial crisis of 2008–2009.

Table 7.8 OPINIONS OF CONSUMER CREDIT USERS CONCERNING EASE OF OBTAINING INFORMATION ON CREDIT TERMS AND ON ADEQUACY OF INFORMATION PROVIDED, SELECTED YEARS, 1977–2012, IN PERCENT

Opinion	1977	1981	1994	1997	2001		2012
					For Self	For Others	
Ease of Obtaining Useful Information on Credit Terms							
Very easy	23	28	23	23	21	11	7
Somewhat easy	39	48	48	49	44	32	39
Somewhat difficult	29	21	23	25	26	36	41
Very difficult	8	4	5	3	6	11	12
Do not know	1	*	1	*	3	9	1
Total[b]	100	100	100	100	100	100	100
Creditors Give Enough Information							
Yes	44	65	62	61	65	49	47
Some do/some do not	13	7	5	9	2	4	*
No	38	27	30	29	31	43	52
Do not know	4	1	2	1	1	4	*
Total	100	100	100	100	100	100	100

For 1977, percentage of families with closed-end installment debt outstanding; for 1981, 1994, and 1997, percentage of families that had incurred closed-end installment debt in the past year; for 2001 and 2012, percentage of holders of bank-type credit cards. Components may not add to 100 because of rounding.
*Less than 0.5 percent.

SOURCE: 1977 Survey of Consumer Finances; for other years, Thomson Reuters/ University of Michigan Surveys of Consumers. The table is from Durkin (2002, 205) and updated from the 2012 source data.

The questioning this year did not also ask specifically about preceptions of the experiences of others.

A related follow-up question produced a similar outcome. When queried in 2001 about whether credit card companies usually provide enough information to enable them to use credit cards wisely, respondents answered affirmatively much more often than when the same question was asked about their perception of the experience of others. The former question elicited almost two-thirds agreement, but the latter found only a bit less than one-half (second panel of table 7.8). The question was asked in this manner not with the expectation of learning something about respondents' view of what was "wise" but rather with the goal of comparing the results with the same question asked in the past of users of closed-end installment credit. Again, responses for credit cards in 2001 were quite similar to recent responses to questioning about closed-end credit, at least after 1977, when Truth in Lending was much newer. There was also falloff in the proportion of affirmative responses to this question in 2012. It will be interesting to see if responses to these two questions return to their previous range if they are repeated sometime in the future as the financial crisis fades further into memory.

Another question explored further the distinction between views about personal experience with credit cards and that of others. This question asked whether general-purpose credit cards with a revolving feature that offered the option of paying part of the balance made managing one's finances easier or more difficult. Almost 90 percent of respondents replied either that such cards made managing finances easier or that there was no difference, and only about 10 percent indicated a perception that managing finances was more difficult (table 7.9). When asked further why credit cards have made managing finances easier, the majority of respondents, not surprisingly, stressed aspects of flexibility, especially expenditure and repayment smoothing, that credit cards permit.

Table 7.9 OPINIONS OF CREDIT CARD USERS CONCERNING THE EFFECTS OF CREDIT CARDS ON PERSONAL FINANCIAL MANAGEMENT, 2001 AND 2012, IN PERCENT

Question and Opinion	2001		2012
	For Self	For Others	For Self
Credit cards make managing finances			
Easier	73	53	82
No different	16	2	8
More difficult	10	40	8
Do not know	2	5	2
Total	100	100	

Components may not add to 100 because of rounding.

SOURCE: Thomson Reuters/University of Michigan Surveys of Consumers. Table is from Durkin (2002, 205) and updated from the 2012 source data.

The smaller proportion who did not find that credit cards made managing finances easier most often noted the dangers of overspending and overextending financial resources. Opinions in this area improved substantially in the 2012 survey.

The generally favorable view concerning the impact of credit cards on their personal financial management contrasted sharply with consumers' views about the experiences of other people in 2001. Just more than half (55 percent) of respondents indicated their view that such credit cards made finances of the "other guy" easier or no different, but two-fifths said that the finances of others were made more difficult by credit cards. The latter proportion is four times the proportion with a negative view of the impact of credit cards on their own finances. The most common reasons for this contention were concern for overspending, too much debt, and a continuing cycle of debt among these unknown other consumers (not in the table).

The generally favorable view of respondents about information availability and their own circumstances is heartening, in that it seems to suggest directly and indirectly that many people are relatively satisfied with the current information situation. This generally favorable attitude contrasts with respondents' perspectives on the experiences of others, whom they appear to regard as more vulnerable. Unknown others are considered less able to obtain and use information or to manage their finances well when using credit cards.

Existence of a generally favorable attitude toward personal experience with credit cards is supported by results of a later segment of the interview in both 2001 and 2012concerning overall satisfaction with credit cards. The final question asked, "Overall, how satisfied are *you* [emphasis stressed by interviewer] with your general-purposes credit card(s)?" The question requested a response on a five-point scale, from "very satisfied" to "very dissatisfied." More than four-fifths in both surveys indicated satisfaction, and fewer than one in ten reported dissatisfaction (table 7.10). Only about 1 percent of respondents in both surveys indicated that they were very dissatisfied. The pattern of responses to this question is much like earlier findings concerning installment credit and home equity credit lines, especially if the very satisfied and those somewhat satisfied are lumped together. The number dissatisfied remains quite small across the years and across credit types.

Credit Card Users and Truth in Lending

Buyer behavior theories contend that knowledge logically precedes attitudes and that both are important for behavior. Thus, an intriguing question about Truth in Lending (TIL) is its long-term impact on consumer awareness, understanding, attitudes, and behavior, if any; this has led to explorations of these issues.

A question in the survey in 2000 indicated that consumer awareness of annual percentage rates associated with credit card accounts, using the procedure for measuring awareness established by the National Commission on Consumer Finance in 1972, had increased dramatically in the three decades since implementation of

Table 7.10 OVERALL SATISFACTION OF CONSUMERS WITH CREDIT, BY TYPE OF
CREDIT, SELECTED YEARS, 1977–2012, IN PERCENT

Question and Opinion	1977	1994		1997		2001	2012
	Closed-End Installment	HELC	Installment	HELC	Installment	Bank-Type Credit Card	
Overall satisfaction with credit							
Very satisfied	77	69	56	75	63	48	47
Somewhat satisfied	18	27	32	21	29	42	37
Not particularly satisfied or dissatisfied	3	2	5	*	4	5	7
Somewhat dissatisfied	2	2	2	*	1	5	7
Very dissatisfied	1	1	5	2	3	1	1
Do not know	*	*	*	1	*	*	1
Total	100	100	100	100	100	100	100

For 1977, percentage of families with closed-end installment debt outstanding; for 1994 and 1997, percentage of families with open home equity lines of credit (HELC, with or without an outstanding balance, first column for each year); for 2001, percentage of holders of bank-type credit cards.

Components may not add to 100 because of rounding.

*Less than 0.5 percent.

SOURCE: 1977 Consumer Credit Survey; Thomson Reuters/University of Michigan Surveys of Consumers. Table is from Durkin (2002, 206) and updated from the 2012 source data.

the law.[14] Awareness under the National Commission's approach had increased from 27 percent before TIL to 63 percent after fifteen months, 71 percent in 1977, and 85 to 91 percent in 2000 for the "narrow" and "broad" definitions of awareness employed in the survey project that year (data on awareness not in table). The 2001 survey confirmed the long-term rise in the awareness level to year 2000, with awareness recorded in 2001 under the same definitions at 82 and 88 percent, within the normal range for statistical variation. Results in 2012 also were very similar (see Canner and Elliehausen 2013, 237, table 6).

14. Fuller explanation of the approach and rationale of the National Commission on Consumer Finance in this area is found in Durkin (2000, 630–631).

The 2001 survey also asked a number of additional questions related to TIL, specifically about consumers' understanding and use of TIL information on bank-type credit cards and their attitudes toward availability of information and the information provided by TIL. The questions employed were the same ones asked in the past to study information use for closed-end credit, although they were not updated in 2012.

The first question stated that the "federal Truth in Lending law requires that credit card companies provide consumers with written statements of credit costs when a new account is opened and as part of the monthly bill." Then the interviewer asked, "Is the Truth in Lending statement helpful in any way?" Three-fifths of consumers with bank-type credit cards indicated in 2001 that the TIL statement was helpful, and almost another three-tenths responded that it was not (table 7.11). These results were similar to past findings, although the former proportion was a bit higher and the latter a bit lower than responses about TIL statements on various forms of closed-end credit in most past measurements. About 11 percent of respondents maintained that they did not know whether the statement was helpful, a bit higher than on earlier surveys.

When quizzed further, "In what way is it helpful?" almost half of those indicating in 2001 that the statement was helpful responded with a generic response that it provided general information on terms and conditions (figures not in table). Thirteen percent specifically mentioned that it provided information on interest

Table 7.11 Opinions of Credit Users concerning Helpfulness of Truth in Lending Statements, Selected Years, 1981–2001, in Percent

Opinion	1981	1994		1997		2001
	Install-ment	HELC	Install-ment	HELC	Install-ment	Bank-Type Credit Card
Helpful	53	60	46	58	58	60
Not helpful[a]	45	32	49	39	39	29
Do not know	2	8	5	3	3	11
Total	100	100	100	100	100	100

For 1981, 1994, and 1997, percentage of families that had incurred closed-end installment debt in the past year; in 1994 and 1997, percentage of families with open home equity lines of credit (HELC), with or without an outstanding balance; in 2001, percentage of holders of bank-type credit cards.

[a]Includes respondents who did not recall receiving statement.

Components may not add to 100 because of rounding.

source: Thomson Reuters/University of Michigan Surveys of Consumers. Table is from Durkin (2002, Table 8, p. 207).

rates or finance charges, and about 10 percent said that it provided a good reference document if problems arose.

Another follow-up question in 2001 asked both those who felt the TIL statement was helpful and those who did not how the statement could be made more helpful. A bit more than two-fifths of those indicating that it was already helpful said they did not know how it could be made more helpful (not in table). Another 15 percent said it could not be made more helpful, but about 28 percent of these favorable respondents mentioned issues of format and clarity: it could be clearer, simpler, easier to understand, in lay terms, or in larger print.

Among the three-tenths of respondents who indicated that the TIL statement was not helpful, again about two-fifths said they did not know how it could be more helpful, but almost half of this group mentioned various format and clarity issues. A number of consumers responded with a variety of other things they considered potentially useful. These answers ranged from sending a representative to one's home to explain account terms to enforcing the laws and making the Truth in Lending Act mandatory reading for all consumers entering into credit contracts.

The 2012 survey next asked cardholders directly for their view on whether the TIL statement had affected their decision to use credit cards in any way. About half of cardholders who sometimes or hardly ever paid balances in full (that is, those who incurred finance charges) reported that the APR or the finance charge affected their decisions. When asked in what way their decision to use credit was affected, most said decisions on whether or not to use credit and how much were affected. But according to Canner and Elliehausen (2013), "only a relatively small share of cardholders changed their spending habits or stopped using cards altogether because of this information, and relatively few cardholders used the information to choose which card to use" (23).

Over the years, consumer surveys also have asked about general perceptions of TIL statements. It is clear from this line of questioning that typical credit users consider TIL statements to be complicated. From around two-thirds to more than three-quarters of consumers have agreed or strongly agree with the statement that TIL statements are complicated, and this measure reached 86 percent in 2012 (table 7.12). Likewise, about three-fifths to more than three quarter recently have agreed or strongly agreed that some information on the statements is not very helpful. On the positive side, a clear majority of respondents has affirmed the view that TIL makes people more confident when dealing with creditors. This seems like a hidden benefit of the law. Consumers may feel that the statements are complicated and that not every element is always useful, but they appear to like knowing that someone is watching the behavior of the creditors.

The only striking difference in the responses of consumers over time to this sequence of questions again appears related to the "other guy" effect. Over the decades, only around three-tenths of consumers have reported agreement with the view that most consumers read their TIL statements carefully. A change in wording in 2001 to focus this question on the individual, rather than on consumers in general, produced the finding that about half of consumers report that they read the statements carefully themselves. While this likely reflects a degree of "yea saying" by respondents to give the interviewer what might be perceived as an answer that is in some sense correct, it probably also mirrors a degree of belief among individuals that they exercise the correct amount of care themselves but that others may be less inclined to do so. Return to the original wording in 2012 again found a low level of agreement.

In sum, survey-based measurements of consumers' attitudes toward credit cards lead to a paradox and a possible explanation. Over the years, a higher proportion of consumers generally and credit card users contend that credit cards are "bad," despite higher use of credit cards. Further questioning, however, reveals

Table 7.12 CONSUMERS' AGREEMENT WITH OBSERVATIONS ABOUT TRUTH IN LENDING STATEMENTS, SELECTED YEARS, 1977–2012, IN PERCENT

Statement and Opinion	1977	1981	1994	1997	2001	2012
Truth in Lending statements are complicated						
Agree strongly	38	31	41	49	45	52
Agree somewhat	35	37	36	32	30	34
Disagree somewhat	11	18	13	11	9	10
Disagree strongly	5	8	5	5	8	3
Do not know	12	6	5	2	8	1
Total	100	100	100	100	100	100
Some information on Truth in Lending statements is not very helpful						
Agree strongly	20	16	21	23	28	33
Agree somewhat	39	41	43	42	38	42
Disagree somewhat	16	23	19	21	18	17
Disagree strongly	5	6	9	10	7	7
Do not know	20	14	8	3	9	2
Total	100	100	100	100	100	100
Truth in Lending makes people more confident when dealing with creditors						
Agree strongly	31	28	24	26	26	15
Agree somewhat	42	44	46	43	41	42
Disagree somewhat	12	14	17	19	15	24
Disagree strongly	5	6	8	10	11	17
Do not know	11	8	5	2	7	1
Total	100	100	100	100	100	1

(Continued)

Table 7.12 (CONTINUED)

Statement and Opinion	1977	1981	1994	1997	2001	2012
Most people read their Truth in Lending statements carefully[a]						
Agree strongly	8	7	9	7	19	6
Agree somewhat	19	24	26	22	30	14
Disagree somewhat	33	38	34	35	22	26
Disagree strongly	31	26	27	34	24	53
Do not know	9	5	4	1	5	*
Total	100	100	100	100	100	100

For 1977, percentage of families with closed-end installment debt outstanding; for 1981, 1994, and 1997, percentage of families that had incurred closed-end installment debt in the past year; for 2001, percentage of holders of bank-type credit cards.

[a]In 2001, this question was asked about th e individual respondent: "I read the Truth in Lending statement carefully."

Components may not add to 100 because of rounding.

* Less than 0.5 percent.

SOURCE: 1977 Survey of Consumer Finances; Thomson Reuters/University of Michigan Surveys of Consumers. Table is from Durkin (2002), 208 and Canner and Elliehausen (2013, 35).

that while overall attitudes toward cards appear to have become a bit worse on average over the past thirty years, part of the explanation may result from the view that credit cards are posing difficulties for the "other guy." Consumers' views of their own experiences with credit cards are much more favorable than their feelings about the experiences of unknown others. In contrast to their views about others, approximately nine in ten respondents holding one or more bank-type credit cards report the following:

- They are generally satisfied in their dealings with card companies.
- Their card companies treat them fairly.
- It is easy to get another card from another company if they are not treated fairly anyway.
- Billing statements are accurate.
- Credit cards have made managing their finances easier.
- Overspending is the fault of consumers and not card companies.
- Card companies provide a useful service to consumers.

Expansion of credit card holding and use since 1970 seems consistent with views of this sort.

Previous Studies of Attitudes toward Credit Cards

Other than the studies discussed above, there are relatively few published studies about consumers' attitudes toward credit cards or, for that matter, about attitudes toward any forms of consumer credit. Concerning credit cards specifically, there likely have been few studies recently in part because card products have now become relatively mature and possibly not as interesting to academic researchers as when they were newer. In past years, when credit cards, and especially three-party credit cards with a revolving feature, were a novel financial phenomenon, there was more interest in studying them generally and especially for studying consumers' motivations surrounding their use of this new product, including attitudes. More recently, except in the legal literature and law reviews, the interest seems to have waned a bit. Another reason, probably of even greater significance, is the inherent difficulty for academic researchers of collecting new data in this area, which typically involves undertaking expensive consumer surveys.

Some exceptions to the paucity of attitude studies exist, but they generally do not attempt to measure attitudes directly, especially concerning credit cards. More commonly, they look for correlations between the relatively limited measures of attitudes in the Surveys of Consumer Finances with various measurements of debt outstanding in the same surveys. Possibly the most noteworthy aspect of such efforts is how the statistical correlations found raise as many questions as they answer, maybe more. A positive or negative correlation of some attitude measurement with a stock outstanding such as consumer debt does not answer any underlying questions about motivation. Causality in such cases could run from attitude to debt use or the other way around, from debt use to attitude, even if economic influences on credit use are otherwise adequately accounted for.

Fundamentally, the decision to use credit or not involves underlying economic motivations and depends on more than favorable attitudes (see chapters 3 and 4). Even though attitude studies typically include "economic variables" in a multivariate equation of some sort, they stop well short of developing an economic decision or buyer behavior model. While attitudes undoubtedly are important in purchase decisions, including choice of brand and product class, there is more to an economic choice than attitudes (pricing, for example). Without a fuller modeling of consumer behavior than normally found in these papers, direction of attitude influence is likely to remain unanswered, despite demonstration of the existence of correlations. A few examples should indicate the flavor of the correlation studies.

A paper by Chien and Devaney offers a good example. The paper begins with a general question in its first sentence, "Do consumers' attitudes toward credit influence their use of it?" which it then proceeds to answer in the second sentence, "Many studies have concluded that the dramatic growth in credit use since the 1980s is due, in fact, to the change in attitude toward credit [references omitted]" (Chien and Devaney 2001, 162). The introduction goes on to argue that maybe this overlooks some important factors, including supply effects and potentially misleading statistical correlations resulting from multicollinearity in the data, and so the issue should be studied once again.

Leaving aside the issue of whether the premise about dramatic credit growth is even correct (see chapter 2 above for extended discussion), it is questionable whether it is possible to say anything definitive about the impact of attitudes on credit growth without fuller discussion of the determinants of credit use behavior, especially the economic aspects. Demand factors including price, tastes, wealth, and demand for the goods often purchased on credit, and many other economic factors likely are also significant, as might be changes over time in the efficiency of credit markets generally.

Attitudes in the context of a buyer behavior model likely *are* important at the margin when all relevant factors are properly taken into account, but correlations by themselves do not demonstrate causality. The Chien and Devaney paper does show that consumer debt outstanding at the micro level is positively correlated with favorable attitudes toward consumer credit (at least as these concepts are measured in the 1998 Survey of Consumer Finances). The need to consider other factors (and direction of influence) is mentioned early in the paper, but the possibility that causality may run in the other direction (from debt experience to attitude) is mentioned otherwise only briefly in the conclusions.[15]

A paper by Kaili Yieh (1996) adopts exactly the opposite view, namely, it uses information on debt outstanding in the 1989 Survey of Consumer Finances (and other variables) to try to explain probability of a negative attitude toward consumer credit. In what appears to be circular reasoning, the paper indicates in the introduction that the reason this is an important question is that attitudes are important in explaining debt growth. As with the Chien and Devaney paper, the attempt to explore the possibility of a correlation between debt and attitude is interesting, but the approach in the second paper does not head toward demonstration of causality, either. In effect, this paper amounts to the statistical reverse of the first paper.

Unfortunately, neither paper demonstrates sufficiently that the variables are measured well enough for the purposes intended or that the demographic and other variables chosen as explanatory variables account adequately for all the economic considerations that undoubtedly are associated with credit use. In the second paper, the impact of debt on debt attitudes is not statistically significant. It may well be that intercorrelations among the lengthy list of independent variables used in the Yieh paper account for this outcome, especially given the findings of a correlation by Chien and Devaney. Likewise, neither paper analyzes how attitudes toward debt that may well have worsened over time can be systematically related to the rapid growth of consumer credit that these papers contend has been taking place.

In another paper, Deborah Godwin (1997) employed the panel data component of the 1983 and 1989 Surveys of Consumer Finances to explore how income,

---

15. It also appears that the Chien and Devaney paper has some definitional difficulties in the concepts of consumer credit that it employs that may call into question some of the correlations it finds. For example, noninstallment credit is not the same as open-end credit, although the paper reports otherwise. Without redoing the analysis, it is not obvious whether definitional problems in the variables might influence reported outcomes in some unknown way.

debt, and attitude toward debt might change for individuals with the passage of time. She rightly points out that the terms *low, middle, upper,* or other designations for income or indebtedness seem implicitly static in connotation, at least in how they are commonly employed. She notes that Duncan (1986) has shown that placement of households in income groups did not prove static for individual families in the 1970s. She hypothesizes that the same may well have been true for income or debt status in the 1980s and for attitudes toward consumer credit. In all three cases, examining static groupings such as income or debt quintiles might well mask substantial migration of individual households across groups.

Using cross-tabulations of income, debt, and debt attitudes placement of households in 1983 and 1989, Godwin showed that there was substantial migration in all three areas in the 1980s, with households in lower income and debt categories moving upward and vice versa. Likewise, there was migration in attitudes toward consumer credit use. She also shows that the migration for debt status and debt attitudes was not symmetric over these years, with more households moving to lower debt status and less favorable attitudes toward consumer credit than toward more debt and more favorable attitudes.

Concerning the movement in debts outstanding and attitudes, it is not clear that Godwin realized that the movement asymmetries she encountered both might well be artifacts of aging by the panel. Everyone in the panel necessarily was six years older in 1989 than in 1983, and older people generally use less consumer credit. They also are probably less favorably inclined toward consumer credit as they age. It is well enough known that as individuals become older, they often become less favorably inclined toward many of the behavioral patterns of their youth.

Economists Thomas F. Cargill and Jeanne Wendel (1996) used the attitude measures in the 1989 Survey of Consumer Finances to examine the relationship between attitudes toward credit and credit card balances outstanding. Employing a regression equation, they found that a positive attitude toward credit in the 1989 survey was associated with a higher balance outstanding on bank-type credit cards, holding a variety of other demand-related variables constant. These authors plainly recognized the bidirectional nature of the correlation they found. In fact, as they pointed out, their methodology and the question they address do not require distinction of direction. Rather than trying to predict either attitude or credit card balance outstanding, they merely posited that a positive correlation is associated with consumer rationality, the issue of importance to them. They suggested that a positive attitude and a higher balance should be positively correlated if consumers are rational, and they accepted the finding of such a relationship as support for their hypothesis of rationality.

In addition to these correlation studies that employ the limited attitude data in the Surveys of Consumer Finances, there are some older studies of attitudes toward consumer credit that attempt to measure attitudes independently. Awh and Waters (1974) used results of a mail survey of customers of a bank to explore whether a measure of attitudes toward credit cards might be related to the distinction between holders of bank-type credit cards who were active users of their cards and those holders who were not. Using a multivariate discriminant function that also included a variety of other variables, they found that their measurement of attitudes toward credit cards was the variable that carried the greatest statistical relationship to active credit card use among holders. Attitude toward credit generally, as they measured it, was less important than attitude toward credit cards. Together, the variables in their discriminant function produced an equation that could classify nearly eight of ten card holders correctly as active users or not. As with the later correlation studies, however, although the Awh and Waters study might have served as the basis for a useful forecasting device at the time, it did not fully explain the underlying motivations, either.

A paper by Danes and Hira (1990) is one of the few exploring consumers' attitudes toward credit use that attempt to incorporate attitudes within a larger theoretical construct contemplating more than an ad hoc listing of other variables of possible interest. The authors provided a simplified model based on theory that tries to take into account both knowledge and beliefs in relation to actual behavior in the use of credit cards. Their model does not assign any potential importance to economic variables of the sort that might influence credit usage, however, and so overall, it probably assigns too much importance to attitudes.

Danes and Hira first explored what previous studies said about relationships among pairs of the concepts of interest: knowledge, attitudes, and behavior (specifically, measures of credit card use). From other studies, they noted that both knowledge and favorable attitudes appeared to be positively related statistically to card use. There's no surprise there but also no indication of direction of causation. Also, they hypothesized that younger and higher-income consumers are also more likely to use credit cards (again, no surprise). They characterized income as a demographic variable, rather than a proxy for an economic concept such as wealth. They found that its relationship to card use in other studies was mixed, which they attributed to confounding of credit users and convenience users among card holders in those studies.

The authors then applied some statistical estimating procedures to a small survey of households in a Midwestern town in 1982. Some of the correlations they uncovered were the opposite of their hypotheses, which may indicate some underlying difficulties of their own within definitions of the variables. The authors contended, for example, that they found a negative relationship between knowledge about credit cards and their preferred outcome: that card knowledge, as they defined it, should be associated with the belief that cards should only be used as convenience devices rather than to generate credit. They did find the preferred negative relationship between this belief and the number of cards held and the propensity to revolve the cards and pay finance charges. They also did not review the possibility of reverse causation previously noted for the other papers.

In sum, it appears that earlier published studies of consumers' attitudes toward credit cards do not add a great deal to our understanding of these attitudes beyond the findings of the more recent studies. It seems that consumers are not destined to be completely happy with credit products generally and with plastic access devices specifically. Nonetheless, as outlined earlier, and differentiating between views of consumers about their own experiences versus perceptions of the condition of others, attitudes toward credit cards have been largely favorable.

This is consistent with growth in use of the product, much as television use and fast-food restaurants have also grown, despite less than universal enthusiasm for them, either.

Public Policy Response to Complaints

Whenever complaining develops about a product or service, public policy investigation and the potential for regulation are usually not far behind. Credit cards are no exception. Congressional committees regularly hold hearings about various aspects of consumers' experiences with credit cards and sometimes propose legislation. Regulatory agencies also watch credit cards, especially in the past the Federal Reserve Board, which has had the responsibility for writing the implementing rules under the Truth in Lending Act and also for monitoring the general health of the financial sector, not an insignificant task as the financial crisis of 2008–2009 clearly showed. In 2011, responsibility for rule writing in this area passed to the new federal Consumer Financial Protection Bureau under provisions of the Dodd-Frank Act of 2010.

After two decades of only minor adjustments of regulatory rules concerning credit cards, policy actions took two controversial tacks beginning in the middle years of the 2000s. They began in late 2004, with Federal Reserve Board development of an agency regulatory proposal on its own authority for lengthy revisions to disclosure rules for credit cards under the Truth in Lending Act. This proposal did not become final until late 2008. At the same time, the Board also approved some new substantive rules affecting specifics of operating methods for granting credit through credit card accounts. Congress then, in effect, ratified the regulatory rules changes in 2009 by passing legislation encoding the regulatory changes into law and added a few tweaks of its own. Adjustments of TIL disclosure rules are fairly common, but federal substantive rules affecting credit-granting operations are less so, and for this reason, the new rules and law in 2008–2009 were quite controversial.

Notably, within a list of technical proposals concerning such things as billing practices and timing of mailing or electronic delivery of credit card bills, one substantive proposal went to the very heart of the nature of the open-end or revolving credit business as it has developed over the years. For decades, credit card issuing companies have maintained that a revolving credit account, unlike installment loans that extend only for a fixed length of time, represents an ongoing credit relationship contemplating further credit extensions in the future in addition to those already made in the past. But because this credit relationship is long-term and may involve new advances of credit long after the initial underwriting and credit analysis occurred, this kind of credit granting is subject to risks that arise from changes in customer financial condition over time. Consequently, card companies have maintained that they must be able to change the finance rates they charge customers when risk increases, if they are simultaneously to be able to charge the lowest possible rates to customers for whom upward risk change does not occur.

Over time, as credit scoring became widely available and credit reporting agencies (credit bureaus) became automated, risk-based pricing of this kind became the norm in the revolving credit industry (see chapters 5 and 6). This means that lower-risk customers, as identified by their credit file at the credit bureau and their mathematical regression credit score, can obtain revolving credit at a lower finance charge rate than those identified as riskier. The idea here is that competition to retain low-risk customers, in addition to fairness, dictates that those who cause risk and higher expense for card issuers be the ones to pay for it, rather than averaging the risk costs over all customers, including those who do not cause these risk-related costs. Further, as discussed at greater length in chapter 5, attempting to charge everyone a single rate can lead to rationing of the riskier customers.

This is the same notion as risk-based pricing in the insurance industry. Insurance companies charge risky drivers more for automobile insurance or smokers more for life insurance, rather than charging everyone the same price. In effect, they do not try to make less risky customers subsidize the riskier ones or subject them to rationing. Not only does this approach prevent subsidization by lower-risk customers, but it also tends to discourage further risky behavior by higher-risk individuals as their price rises (risky driving or smoking, for example).

In this context, card companies have contended that as identifiable risk of individual account holders changes over time, the card issuers also must be able to adjust the rate charged in order for them to continue to maintain portfolio stability and fairness to all customers. This system has generally been satisfactory to low-rate customers, but interest rate increases for those newly exhibiting riskier behavior have generated complaints and a congressional and regulatory agency response.

The difficulty is that without raising rates on existing balances of customers who exhibit riskier behavior such as paying late or going over their credit limits, the riskier customers may not pay their own way. The trade-off then becomes a common one in public policy debates. Should you "protect" consumers who find themselves in some difficulty, such as in this case paying higher rates on their credit card credit because of demonstrated risk, by charging more to the majority who do not exhibit risky behaviors? Further, should the riskier customers be potentially subject to rationing?

The differences in risk and associated costs to card companies are not trivial. For example, one issuer in its comment letter to the Federal Reserve Board on the 2008 regulatory proposal to limit the practice of increasing card holder rates on existing balances noted that customers who pay late twice in a twelve-month period become total losses (charge-offs) *eight* times as frequently as regular customers.

Others submitting public comment letters on the regulatory proposal wrote that prohibiting penalty pricing on existing balances of customers who paid late twice would produce industry-wide revenue effects exceeding $12 billion. This substantial amount would have to be recouped from those paying their bills on time, or card issuers would have to cancel the accounts of the riskier customers. These contentions illustrate well the difficulties of changing public policies in the financial area and why the legislative and regulatory proposals have been controversial.

Despite the arguments of card issuers, in late 2008, the Federal Reserve Board went ahead with its proposal and outlawed raising rates on existing balances (with a few exceptions) even if risk increases were demonstrable. Congress ratified and toughened this decision through legislation in 2009.[16] As a result, credit card issuing banks both raised prices and took steps to limit credit access of riskier customers as 2010 proceeded (see Simon 2010). In 2012, empirical evidence suggested that greater rationing of higher-risk customers had taken place (see Han, Keys, and Li 2012).

CREDIT CARD ACCOUNT PERFORMANCE

Information from consumer surveys shows that card holding and use are widely distributed across the public, but there are still many questions about how consumers actually use their cards and make their payments. For example, do they maintain high or low balances relative to credit limits, or do the balances fluctuate? At the end of the month, do they typically pay all or most of the balance, do they pay little of it, or do they do some of each? On that score, is a given consumer's behavior consistent over time, or do consumers change behaviors concerning proportions of balances typically repaid and revolved? These questions and others can be answered only by examining actual account experience.

For the most part, specific information on experience with individual credit card accounts is available only to the creditors who issue the cards. Only they can review their credit files to ascertain the patterns of card use and repayment. And of course, even they do not know about the experience of customers of their competitors. Fortunately for illustrative purposes, however, a large sample of account information was made available some years ago to the Credit Research Center by a number of large issuers of bank-type credit cards for studying just such questions.

Overall, twelve-month account histories were made available from more than 300,000 randomly selected card accounts during 2001. Originally, the data on individual credit card accounts were collected in three parts: a sample of card accounts from college student marketing campaigns, another sample of accounts of young adults but not from a college marketing program, and a larger sample of more typical accounts not from a college program and not exclusively young adults. Appropriate weighting of the data according to frequency of each kind of account in the underlying population of accounts permits construction and examination of a data set believed to be representative of the relatively new card accounts of five very large issuers of bank-type credit cards. Because of their large size (all were among the top fifteen card issuers by volume of managed credit card receivables), there is every reason to believe that this data set is also representative

16. Credit Card Accountability Responsibility and Disclosure (CARD) Act of 2009. Various parts of the legislation had effective dates in August 2009, February 2010, and August 2010.

of the account experience of card issuers generally. Even if not perfectly representative of the universe of card accounts, the data set is large enough and representative enough to provide interesting descriptions of the card use behavior of millions of consumers at the micro level. The appendix to this chapter contains some more details about the data set and the sample selection process. Data from this sample of card accounts provide information about card use and payment habits of typical consumers that has not been available heretofore, except to card issuers looking at their own portfolios of accounts.

Frequency of Revolving

A question frequently asked is the prevalence of consumers who revolve their bank-type card accounts versus those who regularly pay the accounts in full. The answer to the question depends, of course, in part on the time horizon examined. An individual consumer may well revolve part or most of an account balance this month but pay it in full next month or maybe the following month or the month after. Thus, looking at only an individual month will not provide a complete picture.

Because the data set contains twelve months of information, it is easy to study the prevalence of revolving using the credit card database. To illustrate, table 7.13 shows account payoff experience in the second month of the data set for all the accounts in the sample. (This does not mean February, since the beginning month is not the same among the accounts and the second month of data could be any month for a given account.) Examining the sample of card accounts this way over a one-month horizon reveals that in the given month, approximately 15 percent of active accounts owed nothing (line 1 of table 7.13). Looking at other months in the data set finds that the proportion of active accounts with no outstanding balance in the given month is similar, although not shown in a table.

Using these data, it is also possible to examine the amounts of payments made relative to the amount billed, for example, to find the proportion of consumers paying the bill in full or making minimum payments. This exercise finds that another 20 percent of the accounts paid off their initial balance approximately in full that month, defined as paying 90 percent or more of the outstanding balance (line 2 of the table). Adding this 20 percent to the 15 percent with no initial account balance means that 65 percent of account holders revolved some portion of their account balances that month.

The next question is the proportion of the balance revolved, especially the frequency of making only small or minimum payments. To answer precisely questions about making contractually minimum payments, it would be necessary to know the identity of the card issuers and their policies for the specific accounts of individual card holders, and neither is available. Nonetheless, it is possible to define some amount as approximately a minimum allowable payment and to examine frequencies of behaviors under this definition. For example, if paying 5 percent or less of the balance is defined as making approximately the minimum monthly payment allowable, then about 37 percent of accounts made the

Table 7.13 PAYMENT OF ACCOUNT BALANCES ON CREDIT CARD ACCOUNTS, IN PERCENT OF ACCOUNTS

Payment Experience in Month	Percent
(1) No balance in month	16.3
(2) Paid approximately in full (90% or more)	20.3
(3) Paid more than minimum but less than in full (paid more than 5% but less than 90%)	26.4
Notes for line 3:	
A. Paid more than 5% but less than 10%	8.8
B. Paid more than 10% but less than 50%	13.9
C. Paid more than 50% but less than 90%	3.6
(4) Paid approximately the minimum amount (paid less than 5%)	37.0
Notes for line 4:	
A. And then paid approximately the minimum for the following six months	11.9
B. And then paid off account at least once during the following six months	10.1
C. And exhibited all other payoff behaviors during the following six months	15.0
Total	100.0

Components may not add to 100 because of rounding.

SOURCE: Credit Research Center credit card database.

minimum payment in the month under consideration (line 4 of table 7.13)). This means, then, that about a quarter of accounts made a payment greater than the minimum but less than payment approximately in full (line 3 in the table).

About two-fifths making the minimum payment in a particular month does not mean that they always make minimum payments, however. With additional months of account data, it is possible to track behavior of the minimum payers over a longer time horizon, and it appears that most of them do not always make minimum payments. Notably, a bit less than one-third of minimum payers continue to make minimum payments for another six months after the initial month, while the others at least sometimes pay more than the minimum although not paying in full (see notes to line 4 in the table). This means, then, that only about 12 percent of accounts paid only the minimum for each of the seven months investigated (line 4A of the table).

This proportion making minimum payments continuously for seven months actually is very similar to the 10 percent paying the minimum in the base month but who then pay the account off in full sometime in the following six months (line 4B). Thus, it seems that paying the minimum is chronic for some accounts, but the portion exhibiting this behavior is much less than the 37 percent paying the minimum in a given month. In fact, the majority of the minimum payers exhibit different behaviors in the following months, including full payoff for many of them.

Lengthening the time horizon in this way shows that a fairly high portion of credit card accounts actually pay in full with some frequency. Combining those with no balance in the initial month (line 1) together with those who pay their balance in full in the initial month (line 2) into a group with those who pay in full sometime in the next six months (line 4B) shows that *at least* almost half of accounts (46.7 percent) reduce their balance to zero at some time in a seven-month period. This may well be a proportion higher than the typical assumption that many, or even most consumers, are mired in levels of credit card debt that are almost inescapable.

To know the full proportion who are at least occasional payers in full, it is necessary to add to this 46.7 percent the proportion of those with a balance outstanding in the original month but who do *not* pay either the minimum or in full this initial month (line 3 in the table) but who then pay the balance in full sometime in the following six months. Further study of the credit card database shows that this latter group is about 46 percent of line 3, equal to about 11.1 percent of all accounts (not shown separately in the table). Thus, adding these accounts to the others paying in full shows that the overall proportion who reduced their account balance to zero at least once in the seven-month period actually approaches three-fifths (46.7 percent plus 11.1 percent, or 57.8 percent).

Paying in Full and Not

More generally, it is possible to reorganize table 7.13 and define subsets of account use behaviors, such as minimum payers and other groupings of paying behaviors, as categories. Table 7.14 contains a set of such subsets or categories ranging from "pure convenience users," defined as those who pay their accounts in full five or more times in the seven-month period, through various categories of payers, all the way to "pure minimum payers," those who always pay approximately the minimum amount required each month over the period.

Looking at the accounts this way, the table illustrates that more than one-quarter of the accounts approximately paid in full in all or most months during the seven-month period, defined as paying 90 percent or more of their balance five or more times (line 1). Almost three-fifths of the accounts (57.2 percent) paid down approximately to zero at least once during this time (lines 1–3 combined with line 6). In contrast, only about one-eighth (12 percent) paid approximately the minimum amount all seven months (line 5). Thus, by number of card accounts, those approximately paying off at least once during the examined period outnumbered "minimum payers" by almost five to one.

The finding of a higher proportion of "payers" and "convenience users" than pure minimum payers appears to verify roughly the proportion of payers and pure revolvers found through consumer surveys. Because relatively little has been known about consumers' behavior concerning repayment patterns on card accounts, questioning in this area has been a staple in the Surveys of

Table 7.14 PAYMENT OF ACCOUNT BALANCES ON CREDIT CARD ACCOUNTS, IN
PERCENT OF ACCOUNTS

Groupings of Account Use Behaviors	Percent
(1) Pure convenience users (pay off account in full at least 5 times in 7 months)	26.9
(2) Convenience users (pay off account in full 3 or 4 times in 7 months)	12.3
(3) Payers (pay off account in full 1 or 2 times in 7 months)	14.2
(4) Fluctuators (pay differing amounts monthly but do not pay account in full in 7 months or minimum amount all 7 months)	30.8
(5) Minimum payers (pay minimum amount all 7 months)	11.9
(6) Do not use account in 7 months (although account is active sometime during 1-year period)	3.8
Total	100.0

Components may not add to 100 because of rounding.

SOURCE: Credit Research Center credit card database.

Consumer Finances since 1977, but there has been nothing to use as a standard of comparison to double-check for reasonableness of the consumer survey responses.

These questions in consumer surveys over the years have asked whether respondents "almost always," "sometimes," or "hardly ever" pay the balance in full on their credit card accounts. Responses typically have indicated that about half or a bit more of those asked claim they "almost always" pay their card accounts in full (table 7.15). Without a standard of comparison, but with the (uninformed?) conventional wisdom that many people constantly revolve, this proportion has always seemed high, possibly quite high.

Now, using this credit card database, it is feasible to compare the proportion found in the consumer surveys with actual account experience. The comparison necessarily must remain tentative because of differences in exactness of responses expected from the consumer surveys compared with the precision of the card database. Also, the card database includes only bank-type credit cards, while consumers may also be considering their retail store cards when they answer the survey question, and they may pay their retail cards in full more often, since balances typically are smaller.

Nonetheless, if accounts not used at all in the seven-month period (2 percent) are excluded, and the categories "pure convenience users" and "convenience users" are combined to constitute a group that "almost always" pays in full, and "payers" defines a group that "sometimes" pays in full, then it appears that the estimate of revolving behavior from the consumer surveys and the estimate from account data do not diverge too greatly (compare the last column of table 7.15 with the other columns). If consumer respondents answering the survey question are also thinking about their retail store accounts when they answer the question and they are more apt to pay their retail cards in full monthly, then this might

Table 7.15 CONSUMER SURVEY EVIDENCE CONCERNING PAYMENT PATTERNS ON
CREDIT CARD ACCOUNTS, IN PERCENT

Response from Holders of Bank-Type or Retail Store Cards	Surveys of Consumer Finances								Card Account Survey
	1977	1983	1989	1995	2001	2004	2007	2010	2001
Always/ almost always pay full	50.5	48.6	51.2	51.4	54.8	55.4	55.1	56.2	40.7
Sometimes pay in full	27.8	25.5	21.6	20.0	19.2	20.3	19.6	18.4	14.8
Hardly ever pay in full	21.7	25.9	27.2	28.6	26.0	24.3	25.3	25.4	44.4
Total	100.0	100.0	100.0	100.0	100.0	100.0	100.0	100.0	100.0

Components may not add to 100 because of rounding.

SOURCE: Surveys of Consumer Finances; Credit Research Center credit card database.

explain some of the remaining difference between consumer survey findings and card account experience based solely on bank-type cards.

Account holders in these different payment categories also appear to use their bank-type card accounts differently. Grouping accounts again by payment behavior of the account holder demonstrates a variety of account use differences among the groups (table 7.16). Not surprisingly, looking at accounts this way shows clearly that some accounts seem to serve primarily as sources of credit for their holders, while others serve primarily as transactions devices, with the latter still permitting the holder the choice of revolving the balance or not as needed.

Mean credit lines do not vary dramatically among the different groups of account holders (line 1A of table 7.16), but the way they use their accounts does. "Fluctuators" (those at least sometimes paying more than the minimum but not paying the balance in full in seven months) and "minimum payers" (those paying the minimum seven straight months) have a much higher balance outstanding in a given month at billing time (line 1B). They also repay proportionately much less than others over the period (lines 2A). Paying less is certainly not surprising, since these groups are defined to exclude those who pay their accounts in full. They also pay more in finance charges (line 2D), a further artifact of not paying their accounts in full. Interestingly, they also do not use their cards very much and charge much less on them, also upon reflection not surprising, given that they

Table 7.16 MEAN ACCOUNT CHARACTERISTICS BY PAYMENT BEHAVIOR OF
ACCOUNT HOLDERS, IN DOLLARS, EXCEPT AS NOTED

Mean Account Characteristics	Payment Behaviors					
	Pure Convenience Users	Convenience Users	Payers	Fluctuators	Minimum Payers	All
(1) In initial month						
(A) Credit line	3,414	3,444	3,382	3,041	3,975	3,336
(B) Amount owed (bill received)	466	907	1,322	1,796	3,217	1,362
(C) Utilization of credit line (percent)	16.1	29.8	43.5	67.0	85.1	45.0
(D) FICO score (score points)	718	696	676	656	633	679
(2) Over seven months						
(A) Total of payments	1,932	2,171	2,315	986	460	1,477
(B) Amounts charged	1,734	1,697	1,781	994	310	1,278
(C) Cash advances	93	212	281	140	95	147
(D) Finance charges	10	52	124	202	341	130
(E) Late and over limit fees	6	22	51	99	157	61

SOURCE: Credit Research Center credit card database.

already have a larger fraction of their credit limit already in use (line 1C). Mean credit scores (FICO scores) show that convenience users tend to be the better credit risks (line 1D of the table).

In contrast, those who regularly pay their accounts in full tend to charge much more on their cards. Those who charge the most on their cards on average are the individuals who pay them off frequently, even if not always, defined here as "pure convenience users," "convenience users," and "payers" (columns 1–3 in table 7.16). On average, these groups charged approximately half their credit limits over a seven-month period (line 2B in the table compared with line 1A), and they repaid similar amounts (line 2A). They paid some finance charges (line 2D) but considerably less than those who always revolved their accounts.

The Payment Duration Disclosure

A widely discussed legislative/regulatory issue in recent years asked whether there was a need for a new required disclosure on consumers' monthly credit card bills to inform them of the exact length of time it would take them to pay off their outstanding card balance if they made only the required minimum payment each month. Those who supported such a requirement presumably assumed that consumers did not know that paying only the minimum would produce a long payoff period but also that somehow the precise number of months would be a more meaningful disclosure than just the more generic revelation that the time would be long. Under the proposals most widely discussed and finally passed by Congress in 2005, but not actually implemented for some years afterward, the new required disclosure is for much more than a generic notice. The final implementing rule that went into effect in early 2010 (following the 2009 amendments to this provision) requires for each account monthly calculation and disclosure of a specific number of months such a repayment pattern entails.[17]

For any such initial disclosure on a credit account to be strictly correct over time, it is necessary that the assumptions underlying the calculation hold. On a mortgage loan, for example, the total finance charge and total of payments revealed to the consumer at the outset of the mortgage contract imply that the contract will run to maturity, often thirty years in the future. Most mortgage loans, of course, are refinanced or repaid upon sale of the property, well short of the original maturity. This means that the initial disclosures rarely turn out to be strictly correct, but at least they are based on the declared actual terms of the underlying contract that the consumer signs, and they reflect the terms of the agreement at the time.

In contrast, the difficulty for credit cards (and other forms of revolving consumer credit) is how the underlying contract allows consumers substantial individual discretion in managing their accounts over time. The initial contract does not specify the amount and timing of credit advances, as long as they do not exceed the credit line, or the pace and timing of repayment, as long as payments meet some specified percentage monthly minimum. Thus, a potential requirement for disclosure of account duration given minimum payment raises the empirical question of how often actual behavior of card holding consumers matches the assumptions necessary for reasonable accuracy of the disclosure. This then begs the next question of how great are the errors that arise from cases that do not meet the assumptions about account use.

The credit card database permits exploration of duration questions based on consumers' actual account experiences. Specifically, a required payment duration

---

17. Congress passed this amendment to the Truth in Lending Act as a component of the Bankruptcy Abuse Prevention and Consumer Protection Act of 2005. Rule writing required under the Truth in Lending Act, necessity of public comment required by the Administrative Procedure Act, interaction with other pending Truth in Lending rules, and the need to allow time for card issuers to come into compliance caused the long delay in the effective date until 2010. Originally, the rule was to go into effect July 1, 2010, but in 2009, Congress moved the effective date up to late February 2010.

disclosure for minimum-paying credit card accounts requires three issues for accuracy: (1) the annual percentage rate assumed in the calculation must match the APR that the consumer pays; (2) the card holder must continually make the minimum payment month after month; and (3) the consumer must stop using the card (and, therefore, changing the balance from the one used in making the calculation) while proceeding with the minimum payments. As discussed above, the credit card database shows that constant minimum payment is a feature of the behavior of only about 12 percent of card holders, even over a period as short as seven months. The database permits exploration of the absolute and average error size for a disclosure of the sort proposed over a similar length of time.

Previous information on the reasonableness of the assumptions for calculating the account duration disclosure has only been available from consumer surveys. To learn about two of the necessary assumptions—consumers' behavior with respect to paying balances and the likelihood of their ceasing to use the card after paying only the minimum amount—questions on these subjects, sponsored first by the Federal Reserve and later by the Credit Research Center, were asked in the monthly Surveys of Consumers undertaken by the Survey Research Center of the University of Michigan. Interviewing took place in the summer of 1999 and the following January. In all, two thousand consumers were questioned.

Just more than one-third (35 percent) of holders of bank-type cards in the specialized surveys said they hardly ever paid their balance in full, somewhat higher than the 26 percent found in the 2001 Survey of Consumer Finances (last memo item in table 7.3).[18] When asked further in the specialized surveys for more detail about the payment sizes they actually made, 9 percent of card holders reported that they sometimes paid more than the minimum amount due, and only 7 percent said they hardly ever paid more than the minimum, for a total of 16 percent reporting that they paid the minimum amount at least more than occasionally. This proportion is much like the findings from the credit card database, where 12 percent paid the minimum seven straight months.

Now, as indicated, the proposed disclosure would only be accurate for card users who regularly pay the minimum each month and then do not make additional charges on their cards. Survey questions along this line found that about 9 percent of holders of bank-type cards say they regularly pay only the minimum. Cross-tabulating minimum payers against those who stop using the card when making minimum payments finds only about 4 percent of bank-type card holders jointly in both groups. Thus, based on survey evidence, the proposed new disclosure would be reasonably accurate for only a very small proportion of card holders.

The credit card database shows the reasonableness of the findings from the consumer surveys under this relatively strict definition of disclosure accuracy. If those who pay the minimum for seven straight months are defined as hardly ever paying more than the minimum, then only about 4 percent of card accounts also

18. This proportion is even more in line with findings about minimum payments from the card account database and discussed above than comparison of the card database with the Surveys of Consumer Finances (see table 7.14).

are not further used for purchases or cash advances (data not in a table). This is precisely the same as the measurement from the consumer surveys, one measure representing account holders and the other representing accounts.

The credit card database also permits exploration of the frequency of accurate and inaccurate duration disclosures under less strict definitions of accuracy. Notably, using the credit card database, it is possible to construct a set of disclosures that would be required under some set of assumptions about rates and payments and then to calculate how accurate the disclosures turned out to be based on consumers' actual card use behavior during some time period. This approach can even employ a variety of different definitions of accuracy.

For example, suppose that the annual percentage rate of finance charge on a revolved card accounts is 17 percent. Suppose also that the minimum payment requirement is 2 percent of the balance outstanding, $20, or the full amount owed, whichever is greatest.[19] Under this (or some other) set of assumptions, it is possible to calculate a set of account payment durations that could become required account disclosures if legislated as such. Then, following passage of a month or some other time period, it is possible to calculate another set of payment durations based on the account balance at that time and then to compare the two sets of calculations. The percentage by which the second calculation differs from the initial one (which would be the original required disclosure) could then be defined as the percentage inaccuracy of the initial disclosure over the time period. In similar manner, percentage errors of this sort could be constructed for a variety of time periods, say, every month for a six-month period. Each could be compared with the initial required disclosures according to some standard of accuracy. This would then make each initial disclosure either "accurate" or "inaccurate" according to the chosen standard for the given time period.

For example, an initial payment duration calculation could be undertaken for each card account under the assumptions listed above: 17 percent APR and minimum payment of 2 percent of the outstanding balance, $20, or the full account balance, whichever is greatest. Then the same calculation could be undertaken after one month, and the two calculations could be compared under an accuracy standard of duration at month two not differing by more than, say, 10 percent from the initial disclosure that would be required at month one.

Unfortunately, undertaking such an exercise shows that consumers' intervening actual use of their credit card accounts frequently renders such a duration disclosure inaccurate (often very inaccurate) under such a standard, even over as short a time interval as one month. Using the 10 percent divergence criterion of accuracy, only about half of initial-month disclosures remain accurate one month later, not an especially promising outcome, and the degree of accuracy continues to decline sharply thereafter (table 7.17). After six months, only about a quarter

---

19. For illustrative purposes, this set of assumptions matches those in section 1301 of the Bankruptcy Abuse Prevention and Consumer Protection Act of 2005, which was pending for years and passed both houses of Congress a number of times before passage in final form on April 14, 2005. Any other set of assumptions might also be employed.

Table 7.17 POTENTIAL ERRORS ON PAYMENT DURATION DISCLOSURE ARISING
FROM ASSUMING THAT MINIMUM PAYMENT IS ALWAYS MADE INSTEAD OF
USING ACTUAL HISTORICAL ACCOUNT BEHAVIOR EXPERIENCE, IN PERCENT

Passage of Time Accuracy of Initial Disclosure	After One Month	After Three Months	After Six Months
(1) Accurate (within +10 percent)	51.0	36.1	27.9
(2) Inaccurate (error > +10 percent)	49.0	63.9	72.1
Total	100.0	100.0	100.0
Note:			
(2A) Very inaccurate (error > +25 percent)	37.2	52.2	61.6
(2B) Highly inaccurate (error > +50 percent)	27.8	41.3	50.7

Components may not add to 100 because of rounding.

SOURCE: Credit Research Center credit card database.

of the initial disclosures remain accurate under this criterion. Furthermore, the
magnitudes of the percentage errors also increase. After six months, about half of
the initial disclosures are off by more than 50 percent (that is, a new disclosure
would be at least half or twice the original duration). With a finding of this sort, it
seems difficult to argue strongly that the initial account specific disclosure would
be more useful than a simple generic reminder that constantly paying the minimum could lead to a long repayment period.

Even this dismal accuracy finding may be more optimistic than the facts war-
rant. It is possible that some cases deemed accurate actually are counted as such
by coincidence rather than by fact. For instance, an account whose initial disclosure is still deemed accurate at the six-month point may receive this designation
because its balance outstanding is similar at that time to the initial balance, but
the balance could have varied dramatically (and, therefore, the accuracy of the
initial disclosure also varied widely) within the time interval. Thus, in such cases,
a final designation of accuracy seems more coincidental than actual.

To explore this possibility, calculations were made on another definition of
accuracy that eliminated the chance of "accuracy" in a later month only by coincidence. This second standard of accuracy requires that the original disclosure
be accurate within 10 percent through the whole time period. Thus, disclosure
on an account that is off by more than 10 percent one month later is counted as
inaccurate, even if by coincidence it should again become counted as "accurate"
in some later month.

By this definition of accuracy, the approach of an initial payment duration disclosure appears mostly unpromising—not surprising, because the accuracy definition is stricter than the previous one, since it eliminates coincidental accuracy.
This second definition of accuracy reveals that only about 18 percent of initial
disclosures are accurate after six months (table 7.18). The proportion deemed

Table 7.18 Accuracy of Initial Disclosures of Payment Duration
throughout a Six-Month Period Based on Payment Behavior of
Account Holders, in Percent

Accuracy of Initial Disclosure	Payment Behaviors					
	Pure Conven- ience Users	Conven- ience Users	Payers	Fluctua- tors	Mini- mum Payers	All
(1) Accurate (within +10 percent)	3.1	0.4	3.0	18.9	58.1	17.8
(2) Inaccurate (error > +10 percent)	96.9	99.6	97.0	81.1	41.9	82.2
Total	100.0	100.0	100.0	100.0	100.0	100.0

SOURCE: Credit Research Center credit card database.

accurate also varies sharply by account use behavior. Not surprisingly, almost
no convenience users receive disclosures that are still accurate after passage of
six months. This comes about, of course, because of the nature of accounts used
largely for the purpose of making payments rather than as a credit source, and the
account balances can fluctuate substantially by month. In contrast, about half of
minimum payers, about 6 percent of card accounts, receive an initial disclosure
defined as still accurate after six months. This proportion also is very consistent
with the 4 percent of card holders identified in the consumer surveys as minimum
payers and not further using their cards when they pay the minimum amount.

PROFITABILITY OF CREDIT CARD PLANS

One of the perennial (and sometimes controversial) questions about credit cards
is whether they are somehow an unusually profitable product for the card issuing
institutions. For most of the six decades or so that retail stores have issued credit
cards, they have maintained that their goal was merely customer loyalty to the
store through ease of shopping. If the card operation itself became a profit center,
that was fine, but the motivation was customer loyalty and enthusiasm through
a shopping enhancement, as with convenient parking and attractive in-store displays. In contrast, the goal of bank issuers has always been to produce a profitable
stand-alone product. Experience has been good sometimes but not always.

For many years, the department store industry that issued most of the two-party
cards contended that credit was only an add-on to aid the sale of goods and not
intended to be profitable by itself. But in the 1960s, as retail revolving credit cards
took over the work of charge cards that retailers previously offered, they typically
assessed a monthly finance charge of around 1.5 percent of the outstanding balance (the latter defined various ways), meaning an annual percentage rate of 18 percent in TIL terms. Advocates often claimed that these percentage rates were high

enough to be abusive of consumers. In effect, they argued that the rates should be reduced to some sort of "fair" rate, presumably closer to the convenient "free" parking that many stores offered or the "no cost" return privileges that actually are built into the cost of the merchandise at department stores and paid for by all buyers.

In opposition, retail store card issuers claimed that the finance charges did not even cover the expenses of card issuing, record keeping, billing, collections, funding the portfolio of credit outstanding, and losses, especially since many card holders did not revolve the credit extensions on their cards anyway. In their argument, this meant that cash customers actually subsidized credit customers to an extent, a situation that would only unfairly worsen with any lowering of allowable finance charges.[20]

In contrast to retail store card issuers, there is no doubt about the motivations of the three-party card industry. The miscalculations, false steps, mistakes, losses, and wrecked careers as pioneers tried to reach profitability for the bank-type cards then known as BankAmericard and Master Charge in the late 1960s are legendary in business history.[21] For the banks, and the other pioneering financial institutions such as Diners Club, there was no associated store merchandise to sell to generate additional revenues or sales loyalty to promote for a particular store that might justify the expenses of a credit operation. The credit operation had to be profitable by itself.

The only way for three-party cards to make any profit was for the cards to be used widely. This would generate fees from the merchants and restaurants accepting the cards for payments and finance charges from customers who used the cards as sources of revolving credit. In the early days of bank-type cards, when banks were trying almost desperately to achieve a critical mass of card holders using their products, there generally were no annual card holder fees and so virtually no revenue from that source. Annual fees on bank-type cards did not become widespread until the period of extremely high funding rates and the short-lived federal credit controls program in early 1980. After that period, annual fees largely disappeared from bank-type cards again in the competitive environment of the 1990s.[22] But rather than focusing on the early days, likely a more interesting question today is how profitable are the bank-type card products that have

20. The classic study of the issue is a report without a designated author but typically known as the Touche Ross study (Touche, Ross, and Company 1969). For further discussion of this old controversy, see Shay and Dunkelberg (1975).

21. For a readable, lively discussion of the thinking, triumphs, and missteps in the early days of the three-party card industry, including insights into the personalities of some of the famous pioneers such as Kenneth Larkin of Bank of America and Dee W. Hock of National BankAmericard (later Visa International), see Nocera (1994). For historical discussion of the problems that had to be overcome to establish a truly national and international payment cards system and the economic and technological innovations that overcame them, see Evans and Schmalensee (2005). The latter source also profiles many of the details of how operating systems manage the flow of electronic communications necessary for modern payment cards systems.

22. In contrast, "membership" fees were always a feature of the "travel and entertainment" cards such as American Express Green Cards, Diners Club cards, and Carte Blanche cards. These

survived into the twenty-first century, well after the nerve-racking introductory years when losses sometimes could be extraordinary and funding costs extreme.

Each calendar quarter, all domestic insured banks must file with their federal regulators an extensive "Report of Income and Condition," commonly known as the Call Report. Thousands of banks issue credit cards, but substantial consolidation of card credit portfolios over time has led to the situation where today estimates indicate that more than four-fifths of bank-type card credit outstanding is held by only 10 large card issuing banks that specialize almost exclusively in this area (see chapter 1). Some of these large card issuers offer many banking products (or are part of larger holding companies with other affiliates that engage in a range of related financial businesses), but a group of the large card issuers make their card products available through specialized card banking subsidiaries that concentrate almost exclusively on card products. Consequently, it is possible to say something about the profitability of credit card operations by closely examining the experience of these specialized institutions alone. This is what the Federal Reserve Board does in its annual report on the profitability of credit card operations, which uses data from the Call Reports (see Board of Governors of the Federal Reserve System 2013).[23]

For the purposes of this annual report on profitability, "credit card banks" are defined as banks where consumer loans are at least 50 percent of lending, and revolving credit receivables are at least 90 percent of consumer loans. Some of these institutions also offer credit cards for businesses, and so they are not wholly consumer lenders, but all are primarily credit card lenders. Given the definition of the institutions retained in the sample, it can reasonably be assumed that the profitability of these banks primarily reflects returns from their credit card operations. The first credit card banks were chartered in the early 1980s, and most of these institutions have been in operation only since that time or later. Therefore, to provide a more reliable picture of the year-to-year changes in the profitability of the credit card operations of card issuers, institutions with assets of less than $200 million are excluded. Most of the included institutions have been in continuous operation for some years now, particularly those with assets exceeding $1 billion, and are well beyond the initial phase of their operations. In 2013, fifteen banks with assets exceeding $200 million met the definition of a credit card

---

cards did not generate finance charges for revolving balances, since they were (and for Green Cards still are) charge cards and not revolving credit devices.

23. The quarterly Call Report by banks to their federal regulators provides a comprehensive income statement and balance sheet for each insured bank. It does not allocate revenues and expenses to specific product lines, and so the report is not useful for exploring profitability of all bank products, but existence of specialized card issuing banks makes it possible to study in some detail the profitability of this product. Even for the specialized institutions, however, Call Report accounting does not allow detailed breakdowns of income or expense items because of the securitization of assets and the resulting netting of many revenues and expenses associated with the securitizations, including credit losses. This means that Call Report accounting for components of operations of the various institutions may not be completely comparable, even if totals are.

bank used in the Federal Reserve report. At that time, these banks accounted for approximately two-thirds of outstanding credit card balances on the books of commercial banks or in pools backing securities issued by the credit card banks.

Return on assets invested in credit cards has generally been good during the period since 1990, fluctuating generally around 2 to 4 percent of assets adjusted for credit-card-backed securitization (first column of table 7.19). If securitizations

Table 7.19 RETURN ON ASSETS FOR LARGE CREDIT CARD BANKS, 1990–2010, PERCENT

Year	Percent Return[a]	Percent Return[b]
2012	4.66	4.80
2011	5.25	5.37
2010	2.36	2.41
2009	−3.01	−5.33
2008	1.43	2.60
2007	2.75	5.08
2006	3.34	7.65
2005	2.85	4.40
2004	3.55	6.30
2003	3.66	6.73
2002	3.28	6.06
2001	3.24	4.83
2000	3.14	
1999	3.34	
1998	2.87	
1997	2.13	
1996	2.14	
1995	2.71	
1994	3.98	
1993	4.06	
1992	3.13	
1991	2.57	
1990	3.10	

[a]Discontinuous after 2009 (see Board of Governors of the Federal Reserve System 2012, 1–2).

[b]Excludes securitized credit card from denominator, which overstates ratio but eliminates the discontinuity beginning with 2010 that interferes with illustrating the trend (see Board of Governors of the Federal Reserve System 2013, 1–2).

SOURCE: Board of Governors of the Federal Reserve System (2013).

assets are removed from the denominator of the ratio for return on assets, the totals are somewhat higher, although the pattern is similar (second column of table 7.19). In the past, the Board has focused on the first of these ratios, which includes the securitized assets in the denominator. This approach reflects the view that earnings included in the Call Report reflect revenues and expenses resulting from assets both on the books of the institutions and in off-balance-sheet pools backing securitizations, and so, then, should the denominator of the profitability ratio (return on assets). Accounting changes beginning in 2010 caused the Board to believe that profitability reported for past years may have been somewhat understated in the past relative to what might have been the case under the new accounting rules, and so there would be an inconsistency in comparisons of years beginning with 2010 relative to previous years. This led to release also of a second profitability ratio beginning in 2012 (2011 data), excluding the securitized assets from the denominator (see Board of Governors of the Federal Reserve System 2012, 1–2, for discussion). This ratio probably overstates profitability somewhat, but it is not affected by the accounting change beginning in 2010.

Using the first column in table 7.19, in 2008 returns fell to 1.43 percent of assets. This rate of return was the lowest in the whole data series, which began in 1990, and was sharply below the range that had prevailed for the previous decade. Rate of return then turned negative in 2009, as the recession that year increased credit losses and produced the first full-year loss for the industry in the twenty years of the Federal Reserve's report.[24] There was a bit of a rebound in 2010, reflecting improving economic conditions (in addition to the accounting change), but 2010 was still one of the poorest years on record. Experience from 2008 to 2010 showed that stable, let alone high, returns are by no means automatic in the bank credit card industry. Results in 2011–2012 were much better by both measures.

Among the controversial aspects of bank-type credit card profitability are the sources of the revenue streams. Some observers have contended that a greater reliance on penalty fees imposed on consumers for such things as late payments and charges over credit limits that arise from excess borrowing on the cards has enabled card issuers to earn high profits. It is not possible to break down revenue streams from the Federal Reserve's annual profitability survey, but *PaymentsSource* magazine (formerly *Cards and Payments* and earlier still *Credit Card Management*) has until recently provided some information in its May issue annually (see figure 7.1, constructed from this source).

Figure 7.1 shows that the bulk of revenues from bank card programs arises from interest paid by customers who revolve their accounts, although this proportion declined from about 80 percent to about 60 percent of revenues from 1990

---

24. The 2011 Federal Reserve report details how the 2009 loss would have been 0.46 percent rather than 3.01 percent without a large accounting write-off of accounting goodwill that year by one of the large card issuing entities (FIA Services, owned by Bank of America). The Federal Reserve actually reported the –0.46 percent figure in its 2010 profitability report but revised it in the 2011 report, following the accounting adjustment. Even without the revision, the 2009 experience would still have been the worst in the history of the profitability data series.

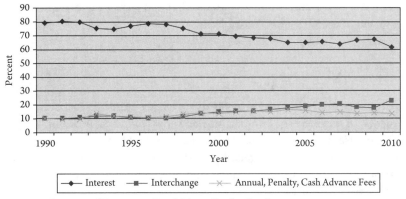

Figure 7.1   Sources of Revenues, Bank-Type Credit Cards.

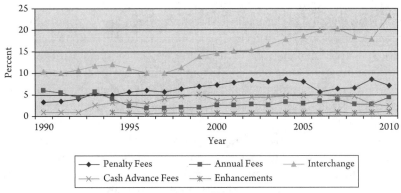

Figure 7.2   Sources of Revenues, Bank-Type Credit Cards.

to 2010. The replacement has come from rising "interchange" revenues, the fees that banks charge to merchants that accept the cards for payments. This does not reflect simply rising fee rates from this source but rather that more consumers are using cards for more purchases, and so there are more fees total. (The interchange amounts are split among the banks that make up the credit card system, with the largest share going to the card issuing banks.)

Revenues from annual fees, penalty fees, and cash advance fees together have remained around 15 percent of revenues over the prior decade (figure 7.1). Figure 7.2 provides more detail in a smaller-scale chart. It shows that the penalty fees component rose over the 1990–2009 period, from about 3.4 percent to about 8.5 percent, but fell off in 2010 as new federal regulations took effect. During the 1990–2009 period, revenues from annual or membership fees declined relatively but rose in 2010. Thus, penalty fees imposed during this period on users who did not meet the terms of their card agreements (contracts) tended to substitute for annual fees imposed in the past on both good and bad risks. This turned around with the new regulations in 2010. Fees for cash advances on the cards have also generally risen over the two decades, from less than 1 percent of revenues in 1990 to a range of 4 to 5 percent in 2001 to 2008 before retreating to 2.7 percent and 2.3 percent of revenues in 2009 to 2010.

CONCLUSIONS

Use of credit cards reflects the growing use of electronic means in making routine payments. In recent years, numbers of electronic payments, including debit and credit card use, have substantially eclipsed numbers of check payments, although check payments are still of larger average size. There are millions of credit cards of various kinds in consumers' wallets and purses, and they accounted for $2.5 trillion in payments in 2012.

Consumers remain wary of card use, however, probably in part because of stories they have heard of how some people armed with credit cards are somehow not able to control their spending habits. Most consumers remain favorably inclined toward credit cards for themselves. Public policy responds to complaints, however, and so the credit card arena has been ripe for continuing policy responses for decades. Most recently, amendments to the Truth in Lending Act in 2009 enlarged and altered the disclosure regime for credit cards and at the same time imposed some new regulations on industry procedures concerning various means of charging rates and fees. All of this came about at a time when bank credit card industry profitability was at the lowest ebb in two decades of record keeping.

Before looking at a variety of other areas of regulation of the consumer credit industry, chapter 8 looks further at the question of whether consumer availability should be open to all, even those whose credit needs are small enough, or risky enough for lenders, that the resulting prices are high. These include payday loan and pawn borrowers and users of other "fringe" financial services. Chapter 9 and 10 then examine federal regulation of consumer credit: Chapter 9 focuses on federal efforts to outlaw discriminatory treatment in credit granting practices in consumer credit through the Equal Credit Opportunity Act, and chapter 10 looks at federal disclosure mandates implemented through the Truth in Lending Act.

APPENDIX: SAMPLE OF CARD ACCOUNTS

To examine aspects of account use behavior, a large pooled random sample of card accounts was assembled in 2001 from the portfolios of five of the fifteen largest credit card issuers at the end of 2000, ranked by managed card receivables. The random selection was done in such a way as to be representative of the relatively new card accounts of the issuer. Together, these accounts likely are quite representative of the universe of domestic new card accounts overall, largely because of the size of the issuers. Accounts selected were restricted to those less than three years old at the beginning of the observation period.

Data from each account are a record of twelve to fourteen months of account activity for each of the approximately 336,000 selected accounts, for a total of close to 4.5 million monthly observations.[25] These monthly observations included accounts open from one to forty-one months. However, the different sampling frameworks adopted by the various companies resulted in some differences in the distribution of accounts by account age (months since initial opening) and also the initial month and subsequent duration of the observation period. To obtain a more uniform data set for analysis, the observation period for each account was restricted to the first twelve months of monthly statement data provided by each issuer. The sample was further restricted to accounts that had been open for thirty-two months or less as of the end of the observation period for each account. Thus, the final data set contains accounts open from one to twenty-one months at the beginning of the observation period and for most of which twelve months of subsequent account information are available. Some accounts in the restricted sample have less than twelve months in the observation period because they charge off or close.

Weights were constructed to reflect the relative size of each issuer's portfolio in the pooled group. Because of varying intervals over which the accounts were sampled across the five companies and different levels of specificity across companies in reporting the underlying population from the different categories of accounts, it was not possible to construct statistically ideal weights. Nonetheless, the weights used can be considered to provide a database of the twelve-month experience of more than 300,000 accounts that were opened at major credit card issuers during the period from mid-1998 through early 2000 and were active during 2000–2001. The restricted sample contains approximately 316,000 accounts with about 3.8 million monthly observations.

All analyses exclude inactive or "dormant" accounts, that is, accounts with no charge activity, payment, positive balance, or other posting of activity at some point during the observation period. Dormant or inactive accounts may reflect a credit card being held in reserve by the individual for an emergency or a credit card that has been discarded or destroyed by the holder without notifying the issuer.

For analysis the following variables were available:

Current balance
Credit line
Payment made
Monthly fees
Finance charges

25. For a fuller description of the data collection, see Staten and Barron (2002). As described there, the data set collected had three components representing accounts as part of the card issuers' college student marketing programs, accounts opened by other young adults, and accounts held by older individuals. For the analysis reported, these components were appropriately weighted so the weighted sample is representative of the age distribution of each issuer's overall portfolio.

Cash advances
Delinquency status (thirty days, ninety days)
Holder's birth date
Date opened
FICO score

Availability of these variables permitted calculation of the following additional variables:

Utilization rate
Proportion with a positive balance
Proportion with a cash advance
Monthly charge activity
Proportion paying in full each month
Proportion of dollars delinquent ninety days
Age of account (months)
Age of holder
And others

8

Credit for All?

Issues and Concerns about Credit Availability

Chapters 3 through 6 examined the demand for and supply of consumer credit and reviewed how credit use and the willingness to provide it both depend on ageless economic motivations. Chapter 7 then looked at the area where change has recently been most obvious and persistent, the ongoing phenomenon of credit cards. Plastic devices to make payments and to generate consumer credit are now employed successfully worldwide, which is not to say that they are no longer controversial. Despite general acceptance of the economic arguments behind consumer credit use, there is still a strong undercurrent of belief that consumer credit is not always a useful product, at least for some population segments, and that credit cards are a big part of the problem. In recent years, credit cards have been at the point of the debate over the benefits of consumer credit, but many other kinds of credit generate heat of their own.

This chapter examines the general issue of credit availability for everyone, focusing especially on the economics of those kinds of consumer credit, other than mainstream credit cards, that are at the center of much of the public controversy. They include high-rate consumer credit in small amounts or for short times, most often used by credit-constrained consumers seeking additional credit sources (for instance, pawnshop loans and payday loans), and credit for younger consumers such as college students. The contention here is that because such products are likely to remain controversial, economic study of their uses and problems can prove beneficial. Economics is hardly determinative in modern society, but it often can shed some light on phenomena that otherwise may appear anomalous.

After examining the economics of high-rate credit and looking briefly at credit use by college students, the chapter closes with a brief review of the recent public debate over "predatory lending." Much of the public discussion involving this subject concerns questions of fraudulent, purposely misleading, or otherwise inappropriate practices in mortgage lending rather than consumer credit, the main subject here. Nonetheless, it is still useful to examine this area at least briefly, since it recently has been such an important area of policy concern.

USE OF CREDIT PRODUCTS WITH HIGH ANNUAL PERCENTAGE RATES

Some consumer credit products have gained special notoriety in recent years because of their apparently high prices, as evidenced by high annual percentage rates and their use by lower-income, credit-impaired, or other less fortunate consumers. The products in question include pawnbroker loans, some kinds of small personal installment loans, payday loans, subprime credit cards, automobile title loans, and income tax refund anticipation loans. Although they are sometimes called "fringe" products because of the relatively small amounts of money typically involved, they are used by millions of people every year. John Caskey (1991, 1994, 2005) has written extensively about these financial services and is generally acknowledged as the popularizer, if not the originator, of the terms *fringe products* and *fringe institutions*. Some other researchers have referred to them as alternative financial services (AFS). Whatever the terminology used to describe this collection of financial services, policy concerns over them have extended considerably beyond only academic study.

Prices for these fringe credit products are indeed high when expressed in terms of annual percentage rates required under Truth in Lending. Finance charges are large relative to loan amounts, and terms to maturity are short. Annual percentage rates often exceed 100 percent. Certain short-term leases with purchase options, called rent-to-own transactions, have also been singled out in policy discussions, because the purchase option inherent in the rental contract has a relatively high price when compared with the price of a mainstream credit purchase. Although, strictly speaking, rent-to-own transactions are not credit, they serve as credit substitutes in some cases, and many people lump them together with high-rate credit products.

Not surprisingly, triple-digit interest rates invite widespread criticism. The critics of high-rate credit products often contend that consumers would be better off without such borrowing opportunities. They see little or no benefit to using high-rate credit and assert that high-rate credit products contain great potential to harm consumers. They declare further that consumers using such products often are uninformed or sometimes misled, often supporting these views using anecdotes and stories. There clearly are instances when consumers have suffered harm and have been uninformed or misled when they used these products, but systematic evidence on frequency of problems or the extent to which use of high-rate credit may be informed has been very limited. That these products visibly remain in demand, and even seem to be gaining in popularity, suggests the usefulness of further analysis.

This chapter section examines available evidence on consumers' employment of high-rate credit within the context of their credit situations and their decision processes analyzed in earlier chapters. The first subsection describes these credit products in more detail. The second subsection begins examination of the decision framework underlying use of these products. The review starts with the economic intertemporal consumption and investment decision model from chapter 3 originally developed by Irving Fisher (1907 and 1930) and expanded by Seligman

(1927), Hirshleifer (1958), and Juster and Shay (1964). This economic model of consumer credit use predicts the characteristics of consumers that may benefit from high-rate credit. The third subsection compares the predictions with characteristics and credit experiences of users of high-rate credit services.

In the remaining three subsections, this basic framework extends to the insights from the psychologists' cognitive model of the decision framework found in chapter 4. The economists' model helps answer the question of whether actual users of high-rate credit fall into groups that the theory predicts might benefit from use of such credit. The psychologists' model of the decision process then provides criteria for assessing the extent to which these consumers' behavior is purposive and intelligent.

To preview, the findings in this part of the chapter indicate that high-rate credit users generally are those who economic theory predicts may benefit from such credit, and many of them are fully aware of what they are doing, even as critics see their choices as outrageously shortsighted. The final subsection of this first part of the chapter examines decision processes for several specific high-rate credit products for which information is available and provides a summary and conclusions concerning the markets for credits of this kind.

The Products Described

High-rate products actually are quite diverse. Many are small single-payment loans with relatively short terms to maturity, but a few involve larger amounts and installment payments over a year or longer. The characteristic that makes these sorts of loans distinctive, other than their relatively high price, is their availability to consumers who have difficulty qualifying for many other types of credit. The diversity of the products, at least in part, reflects efforts of various lenders to find ways of making credit available to such consumers. This characteristic of these markets also differentiates high-rate loans from the mainstream credit products, which are the ones more familiar to most consumers.

PAWNBROKER LOANS
Pawnbroker loans are among the oldest forms of credit, stretching back to antiquity.[1] In a pawn transaction, the borrower brings an item that secures the loan to the pawnshop. The most frequently used security in a pawnbroker loan today is jewelry, but consumer electronic equipment, firearms, tools, and musical instruments also often serve as security for pawn loans. A pawnshop employee inspects the item and estimates its value.[2] Based on the estimated value, a loan amount will be determined.

---

1. Exodus 22:25–26 and Deuteronomy 24:12–13, for example, state that a lender who held a garment in pledge should restore it to the borrower at night so that the borrower would have protection from the cold. Finley (1981) pointed to the operation of pawnbrokers in ancient Greece. And Yang (1950) noted that in China, pawnbrokers can be traced back to the fifth century.

2. The inspection may include a request for the borrower to demonstrate how an item works. The purpose of the demonstration is twofold. The demonstration shows not only whether the item

The borrower leaves the item with the pawnbroker, and at the end of the term of the loan, commonly one month, the borrower may repay the loan amount plus a finance charge to redeem the item. The borrower may also extend the loan for an additional month or two, paying additional finance charges for extensions. If the borrower does not redeem the item at the end of the term, the item is forfeited to the pawnbroker/lender or, in some places, to the state, for resale.

Pawnbroker loans generally are quite small. In 1997, pawn loans typically ranged from $35 to $260, with an average size of about $70 (see Johnson and Johnson 1998). The National Pawnbrokers Association, the trade organization for the industry in the United States, reported an average loan amount of $100 in 2009 (www.nationalpawnbrokers.org/2010/year-in-the-life-of-a-pawnshop). In 2013 the Association reported that a typical loan is less than $150 for thirty days (see National Pawnbrokers Association 2013. The finance charge consists of interest and a storage and security charge for the pawned property. The finance charge on a $70 loan, for example, might be $9.40, with $1.40 (2 percent per month) in interest and an $8 charge for storage and security. The annual percentage rate for this example is ($9.40 ÷ $70) × 12 = 161.14 percent.

A pawnbroker loan is based on the value of the item pledged as security and, perhaps, the borrower's history of previous redemptions. The loan does not depend on the borrower's income or credit history. The borrower's performance on a pawnbroker loan is not sent to a credit reporting agency (credit bureau). For most loans, default is not possible, because the contract permits the pawnbroker to sell the collateral to pay off the loan.

Because the pawnbroker takes physical possession of the security item, the pawnbroker must protect pawned items. The pawnbroker is liable for replacement value of any pawned item that is lost, stolen, or damaged. In the past, this sometimes encouraged consumers to pawn seasonal items such as expensive fur coats (where larger loan size also meant lower rates) as a means of acquiring out-of-season secured storage. Pawnbroker personnel must be knowledgeable about jewelry, appliances and equipment, electronics, firearms, musical instruments, tools, and many other segments of the used goods market to assess the market value of a wide variety of items. Since a borrower is unlikely to redeem an item worth less than the loan amount, a pawnbroker lending too much on an item then faces the likelihood of a loss on the transaction when it is not redeemed. Pawnbrokers also need to be able to identify and note defects in pawned items, distinguish genuine items from imitations, register items with the local police as needed to prevent fencing of stolen property, and be watchful that the customer does not substitute an item of lesser value for one that is inspected. All of this makes pawn lending an expensive form of credit for the pawnbroker to engage in, especially considering the generally small amounts usually borrowed.

indeed works but also whether the borrower knows how the item works. Not knowing how an item works raises a question of whether the borrower actually owns the item. One of the costs of modern pawnbroking is the necessity of complying with rules in various jurisdictions designed to prevent sale by criminals of items they have stolen (often called fencing).

Small Consumer Finance Installment Loans

The consumer finance industry emerged early in the twentieth century after states enacted laws establishing special interest rate ceilings for relatively small loans to consumers (see Michelman 1966, Chapman and Shay 1967, Rogers 1974, and Calder 1999).[3] With the goal of promoting public relief from illegal lenders (loan sharks), these laws required lenders operating under the special rate ceilings to obtain a license from the state. The laws established rate ceilings that were high enough to enable licensed lenders to lend small amounts profitably. The interest rate ceilings in these laws came to be graduated by size of loan, with higher rates being allowed for smaller loans. The laws also often regulated other loan terms, such as maximum loan sizes and term to maturity. These laws gave rise to the regulated small loan company or consumer finance company industry. The small consumer loans from these companies are typically repaid in monthly installments. The loans are amortized, with a part of each payment repaying principal so that the loan is paid in full by the last scheduled payment. The loans are often unsecured.

The Texas Finance Code Chapter 342-E is an example of a law with a graduated interest rate ceiling and limits on term to maturity and maximum loan size. The maximum interest rate is 18 percent per year (add-on) for loan amounts up to $1,800 and 8 percent per year (add-on) for loan amounts from $1,800 to $15,000.[4] The maximum term to maturity is thirty-seven months for loans of $1,500 or less, forty-nine months for loans from $1,501 to $3,000, and sixty months for loans more than $3,000. The rate ceiling can be converted into an annual percentage rate in Truth in Lending terms when loan size and term to maturity are specified. For example, the rate ceiling for a twelve-month $1,000 loan is 31.71 percent per annum, and the rate ceiling for a twenty-four-month $3,000 loan is 23.40 percent per annum.[5]

The Texas Consumer Finance Code is of particular interest because it specifies in Chapter 342-F special interest rate ceilings for very small loans. Rate ceilings

3. See also chapter 11 below for further discussion of the emergence of the modern consumer finance industry.

4. An add-on rate is a rate applied to an initial credit balance, multiplied by the number of years (or fractions of a year, as needed), with the product then added to the initial balance to determine the total of the payments expected over time. Division of this total by the number of months produces the monthly payment. When the credit is repaid in installment payments, however, the average effective credit balance outstanding is about half the beginning balance, and so the add-on rate is about half the effective annual percentage rate required for Truth in Lending disclosures. Add-on rates were popular in the past, when calculators and computers were expensive or unknown, because of the ease of doing the calculations with pencil and paper, and for this reason, they often became enshrined in state laws. Today add-on rates are still found in some state rate laws, and they sometimes are still used for calculations, typically with a computer, but they may not be used in disclosures to consumers. Consumer rate disclosure must be the Annual Percentage Rate defined in Truth in Lending.

5. The graduated rate ceiling reflects loan size bracket adjustments in the Texas Office of Consumer Credit Commissioner, Texas Credit Letter 28 (March 10, 2009).

in this loan size range under a complicated legal formula are considerably higher than the ceilings for the larger small loans and can range upward to more than 100 percent for the smallest loans with the shortest maturities.

The maximum term to maturity is one month for each $10 up to a maximum of six months for loans of $100 or less and one month for each $20, up to a maximum of twelve months for loans of $101 or more. The average size of Chapter 342-F loans was $546 in 2009, far less than the average loan size of $7,578 for regular Chapter 342-E loans.[6]

Consumer finance companies generally serve consumers whose income or past debt payment performance prevents them from qualifying for prime credit, although the main consideration in making the loan remains the consumer's ability to make the payments, unlike pawn loans, where the main concern is the value of the collateral. Lenders look for a reliable source of income for the borrower and attempt to arrange a loan with a relatively low monthly payment, which the borrower can afford to pay with ease. Thus, the term to maturity tends to be at the maximum allowed, and loan amounts may be limited to keep monthly payments low. A history of previous payment problems does not necessarily disqualify a consumer in this market, but previous problems at the same lender may preclude further borrowing there.

The Texas Chapter 342-E rate ceilings are similar in structure to rate ceilings in many other states, although the level of ceilings in some other states may be somewhat higher. The Texas Chapter 342-E and many other state rate ceilings are not sufficiently high to allow lenders to make the very smallest loans profitably, leading to the special provision in Texas and in some other states. In contrast, the Texas Chapter 342-F rate ceilings are among the highest for consumer finance installment loans. Rates in this loan size range are lower than typical rates of pawnbroker and payday loan companies, and the loans are installment loans payable over a longer time than a few weeks or a single month.

Payday Loans

While pawn loans date back to antiquity and small cash installment loans existed at least in the nineteenth century and legally since about 1910 to 1920 in many states, the payday loan industry developed only during the 1990s. A payday loan is a small, short-term, single-payment consumer loan. The part of this lending approach that is new is that the customer writes a personal check for the sum of the loan amount and finance charge and leaves it with the lender at the time of receiving the cash.[7] The payday loan company agrees in writing to defer presentment of the check until the customer's next payday, which is often ten to thirty days later.[8] At the next payday, the customer may redeem the check by paying the

---

6. Texas Office of Consumer Credit Commissioner, Calendar Year 2009 Regulated Lender Consolidated Lender Report, available at http://www.occc.state.tx.us/pages/publications/consolidated_reports/RegulatedLender2009ConsolidatedReport.pdf.

7. Internet payday lending has grown in recent years. Electronic payments replace checks in Internet lending.

8. Payday loan companies may provide only payday loans, or they may provide payday loans and other services, such as check cashing, pawnbroker loans, and wire transfers.

loan amount and the finance charge, or the payday loan company may deposit the check in its account. In some states, the customer may extend the payday loan by paying only the finance charge and writing a new check. Most state laws that allow such extensions or renewals limit the number of renewals during the year. Payday loan companies may offer an extended payment plan, which allows the borrower to repay the loan in a small number of installments. A few states require payday loan companies to offer extended payment plans.

Payday loans typically range from $100 to $500, although some states permit payday loans up to $1,000 (see Elliehausen 2009). Finance charges are typically between $15 and $20 per $100 of the loan amount. The calculation of the cost of a payday loan is straightforward. For example, a customer borrowing $200 for fourteen days where the finance charge is assessed at a rate of $15 per $100 borrowed would owe a finance charge of $30 (2 × $15 = $30). The annual percentage rate for this transaction is 391.07 percent, which is the periodic rate ($15 ÷ $100 = 15.00 percent) multiplied by 26.07, the number of fourteen-day periods in a year.

The underwriting process for payday loans consists primarily of verifying the applicant's income and the existence of a bank account. Payday loan companies typically request that applicants provide their last bank statement and pay stub, identification (e.g., social security number and driver's license), and sometimes proof of residence. Companies generally limit the maximum amount of the loan to a specified percentage of the customer's take-home pay. Unlike mainstream lenders, payday loan companies do not obtain a credit bureau report, but some companies do subscribe to a risk assessment service that provides information on recent payday loan use by the applicant. Also, in some states the payday loan company must check a realtime database to verify that a loan is in compliance with state restrictions on renewals, number of loans per year for the customer, or concurrent loans with different companies.

Taking a postdated check helps reduce the costs of collection for the payday loan company.[9] If the consumer fails to redeem the check, the payday loan company has a relatively low-cost method of collection: the company can deposit the check to obtain payment of the loan amount and finance charge. Depositing the check does not ensure payment, of course, since the customer may not have sufficient funds in the account. But not having sufficient funds in the account subjects the customer to overdraft fees, which makes failure to repay the payday loan more costly to the customer. Thus, the postdated check provides an incentive for the customer to repay the payday loan, thereby reducing the probability of default and the expected value of collection costs for the lender.

Subprime Credit Cards
Subprime credit cards are credit cards intended for consumers who have serious delinquencies or other credit problems in their credit histories. Subprime credit

---

9. For further discussion of fees, costs, and profitability of payday lending, see Flannery and Samolyk (2005). Also see discussion of payday loan costs in chapter 5 above.

cards have low initial credit limits, $300 to $500 (Andriotis 2011), to limit losses from delinquencies and defaults. Annual percentage rates for subprime credit cards (on average, about 20 percent) are substantially higher than the industry average but do not reach the triple-digit levels of other small loan products. The notable feature of subprime credit cards is that their annual fees are quite large, $39 on average, relative to credit limits. They may also charge an initial account processing fee and a monthly fee.

These fees are deducted from the credit line, leaving the customer initially with little available credit. For example, before the Credit Card Accountability Responsibility and Disclosure (CARD) Act of 2009 limited initial fees to 25 percent of the credit limit granted, initial available credit on a $300 credit line might be restricted by a $19 processing fee and a $75 annual fee, leaving available credit at $206. Fees for some subprime credit cards were higher. Initial and monthly fees are not included in annual percentage rates under Truth in Lending, but they make subprime credit cards costly relative to the amount of the credit line.[10] Restrictions in the 2009 CARD Act made many subprime credit card programs unprofitable, however, and subprime credit card issuers responded by discontinuing programs or substantially raising minimum credit standards. By 2012, subprime credit card lending had not recovered from the effects of the prior recession (see Han, Keys, and Li 2012).

The low credit line and fee structure for subprime credit cards can be explained by customer risk. Large percentages of customers defaulted within two years of account opening or were chronically delinquent, but a significant percentage of customers had been able to improve their credit bureau scores and qualify for prime credit after a short period of time. The low credit limits limit losses from defaults.[11]

The one-time initial processing fee helps provide revenue to cover origination expenses and losses on accounts that default. Recurring annual and monthly fees help compensate for collection costs for chronically delinquent accounts. The amount of interest income generated on these low-balance accounts is insufficient

---

10. Because credit card balances can fluctuate rapidly and unpredictably and sometimes equal zero, factoring such fees into the APR is not practical. Such APRs would be highly volatile and sometimes even infinite. Moreover, such APRs could only be calculated retroactively, because future charges and payments are unknowable. For discussion, see chapter 6 in Durkin and Elliehausen (2011).

11. Only limited pre–CARD Act data on subprime credit card performance are available. One subprime credit card issuer indicated that about half of subprime accounts had one or more delinquencies of ninety days or more in the first twenty-four months after account opening, and 30 percent charge-off all or part of balances owed (Beacom 2008). This performance resulted despite screening that rejected about two-thirds of applicants. The company also reported that 23 percent of its customers improved their credit bureau scores and obtained higher-limit (near prime or prime) credit card accounts within twenty-four months. Turner and Walker (2008) examined 2007 data from three issuers and reported that defaulting borrowers used virtually all of the available credit (98 percent) and defaulted early (about three-fourths of charged-off accounts were delinquent within the first three months).

to cover costs of default and delinquency. Because of the low balances involved, sharply higher rates than the rates actually charged likely would still be insufficient to cover the costs.

Automobile Title Loans

Automobile title loans, sometimes called title pawns, typically are one-month loan contracts secured by a first lien on the borrower's automobile or truck. The borrower gives the lender the title to the vehicle as collateral for the loan. The borrower also gives the lender a copy of the keys or allows the lender to install a device to disable the ignition, which facilitates seizure of the collateral in the event of default. The entire balance of the loan plus finance charge is due at the end of the month. The borrower may extend the loan by paying the finance charge at the end of the month. Borrowers commonly extend loans by paying the finance charge and a percentage of the amount borrowed, often for three to five months. Automobile title loans range from $100 to a few thousand dollars, but the typical loan size is from $400 to $600. A typical monthly finance charge would be $25 per $100 borrowed. In that case, the annual percentage rate would be 300 percent.

Automobile title loan lenders typically require applicants to provide information on the vehicle, income, proof of employment (such as a pay stub), proof of residence, and information on the title and insurance. Loan evaluation consists of an examination of the condition of the automobile or truck, determination of its value, and evaluation of the borrower's ability to repay. Lenders may verify employment and obtain a credit report. However, some automobile title loan lenders will lend even to consumers who are not employed or have a bad credit history.

Vehicles used as collateral for automobile title loans tend to be older, as the borrower must have clear title. About 14 percent to 17 percent of automobile title loans default, but only a fraction of these defaults lead to repossession. The need for expensive repairs on older vehicles or accidents often triggers default. In many such cases, lenders do not repossess the vehicle pledged as collateral. Title loans generally are nonrecourse loans, so the lender cannot sue the borrower for the difference between the amount owed and the value of the vehicle.[12]

Income Tax Refund Anticipation Loans

A refund anticipation loan (RAL) is a short-term loan to a consumer that is based on the amount of the consumer's expected income tax refund. The consumer receives the loan amount up to the expected refund due minus the loan fee. The proceeds of the RAL may be paid to the consumer by check, deposited in a bank account, or disbursed through a prepaid cash card, within one to three days of filing the tax return. The RAL and fee are normally repaid by the tax refund. The loan functions like an acceleration of receipt of the tax refund due, but because there is an advance of funds to the consumer, it is also a loan of money and must be booked under a variety of laws as an advance of consumer credit.

---

12. See Zywicki (2010a) for further discussion.

Tax refund anticipation loans are typically arranged through tax preparation services, which act as middlemen between borrowers and the lenders. The lender makes the credit decision and funds the loan through the services of the tax preparer. Until quite recently, a small number of banks provided the loans in conjunction with tax preparers. Federal bank regulators forced the larger of these banks to discontinue offering RALs in 2010 and the remaining three smaller banks to discontinue offering such loans in 2012 or 2013 (see Johnson 2010, Aspan 2011, Barba 2012b).[13] Some smaller tax preparers are looking to provide RALs through nonbank lenders (Hochstein 2012, Barba 2012a).

Tax refund anticipation loans typically range from $200 to $7,000, and available evidence suggests most exceed $2,000 (see Elliehausen 2005). Lenders may make loans up to the amount of the claimed refund, but some lenders limit the loan amount regardless of the size of the refund or lend only up to a specific percentage of the refund amount if they have had no previous experience with the customer. The RAL fee ranges from $10 to $100, depending on the size of the loan.[14]

The term of the loan depends on the time the Internal Revenue Service takes to process the refund claim, generally between ten and fourteen days in 2005. Annual percentage rates for tax RALs are relatively high. For example, a $2,000 tax refund anticipation loan might have a loan fee of $89, which is 4.45 percent of the loan amount. If the loan is outstanding for ten days, the annual percentage rate would be 4.45 percent multiplied by 365/10, 36.5 periods per year, or 162.43 percent.

Making a tax refund anticipation loan is not risk free for the lender. The borrower is obligated to repay an RAL but may not actually receive all or part of the anticipated refund expected to repay the loan. The Internal Revenue Service may reduce a request for a refund for any number of errors or omissions in the borrower's tax return or may also apply funds from a refund to offset unpaid federal income tax obligations from previous years, student loans, other federal agency debts, state taxes, or child support.

The lender collects or may collect information on an applicant's name, address, telephone number, and social security number; amount of income, deductions,

13. In the early 1990s, the Internal Revenue Service provided notice of the existence of an offset (but not the amount of the offset) against a tax filer's refund for previous taxes, student loans, or child support owed on the acknowledgment of the electronic tax submission transmission. The IRS discontinued the notice in 1994 because of concerns about fraud in electronic filings with refund anticipation loans but reinstated the notice in 2000 in order to encourage electronic filings. The IRS again decided to discontinue the notice for the 2011 tax season, because it believed that the notice was no longer needed to promote electronic filing. See Theodos et al. (2010). The federal bank regulators have argued that without the IRS offset notice, offering a refund anticipation loan is an unsafe and unsound banking practice (Horwitz 2012, Barba 2011).

14. Other fees, such as electronic filing and deposit account setup fees, may be charged in conjunction with a refund anticipation loan. Whether or not such fees are included in the finance charge and annual percentage rate under Truth in Lending rules depends on whether the charge would be incurred in comparable cash transactions.

and refund from the tax return; debts or liens owed to the government; other debts and assets; previous RALs; employment; and credit history. Most applications for a tax refund anticipation loan are accepted. Some lenders advertise that they accept nearly 90 percent of applications. As indicated, many RALs are for the full amount of the refund minus the amount of fees deducted, although in some situations, lenders may limit loan amounts to control risk. Lenders may limit the dollar amount of an RAL or the percentage of the refund financed if the customer had no previous RAL or an RAL from another lender. Lenders may also limit the amount or percentage of the RAL covered by an earned income tax credit or limit loans that rely on income from federal Form 1040 Schedule C (sole proprietorships). And lenders may limit or refuse applications if the consumer owes delinquent child support or government debts or liens.

ILLEGAL LOANS

With passage of small loan laws in the early twentieth century, many of the firms that previously made small loans illegally (that is, at interest rates well above legal rate ceilings, "usury ceilings") became licensed and constituted a large part of the new consumer finance industry. The small loan laws did not eliminate unmet demand for legal small loans, however. Not all jurisdictions passed small loan enabling legislation at the same time, and the ceilings were not generally high enough to allow lenders profitably to extend very small loans.[15] Illegal lenders continued to operate in states that had not passed legislation. With the change in laws that permitted rates sufficient for profitable lending at some loan sizes, most firms that had specialized in making very small loans changed their business plans and made larger loans under the new ceilings or exited the state (Robinson and Nugent 1935, Haller and Alviti 1977).

In the 1920s, a new source of illegal lending emerged in New York (which did not pass small loan legislation until 1932). Criminal organizations entered the loan business, first lending to gamblers and local businesses and then, by the early 1930s, to consumers who previously had been served by salary lenders. By the 1950s, consumer lending was a standard business activity of criminal organizations operating in many major metropolitan areas across the United States

---

15. At that time, two types of firms supplied illegal loans: chattel lenders, which took security interest in household goods, and salary lenders, which included wage assignment provisions authorizing payments to the lender directly from a borrower's employer in the event of default. The chattel lenders made larger loans than the salary lenders and could operate profitably under rate ceilings established by the new small loan laws. The smaller loans extended by salary lenders, however, generally were not profitable. Robinson and Nugent (1935) reported that state regulatory agencies and the Russell Sage Foundation knew that salary lenders were unable to make small loans at ceiling rates but made no effort to do anything about the problem despite recognition that a demand for such small loans existed. There is further discussion of the activities of the Russell Sage Foundation and licensed small loan lenders to eliminate illegal lending in chapter 11 below.

(Haller and Alviti 1977). Racketeer loan sharking still exists today despite the growth of legal high-APR credit alternatives since the 1990s.[16]

Unlike the firms that made illegal loans before small loan laws, the racketeer lenders operated informally, relying on personal acquaintance and local connections at the workplace or in the local community. Because of the informal nature of the illegal loan market, few reliable statistics on the nature or the extent of these loan transactions exist. Available evidence from the mid-1960s suggests that typical racketeer loan shark loans ranged in size from $50 to $1,000, with an average probably between $150 and $400 (Seidl 1968, 1970). The customary interest rate was 20 percent per week, which amounts to 1,040 percent per annum. Interest charges were due each week as long as the principal was outstanding. Principal could be reduced only in lump-sum or, sometimes, half-lump-sum payments.[17] Loan sharks typically used the threat of force or violence to enforce payment. Instances of actual violence tended to be limited, however. Violence discourages new or continued borrowing by making customers more apprehensive, and some forms of violence (murder, for an obvious example) make it difficult for the borrower to repay and the lender to recover loan principal.[18]

Illegal lenders often have operated in low-income neighborhoods (Venkatesh 2006) or immigrant communities (Filkins 2001). It is likely that not all illegal lenders are associated with organized crime, and some rely on repossessing assets (business equipment, cars, electronic equipment, or household goods, for example) rather than threats or violence to collect loans (Venkatesh 2006). Available evidence suggests that these illegal lenders charge high rates of interest similar to those charged by racketeer lenders.

Illegal lending probably accounts for only a small part of high-price lending today. Most consumers with unmet demand for small loans likely would not turn to illegal lenders if legal high-cost loans were not available.[19] Nevertheless, illegal lending is worth mentioning, because its existence is a reminder that there are

16. For recent instances, see, for example, "22 Held in Staten Island Betting and Loan Sharking Raids" (Associated Press 2009), "Authorities Accuse 13 in Philadelphia of Mob Charges" (Warner 2011), or "In Court, 'Frankie the Fixer' Describes Collecting Loan Sharking Debts" (Roebuck 2014).

17. Seidl reported some variation in rates across markets. In several markets, the rate was 20 percent add-on for a six- or ten-week period, with interest and principal paid in equal weekly installments. Interest rates would be 284.53 percent and 179.93 per annum, respectively.

18. Seidl identified three other market segments in addition to the small consumer loans: small businesses needing working capital, speculators seeking venture capital, and individuals needing funds to satisfy spending habits (gambling or drug consumption, for example) or finance illegal business activities. Loan terms in these other market segments differed from those in the small consumer loan segment.

19. Even if legal alternatives are available, some consumers might turn to illegal lenders because they ask few questions of the borrower, are willing to provide credit immediately, and are often also available outside of normal business hours.

sources willing to provide high-price credit even if the provision of such credit is illegal.[20]

BANK PAYDAY LOAN PRODUCTS AND THE FDIC's
SMALL DOLLAR AMOUNT LOAN PILOT PROJECT

A few banks offered deposit advances, a payday product that resembles an automated version of payday loans made by payday lenders. In early 2014, however, all of the banks offering deposit advances decided to withdraw the product from the market (see Wack 2014). The banks decisions followed issuance of supervisory guidance by two federal banking regulatory agencies, Office of the Comptroller of the Currency (OCC) and the Federal Deposit Insurance Corporation (FDIC), that found that the high rate short term deposit advance product was difficult to repay and consequently posed significant safety and soundness and consumer protection risks. A brief discussion of the deposit advance product is nevertheless useful because it was an economically tenable attempt by the banking industry to compete in the small, short term loan market.

To be eligible for this product, the customer needed a direct deposit of a paycheck or other recurring payment into a checking account (social security, for example). The credit limit on this type of account was based on the size of the direct deposit and commonly has a maximum between $500 and $750.

The customer initiated the advance by telephone, at an ATM, or through the Internet. The advance was repaid from the customer's next direct deposit. These automated procedures likely make the operating cost of the bank payday loan product less than that of the standard payday loan.

The finance charge for the advance was 10 percent of the advance amount, regardless of the time the loan was outstanding. Thus, the finance charge on a $300 advance would be $30. The annual percentage rate depends on when the advance is obtained relative to the upcoming direct deposit. If the loan was obtained two weeks before the deposit, for example, the number of two-week periods in a year is 26.07, and so the annual percentage rate would be 10 percent × 26.07 = 260.70 percent.

The banks offering this product marketed it as short-term credit. To enforce the short-term intent, these banks limited the number of consecutive checking account statement periods in which an advance can be obtained. Limits ranged from six to twelve statement periods. After reaching the limit, the customer was ineligible for advances for a specified period of time, or the bank reduced the credit limit until it reaches zero.[21]

---

20. In a study of credit market regulation in the United Kingdom, Germany, and France, Policis (2006) found that borrowers in Germany and France, where low rate ceilings restrict credit availability, were much more likely to turn to illegal lenders than borrowers in the United Kingdom, where high-rate credit is readily available from a variety of different sources. See chapter 11 below for further discussion of rate ceilings and illegal lending.

21. Many more banks offer lines of credit on checking accounts, but most of these accounts are similar to credit card accounts. Results of a survey of banks supervised by the Federal Deposit Insurance Corporation indicated that the median credit limit of checking account lines of credit

Noting the demand for payday loans and use of fee-based check overdraft programs but critical of their cost, the Federal Deposit Insurance Corporation initiated in 2008 a pilot project to stimulate development of low-APR small dollar loan products at banks (Miller et al. 2010). For the pilot project, the FDIC specified certain guidelines for product designs:

- Loan amounts of up to $1,000.
- Payment periods that extend beyond a single paycheck cycle.
- Annual percentage rates less than 36 percent.
- Low or no origination fees.
- No prepayment penalties.
- Streamlined underwriting.
- Prompt loan application processing.
- Automatic savings component.
- Access to financial education.

Because the pilot project was intended to encourage experimentation, the guidelines were not rigid requirements for participation in the pilot project. The FDIC required that the products be designed to be profitable and not be contrary to bank safety and soundness.[22]

One of the preliminary results of the pilot project was that some banks also relied on somewhat larger loans to make their entire program profitable. These banks reported that some customers qualified for larger loans and that the larger loans provided greater revenue for the same operating cost as the smaller loans ($1,000 or less).[23] This result caused the FDIC to expand the pilot to track larger loans of $1,001 to $2,500 (sometimes called "nearly small dollar loans").

Twenty-eight banks participated in the pilot program as of its completion at the end of 2009. All of the pilot project products were closed-end loans. The overall average size of "small dollar loans" ($1,000 or less) was $724, and the smallest loans made were around $445. The average "nearly small dollar loan" ($1,001 to $2,500) was $1,727. The average term to maturity was twelve months for small dollar amount loans and fifteen months for nearly small dollar amount loans.

The most common interest rate charged for both loan size categories was 18 percent. About half of the banks also charged initial fees, which were larger for nearly small dollar amount loans ($46 on average) than for small dollar amount loans ($31). Annual percentage rates, which include both fees and interest, for all products were less than 36 percent, as specified in the initial guidelines.

was $5,000, and the median annual percentage rate was 18 percent (Federal Deposit Insurance Corporation 2008).

22. A press release announcing the pilot project can be found on the FDIC website at www.fdic. gov/news/news/press/2007/pr07052a.html. The press release explains the purpose of the pilot project and discusses the guidelines for product designs.

23. This finding is consistent with relationships between costs and loan size discussed in chapter 5 and historical experience in regulating small loans discussed in chapter 11.

Thirty-day delinquency rates for both small dollar amount loans (9 to 11 percent, depending on quarter) and nearly small dollar amount loans (6 to 11 percent) were at least three times higher than for other types of unsecured loans (2 to 3 percent) in 2009. In contrast, charge-off rates for pilot project products were in line with industry averages. The cumulative charge-off rate was 6 percent for small dollar amount loans and 9 percent for nearly small dollar amount loans. These compare with charge-off ratios of 5 percent for unsecured loans to individuals and 9 percent for credit cards in the fourth quarter of 2009.

Because the small dollar amount products are not established products, some further comment on their commercial viability seems appropriate. The FDIC did not have reliable data on the profitability of the pilot project small dollar amount products but was able to report qualitative information provided by the banks participating in the program. The banks indicated that the costs of launching and marketing small dollar loan amount programs and originating and servicing the loans were similar to those of other consumer loans. However, because of their small size, the interest and fees from these loans were not always sufficient to achieve robust short-term profitability. Most bankers participating in the pilot project said that they sought to generate long-term profitability through volume and by using small dollar loans to cross-sell additional products.

The FDIC saw the products developed in the pilot program as possible alternatives to payday loans, but whether the small dollar amount products are indeed substitutes for payday loans is not clear.[24] The average size in the small dollar program ($445) was larger than most payday loans. Elliehausen (2009) reported that only about a quarter of payday loans were greater than $400. The larger loan sizes of the small dollar loans may reflect greater ability of pilot project borrowers to service debts, because of lower interest and longer time to repay, or simply different loan demand. That most banks used credit reports in underwriting suggests that a significant number of payday loan customers might have difficulty qualifying for one of these bank loans, so different (although perhaps partly overlapping) market segments for the bank and payday products seem plausible. Moreover, the marginal profitability of these bank small dollar amount products suggests that they are unlikely to displace the payday loan industry.

RENT-TO-OWN TRANSACTIONS

Rent-to-own transactions are short-term rentals, not credit.[25] However, consumers often rent long enough to obtain items through the rent-to-own program,

---

24. Based on the experience gained from the pilot project, the FDIC proposed the following template for bank small loan amount lending products: (1) a maximum loan size of $2,500, (2) a minimum term to maturity of ninety days, (3) interest rate and fees not exceeding 36 percent, and (4) a streamlined underwriting process in which proof of identity and residence is required, loan amount is based on income verification and an assessment of ability to pay, and credit reports are obtained.

25. Rent-to-own transactions are not covered by the federal Truth in Lending Act (Regulation Z) or Consumer Leasing Act (Regulation M). According to the Association of Progressive Rental Organizations, a trade group, in 2011, forty-seven states had state laws that defined

either intentionally or unintentionally; rent–to-own companies make heavy use of the purchase option to market their products. The implicit APR of the rental purchase justifies their inclusion in this discussion.

The rent-to-own industry consists of dealers that rent furniture, appliances, home electronics, and jewelry to consumers on a week-to-week or month-to-month basis. Rent-to-own companies do not check credit reports, but they do require verification of applicants' identity, residence, and employment. In a typical rent-to-own transaction, the customer enters into a self-renewing weekly or monthly lease for the item. The customer is not obligated to continue payments beyond the current weekly or monthly period. At the end of the period, the customer can continue to rent by paying for an additional period or can return the item. Customers having difficulty making payments may return items voluntarily, but in many cases, rent-to-own companies incur collection costs to recover payments or repossess items. In some cases, the rent-to-own company charges off the item, either because the item is damaged or because the customer disappears without returning the item (Anderson and Jaggia 2009).

The rental agreement provides an option to purchase the item. The customer can accomplish purchase by continuing to pay rent for a specified period of time, by paying a specified percentage of the rental payments that remain to be paid before the item is purchased, or by some other formula that depends on factors such as the number of payments made and the value of the item.

The rent-to-own transaction differs from transactions involving an installment purchase or a multiperiod financial lease in that the rent-to-own company, not the consumer, bears the risk of ownership. The rent-to-own company incurs the costs of delivery, setup, repair, loaner services, pickup, refurbishing, and rerental. Installment sellers generally do not deliver and set up items without charging for the services. Sellers also do not normally repair items or provide a loaner during the repair period, although they may for an additional charge sell a customer a service package. The rent-to-own customer can return the item without penalty at the end of the week or month if he or she is dissatisfied, no longer needs the item, or has difficulty making payments. A consumer who purchases an item would have to seek a buyer in the secondhand market or otherwise dispose of an unwanted item, and a consumer who uses a financial lease normally would pay an early termination fee. These features make rent-to-own purchases more costly to the provider than an installment purchase or a multiperiod financial lease.

The terms of a rent-to-own transaction can be illustrated by considering the rental of a large high-definition television with the following terms. The rental cost for the television is $99.99 per month, and the customer owns the television after twenty-four months. If the customer wants to purchase the television earlier than twenty-four months, he or she would have to pay the difference between the rent-to-own company's specified cash price of $1,329.99 and a percentage of the

rent-to-own as a lease and regulated the terms of rent-to-own transactions (http://www.rtohq. org, accessed June 2011).

sum of rental payments made. The customer can also purchase the television by paying the company's cash price within the first ninety days of the rental.

Determining the cost of credit when a product is purchased jointly with financing and also possibly with other services is not always straightforward. The calculated cost of credit depends on the allocation of costs among the items purchased jointly; but the allocation of costs may be arbitrary if the product and other services are not also sold separately for cash, which is normally the case for parts of rent-to-own transactions.[26]

For example, it is possible to use the retail price for the same television to attempt to measure the credit cost. Suppose the same television has a list price of $849.95 and retails for $528.00. The seller does not calculate and collect sales tax for items ordered through the Internet. The shipping cost is $102.85. A three-year extended warranty may be obtained for $139.99. Including these additional costs yields a cash purchase price of $770.84. The periodic rate that equates this purchase price and the twenty-four payments of $99.99 is 7.30 percent, which is 145.71 percent on an annual basis.[27]

The 145.71 percent annual rate for this transaction would not include setup, however, nor, more important, does it include the value of the option to return the item at any time or the repair and loaner features available in the rent-to-own situation. Presumably, the value of these features would be included in the rent-to-own company's cash price of $1,329.99, although there is no assurance that this aspect of the price would be a market price. Equating the company's cash price and the twenty-four payments of $99.99 yields a periodic rate of 5.38 percent, or 64.57 percent annually.[28] Regardless of the choice of product price, this example suggests that renting to own is a much more costly method for financing the purchase of a consumer durable than installment credit.[29]

High-Rate Credit and the Economic Model of Consumer Credit Use

In their economic analyses of the consumer's credit decision, Juster and Shay (1964) explained why consumers are sometimes willing to borrow at high rates of interest (see chapter 3 above). To summarize, they argued that many durable

26. See Durkin and Elliehausen (2011, chapter 4) for discussion of the difficulties of determining annual percentage rates in joint purchases.

27. These terms were available from a vendor on Amazon.com in early June 2011. The vendor did not calculate or collect sales tax. The item shipped within two days of the order. Faster shipping was not available. The warranty was for thirty-six months.

28. The rent-to-own company also offers a contract with weekly payments of $24.99. The customer owns the television after 104 payments. The annual percentage rate for this contract would be 161.59 percent at the retail price and 76.17 percent at the rent-to-own company's cash price.

29. For further discussion of the economics of renting to own, see Beales, Eisenach, and Litan (2012).

products purchased using credit provide benefits over a period of time and that for some families, the implied rates of return for these benefits can be quite high. Because income and accumulated savings are finite, lenders limit the amount of credit they are willing to offer any consumer. Consequently, the rate of return from additional investment in durables may exceed the marginal borrowing cost from primary lenders but be less than the sacrifice of current consumption or reduction in savings necessary to acquire additional durable goods. When this situation occurs, consumers are said to be credit constrained or rationed. Specialized secondary lenders willing to lend small amounts at relatively high rates can relax the credit constraint and increase utility.

Consumer Characteristics Associated with Credit Rationing

Reviewing discussion from chapter 3 further, rationed borrowers are likely to be in early family life cycle stages. For them, rates of return on household investment tend to be high. They tend to have relatively low or moderate current incomes and little discretionary income, making the sacrifices in current consumption to pay for large expenses personally costly. And because of their moderate incomes and young age, rationed borrowers generally would not have accumulated large amounts of liquid assets. At this stage in the life cycle, their liquid asset holdings have a high subjective yield because of precautionary savings motives.

Unrationed borrowers, in contrast, typically are in later family life cycle stages or have relatively high incomes. Unrationed borrowers in later life cycle stages may have relatively few high-return household investment opportunities. For them, high income may provide discretionary amounts that allow for relatively large expenditures without costly reductions in current consumption. Moreover, their age and income may allow them to accumulate some discretionary savings. Consequently, subjective yields on liquid assets can be substantially lower for unrationed borrowers than for rationed borrowers. Availability of low-cost discretionary income and liquid assets for acquisition of durable goods would make unrationed borrowers generally unwilling to pay high interest rates for additional credit.

Based on this theory, users of high-APR credit products would be expected to have characteristics of rationed borrowers. Unrationed borrowers generally would not find high-APR credit products attractive. A large, disproportionate percentage of unrationed borrowers using high-APR credit products would raise a question of whether the credit use is irrational, as marginal borrowing rates for unrationed borrowers are normally relatively low. Within this theoretical context, Juster and Shay identified characteristics that likely distinguish rationed and unrationed borrowers. This distinction is useful in assessing consumers' use of high-APR credit products.

New High-Cost Borrowing Opportunities for Rationed Consumers

Consumer credit markets have changed considerably since Juster and Shay's study. Advances in information availability and in the technology to manage and analyze large amounts of information have improved lenders' ability to assess risk.

Credit reporting through automated credit reporting agencies (credit bureaus) is now close to comprehensive. Credit reports thus reflect a consumer's complete credit history, making information in credit reports more useful for predicting future payment performance. In addition, the development of credit bureau scores has made statistical credit evaluation available to all lenders.

Such changes have loosened the credit limits of primary lenders. Equity requirements have also relaxed, as terms to maturity have lengthened for most closed-end installment credit, and down payment requirements have also been reduced. Furthermore, home equity lines of credit and cash-out refinancing of mortgage loans have developed to allow consumers to finance acquisition of durable goods using savings from equity in their homes. Thus, today many consumers are more able to finance a greater proportion of their household investment through primary lenders.

Nonetheless, higher-cost credit products from secondary lenders have also proliferated. Unsecured credit is now widely available through bank credit cards, and many borrowers today use bank credit cards in much the same way as Juster and Shay described borrowers using unsecured personal loans (see Bizer and DeMarzo 1992, Brito and Hartley 1995). Competition has extended availability of bank credit cards to many consumers who previously would have had difficulty qualifying for them. As a result, unsecured credit is now available to more consumers at a lower cost than in the past.

There also are various "subprime" versions of credit cards, automobile financing, and mortgages. Such products are mostly used by those who exhibit greater amounts of credit risk than mainstream consumers. These subprime products allow consumers to finance a larger share of the value of household durable goods and services, borrow more heavily against future income, and obtain credit despite previous problems repaying debts. The financial crisis of 2008–2009 disrupted subprime credit markets, but after necessary reevaluation and restructuring, these credit sources are unlikely to go away.

Further, as outlined earlier in this chapter, there also are new short-term credit products to go with the small loan industry, which has existed for decades, and pawn lenders prevalent for centuries. The payday lending industry allows consumers to obtain an advance on their next paycheck, automobile title lenders offer small loans secured by consumers' automobiles, and income tax refund anticipation loans enable consumers to obtain an advance on expected tax refunds. Short-term credit products can facilitate the accumulation of household assets even when they are not used directly to finance the household investment by enhancing overall liquidity, even at high cost. The availability of short-term credit may reduce consumers' vulnerability to unexpected expenses or reductions in income when consumers use relatively large amounts of debt to finance household investment. Although these short-term credit products may be very costly, consumer losses resulting from a lack of liquidity may be quite large. Late payments of utility bills, for example, can cause a consumer to incur late payment fees, deposits of one or more average monthly utility bills, and reconnect fees. Thus, short-term credit products may also have expanded the opportunities for rationed consumers to finance household investment.

THE SHORT-TERM CREDIT DECISION

It is possible to examine this common consumer problem with the standard tools of financial economics as found in any textbook (see, e.g., Brealey, Myers, and Allen 2010). The net present value rule for evaluating investments is the theoretical core of modern financial analysis, as discussed in chapter 3. It holds for consumer investment decisions in addition to corporate finance and is consistent with the work of Juster and Shay.

Net present value (NPV) is calculated as follows:

$$NPV = -C + \sum_{t=1}^{n} \frac{S_t}{(1+r)^t}$$

(8.1)

where C is the cost of an expenditure, S_t is a periodic benefit for n periods from making an expenditure, and r is the periodic discount rate. An expenditure is utility increasing when the present value of its benefits exceeds its cost. As noted by Juster and Shay, the benefits from durable goods acquisitions can often be measured in dollars as saved costs. The benefits of using a short-term loan may also be expressed in terms of the costs of some market alternative. For example, a short-term loan may be used to avoid a late payment, take advantage of a one-time sale, or avoid some other costly outcome.

Payday Loan Example

Elliehausen and Lawrence (2001) provide an example of a net present value calculation of the kind familiar in economic and financial analysis but evaluating use of a payday loan to repair an automobile. In their example, a consumer needs $200 to repair the automobile. The consumer can obtain a $200 payday loan for a $30 fee due on the next payday in two weeks or take public transportation until the next payday and obtain repairs then.

Their example is based on commuting from a Washington, DC, suburb to the city. They used the US government mileage rate for calculating automobile fuel and depreciation cost. Opportunity cost for extra time for commuting by public transportation was calculated for a $10.00-per-hour wage rate. Parking was provided by the employer, so use or not did not affect the consumer's cost. They assumed that the automobile was used only for commuting between the consumer's residence and place of employment and not for additional useful or pleasurable purposes. The upper panel of table 8.1 summarizes the calculation of the daily cost of using public transportation as an alternative means of commuting.

The second panel of table 8.1 summarizes the cash flows and calculates the net present value of using a payday loan to pay for the repair. The cost of the repair C is the net cash flow on day 0. The cost of public transportation is the periodic savings, S_t, which are $4.56 per day on weekdays and $0.00 on weekends. In addition, the consumer incurs the cost of repairing the automobile at the end of two weeks.

The column on the right provides the discounted value of the cash flow. The periodic discount rate is 1.07 percent per day, which is the finance charge of $15 per $100 borrowed divided by the 14 days (the term of the payday loan). The net present value is the sum of discounted cash flows $14.55. The positive net present

Table 8.1 Cash Flows for Using a Payday Loan to Repair an Automobile

A. Daily cost of public transportation	Dollars	
Bus and subway fare (2 × $3.50)	7.00	
Minus: Automobile mileage (2 × 12 miles ×.31 per mile)	7.40	
Plus: Opportunity cost for commuting (2 × 0.25 hours × $10 per hour)	5.00	
Equals: Daily cost	4.56	
B. Cash flows	**Undiscounted cash flow (dollars)**	**Discounted cash flow (dollars)**
Day		
0 Tuesday (repair car)	−200.00	−200.00
1 Wednesday (daily cost)	4.56	4.51
2 Thursday	4.56	4.46
3 Friday	4.56	4.42
4 Saturday	0.00	0.00
5 Sunday	0.00	0.00
6 Monday	4.56	4.28
7 Tuesday	4.56	4.23
8 Wednesday	4.56	4.19
9 Thursday	4.56	4.14
10 Friday	4.56	4.10
11 Saturday	0.00	0.00
12 Sunday	0.00	0.00
13 Monday	4.56	3.97
14 Tuesday (daily cost and car repair)	204.56	176.24
Sum of cash flows	45.60	14.55

SOURCE: Elliehausen and Lawrence (2001).

value indicates that borrowing at 1.07 percent per day, a 309.00 percent annual percentage rate, leaves the consumer with greater wealth than waiting and using public transportation.

It is worth noting that the undiscounted net value of using the payday loan equals the $45.60 sum of net cash flows from the table minus the $30 finance charge for the payday loan or $15.60. That result, $15.60, is not much different from the $14.55 discounted net present value. Despite the high discount rate, the effect of discounting is small because of the very short term to maturity. The short term to maturity for many of the high-price credit products simplifies the consumer's decision. There is not any great need to think in terms of discounting cash flows, even in theory, because the time is so short that the undiscounted cost serves as a good proxy for the discounted costs, even if the discount rate is very high. This would not be the case for a long-term loan, of course. Extended use of this sort of credit is where it becomes most highly controversial.

This example is obviously hypothetical. Different assumptions might lead to different decisions. A more costly repair or daily parking fees would reduce net present value and might produce negative net present values. Additional trips using public transportation or a higher opportunity cost rate would increase net present value and might produce a positive net present value even for a more costly repair or including daily parking fees. Data that permit calculation of net present values for actual payday loan decisions are not available. Nevertheless, the example illustrates that there are plausible situations in which use of high-price credit is rational.

Income Tax Refund Anticipation Loan Example

Elliehausen (2005) calculated the net present value of using income tax refund anticipation loans to obtain a benefit a short time earlier by various loan sizes and benefit amounts. This type of transaction might involve using the proceeds of the RAL to pay bills now rather than paying bills late plus late payment fees for failure to make timely payment. A more positive example might be buying an item on sale now rather than paying full price later. Because a RAL is a single-payment loan, equation 8.1 simplifies to

$$NPV = -C + \frac{F}{1 + r} \tag{8.2}$$

where C is the current cost (the amount of the bill or the sale price), F is the future cost (the amount of the bill plus avoided late payment fee or the regular price of the item), and r is the discount rate. Net present values are calculated for selected undiscounted benefits (that is, avoided fees or regular price), amounts ranging from \$25 to \$125. The discount rate for a ten-day period, based on an actual refund anticipation fee schedule at the time of the study, was calculated by dividing the RAL fee by the loan amount.[30] A positive net present value indicates that the benefit exceeds the cost of the transaction.

As an example, Elliehausen considered a consumer who has a choice between purchasing an appliance for \$2,000 in a limited time period sale and waiting ten days or longer (until receipt of a tax refund) to purchase the appliance at the regular price of \$2,100. The net present value of using an RAL to take advantage of the sale is obtained by subtracting the sale price from the full price discounted at the periodic 4.50 percent rate for a \$2,000 RAL. That is,

$$NPV = -\$2,000 + \frac{\$2,100}{1 + 0.0450} = \$10.53 \tag{8.3}$$

30. The 4.50 percent rate for ten days implies an annual percentage rate of 164.25 percent (4.50 percent per 10-day period × 365/10 periods per year).

Table 8.2 Net Present Value and Undiscounted Net Value of Refund
Anticipation Loan (RAL), by Size of Refund Anticipation Loan and
Amount of Savings or Avoided Loss

RAL Amount	RAL Fee	Periodic Rate	Benefit (Savings or Avoided Loss)				
			$25	$50	$75	$100	$125
A. Net present value (dollars)							
$300	$34	11.3%	−8.08	14.37	36.83	59.28	81.74
$750	$49	6.5%	−22.53	0.94	24.41	47.87	71.34
$1,250	$59	4.7%	−32.47	−8.59	15.28	39.15	63.03
$1,750	$74	4.2%	−47.01	−23.03	0.96	24.95	48.93
$2,000	$89	4.5%	−61.27	−61.27	−13.40	10.53	34.47
$4,000	$89	2.2%	−62.61	−38.15	−13.70	10.76	35.22
B. Undiscounted net value (dollars)							
$300	$34	11.3%	−9.00	16.00	41.00	66.00	91.00
$750	$49	6.5%	−24.00	1.00	26.00	51.00	76.00
$1,250	$59	4.7%	−34.00	−9.00	16.00	41.00	66.00
$1,750	$74	4.2%	−49.00	−24.00	1.00	26.00	51.00
$2,000	$89	4.5%	−64.00	−39.00	−14.00	11.00	36.00
$4,000	$89	2.2%	−64.00	−39.00	−14.00	11.00	36.00

SOURCE: Elliehausen (2005); authors' calculations.

This result means that using an RAL to purchase the appliance on sale is less costly than waiting for a tax refund and paying the regular price, even taking account of the RAL fee through the discount rate.[31]

Other situations would produce different results. Panel A of table 8.2 shows net present value calculated for different loan sizes and benefits. In the example just discussed, the net present value of the $2,000 RAL to obtain the item with a regular price of $2,100 ($100 saving) is found in the second from last row of the $100 column. If the savings from purchasing the appliance on sale were only $75, a negative net present value, −$13.40, would be obtained (second from last row of the $75 column). In this case, the consumer would be better off waiting for the tax refund and paying the regular price than using an RAL to purchase the appliance on sale.

As in the payday loan example, the effect of discounting is very small, even at discount rates that are relatively high when stated on an annual basis. For the RAL example shown in equation 8.3, the undiscounted net value is the $100 savings

31. The calculation does not include any flow of services from the purchase during the time interval, nor does it consider any nonpecuniary benefits such as convenience or reputation of sales outlet.

from purchasing at the sale price minus the $89 RAL fee. The undiscounted net value of $11 is just $0.47 greater than the net present value of $10.53.

Over a broad range of plausible values of loan amount and savings, the difference between the net present values and undiscounted net values are small. Panel B of table 8.2 provides undiscounted net values for the RAL amounts and savings amounts from panel A. In nearly all cases, the undiscounted present value is within a few dollars of the net present value. In no case would the undiscounted net value rule lead to a different decision from the net present value rule. This example suggests that an undiscounted net value heuristic would probably perform about as well as the optimizing net present value rule in evaluating choices involving short-term credit.

High-Rate Credit Customers

The economic model of consumer credit predicts that users of high-price credit products would be consumers in early family life cycle stages who have limited discretionary income for servicing debt and face constraints to additional credit use. An examination of demographic characteristics of high-price credit users suggests they generally have the characteristics that economic theory predicts.

AGE AND LIFE CYCLE STAGE

Consistent with the predictions of the economic model, users of high-price credit products generally are young. Available evidence shows that more than half of pawnbroker, rent-to-own, and refund anticipation loan customers are younger than thirty-five, and more than 36 percent of payday loan customers are younger than thirty-five (table 8.3). These percentages are considerably higher than the 28.6 percent of householders younger than thirty-five across all households.[32]

The thirty-five-to-forty-four age group also shows greater than proportionate percentages of pawnbroker loan, payday, rent-to-own, and refund anticipation loan customers. Although the percentage of automobile title loan customers who are younger than thirty-five is the same as in the population as a whole, the percentage of automobile title loan customers who are between thirty-five and forty-four is nearly twice the percentage of the population in that age group. Older consumers generally have less demand for credit than younger consumers, and so older consumers also would be less likely than younger consumers to be in situations in which mainstream credit would not be available.

---

32. The surveys for demographic information on high-rate credit users in this table were conducted between 1997 and 2005. The statistics are from the following sources: pawnbroker loans, Johnson and Johnson (1998); payday loans, Elliehausen and Lawrence (2001); rent-to-own transactions, Lacko, McKernan, and Hastak, (2000); income tax refund anticipation loans, Elliehausen (2005); and automobile title loans, Verant (2000). For approximate comparison, statistics for bank credit card revolving credit users are from the University of Michigan Survey Research Center's January 2000 Survey of Consumers. The comparative statistics for all households are from an omnibus telephone survey of adults conducted in 2004 (Elliehausen 2005).

Table 8.3 DEMOGRAPHIC CHARACTERISTICS OF HIGH-RATE CREDIT
CUSTOMERS (PERCENTAGE DISTRIBUTIONS)

	Pawnbroker loan	Payday loan	Rent to own	RAL	Auto title loan	All households
A. Age of customer						
Younger than 35	53.1	36.4	50.8	61.0	28.6	28.6
35–44	31.1	31.9	28.6	25.4	39.2	21.3
45–54	11.6	21.7	15.9	10.4	17.1	18.4
55 or older	4.3	10.1	4.5	3.3	15.1	31.7
Total	100.0	100.0	100.0	100.0	100.0	100.0
B. Life cycle stage						
Younger than 45						
Unmarried, no children	11.1	8.1	NA	NA	NA	13.7
Married, no children	7.2	4.8	NA	NA	NA	8.0
Married, children	35.2	47.2	NA	NA	NA	19.2
45 or older						
Married, children	5.0	2.0	NA	NA	NA	5.1
Married, no children	9.4	4.2	NA	NA	NA	20.2
Unmarried, no children	8.9	5.4	NA	NA	NA	22.3
Any age						
Unmarried, children	23.3	28.3	NA	NA	NA	11.5
Total	100.0	100.0	NA	NA	NA	100.0
C. Family income						
Less than $15,000	38.5	7.3	27.0	18.6	11.9	19.3
$15,000–$24,999	26.4	17.0	33.5	27.9	17.4	15.1
$25,000–$49,999	29.1	50.5	33.2	38.8	40.8	30.6
$50,000 or more	7.1	25.2	6.3	14.8	30.2	34.9
Total	100.0	100.0	100.0	100.0	100.0	100.0

NA: not available.

Elliehausen and Lawrence (2001) and Elliehausen (2005) also provide information on life cycle stage of high-price credit customers; life cycle stage involves consideration of marital status, children, and age. These studies found that both payday loan and RAL customers are concentrated in two life cycle groups: younger than forty-five, married, with children; and any age, unmarried, with children (part 2 of table 8.3).

It is notable that these two life cycle groups are also more likely than households overall to be credit card revolvers, another source for borrowing small amounts for short periods of time. Such families are the ones that Juster and Shay hypothesized would be most likely to turn to high-price credit to finance additional household investment, in large part because they have not yet accumulated substantial stocks of household durable goods and because their families are growing. This would mean that the return on additional durable goods and services could be quite high, leading both to credit use and to concerns over liquidity.

HOUSEHOLD INCOME

High-rate credit customers are also disproportionately drawn, not surprisingly, from low- or moderate-income segments of the population. These individuals are more likely than those with higher incomes to have limited discretionary income after necessities and to be more vulnerable to unexpected expenses (part 3 of table 8.3). This characteristic of high-price credit customers suggests both greater likelihood of being rationed and that liquidity sources may be important to them.

Differences in the income distributions across high-rate credit products argue that the submarkets within high-rate credit products may be somewhat segmented. For example, most pawnbroker and rent-to-own customers are drawn from the lowest income groups (less than $15,000 and $15,000–$24,999). Only small percentages of pawnbroker and rent-to-own customers are in the highest income group. In contrast, most tax refund anticipation loan customers are in lower, but not the lowest, income groups ($15,000–$24,999 and $25,000–$49,999). The majority of payday loan customers and almost two-fifths of automobile title loan customers are in the moderate income group ($25,000–$49,999). Only small percentages of payday loan and automobile title loan customers are in the lowest income group, but a quarter of payday loan customers and 30.2 percent of automobile title loan customers are in the highest income group in the table.

CREDIT EXPERIENCES

High-price credit customers are less likely to have a credit card than households generally (not in table). Only 57.0 percent of payday loan customers have a bank credit card, and 61.6 percent have any credit card, compared with 68.0 percent of all households having a bank card and 73.0 percent with any credit card. Other high-price credit customers are even less likely than payday loan customers to have credit cards. Fewer than half of pawnbroker, rent-to-own, and refund anticipation loan customers have credit cards. Thus, many high-rate credit customers are unable to turn to open-end credit for short-term borrowing.

Information on closed-end credit use is also available for payday loan and RAL customers. In contrast to open-end credit, both payday loan and RAL customers are more likely than all households to owe automobile and other closed-end credit. Moreover, when they owe debt (regardless of whether it is closed- or open-end), payday loan and RAL customers are apt to have higher monthly debt service payments compared with income than all households (not in table). These findings are consistent with these customers being predominantly in early life cycle stages, where heavy debt use is more prevalent, than in later life cycle stages.

Many high-rate credit customers exhibit characteristics that make qualifying for additional credit difficult. Pawnbroker, payday, and refund anticipation borrowers are more than several times more likely than all families to have had a recent bankruptcy or serious delinquency (data not in table). Twelve percent of pawnshop borrowers had filed for bankruptcy in the last ten years. More than a quarter of payday loan customers were sixty days or more past due on a payment sometime in the last year, and 15.4 percent had filed for bankruptcy in the last five years. Twenty-six percent of tax refund anticipation loan customers were sixty or more days past due sometime in the last year. In contrast, among all households, just 5.8 percent were sixty or more days past due sometime in the last year, and 3.7 percent had filed for bankruptcy in the last five years.

Further, large percentages of pawnbroker, rent-to-own, and refund anticipation loan customers do not have a checking or any bank account (data not in table). More than half of pawnbroker customers and a third or more of rent-to-own and refund anticipation loan customers do not have a checking account. Payday loan customers are the exception, since having a checking account is a requirement for obtaining a payday loan. It is notable that the use of mainstream credit products by income tax refund anticipation loan customers with bank accounts is similar to that of payday loan customers. They are more likely than all families to owe closed-end credit (not in table). In contrast, tax refund anticipation loan customers with no bank account are less likely than all families to owe closed-end credit.

Consistent with relatively high debt use, credit payment problems, and the frequent lack of a banking relationship, many high-price credit customers experienced or perceived limitations in credit availability. Of the 32.2 percent of pawn loan customers who applied for other credit in the previous twelve months, 50.2 percent experienced a turndown. Seventy-three percent of payday loan customers and 46.5 percent of RAL customers were turned down or limited in the last five years (part 6 of table 8.3). Almost half of payday loan customers and three-fourths of RAL customers said that during the last year, they thought about applying for credit but did not because they thought that they would be turned down.

Further evidence of credit constraints is available for payday loan and RAL customers with bank credit cards, which consumers might use for short-term borrowing of small amounts. Sixty-one percent of payday loan customers with a bank card and a third of RAL customers with a bank card reported that they refrained from using a bank card in the last year because they would have exceeded their credit limit.

In sum, consumers using different types of high-rate loans tend to be in age, life cycle, and income groups that are associated with strong demand for credit and are often rationed. They are relatively young, are in early family life cycle stages, and have lower or moderate incomes, depending on the product. Some of these consumers (payday loan and tax refund anticipation loan customers with bank accounts) are more likely to use closed-end credit than all families and are apt to have higher debt burdens than families with debt generally. Others (pawnbroker, tax refund anticipation loan customers without bank accounts, and rent-to-own customers) are less likely than all families to use mainstream credit products. Regardless of their use of mainstream credit products, many high-rate credit customers have characteristics that limit their access to credit, and most have experienced turndowns or perceive that they are constrained. Thus, the consumers who use high-rate loans are generally ones who economic theory predicts might benefit from relaxation of credit constraints.

That consumers using high-rate credit products tend to have demographic and economic characteristics that are associated with credit rationing and rational use of high-rate credit does not in itself, of course, indicate that their use of such credit is rational, but it does suggest that their circumstances are such that use of high-APR credit may be utility-increasing. In the next sections of this chapter, we will look for evidence that these consumers understand the high-rate products that they obtained and showed signs of deliberation in their decisions.

Are Consumers' Choices Involving High-APR Credit Products Purposive and Deliberative?

As this discussion indicates, the standard economic analysis of consumer behavior focuses on the outcome of decisions, for example, using credit or not. While this approach has been highly successful in predicting outcomes, it provides little insight into the actual decision process itself.

To understand consumers' choices involving high-rate credit products, researchers have turned to cognitive models of consumers' decision processes from psychology. As discussed in chapter 4, the consumer's decision is a process that occurs over several stages: problem recognition, internal and external search for information, choice, and outcome evaluation. These stages are interrelated, with feedback occurring throughout the process. Developments during each stage may cause the process to stop, move to the next stage, or proceed immediately to the purchase. Consumers may simplify, use heuristics, or take shortcuts during the decision process.[33]

DETERMINANTS OF THE EXTENT OF THE DECISION PROCESS
Empirical evidence on consumer behavior suggests several things that can affect the extent of the decision process: situational factors, product characteristics, consumer characteristics, and environmental factors. For instance, among the

---

33. Economists also recognize that consumers may not obtain complete information about alternatives before making decisions. In the economist's framework, acquisition of information may be costly. A consumer will acquire additional information only if its expected benefit exceeds the cost (see Stigler 1961).

situations that might lead to extended decision processes is the possibility that the consumer has little or no relevant experience in the area. This situation might arise if the consumer has never purchased the product before, the product is new, past experience is obsolete because the product is purchased infrequently, or the purchase is considered discretionary rather than necessary.

Several product characteristics are associated with extended decision processes. Examples include products that commit the consumer for a long period of time, have a high price relative to the consumer's income, and have substitutes with both desirable and undesirable characteristics relative to the product.

Many socioeconomic characteristics of consumers are correlated with the extent of the decision process. Some of the characteristics probably reflect cognitive ability and the opportunity cost associated with search time. Others may reflect experience or attitudes. Decision processes are more likely to be extended than limited when, other things being equal, the consumer has a college education, has moderate rather than high or low income, is younger than thirty-five, enjoys shopping, and perceives no urgent or immediate need for the product.

Finally, environmental factors include family and cultural influences. An extended decision process may be stimulated by differences between a consumer's attitudes and those of his or her family or personal reference groups.

HYPOTHESES ON THE EXTENT OF DECISION PROCESSES FOR HIGH-RATE CREDIT PRODUCTS

In general, these hallmarks of extended decision-making processes do not describe the circumstances typically involved in choosing high-rate credit products; high-rate credit products have characteristics associated with limited decision processes. Concerning product characteristics, most are relatively short term. Also, because loan amount is usually small, the finance charge is high relative to loan amount but not generally relative to the borrower's monthly income.

Further, situational factors may also limit decision processes. A short term to maturity makes high-price credit products more suited to addressing temporary shortfalls in funds than financing investment in durable goods that might last years. Temporary shortfalls may often be the result of unexpected expenses and may therefore be viewed as urgent. Moreover, short-term use to address temporary shortfalls in cash may involve relatively short time periods since previous decisions. In such situations, consumers may perceive that information obtained from previous decisions is not obsolete.

The buyer behavior model suggests that extensive collection of information and weighing of all available alternatives may not always be necessary for purposive and intelligent decisions (see chapter 4). Focusing on the psychological aspects of the decision to use credit for purchasing durable goods on credit, Katona (1975) noted that if careful deliberation were defined as including all features of decision making—consideration of alternatives and consequences, discussion with family members, information seeking, and concern with price, brand, quality, performance, special features, and gadgets—the conclusion would emerge that almost all people proceed in a careless way in purchasing large household goods. This conclusion, however, seems unwarranted, especially for shorter-term purchases of a more urgent nature. Deliberation for such purchases may be strongly focused on one aspect of the purchase to the exclusion of others. Therefore, it may be considered as careful deliberation if some, but by no means all, of the features of problem solving and thinking are present.

Decision Processes of High-Rate Credit Customers

With this background, it seems useful to examine in more detail available evidence concerning thought, understanding the transaction, and the decision involving purchase of high-cost credit products.

SMALL CONSUMER FINANCE LOAN DECISIONS

In 1972, Durkin (1975) conducted for the National Commission on Consumer Finance a study of consumers obtaining very small consumer finance loans in Texas (Chapter 301-F, subchapter 201; formerly Article 3.16 loans).[34] The maximum loan size at this time was $100. Customer and loan information was obtained from lender files. Customers were also directly surveyed about their loans. The survey included questions about reasons for borrowing, awareness of loan price, and satisfaction with the loan.

Responses to the question on reasons for borrowing suggest some urgency for many consumers. The single greatest reason for borrowing was to pay old bills or consolidate debts. The next most frequently mentioned reasons were medical expenses and automobile purchase or repair. Together, these three responses accounted for nearly two in five reported reasons. Adding other responses such as utility bills, food, and taxes or insurance suggests that most customers faced an urgent need for funds, which may have limited their decision process.

Information from lender files included the annual percentage rate and finance charge, which permitted a comparison with reported APR and finance charge from the consumer survey. Only 2.4 percent of customers were able to report an interest rate that indicated that they were aware of the APR. Thirty-nine percent said that they did not know, and 27.2 percent reported dollar charges. Virtually all of the remaining 31.1 percent of customers reported rates that were too low.

In contrast, two-thirds of customers reported a finance charge that indicated that they were aware of the finance charge. Thirty-eight percent reported the exact amount of the finance charge; another 8.3 percent reported an amount that was close (plus or minus 20 percent) to the exact amount; and 20.1 percent reported an accurate finance charge for a different contract, which may have been a refinancing that occurred between the sampling and interview dates or a generalized price ($34 per $100 borrowed for six months, for example). Nearly all of the remaining one-third said that they did not know the finance charge or reported amounts that were too high or too low.

---

34. Durkin and McAlister (1977) provided a similar analysis of customers obtaining larger, Chapter 342-E, subchapter 201, consumer finance loans.

The relatively high level of awareness of the finance charge suggests that many consumers may have considered the finance charge in their decision.[35] Even if they did not use information on finance charges to shop for credit, it would be difficult to conclude that these consumers made uninformed decisions. In contrast, the lack of awareness of APR suggests that these consumers were unlikely to have used the APR in making their decisions.[36] The failure of virtually all customers to consider the effect of time discounting generally would not cause serious errors because of the very small loan size and short term to maturity for these loans.

Most borrowers also were aware of cost differences across types of lenders. That is, they were aware that finance company loans were more expensive than bank loans. About two-thirds of borrowers said that borrowing from a finance company was more expensive than from a bank. The decision to borrow from a finance company apparently was often influenced by consideration of credit availability. About half of customers who said that borrowing from a finance company was more expensive reported that they borrowed from a finance company because they could not get a similar loan from a bank. Twenty-three percent of customers reported that they had actually been turned down by a bank or finance company in the last five years.

Consumers using very small consumer finance loans generally evaluated their purchase decision positively. When asked to evaluate whether the loan was worth it or not, 84.8 percent of customers said that the loan was worth it. Most customers gave reasons related to the need for funds as the reason for their satisfaction. Of those who said that the loan was not worth it, about half cited the high price as the reason for dissatisfaction. Seventeen percent of dissatisfied customers reported difficulty of getting out of debt as the reason for dissatisfaction, but these customers accounted for just 2.6 percent of all customers.

In sum, most customers used small consumer finance loans because they had an urgent need and did not have better alternatives. They were aware of the finance charge and were thereby able to make informed decisions on this dimension, regardless of whether or not they shopped or had alternative sources of credit. Customers generally evaluated their decisions positively, saying that the loan was worth it because it provided needed funds.

Payday Loan Decisions

Elliehausen and Lawrence (2001) surveyed a representative sample of payday loan customers at companies belonging to the industry trade association. Companies belonging to the association operated about half of the offices offering payday

---

35. Consumers using very small, short-term consumer finance loans had a greater level of awareness of the finance charge than consumers using mainstream credit. Day and Brandt (1973), in another study for the National Commission, found that a little more than half of consumers using mainstream credit products were able provide estimates of the finance charge.

36. Durkin (1975) hypothesized that respondents may have disregarded APR as unimportant because they did not understand APRs and saw no relationship between the APR and the finance charge.

loans at that time. Customers were asked about their use of payday loans, recent payday loan decisions, other credit use, and perceptions of credit availability.

The survey results showed that payday loans were often used to address urgent needs. Nearly two-two thirds of payday loan customers obtained their most recent new advance (not renewal) because of an unexpected expense or shortfall in income. Only 11.9 percent used a payday loan for a planned expenditure. The remaining 22.5 percent of customers used payday loans for various other purposes, some of which likely also were urgent.

Like the installment loan borrowers, payday loan customers were generally aware of finance charges but not APRs. Eighty-five to 96.1 percent of payday loan customers reported accurate finance charges paid for their most recent payday loan.[37] In contrast, only 20.1 percent of customers were able to report an accurate APR, although 78.0 percent of customers recalled receiving information on the APR. Thus, payday loan customers appear to use the finance charge rather than the APR in their decisions.[38]

Thirty-eight percent of customers reported that they considered another source of credit before obtaining their most recent payday loan. Nearly all of the customers considering another source considered a depository institution or a finance company. That payday loan customers considered these sources is not surprising, since their ownership of a checking account and relatively frequent use of mainstream credit suggest that they are familiar with these sources. In contrast, only 0.6 percent considered a pawnbroker, and 2.5 percent considered an automobile title loan company. Thus, pawnbroker and automobile title loans do not appear to be very close substitutes to payday loans in the minds of payday loan customers.

About half of payday loan customers had been using payday loans for a year or less. Most use was short-term, which is consistent with the design of the product. More than a quarter of payday loan customers' longest sequence of consecutive loans (new loan and renewals) was two weeks or less, and 56.6 percent of customers' longest sequence of consecutive loans was six weeks or less. Customers may have resorted to payday loans several times during the year, however. While a little more than a third of payday loan customers had four or fewer loans during the last twelve months, 27.2 percent had five to eight payday loans, and 38.1 percent had nine or more payday loans during the last twelve months. Most customers with a large number of loans had intervals between borrowings, but some had payday loan sequences lasting fourteen weeks or longer. Obtaining a relatively large number of payday loans during the year or renewing existing loans

37. Because actual finance charges and APRs were not known, consumers' knowledge of costs was assessed based on awareness zones. An awareness zone is a range of finance charges or APRs that are available in the market. Respondents who report a value that falls within the awareness zone are classified as aware. For discussion of awareness zones, see Durkin (2000).

38. For discussion of the use of the finance charge as a measure of the costs of short term loans, see Durkin and Elliehausen (2013).

frequently is expensive but not necessarily evidence of a problem of understanding.[39] Consumers living from paycheck to paycheck may experience several unexpected emergencies during a year, causing them to need funds more frequently than initially expected. However, such frequent payday loan use undoubtedly did not help some borrowers to manage their finances, and it may well have exacerbated the difficulties of others.[40]

Nonetheless, by far most customers were satisfied with their most recent advance. Of the 12.2 percent of customers who were dissatisfied, 61.6 percent cited the high price as the reason for dissatisfaction. Difficulty of getting out of debt (which might indicate that customers did not understand that the product was designed for short-term use) and lack of information about the product were rarely mentioned as reasons for dissatisfaction.

Conclusions about the payday loan decision are similar to those about the small consumer finance loan decision. Most customers used payday loans because they had an urgent need and had few alternatives. Customers generally used payday loans over relatively short time intervals consistent with the design of the product. They were aware of dollar cost of payday loans and evaluated their decision to use payday loans positively.

REFUND ANTICIPATION LOAN DECISIONS

Elliehausen (2005) surveyed a nationally representative sample of refund anticipation loan customers about their RAL decision, other credit use, and perceptions of availability. Forty-one percent of refund anticipation customers reported using RALs to pay Christmas, credit card, or other bills; 21.2 percent reported unexpected expenditures; 12.9 percent reported planned purchases; and the remaining 25.0 percent reported various other reasons. Need may have played a role in customers' decision to use RALs, but many customers may also have had another motive. Many of them apparently used RALs as part of a precommitment strategy to force saving during the year. About a third of refund anticipation customers said that they had extra amounts withheld from their paychecks in order to get a refund.[41] The uses of the funds were often foreseen. More customers mentioned paying Christmas bills or planned expenses than unexpected expenses as the reason for obtaining a RAL. And the behavior appears to have become a habit for many customers. Less than a third of RAL customers were first-time customers. Of

---

39. Payday loan renewals are sometimes seen as a sign that consumers have unrealistic expectations about their ability to repay (see, for example, Pew Charitable Trusts 2012). However, Mann (2013) has provided evidence that most payday loan borrowers accurately assess how long they will need to repay their loan.

40. Factors associated with difficulty in managing finances such as not saving, relatively heavy credit card indebtedness, and overdrawing checking accounts are associated with frequent use of payday loans (Lawrence and Elliehausen 2008, Elliehausen 2009).

41. For evidence of use of tax withholding for saving among low- and moderate-income consumers, see chapters 9 and 10 in Barr (2012).

the more than two-thirds of RAL customers with previous experience, 72.3 percent had three or more previous RALs.

About half of RAL customers were classified as aware of the RAL fee. Only about a quarter of them recalled receiving an APR, and hardly any reported an accurate APR. The levels of awareness of RAL fees may have been influenced by the greater complexity of the transaction. The RAL was purchased jointly with tax preparation and possibly other services. Customers may not have recalled finance charges because they focused on other aspects of the transaction that they considered more important or more difficult. The level of awareness may also have been influenced by previous experience. As mentioned, many customers had obtained RALs three or more times in the past. Customers who were satisfied with previous experience may make decisions with little information gathering or deliberation.

Most customers recalled other details of the transaction. Virtually all were aware of an electronic filing option, and 64.8 percent of customers reported discussing other options for obtaining funds faster before obtaining the RAL. Most customers not recalling the RAL fee were able to report other information about the transaction. Half reported the tax preparation fee, nearly three-fourths reported the cash advance amount, and a third reported both the loan fee and the cash advance amounts. Thus, customers may have considered some information in decisions about RALs.

Considering the high level of repeat usage, it is not surprising the RAL customers generally were also satisfied with current loans. Eighty-five percent of customers said that they were satisfied with their last RAL. Virtually all satisfied customers reported the quick receipt of needed money as a reason for satisfaction. Of the 14.0 percent of customers who said that they were dissatisfied, 70.2 percent cited the high price as a reason for dissatisfaction. Lack of information was not perceived as a problem by most dissatisfied customers. Eleven percent of dissatisfied customers mentioned inadequate information as a reason for dissatisfaction.

Although only about half of customers were aware of RAL cost on their most recent loan, it is not clear that decisions were not purposive and intelligent. Customers were able to report information about their loans. Virtually all were aware of electronic filing, and more than half discussed other options for receiving funds faster before obtaining an RAL. Evidence also suggests that for some customers, RALs are part of an annual forced saving plan, in which they use tax withholding to accumulate funds for large purchases or paying Christmas, credit card, or other bills.

RENT-TO-OWN DECISIONS

Lacko, McKernan, and Hastak (2000) surveyed a nationally representative sample of rent-to-own customers about their experience with rent-to-own stores. A major focus of the survey was to ascertain the extent to which rent-to-own transactions result in the purchase of rented items. Survey responses indicated that 69.9 percent of customers purchased items that they rented. Two-thirds of customers initially intended to purchase the rented item, and so purchases were generally consistent with customer purchase intentions.[42] Eighty-seven percent of customers intending

---

42. Analyzing transaction data from a rent-to-own chain, Anderson and Jaggia (2009, 2012) observed a lower purchase rate even after accounting for some customers having more

to purchase actually did purchase. About half of purchases were rented for a year or less, suggesting that many customers exercised the early purchase option. Nearly all items on which customers made substantial payments toward ownership were purchased by the customer.

A quarter of rent-to-own customers intended a temporary rental, and 90 percent of these customers returned the item.[43] Most returned the items after a relatively short period, averaging five months. The relatively short rental period is consistent with these customers' initial intentions.[44]

By far most were satisfied with their rent-to-own experiences. Seventy-five percent of customers said that they were very or somewhat satisfied, 8 percent said that they were somewhat dissatisfied, and 10.5 percent said that they were very dissatisfied. The remaining 6.5 percent were neither satisfied nor dissatisfied or said that they did not know.

Lacko, McKernan, and Hastak did not question respondents about costs, but responses to questions about satisfaction with rent-to-own experiences suggest that many respondents were aware that the price was high. High price was the most commonly reported reason for dissatisfaction with the transaction. Two-thirds of dissatisfied customers said that they were dissatisfied with their rent-to-own experience because of high prices.

Satisfied customers typically reported characteristics of the item being rented or services provided by the rent-to-own company as a reason for satisfaction. However, 16.1 percent of satisfied customers said that because of high prices, they were only somewhat satisfied. The percentage of satisfied customers mentioning high prices is far greater than the 3.5 percent of satisfied customers who cited low price as a reason for satisfaction (and who, therefore, appeared uninformed about transaction details).

Very few customers gave inadequate cost information as a reason for their evaluation. Five percent of dissatisfied customers (1.0 percent of all customers) reported hidden or added costs as a reason for dissatisfaction.

The consistency of purchase intentions with actual behavior suggests that rent-to-own customers generally know whether they will purchase the item at the beginning of the rental period. The survey evidence indicates directly that at least a quarter of customers believed that rent-to-own prices are high. The actual

than one rental, but their analysis using a competing risk model of rental outcomes indicated that renting to own was an important means of obtaining ownership for "working poor" consumers. Anderson and Jaggia noted that survey response issues may have contributed to some of the differences from the survey. In the survey, exchanges of items may be reported as one transaction, for example, and involuntary returns and customer fraud may be underreported. In addition, the customers of the rent-to-own chain may not be nationally representative, although the demographic characteristics of the firm's customers are broadly similar to those of survey respondents.

43. The remaining 8.1 percent of customers were not sure or did not know their intentions. About half of those who were not sure or did not know their intentions eventually purchased the items.

44. Anderson and Jaggia (2009) found that customers who returned items generally made a small percentage of the total of payments required to own before returning the item.

proportion of customers believing that rent-to-own prices are high likely is actually greater. Customers may have been aware that purchasing items by renting to own is relatively expensive but did not volunteer this information when responding about their reasons for satisfaction or dissatisfaction. Consequently, it is likely that many consumers who intended to purchase were aware that rent-to-own purchases were expensive. Nonetheless, most customers evaluated their rent-to-own decisions positively. Customer characteristics discussed earlier suggest that limited availability of credit from other sources likely played a role in their decisions.

Do Consumers Benefit from Access to High-Rate Credit Products?

And so the review of available empirical evidence indicates that users of high-rate credit products typically are rationed consumers, those who theory suggests may benefit from availability of high-rate credit. Evidence also shows that users of high-rate credit, to varying degrees, demonstrate signs of deliberation in their decisions, although decision processes tend not to be extensive. The ultimate question is whether consumers benefit from the use of such credit. A few recent researchers have attempted to test empirically whether consumers benefit from access to high-rate credit, specifically to payday loans, using a variety of different ways to measure possible benefits. These studies are interesting, but to a large degree, they are only that and not completely convincing because of the macro nature of the potential impacts investigated (recovery from natural disasters, bankruptcies, or total amounts of debt used, for example, each of which is also subject to other influences and explanations). There clearly is room for more micro-oriented research into specific effects of availability of high-rate credit, although such studies can be very expensive and difficult if they involve survey work.

COMMUNITY WELL-BEING IN THE AFTERMATH OF NATURAL DISASTERS

Morse (2011) examined the effect of availability of payday loans on measures of community well-being after the occurrence of floods, fires, or other natural disasters. Natural disasters, she argued, create a natural experiment in which financial distress is exogenously induced on communities with and without access to payday loans. She hypothesized that if payday loans increase welfare, their availability would mitigate negative effects of disasters and hasten a return to normal life following distress.

Morse's regression analyses indicated that areas with payday lenders recovered more quickly following a natural disaster—with fewer foreclosures, larcenies, vehicle thefts, and burglaries.—than areas without payday lenders. For each measure of well-being, the estimated coefficient for the effect of payday loans (that is, the interaction of treatment, post-disaster time group, and availability of payday loans) had the hypothesized negative sign and was, with the exception of vehicle thefts and burglaries, statistically significantly different from zero. On the basis of these findings, Morse concluded that despite its high price, payday lending increases welfare by increasing communities' resiliency to financial difficulties.

FINANCIAL DIFFICULTIES AND AVAILABILITY OF PAYDAY LOANS

Morgan and Strain (2008) examined changes in the number of returned checks, complaints about collection behavior against lenders and debt collectors, and bankruptcies following legislation in Georgia and North Carolina that permanently closed all payday lenders operating in those states.[45] They hypothesized that if payday loans exacerbate financial strain, then their availability would be expected to increase problems with returned checks and debt servicing. If, instead, payday loans help manage financial strain, then availability of payday loans would be associated with lower levels of such problems. They examined post-payday-loan-ban changes in Georgia and North Carolina relative to other states not experiencing a change in payday lending laws.

Morgan and Strain's findings indicated that consumers' problems in these areas generally increased significantly in Georgia and North Carolina relative to other states following the payday loan bans. The number of returned checks increased, although the increases for North Carolina were not statistically significant. Complaints about behavior of debt collectors increased in both states following the bans. Complaints against lenders, which were far less numerous than complaints against debt collectors, increased in Georgia but declined by a small amount in North Carolina following the payday loan bans.

Consumer bankruptcies filed under Chapter 7 of the federal Bankruptcy Code increased significantly in both states after the ban on payday loans (see Chapter 13 in this book for further discussion of bankruptcy). Bankruptcies under chapter 13 of the Bankruptcy Code, which involve continued payments to creditors rather than debt discharges, decreased in Georgia and North Carolina relative to other states after payday loans were banned. In both cases, the effect might be explained by greater difficulty in managing finances when payday loans are no longer available: removing a means of managing finances might prompt a debt-strapped borrower to choose a Chapter 7 debt discharge rather than seek a workout under a Chapter 13 plan.[46]

In a later paper Morgan, Strain, and Seblani (2012) extended Morgan and Strain's analysis of changes of payday loan access to other states. They found robust evidence that the number of check returns and overdraft fee income at banks

---

45. Georgia passed legislation making payday lending a felony subject to class action lawsuits and prosecution under racketeering laws, effective May 2004. The office of the North Carolina Commissioner of Banks effectively ended payday lending when it ruled that payday lending through a local agent of a national bank, which was the method for payday lending in North Carolina after the 2001 expiration of the payday loan exemption to the state's usury limits, was a violation of North Carolina law.

46. For two of the three types of problems, Morgan and Strain also considered liberalization in Hawaii's payday loan law (an increase in the maximum loan size for payday loans from $300 to $600 in July 2003), which would have the opposite effect of a ban. (They were unable to consider changes in check returns, because Hawaii does not have a Federal Reserve check processing center.) Relative to other states, complaints about collection behavior of debt collectors and lenders in Hawaii decreased, and bankruptcies fell significantly (chapter 13 bankruptcies rose, and chapter 7 bankruptcies fell by more than chapter 13 bankruptcies rose) after Hawaii increased the payday loan size limit.

increased following payday loan bans. They also found that complaints against lenders and debt collectors increased after bans and that Chapter 13 bankruptcies decreased. These results largely confirmed the findings of the earlier paper.

Zinman (2010) provided further evidence on effects of restrictions on payday loans. He examined panel data from surveys of payday loan customers before and five months after Oregon imposed a restrictive rate ceiling that caused many payday loan companies to leave the state.

Zinman found that the use of payday loans in Oregon fell relative to the state of Washington, the comparison group state for his analysis, but use of several other types of short-term credit (automobile title loans, credit card advances, and bank overdraft credit lines) did not increase significantly in Oregon relative to Washington. Apparently, these loan products either were not available to former payday loan customers or were not generally viewed as close substitutes for payday loans. The incidence of returned checks and late payments of bills did not change significantly, either. Taken together, however, the use of *any* short-term credit (including payday loans) in Oregon declined significantly relative to Washington, but the decline was smaller in size than that for payday loans alone. Thus, collectively, the nonpayday forms of short-term credit appeared to make up for some of the loss in payday loan credit, even if no one product was an especially close substitute for payday loans.[47]

Zinman also examined customers' perceptions of credit availability and their own financial situation. Five months after Oregon's restrictive rate ceiling became effective, payday loan customers in Oregon reported more frequently relative to customers in Washington that short-term credit was more difficult to obtain in the preceding three months. After the rate ceiling became effective, customers in Oregon did not more frequently report a worsening of their financial situation in the preceding six months, but a greater proportion of customers in Oregon said that they expected their financial situation to get worse in the future. Whether customers' assessment of their financial situation was directly related to availability of short-term credit was not examined.

Melzer (2011) analyzed data from the Urban Institute's 1997, 1999, and 2003 National Survey of America's Families for households in Massachusetts, New York, and New Jersey, states that because of restrictive laws had no payday loan company offices during the study period. Each of these states bordered other states that had payday loan offices, however. Melzer compared different measures of financial distress for households in border counties that were near payday loan offices in other states to those of households in counties that did not have proximate availability of payday loans. Measures of distress included inability to pay rent or bills in the past year, moving residence for financial reasons, reducing meals for financial reasons, doing without telephone services, and delaying medical treatment because of lack of insurance or money.

---

47. Zinman did not consider pawnshop, noncash advance credit card borrowing, and loans from friends or relatives, which may also be substitutes for payday loans in some cases.

Melzer's regressions predicting the incidence of different types of financial distress in the past twelve months indicated that payday loan access (that is, living in a county that is near out-of-state payday loan offices) was associated with higher, generally statistically significantly higher, incidence of distress for households with incomes in the range where payday loan use is concentrated ($15,000–$50,000). Access to payday loans was not significantly related to distress for lower-income households (which often did not qualify for payday loans because they did not meet lenders' checking account ownership or regular income requirements) or higher-income households (which generally have access to lower-cost sources of credit).

In contrast, Bhutta (2012), using a methodology similar to that of Melzer to analyze credit reporting bureau data from the Federal Reserve Bank of New York's Consumer Credit Panel (Lee and van der Klaauw 2010), found little or no effect of payday loan access on credit bureau scores of individual consumers in the late 2000s, leading him to conclude that payday loans appear to be neither financially destabilizing nor greatly beneficial.[48] A possible explanation for the lack of effect (either negative or positive) is that the alternatives used by consumers with no payday access (e.g., check overdrafts, pawnbroker loans, borrowing from family or friends) have similar effects or that the relatively small size of payday loans limits their benefits or harm. Bhutta further noted that his findings need not be inconsistent with other studies, because other studies considered different outcomes. Consumers having access to payday loans in Melzer's surveys, for example, might have experienced stress in paying bills, moving, cutting meals, or postponing medical treatment without becoming delinquent on reported debts.

Skiba and Tobacman (2011) investigated whether a borrower's use of payday loans was associated with greater likelihood of bankruptcy filing. The data for their analysis were from loan applications at a payday loan company's Texas offices. The applications were matched with public records on bankruptcy filings, which allowed Skiba and Tobacman to identify payday loan applicants whose subsequent credit problems led them to file for bankruptcy.

Skiba and Tobacman used a statistical model to estimate the effects of payday loans on marginal customers. The margin was a threshold payday loan risk score. The risk score was developed by a credit reporting firm that specializes in nontraditional credit performance data. The risk score is a prediction of credit risk specific to payday lending. Individuals just above the threshold were offered payday loans. Individuals just below were rejected, but because their scores were nearly equal to those of marginal accepted applicants, Skiba and Tobacman argued, their unobserved financial characteristics were similar to those of accepted applicants, making marginally rejected applicants suitable as a comparison group.

---

48. Bhutta estimated effects of payday loan access on the credit scores of three groups: consumers between the ages of twenty-five and forty-nine, consumers with total revolving credit lines of less than $10,000, and consumers with total revolving credit lines of less than $10,000 who were denied credit in the past twelve months. He also estimated effects on the probability of discrete declines of 10 percent and 20 percent between 2008 and 2010.

In regression analyses for the probability of bankruptcy filing, Chapter 7 bankruptcy filings were not significantly different for applicants whose first application was approved and applicants whose first application was not approved, but Chapter 13 bankruptcy filings were significantly higher for applicants whose first application was approved. The statistical association between payday loan approval and Chapter 13 bankruptcy filing does not imply that payday loan approval caused bankruptcy filing, however. Payday loan use is typically a response to financial distress, which may ultimately end in bankruptcy.

Skiba and Tobacman were able to provide information on the financial condition of the applicants who subsequently filed for bankruptcy. These applicants had substantial debts. Applicants whose first applications for payday loans were approved reported on average $103,783 in secured debt and $34,171 in unsecured debt. In total, this was 1.7 times their total assets.[49] Twenty-three percent of the applicants who filed for bankruptcy had payday loans outstanding at the time they filed for bankruptcy, sometimes at more than one payday loan company, but payday loans made up a very small fraction of applicants' $34,171 of unsecured debt. It seems likely that payday loans hastened the decision of some of these consumers to file for bankruptcy, but it is not clear that payday loans were what drove most of these consumers into bankruptcy.

Bhutta, Skiba, and Tobacman (2012) matched payday loan applicant data from Skiba and Tobacman (2011) with credit bureau history from the Federal Reserve Bank of New York's Consumer Credit Panel (Lee and van der Klaauw 2010). The match allowed them to observe applicants' use of and payment performance for mainstream credit in periods before and after obtaining a payday loan. Focusing on marginal applicants—those whose payday risk score was close to the payday lender's threshold for approval—they found that initial payday loan applications occurred at a time when applicants' access to credit from mainstream lenders was low. Average debt of applicants rose sharply before application. Of the applicants with credit cards, 80 percent had no credit available at the time of application, and another 10 percent had less than $300 available credit.

The credit bureau data suggest that applicants were experiencing financial difficulties. The average percentage of accounts that were delinquent increased steadily in the months before the payday loan application. The credit data also suggest that applicants were seeking mainstream credit before they applied for a payday loan. Credit inquiries rose sharply just before the date of application. These efforts were largely unsuccessful. The average number of new accounts did not rise.

Not surprisingly, rising debt levels, high utilization of credit card limits, increasing delinquencies, and more frequent credit inquiries caused applicants'

---

49. Nearly 1 percent of the applicants filed for chapter 7 bankruptcy within two years of the first application, and 1.56 percent applied for chapter 13 bankruptcy. Applicants whose initial payday loan applications were rejected and subsequently filed for bankruptcy had on average $145,317 in secured debt and $32,221 in unsecured debt. Total debt was on average 93 percent of total assets, but more than half of these applicants reported debts greater than assets.

credit bureau scores to fall in the period leading up to the initial application. The patterns for marginally accepted and marginally rejected payday loan applicants were nearly the same.

Using the credit bureau score to measure the effect of payday lending on the financial situation of applicants, Bhutta, Skiba, and Tobacman found that average credit bureau scores of both accepted and rejected applicants followed an almost identical pattern, falling slightly in the quarter after application and then rising slowly. Average credit bureau scores for accepted applicants fell a little more than average credit bureau scores for rejected applicants, but this result was influenced by differences in preapplication scores. After accounting for preapplication scores, the difference between accepted and rejected applicants was not statistically different from zero. In other words, use of payday loans appears to have had no effect, positive or negative, on applicants' credit performance. Overall, payday loans neither helped consumers improve their creditworthiness nor led to further deterioration. Bhutta, Skiba, and Tobacman speculated about why payday loans would not have any significant effect. One explanation is that the size of payday loans, typically $300 to $400, is too small to matter. Another explanation is that rejected applicants were able to obtain credit somewhere else—another payday lender, a pawnbroker, or a small loan company, for example—and that loans from these other sources had similar effects on rejected applicants' performance. Also possible is that payday loans had an effect on some other financial outcome.

Mayer (2004) provided additional evidence supporting a conclusion that payday loans may contribute to but do not play the definitive role in bankruptcy filing decisions. Mayer examined a sample of 3,600 bankruptcy petitions in three counties in different parts of the country. Payday loans were listed in 9.1 percent of the petitions. For petitioners with payday loans, payday loans were a very small percentage of total unsecured debt. The median percentage of payday loans to total unsecured debt was 6 percent. The percentage of credit card debt was more than five times greater.

In many cases, payday loans may have contributed to petitioners' financial difficulties. Sixty percent of petitioners with payday loans owed more than one payday loan. The distribution of number of payday loans varied widely. In a few cases, petitioners accumulated a substantial number of payday loans. Mayer reported that the largest number of payday loans owed by a petitioner was twenty-three, for a total of $5,675, and that another petitioner owed twenty-one payday loans, totaling $5,985.[50] In these cases, the total amount of payday loans was greater than net monthly income. These two examples are extreme cases and not usual. The median number of payday loans was two. The median amount of payday debt was $880, which was 46 percent of net monthly income. These petitioners

---

50. One case involving an accumulation of seventeen payday loans appeared to be fraudulent. Using a closed checking account, the petitioner obtained fourteen of the loans at different branches of the same company in a two-week period before filing for bankruptcy. The payday loan company challenged the discharge of debt and eventually obtained an agreement with the petitioner for repayment of the principal.

had substantial debts and probably would have ended up filing for bankruptcy anyway, but payday loans likely hastened the outcome. That these cases often involved different payday lending companies and frequent renewals underscores the risk of such behavior to both customers and lenders.

For the 40 percent of petitions with payday credit but just one loan, the average amount of the payday loan was about $350. This was 1.3 percent of the average amount of unsecured debt of petitioners with payday loans. The typical finance charge on a $350 payday loan ($52.50) would be about 2.4 percent of the average net monthly income of unsecured debt of petitioners with payday loans. It is unlikely that these payday loans were what drove these petitioners to bankruptcy.

PAYDAY LOANS AND THE MILITARY

Carrell and Zinman (2008) investigated the effect of payday loan access on indicators of performance of US Air Force personnel at all sixty-seven bases in thirty-five states. They noted that base assignments of personnel are at the discretion of the Air Force and are based on airmen's and women's occupation and experience satisfying the personnel needs of the Air Force. Thus, those vulnerable to financial distress do not have a choice in locating where payday loans or any other types of credit are readily available or not. As a result, access to payday loans is random. As measures of performance, Carrell and Zinman considered forced enrollment in a weight loss program, presence of an unfavorable information file, and eligibility for reenlistment. Eligibility for reenlistment depends on job performance, and the first two measures influence that eligibility. Performance measures used were outcomes aggregated by occupation, enlistment term, base, and year.

Regression analyses indicated a statistically significant relationship between availability of payday loans and two measures of performance (presence of an unfavorable information file and eligibility for reenlistment) for first-term personnel. Availability of payday loans was not significantly related to any measure of performance for more experienced second-term or career personnel. Carrell and Zinman found that the positive relationship was mostly limited to personnel with nonfinance/acquisition occupation specialties and lower Air Force Qualifying Test scores. (There was an exception in that for high test score personnel, availability of payday loans was positively related to enrollment in a weight loss program, a puzzling finding.) The findings suggest that any unfavorable effects of payday loans on performance were largely among inexperienced and financially unsophisticated personnel.

EXPERIMENTAL STUDIES

Wilson et al. (2010) conducted an experimental study investigating how availability of payday loans and overdraft protection affected subjects' ability to manage a hypothetical household budget over a thirty-month interval. The project was implemented by a computer simulation. The budget consisted of monthly bills and income that placed subjects in tight financial situations. The subjects were university students who were paid to participate, with the amount of payment depending on the students' performance. Subjects were required to maintain a minimum level of consumption and were offered optional discretionary consumption opportunities. Monthly bills included regularly recurring payments and unexpected expenses. Failure to pay bills resulted in penalties that were deducted from consumption. Subjects were required to pay any missed bills and late fees in order to continue to the next month. Some subjects used payday loans or overdraft protection as alternatives to missing bills.

An analysis of subjects' performance indicated that their likelihood of surviving to month t (that is, to satisfy obligations while maintaining the minimum required consumption level up to month t) was inversely related to the level of average monthly consumption to income. That is, subjects who consumed a larger share of their monthly income were less likely to survive financially. Availability of payday loans increased the likelihood of survival by 31 percent, but a greater number of payday loans reduced the likelihood of survival by 3 percent for each additional loan. This finding suggests that availability of payday loans potentially could increase consumers' well-being but that benefits likely diminish as use becomes more frequent. Whether the performance of university students in managing hypothetical budgets reflects the ability of distressed consumers to manage actual budgets is not beyond doubt, however.

Karlan and Zinman (2010) analyzed data from a field experiment in South Africa. A lender randomly reconsidered applicants for short-term, high-rate small loans to consumers who would otherwise marginally be rejected under the lender's standard underwriting criteria. Reconsidered applicants, who formed the treatment group, were offered a four-month installment loan with an annual percentage rate of 200 percent. The control group consisted of applicants still rejected.

The researchers evaluated consequences of providing the loan over the medium term using data from a survey conducted six to twelve months after the application. For examination over the longer term, they used credit scores thirteen to fifteen months and twenty-five to twenty-seven months after the application. Although the loan product in this study is not a payday loan, the results provided evidence on whether short-term borrowing at triple-digit interest rates increases rationed consumers' well-being.[51]

Analysis of the data indicated that the control group of rejected applicants did not obtain a loan elsewhere and that overall, the treatment group increased its total borrowing and shifted much of its borrowing from informal to formal sources in the six to twelve months following the initial loan. Moreover, the percentage of applicants in the treatment group with available credit scores increased relative to the control group one and two years after the initial loan. The increase in the percentage with credit scores indicates increased credit use, since having little or no credit history is usually the reason for lack of a credit score. Thus, differences between treatment and control groups can be interpreted as effects of relaxation of credit constraints among rationed borrowers.

---

51. The experiment was part of the lender's evaluation of its underwriting criteria for short-term, high-price loans.

Karlan and Zinman considered a variety of tangible and subjective measures of well-being for the six to twelve months following the initial loan. They found positive effects on job retention, income, food consumption, and mental outlook for the treatment group relative to the control group. They found one negative effect on mental health (principally stress), however. Over the longer term, Karlan and Zinman found no deterioration in credit scores for the treatment group relative to the control group one and two years after the initial loan. These findings suggest that access to high-rate credit produced benefits in the medium term without a deterioration in applicants' performance in using and servicing debt.

Conclusions

This discussion of high-rate credit products has employed an economic model of the consumer's credit decision and a psychological model of the decision process to evaluate consumers' decisions to use high-rate credit products. The economic model is a framework to assess the question of whether borrowers using high-rate loans are likely to benefit from use of such credit and predicts circumstances in which high-rate credit permits a consumer to increase utility or wealth. The psychological model is a cognitive model describing the decision process from the recognition of a problem through information gathering to the postpurchase evaluation of the decision. This model helps answer the question of whether borrowers' decisions are purposive and intelligent.

Evidence indicates that customers of high-rate credit products disproportionately have characteristics of groups that economic theory predicts might benefit from use of higher-rate credit. Customers are concentrated in relatively early life cycle stages and have children. Customers have low or moderate incomes, depending on the product, and customers are credit-constrained (rationed). Some (payday loan customers and refund anticipation loan customers with bank accounts) tend to use more credit than all families and have experienced credit problems. Others (pawnbroker loan customers, refund anticipation loan customers with no bank accounts, and rent-to-own customers) have characteristics that make qualifying for credit difficult elsewhere and are less likely than all families to use mainstream credit products.

Most consumers using high-rate credit products are aware of the cost of such credit. They generally are able to recall reasonably accurate finance charges but are largely unaware of annual percentage rates for recent loans. Because most high-rate loan products have a short term to maturity, knowledge of the finance charge is generally sufficient for making informed decisions. Under this circumstance, consumers can evaluate costs and benefits without consideration of their timing. Net undiscounted benefits will not differ much from net present value of benefits.

Many customers show signs of deliberation in their decisions, but most probably do not have an extended decision process. Many customers have previous experience with the product and may not exert much effort in subsequent decisions. Relatively low loan amounts and short terms to maturity also may contribute to lack of awareness and lack of deliberation. Customers are largely satisfied with their decisions and generally do not believe that they have insufficient information. Decision processes for high-price credit products do not appear to be much different from decision processes for mainstream credit products. The decision to use high-price credit typically is a result of the consumer's situation rather than a lack of knowledge or information.

Efforts to determine whether consumers actually benefit from high-rate credit products have focused largely on payday loans. They have examined a wide variety of outcomes, many of which are quite far removed from the circumstances of the payday loan decision. That a $300 two-week loan used by a very small proportion of the population could significantly influence outcomes such as property crime rates, bankruptcy rates, job performance, or check returns seems almost incredible. To be convincing, these studies must ensure that the differences in outcomes are caused by differences in payday loan access rather than something else and that the consumers who have access to payday loans are similar to consumers who do not.

It is not clear that these studies have succeeded. State laws that regulate payday lending are the product of a political process that also produces laws affecting many other aspects of the local economic and social environment, including the availability of other financial services, quality of educational services, and types of employment opportunities. A state that sharply limits personal or auto loan rates, for example, would hardly be inclined to authorize rate ceilings that permit payday lending. Geographic proximity or accounting for differences in a limited set of economic or social variables is unlikely to eliminate entirely the effects of other influences on outcomes. Thus, while suggestive, these studies are not fully convincing.[52]

The most convincing evidence to date on the effects of high-rate credit is from Karlan and Zinman's (2010) experimental study, which granted small, short-term, high-rate installment loans to a random sample of marginal rejected applicants at a South African lender. Greater levels in various self-reported measures of well-being and longer-term improvements in credit scores for applicants who obtained the loans than for applicants who did not receive loans suggest that access to high-rate credit produced benefits in the medium term without a deterioration in applicants' performance in using and servicing debt. Further evidence for different lenders and other types of high-rate credit is necessary to generalize beyond this one experiment.

CREDIT USE AND YOUNGER CONSUMERS

Another form of consumer credit that sometimes generates controversy is credit extended to younger consumers, especially college students. Generally, two kinds of credit enter the discussion: student loans and credit card credit. Most

---

52. See Caskey (2010) for further discussion of these studies.

observers agree, or at least acknowledge, that student loans for the purpose of attaining a college degree or for further career training can be a useful, or at least an acceptable, employment of consumer credit, although some students may still find themselves overburdened with remaining debt when they graduate. For most college graduates with debt, student loans constitute the bulk of their outstanding obligations.

In contrast, some observers contend that credit card credit use by students is another story. A fair amount of political activism in recent years has questioned the usefulness of credit card use by college students who sometimes have limited employment or ability to repay debts on their own. Press reports of college students unable or unwilling to pay their debts have sometimes led to the contention that dissemination of credit cards to younger consumers should be restricted in some manner.

Student Loans

The use of loans by college students or their parents to finance higher education is a straightforward use of consumer credit, albeit sometimes generating substantial amounts of debt. In the student loan case, families estimate that higher future earnings and/or better future quality of life of college graduates are sufficient to justify the substantial expenditures necessary to become a college graduate. This means that borrowing for educational purposes is a straightforward application of the standard investment/consumption model of chapter 3: current investment produces a return over time sufficient to produce a positive net present value of the investment, and borrowing now to achieve this goal permits a preferred consumption time schedule (see chapter 3).

Each year, the College Board, a nonprofit membership association affiliated with many universities and other educational organizations, collects and releases statistics on a variety of aspects of higher education, including financing. The College Board's annual surveys report that in 2011–2012, about 60 percent of bachelor's degree recipients graduated with student debt, and the average amount was $26,500 (see College Board 2013).

The US Department of Education has provided through its Center for Educational Statistics some interesting analyses of student loan use and how it has changed in recent decades. In particular, the Education Department provides ongoing review of student lending through the Center for Educational Statistics' Baccalaureate and Beyond program. The Baccalaureate and Beyond database consists of results of surveys of more than 10,000 graduating colleges students and then reinterviews of the same graduates after one year. In 2005, the Educational Statistics Center released comparative figures for 1992–1993 and 1999–2000 which offers perspective both on the use of consumer credit for educational purposes and the trend in use over time (Choy and Li 2005). In 2006, the Center provided a ten-year look at the experience of graduates in 1992–1993 (Choy and Li 2006). As of early 2014, these studies had not been further updated, although presumably such analyses will be forthcoming.

In their 2005 report, Choy and Li point out that changes in the federal Higher Education Act in 1992 expanded eligibility for federal student loans and led to an expansion of credit through federal programs since that time. Higher salaries of graduates and lower payments relative to amounts borrowed kept the median debt burden, defined as monthly payments as a ratio of monthly salary a year after graduation, about the same in 1999–2000 as they had been in 1992–1993, however.

They found that 49 percent of graduates in 1992–1993 had borrowed from any source to finance undergraduate education, a proportion that rose to 65 percent in 1999–2000. The average amount borrowed increased from $12,100 to $19,300 (in constant 1999 dollars) over the period. They noted that the increase in the percentage of those borrowing occurred across type of school and degree, length of time it took to earn the degree, and racial/ethnic designation and age of student, for both independent and dependent students, and for all income groups of families of dependent students.

They also pointed out that higher debt levels did not appear to be discouraging graduate study (21 percent had enrolled in a graduate or professional program within a year, versus 16 percent in the earlier period). About 5 percent of those planning graduate school later cited debt level as the primary reason for the delay, lower than other reasons such as desire for work experience (37 percent) or desire for a break from school (17 percent). About 17 percent gave financial reasons unrelated to debt.

Individual debt levels rose between the dates of the two survey projects, but lower interest rates and higher marketplace salaries kept the median debt repayment burden about the same, around 7 percent. For some individuals, a combination of higher debt and lower salary would, of course, produce a higher debt burden than the average, but average debt burden of those in the lowest salary bracket in 2001 at 15 percent was down from 18 percent in 1994. There is no specific mention of any amounts of credit card debt in the study, but the report does indicate that those with low student debt burdens at graduation are more likely to have taken on other debts within a year than those with higher student debt burdens: "For both cohorts, among graduates repaying their loans, those with a debt burden of less than 5 percent were more likely than those with a debt burden of 17 percent or more to have mortgage, rent, or auto loan payments, and when they did, the amounts they paid were generally larger" (Choy and Li 2005, vii). This finding is not especially surprising: those with little or no debt upon graduation are likely both more able and more willing to take on new obligations after graduation, while others must focus on repaying their student loans.

In their longer-term 2006 study, Choy and Li found that ten years after graduation, the 1992–1993 cohort who graduated with undergraduate debt but no further student loans had mostly repaid their college debt. Among this group, 74 percent had repaid their student loans, and among the remaining 26 percent, remaining debt burden (debt to income ratio) averaged 3 percent. They found that most students were able to repay their loans without repayment deferrals or defaults. Among the approximately 10 percent who defaulted at some point, about 45 percent were able to begin payments again.

In a review article discussing the effects of credit availability on investment in human capital, Lochner and Monge-Naranjo (2011) argued that credit constraints have become an important consideration in education decisions. Increases in the costs and returns to college have increased the demand for credit beyond the supply available from government programs. Private student loans supplement government loans, but weaker payment enforcement mechanisms and information and incentive problems for private loans may limit availability. As a consequence, some individuals may not invest as much as they like in education. Empirical evidence on the extent to which market imperfections limit education is inconclusive, however.

The amount of student indebtedness may affect individuals' decisions in other ways. Rothstein and Rouse (2011) examined the effects of a "no-loans" experiment, in which a university phased in a financial aid package that substituted grants for loans over a period of years, to investigate the effect of debt on students' post-graduation job choices. They employed a variety of control and instrumental variable strategies to distinguish the effect of debt on academic outcomes and job choices across cohorts using debt and those otherwise identical but who were financial aid recipients. Their statistical analysis indicated that students with more debt were less likely to accept jobs in low paying industries and accept higher paying jobs more generally than students with less debt. This outcome did not appear to have much effect on employability (GPA or major). Rothstein and Rouse also examined the effect of debt on student donation pledges and subsequent contributions. The level of debt did not have much effect on pledges, but it had a negative effect on actual gifts, results suggesting that individuals may not have fully realized the effect of debt payments on their subsequent budgets.

Credit Card Use by College Students

Credit card companies are, of course, in business to make money on their card products, and to do this, they try to find ways to insert their cards into the wallets, purses, hands, and spending streams of new customers, including college students. Sometimes they are aggressive in their marketing tactics, maybe too aggressive in some contexts. Along with purveyors of many other products, credit card issuers are not immune from this criticism. But because today's college students include the likely leaders (and middle- and high-income spenders) of the next generation, it is hardly surprising that the card-issuing companies have targeted them for special attention. The view from the card companies is to grant younger consumers small credit lines until they prove their creditworthiness, at which time the lines can be increased and loyalty to the issuing bank and brand become likely.

The problem is that, like almost any group of consumers, including the parents of today's students, any group of individuals contains some who are irresponsible. Emotional and intellectual immaturity of some (but certainly not all) students can exacerbate certain kinds of problems associated with newfound freedoms. It is obvious that some students do not study as much as they know they should, and some undoubtedly devote more of their time to fraternity and sorority parties than the importance of these activities warrants. But even more than these self-destructive foibles, students' mistakes in using credit cards seem to promote a form or moralizing outrage among some observers. Sometimes the vilifications seem to approach a medieval-inspired threat of just deserts to follow. The difference is that in these observers' view, it seems that the modern sinner is not the actual perpetrator of the sin, but rather the new evildoer is the issuer of the means: the offending credit card company that, like a snake in a garden, somehow enticed the innocent student to borrow. Certainly, use of credit cards by students and other young consumers who have had subsequent debt difficulties has brought about journalistic excess.[53]

There is only limited systematic information available on credit card use specifically by college students. What data are available indicate that some college students take on credit card debt, but others do not; some repay in full on time, but some do not. In this, they mimic the behavior of older members of the population. Probably the greatest difference between college student debtors and others (apart from their age) is that the credit lines of college students are lower, reflecting

---

53. It is tempting to review some of the best journalistic nuggets but likely not worth the time or the trouble; most of the frequent readers of the genre have collected their own favorite examples. In general, they tend roughly to follow a simple format. They begin with a couple of examples of young individuals who have found themselves in debt difficulty, which the authors use to generalize about the wide extent of the problem. They then quote one or two morally outraged opponents of the credit card industry, and they close by saying that it has not always been this way and maybe that some favored politician is working on the problem. The report usually also includes some mention of a credit counselor who reports that many of his or her clients are young, which actually is not especially surprising, since, as discussed in chapters 2 and 3, most credit users are drawn from the younger end of the adult age spectrum.

A favorite report of this kind for one of this book's authors is Dugas (2001). This article begins with the sagas of Jennifer Massey, Paige Hall, and Mistie Medendorp, who have debt difficulties. This allows a generalization, also vaguely attributable to others: "Like no other generation, today's 18 to 35 year olds have grown up with a culture of debt—a product of easy credit, a booming economy and expensive lifestyles. They often live paycheck to paycheck, using credit cards and loans to finance restaurant meals, high tech toys and new cars they otherwise couldn't afford, according to market researchers, debt counselors, and consumer advocates."

But before turning to the necessary quotation from a counselor, Dugas looks to Medendorp to keep the article from bogging down. In the process, this unfortunate individual also illustrates the origin of her debt difficulty: " 'I knew for a while that I had a problem. I wouldn't say I was living high on the hog, but when I wanted clothes, I'd buy a new outfit,' says Medendorp, an Atlanta resident. 'I'd go out to eat, and charge it on my cards. There were a bunch of small expenses that added up and got out of control.' "

A favorite part of the article is the direct affirmation of cultural historian Lendol Calder's contention that observers in each generation report how the fall from virtue is recent; the previous generation did not behave this way. According to Dugas, "Unlike the baby boom generation, raised by Depression-era parents, young Americans today are often unfazed by the debt they carry." Calder calls contentions that earlier generations were more frugal and less likely to use credit "The Myth of Lost Economic Virtue" (see Calder 1999, especially 23–26).

the trial run nature of the credit lines advanced by the card issuers. This means that amounts of credit outstanding to them are smaller, even though utilization rates of credit lines are higher, because of their small size. And of course, some students show irresponsibility or run into unexpected debt difficulties beyond their control, also like those in the generations that have gone before them.

THE GAO REPORT

In response to a congressional request, in 2001, the federal General Accounting Office (GAO, now the Government Accountability Office) reviewed and summarized the issues surrounding use of credit card credit by college students (General Accounting Office 2001). In the process, it examined and summarized the relevant data collection and statistical studies on the subject available at that time. Since that time, there have not been many additions to the list.[54]

The cover letter accompanying the GAO report to its congressional requesters noted that the objectives of the report were to describe (1) advantages and disadvantages that credit card use presents to college students, along with available data on bankruptcy trends; (2) results of key studies showing how college students acquire and use credit cards and how much debt they carry; (3) universities' policies and practices related to on-campus marketing; and (4) the business strategies and educational efforts that credit card issuers direct at college students. While the sections on marketing and education efforts are interesting, our purpose is to examine discussion of card use and debt outstanding as revealed in the statistical studies. This means the focus here is mostly on the second item on the GAO's list of objectives.

At the time it prepared its report, the GAO noted six available studies reporting survey results on how students acquire credit cards, how they use them, and how much debt they incur. The GAO relegated three of the six studies to an appendix of the report, "because the survey methodology of these studies did not employ random sampling techniques that would allow us to draw inferences about the student population as a whole or even about a specific subset of students" (General Accounting Office 2001, 67). For the same reason, the relegated reports also are not mentioned further here (except in the next footnote), even though one of them has become fairly well known and features a set of followers and supporters despite its methodological limitations.[55] In addition, few other

---

54. The GAO report also extensively reviewed the status of state legislative efforts in this area in its lengthy Appendix II, "State Legislation regarding Credit Card Solicitation at Institutions of Higher Education 1999 to 2001."

55. Two of the relegated reports, "Credit Cards on Campus: Social Consequences of Student Debt" and "Credit Cards on Campus: Current Trends and Informational Deficiencies," are posted on an Internet website by Robert D. Manning (www.creditcardnation.com). According to the GAO commentary on this website, "The report covered more than 350 interviews and 400 surveys; some of the surveys were from students walking past one campus building, and others were given to students taking an Introduction to Sociology class" (General Accounting Office 2001, 68).

limited studies exist but were not mentioned at all by GAO in its report.[56] The GAO noted that by "college students" it meant full-time undergraduate students at four-year colleges and universities. As it turns out, sometimes differences in the meaning of "college students" can mean differences in card holding and debt use across surveys.

The GAO reported findings from two interview studies designed to be representative of the national student population (TERI 1998 and Student Monitor 2000). The agency quoted the sources as indicating that 64 percent and 63 percent of college students had credit cards they had acquired in their own names. The GAO said that the studies found that most of the students (59 percent and 58 percent in the two studies) reported that they regularly paid off their balances in full. One of the studies found that the other 42 percent of the students interviewed maintained an average balance of $577, and the two studies found that 14 percent and 16 percent had balances of more than $1,000. The students reported using the cards for a variety of expenses, including books, supplies, food, clothing, entertainment, school fees, and tuition.

A third study arose from a sample of students who did not qualify for federal loans for educational expenses or had already received the maximum amount of loans available to them (Nellie Mae 2005). This study indicated a higher proportion of students with credit cards and higher average balances, but it seems, and the GAO noted, that the sample probably is not representative of college students as a whole, but the GAO reported its findings anyway.

The two nationally representative studies and the study of students not qualifying for federal loans are examined in a bit more detail below. A few observations about the GAO report are notable. Most of the report consists of a review of arguments for and against college students having credit cards and discussion of experiences of the colleges themselves with the marketing process. There are fairly wide divergences in views concerning the usefulness of cards for students and about how colleges or their enterprises such as bookstores, athletic departments, and alumni associations may themselves profit from advertising and marketing agreements or contracts with credit card companies. The GAO indicated the resulting ambivalence on its part within the opening pages of its report:

> For those students who manage their credit responsibly, credit cards provide access to credit and payment convenience. For those college students who do not manage credit responsibly, and have trouble repaying debt, the disadvantages of credit cards can outweigh the advantages, and their credit card debt may be costly and difficult to repay. Card issuers have used lower credit limits and other techniques on a per card basis to constrain the amount of debt that college students can accumulate. (General Accounting Office 2001, 8)

56. For example, Warwick and Mansfield (2000), which reports on a limited survey "at one Midwestern campus," and Austin and Phillips (2001), which reports on a limited survey "from a large university in the southeast USA."

THE TERI AND STUDENT MONITOR STUDIES

The GAO noted that two of the interview studies mentioned above used similar methodologies and had similar findings and limitations. Chief among the limitations was their status as self-reports by interviewed students. To the extent that the students wanted to hide certain information, they might not be completely accurate though nationally representative. The GAO reported its view that both surveys "drew statistically valid samples and were representative of a broad college student population in the United States" (General Accounting Office 2001, 15). Neither study specifically reported its survey response rate.

One of the surveys was commissioned by the Educational Resources Institution (TERI), a not-for-profit organization headquartered in Boston that "functions as a private guarantor of student loans and engages in a variety of education policy and research activities" (TERI 1998). The study noted that earlier studies had found that the majority of college students had credit cards and many carried balances, but there was little available information about how extensively students used credit cards for education expenses, living expenses, and payments convenience, among other things. To answer such questions, TERI commissioned an interview study using a stratified random sample taken from a nationally representative listing of 2 million college students, including graduate students. The project involved 750 interviews completed in March and April 1998. Among the students interviewed, 86 percent were full-time students, and 11 percent were graduate students.

Findings from the TERI study may be somewhat dated today, and some of the questions asked did not adequately differentiate between use of credit cards for making payments and use to generate consumer credit, also a problem with the other studies reported by the GAO. But much of the survey results indicate that, after taking into account much of the special nature of college life, where books, supplies, and tuition loom large in a student's expenditure requirements, the experience of college students is in many ways like that of other consumers who use credit cards. For example, the study found that 64 percent of college students had one or more credit cards, somewhat less than the estimated proportion of 74 percent with any credit card and 68 percent with bank-type credit cards in 1998 but not dramatically different (see chapter 7, table 7.3).

Among students with credit cards, the TERI surveys found that 41 percent said they carried over balances at the end of the month. This is somewhat less than the corresponding 58 percent among all card holders in 1998 (table 7.3). About 82 percent of students who could estimate average monthly balances had typical monthly balances of less than $1,000, and slightly more than half reported a credit limit of less than $3,000. The report noted that a minority of students did not fit the general mold and used their credit cards more, suggesting greater financial risk to themselves. This section of the report maintained, however, "All of these factors indicate that the majority of students use credit cards responsibly" (TERI 1998, 11).

The report also noted that nontraditional undergraduate students, defined as those who were independent or part-time (about 29 percent of the undergraduates surveyed), were more likely to be older, to be married, to have children, and to attend college part-time. Their financial circumstances also differed from those of traditional undergraduates, in that they were more likely to have more credit cards, higher credit limits, and higher average balances and to revolve the balances more frequently, and they were more likely to have other debt. The report contended that the situation of nontraditional students was worthy of further study. For at least some of them, it seems that the burdens of the early family formation life cycle stage might well be exacerbated by additional burdens associated with college attendance, leading to greater credit use.

The TERI study further suggested the potential for interaction of credit card balances and repayments with the burdens of repaying student loans. The study noted that about half of the students surveyed had student loans outstanding. The survey found that about 10 percent of students (one-third of the third who had both student loans and credit cards) had used their credit cards while awaiting disbursement of their student loans.

The second interview study reported by the GAO actually derives from an ongoing series of periodic interviews of college students on a variety of issues undertaken semiannually by a marketing research company for resale to clients (Student Monitor 2000). The GAO examined the 2000 report, but a more recent issue updates the findings (Student Monitor 2005). This report indicates that it is based on a representative sample of 1,200 full-time students at four-year undergraduate institutions on one hundred campuses.

The report indicates that 44 percent of the interviewed students had a credit card in their own name, down from 53 percent only two years before and 57 percent in 2001. The decline in credit card holding possibly reflects the growing popularity in recent years of ATM cards and other debit cards for making routine payments. About 57 percent of those interviewed said they had an ATM card, and 70 percent said they had a debit card, up from 51 percent and 68 percent the previous year. The 70 percent with debit cards was up from 33 percent in 1998. Many students now also have university ID-based stored value cards usable for purchases at a variety of campus and neighborhood outlets.

Among the 44 percent with credit cards, 75 percent said they had one card, and 19 percent had two. Only about 6 percent of students interviewed reported having three or more credit cards. A bit less than one-third of card holders (32 percent) said they revolved account balances, with an average revolving balance of $523, down from 37 percent revolvers with an average balance of $546 the previous year. Average credit limits were relatively low, at $1,662 on Discover and $2,671 on American Express, with indicated mean of $2,102.

Half of the student respondents to the Student Monitor (2005) project who held credit cards said they felt they were "very prepared" for the responsibility of a credit card. Another 36 percent said they felt they were "somewhat prepared," and the remaining 14 percent were closely divided between "not very prepared" and "not at all prepared" in their estimation. If the survey asked any questions about defaults or delinquencies, the responses are not indicated in the report, but the report does indicate that a bit less than one-quarter of students with credit cards said they had paid a late fee at least once in the previous year. About half of this group said they had done so more than once.

THE SALLIE MAE/NELLIE MAE REPORTS

Beginning in 1998, national student lender Sallie Mae/Nellie Mae conducted a series of five studies of credit card use by students applying for its credit-based alternative student loans.[57] The studies were prompted by concern over perceived increases in credit activity of its customer base (Nellie Mae 2005). The initial three studies were based entirely on credit bureau data for a sample of applicants. The 2004 and 2008 studies used credit bureau data but were supplemented by survey data collected from sampled applicants (Sallie Mae 2009). The 2008 study was conducted at a different time in the school calendar from the earlier studies, which affects its comparability with the earlier studies.[58] Because the Sallie Mae reports seem to have received a bit more attention than the other surveys, it is also worth looking at their findings.

The sample frame of applicants for "alternative loans," a product for those who have exhausted their eligibility for federal loans or are otherwise ineligible for government sponsored loans, is unlikely to be representative of the population of all college students. This sample frame does not include students with no student loans, students with only federal Stafford loans, and students with loans made only to parents. The GAO noted that the Sallie Mae studies are "restricted to a special subpopulation of loan applicants, and the results are probably not representative of a larger and typical college-student population as a whole" (General Accounting Office 2001, 48). In particular, having exhausted their eligibility for federal loans, students in this specialized group are likely to have larger amounts of debt outstanding than students as a whole. Further, the Sallie Mae approach of using credit bureau data probably overstates the extent of these students' reliance on debt, because the data include transaction balances that are to be repaid upon receipt of the bill.

With these caveats, the Sallie Mae/Nellie Mae reports are not completely inconsistent with the survey sources of information on student use of credit cards. Notably, the Nellie Mae study for 2004 reported, as did the TERI and Student Monitor studies for somewhat different time periods, that the majority of college students in their sample had credit cards. The Nellie Mae and TERI studies appear to include cards issued by both retail stores and banks, and so the proportion of students reported in these studies as holding credit cards is higher than in the Student Monitor study, which focuses on bank-type credit cards. Also, Nellie Mae found in 2004 that the proportion of students with credit cards and the proportion with multiple cards had declined somewhat since its previous report in 2001. Student Monitor also reported these declining trends.

But the amounts of credit outstanding among its sampled students is much higher for Nellie Mae, probably reflecting the nature of its specialized sample of

---

57. The first four reports were issued by Nellie Mae, a wholly owned subsidiary of Sallie Mae.

58. The earlier studies were conducted at the beginning of the school year, and the 2008 study was conducted in the middle of the school year. Consequently, more freshmen had cards and outstanding balances were higher in the 2008 study than would be the case if the study had been conducted at the beginning of the school year.

students more likely to be heavier debt users. In its conclusion, Nellie Mae even provides a solution for their needs: "Finally students particularly need to understand that there are other, less costly financing options for purchasing big ticket items, especially for costs associated with college attendance" (Nellie Mae 2005, 11). Presumably, this includes loans from Nellie Mae.

The Staten-Barron Study

Since publication of the GAO report in 2002, there have been only a few additional research sources of information on use of credit cards by college students, including subsequent Student Monitor and Nellie Mae studies. One of the studies is in a large sense related to the GAO study, because it undertook a phase of the project planned by the GAO but not accomplished because of insufficient available staffing budget and the press of other priorities.

The Staten and Barron (2002) study differs from other reports on student credit card use because the authors were able to assemble account level data for more than 300,000 credit card users at five of the largest credit card issuers. Consequently, it consists of review of account use behavior rather than interviews of account users. The analysis compares behavior on three types of accounts: those opened by college students through college-related marketing programs, those otherwise opened by young adults ages eighteen to twenty-four but not through college-related marketing efforts, and those opened by older adults through normal marketing channels. All accounts examined in the study were opened during the period from mid-1998 until early 2000 and observed over twelve-month periods during 2000–2001. The report specifically indicates that it follows a study plan originally proposed to card-issuing companies by the GAO but never undertaken because of budget constraints, to compare activity of recently opened student accounts with experience of accounts recently opened through other marketing channels. The authors employed statistical weighting methods to account for sampling differences among the three populations of accounts from the three groups. Because of the weighting and the size of the five card issuers sampled, the authors reported their belief that the data set as a whole was representative of accounts opened at major credit card issuers during the period from mid-1998 through early 2000 that were active during the 2000–2001 period.

Staten and Barron report findings in a number of areas. First, concerning balances, limits, and utilization rates, they found that the average balance of an account opened through the college marketing channel (called an active student credit card account or a student account) was $552, about the same as found by Student Monitor. The student balance was approximately one-third the $1,465 mean balance of an account of a young adult not acquired through the college marketing channel (which they called a nonstudent young adult account) and less than one-fourth the size of the average balance for a new active account of an older adult ($2,342).

The mean credit limit for student accounts was $1,395 in 2001, a bit less than the credit limit for Discover cards reported by Student Monitor for 2005. This limit in 2001 was less than 40 percent of the mean for a nonstudent young adult account ($3,581) and less than 20 percent that of adult accounts ($7,436) at that time.

Staten and Barron also found that lower credit limits for student accounts generally led to higher utilization rates. Among card holders with credit limits of more than $1,000, student accounts tend to have the lowest utilization rates, however.

Concerning account usage, Staten and Barron found that student account holders were more likely than others to pay the balance in full in a given month and less likely to record a cash advance in a given month. Accounts of both groups of young adults are more likely to be used in a month than accounts of older adults, however. When used, student accounts are likely to show smaller monthly charges and cash advances. This pattern seems reasonable. Younger adults who grew in a world where credit cards were common are more likely to adopt this relatively recent technology for making routine payments than their older counterparts. Older adults on average have more income and may make many larger purchases, but they also may be more likely to save their credit cards for use in making the occasional large purchase rather than more common use for smaller day-to-day transactions.

They also found that a student account was somewhat less likely to incur finance charges in a given month but somewhat more likely to incur fees, either for being late or for being over the credit limit. They found that only 5 percent of student accounts incur a finance charge greater than $26 in a given month.

Concerning delinquencies, they found that delinquency rates on both student accounts and young adult nonstudent accounts were higher than on accounts held by older adults, but student accounts with relatively large balances (more than $1,000) have lower delinquency rates than young adult nonstudent accounts. About 3.6 percent of student accounts charge off annually, compared with 2.8 percent of young adult nonstudent accounts and 1.6 percent of older adult accounts. As might be expected, large-dollar charge-offs are not common among student accounts because of their substantially lower average credit limits and balances. Very large charge-offs that exceed $5,000 are rare on student accounts. For every 10,000 accounts of each type, the data set indicates that there would be 77 adult accounts with charge-offs exceeding $5,000 over a one-year period, 58 such charge-offs for nonstudent accounts of young adults, but only 2 such charge-offs for student accounts.

Staten and Barron found that over time, student accounts mature and performance converges to that of young adult nonstudent accounts. More specifically, a student account approaching the end of its second year has a frequency of delinquency and a likelihood of charge-off quite similar to that of nonstudent accounts held by people younger than twenty-five.

All of this led Staten and Barron to conclude that although recently opened student accounts are more likely to be delinquent and have a higher likelihood of a charge-off compared with other groups, the dollar amounts at risk on delinquent accounts and the actual losses on charged-off accounts are substantially lower. Further, the delinquency and charge-off experience for student accounts becomes similar to that for nonstudent accounts of young adults for accounts open more than a year and a half. They contended that these findings were consistent with statements of card issuers that they establish student accounts with relatively low credit limits with the expectation that the large majority of new, young card holders will learn how to manage a credit card, establish a credit history, and become longer-term customers.

The Attitude Studies

Chapter 7 pointed out that there were relatively few recent studies of consumers' attitudes toward credit cards. As discussed there, credit cards have become mature products that may no longer be as interesting to the academics who do studies than newer products, and there are difficulties and substantial expenses for collecting new, representative data on previously explored issues. Possibly because of political interest, there have been a few studies focusing on attitudes of college students and their use of credit cards. For the most part, the limited nature of the behavioral models explored and the corresponding data gathered makes it difficult to have a great deal of confidence in the conclusions rendered, regardless of the importance of the issues raised or the sophistication of the statistical procedures used.

For example, a series of studies by Hayhoe and colleagues relied on a mail survey of five hundred college students at each of six universities (Hayhoe, Leach, and Turner 1999; Hayhoe et al. 2000; and Hayhoe 2002). Response rate was 16 percent for the first survey and only about one-quarter of this already small group in the follow-up. There was no way to compare credit card use of these small fractions of college students at a few universities with the broader experience of students generally; consequently, resulting sampling and response biases are unclear but very well may be substantial.

Also, some of the questions used in the survey seem not well defined, and others are not adequately described in the sections of the papers on survey results. For example, "number of cards with a balance" is used as a key variable for prediction in a main equation in one of the papers and is mentioned in all of them, but it is not defined. It reasonably could refer to recent use of a card for transactions that creates a balance to be repaid at the end of the month, to a revolving balance of short or long duration, or to elements of each. Further, unless carefully worded, students' answers to such a question may depend on their variable interpretations of the wording. Without information on question wording or these definitions, it is hard to argue in favor of relying on the resulting statistical findings.

That said, the surveys indicate about 62 percent of the sample of college students with credit cards "individually owned," presumably meaning in their own names, similar to the 64 percent found by the TERI study. The attitude studies do not report much further about financial and credit experiences of the sample of students, preferring to focus on measures of attitudes constructed in various ways. The authors indicate their belief that behavior with respect to card use is dependent in some way on attitudes, although there is no discussion of a more complete economic or behavioral model that includes attitudes.

Ultimately, the decision to use credit or not involves underlying economic motivations and depends on more than favorable attitudes, as discussed more fully in chapters 3 through 5 and earlier in this chapter. Although attitudes undoubtedly are important in purchase decisions, without a fuller modeling of consumer behavior than normally found in the attitude papers (pricing, for example), direction of attitude influence is likely to remain unanswered, despite demonstration of the existence of correlations.

Potentially the greatest concern is imprecision in definition of the criterion behavioral variables. "Carrying a balance" has already been mentioned, but there also is no clear distinction between using a credit card to simplify transactions on the Internet or at the gas station or Best Buy and using it for "living beyond one's means" (phrase used in Hayhoe, Leach, and Turner 1999, 647). One paper indicates formation of a "variety of purchases index" by "summing the number of yes answers to seven questions dealing with items purchased with credit cards: (1) clothing, (2) electronics, (3) entertainment, (4) travel, (5) educational expenses, (6) food away from home, and (7) gas and automobile expenses." It is not clear how this list serves as the basis of an index of variety of purchases that somehow might statistically be related to credit use. Most middle-class consumers (and presumably also many college students) regularly use credit cards as transactions devices for making routine purchases and likely normally use credit cards in purchasing all of these items. Such use may be completely independent from any credit use, except in correlations of unrelated variables. Consequently, without significant additional information about their purchases and their use of credit, how can this index basis serve in exploring credit use? The index would be identical across middle-class consumers, and the relationship would depend solely on the proportion of credit users, however defined but not likely related behaviorally, in the sample.

The Credit Card Accountability Responsibility and Disclosure Act of 2009 (the CARD Act) contains several provisions governing issuance of credit cards to young consumers and college students. The act restricts marketing and underwriting practices regarding cards issued to consumers under 21 years of age. A credit card issuer must obtain documentation that an applicant under 21 years has the means to repay any debts incurred on the account. If the applicant does not have the means to repay, he or she must provide a cosigner 21 years of age or older who does have the means to pay any debts incurred in connection with the account. In the latter case, the issuer must obtain approval from the cosigner for any increase in the credit line. The act further restricts prescreened solicitations of consumers under 21 years of age.

Furthermore, educational institutions must publicly disclose any arrangements with credit card issuers for marketing credit cards to students. In marketing student credit cards, issuers may not offer any tangible item to induce students to apply for a credit card. In addition, credit card issuers must submit an annual report to the Federal Reserve Board on the terms of all marketing agreements, conditions, and terms for student and affinity credit card programs with institutions of higher education or alumni associations.

OVERREACHING AND "PREDATORY LENDING"

The rise and fall of home purchase and home mortgage loan opportunities for consumers with blemished credit histories or other indicia of greater credit risk for lenders have been one of the recent high-profile stories of consumer lending in the United States. In the past, such applicants most likely would have been rejected by mortgage lenders, but development of below-prime or "subprime" mortgage products at the end of the twentieth century greatly enhanced the borrowing opportunities of potentially riskier consumers. Mortgage lending is generally not within the scope of this book, but because the term *subprime* sometimes also attaches to some users of consumer credit and to some consumer credit products, it seems appropriate to round out discussion of special issues of credit availability by looking at least briefly at some of the controversies that recently emerged in the area described particularly as subprime. The term typically is applied to mortgage credit to certain borrowers or with certain characteristics, but it also is used elsewhere. Subprime credit cards have already been mentioned.

Subprime lending has no strict definition, but in common usage, it is often defined in terms of borrower circumstances or specifics of the kind of loan itself. For example, loans to riskier consumers such as those with prior credit difficulties or with volatile income sources are often deemed subprime loans, and mortgage loans exhibiting large loan size relative to the value of the property serving as collateral (high loan to value lending or high LTV) are subprime loans. Borrowers of subprime loans then become known as subprime borrowers. Beyond certain mortgage loans, pawnbroker loans, payday loans, and the other kinds of credit discussed in this chapter also fit within the loose definition of subprime credit. These loans are available to individuals with past credit problems or low income and no credit history and to those with large amounts of other credit outstanding relative to their income or assets. By volume, subprime mortgage credit was by far the largest component of subprime lending. The publication *Inside B&C Lending* reported that subprime mortgage lending rose from about $34 billion of originations in 1995 to more than $665 billion of originations at its peak in 2005. Subprime mortgages declined to $640 billion in 2006 and then fell precipitously in the following years. By 2008, subprime mortgage lending practically ceased.[59]

Difficulties arose because instances of fraud and misrepresentation sometimes diminished the benefits of additional credit availability through subprime credit markets. Because of greater risk, subprime mortgage loans typically were structured differently from prime loans. Subprime loans were subject to higher pricing than prime loans through higher interest rates and fees, and many subprime loans had terms not commonly found in prime loans, such as prepayment penalties and large final payments called balloon payments. Customers with balloon mortgages typically must refinance the large final payment, which may cause difficulties for some subprime borrowers. These terms and the relatively high market share of subprime loans in lower-income and minority neighborhoods elevated concerns among activists and regulators about possible incidences of abusive lending tactics and the targeting of particularly vulnerable borrowers. Activists, journalists, and regulators used the term *predatory lending* to describe abusive loans, although there is even less agreement on a strict definition of this term than for *subprime lending.*

With inexactness of definition in mind, predatory lending typically is defined according to specific features of individual credit accounts (e.g., especially high

59. *Inside B&C Lending,* February 17, 2006; February 9, 2007; March 14, 2008; February 27, 2009.

interest rates or loan fees, high prepayment penalties) or specific practices of the creditor in individual cases (e.g., high-pressure marketing, a focus on available equity in property owned by unsophisticated borrowers rather than on their ability to pay, frequent refinancing of the loans on a property with terms unfavorable to the borrower leading to loss each time of some equity in the property by the borrower, and illegal practices such as failure to credit payments). Many practices associated with predatory loans under this description are illegal under state laws (e.g., deception, fraudulent failures to account for payments or refunds properly, falsification of documents, etc.). Some other possible loan terms, such as prepayment penalties, balloon payments, or loans based on collateral rather than the ability to repay, may be perfectly fine for borrowers who understand their uses and how agreeing to such terms may be useful in bargaining for more favorable interest rates or other terms. But the same terms on mortgage loans not understood fully by unsophisticated borrowers may be predatory in both intent and effect.

Most observers and commentators contend that subprime lending is a necessary but not sufficient condition for predatory lending. Thus, to most observers, not all subprime lending is predatory, but most or all predatory lending is subprime. They often argue that the reason predatory lending occurs mostly in the subprime area is that there is less competition in the subprime market, many borrowers of subprime loans are not financially sophisticated, and some of these borrowers are in difficult financial circumstances and may be taken advantage of more easily. Frequently, there is an accompanying contention that the reason for lower levels of competition in subprime lending is insufficient presence of prime lenders in local markets where subprime lending is common. The danger with attempting to eliminate with restrictions or other policy initiatives any possibility of predatory lending among subprime loans is to do so without also restricting the availability of legitimate subprime loans and undermining the benefits that arise from subprime lending. The problem is that without detailed knowledge of the circumstances of a transaction, it is difficult to judge whether a loan is predatory, which complicates the task of crafting effective legislation or regulation to curb abusive cases only.

Congress first addressed the issue of predatory lending in 1994, with the enactment of the Home Ownership and Equity Protection Act (HOEPA), which amended the Truth in Lending Act. It imposed additional Truth in Lending disclosures and certain restrictions on contract terms for refinance mortgage loans and closed-end second lien mortgages. Included loans became subject to these additional disclosures and restrictions if the interest rate or fees charged exceeded certain thresholds. Because the thresholds for inclusion have always been fairly high, included loans are often designated as high-cost loans or simply HOEPA loans. Using its authority granted by the statute, the Federal Reserve Board tightened the thresholds and requirements somewhat in 2001.[60]

60. After the adjustment in 2001, HOEPA loans include first lien refinance mortgages where the annual percentage rate charged exceeds the interest rate on US Treasury securities of comparable maturity by eight percentage points or more or second lien closed-end mortgages where

Since that time, states, cities, and counties have enacted further restrictions using a HOEPA-like approach. These laws often contain thresholds for mortgages subject to their restrictions that are lower than those in HOEPA, therefore including more loans automatically, and they sometimes impose certain restrictions on broader classes of mortgages than those covered by HOEPA, such as real estate purchase loans or prime loans.[61] The question in each case has been whether these additional limitations have also restricted the availability of subprime credit to certain borrowers because of a tendency to decrease the willingness of lenders to make these loans. A related questions is whether these laws may actually raise credit prices as a result of passing on to consumers regulatory burdens that the laws might generate.

Evidence from Previous Studies

As of spring 2006, statistical evidence concerning the effects of HOEPA-like laws at the state and local government level was limited. Most evidence available at that time concerned North Carolina's 1999 law, the first state law to impose stiffer standards than the federal HOEPA. Regardless of point of view about the efficacy of the law of the various authors or the particular data set used to analyze its effects, the findings of the North Carolina studies indicate that the volume of subprime mortgage lending in the state declined relative to neighboring states after its law become effective. The decline centered especially on loans to the lower-income end of the spectrum. In general terms, the studies indicate that much of the impact of the state law seems to result from reduced marketing efforts by lenders. Rather than reduced lending because of increased lender rejection of borrowers, lower levels of both applications and acceptances appear to indicate less attention to these markets among affected lenders. Beginning in mid-2006, studies with somewhat broader geographical range began to emerge, as more state-based HOEPA-like laws had then been in effect long enough to analyze their impacts, too.

Specific Studies concerning Impact of the North Carolina Law
Five early studies of the impact of the North Carolina law on subprime mortgage credit availability using three separate sources of data all found contraction of credit availability on mortgage refinance loans relative to comparison states. Harvey and Nigro (2004) used multivariate statistical techniques to investigate subprime loan originations in North Carolina and four neighboring comparison states from 1998 through 2000, with data collected by government agencies

---

the APR exceeds the comparable Treasury rate by ten percentage points or more. HOEPA also extends to the same sorts of mortgage loans where initial points and fees exceed the greater of 8 percent of the loan amount or a dollar amount that adjusts every January according to the Consumer Price Index ($528 in 2006).

61. For a summary of the state laws, see Ho and Pennington-Cross (2005).

under the Home Mortgage Disclosure Act (HMDA). They found that the North
Carolina law reduced the overall level of mortgage originations by subprime lenders in that state relative to the comparison states. Low-income and minority borrowers were less likely to receive loans after passage of the law, primarily as a result
of a decrease in applications. Ernst, Farris, and Stein (2002) used the same data in
a similar analysis and found, not surprisingly, similar results. They argued, however, that the decline occurred only in predatory loans, a conclusion that goes
beyond the data they employed for the project. The HMDA data they used actually contain insufficient information about the characteristics of the individual
loans in the data set to permit this to be more than an assertion.

Burnett, Finkel, and Kaul (2004) also used HMDA data to analyze lending
in North Carolina, but their study extended through 2002 and permitted more
time for a before-and-after analysis. Overall, they found a 16 percent decline in
originations by subprime lenders in North Carolina after the law relative to comparison states. In contrast, they ascertained that relative decline in prime loan
originations was negligible. They found that originations of both subprime home
purchase and refinancing loans declined relative to other states, and, like Harvey
and Nigro, they determined that it was a result of a decline in applications. They
were careful to point out that the HMDA data set they used did not permit separation of reductions in predatory loans from unintended reductions in access to
legitimate subprime credit.

Elliehausen and Staten (2004) investigated the impact of the law using a specialized database containing all mortgage originations in the portfolio of nine
large subprime lenders. They determined that originations per county in North
Carolina using these data fell 14 percent relative to three neighboring states following passage of the lending law, similar to Harvey and Nigro's results using different data. They also found that the declines occurred only among lower-income
consumers.

Finally, Quercia, Stegman, and Davis (2004) employed a third data set, this
one from a large proprietary database of securitized subprime loans originated
between 1998 and 2002 and contained in Loan Performance System's Asset
Based Securities Dataset. Like Ernst, Farris, and Stein, they asserted that the relative decline they found in securitized subprime refinance loans in North Carolina
was a result of a decline in loans with abusive or predatory terms. Since the decline
they note is in loans with terms specifically proscribed by the act, this is little more
than the assertion of a definition. It is hard to say whether the loans would have
been beneficial to individual consumers with their specific circumstances, but
they are correct that the law made loans with the outlawed terms illegal. Their
finding of a relative decline in North Carolina after the effective date of the law is
consistent with the other studies.

BROADER STUDIES
By mid-2006, enough time had passed following enactment of HOEPA-based
predatory lending laws in other states to permit some multistate studies. The
first two of them continued examination of the issue of lending volume after

HOEPA-based laws went into effect, and the third concerned the relationship of these laws to the interest rates on subprime loans.

Bostic et al. (2008), extending earlier work by Ho and Pennington-Cross (2005, 2006), examined the effects of forty-eight state and local laws through 2005. Interestingly, they devised an index of the strength of each law in terms of scope of coverage, severity of restriction, and scope of enforcement relative to HOEPA. They used the HMDA data set for their estimations and found, similar to the North Carolina studies, that overall, without considering the strength of the laws, the measured impact was a decline in applications and rejection rates with little overall impact on originations. They found, however, that that the decline in applications and rejection rates was more pronounced in the states with the strongest laws, and this also produced a decline in originations. Variation in enforcement was not consistently related to applications or originations, but stronger enforcement was associated with fewer rejections. Overall, the broader studies are largely consistent with earlier ones. They suggest that when faced with the new laws, subprime lenders become less aggressive in marketing to higher-risk applicants, leading to a falloff in credit availability where the laws are strong. In a related study using the Loan Performance System's Database, Pennington-Cross and Ho (2008) found that severity of the state's predatory lending law also affected interest rates on subprime mortgages. They found that presence of state laws was statistically associated with moderate increases in interest rates but that stronger laws produced greater increases than weaker laws. Using their specialized database of loans from nine large subprime lenders, Steinbuks and Elliehausen (2014) obtained similar results on loan originations. Specifically, they found that the volume of covered loans declined in the states with more restrictive lending laws but generally less or not at all in the states with more moderate laws.

In sum, findings concerning the impact of predatory lending laws appear consistent with what one might expect: additional broad-based regulation for the purpose of eliminating specific practices runs the risk of having a negative impact on volume and price. So far, the studies have examined the state and local laws that build on the federal HOEPA and have an impact on volume in the markets where the laws are strong enough to be binding. This includes North Carolina, the first state to add further restrictions to the HOEPA base, but also applies to other states.

2008 Changes in Rules Implementing the HOEPA

On July 14, 2008, the Federal Reserve Board adopted new, more stringent rules implementing the HOEPA. They included the following provisions:

1. Prohibiting lenders from making loans without regard for borrowers' ability to repay.
2. Requiring lenders to verify the income and assets on which they rely to determine repayment ability.

3. Prohibiting prepayment penalties for loans on which the payment can change during the first four years and limiting prepayment penalties to the first two years for all other higher-price loans.
4. Requiring lenders to establish escrow accounts for property taxes and home owners' insurance for all first lien mortgages.

In addition, the Board revised the definition of high-price loans to include virtually all subprime loans. The previous definition covered far fewer subprime loans. The Board further amended its rules for all loans, whether higher-price or not, secured by consumers' principal dwelling. The amendments involved appraisals, pyramiding of late fees, and good-faith estimates of loan costs.

The Board intended its actions to address perceived problems in mortgage markets that were later believed to have contributed to the financial crisis. The later rule changes affected the broader mortgage market, but the subprime mortgage market had already shut down before the rules for higher-price loans took effect.

The Dodd-Frank Wall Street Reform and Consumer Protection Act (Dodd-Frank Act), signed into law in 2010 in response to the financial crisis of 2008–2009, introduced a number of restrictions that affected loan contract terms and provisions, previously widespread in the risky segments of the mortgage lending market. Among the most significant provisions are the "ability to repay" rule, the expansion of the definition and restrictions of "high-cost" loans, and restraints on prepayment penalties.

The "ability to repay" rule prohibited creditors from making residential mortgage loans unless a creditor was able to verify that a consumer had a reasonable ability to repay a loan according to its terms. The Dodd-Frank Act (Section 1412) defines "qualified mortgages" as the low-risk loans that met income documentation requirements and underwriting standards consistent with statutory and regulatory requirements. Qualified mortgages are presumed to meet "ability to repay" requirements. This rule has significantly impeded origination of non-qualified mortgage loans and has effectively banned low- and no- income documentation mortgages.

"High-cost" loans are defined and regulated by the Home Ownership and Equity Protection Act (HOEPA) signed into law in 1994. The Dodd-Frank Act (Sections 1431, 1432, and 1433) expanded the coverage of HOEPA and imposed additional Truth in Lending disclosures and restrictions on contract terms for "high-cost" mortgages.

Prepayment penalties inhibit a borrower's ability to prepay the loan. Lenders and investors in the mortgage market used this term to manage the mortgage prepayment risk by charging fees when the mortgage was paid before the due date in exchange for a lower contract interest rate at origination. Prepayment penalty terms were more common for subprime than for prime loans, and the refinance lock-outs were usually in effect for two to five years. The Dodd-Frank Act (Sections 1414 and 1432) prohibits prepayment penalties for mortgages that are "not qualified" mortgages and also significantly restricts application of prepayment penalties to "qualified" loans.

9

Federal Regulation of Consumer Credit

Credit Granting Discrimination

Chapter 1 noted that credit for individuals is as old as recorded human history; so is the ongoing interest of governments in controlling it. The ancient laws of Babylon, Greece, and Rome all contained regulation of lending and borrowing by individuals. Because credit regulations were well-developed features of these earliest written legal traditions, some historians have conjectured that centralized tribal control of credit extends even deeper into antiquity, possibly to the earliest days of the development of borrowing and lending in Neolithic times. Much later, in the Middle Ages, the Christian church contended that charging interest on loans was a moral evil (usury) and therefore prohibited, ultimately based on restrictions found in its own antiquity, the ancient books of the Hebrew Bible.[1] Overlaps between religious and civil authority during the Middle Ages guaranteed that development of lending and borrowing relationships in western Europe remained complicated for centuries, producing legal difficulties extending even into modern times.[2]

Religious opposition to lending at interest gradually faded with development of more robust commerce and trade during the Renaissance/Reformation/Enlightenment centuries and later, but widespread cultural and governmental anxiety over personal lending and borrowing has never completely gone away, even as secularization of economic and commercial affairs has advanced. At least some of modern governmental concerns over consumer credit appear to arise from society's remaining basic ambivalence about whether credit use by individuals is good for them, perhaps a modern vestige of the ancient and medieval view that credit use is questionable or even immoral. Modern economic analysis has

---

1. Specific verses of the Old Testament are cited in chapter 1.

2. For discussion of the development of religious and economic thought about lending, borrowing, and their regulation in antiquity and the Middle Ages, see Homer and Sylla (1996) and Gelpi and Julien-Labruyere (2000). Rasor (1993) examines the parallels between the biblical codes and modern consumer credit laws.

shown that there are many situations where credit use is beneficial to consumers (see chapter 3), but the issue is still not settled completely to the satisfaction of everyone. Nonetheless, it is obvious that there has been a strong, long-term trend toward greater acceptability of credit use by individuals as a feature of modern life.

CONSUMER PROTECTION

As notions of morality based on religious principles have faded over time as a foundation for commercial restrictions, concern has developed in some quarters that individuals still need government protection in their credit relationships for two further reasons: to shield them from inability to understand fully the implications of the credit transactions they enter into and to help them avoid possible inappropriate behavior by questionable credit vendors in the marketplace. In this view, the term *consumer protection* in credit matters refers to various governmental means of altering prevailing conditions and practices in the credit marketplace rather than absolute prohibition of credit relationships.

According to many modern supporters of credit regulation of this kind, the inherent imbalance in market power and understanding between lenders and borrowers requires government to help consumers protect their interests. Extreme adherents to this position argue that virtually every aspect of consumer credit should be carefully regulated by government officials, even up to, as needed, precluding an individual's right to use credit at all, as in the Middle Ages. Those who take the opposite position frequently argue that competition in the marketplace protects consumers more effectively than regulation. In this view, if markets are competitive, then malefactors and unsavory practices ultimately will lose out to better ones, and governments will not have to make decisions about how markets should operate or tell consumers what they can and cannot choose to do. In this approach, consumers will be protected and easily able to make good choices about using credit, because good actors will win the competitive battles, and the battles themselves will provide that necessary information about the quality of products and producers is widely disseminated. Since strong adherents to this position typically also contend that markets are quite competitive, they often argue that there is little need for government intervention beyond basic rules establishing a legal system that recognizes the validity of contracts between willing parties.

Somewhere in between the extreme positions, most observers of consumer credit markets believe that they are neither perfectly competitive nor perfectly uncompetitive; consequently, many individuals recommend regulatory roles for both competition and government. In their view, good actors may on balance win the competitive battles for survival, and they may also, for the most part, make necessary information about the terms and features of their products readily available to consumers. Nonetheless, in this view, markets and market information still may not function perfectly, necessitating a corrective or market-enhancing role for government. Intermediate preferences of this kind have accompanied what sometimes has appeared in recent decades to be a simultaneous increase in both competition and government regulation of consumer credit in the United States. Overall, it does seem that market forces increasingly have forced financial institutions to gain new customers by competing actively for them, especially by making their products less generally mysterious and more attractive in the marketplace. At the same time, government protection has also expanded in various ways, particularly at the federal level.

Whatever the influences, reasoning, and circumstances leading to current conditions, it is apparent that few areas of the American economy are as closely regulated as consumer credit. Until the late 1960s, governmental consumer protection in credit markets was mostly the province of state agencies, but today both federal and state authorities are involved. Consumer credit regulation evolved during a time when the federal system of governing left most aspects of local commerce as the province of state governments, and so early forms of regulation were at the state level. Federal activities for consumer protection began in 1968, with enactment of the federal Consumer Credit Protection Act on May 29 that year, and with its most important provision, the Truth in Lending Act, effective July 1, 1969. By 2010, the growth of federal regulation led to establishment of a new federal Consumer Financial Protection Bureau (CFPB), with official opening date July 21, 2011.[3]

This chapter and the next two chapters look at the role of consumer credit regulation as it has evolved in the United States, especially in the post–World War II era. Chapter 6 already examined federal rules in the area of creditors' use of information about consumers through regulation of credit reporting agencies under the Fair Credit Reporting Act and its amendments. This chapter focuses on another important area of federal action: restriction of credit discrimination on socially unacceptable bases, such as sex of borrower, marital status, and race. This is the domain of the Equal Credit Opportunity Act and some related laws specifically concerning housing discrimination. Chapter 10 then examines the other

---

3. The federal government first entered into regulating consumer credit during World War II and its aftermath and during the Korean War, when the federal government restricted consumer credit growth (Regulation W). At that time, however, the federal restrictions were intended to dampen aggregate domestic demand to meet wartime necessity, rather than for consumer protection. During World War II, consumer durable goods such as automobiles were not produced because of the shifting of materials and production lines to the war effort. Further, there was general macroeconomic anxiety at the time and for a period after the war and during the Korean War that a highly stimulated wartime economy with little production of consumer goods could become very inflationary. The proposed solutions included controls on consumer credit for economic stabilization reasons to supplement the monetary and fiscal policies at the time. The wartime debate about whether specific controls on some segment of financial markets such as consumer credit might usefully supplement more general economic policies is an issue largely of historical concern today, although selective controls on consumer credit were tried again for a few months as supplemental policy as recently as early 1980. For discussion of the issues surrounding macroeconomic consumer credit controls during World War II and afterward (known then as Regulation W), see generally Board of Governors of the Federal Reserve System (1957) and especially the papers by Friedman (1957), Nadler (1957), Shay (1957), and Simmons (1957) within the larger study. See also Shay (1953).

historically important area of federal intervention: providing for availability of transactional information about credit and financial products tailored to individual consumers. This is the domain of the Truth in Lending Act and other federal disclosure laws. And Chapter 11 looks at state regulation. Historically, the states have regulated an array of features of consumers' credit arrangements, especially pricing terms such as interest rates and specific practices of credit granting institutions. It is possible that in the future, the CFPB may take over many of these areas of state action in the past.[4]

FAIRNESS IN CREDIT GRANTING: EQUAL CREDIT OPPORTUNITY

As indicated, compared with federal wartime macroeconomic controls and state mandates aimed at consumer protection, federal consumer protection in the credit area began only relatively recently with passage of the federal Consumer Credit Protection Act (CCPA) in May 1968. At its outset, this act consisted mostly of Truth in Lending, but over the intervening years, Congress has added whole new areas of federal regulation to the CCPA, including the Equal Credit Opportunity Act (ECOA) in 1974. As Congress enacted each additional federal consumer credit protection law, it made the new law structurally a new section ("Title") of the CCPA, so that now most federal credit regulations are collected in this location. Regardless of structure of the legal books, each new section of the CCPA is usually still best known by its own name and its specific area of regulation, such as the Truth in Lending Act (Title I of the CCPA), the Equal Credit Opportunity Act (Title V), and the Fair Credit Reporting Act (Title VI).

Certainly, the ECOA is one of the most significant sections of the CCPA.[5] As an important component of more than a decade of sharply intensified federal

4. Future details of actions of the new agency are not known with any certainty, probably not even by its own insiders. Much of its early years were given over to administrative matters such as hiring staff, taking over rule-writing responsibilities for Truth in Lending and other federal laws from other agencies, notably from the Federal Reserve Board, and preparing and implementing rules mostly in the mortgage credit area required under the Dodd-Frank Act that established the CFPB (Public Law 111-203).

Even so, the CFPB's early days have been controversial, with critics contending that the agency has inherent structural flaws involving (1) its exemption from the federal budgetary process through monetizing its expenses through the Federal Reserve System; (2) operation through a single director, unlike the boards of directors at other regulatory agencies such as the Federal Reserve, the Federal Deposit Insurance Corporation (FDIC), the Securities and Exchange Commission (SEC), the Federal Trade Commission (FTC), and others; and (3) the extent of its legal interpretive and enforcement authority. Opponents have introduced legislation to make changes, but others have vehemently opposed the proposals. For extended discussion of the origins of the agency and its early days, see Zywicki (2013).

5. Elliehausen and Durkin (1989) discussed its origins and background at some length, and this section and the next draw upon their paper.

efforts beginning in the 1960s to promote civil rights in various aspects of domestic life, Congress extended civil rights legislation to credit markets by passing this law in October 1974 (Public Law 93-495, Title V) and by substantially broadening its coverage in March 1976 (Public Law 94-239). Not limited exclusively to credit for individuals, although both proposers and enforcers have devoted most of their attention to consumer and mortgage credit, the original Equal Credit Opportunity Act of 1974 made it "unlawful for any creditor to discriminate against any applicant on the basis of sex or marital status with respect to any aspect of a credit transaction."

Only five months after the effective date of the original act, Congress expanded coverage in early 1976 to outlaw discrimination on the basis of "race, color, religion, national origin, sex or marital status, age (provided the applicant has the capacity to contract); because all or part of the applicant's income derives from any public assistance program; or because the applicant has in good faith exercised any rights under the Consumer Credit Protection Act." Again allowing one year for necessary drafting of implementing regulations, the revised act and regulation became effective on March 23, 1977.

Congress believed that the ECOA would provide consumers with two significant benefits: enhanced credit access and consumer education. Of these, the major intended benefit involved easier access to credit for those classes of potential borrowers protected by the legislation. Congress stated this goal in the original act's statement of purpose and findings. Congress did not change this particular wording when it extended the act's coverage to include the other protected classes, but the legislative history and the text of the revised act as a whole make it amply clear that Congress viewed enhanced credit availability for all protected classes as the major goal of the revised law:

> The Congress finds that there is a need to insure that the various financial institutions and other firms engaged in the extensions of consumer credit exercise their responsibility to make credit available with fairness, impartiality, and without discrimination on the basis of sex or marital status.. . . It is the purpose of this Act to require that financial institutions and other firms engaged in the extension of credit make that credit equally available to all creditworthy customers without regard to sex or marital status. (Public Law 93-495, 15 USC 1691, section 502)

The second intended benefit involved consumer education. Although this purpose was not as fully defined and carefully articulated in the law, review of the legislative history and the text of the act itself clearly reveals that Congress also intended an educational benefit. As set out in section 701(d) of the revised act, Congress mandated that creditors provide applicants with notification of actions taken on credit applications and, most notably, with "specific reasons" for any "adverse actions" taken. According to the Senate Committee on Banking, Housing, and Urban Affairs, which drafted the initial version of this provision, this section was to be "a strong and necessary adjunct to the antidiscrimination purpose of the legislation" (US Senate 1976, 4). In the committee's view, this requirement would discourage creditors from discriminatory denials, since reasons for denials must be revealed. In addition, the committee believed this provision would satisfy wider educational goals. According to the committee's report on the pending bill, "Yet this requirement fulfills a broader need: rejected applicants will now be able to learn where and how their credit status is deficient and this information should have a pervasive and valuable educational benefit" (US Senate, 1976, 4).

Background and Intent of the ECOA

Ultimately, the ECOA grew out of hearings on credit discrimination against women held by the National Commission on Consumer Finance (NCCF) in May 1972. The NCCF did not recommend federal legislation in this area, although it did urge the states to examine their laws for constraints, such as prohibition of loans to both a husband and a wife by one lender, that could limit credit availability to creditworthy women. Beyond this, the NCCF apparently preferred to let changing times and competitive markets work to reduce the extent of any discriminatory practices that may have existed at the time:

> Many practices to which witnesses have objected have been inherited from past decades, if not centuries. They fail to reflect the times. The extensive publicity that accompanied the Commission's hearings has caused many credit grantors to re-examine their policies with respect to the existence of sex discrimination. In a competitive market, creditors responsive to these complaints will capture business from their more archaic competitors. (National Commission on Consumer Finance 1972, 153)

Even though it did not recommend federal legislation in its report, the NCCF recalled that witnesses had presented it with numerous documented accounts of difficulties women faced in obtaining credit. Characterizing the evidence as "anecdotal" (presumably as opposed to "systematic"), the NCCF listed five points in its summary of the hearing record:

1. Single women have more trouble obtaining credit than single men (this appeared to be more characteristic of mortgage credit than of consumer credit).
2. Creditors generally require a woman upon marriage to reapply for credit, usually in her husband's name. Similar reapplication is not asked of men when they marry.
3. Creditors are often unwilling to extend credit to a married woman in her own name.
4. Creditors are often unwilling to count the wife's income when a married couple applies for credit.
5. Women who are divorced or widowed have trouble reestablishing credit. Women who are separated have a particularly difficult time, since the

accounts may still be in the husband's name. (National Commission on Consumer Finance 1972, 152)

Less than six months after publication of the NCCF's report, the Senate Committee on Banking, Housing, and Urban Affairs quoted the NCCF's summary as an important element of the committee's analysis of the need for legislation (US Senate 1973, 16–18). The committee also provided a long list of examples of other actions that, in its view, constituted discrimination on the basis of sex or marital status. Eventually, the bill developed by the Senate committee became Title V of an omnibus bill amending a variety of financial regulatory acts. The bill passed both houses of Congress in October 1974 and was signed by President Ford on October 28.

In April 1975, only six months after passage of the initial law and well before its effective date, the Subcommittee on Consumer Affairs of the House of Representatives Committee on Banking, Currency, and Housing held the first hearings on expanding the Equal Credit Opportunity Act. In its report, the full committee stated that new legislation was needed because the original ECOA was enacted in the waning days of the 93rd Congress, when "it was impossible to achieve legislation that would have covered all forms of credit discrimination" (US House of Representatives 1975, 3). The committee indicated that "numerous instances of denial of credit for reasons other than a person's creditworthiness" had been brought to its attention during its hearings and that these and "further examples ... contained in the Committee's files" suggested the need for additional legislation.

The revised version of ECOA prohibiting discrimination on the basis of age (provided the applicant has the capacity to contract), race, color, religion, or national origin, in addition to sex or marital status, passed the House first and was amended by the Senate to include prohibitions of discrimination based on receipt of public assistance benefits and good-faith exercise of rights under the Consumer Credit Protection Act. The Senate also added a requirement for disclosure of reasons for adverse action. The Senate amendments in both areas were accepted by the House, and both houses of Congress agreed to the amended act on March 9, 1976; President Ford signed the act on March 23. Like the original ECOA, the revised act required the Board of Governors of the Federal Reserve System to issue the necessary implementing regulations. After public comments and necessary drafting periods, the Board issued the revised regulation (Regulation B, 12 CFR 202) in December 1976, to be effective March 23, 1977.

Some Difficulties of Transforming Intentions into Effective Regulation

As indicated, Congress intended two benefits from the ECOA: enhanced credit opportunity for protected classes and consumer education. To promote these twin goals, the law that emerged from the congressional process is a hybrid containing both civil rights elements and disclosure requirements. Unfortunately, both areas have illustrated the difficulties of transforming laudatory ideas and goals into an effective regulatory structure. The focus here will be on the civil rights aspect of the ECOA. Although the legal preparations and procedural changes necessary for compliance took some time and effort at the outset, subsequent legal difficulties have been quite limited, at least in comparison with Truth in Lending, which has never really settled down legally (see chapter 10).

To enhance credit opportunity for classes of protected borrowers, the ECOA prohibits "discrimination" on the basis of any of a group of specified criteria. The problem was that it proved difficult to define discrimination narrowly enough to outlaw all socially unacceptable differential treatment while permitting all legitimate efforts of creditors to screen bad risks at reasonable cost. The legislative history of the act shows quite clearly that Congress did not intend to bar legitimate credit screening.[6] Always the challenge has been to produce an operational regulatory structure that enhances the credit opportunities of protected classes while permitting creditors to exclude poor credit risks legitimately. In the remainder of this discussion, the term *discrimination* is used in its pejorative sense to mean socially unacceptable differential treatment.

Congress itself avoided the sticky issue of how to make its civil rights objective operational by not defining "discriminate" in the text of the law, leaving this important decision to the Federal Reserve Board. In section 202.4 of Regulation B, the Board stated the general rule implementing the civil rights portion of the act: "A creditor shall not discriminate against an applicant on a prohibited basis regarding any aspect of a credit transaction." The term *discriminate against an applicant* was defined in section 202.2(n) as meaning "to treat an applicant less favorably than other applicants." Thus, in Regulation B, the Federal Reserve Board articulated the major civil rights protection of the act as prohibiting treatment of any credit applicant less favorably than any other on a prohibited basis in any aspect of a credit transaction. By itself, however, the rule as formulated this way still does not offer an unquestionably unambiguous operational definition of socially unacceptable discrimination in a screening context, where limited selections are continually being made from a longer list of applicants. In fact, there are at least three alternative regulatory approaches. Because of its rule-writing obligation, the Federal Reserve had to examine the merits of each.

The first approach might be characterized as the "effects approach." Such an approach would emphasize the effects of credit screening, holding illegal any credit screening method that has the effect of treating a protected class less favorably, regardless of reason for this effect. An extreme form of the effects approach might require credit allocation based on population proportions or shares of credit applications. If amounts of credit supplied to protected groups were less

---

6. See, for example, US Senate (1973, 18). In discussing the definition of discrimination, the committee reported: "the Committee recognizes that credit should be granted only to creditworthy individuals; valid and reasonable criteria used to determine creditworthiness must be determined by the members of the credit industry who bear the risk of extending credit."

than proportional to their share of the population or of credit applications, there would be a violation under a pure effects standard.

The legislative history of ECOA demonstrates clearly that Congress never intended such an extreme form of credit opportunity. Based on its discussion of the subject, it appears Congress did envision, however, a more limited effects approach, the "effects test."[7] Under the effects test, evidence of disproportionate credit granting would not, by itself, establish a violation. Nevertheless, such evidence could be used to establish a prima facie (rebuttable) case of discrimination, which creditors might defend by showing that the criteria they used in analyzing applications had a manifest relationship to creditworthiness. In general, Regulation B does not take the effects approach, although it does mention the effects test in a footnote to section 202.6(a). In 2013, however, the CFPB began to investigate rates of charge on automobile lenders using an effects test approach, which may signal a new federal enforcement method. As of early 2014, this effort was still mostly at the discussion stage.

The second approach might be called the "intent approach." Under this view of compliance and enforcement, a creditor firm would be judged in violation if it *intended* to treat applicants less favorably because they were members of some protected class. For example, any creditor intending to deny credit to applicants of a particular nationality regardless of creditworthiness would be in violation under this standard. Presumably, violations of a pure intent standard would be less frequent than violations of a pure effects standard. Violations of an intent standard would come about only through intentionally discriminatory acts, but disproportionate effects could also arise in many other ways. For example, disproportionate amounts of credit granted to different population segments might arise from different employment, income, wealth, and other factors affecting creditworthiness and also from different purchasing and saving habits affecting credit demand and credit applications.

A third approach to ECOA compliance and enforcement might well be characterized as the "practices approach." Under this method, compliance efforts would not be judged on either effect or intent. Instead, both creditors and regulators would measure compliance by comparing practices with a mandatory list of do's and don'ts. Essentially, this approach makes the basic assumption that complying with the list of requirements produces results that satisfy the act's goals. In large degree, this is the approach of Regulation B. Rather than focusing on intent or ultimate effect, Regulation B provides a long list of required and prohibited practices. They range from mandatory requirement of separate credit histories for married women (section 202.10) to prohibitions on requesting designation of courtesy titles (such as Mr. or Ms.) on application forms unless the forms "appropriately disclose that the designation of such a title is optional" (section

---

7. See US House of Representatives (1975, 4-5) and US Senate (1976, 4). The effects test grew out of US Supreme Court decisions in the employment area. See *Griggs v. Duke Power Co.*, 401 US 424 (1971), and *Albemarle Paper Co. v. Moody*, 422 US 405 (1975). For discussion of applicability in the credit area, see Board of Governors of the Federal Reserve System (1977) and Hsia (1977).

202.6[d][3]). Enforcement is inherently easier under this approach than under effects or intent standards, since examiners can be dispatched armed with simple checklists. The problem, of course, is the question of whether the assumption is valid that compliance with any particular checklist satisfies the act's goal of enhanced opportunity.[8]

Beyond these fundamental definitional problems associated with ECOA's civil rights provisions, difficulties have also arisen in the education area. Essentially, the non–civil rights protections of ECOA require creditors to follow certain procedures, and especially to make certain disclosures, in the handling of credit applications. Section 701(d) of the act specifies requirements in two areas. First, creditors must notify applicants of actions taken on applications within thirty days of receipt of an application for credit (except for classes of credit transactions for which the Federal Reserve Board was permitted to specify longer "reasonable" times). Second, if the creditor takes "adverse action" on an application, then the applicant must be given notice of the "specific reasons" for the adverse action.

Congress clearly regarded provision of specific reasons for adverse action as an important tool for educating credit applicants about the credit process. Problems arise, however, because acceptance or rejection of credit applications (whether judgmentally or by numerical credit scoring) normally involves simultaneous consideration of the effects of many variables resulting in acceptance or rejection of the entire profile. Consequently, specifying any subset as the "specific reasons" for acceptance or rejection is not theoretically possible in most cases. Federal Reserve attempts to wrestle with this problem by interpreting Regulation B produced a lengthy regulatory proceeding lasting from April 1979 until October 1982.[9]

By themselves, adverse action notices have not turned out to be especially controversial over the years. Rather than the specifics of information in the notices, the question of what actually constitutes "adverse action" has been the more divisive issue. Is adverse action only a credit denial, or might it arise more frequently when consumers actually are granted the credit in question but possibly on less favorable terms than given to some other consumer applying for the same credit or through the same channels? For many years, adverse action referred to credit denials, but Congress changed this a bit regarding credit bureau reports with passage of the Fair and Accurate Credit Transactions (FACT) Act of 2003, which amended the Fair Credit Reporting Act (see chapter 6).

Following a lengthy rule making, the Federal Reserve and the Federal Trade Commission announced in December 2009 the final rules implementing this amendment. The rule making requires a creditor to issue a "risk-based pricing notice" whenever, based on information on the individual's credit report, it provides credit to an individual on less favorable terms than it asks of a substantial proportion of others. The risk-based pricing notices and certain alternative

8. For further discussion of this point, see Chandler and Ewert (1976).

9. For extended discussion of this problem, see Eisenbeis (1980).

approaches allowable under the rule involve free credit reports and additional education for the individuals affected. These rules went into effect on January 1, 2011.[10]

ECONOMIC THEORY OF DISCRIMINATION

The theoretical framework for analyzing discrimination in consumer credit markets is based on economic models developed originally for studying discrimination in labor markets.[11] In general, these models adopt the intent approach to defining discrimination. The models themselves are representations of assumptions, hypotheses, and theory, usually in mathematical form, which are used to delineate conditions when intentional discrimination might be expected or not. Within the frameworks established, analysts then employ empirical methods to test theoretical conclusions against actual market results.

Fundamentally, there are two types of labor market discrimination models that have been used to examine consumer credit discrimination issues. The first postulates that individuals or firms have a preference (or "taste") for discrimination and derives implications of this assumption using traditional neoclassical economic theory. A fundamental conclusion of these theoretical studies is that intentional discrimination will not exist in equilibrium in a competitive market. The second approach appends to traditional neoclassical economics a newer branch of theory known as the economics of information. This approach points out that obtaining information about market participants may be costly in many cases. In these cases, group membership may be an imperfect but less costly source of information on the performance of market participants. As a result, intentional discrimination can exist under such circumstances, even if firms themselves do not exhibit a taste for discrimination.

Models postulating a "taste" for discrimination are based ultimately on the work of Nobel laureate Gary Becker (1971). According to Becker, an individual has a "taste for discrimination" if that individual acts as if he or she were willing to pay something, either directly or indirectly in the form of reduced income, to be associated with some people rather than others. Becker explored this willingness to pay for discrimination by using a statistic he developed, the "discrimination coefficient." The discrimination coefficient reflects the relative difference between the potential money costs of a possible transaction and the (higher) net costs of the same transaction where the cost of discriminating is included as part of net costs. Specifically, the discrimination coefficient is the difference between money costs and higher net costs expressed as a proportion of money costs. For

10. See Final Rule: Fair Credit Reporting Act Risk Based Pricing Regulations, 75 *Federal Register* (January 15, 2010), 2724. The Federal Trade Commission discussed this rule making a bit further in its congressional testimony on March 24, 2010 (see Federal Trade Commission 2010).

11. Labor market models have also been widely used in studying the theory of credit rationing, For further discussion in this area, see Milde (1974), Baltensperger (1978), and chapter 5 above.

example, suppose that an employer would employ white workers at a wage rate w_w but would be willing to employ equally productive black workers only at a lower wage rate w_B. In this case, the employer's taste for discrimination would cause him or her to pay an amount $w_w - w_B$ per worker to avoid employing black workers. Becker's discrimination coefficient, DC, is defined as $DC = (w_w - w_B)/w_B$.

This example can be used to illustrate an individual employer's behavior. Suppose that discrimination in the market establishes a higher equilibrium money wage rate for white workers than for black workers. The relative difference between these wage rates is the market discrimination coefficient DC_M. However, an individual employer acts on the basis of his or her own discrimination coefficient rather than the market coefficient, or, in other words, on the basis of (subjective) *net* wage rates rather than money wage rates. Thus, if the employer's own coefficient is less than the market coefficient (that is, this employer would not be willing to pay as much to discriminate as the market would pay on average), then this employer would hire only black workers, because the savings in money wages would exceed the disutility of employing black workers. Similarly, an employer with a discrimination coefficient greater than DC_M would hire only white workers, because the disutility of employing black workers exceeds the additional cost of paying the extra wage for white workers. Obviously, the distribution of individual firms' discrimination coefficients is an important factor in determining the extent of their discrimination in the market.

Becker argued that under a wide range of circumstances, market forces would push market discrimination coefficients toward zero or, in other words, that under these conditions, discrimination would not exist in equilibrium. He divided the discussion into two fundamental cases: competitive and imperfectly competitive output markets. First, he showed that in competitive markets, if the industry is characterized by either constant or decreasing unit costs as output expands, then the firm with the smallest discrimination coefficient would have the lowest unit cost, and it could undersell all other firms. As a result, the least discriminating firm would produce the total output, and ultimately, the market discrimination coefficient would equal this firm's discrimination coefficient. Moreover, if even only one employer does not have a taste for discrimination (that is, its discrimination coefficient is zero), then the equilibrium market coefficient would be zero.[12]

---

12. These conclusions would not necessarily follow if firms' production functions were characterized by decreasing returns to scale (increasing costs). In this case, the less discriminatory firms would not produce total output. Firms with smaller discrimination coefficients would have larger profits and would tend to expand relative to other firms, but in this case, rising unit costs would limit the levels of output for which firms have a cost advantage. The limited expansion of firms with smaller discrimination coefficients would force the wage rate for black workers to rise relative to the wage rate for white workers and reduce the market discrimination coefficient. But in this case, decreasing returns to scale would prevent the least discriminatory firm from producing the total output, and the resulting market discrimination coefficient would be greater than the lowest firm's coefficient. This case does not appear important for consumer credit markets, however, because statistical cost studies suggest that consumer credit costs are constant or slightly decreasing over normal output ranges. See Benston (1965, 1972, 1977a), Bell and Murphy (1968), Mester (1987), and Durkin and Elliehausen (1998).

Second, Becker suggested that even in imperfectly competitive output markets, the equilibrium market discrimination coefficient would also equal zero if capital markets are competitive, firms' assets are transferable, and at least one producer has no taste for discrimination. A firm in an imperfectly competitive market with a relatively large discrimination coefficient would have higher net costs and receive a lower net income than other potential producers. However, the owner of the firm could receive a larger net income by selling the firm to an individual with a lower discrimination coefficient than by keeping the firm. It follows, then, that if capital markets are competitive and assets are transferable, the firm would be sold to the bidder with the lowest discrimination coefficient, since this firm would make the highest bid. Again, if at least one potential employer had a discrimination coefficient of zero, then the equilibrium market coefficient would also be zero.[13]

Peterson and Peterson (1978) and Peterson (1979 and 1981) adopted Becker's model as a framework for studying possible discrimination in consumer credit markets. Following Becker, they proposed that a creditor with a taste for discrimination would adjust the expected costs of a requested loan by adding a discrimination coefficient. Thus, because this adjustment would make these loans subjectively more costly to creditors, the Petersons argued that creditors would treat those discriminated against differently before they would grant them credit. In particular, the Petersons contended that discriminating creditors would apply higher standards of creditworthiness, charge higher interest rates, or impose more stringent nonprice credit terms on credit to unfavored applicants than they would require on credit to equally creditworthy favored borrowers. However, the Petersons argued that even if creditors have preferences for discrimination, competition in both output and capital markets would act to reduce or eliminate equilibrium discrimination coefficients, as predicted by Becker's model.

Within the Becker framework, the Petersons also maintained that important other conditions in credit markets suggested that discrimination there would likely be less than in labor markets. For example, unlike the labor market, where contact between an employer and an employee is frequent, the usual contact between a creditor and an applicant is limited to a short period of time when the application is made. In many modern credit transactions, the creditor never even sees the borrower. Consequently, according to the Petersons, discrimination coefficients resulting from a creditor's aversion to contact with members of another group are likely to be much lower in credit transactions than in the work environment. As a result, they predicted that there would be less discrimination in credit markets than in labor markets.

Of course, by itself, this argument is not entirely satisfactory for drawing conclusions about the likely extent of discrimination. Arrow (1972), another Nobel laureate, has suggested that dislike of association with certain groups depends

---

13. In contrast, if a firm's assets were not transferable, then there would be no market incentive reducing the market discrimination coefficient. For discussion of all the possible conditions, see Becker (1971). In general, completely nontransferable assets are not found in most industries.

CONSUMER CREDIT AND THE AMERICAN ECONOMY

on the nature of the association and that physical proximity may be significant only in some contexts. For example, unlike race, it seems unlikely that physical proximity would be a reason for creditors to discriminate on the basis of attributes such as sex or marital status. Other considerations would have to explain these kinds of discrimination. Thus, limited contact between parties in credit markets does not necessarily imply that lenders' preferences for discrimination would be relatively weak in all cases. In many situations, other social considerations might be important instead. However, as noted, the Petersons did not rely solely on the proximity argument. Their empirical findings, which supported their theoretical discussion, are reviewed in the next section.

In contrast to Becker, Alchian and Kessel (1962) suggested that public regulation could provide conditions conducive to discrimination in imperfectly competitive product (output) markets, even if capital markets are competitive and firms' assets are transferable. Public regulation often protects monopolists from competition, but at the same time, it often fixes prices to prevent rates of return above competitive rates. Monopolists who appear to be too profitable are likely to face pressures to reduce prices, and consequently, they may prefer to take potential excess profits in nonpecuniary forms that can be treated as costs.[14] For example, a profit-maximizing public utility monopolist with only a small taste for discrimination might prefer to hire only higher-wage white workers, because the firm would not be allowed to keep the additional profits from hiring black workers at a lower wage. In the credit area, creditors with even a small taste for discrimination might be induced to ignore profitable loans to unfavored groups and to prefer loans to more marginal risks among favored classes. Ultimately, the restriction on pecuniary income caused by public regulation or its threat could prevent potential producers with lower discrimination coefficients from making a sufficiently large enough bid to induce relatively more discriminatory monopolists to sell their firms.

Historical chartering and branching restrictions on commercial banks, convenience and advantage licensing of finance companies, and historical differential rate ceilings and loan size limits by institutional class potentially could have limited entry and restricted competition in consumer lending.[15] Thus, if no other information were available, the presence of these regulatory constraints on entry and prices in the past might suggest that Alchian and Kessel's model could be applicable to consumer credit markets, especially historically.[16] However, a variety of empirical studies has found evidence of strong interinstitutional competition

14. Alchian and Kessel suggested that any large firm may manifest the behavior of a regulated monopoly. If an unregulated large firm appears too profitable, the firm bears the risk that the state may subject it to explicit regulation or destroy it through antitrust action.

15. For discussion of entry barriers and rate ceilings in consumer lending at the time of passage of the ECOA, see National Commission on Consumer Finance (1972, chapter 7). See also chapter 11 of this book.

16. See Fand and Forbes (1968), Shay (1970 and 1974), Sartoris (1972), Smith (1973), Boczar (1978), and Johnson and Sullivan (1981). For further discussion, see chapter 11 below.

in consumer credit markets. These studies suggest that regulation may not constrain lenders' behavior in at least the portions of the markets studied, and, based on Becker's model, they imply that competition will reduce discrimination in consumer lending.

In sum, neoclassical theoretical models show how a firm's tastes for discrimination may result in discriminating behavior in the market and suggests that over time, competition will tend to eliminate intent-based discrimination unless constrained by regulation. However, the neoclassical approach has a number of limitations. First, the neoclassical models offer no insights about timing of events, such as how long it will take for competition to have its predicted effects. If time periods are long because competition works slowly, then discriminating firms may exist for a time, even if they continuously lose ground and ultimately are eliminated from the market as theory predicts. To explore this possibility, empirical work seems in order. Second, the neoclassical models do not give reasons for existence of the taste for discrimination, which is costly to those that have it. Costly preferences for discrimination are simply postulated for theoretical purposes, and their implications are explored, leading to the conclusion that markets will eliminate such tastes. As will be discussed further in the next section, the information-cost models analyze the implications of another possibility, that discriminatory behavior arises because in some cases, it might reduce costs. Obviously, these implications might be different from those of the neoclassical models.

Nonetheless, despite their limitations, the neoclassical models are important for producing conclusions about possible discrimination arising from tastes, and the timing issue raises three fundamental empirical questions for study:

(1) Extent of discrimination against protected classes before passage of the law.
(2) Impact of the law in increasing credit opportunity of protected classes.
(3) Other effects of the law, if any.

Information Cost Models of Discrimination

As indicated above, other economists have used a newer branch of theory called the economics of information to add to neoclassical theoretical models of discrimination. The information theory approach goes beyond the neoclassical approach to explore in more detail possible reasons for discrimination. But rather than assuming that discrimination arises from tastes and is costly, the information approach argues that discrimination can arise instead from attempts to reduce costs. Under these circumstances, there are cases in which discrimination may be economically rational. As it turns out, the theory suggests that competitive markets may not always eliminate such discrimination.

For example, in the labor market, an employer does not know the performance of a job applicant until after the applicant is hired. The employer could hire every applicant and dismiss those who were unqualified, but this would require the employer to incur an investment cost in each applicant. Alternatively, the employer could find some less expensive source of information that is related to job performance, such as an education criterion, and could base decisions on this information. Similarly, a creditor does not know beforehand whether a loan applicant will be able and willing to repay as promised. The creditor could extend credit to all applicants and incur losses on credit to unqualified borrowers, or the firm could evaluate applicants on the basis of more inexpensively observed attributes—such as occupation or credit score—that are related to repayment performance. In both cases, discrimination may result if membership in some demographic group is related to (provides information about) market performance.

An early information theory model of discrimination was developed by Edmund S. Phelps (1972).[17] In Phelps's model, an employer administers a test to job applicants and uses the test to predict an applicant's job performance. In the absence of any further information about applicants, performance would be predicted solely on applicants' test scores. However, employers fully realize that test scores are not a perfect predictor of performance; some employees will perform better than predicted by their scores, and some will not perform as well.[18] As a result, employers are interested in obtaining additional information about potential employees before going to the expense of hiring them.

For discussion, Phelps assumed that employers also are able to observe whether applicants are members of particular groups (to use some simple examples, say, whether they are law school graduates, veterans, athletes, born in New Jersey, and so forth) and that membership in some groups is somehow related to performance. Thus, based on prior experience, if the employer knows that applicants who are members of some groups perform better on average than nonmembers, even if their test scores are the same, then the employer has additional information that may be useful in hiring.[19] Of course, using such information for making hiring decisions could lead to socially unacceptable differential treatment (discrimination) if the group criterion used is socially sensitive, such as a social or religious criterion.[20]

Phelps discussed two possible cases in which group membership provides additional information. In the first case, the impact of group membership on performance is independent of level of test score. In this case, it is always better to

---

17. Arrow (1972) independently developed a similar model. Both Phelps and Arrow received the Nobel prize for their significant contributions to economic science.

18. In formal terms, the test score measures the applicant's expected job performance with random error e_i. That is, $y_i = q_i + e_i$, where e_i is a random variable with mean zero.

19. In econometrics, models of this general form are known as errors-in-the-variables models. For general discussion of models of this type, see Johnston (1972, 281–283).

20. If beliefs about group differences are not based on fact, then the effects of Phelps's model are similar to models based on tastes, even though the genesis is different. For discussion, see Arrow (1972, 97).

be a member of the favored (high-performing) group, regardless of level of test score. If employers planning to hire additional workers require some minimum (threshold) level of expected performance, they would tend to favor members of the favored group at every test score level. Examined from the other perspective, applicants who were not members of the favored group would have to exhibit higher test scores before they would be hired. Clearly, depending on the group membership variable, unacceptable discrimination could result.

Under the conditions that group membership provides additional information about performance and that the group membership effect is independent of test score, any legal limitation on using this additional information would tend to benefit members of the disadvantaged (lower-performing) group relative to the advantaged class. If, for example, being born in New Jersey were an indication of good job performance and were, therefore, a positive factor to prospective employers, prohibiting employers from using this information would benefit relatively those not born in the state. Of course, relative gains might not translate into absolute gains. If, for example, limitation or prohibition on using group membership information significantly worsened the quality of hiring decisions (that is, made the decisions significantly more costly), then fewer might be hired from both groups despite relative improvement in the position of the lower-performing group.

In his second case, Phelps added an additional complexity. Instead of assuming a group effect that is independent of test score, Phelps explored the possibility that variability of performance (and, consequently, the credibility of test scores as a predictor of performance) depends on group membership. In this case, group membership might have a widely different impact at different levels of test score.[21] For example, being from New Jersey might be a large negative factor at low test scores, but it might be only a small negative factor or even a positive factor at high scores. Furthermore, if test scores of applicants from New Jersey are less reliable than scores of other applicants (that is, they measure performance with greater error), then being from New Jersey might be a positive factor or only slightly negative at low test scores, but it might be a large negative factor at high test scores. Obviously, the impact of group membership is ambiguous in this case. At low test scores, there may be one impact, and at higher scores, there may be another.

From a public policy standpoint, Phelps's second case poses the special problem that prohibitions on using group membership information in selection procedures may not always help "protected" classes, even relatively. Because the group effect is not independent of the test score, prohibiting use of group membership information may help protected classes at one level of test score. But at other levels of these scores, such a prohibition may actually relatively disadvantage them. Thus, to determine the (possibly ambiguous) effect of prohibiting use of group membership information, empirical work seems necessary.

---

21. Econometrically, the slope of the regression of performance on test score depends on group membership.

Phelps's model can readily be applied to consumer credit markets. Instead of administering employment tests, a creditor examines applicants' characteristics that have proven to be reliable indicators of creditworthiness. The creditor's evaluations are summarized by an index or credit score that imperfectly predicts applicants' likely performance.[22] But, as in the labor market, the creditor's previous experience indicates that on average, one group's performance is better or worse than that of another group. In this case, other things being equal, creditors would tend to favor the better-performing group. Consequently, prohibiting use of this information should improve the position of the disadvantaged class relatively, other things being equal. However, the relative gain might not translate into an absolute benefit if costs rise. Moreover, if group membership has a different relationship to performance at different levels of credit score, prohibiting creditors from categorizing applicants into these groups could have differing impacts depending on score.

Empirically, Phelps's information theory model adds some questions for investigation to the three listed above suggested by the neoclassical models. In summary, these involve the usefulness of information in making judgments and the impact on protected groups of eliminating use of the information:

(4) Extent, if any, to which demographic group membership provides information about market performance.
(5) Whether the group membership effect, if any, is independent of credit evaluation test score.
(6) Whether any relative benefits resulting from prohibiting group membership information translate into absolute gains for any group.

Avery (1981b) developed a model of credit screening under imperfect information that is based on the Phelps approach. Actually, the Avery model is a generalization of the Phelps approach to a wider variety of cases. In Avery's model, the creditor collects information on financial and economic characteristics of the applicant (the "economic variables" in Avery's terminology or the "test scores" in the Phelps model) and summarizes this information as a probability distribution of rates of return. The creditor also observes group membership and notes that group membership provides information about the probability distribution of returns. However, no matter whether performance expectations are based on economic or both economic and group membership variables, the creditor's decision rule is to grant credit if expected return is greater than expected costs (including a provision for possible default costs).

Avery considered two possible ways group membership information might be related to the distribution of returns. In the first case, both the distribution of

---

22. Although the term *credit score* is generally associated with statistical evaluation systems, this discussion also applies to judgmental credit evaluation systems. Both statistical and judgmental systems are based on the same principle; the only difference is the method by which creditworthiness is estimated. For further discussion, see Chandler and Coffman (1979) and Eisenbeis (1980).

economic variables and the related distribution of rates of return are uniformly higher for one group than they are for the other. Using the previous example and assuming that the only economic variable is income, then this case postulates that the income distribution and the related expected return are uniformly higher for credit applicants born in New Jersey than for credit applicants born outside the state. As a result, random credit applicants are more likely to be accepted if they are from New Jersey—not because of their group membership but because if they are from New Jersey, they are more likely to be higher-income and more likely to produce an acceptable return. Consequently, even for equal numbers of random applicants from the two groups, the acceptance ratio and the number accepted would be higher for the New Jersey group.

Avery called this possibility the "endowment effect." It would not constitute discrimination under the intent or practices approaches discussed earlier, because the differential acceptance rates arose from unlike distributions of the economic variables between groups, not from group membership itself.[23] Realistic examples of possibilities for an endowment effect abound. If whites, for example, earn higher incomes than blacks, then to the extent that creditworthiness is related to income, whites would be more likely than blacks to be granted credit.

Avery's second possibility is the case in which group membership itself provides information about expected returns beyond the information provided by the economic variables alone. In particular, in this case, creditors observe group membership and believe that the expected rate of return given the economic variables and group membership differs from the expected rate of return given only the economic variables. This is the first case explored by Phelps.[24] Again using the New Jersey example, in this case, applicants from New Jersey are better risks for any given level of income than applicants not from New Jersey. Thus, group membership provides additional information; in effect, it becomes another economic variable. Avery called this possibility the "mean shift effect." Under this assumption, any consideration of group membership reduces the probability of acceptance for applicants from the low-return group and raises the probability of acceptance from the high-return group. For example, in the past, some creditors have contended that marital status is a group membership variable that provides information about creditworthiness. If married applicants are, in fact, better credit risks on average than divorced applicants, then marital status provides information beyond that supplied by other available variables.

After developing his two cases (endowment effect case and mean shift effect or "Phelps" case), Avery used the model to examine how a creditor might react to two of the ECOA approaches mentioned earlier, the practices approach and the effects approach. Thus, in all, Avery considered four situations, each of two ECOA approaches under each of two information cases.

23. The different acceptance rates would constitute discrimination under the effects approach also discussed above.

24. Econometrically, it is the errors-in-the-variables model.

First, under the practices approach, ECOA prohibits use of group membership information in the credit screening process. Avery's model shows that this
would have no effect on the credit screening process if group differences arise
solely from an endowment effect. Simply stated, if group membership provided
creditors with no additional useful information, then prohibiting its use has no
particular impact on credit screening.[25]

However, the situation is different under the practices approach to ECOA
when there is a mean shift effect (the "Phelps" information case). In the mean
shift case, group membership provides additional information; consequently,
prohibiting its use has an impact. In particular, prohibiting use of group membership information raises the probability of acceptance for a random applicant
from the low-return group, and it reduces the probability of acceptance for a random applicant from the high-return group.[26] However, the prohibition also makes
the credit screening process less accurate and probably more costly overall. As a
result, credit is more costly, because default losses increase, potentially profitable
applicants are rejected, or a more costly screening process must be used.

Next, Avery examined implications of ECOA under the effects approach to
defining unacceptable discrimination.[27] As defined earlier, the effects approach
would prohibit any credit screening that leads to significant differences in
credit rejection rates for different groups. In other words, the effects approach
would require that the probability of acceptance be the same for members of the
low-return and high-return groups.

In this case, Avery's model produces the not very startling result that the pure
effects approach will have an impact on credit markets, regardless of whether
group differences are associated with an endowment effect or a mean shift effect.
In particular, the effects approach will produce a higher acceptance rate for the
low-return group, a lower acceptance rate for the high-return group, and a less
accurate and more costly credit screening process.[28] In addition, if an endowment
effect is present (with or without a mean shift effect), the model shows that the
effects approach also produces reverse discrimination. Applicants would have to
be treated unequally to achieve an equal probability of acceptance for low- and
high-return groups. Specifically, the creditor would have to set a higher threshold
rate of return for high-return applicants than for low-return applicants. As a practical matter, the implication of reverse discrimination under the effects approach
with an endowment effect need not be overemphasized, since, as mentioned

25. There may be, of course, an impact on costs as creditors comply with regulatory requirements.

26. This is the relative gain predicted by the Phelps model. Of course, this may not generate
an absolute gain. Also, if the second Phelps case were present (group effect not independent of
score), even relative impact could be ambiguous, as discussed above.

27. Avery used slightly different terminology than employed here, using "effects test" for what is
referred to here as the pure "effects approach."

28. This is the same impact as the practices approach with a mean shift effect, discussed above.

earlier, the basic thrust of ECOA through Regulation B involves the practices approach rather than the effects approach.[29]

Nevertheless, since the practices approach produces an impact on markets when there is a mean shift effect, presence or not of this effect is a major empirical issue raised by the Avery model.[30] If group differences are caused solely by an endowment effect, then the practices approach will have no impact except to cause some compliance costs among creditors if they must change procedures, reprint forms, keep additional records, and so on. If, in contrast, group differences are caused by a mean shift effect, then Avery's model predicts that the practices approach prohibiting use of group membership information would change acceptance probabilities in addition to making the credit screening process less efficient and more costly.

In sum, consistent with the Phelps model, Avery showed that the practices approach to ECOA adopted in Regulation B could increase credit acceptance rates among protected classes if denials arose from a mean shift effect (the Phelps case). Under the effects approach, higher acceptances would result if either the endowment or mean shift effects were present. Unfortunately, in either case, the higher acceptance rates would be achieved only at higher cost and with greater inefficiency in the screening process.

There is no reason to assume that creditors will simply accept higher costs, however. Instead, it seems likely that creditors would take subsequent actions to reduce costs. Indeed, economic theory suggests that in a competitive market, firms must take all available options of reducing production costs, or they will be driven from the market in the long run. For this reason, in a final major section of his paper, Avery extended his model to the situation in which creditors economize on screening costs by controlling which potential applicants actually apply. The basic idea of the extended model is that the creditor performs an initial screening of potential applicants using a limited subset of information (which, for simplicity, Avery assumed could be collected without cost). The creditor's decision rule is to take an application if the expected rate of return based on this first subset of information exceeds a threshold rate of return that reflects the cost of processing applications. Simply stated, if a (costlessly collected) subset of information suggests that it is worthwhile to take an application, the creditor firm will do so; otherwise, it will not. If the decision is made to take an application, then the creditor will collect additional (costly) information and decide whether to grant credit based on expected returns from doing so. Avery called the initial screening of potential applicants "indirect screening," to distinguish it from the screening of actual loan applications, which he called "direct screening."

29. This could, of course, change in the future if the courts extend the effects test approach to credit markets in a significant way or the Consumer Financial Protection Bureau extends the importance of the effects approach, as it indicated in 2013 that it may do.

30. This question of the extent to which group membership provides (i.e., presence or not of Avery's "mean shift effect") was also raised by the Phelps model.

In the context of his extended model, Avery showed that if indirect screening using group membership information is possible, the ECOA will cause the creditor to raise indirect screening thresholds. This would happen because the ECOA-prescribed restrictions on information use reduce the profitability of credit (since if Regulation B has any impact, more unprofitable low-return applicants and fewer profitable high-return applicants will be accepted). Moreover, Avery's analysis also showed that the threshold for the low-return group will be raised relatively more than the threshold for the high-return group. Thus, even if ECOA raises the probability of obtaining credit among applicants in the low-return group (through the act's restrictions on using group membership information as a direct screening variable), the higher costs that result will encourage greater indirect screening, which reduces the number of applicants from both groups. Furthermore, the impact of indirect screening will be greater on the low-return group, presumably the group the act is designed to protect. In effect, the impact of prohibitions on information use in the direct screening process may be counteracted in large part by the effects of indirect screening that arise as a substitute for direct screening.

In practice, indirect screening is likely to take the form of activities by the lender to make it more costly for certain potential applicants to apply for credit rather than an explicit refusal to accept applications. For example, if prospective debtors are more likely to apply for credit in their own neighborhoods, a creditor could indirectly screen potential applicants by the selection of the neighborhoods in which stores or branches are located. Because potential debtors are discouraged from applying, it may be difficult to distinguish indirect screening from differences in the demand for credit. In the example given above, a lack of offices in certain neighborhoods might also be explained by insufficient credit demand in these neighborhoods. Thus, the possibility of indirect screening increases the difficulty of assessing the impact of ECOA, since the applicant pool itself may change as a result of the law.

In sum, unlike the neoclassical models, Phelps's and Avery's information theory models suggest that there are some plausible conditions under which ECOA will have an impact on markets. In particular, under the practices approach adopted in Regulation B, ECOA can be expected to have an impact if group membership provides information about creditworthiness beyond the information provided by other variables (Avery's mean shift effect). Of course, the presence or not of a mean shift effect and the degree of resulting impact of ECOA are empirical questions. However, the models predict that if there is an impact, it would be to raise the acceptance probabilities of protected groups but at a higher level of cost and inefficiency. Greater inefficiency would then lower the acceptance probabilities of all groups, possibly disadvantaging everyone absolutely.

Beyond Phelps and Avery, A. Michael Spence (1973 and 1974), another Nobel laureate, developed a third information theory model with implications for ECOA. The Spence model suggests that under certain circumstances, the practices approach to ECOA may have negative impacts on protected groups even relatively. This anomalous result comes about if members of protected groups use different information to "signal" their creditworthiness to creditors, but the law and regulation prevent creditors from "seeing" the signal.

In both the Phelps and Avery models, employers or creditors predict applicants' performance based on previous experience with applicants exhibiting similar characteristics, where "characteristics" refers to all relevant variables, including group membership. However, neither model attempts to explain the reasons that applicants' characteristics may be related to performance. Spence examined this issue. Concentrating on labor markets, Spence focused on the possibility that at least some characteristics are related to performance, because job applicants choose to use alterable characteristics to reveal or "signal" future performance to prospective employers. Within this context, where some characteristics are signals, Spence then explained why group membership might be an important dimension to employers, even if group membership is not alterable and, by itself, provides no information about performance.

In Spence's model, the employer observes the relationship between performance and individual characteristics for recently hired employees and expresses the relationship as a conditional probability distribution. In other words, there is a probability distribution of possible performance levels conditional on the states of individuals' characteristics. To use an example, an employer might realize that the distribution of workers' productivity levels is conditioned on their education levels. If so, then employers would be prompted to consider variable wage offers based on education level. As long as a higher wage to better-educated employees was more than offset by greater productivity, then the employer would be better off hiring applicants with more education.

Potential employees would, of course, quickly notice higher wages to better-educated applicants and invest in education if there is sufficient return to acquiring the education. In this way, potentially productive employees would signal their greater potential productivity to employers. However, it is easy to see that a characteristic cannot effectively serve as a signal if everyone can acquire it easily (i.e., acquire it at low cost). Thus, a decision to acquire a characteristic can serve as a signal only as long as the costs of acquiring the characteristic (the "signaling costs") are inversely related to performance. For example, education can serve to signal performance as long as high-performance individuals can acquire education more easily than low-performance individuals. If high-performance individuals can acquire, say, a high school diploma or a college degree more easily than low-performance individuals, then education can serve to signal performance. If this inverse cost relation exists and the difference in wages is sufficient to induce high-performance (but not low-performance) individuals to invest in education, then education can serve as a signal of performance.[31]

31. This process is part of what is known as an information feedback loop. After hiring and subsequent observation of how signals relate to performance of signaling employees, the employer will adjust the conditional probabilities, and a new round will begin. In general, the conditional probability distribution for the new group will differ from the distribution for the previous group. However, a stable signaling equilibrium will exist if the employer starts out with a conditional probability distribution that is not disconfirmed in the next round by the incoming data. For further discussion and mathematical analysis of signaling equilibrium, see Spence (1974).

Spence's signaling theory presents the possibility that group membership might be an important evaluative criterion, even if group membership itself is completely uncorrelated with performance. The reason is that unalterable characteristics might have the effect of defining groups with different signaling capabilities. In this case, signaling information of one group could be independent of signaling information of other groups. Under these circumstances, observers' assessment of conditional probabilities of performance would depend on both group membership and signaling variables, even though group membership is totally uncorrelated with performance.

Suppose, for example, that in the bank credit card market, the proportion of high-performance men (those who always pay on time) is exactly the same as the proportion of high-performance women. Assume also that card issuers have discovered through experience that time on the job is a useful signal of creditworthiness. Now, suppose that, on average, creditworthy women have fewer years on their jobs (because of past employment discrimination or some other reason). The result is that a particular number of years on the job will potentially signal different levels of creditworthiness among men and women. Under the circumstances, because the signals are different, properly assessing creditworthiness among both men and women would depend on the signals and group membership, even though performance itself is uncorrelated with group.[32]

Spence's signaling approach to the impact of group membership variables has potential implications for administration of the ECOA. A practices approach that forbids use of group membership variables in a credit evaluation scheme essentially assumes that the relationship between performance and alterable characteristics of applicants (i.e., signals) is the same for all groups. If this is true, then the impact of ECOA will be to make differential treatment more difficult for those who intend to discriminate on a prohibited basis. However, if signals are not the same among groups, then the impact could be quite different. In this case, allowable credit criteria would be based on experience with the dominant group, to the possible disadvantage of others.

In conclusion, it seems that neither neoclassical nor information theory models predict much success for the ECOA. Neoclassical models of the Becker type do not predict the existence of discrimination as long as output markets are competitive or firms' assets are transferable, both of which conditions seem to characterize consumer credit markets. Thus, if no one discriminates, then ECOA will not wipe out any discrimination, although it may raise operating costs. In contrast, information theory models specify some plausible conditions under which differential treatment may occur, namely, when group membership provides some information potentially useful in predicting applicants' scores. Under these conditions, both the practices approach and the effects approach to ECOA would have an impact on markets, although the impact on protected groups is unclear from theory alone and may be detrimental. In all, the theoretical models

---

32. In general, any factor that causes groups to invest differently in signals will cause this result. Moreover, if resulting conditional probability assessments are not disconfirmed in the subsequent round, different stable signaling equilibria will be obtained for each group.

raise at least six interesting empirical questions, which may be grouped into three classifications:

I. Group membership and information about market performance.
   (1) Extent, if any, to which demographic group membership provides information about market performance.
   (2) Whether the group membership effect, if any, is independent of credit evaluation test score.

II. Existence of discrimination.
   (3) Extent of discrimination against protected classes before passage of the law.

III. Effects of ECOA.
   (4) Impact of the law in increasing credit opportunity of protected classes.
   (5) Whether any relative benefits derived from prohibiting group membership information translate into absolute gains for any group.
   (6) Other effects of the law, if any.

Empirical Evidence concerning Consumer Credit Discrimination

As discussed in the preceding subsection, theoretical models of discrimination raise some important questions that can be answered only with empirical methodologies. At the time of enactment of the Equal Credit Opportunity Act, empirical evidence on these questions was largely anecdotal; not much statistical evidence was available. Unfortunately, passage of time has done little to change this situation. Empirical information is limited, although a few empirical studies have been done, and some statistical evidence has been produced. As time has passed, undertaking studies of issues of discrimination involving credit other than mortgage-related credit has become increasingly difficult for lack of data. Statistical systems do not capture prohibited data (for obvious reasons), which also makes direct economic research on these questions impossible. In contrast, the Home Mortgage Disclosure Act *requires* collection of racial data on mortgage-related transactions, which has encouraged studies of discrimination in the housing area. The following section reviews available empirical studies in the (nonmortgage) consumer credit area.

GROUP MEMBERSHIP AND INFORMATION
ABOUT MARKET PERFORMANCE
The first question is whether knowledge of credit applicants' (protected) group membership provides creditors with information about their market performance (creditworthiness). If group membership does not provide information about performance, then theory predicts that ECOA will have no impact

(except perhaps to raise costs) unless tastes for discrimination exist that the market has not had time to eliminate. In contrast, if group membership does provide information, then ECOA could change acceptance probabilities in addition to costs.

The relationship between personal characteristics and creditworthiness was first studied statistically by Durand (1941). Exploring data from twenty-one commercial banks and twelve industrial banks and finance companies, Durand concluded that women and older borrowers were better credit risks than men and younger debtors. In contrast, he found little difference among consumers of different marital status. While the findings for sex and age might have arisen as a consequence of earlier discrimination that eliminated women and elderly borrowers with less than impeccable credit credentials, they suggest that economic forces would have been on the side of finding ways of lending more to women and older borrowers, not less.

In a review of thirteen credit scoring models for consumer loans developed before ECOA, Altman et al. (1981) noted that eight of these models included ECOA-prohibited variables, with sex, age, and marital status being the most frequently occurring prohibited variables.[33] Most models tended to find women and older borrowers less risky than other borrowers. In contrast to Durand, however, several studies detected a relationship between marital status and creditworthiness.

Later findings concerning the relationship of sex, age, and marital status to creditworthiness are largely consistent with Durand's conclusions.[34] In a statistical study of 2,000 credit card applicants and account holders at a major bank between 1971 and 1974, for example, Chandler and Ewert (1976) found that being female was positively related to creditworthiness. Using data from a large bank credit card issuer, Boyes, Hoffman, and Low (1986) again found that older borrowers were less likely than younger borrowers to default and that being married appeared to be unrelated to creditworthiness. And in a study of a large number of accounts at a single consumer finance company, Avery (1982) found that older customers appeared to be better risks. However, Avery also found evidence suggesting that marital status was related to creditworthiness.

---

33. The credit scoring studies using ECOA-prohibited variables are Durand (1941); Myers and Forgy (1963); Smith (1964); Pratt and McGhee (1967); Boggess (1967); Chatterjee and Barcun (1970); Apilado, Warner, and Dauten (1974); and Sexton (1977).

34. The credit scoring models reviewed by Altman et al. (1981) were developed from samples that contained only approved applicants. Such samples, which exclude rejected applicants, are subject to selection bias. In order to counteract the effects of creditors' current credit policies, studies by Chandler and Ewert (1976); Avery (1982); and Boyes, Hoffman, and Low (1986), discussed below, attempt to correct for this bias using statistical methods. Chandler and Ewert used a method based on sampling theory called augmentation, which weights each accepted account by the reciprocal of its probability of being accepted (see Cochran 1963, 371–374). Avery and Boyes, Hoffman, and Low used a method developed by Heckman (1979), which follows a similar weighting procedure to adjust for selection bias.

Obviously, more evidence would be useful, especially from controlled experiments that freed results from any influences of credit screening processes. But at present, there is no available information suggesting that women or the elderly are worse credit risks than others, other things being equal, or that marital status might be an especially important criterion. As a result, there is no reason to conclude that credit discrimination against these protected groups would arise from rational courses such as Avery's mean shift effect.

Two important implications stem from the tentative conclusion that some ECOA protected variables do not provide information anyway. First, any credit discrimination that does arise would ascend from "tastes" for discrimination as discussed by Becker (1971). And this is the kind of discrimination that markets would eliminate. Whether markets operate speedily enough to have accomplished this task acceptably is an additional empirical question that will be discussed further in the next subsection. Second, if ECOA supports market forces rather than opposing them, benefits to protected classes may not be as great as envisioned by proponents. However, if, as limited evidence suggests, some protected classes are actually *more* creditworthy than some nonprotected groups, ECOA could work in the long run to the *disadvantage* of these protected groups. This possibility is also discussed further below.

The one potential problem area from the very small number of ECOA-related empirical studies concerns race. In his study using data from a single consumer finance company from the period before ECOA, Avery (1982) found that blacks and young applicants appeared less likely than other applicants to pay off their accounts as scheduled, even after controlling for applicants' financial and credit characteristics. Similarly, Boyes, Hoffman, and Low (1986) found in their study of a bank card issuer's accounts that blacks were somewhat more likely than whites to default, other things being equal. While two very old studies involving only two creditors can hardly be regarded as conclusive of anything, they do suggest the need for care in examining creditors' behavior toward protected groups for evidence of differential treatment apart from the effect of normal credit granting criteria.

EXISTENCE OF DISCRIMINATION IN CONSUMER CREDIT MARKETS
After passage of ECOA, a number of researchers attempted to examine credit market conditions before passage of the antidiscrimination law. Unfortunately, their efforts have been hampered by unavailability of useful data on market conditions many years ago. Nevertheless, a few studies have become available.

In one study, Marshall (1979) compared credit rejection rates between unprotected and ECOA-protected classes of consumers. Using data from two large finance companies collected before and after enactment of ECOA, he constructed a logistic model to estimate the probability of loan approval conditional on three factors: sex, age, and credit score.

Only one firm could provide information on sex of credit applicants, but through his statistical work, Marshall found that sex of applicant appeared to have no impact on the credit granting decision at this firm either before or after ECOA. Although, obviously, the study universe is very limited, this finding is not consistent with the hypothesis of sex discrimination in credit granting. In contrast, Marshall found that age of applicant did appear to have some impact on credit decisions. At one company, rejection of older applicants before ECOA was higher than would be predicted by credit score alone, a phenomenon that disappeared after ECOA. At the other company, he observed this finding both before and after ECOA, evidence of possible age discrimination at this company.

A search for evidence of credit discrimination using a larger database was undertaken by Peterson and Peterson (1978) and Peterson (1979 and 1981). Data consisted of account information on 37,000 consumer loans at thirty banks over the period from 1965 to 1971 collected by the Federal Reserve Board for a study of bank consumer credit practices. As described above, the Petersons used these data to test a model of credit market discrimination based on Becker's (1971) model of labor market discrimination.

From their model, the Petersons argued that if creditors discriminated against some groups of people, results of the discrimination would show up in the form of higher standards of creditworthiness required of these people, higher interest rates charged, or more stringent nonprice credit terms. Higher credit standards would manifest themselves in the form of lower default rates among the group discriminated against, since they would be forced to exhibit higher degrees of creditworthiness before being accepted.[35] These conclusions from their theoretical model gave the Petersons testable hypotheses for checking against the data.

Because they had information on the sex of applicants, Peterson and Peterson focused their analyses on sex discrimination. They found no significant differences in default rates between men and women for most types of loans, which caused them to reject the hypothesis of systematic discrimination. But in two cases, differences in default rates between men and women were significant. Women defaulted at a disproportionately higher rate on used car loans, suggesting that discrimination may have existed against men in granting used car loans. One interpretation of this finding is that banks may have been overly conservative in granting used car loans to men, erroneously judging men to be poorer credit risks because they tend to be greater automobile insurance risks than women. On the other hand, women defaulted at a disproportionately lower rate on home improvement loans. This result may indicate discrimination against women, but other evidence suggests a weaker interpretation. The ratio of loan loss to credit advanced on home improvement loans was higher for women than

---

35. The Petersons assumed that the basic risk distributions of male and female applicants were similar, so that average default rates reflect marginal credit standards. In contrast, if the assumption of similar risk distributions is not correct, then discrimination against one group or the other could exist even if average default rates were the same. For example, if the Durand suggestion is correct that women are better credit risks, all other things being equal, then equal default rates would indicate discrimination in favor of women (against men). For further discussion of the assumption of similar risk distributions among applicant groups, see Peterson (1981, 556–559).

for men. Bankers may have applied higher credit standards on home improvement loans to women in order to compensate for larger loan losses on home improvement loans made to women. Consequently, no unambiguous conclusions could be drawn about evidence of discrimination against women on home improvement loans.

In the second study, Peterson followed a similar approach to test for discrimination by sex in direct consumer lending from 1966 to 1971. This study differed from the earlier study by Peterson and Peterson which used the same database, in that it considered only direct loans and analyzed interest rate, charge-off, and loan loss data. Peterson found no statistically significant difference in ratios of loan loss to credit advanced or in charge-off ratios for male and female borrowers. To test for differences in interest rates, Peterson regressed the interest rate on the borrower's sex, life cycle stage and financial attributes of the borrower, loan terms, and a variable representing whether the borrower is a former customer. In all but one case, the sex variable was not significantly related to the interest rate, and in that case (household goods loans), the sign of the sex coefficient indicates that women paid significantly less for household goods credit at banks than men. In sum, none of this group of studies produced rigorous statistical evidence of systematic discrimination against women before ECOA.

Evidence concerning racial discrimination before ECOA is more mixed, although on balance, it suggests that discrimination probably was not pervasive. Avery (1982), in his study of a consumer finance company, found that black, single, and young applicants were less likely than other applicants to be accepted. This is the same study in which he found that black and young applicants who were accepted also appeared to default more often, other things being equal. Using a different approach in another study, Avery (1981a) also found evidence of possible credit discrimination against blacks and Hispanics. Using data on 1,300 low-income households that participated in the New Jersey negative income tax experiment from 1968 to 1972, he estimated a cross-section, supply and demand model for consumer credit. The estimated supply function, which was based on the assumption that creditors face a fixed interest rate and ration households at that rate, indicated that after taking financial and credit characteristics into account, blacks and Hispanics had significantly lower levels of consumer debt than non-Hispanic whites. Since his analysis showed that blacks and Hispanics did not demand less debt, Avery concluded that race appeared to play a role in creditors' lending decisions at that time.

Other evidence, however, is not consistent with this conclusion. Using survey data from a single city (Atlanta), Lindley, Selby, and Jackson (1984) found little evidence to support the hypothesis of racial discrimination in credit granting either before or after extension of the ECOA to cover race. The authors felt so strongly about the findings of their probit analysis that they suggested that "the legislation was not only ineffective, but also unnecessary" (740), which is probably an overstatement. In a study of 2,000 finance company borrowers, which the authors believed was representative of Texas borrowers in 1973, Elliehausen and Lawrence (1990) also failed to find evidence of racial discrimination. Basing their analysis on the Becker (1971) model and using the canonical correlation statistical technique, they found no relationship between race and credit terms.[36] Absence of racial discrimination before ECOA is also suggested by survey findings (discussed below) that find similar debt levels held by similarly situated blacks and others.

Even if researchers have not uncovered much evidence of systematic discrimination, though, this does not prove that discrimination does not exist. For this reason, analysts have also used survey methods to study consumers' perceptions of discrimination. Although, of course, perceptions of discriminatory treatment cannot be regarded as proof that discrimination exists, perceptions may reflect consumers' experiences and provide some information about the market and the extent of the problem.

To provide benchmark information on perceptions, a number of questions on credit discrimination were asked as part of the federal banking agencies' 1977 national consumer credit survey (see Durkin and Elliehausen 1978). In the survey, respondents were first asked whether they felt that they had ever been treated unfairly in credit transactions. Approximately 24 percent of the respondents had some experiences that they regarded as unfair; however, fewer than 5 percent of respondents reported problems related to sex, marital status, age, or race. These responses may reflect consumers' belief that personal characteristics are not very important factors in creditors' lending decisions. In another question, respondents were asked to indicate which factors they thought creditors considered most important in deciding to grant credit. Respondents viewed financial variables such as credit history (64 percent) and income (62 percent) as the most important credit criteria. Of the criteria governed by ECOA, age (9 percent) and marital status (6 percent) were most frequently mentioned, while sex and race (less than 2 percent) were among the factors mentioned least often. The pattern of responses did not change significantly when membership in protected classes was taken into account. Although protected groups mentioned protected variables more frequently than other consumers, only one factor (age) was reported by more than 10 percent of respondents of the group.

To study perceptions more closely, respondents to the 1977 survey who had experienced a credit denial or limitation in the previous five years were asked a number of direct questions about that experience. In all, about one-fifth of the respondents reported being either turned down or unable to obtain the desired amount of credit. Of these, when asked directly, 64 percent reported that they believed that age, race, nationality, sex, or marital status was *not* a factor in denial or limitation of credit. Of those who believed that one of these factors may have contributed to denial or limitation (36 percent of those turned down or limited), most mentioned age or marital status as the discriminatory reason they perceived. Only a few respondents mentioned sex or race.

36. Elliehausen and Lawrence did find possible differential treatment of widowed females, but they attributed the difference in credit terms to demand factors. They found no other apparent impact of sex or marital status.

In another study, Shay and Brandt (1979) examined both perceptions of discrimination and the relationship of perceptions to credit availability. Data for this study were from two consumer surveys, one conducted in 1977 and the other in 1970. The 1977 survey was based on three probability samples of 967 households across the United States.[37] The 1970 survey was based on two probability samples of 793 California households (see Day and Brandt 1973 for description).

With respect to perceptions of discrimination, 13 percent of the respondents to the 1977 survey reported perceiving discrimination. Age, sex, and marital status were the most frequent bases for discrimination reported, but 28 percent of responses were reasons not related to the ECOA. Not surprisingly, perceptions of discrimination were strongly associated with credit denials. One-third of the respondents who were denied credit in the last two years believed that discriminatory treatment may have been involved, while fewer than 5 percent of respondents who were not denied credit perceived discrimination.

Shay and Brandt used regression analysis to look at the relationship between measures of credit availability, perceptions of discrimination, and protected class membership while holding other borrower characteristics constant. They estimated two regression models, the first using an ordinally scaled variable reflecting perceived difficulty in obtaining credit as the dependent variable and the second using the level of nonmortgage debt as a dependent variable. Both models contained the same independent variables: a variable indicating whether the respondent perceived discriminatory treatment, variables indicating membership in protected groups, and other financial and life cycle characteristics of the respondent. Estimated regression equations showed that perceived greater difficulty in obtaining credit was associated with perceived discriminatory treatment, but perceptions of discrimination were not significantly related to lower levels of nonmortgage debt. Single males and minorities perceived significantly greater difficulty in obtaining credit, but these groups did not have significantly lower levels of nonmortgage debt. Of the groups protected by ECOA, only respondents age sixty-two and older had significantly lower levels of nonmortgage debt. However, discrimination is not necessarily involved, since this group also tends to demand less credit.

Similar procedures were used to analyze results of the 1970 survey, although the 1970 survey had not asked direct questions about discrimination. However, the methodology and a number of questions in the 1970 survey were similar to the 1977 survey. Regression analysis showed that female family heads, single males, and minorities perceived significantly greater difficulty in obtaining credit in 1970. Respondents age sixty-two or older had lower levels of total debt, but

---

37. Samples consisted of surveys of all households, unmarried women who are heads of households, and residents of disadvantaged areas in central cities. The latter two surveys were required to obtain a sufficient number of cases of individuals belonging to protected groups. Research by Kosobud and Morgan (1964) indicates that combining the subsamples does not seriously bias the results where the focus is on between-group differences.

minorities had significantly higher levels of total debt despite perceptions of greater difficulty in obtaining credit.[38]

In sum, the 1977 Consumer Credit Survey and Shay and Brandt's survey work suggest that most consumers did not believe that they had received discriminatory treatment in the credit market. When discrimination was perceived, marital status and age were the most frequently mentioned problems. Regression analysis indicated that perceptions of discrimination were related to perceptions of credit availability. But neither perceptions of discrimination nor those of protected group membership appeared to be associated with levels of nonmortgage debt. Of course, it might be possible that protected groups obtained comparable levels of debt at less favorable terms. Limited evidence from the 1970 survey analyzed by Shay and Brandt suggested that protected groups perceived greater difficulty in obtaining credit before the ECOA. However, despite these perceptions, most protected groups did not owe significantly less total debt at that time, either. In all, after considering these studies, which admittedly and purposefully ignore issues associated with housing discrimination by focusing on credit not related to housing, there is nonetheless still little available statistical evidence of systematic credit discrimination either before or after passage of ECOA in the area of consumer credit.

Effects of the ECOA on Consumer Credit

Discussion above could lead to the conclusion that ECOA has had ultimately little impact on consumer credit markets. If (protected) group information rarely provides creditors with detrimental information, then prohibiting its use should not change acceptance probabilities materially. And if available evidence is correct that credit discrimination has not been widespread, then ECOA should not affect things very much.

Unfortunately, another group of empirical studies suggest that conclusions about the impact of ECOA may not be so simple. As pointed out earlier, Spence's (1973 and 1974) information model suggested that group identification could be an important decision variable, even if it were unalterable and, by itself, it were uncorrelated with market performance. According to Spence's hypothesis, this anomalous result could come about if the relationship of alterable characteristics to market performance differed between distinct groups. Under these circumstances, prohibitions on considering group membership could have profound impacts by subordinating the signals generated by a minority to the stronger

---

38. In the regression model for total debt, the signs of the age (older than sixty-two) and sex (female) coefficients are reported negative in the text and positive in the table. Since older consumers tend to demand less credit, the negative age coefficient reported in the text is probably correct. If the negative sex coefficient reported in the text is also correct (significant only at the 10 percent level), then women had lower levels of debt. This result may indicate that lenders discriminated against women in granting credit in 1970.

signals characterizing the majority. A few empirical studies indicate that such an unintended result may have come about after ECOA.

For example, Chandler and Ewert (1976) estimated four multiple regression credit scoring models, which differed only in their treatment of sex. Model 1 was in full compliance with the ECOA and Regulation B. Model 2 contained the same applicant characteristics as model 1, plus a dummy variable to account for sex. Models 3 and 4 also contained the same applicant characteristics as model 1, but model 3 was estimated solely on the basis of female applicants and model 4 solely on the basis of male applicants. Each of the four credit scoring models was then used to classify a holdout sample consisting of one-third of the original sample.

Through their statistical work, Chandler and Ewert found that ECOA appeared to disadvantage rather than benefit female credit card applicants. Their models 2 and 3, which took sex into account, each accepted a larger proportion of women than model 1, which complied with ECOA. The difference was most striking for model 3, which accepted a considerably larger proportion of historically rejected female applicants than either model 1 or 2. This result suggests that risk profiles for male and female borrowers differ markedly and that separate models for evaluating male and female applicants may identify credit risk more precisely than a model that ignores applicants' sex or one that allows for only limited differences in male and female risk profiles.

Shinkel (1980) also studied the effect of limiting information in credit scoring models (this is the same database used by Avery 1982). With a sample of about 9,900 new applicants at a major finance company from 1968 through 1970, Shinkel developed eight discriminant models.[39] Seven models were constrained to exclude consideration of attributes prohibited by the ECOA or state statutes concerning discrimination, and one model was not constrained to exclude prohibited variables. Each model was used to classify applicants in a holdout sample. Results indicate that exclusion of prohibited variables reduced the number of good loans accepted in the various models (by 0.3 percent to 2.3 percent) and increased the number of bad loans accepted (by 0 to 2.6 percent), with a reduction in profitability of 2 to 16 percent.

Shay and Sexton (1979) examined credit applications from a national retailer and a large finance company made before the ECOA to determine whether information on sex, marital status, and age improved the accuracy of credit scoring models. Using discriminant analysis, they estimated two credit scoring models for each set of applications. The first model contained variables for sex, marital status, and age; the second model excluded these variables.[40] Unlike Chandler

---

39. Shinkel used a method called reclassification to account for rejected applicants. In reclassification, a credit scoring model developed for accepted good and bad accounts is used to classify rejected applicants. Chandler and Coffman (1979) concluded that reclassification and augmentation have about the same predictive ability to separate past good and past bad accounts but that augmentation accepts more rejected applicants. They cautioned, however, that these conclusions were based on analysis of one set of data.

40. Prohibited variables considered by Shinkel were race, marital status, and age.

and Ewert (1976) and Shinkel (1980), they found that classification of holdout samples revealed no significant differences in the predictive accuracy of the two models. Unfortunately, both Shay and Sexton data sets may suffer from selection bias, since they excluded rejected applicants from their analysis.

Nevin and Churchill (1979) attempted to determine whether marital status and age were useful in differentiating good accounts from bad accounts at two large finance companies. They found that consideration of marital status and age reduced classification errors 12 to 14 percent below those based on sample proportions but that marital status and age had a negligible impact on predictive accuracy in a discriminant model that included predictor variables such as discretionary income, occupation, and years on the job. However, again, both samples may be subject to selection bias, because rejected applicants were excluded.

In sum, Chandler and Ewert presented evidence suggesting that male and female bank credit card applicants possessed different characteristics (perhaps reflecting discrimination in other areas such as employment) and that their characteristics related differently to credit performance. Shinkel found that variables for marital status, age, and race increased the predictive accuracy of his credit scoring model for finance company applicants. In both of these studies, classification results suggest that inclusion of prohibited variables would increase the availability of credit to protected groups. Studies by Shay and Sexton and by Nevin and Churchill, on the other hand, concluded that consideration of sex, marital status, and age were not useful for distinguishing good credit risks from bad credit risks, although results may be influenced by sample bias. Regardless, it is still correct to say that there is no specific empirical study showing that ECOA has increased consumer credit availability for anyone.[41]

Conclusions on Consumer Credit

In conclusion, although they have merely touched the surface of the empirical questions raised by the Equal Credit Opportunity Act, available statistical studies do not offer any more grounds for optimism about the law's impacts than the theoretical ones. Clearly, more study on the six empirical questions derived from the theoretical work would be useful. However, pending more study, a few tentative conclusions have emerged.

First, there is little available evidence that membership in some now protected groups provides information about lack of creditworthiness, other things being equal. If anything, limited evidence about women and older consumers suggests the opposite. For this reason, it seems unlikely that rational creditors would arbitrarily exclude members of protected groups, although ones with a taste for discrimination might do so in markets slow to eliminate such behavior. Thus, ECOA would not have a substantial impact in changing acceptance probabilities unless

41. A group of studies does show that ECOA and Regulation B increased costs for financial institutions. See Smith (1977), Murphy (1980), and Elliehausen and Kurtz (1988).

tastes for discrimination are widespread and markets are slow to react. On their face, these do not seem like good assumptions.

Second, available studies (again, albeit old and limited) have failed to produce much evidence of systematic discrimination despite persistent complaints. The reason for the apparent inconsistency is that there is probably some truth on both sides: some creditors probably did discriminate, but the market as a whole probably did not. As a result, those persistent enough not to be discouraged may have always been able to obtain credit on terms reflecting their creditworthiness.

Third, equal credit opportunity legislation probably has done little to enhance credit opportunities overall. Although society has now given itself a club to use on creditors with tastes for discrimination, it has also, in effect, required each creditor's acceptance criteria to reflect characteristics of the firm's majority customers. Although Regulation B permits special credit programs for protected groups, there is little doubt that the law has complicated signaling of creditworthiness by minorities. Even if Chandler and Ewert and Shinkel were not correct that ECOA has absolutely decreased credit availability for protected groups, ECOA apparently has raised costs and made credit evaluation more bureaucratic. And, unfortunately, there is no evidence currently available that ECOA has actually improved credit availability for anyone.

Thus, rather than having profound impact on credit markets, the ECOA stands as a monument to principles. The principles, of course, are the ones dearest to all Americans: freedom, equality, and justice. Who would, or why would anyone, say that such principles are unimportant?

FAIR LENDING IMPACT OF CREDIT SCORING

One question that has been especially controversial over the years is whether credit scoring may actually have reduced credit availability to protected classes in some cases, despite score calculation without considering information on inclusion of the individual within a protected class (as required by Regulation B). The reasoning is that use of certain variables in credit scoring systems that on their face are not discriminatory may still have a discriminatory effect, because they are correlated with personal characteristics that under Regulation B are illegal to use as credit criteria.

This question has been discussed as long as the concept of ECOA (see Eisenbeis 1980, Sonntag 1995, and Dennis 1995), but in 2003, Congress requested a more substantial answer than theory or speculation. As part of the amendments to the Fair Credit Reporting Act (FCRA) that year, widely referred to as the FACT Act, Congress asked the Federal Reserve Board and the Federal Trade Commission to address a variety of questions about the relationship of credit scoring to equal credit opportunity and to the sale of insurance.[42] The Federal Reserve Board,

---

42. The Fair Credit Reporting Act amendments that year were called the Fair and Accurate Credit Transactions (FACT) Act. For discussion of the importance of the FACT Act to credit reporting, see chapter 6.

which had the rule-writing responsibility under the ECOA, answered the congressional request with an extensive research report in 2007 (see Board of Governors of the Federal Reserve System 2007).

Specifically, section 215 of the FACT Act asked the Board to investigate, among other things, "the extent to which the use of credit scores and credit-scoring models may affect the availability and affordability of credit to protected populations under the Equal Credit Opportunity Act (ECOA)." In approaching this and other specific questions asked by Congress, the Board undertook an expansive research effort that included a variety of aspects and approaches. Among other things, the Board staff acquired hundreds of thousands of extensive credit reports (without any identification of the individuals) from a credit reporting agency (credit bureau). The credit reports included credit scores for the individuals, but the researchers used these credit reports to construct their own scoring models. Unlike with standard credit reports that must comply with Regulation B, the research staff, with the help of the Social Security Administration and private firms, was able to enhance the credit reports by adding demographic information. This was done through an elaborate set of procedures designed so that no one ever had access to the credit information or demographic information together with the identity of any of the individuals in the credit reports. Two credit reports on each individual eighteen months apart allowed consideration of credit experience over the period along with credit characteristics and credit scores at the outset of the time interval.

Among other research approaches with this database, the staff could add and subtract variables to and from credit scoring models in ways that would not be legal if done by creditors for credit granting purposes. The research project probably went beyond what would have been necessary to satisfy the congressional request, and the report included for reference hundreds of pages of tables and charts.

Within the extensive report, the basic conclusions on the long-standing questions of the interaction of credit scoring and the ECOA are straightforward: from this research, it does not appear that information routinely included in multivariate scoring models used by creditors employs variables that are correlated with individual characteristics in ways that might make the variables unacceptable for use as credit characteristics under the ECOA or Regulation B.

In particular, the Federal Reserve report highlights a number of important conclusions from the multiyear research effort that are directly relevant to concerns over credit scoring and the ECOA:

1. The credit history scores evaluated here are predictive of credit risk for the population as a whole and for all major demographic groups.. . .
2. Results obtained with the model estimated especially for this study suggest that the credit characteristics included in credit history scoring models do not serve as substitutes, or proxies, for race, ethnicity, or sex.. . .
3. Different demographic groups have substantially different credit scores, on average. For example, on average, blacks and Hispanics

have lower credit scores than non Hispanic whites and Asians, and individuals younger than 30 have lower credit scores than older individuals.. . .

4. Evidence provided by commenters, previous research and the present analysis supports the conclusion that credit has become more available over the past quarter century. Credit scoring, as a cost- and time-saving technology that became a central element of credit underwriting during that period, likely has contributed to improved credit availability and affordability.. . . The increase in credit availability appears to hold for the population overall as well as for the major demographic groups, including different races and ethnicities. (Board of Governors of the Federal Reserve System 2007, S1–S2)

These basic findings would seem to answer the long-standing concerns that credit scoring might through statistical legerdemain produce a disparate outcome in credit granting to protected groups that ECOA would otherwise ban.

EVIDENCE FROM MORTGAGE CREDIT MARKETS

In recent years, the possibility of socially unacceptable discriminatory practices in mortgage credit markets has led to a substantial body of research work in this area. Part of this interest arises because mortgage credit often involves loans for house purchase, and the potential for housing discrimination through mortgage lending practices is another issue of public policy focus. In addition, researchers have been active in this area because as a result of concerns about housing and mortgage lending discrimination, collection of information on race of borrower is required under the Home Mortgage Disclosure Act (HMDA). This has led researchers to study the relationship of race and mortgage lending using a variety of empirical methodologies. It almost goes without saying that these studies have been controversial. Those who believe that inappropriate discrimination exists generally are not satisfied when a study does not find inappropriate discrimination. Conversely, those who do not believe that such discrimination exists or who believe that it is not widespread tend to be critical of incompleteness of studies that contend it does exist.

Extended discussion of controversies in the area of mortgage credit are beyond the scope of this book, for the most part, but it seems appropriate to end the discussion of unlawful discrimination in credit markets with a brief look at some of the methodological controversies that have arisen in mortgage studies and are in many ways at the heart of the arguments over policy.

Not surprisingly, availability of personal characteristics such as a racial indicator for mortgage credit has meant that these studies have been quite numerous. Methodological studies in the mortgage area have also investigated pitfalls in statistical testing for discrimination. Statistical difficulties can lead to false positives (finding discrimination when there really is none) or false negatives (finding no discrimination when it really exists).

For further discussion of these statistical issues, see papers by Yezer, Phillips, and Trost (1994); Phillips and Yezer (1996); Yezer (2010); and LaCour-Little 2001. The first three of these papers examine econometric difficulties arising from self-selection, omitted variables, and simultaneity in empirical tests of discrimination in mortgage markets. The authors argue that the single equation models of some authors who believed they found discrimination actually produced biased and inconsistent parameter estimates, which can lead to incorrect conclusions on borrower and lender behavior. In a related paper, LaCour-Little found that reduced form estimates of discrimination in mortgage lending may be biased by group membership differences in loan demand.

That simple models sometimes produce false positives can also be seen from analyses of fair lending bank examinations. Bank examiners use statistical models to identify discrepancies to investigate for possible discrimination. Calem and Longhofer (2000) and Dietrich and Johannsson (2005) examined discrepancies in lending outcomes that examiners investigated further. Examiners have access to entire loan files, and so false positives from faulty statistical methodology are not an issue at this stage. These studies found that there typically are legitimate reasons behind what statistically may look like a discrepancy. Zhang (2010) further found that sample selection bias and estimation are subject to omitted variables.[43]

Sometimes theoretical models can help identify possible discrimination. Berkovec et al. relied on market structure to identify possible discrimination. As discussed earlier, Alchian and Kessel's (1962) theory indicates that prejudicial discrimination could persist in an imperfectly competitive market (because monopoly profit can be taken in the form of taste for discrimination) but not in a competitive market. The theory helps identify potential areas to study for discrimination from effects of omitted variables associated with race.

Studies for labor markets are also useful here (see, e.g., Heckman 1998). Heckman assessed the audit pair method for detecting discrimination. He found that audit pair tests are sensitive to alternative assumptions about unobservable variables and the way in which markets work. Such tests can find discrimination when none exists or fail to find discrimination when it occurs. Heckman considered discrimination in the labor market, where the audit pair method has been authorized by the Equal Employment Opportunity Commission and is widely used. Heckman's analysis is relevant because the audit pair method has also been proposed for consumer lending. Notably, Heckman is a recipient of the Nobel Prize in economic science for his work in various areas of statistical methodology.

---

43. He also found statistical evidence of sample selection bias, suggesting an interaction between underwriting results and pricing differences among minority and nonminority borrowers.

10

Federal Regulation of Consumer Credit

Disclosures

As outlined briefly in chapter 9, the era of federal consumer protection in the credit area began in 1968 with signing of the Consumer Credit Protection Act (CCPA) by President Johnson on May 29. The most significant component of the original CCPA was Title I, the Truth in Lending Act, effective July 1, 1969. Even at the time of passage, it was easy to see that Truth in Lending was a watershed piece of legislation. Not only was it the first federal foray into consumer protection for credit users, but it also initiated a fundamentally new approach to financial consumer protection, now still growing and evolving after more than four decades: extensive required disclosures to consumers of transaction-specific information.

Before that time, consumer protection in the credit area had been state responsibility, and states had been interested primarily in establishing and enforcing credit price ceilings within their boundaries (usury laws) and in licensing the providers of credit and circumscribing certain practices considered objectionable (both discussed in chapter 11). Subsequently, information disclosure became one of the two main thrusts of federal consumer protection efforts for credit, joining with civil rights protection efforts of the kinds discussed in chapter 9. Over the decades, required disclosure has become the common element uniting virtually all federal financial consumer protection, not just credit regulation. Even when direct regulation of some practice has been the main thrust of some initiative (such as providing for equal credit opportunity or controlling credit reporting), disclosures have been an important aspect of the resulting legislation or regulation.

This chapter discusses the growth of federal disclosure requirements for credit, particularly Truth in Lending. Much of the growth over the decades is a result of specific congressional amendments to Truth in Lending and the implementing rules written by the Federal Reserve Board (Regulation Z). The actual mechanics of regulation in this area are now changing. In August 2011, the Consumer Financial Protection Bureau (CFPB), a federal agency with immense new powers in the financial consumer protection area, took over most of the responsibility in this area. Established under the Dodd-Frank Wall Street Reform and Consumer Protection Act of 2010, the new agency has devoted much of its time so far to organizational and transitional matters. The full scope of its future actions is unknown, but it seems likely that the importance of both disclosures and civil rights will remain.[1]

Over the years, information disclosures have been so central to the regulatory methodology in some areas of federal financial consumer protections that we might properly call the efforts "disclosure protections" or "information protections." Truth in Lending is probably the most notable example, but others include the Real Estate Settlement Procedures Act (RESPA, 1974), the Consumer Leasing Act (CLA, 1976), the Electronic Fund Transfer Act (EFTA, 1978), and the Truth in Savings Act (TISA, 1991). The main thrust of each of these laws is mandatory, designated disclosures. For consumer and mortgage credit, Truth in Lending has been a key federal consumer protection measure (along with the ECOA), and it governs almost all consumer transactions involving credit.[2]

This chapter explores the method of disclosure as a consumer protection and reviews experience with credit disclosures for this purpose, especially with Truth in Lending. The next section looks at some reasons disclosure has become a favorite means of protecting consumers and the range of disclosures that Truth in Lending actually requires. The following section then examines some reasons the list of disclosures has become so lengthy, and the section after that reviews evidence on the impact of this important disclosure law. A final section briefly looks at other areas of federal financial disclosure requirements, before suggesting some conclusions about disclosures as a consumer protection in the credit area. A companion book to this one reviews disclosure as a consumer protection in considerably more detail than possible here (Durkin and Elliehausen 2011).

1. Initial organizational matters for the CFPB through 2013 included hiring employees, taking over rule-writing responsibilities for Truth in Lending and other federal laws from other agencies, notably from the Federal Reserve Board, and preparing implementing rules, mostly in the mortgage credit area, required under the Dodd-Frank Act that established the CFPB (Public Law 111-203).

2. RESPA concerns only mortgage credit, and EFTA and TISA involve consumers' deposit accounts. Structurally, the CLA is part of Truth in Lending, even though some observers consider leasing a different sort of financial transaction from credit, since ownership of the leased item does not pass to the consumer absent a subsequent sale of the item to the consumer. Nonetheless, because consumer leasing of such movable items as automobiles is in many cases a substitute for purchasing them on credit, Congress has subjected consumer leasing to its own section of Truth in Lending known as CLA.

Even those federal financial consumer protection laws that are not primarily information protections contain significant disclosure provisions. Statutes such as the Fair Credit Reporting Act (FCRA, 1970), the Equal Credit Opportunity Act (ECOA, 1974), the Community Reinvestment Act (CRA, 1977), the Expedited Funds Availability Act (EFAA, 1987), and the sections of the Gramm-Leach-Bliley Act (1999) concerning consumer privacy largely entail direct regulation of the market behavior of institutions, but they also rely on information disclosures to advance their objectives.

FEDERAL FINANCIAL DISCLOSURE LAWS

As indicated, disclosure of transactional information has become central to federal financial consumer protection efforts. Specific required disclosures are not the only possible methods of government regulation, however, and disclosure is not even the only information enhancement method. Somewhat less specific information methods include efforts to influence and improve general information conditions in markets of interest, not just in some limited area where specific disclosures are mandatory. General efforts encompass such tactics as attempting to free the marketplace from any information flow impediments that might otherwise arise, so that information can flow more freely. Encouraging removal of constraints on advertising by professionals such as accountants and lawyers is an important example.

Somewhat more targeted approaches encompass direct efforts to enhance specific information availability, for example, by publishing comparative price information in the newspaper or on the Internet. Affirmatively suppressing information regarded as misleading or otherwise harmful, including attacking false advertising, is another active approach affecting general information availability and quality. Beyond general information approaches of this kind is, of course, the method so often chosen: transaction-specific disclosures.

Advantages of Disclosures

It seems that the importance of required disclosures in federal policy stems ultimately from at least four potential advantages over other methods of regulation. First, information protections often are compatible with existing market forces already at work to protect consumers. Financial services providers with good reputations and favorable pricing have an incentive to make these facts known, and required disclosures can provide for common standards and terminology, such as the finance charge and annual percentage rate (APR) under Truth in Lending. Mandatory standards can then enhance the power of existing market incentives to provide information, advancing consumers' learning process, lowering its cost, and making it more efficient. Under the circumstances, required disclosures in a standard format help highlight the performance of the best institutions and expose the inadequacies of the poorer ones.[3]

Second, if what consumers really lack is information in particular areas, then it seems logical that consumer protection should focus on providing what is missing, rather than engaging in some other protection method. If consumers need information about pricing or terms of consumer credit contracts, for example, then it seems more reasonable to require disclosure of the information than to

3. For discussion of the theoretical underpinnings of Truth in Lending and the other federal financial disclosure protections, see Durkin and Elliehausen (2011, chapters 2 and 3), which this section draws on.

regulate prices or contract terms. Providing information rather than directly intervening does not require that the government know, or presume to know, the product feature preferences of all consumers. With disclosures, consumers can decide for themselves what their own preferences are for the trade-off between price and product features, and success of the disclosure approach does not depend on consumers' preferences being the same.

Third, disclosures as federal consumer protections do not require preemption of, or even fundamental interference with, the basis of much state law: contract and property law. Disclosure laws have become a way of enhancing consumer protections without needing substantial revisions to contract laws in the fifty states. It seems probable that federal legal theories generating substantial need to rewrite state statutes would have engendered more questioning and potential for political opposition in a variety of areas.

Fourth, required disclosures may be relatively lower in cost, in terms of both market disruption and out-of-pocket government expenditures, than other approaches to consumer protection, although some observers may argue this point. Lower expected costs of this sort from disclosure schemes undoubtedly have been instrumental in encouraging their adoption as political compromises between those demanding greater consumer protection and those arguing that more substantive market interference is too wrenching and costly or too harmful to the benefits that arise from a market-based system.

Regardless of the reasons behind disclosure requirements (or the arguments and evidence supporting them), mandatory disclosure, as noted, has become the overarching financial consumer protection approach in the United States at the federal government level, along with civil rights provisions. In broad outline, federal statutes specify disclosures for credit prices and terms, real estate settlement, credit denials, credit reporting, consumer leasing, deposits, electronic fund transfers, securities purchases, privacy policies, and geographic lending patterns of financial institutions. In each area, the requirements are extensive and often complicated, sometimes involving multiple laws and rules. Taken together, the disclosure requirements involve hundreds of pages of detailed regulations.

Among the federal financial disclosure laws, undoubtedly the most significant for consumer credit is the Truth in Lending Act. Basically, Truth in Lending (TIL) covers all consumer credit (noncommercial or nonagricultural credit) in amounts of $50,000 or less (adjusted after December 31, 2011, for changes in the consumer price index for urban wage earners and clerical workers), plus other credit transactions of any size undertaken by consumers if secured by real property (mortgage credit).[4] Besides mandating the specific disclosures, the act and its regulation

---

4. Federal Reserve Regulation Z has been the implementing regulation for TIL since 1969, but in July 2011, authority over Regulation Z passed to the new Bureau of Financial Consumer Protection. Regulation Z, 226.1(c), defines coverage as follows:

  (1) In general, this regulation applies to each individual or business that offers or
       extends credit when four conditions are met:
       (i) The credit is offered or extended to consumers;
       (ii) The offering or extension of credit is done regularly [footnote omitted];

(known as Regulation Z, Consumer Protection 6500, formerly 12 CFR, Part 226) specify precise definitions and calculation methods to ensure uniformity. The act also contains some nondisclosure regulations of creditor behavior, sometimes called "behavioral" or "substantive" regulations, but disclosures have always been its main purpose. The main substantive provision in the original act involved the right of rescission on non–purchase money consumer credit secured by the consumer's principal dwelling. Since 1968, amendments to TIL have added many additional substantive requirements, particularly in the areas of credit card solicitations, credit card billing and practices, and credit secured by dwellings.

Truth in Lending Disclosure Requirements

Table 10.1 lists in outline form the main required Truth in Lending disclosures. This table hardly begins to indicate the complexities of the disclosure process, because it omits considerations of timing, formats, sequencing, groupings, and so on (see Regulation Z, 226.5, 226.17, and many other sections). The first section of the table lists requirements on closed-end consumer credit. As outlined in chapter 1, closed-end consumer credit arrangements typically involve one extension of credit and a fixed schedule of payments (consumer automobile credit, for example). The list of disclosures for closed-end credit is quite comprehensive, including written notification of amounts of credit extended, finance charges, and annual percentage rates (APRs), plus information on payment schedule, security interests, default events, and rescission rights for credit that establishes a security interest in a debtor's residence.

      (iii) The credit is subject to a finance charge or is payable by a written agreement in more than four installments; and

      (iv) The credit is primarily for personal, family, or household purposes.

(2) If a credit card is involved, however, certain provisions apply even if the credit is not subject to a finance charge, or is not payable by a written agreement in more than four installments, or if the credit card is to be used for business purposes.

(3) In addition, certain requirements of § 226.5b apply to persons who are not creditors but who provide applications for home-equity plans to consumers.

(4) Furthermore, certain requirements of § 226.57 apply to institutions of higher education.

The regulation also enumerates some exceptions or exemptions in section 226.3, each one defined there in more detail than given here: (a) business, commercial, agricultural, or organizational credit; (b) credit over the threshold amount ($25,000 before 2011, $50,000 after December 31 that year and adjusted by the consumer price index) for loans not secured by real property or a dwelling (many creditors tended to ignore the $25,000 exemption, which was instituted in an earlier time when price levels were much lower, because to avail themselves of this exemption typically would require two complete systems for much of consumer credit generation; the adjustment in 2011 may cause them to rethink this matter: the savings, if any, from not making TIL disclosures on some transactions often was not worth the trouble associated with having a second system); (c) public utility credit (such as electric and water company billing); (d) securities or commodities accounts; (e) home fuel budget plans; (f) certain (limited) student loan programs; and (g) employer sponsored retirement plans.

Table 10.1 DISCLOSURES REQUIRED BY THE TRUTH IN LENDING ACT

I. Closed-end consumer credit
(a) Identity of the creditor
(b) Amount financed
(c) Itemization of amount financed
(d) Finance charge
(e) Finance charge expressed as an annual percentage rate (APR)
(f) Total of payments
(g) Payment schedule
(h) Demand feature
(i) Total sales price (if applicable)
(j) Prepayment rebate or penalty (if applicable)
(k) Late payment fees (if applicable)
(l) Security interest charges (if applicable)
(m) Insurance and debt cancellation features
(n) Certain security interest charges
(o) Statement referring customer to contract concerning defaults, nonpayment, right of acceleration, and prepayment rebates and penalties
(p) Assumption policy (for purchase money mortgages)
(q) Required deposit (if applicable)
(r) Interest Rate and Payment Summary for mortgage transactions (if applicable)
(s) No guarantee to refinance statement for transactions secured by real property or a dwelling (if applicable)
(t) Statements about right of rescission when there is a security interest in debtor's residence and the credit is not for purchase of the property (if applicable)
(u) Variable rate features (if applicable)
II. Open-end consumer credit, including credit card accounts
(a) Finance charges
(b) Other charges
(c) Security interest (if applicable)
(d) Statement of billing rights and error resolution policy
(e) Home equity plan information (if applicable)
(f) Previous balance
(g) Identification of each credit transaction
(h) Credits to account
(i) Periodic rates
(j) Rate changes not because of index or formula
(k) Balance on which finance charge is computed

Table 10.1 (Continued)

(l) Amount of finance charge
(m) Annual percentage rate (APR)
(n) Closing date of billing cycle and new balance
(o) Due date and late payment costs
(p) Free ride periods without finance charge
(q) Address for notice of billing errors
(r) Minimum payment repayment and total cost estimate
(s) Supplemental credit devices and additional features with a different finance charge
(t) Change in terms and increased penalty rate summary
(u) Notice of fee to renew credit or charge card
(v) Change in credit card account insurance provider
(w) Increase in rates caused by delinquency or default or as a penalty
(x) Fees for issuance or availability
(y) Minimum interest or fixed finance charge
(z) Transaction charges
(aa) Name of the balance computation method
(bb) Statement that charges incurred by use of charge card are due when periodic statement is received
(cc) Cash advance fees
(dd) Late payment fees
(ee) Over the limit fees
(ff) Balance transfer fees
(gg) Returned payment fees
(hh) Required insurance, debt cancellation or debt suspension coverage
(ii) Available credit (if applicable)
(jj) Website reference
(kk) Statements about right of rescission when there is a security interest in debtor's residence and the credit is not for purchase of the property (if applicable)
(ll) Grace period
III. Closed-end consumer credit: certain residential home mortgage transactions, including transactions with variable rates
(a) Redisclosure required if the APR at the time of consummation varies from the APR disclosed earlier by more than $\frac{1}{8}$ of 1% in a regular transaction or more than $\frac{1}{4}$ of 1% in an irregular transaction
(b) Variable rate transactions (if APR may increase after consummation in a transaction secured by the consumer's principal dwelling with a term greater than one year):

Table 10.1 (Continued)

(1) Booklet titled *Consumer Handbook on Adjustable Rate Mortgages* or a suitable substitute
(2) The following loan program disclosures for each variable rate program in which consumer expresses interest:
i. Interest rate, payment, or term of loan may change
ii. Index used in making adjustments and source of information about this index
iii. Explanation of interest rate and payment determination and how index is adjusted
iv. Statement that consumer should ask about current margin value and interest rate
v. Interest rate will be discounted, and consumer should ask about amount of discount
vi. Frequency of interest rate and payment changes
vii. Rules relating to changes in index, interest rate, payment amount, and outstanding loan balance
viii. An example of a $10,000 loan illustrating the effect of interest rate changes
ix. Explanation of how consumer may calculate payments for the loan amount to be borrowed
x. Loan contains demand feature
xi. Type of information that will be provided in notices of adjustments and timing of such notices
xii. Statement that disclosure forms are available for creditor's other variable rate loan programs
(c) In an assumption, new disclosures must be made to consumer based on the remaining obligation
(d) Variable rate adjustments subject to (b) above:
(1) Current and prior interest rates and the index on which these are based
(2) Extent to which the creditor has forgone any increase in interest rate
(3) Contractual effects of the adjustment
(4) Payment required to fully amortize the loan at the new interest rate over the remainder of the term
IV. Open-end consumer credit secured by consumer's dwelling, in addition to the open-end credit requirements in section II above
(a) The length of the draw and repayment periods
(b) Explanation of determination of minimum payment
(c) Information about balloon payments (if applicable)
(d) Fees imposed by the creditor and by third parties
(e) Statement concerning negative amortization (if applicable)

(Continued)

Table 10.1 (Continued)

(f) Limitations on number of extensions or amount of credit
(g) Any minimum balance and minimum draw requirements
(h) An example based on a $10,000 outstanding balance and a recent APR, showing the minimum periodic payment, any balloon payment, and the time it would take to repay the $10,000 outstanding balance if the consumer made only those payments and obtained no additional extensions of credit
(i) Advice to consult a tax advisor regarding deductibility of interest
(j) Statement that the consumer should retain a copy of the disclosures
(k) Statement of the time by which the consumer must submit an application to obtain specific terms disclosed
(l) Statement that if a disclosed term changes prior to opening the account and therefore the consumer decides not to open the account, then the consumer may receive a refund of all fees paid in advance
(m) Statement that the security interest may result in loss of dwelling if default occurs
(n) Statement that the creditor may terminate the plan under certain circumstances and require payment of the outstanding balance in a full single payment and impose fees, prohibit additional credit extensions or reduce the credit limit, or implement certain other changes and that the consumer may receive information about the conditions under which such actions can occur
(o) Home equity brochure explaining the nature of home equity lines of credit including benefits and disadvantages
(p) Statement that the APR does not include costs other than interest and recent APR imposed under plan
(q) For variable rate plans:
(1) APR, payment, or term subject to change
(2) APR includes only interest costs
(3) Index used in making rate adjustments and source of information about the index
(4) Information about how the APR will be determined and how the index is adjusted
(5) Statement that consumer should ask about current index value, margin, discount or premium, and APR
(6) Statement that initial APR is not based on the same information as later rate adjustments and period of time such initial rate will be in effect
(7) Frequency of changes in APR
(8) Rules regarding changes in the index value and APR and resulting changes in the payment amount
(9) Statement of limitations on changes in the APR
(10) Statement of the maximum APR

(Continued)

Table 10.1 (Continued)

(11) Statement of minimum payment required and maximum APR for a $10,000 outstanding balance
(12) Statement of the earliest date or time the maximum rate may be imposed
(13) Historical example based on $10,000 extension of credit and past APRs
(14) Statement that periodic statements will include rate information
V. Home Ownership and Equity Protection Act of 1994 (HOEPA Requirements), in addition to other truth in lending requirements, for non-purchase money, closed-end loans secured by residential real estate with rates or fees above specified amounts
(a) Statement that the consumer need not complete the transaction even though the disclosures have been received and that consumer must meet loan obligations to avoid losing home
(b) APR
(c) Regular payment and balloon payment
(d) For variable rate plans, interest rate and monthly payment may increase
(e) For a mortgage refinancing, disclosure of the amount borrowed, which consists of the amount financed plus prepaid finance charges (if any), in early disclosures
VI. Reverse mortgages, in addition to other required disclosures on mortgages
(a) Statement that the consumer need not complete the transaction even though the disclosures have been received or has signed an application for a reverse mortgage loan
(b) Good-faith projection of the total cost of credit, expressed as a table of "total annual loan cost rates"
(c) Explanation of the "total annual loan cost rates" table
(d) Itemization of loan terms, charges, age of the youngest borrower, and appraised property value
VII. Consumer leases of personal property
(a) Description of leased property
(b) Total amount of any initial payments
(c) Payment schedule and total amount of periodic payments
(d) Itemized amounts of any other charges
(e) Total amount to be paid
(f) Payment calculation
(g) Early termination conditions, charges, and notice
(h) Identification and details of maintenance responsibilities
(i) Statement concerning option to purchase property
(j) Statement that lessee should consult lease for additional information

(Continued)

Table 10.1 (CONTINUED)

(k) Statement of and information concerning lessee's liability, if any, at end or termination of lease
(l) Statement concerning independent appraisal of value at end or termination of lease
(m) Description of liability at end of lease term based on residual value, if necessary
(n) Total fees and taxes
(o) Identification of any insurance
(p) Identification of any warranties
(q) Amount or method of determining any default or delinquency charges
(r) Description of security interest
(s) Rate information disclaimer

See Title I of the Consumer Credit Protection Act, starting at 15 USC 1601, and Federal Reserve Regulation Z, 12 CFR Part 226. For consumer leasing, see the Consumer Leasing provisions of the Truth in Lending Act and Federal Reserve Regulation M, 12 CFR Part 213. In July 2011, the Bureau of Financial Consumer Protection took over the responsibility for the Truth in Lending regulations, and the CFR citations may change slightly over time.

Open-end credit, such as typical credit card credit and check overdraft credit that permit multiple credit advances and variable payments, has its own set of disclosure requirements, found in the second section of the table. The open-end credit list is also lengthy, requiring disclosures of individual transactions under the open-end plan, outstanding balances, finance charges, fees, APRs, and error-resolution policies. An amendment in 1988 substantially expanded disclosure requirements for credit card applications and solicitations. Disclosures are now required in solicitations and at account opening and with periodic billing statements. Any change in terms generates special disclosure requirements. TIL has also always contained provisions governing advertising, but these mandates are not included in table 10.1 because advertising is not required.

Beyond these basic disclosures for closed-end and open-end credit, TIL also provides for extensive additional disclosures on credit associated with consumers' dwellings, especially concerning transactions with variable interest rates (third section of table 10.1). The variable rate provisions were added in 1988. Another important TIL amendment in 1988 also greatly expanded the number of required disclosures on open-end credit secured by a consumer's residence (fourth section of the table). This revision also requires disclosures when (or shortly after) a consumer receives an application, with additional disclosures at account opening. Thus, after November 7, 1989, when the revisions took effect, those who open an open-end credit account secured by a dwelling receive two sets of required TIL disclosures. The new requirements in this fourth part of the table include extensive details about the account plus examples and historical experience with interest rates on similar, hypothetical accounts.

The fifth section of table 10.1 contains the disclosure requirements that arose from an amendment to TIL in 1994 called the Home Ownership and Equity Protection Act (HOEPA). These provisions resulted from the view in Congress at that time that consumers who enter into "high-cost" mortgages need additional protections beyond the normal TIL mortgage disclosure requirements. Beside additional disclosures, the HOEPA mandated different timing rules and more precision for disclosures on mortgages judged to be high-cost.[5] The HOEPA also contained new provisions for "reverse mortgages," a product normally intended for older, retired consumers who prefer to stay in their homes after retirement. This product, typically packaged with an annuity, permits consumers to receive payments from a financial institution, usually monthly, with the payments added to a mortgage balance until the property is sold (or, in some cases, the consumer passes away). Because of the complexity of this product, Congress believed that additional disclosures were appropriate (sixth section of the table).

The final section of the table lists disclosures required for consumer leases, especially automobile leases. Disclosure requirements for leases are somewhat different from those for credit transactions, but Congress believed that leases should also be included within TIL requirements because leases often can serve as substitutes for purchases on credit, especially long-term automobile leasing arrangements. In 1976, the Federal Reserve Board separated the implementing rules for leasing from Regulation Z and gave consumer leasing its own regulation, Regulation M (12 CFR Part 213). In July 2011, authority over Regulation M passed to the federal Consumer Financial Protection Bureau, along with Regulation Z.

GROWTH OF TRUTH IN LENDING

Even a casual glance at table 10.1 shows that consumer credit (and leasing) requirements are much broader than only credit cost (the finance charge) and its percentage summary, the APR. The reason TIL requires so many other disclosures in addition to credit cost is likely based on two causes: (1) the difficulty of separating the totality of transactions into components so that the components can be disclosed separately and (2) uncertainty about the future. Since it is often difficult to separate parts of transactions or to predict the future completely accurately, TIL and Regulation Z have come to require consistency of disclosure for all aspects of information that might conceivably have an impact on a transaction's outcome, in other words, all information items that might conceivably be useful to someone, sometime. In conjunction with the diversity of consumer credit transactions and the penalties for violating the law or regulation, the guiding principle of full

5. Despite common identification of the HOEPA revisions to the Truth in Lending Act as the "high-cost mortgage" section, neither the HOEPA nor the implementing section of Regulation Z uses this term. For review of the nondisclosure provisions of this 1994 amendment to TIL affecting "high-cost" mortgages, see Ornstein (1996).

disclosure of everything undoubtedly has contributed substantially to the extent of TIL's requirements and to its operational complexity. And then the resulting complexity has generated calls for more disclosures to clarify the complexities. Proposals for layering of disclosures have been especially prevalent if there is any evidence or belief that some population segment does not fully understand some aspect of existing disclosures. The ensuing demand for summaries, explanations, and more details has produced a constantly expanding regulatory structure to help consumers try to understand.

This progression of disclosures leading to more disclosures is visible throughout the history of TIL but probably nowhere more obviously than in the example of credit cards. Disclosures for revolving credit, including credit cards, were not part of the earliest form of TIL, the draft Consumer Credit Labeling Bill in 1960, but after almost a decade of consideration in Congress, credit card related disclosures found their way into the original Truth in Lending Act passed in 1968. Apparently not satisfied with the outcome, two decades later, in 1988, Congress provided for summary disclosures of existing requirements in the Fair Credit and Charge Card Disclosure Act (Public Law 100-583, November 3, 1988). After almost another two decades of experience, the Federal Reserve Board in 2007 proposed further revamping and more summaries of the information previously provided, portions of it already in summary form. These rules were to become effective in 2010, but in 2009, Congress passed further amendments to TIL in this area, necessitating further adjustment in the rules in 2010 (Credit Card Accountability and Disclosure, or CARD, Act, Public Law 111-24). And so the beat goes on for credit cards, now in their fifth decade of disclosure evolution.

The Conceptual Stumbling Block: What Is a Credit Cost?

Since implementation of Truth in Lending in 1969, most credit disclosure questions and controversy have arisen not from the mathematical requirements for calculating the mandated disclosures but rather from a central conceptual matter: what cost items constitute the cost of credit, called the finance charge, and what parts of the cash flows are something else. Since isolating the finance charge is necessary for disclosing it properly and calculating the annual percentage rate correctly, this issue is a core concern for TIL. At first glance, the question might seem archaic more than four decades after passage of the act, but as credit markets evolve, it has remained remarkably unsettled. Ultimately, what constitutes the finance charge for required disclosures is the key operational question for TIL as a consumer protection, maybe the only really significant one. With a clear answer, disclosure of the other required measures, including the APR, becomes much simpler, even if not completely so because of accompanying uncertainty and wrangling over legal details in other areas, including mathematical methods and what else should be disclosed, how, and when. Each of these issues is discussed in greater detail in Durkin and Elliehausen (2011).

This central conceptual uncertainty manifests itself in three groupings of specific issues associated with finance charges and their interdependent APRs. First is the "outlay" issue (these are the authors' terms; they are not part of TIL proper). This is the problem that arises because not all outlays in conjunction with a credit transaction are credit costs, and this frequently generates confusion over which outlays constitute such costs and which are something else. For example, outlays in a credit transaction also can include down payments, expenditures for other products, repayments of principal due on a prior transaction, and other outlays for a variety of ancillary services and taxes. Under full disclosure, everything must be accounted for correctly, however, added and subtracted correctly, and disclosed as necessary in the right boxes and formats "clearly and conspicuously" (Regulation Z 226.5[a][1] and 226.17[1]).

Second is the "unknown future events" issue. It arises because both the amount of credit costs and the cash flows arising from credit arrangements always depend on future actions and typically are unknown at the outset of the transaction when initial disclosures are due. Consequently, there must always be some assumptions in order to make initial disclosures. But assumptions necessarily introduce an element of arbitrariness into any proceeding, and there often are good arguments for employing some other reasonable assumptions. This means there is potential for ambiguity and mistakes in determining proper finance charges and APRs, sometimes leading to arguments over policy and to legal disputes.

Third is the "compliance" issue, which concerns the effects and implications of compromises, deviations from rules, and special rules generated to help creditors comply. Over the years, the operation and evolution of credit markets, products, and the uses of credit products, together with the range of size, sophistication, and technical skills of creditors, have produced demand for simplifications, exceptions, shortcuts, and compliance aids. This demand has focused especially on the mathematical conception of the APR itself and has produced a host of special provisions.

At the heart of the controversy over each of these three groupings of concerns about the finance charge is an inherent conflict of basic objectives. On one side is the laudable search for exactitude, completeness, consistency, and comparability in a complicated area, despite complex and changing markets and an unknown future ("Truth" in Lending, after all). Against this is the difficulty for consumers to understand all the necessary concepts, along with the equally praiseworthy goal, at least to those regulated and to the political figures who make up the Congress, of reasonable compliance ease for regulated institutions, especially smaller and less sophisticated ones and larger ones with a wide range of products. As is so often the case in legislative matters, a clear solution that is acceptable to everyone is not instantly obvious.

The Extent Issue: How Much Disclosure Is Enough?

Ultimately, the conceptual difficulties caused by these issues have led to a good deal of the demand for extensive disclosures of calculating details, summaries, and explanations of cost and cost-related information, in addition to the basic finance charge and APR, that has become inherent in the TIL disclosure rules as they have developed. But the approach of working around the difficulties by disclosing extensive details and related information has produced problems of its own, which might be characterized as the "extent issue." Table 10.1 shows that the finance charge and the APR may be the key disclosures, but they are very far from being the only ones. What other disclosures might also be useful or necessary has been a subject of debate all the way back to the hearings in the 1960s before initial passage of the law.

To cite an example, in section I of table 10.1, it is easy enough to spot the key cost disclosures (finance charge and APR) in the first half-dozen lines. The table also shows that there are many other requirements, though, and some of them raise questions. For instance, it seems reasonable to require disclosure of the payment schedule, line I(g) in the table, but the total of payments is also required, line I(f). The total of payments is merely the periodic payment from the payment schedule multiplied by the number of payments, also part of the payment schedule. Likewise, the total of payments is also the sum of the amount financed and the finance charge. In effect, the disclosures include three ways of looking at the same information: once as components, once as the product of two components, and a third time as the sum of two others. While no one disputes that all three disclosures potentially provide information useful at times to certain recipients, the mathematical redundancy also naturally raises the question of what is gained and what is lost by requiring all the detail.

There also are other questions. For instance, although the amount financed is a required disclosure and is also necessary mathematically for solving the APR equation for closed-end credit, some observers have asked whether the concept is meaningful to consumers, especially if the credit finances certain prepaid finance charges or insurance premiums. A report by two federal agencies in 1998 raised the question of whether this disclosure should be replaced with something new called the "loan amount" (see Board of Governors of the Federal Reserve System and Department of Housing and Urban Development 1998). Then, should both loan amount and amount financed remain required disclosures? Would consumers understand the distinction?

Another ongoing question is how much of the contractual detail should be left in the contract and how much should become additional, separately required disclosures. What about name of the creditor, for example? The answer is mostly a legal issue but one subject to much TIL litigation in the past. Is this important to consumers other than where and to whom the payments are due? To cite another example, provisions for late charges might be important if a consumer defaults, but how many consumers shop for this term? All such concerns cloud the answer to the extent question.

The extent of requirements on open-end credit is at least equally problematic. As discussed earlier, even the key disclosures are lengthier for open-end credit. In addition to finance charges, there have been required disclosures for "other charges." There even has been more than one conception of the APR required in open-end disclosures (prospective and retrospective; see Durkin and Elliehausen 2011, chapter 6).

Much of the debate over TIL disclosures has involved whether all the required disclosures are really needed as required disclosures in addition to their presence as contract provisions; that is, what should be the proper extent of the disclosure requirements? Equally important but more forward-looking, are new disclosures sometimes needed, and if so, what and when? Does this mean that others should be eliminated?

To a large degree, the answer in all cases depends on the underlying goals of the disclosure program in the first place. If, for example, the intent of the disclosures is to provide information necessary for shopping, then maybe something useful at the point of sale would be more valuable than the current formidable TIL forms after the fact. In contrast, if the goal is a full record of underlying transactions for record, tax, and dispute resolution purposes, then maybe a fuller listing is appropriate. If it is both of these things at different times, then maybe different disclosures would be useful at different times, rather than the current compromise single approach now mandatory.

The issue of goals of TIL is discussed further in the next section of this chapter; suffice it to say here that the goals of disclosure programs have not always been as well articulated as one might hope. The result has been that the extent of the disclosures required has remained controversial and probably will continue that way until a firmer conception of goals emerges.

In sum, despite the obvious advantages of disclosure of credit costs in dollars and as a unit price, the experience of TIL illustrates the difficulties of trying to compress all the information that a consumer might need into key summary disclosures. Even apart from the extent question about what other disclosures are also useful enough to be required for everyone, it seems consumers are going to have to be at least somewhat knowledgeable about what the numbers they receive stand for and mean, if they are to be adequately informed. Both the issue of joint purchases (the outlay issue) and the assumptions necessary to make TIL manageable (the unknown future events issue) are significant. They illustrate the fundamental complexities of disclosing costs in a meaningful way when they depend either on difficult distinctions among categories of outlays or on unknown and unpredictable future behavior. Beyond this, the history of TIL involves a succession of compromises made for the sake of clarity, computational ease, and "simplification," especially from the time when computer systems were much less common than today. All of these problems make the finance charge and the associated APR as the unit price a bit less uniform and accurate than might be hoped for in some imaginary world where there are no complexities.

All of the compromises and difficulties taken together have not returned credit cost disclosures to the chaotic condition that existed before TIL, however, or taken away its basic thrust or intent. For this reason, it seems probable that despite residual ongoing difficulties that should have been expected and probably cannot be avoided completely, the Truth in Lending Act has had a favorable impact on consumer credit markets by improving information conditions overall. There are implementation difficulties to be sure, and many aspects of the program over the years are possibly unnecessarily costly, but it is still true that the act has developed for consumers a relatively consistent set of definitions for credit costs, albeit within the confines of assumptions necessary to make the disclosures workable. There certainly is improvement relative to the situation before mid-1969.

Furthermore, disclosures must be made available upon account opening (and sometimes periodically, depending on account type), and it is difficult for creditors to hide anything significant.

There still are legitimate questions about consistency and comparability of methods of finance charge and rate calculation, but under reasonable assumptions about account features and consumers' behavior, the information disclosed on charges and rates likely is helpful in many cases. Various consumers may well employ the information differently (or not at all), and the extent of other disclosures may or may not be useful, but information is certainly accessible. Consumers undoubtedly know that low APRs are better for them than high APRs, and both they and marketplace competitors can monitor market conditions if they desire. It seems likely that all of these things have the potential for a favorable market impact, but this is ultimately an empirical question.

Nonetheless, the ongoing search for resolution of the conflict among exactness, understanding, and reasonable compliance ease has produced decisions and compromises leading to multiple regulatory approaches in some areas, anomalies, various inconsistencies, and lots of disputes, along with mind-numbing complexity in the law (table 10.1), the regulation, and the commentary, which is itself the compilation of the set of annual official interpretations felt necessary. This complexity, in turn, has produced simultaneous criticism that the regulation is not exact enough to constitute "truth" but also that the current regulatory structure is unworkable to the point where compliance is impossible. With more than four decades of hindsight, it seems clear that before there ever would be any really substantive changes to the current structure (further dramatic simplification, for example), there would need to be a firmer decision on the fundamental question of exactitude, completeness, understanding, and consistency versus reasonable compliance ease. For many years, it has seemed as if there has existed enough of a political equilibrium on this question that the underlying fundamental approach of TIL has really not changed much at all since inception, despite all the ongoing discussion, tinkering, and sometimes bickering.

EVALUATING TRUTH IN LENDING AS A CONSUMER PROTECTION

To evaluate any consumer protection, the first concern is to identify a useful yardstick. Congressional intent is clear enough; the central goal of TIL is stated clearly in the act's Statement of Findings and Purpose (section 102). The research question is whether the act had its intended effect:

> The Congress finds that economic stabilization would be enhanced and the competition among the various financial institutions and other firms engaged in the extension of consumer credit would be strengthened by the informed use of credit. The informed use of credit results from an awareness of the cost thereof by consumers. It is the purpose of this title to assure a meaningful disclosure of credit terms so that the consumer will be able to

compare more readily the various credit terms available to him and avoid the uninformed use of credit.

But while enhanced competition through avoiding the "uninformed use of credit" is undoubtedly the act's central purpose and is certainly a goal consistent with market efficiency, stating this view in the act still does not offer a convenient evaluative criterion for the effects of the law. Filling this gap in the years before and since passage, observers of consumer-oriented financial markets have suggested many other, more specific goals for TIL. Examining the economic, legal, and behavioral science literature, in addition to congressional hearings and statements, reveals that observers have articulated a wide variety of objectives for TIL. It seems worthwhile to look at these goals more closely.[6]

The Goals of Truth in Lending

Some of the goals offered for TIL concern broad aspects of economic efficiency, but most involve knowledge and behavior of individuals. Congress itself apparently believed that TIL would influence competition and individual consumer behavior directly (see discussion in Landers and Rohner 1979). Other TIL objectives include regulating macroeconomic conditions and influencing general educational and philosophical aims. Some even involve totally extraneous matters, including controlling specific behaviors of financial institutions in the marketplace; the latter objectives mostly do not concern the usefulness of information per se.[7]

6. Taking a considerably more limited view of TIL's goals based only on the wording of the act itself about its purpose, Rubin (1991) contended that Truth in Lending was largely a failure. His discussion of success or failure of the act is so brief, however (it is limited to three paragraphs referring to a very few old research papers), that it amounts more to an assumption of failure for illustrative purposes than a real analysis of the act's effects. It seems his criterion was too strict, and he dismissed TIL too rapidly, but the purpose of his interesting paper was less to evaluate the success or failure of TIL than to use it as motivation for a case study on developing good legislative "methodology." He felt that good developmental methodology was absent in the TIL case (he argues this convincingly), and he calls for a better legislative approach.

In contrast, this chapter is a bit more optimistic, in that it allows more room for TIL to be successful. It does not hold TIL to a handful of goals specified only within the body of a single paragraph in the act titled "Purpose," although it acknowledges the importance of this congressional expression. Instead, it outlines goals for TIL suggested by a variety of sources in a range of contexts, measures them against the available (albeit meager) data, and tries to review what are essentially empirical questions, whether and where TIL has "worked." See Durkin and Elliehausen (2011, chapter 7) for expanded discussion of the goals of TIL.

7. Even some behavioral scientists have expressly argued that goals of disclosure necessarily must go beyond impact on individuals, because, in their view, it is so difficult either to understand or to evaluate the likely impact of disclosures on behavior: "The adoption of a new requirement is less likely to be influenced by arguments that the consumer will or will not use the information or make better purchase decisions because so little is known about these questions. The uncertainty about possible effects typically persists after the policy has been implemented, in part

Table 10.2 lists thirty-eight objectives for TIL that various analysts and interested parties have advanced at one time or another in eight separate categories. There probably are additional goals that might be added to the list. By itself, the length of the table shows the difficulties of fully evaluating TIL and other information protections to the satisfaction of everyone. Nonetheless, with this lengthy listing of possible goals for the legislation in mind, it is possible to articulate a few general principles or guideposts for evaluating TIL.

The first has already been stated: because there are many objectives of TIL, evaluating the law on the basis of a single objective is not going to be sufficient to satisfy everybody.[8] For example, improvement in the functioning or efficiency of credit markets (category I in the table), which economic theory and the economics of consumer protection suggest should be the central objective of TIL and other information protections, directly involves only one of the eight general categories of goals. Clearly, some observers will focus on the other objectives.

Table 10.2 provides many candidates. Categories II, III, and IV in the table involve buyer behavior goals, including consumer knowledge, attitudes, behavior, and decision making. These goals are easier to understand than overall condition of the marketplace, and they are important to many observers for that reason alone. Individual goals among them are very important to some observers. (For further discussion of buyer behavior theory, see chapter 4 above and Durkin and Elliehausen 2011, chapters 3 and 7).

Following the buyer behavior goals is a listing of general philosophical and education goals (category V). These objectives involve a long-term improvement in consumers' understanding and abilities, apart from and beyond any immediate impact on knowledge and behavior concerning a particular purchase. Following them is the goal of influencing the macroeconomy (category VI). This was an important aspect of the TIL hearings in the 1960s, although not mentioned frequently in more recent years.

The remaining groups of objectives in the table are the ones that go beyond information protections. Category VII concerns direct control of institutions themselves, to gain leverage for consumers, such as by providing legal defenses to creditors' collection actions. To a large extent, these objectives were minimized in the debate over passing TIL in the 1960s, but they have become more important since then. The final group (category VIII) memorializes some specific provisions of TIL that are not information protections. The goals in this grouping were fully intentional all along, but they do not involve information per se. These goals include delays or "cooling off" periods to be built into the processing of certain kinds of

---

because the impact of the policy is difficult to separate from other changes and influences in the marketplace" (Day and Brandt 1974, 21).

8. A published transcript of a panel discussion at a meeting of the Committee on Consumer Financial Services, American Bar Association Section of Business Law, offers a useful illustration. Each of the panel members appeared frustrated with TIL and seemed to contend that it was not working as well as possible, but each also seemed to base this contention on a different view of the purpose of TIL (see Golann et al. 1998).

Table 10.2 GOALS OF TRUTH IN LENDING

I. Credit market goals
1. Enhance competition in consumer credit markets
2. Improve understanding of differences among classes of institutions
3. Drive out high-cost producers
4. Encourage industry to reform
5. Improve credit market products
6. Discourage risk shifting by institutions
7. Discourage *in terrorem* boilerplate clauses in contracts
8. Provide vehicle for legal reforms
9. Protect legitimate businesses from unethical competition
II. Cognitive goals: awareness and understanding
10. Improve awareness of credit costs
11. Improve consumers' understanding of the relationships among credit cost terms
12. Improve awareness of noncost credit terms
13. Simplify information processing
III. Attitudinal goals
14. Improve consumer satisfaction
15. Improve consumer confidence
IV. Behavioral goals
16. Reduce credit search costs
17. Show consumers where search can be beneficial
18. Encourage credit shopping
19. Improve consumers' ability to make comparisons
20. Enable consumers to match products and needs
21. Enable consumers to decide between using credit and using liquid assets
22. Enable consumers to decide between using credit and delaying consumption
V. General philosophical and educational goals
23. Satisfy consumers' right to know
24. Enhance consumer education
25. Enhance consumers' general understanding of the credit Process
26. Promote long-term rise in consumer sophistication
27. Promote the informed use of credit
28. Promote wiser credit use
VI. Macroeconomic goal
29. Enhance economic stabilization

Table 10.2 (Continued)

VII. Institutional control goals
30. Promote control of institutions through compliance requirements
31. Improve consumers' bargaining position relative to institutions
32. Provide defenses for consumers
33. Provide leverage for hard-pressed debtors
VIII. "Behavioral" or "market protection" goals
34. Require procedures for credit card billing error resolution
35. Provide end-of-lease liability limits for consumer leasing
36. Provide "cooling off" period for credit secured by residence
37. Provide for limited liability on lost or stolen credit cards
38. Eliminate unsolicited credit cards

credit and a variety of requirements concerning issuance and billing of credit card credit.

With such a lengthy list of objectives, it becomes obvious that even if economic information theory provides the fundamental economic underpinning for information protections, this does not indicate that a favorable outcome in this area will necessarily satisfy all interested observers of TIL. Accordingly, TIL as a consumer protection must withstand examination from many viewpoints and, indeed, even evaluation according to a single perennially favorite goal such as credit shopping (goal 18 in table 10.2) is not going to satisfy everyone. Even apart from the general issue of whether specific behavioral goals such as credit shopping are important in themselves or whether they are simply a means to some other end (such as enhancing efficiency of markets), specific behavioral goals are only one of eight categories in table 10.2, and encouraging shopping is only one among thirty-eight suggested objectives.

As a corollary to this first evaluation guidepost, that not everyone is going to be happy with someone else's single criterion, if it is not sufficient to evaluate TIL on only one criterion, then it also seems questionable to recommend wholesale changes in the protection based on a single criterion. At a minimum, any proposed changes to the law should be examined in terms of the likely effects on a variety of goals. Again, the shopping criterion provides a useful example. It simply may not be reasonable to make wholesale changes in the regulatory structure to encourage one goal such as shopping unless it is clear that the market is inefficient or the changes simultaneously also encourage other goals, or the beneficial changes can be made at small cost. If the market is relatively efficient so that most consumers are receiving a price commensurate with risk, or if costs of change to the law are large relative to the benefit, or if the impacts of reforms on other goals are small, then there exists the possibility of achieving small or no gains in allocational efficiency from additional shopping of a few individuals at the expense of large losses of operational efficiency. This could produce a net loss for society as a whole. This is a serious risk with every episode of TIL tinkering; the larger the proposal, the greater the risk.

As a second guidepost, some goals do not suggest any directly measurable evaluative criteria and must be evaluated indirectly. The general philosophical and educational goals in category V of the table offer good examples. The six goals listed there (such as satisfying consumers' "right to know" and enhancing their general sophistication) are almost universally recognized as important aspects of TIL, but they largely appear too general for direct analysis and invite only indirect conclusions. In this context, it might be worth noting again that if two disclosure programs both appear designed to satisfy these general goals but one also appears likely to satisfy other goals or to satisfy the general goals at lower cost, then this method is preferable, other things being equal.

Third, while some goals do offer evaluative criteria, the measured effects may differ among individuals, making it difficult to draw general conclusions. Many of the goals associated directly with consumer decision making at the individual level in category IV illustrate this phenomenon. Goal 20, for example, improving ability to match products and needs, might be examined by studying choices made in the marketplace. But consumers' needs differ, and consequently, so will the choices made even under conditions of perfect information. Likewise, consumers faced with deciding between using credit and paying cash (goal 21) will not all reach the same conclusion. In a world of perfect information, some people will choose cash, and others will choose credit, depending on their individual circumstances (that is, depending on their own preferences, constraints, and resulting demand functions).[9] Consequently, a simple criterion related solely to likelihood of taking one behavioral path or another cannot be expected to produce useful analytical conclusions.

Fourth, some goals may be more costly than others to achieve and may become especially problematic if special attempts are made to reach them without sufficient regard to costs. Encouragement of credit shopping (goal 18) has already been mentioned, but there are other examples. These include, for instance, goal 12, improving consumers' understanding of the relationships among credit cost terms. Much of the complexity, litigation, and costliness of the original Truth in Lending Act and Regulation Z arose, in a large sense, out of attempts to satisfy this goal with extensive, detailed TIL disclosure statements. Possibly a better approach might have been to consider whether all the details were necessary to enhance market efficiency and the other thirty-seven goals or whether a simpler, less costly approach might have been sufficient. This question is an ongoing concern.

Survey Evidence on the Impact of Truth in Lending

Durkin and Elliehausen (2011, chapter 7) review available evidence on the effects of TIL on these goals, largely from consumer surveys that allow some comparisons over time. Although the time dimension means the evidence is always subject to

---

9. Juster and Shay (1964) evaluate the economics of this decision more fully. For extended discussion, see chapter 3 of this book.

potential methodological problems, particularly that alternative explanations of the changes over time may well be available (such as changes in the effectiveness of consumer education), it is still possible to discuss general findings concerning some of the goals in the table.[10]

Survey evidence on some of these questions is consistent with a favorable outcome from the disclosure law. One issue is the importance that consumers attach to the information disclosed. If required disclosures highlight or make more understandable the information most desired by consumers, then the regulations can lower information acquisition costs and encourage positive impacts on the marketplace. TIL mandates many disclosures, but foremost are cost disclosures.

Available evidence immediately suggests that consumers regard cost terms as the most important credit terms. This is clearly visible from the results of surveys that have explicitly asked consumers which credit terms they regard as most important. For example, in response to an open-ended question concerning credit terms they regarded as most important on automobile credit, 62 percent of consumers in a national survey in 1977 mentioned "interest rates" or "annual rates" first, and monthly payment size and size of finance charges followed in importance (see Durkin and Elliehausen 1978, table 4-3). These three terms were also the ones receiving the highest places in a follow-up, closed-end question asking specifically for rankings of importance of cost and other credit terms (Durkin and Elliehausen 1978, table 4-5). A smaller national survey in 1984 produced similar results for both questions. Again, 62 percent of consumers mentioned interest rates first, and rates, payments, and finance charges again were most important in the ranking question (1984 findings are unpublished Federal Reserve survey results available from the authors).

More recent survey results concerning important terms on credit card accounts are similar, in that consumers continue to report that they focus on cost terms as most important. In 2001, those both with and without credit card accounts were asked about information they would like to have if they were shopping for a new general-purpose, bank-type credit card account such as Visa or MasterCard. Although respondents offered a variety of answers concerning important credit terms, cost items again predominated, notably percentage rates and finance charges. About two-thirds of those both with and without bank-type credit cards indicated that interest rates or finance charges were the most important terms (see Durkin 2002, tables 2 and 3 and accompanying text).

Other survey results indicate that consumers believe that obtaining cost information is relatively easy and generally adequate (see Durkin and Elliehausen 2011, table 7.2 and related discussion). Beyond these attitude expressions, most consumers also report that they frequently peruse the disclosures made, at least on credit card accounts, which sometimes are controversial because they are so easy to use. A survey of card holders in early 2005 found that more than three-fifths of holders of general-purpose revolving cards such as Discover, MasterCard, or

---

10. For discussion of some of these methodological issues, see Phillips and Calder (1979 and 1980).

Visa reported that they examined the APR on their cards at least four to five times per year, defined in the study as "frequently" (see Durkin 2006, table 1). Not surprisingly, the frequency of examination of the APR on credit cards appears to vary directly with the use of cards as credit, rather than transactions, devices. The survey found that the likelihood that the holder reported examining the rate frequently rose as the outstanding balance on the card increased. Only about two-fifths of card holders with no balance outstanding reported that they examined their APRs frequently. In contrast, about four-fifths of those with a balance outstanding of $4,500 or more reported that they examined the APRs frequently. Consumers reported examining the descriptive material on the bill somewhat less frequently, but again, the likelihood of doing so rose with the balance outstanding on the card.

Concerning the particular behavior of credit shopping, available consumer surveys indicate that credit shopping by consumers was not universal either in the years immediately following implementation of TIL or more recently, but it does take place. For example, the nationwide survey in 1977 found that about one-quarter of those with outstanding closed-end credit accounts had tried to obtain information about other creditors or credit terms before obtaining the credit, the same proportion found in 1981. The proportion who tried to obtain information about this sort of credit arrangement was a bit higher in later surveys, reaching about a third of closed-end installment credit users in the 1990s (see Durkin and Elliehausen 2011, table 7.7).[11]

In each of the surveys, respondents were also asked open-ended follow-up questions about what they had done to obtain information about creditors or credit terms and the kind of information they wanted. A difficulty of this approach is that with repetitions of open-ended questions over time, there is always concern about consistency of coding of the responses, especially, as in this case, where the work was done over many years by many different coders. This means that there should not be much attention given to small differences or small changes over time, although overall, the broad pattern of responses should be indicative.

The notable thing about the pattern of responses to the questions about credit shopping is their general consistency over time. In all survey years, the most common action taken has been to shop institutions, including calling them (line 2 of the table). It is possible that frequency of shopping or contacting individual institutions may have fallen off a bit in the more recent years in favor of other actions (indicated by vaguer responses such as "calling around" or "checking around," but this may be more an artifact of the coding than a real trend. There also are more sources of information about credit today, including better-informed friends and

11. The findings reported are broadly consistent with those from other surveys. See, for example, Day and Brandt (1973), who reported on their 1970 California survey for the National Commission on Consumer Finance; Board of Governors of the Federal Reserve System (1987), which examined experiments concerning shoppers' guides for credit; and Chang and Hanna (1991), who used data from the 1983 Survey of Consumer Finances. Shay and Brandt (1979) used a different shopping criterion, but results from their survey were consistent, in that they found that shopping was fairly common but much less than universal.

advisers and, of course, the Internet. In any case, shopping for credit information seems reasonably common, and shopping individual institutions seems, by whatever means, to be the most frequent approach.

The finding of less than universal credit shopping is not especially surprising. Day and Brandt (1973) discussed how, for consumers in the process of purchasing durable goods such as automobiles and appliances, details of the credit contract involve only one component of the purchase and not necessarily the most important one to the consumer. There are decisions to make concerning amount to spend, features or model of the purchase, brand or make, store or dealer, cash or credit, and credit source. They found that most consumers ranked the product decisions in this list as more difficult to make than the credit decisions (see Day and Brandt 1973, table 3-12). This was especially true among consumers without sufficient cash to make the purchase without using credit. It does not seem surprising that the product decisions loom large, since the amount of expenditure on the product dominates the amount for credit in the typical purchase of durable goods. According to Day and Brandt:

> If the last three decisions in Table 3-12 [listed above] are defined as part of the overall credit decisions, for in many cases the store choice obviated the need to choose a credit source, we discover that even in this broad context the credit decision was considered as one of the *two* most difficult decisions by less than 25 percent of credit users in the study. The other three decisions, which might be labeled as product decisions, were considered far more difficult to make by more than three fourths of the respondents. (Day and Brandt 1973, 42; emphasis in original)

One significant market change in the years since the Day and Brandt study is the widespread use today of general-purpose or bank-type credit cards, but it is not clear that this change would alter their conclusions if the study were redone. It seems unlikely that today's consumer armed with a bank card (or a pocket full of them) would spend more effort analyzing the credit decision at a retail store. Instead, knowing that credit is already available, consumers might well spend relatively even more time today analyzing the product decision. For durable goods such as automobiles and boats, where credit cards are less useful, it is still not clear that product decisions have become easier relative to the credit decision.

When consumers do seek information about credit terms, percentage rates are the most commonly sought information (see Durkin and Elliehausen 2011, table 7.7). About three-quarters to four-fifths of those who indicated that they sought some information said they wanted "interest rates," "best rates," or something similar that showed that they were looking for percentage rates. Respondents also gave a variety of other answers, including fees and charges, payment sizes and maturities, and other credit information. There may be some indication from the responses that availability of credit is less of a concern among respondents in recent years than it was in the past, at least for closed-end financing.

More important than information sought is whether those who try to obtain information are generally successful. Consequently, respondents also were asked whether they were able to obtain the information they sought. In each year, approximately nine-tenths of those who inquired about creditors or credit terms were able to find the information. Although this outcome cannot be attributed solely to TIL, it is not clear that there is a groundswell of opinion asking for disclosure of more information in the years since passage of the law.

In 1993–1994 and 1997, interviewers asked the same questions of users of home equity credit, either in the form of home equity lines of credit or traditional second mortgage loans (for discussion of these surveys, see Canner, Durkin, and Luckett 1994 and 1998). Findings of the home equity surveys are generally similar to results from the other surveys (see Durkin and Elliehausen 2011, table 7.8). Notably, about two-fifths of home equity credit users indicated that they had searched for information about these credit products, with shopping other institutions being the most common action and interest rates being the typical piece of information sought. A couple of differences are also worth noting. It appears that searching for information about "fees" (probably closing costs) is more common for home equity credit, and there is evidence of relatively more use of media and printed sources. The latter may be true because there have been considerable amounts of print advertising of home equity credit plans in the past, along with more credit rate advertising generally in recent years when these surveys were undertaken. Again, more than 90 percent of those with either home equity loans or traditional second mortgages and who sought additional information indicated that they were able to obtain the information they looked for.

While certainly not conclusive, this finding of a measurable proportion of consumers shopping for credit cost information and a large portion of those individuals being able to obtain the information sought recalls the views of the National Commission on Consumer Finance that a portion of consumers shopping for credit would likely make the marketplace competitive: (National Commission on Consumer Finance 1972, p. 176)

> An individual creditor cannot know whether a consumer is "aware" or "unaware." If, as in the general market somewhere between one third and one half of the prospects are aware,[12] and if some portion shop for credit, a credit grantor is likely to offer each prospect a given package of credit terms for the same price. Most important, if the price is not competitive with similar packages offered by other creditors, the credit grantor faces the ever-present risk of losing the customer to a competitor. Indeed consumers' shopping is supplemented by comparison shopping of creditors. Credit grantors in the general market must comparison shop if they are to maintain competitive rates because of the threat that many potential customers aware of APRs and differences in rates may shop around for the best rate. (National Commission on Consumer Finance 1972, 176)

---

12. These were the proportions classified as "aware" in the NCCF's studies fifteen months after the effective date of TIL. The proportions classified as aware under the same definitions in 1977 were higher (see Durkin and Elliehausen 1978, chapter 2).

Not all consumers shop extensively for credit, of course, and the NCCF was careful to point out (twice) in the paragraph quoted above that its contentions applied only to the general market where consumers have shopping skills, not to the low-income market it discussed elsewhere. Lack of shopping skills certainly is one reason credit shopping is not universal, but there is more to the issue. The general reason is that shopping is costly; and, as both economists and other behavioral scientists have pointed out, the costs of shopping can easily outweigh the benefits. This is especially true for those generally aware of credit costs, for whom much additional credit shopping can be largely redundant. Regardless, it seems that those with higher education and income are the ones most likely to shop for credit. These individuals also are the customers likely to be of most interest to the credit grantors and the ones for whom competition is most fierce.

Lack of shopping does not necessarily indicate unreasonable or irrational behavior. On the contrary, failure to shop could indicate an awareness of credit costs on the part of the consumer and may reflect the view that further shopping is unwarranted. Consumers may be wrong in their judgments sometimes, but by itself, failure to shop for credit terms does not indicate a failure of TIL. Probably more important for TIL evaluation are the questions of whether the regulatory structure increases cost awareness and whether it permits effective shopping, if desired. The first of these questions has already been answered affirmatively, and the second answer also seems positive. By establishing a consistent unit price and standards of terminology, TIL permits consumers to shop for credit to whatever extent they feel is appropriate.

Although survey evidence indicates that relatively few credit users are influenced directly by disclosures in their decision to take on debt, some unanswered questions may be as important. These include the extent to which cash buyers are dissuaded from using debt by its cost and the extent to which consumers' attention and sensitivity to finance rates has changed over time. Regardless of answers to these questions, it seems that TIL has provided consumers with the necessary tools for whatever purpose they want to use them.

One additional line of questioning employed in surveys a number of times in the past decades stated that the "federal Truth in Lending Law requires that credit card companies provide consumers with written statements of credit costs when a new account is opened and as part of the monthly bill." Then the interviewer asked, "Is the Truth in Lending statement helpful in any way?"

Three-fifths of consumers with bank-type credit cards indicated in 2001 that the TIL statement was helpful, and almost three-tenths responded that it was not (see Durkin and Elliehausen 2011, table 7.9). Most of those who said it was helpful gave a generic reason that it provided information on interest rates or finance charges, and about 10 percent said it provided a good reference document if problems arose.

These results are similar to past findings about closed-end credit, although the favorable proportion is a bit higher and the unfavorable somewhat lower than earlier responses about TIL statements on various forms of closed-end credit in most past measurements. When asked in a follow-up question for their views on whether the TIL statement had affected their decision to use credit cards in any way, about 18 percent of card holding respondents indicated that the statement had affected their decisions, and 77 percent said it had not. About 5 percent said they did not know. Among the minority of consumers who reported that the TIL statement had affected their credit decision, about half said it helped in deciding whether to use a card and, if so, which card. A bit more than one-quarter of this group said it made them more cautious in using credit. The proportion of users of home equity credit who reported being specifically influenced by their TIL statement was even smaller (see Canner, Durkin, and Luckett 1998, 245).

Conclusions about Disclosures

In sum, a variety of pieces of information suggest that credit cost information is readily available to consumers, that TIL has had a positive impact on this outcome, and that competition in markets for mainstream consumer credit likely is enhanced as a result (competition is discussed further in chapter 11). Survey studies suggest that consumers regard cost information as the most important information about credit terms, they do not believe that credit information is difficult to obtain, they believe that creditors supply enough information for them to make good credit decisions, they examine APRs on credit card monthly statements, and they appear to supplement cost information with knowledge of differences among classes of institutions. Each of these indications is consistent with, although, of course, does not prove, existence of both a competitive market for consumer credit and a positive impact of TIL on market efficiency, at least in the market for mainstream credit products. But as the list of goals in table 10.2 suggests, there is also more to the story of TIL.

OTHER FINANCIAL CONSUMER PROTECTIONS

Truth in Lending is the first and undoubtedly the preeminent set of federal financial disclosure requirements for consumers, but after almost four decades of development of the genre, it is also certainly not the only one. In fact, as indicated above, Congress has included disclosure mandates in all of the federal financial consumer protection laws, but disclosure is so central to five of them that they are designated in the companion book to this one as financial "information protections" (Durkin and Elliehausen 2011). After TIL and listed in an order that roughly (but subjectively) ranks them according to the centrality of disclosure to their intended purposes, the other information protections are the Consumer Leasing Act (CLA, 1976), the Real Estate Settlement Procedures Act (RESPA, 1974), the Truth in Savings Act (TISA, 1991), and the Electronic Fund Transfer Act (EFTA, 1979). Two appendices in Durkin and Elliehausen (2011) discuss them and the other federal financial disclosure requirements in some detail. The first appendix discusses the lengthy list of financial disclosure requirements in federal consumer protection statutes, and the second evaluates the record of the other information protections listed above.

For the most part, these laws are not as well known to the public at large as TIL, and they generally have not posed TIL's compliance and litigation difficulties for regulated institutions. Among them, Consumer Leasing, Truth in Savings, and Electronic Fund Transfers have been relatively quiet areas of law and practice in recent years, with Real Estate Settlement Procedures somewhat less so. In 2002, the Department of Housing and Urban Development began a lengthy rule making to revise disclosures required under RESPA, but the effort became highly controversial and bogged down for some years before resurfacing again from 2008 to 2013. In late 2013 the Consumer Financial Protection Bureau released hundreds of pages of new regulations combining elements of TIL and RESPA. Because experience with these important statutes has been reviewed and discussed at some length in Durkin and Elliehausen (2011), they are not discussed again here.

11

State Regulation of Consumer Credit

Until passage of the federal Truth in Lending Act in 1968, the states were the primary regulators of consumer credit in the United States. When the federal government entered the field, its chief areas of interest were "fairness" in credit granting, as demonstrated by passage of the original Equal Credit Opportunity Act in 1974, and complete disclosure of costs to borrowers, as required by the Truth in Lending Act of 1968. Each of these areas of regulation has received its own chapter of discussion here, chapters 9 and 10, respectively.

In contrast, at the state level, the primary concerns historically were the cost (pricing) and characteristics of credit services. States acted to regulate credit costs through interest rate ceilings. Credit price ceiling laws were known as usury laws or usury ceilings. States also hoped to influence other significant characteristics of credit offerings in the marketplace by restricting market entry only to "legitimate" lenders through licensing and other requirements. States further provided for limits on credit terms involving creditors' rights in the case of default. The latter kinds of regulations have come to be known collectively as restrictions on creditors' "remedies."

State regulation of interest rates, in particular the establishment of usury ceilings for interest rates, has unquestionably exerted a tremendous influence on development of consumer credit institutions and markets in the United States. Restrictions on entry and creditors' remedies were always closely connected and justified in the same way as rate ceilings, as part of a regime of controlling price and character of credit service. The underlying rationale for the regulations included, first and foremost, attempting to protect unsophisticated borrowers from unneeded credit, uninformed use of credit, and harsh credit terms. They also were intended to redress unequal bargaining power arising from borrowers' urgent need or lenders' market power and to discourage prodigal spending and excessive indebtedness.[1]

---

1. See, for example, discussion in Bentham (2009 [1787]), Blitz and Long (1965), and National Commission of Consumer Finance (1972, 95). For centuries in the Western world, usury laws (either a complete prohibition on the charging of interest or prohibiting the charging of "unreasonable," "unfair," or "unconscionable" rates of interest) were justified primarily on

Chapter 5 discussed the fundamental economic theory of interest rate restrictions and their important result: rationing in the marketplace. Interest rate ceilings have no effect when ceilings are higher than market rates but lead to rationing when the ceilings are below market rates of interest. This chapter examines origins of interest rate regulation, the evolution of interest rate regulation over time at the state level in the United States, and specific outcomes that have occurred. It then looks at evidence on the effects of a closely related area of state regulation, restrictions on creditors' actions known as creditors' collection remedies. These are the actions that creditors sometimes undertake to recover their money when default or slow payment occurs.

INTEREST RATE CEILINGS

Before turning to the specifics of state regulation of interest rates, it is appropriate first to examine briefly the origins of interest rate regulation in antiquity and through later stages of history. There are few areas of government regulation with as long a period of gestation.

Origins of Interest Rate Ceilings

Government limits on interest rates and other terms of credit are ancient and ubiquitous although varying in impact by time and location.[2] Laws (political and religious) regulating interest charges on loans date back at least to the Babylonian Code of Hammurabi (1750 BC), which limited interest charges to 33.3 percent on loans of grain repayable in kind and 20 percent on loans of silver. Hammurabi's

moral grounds (see Gelpi and Julien-Labruyere 2000). While remnants of this moral thinking continue today, proponents of usury laws more recently have attempted instead to justify them on political or economic grounds. Among economists, however, regardless of their political views on other matters, interest rate ceilings have received almost uniform disapprobation. For instance, free market oriented economist Milton Friedman (1970, 79) wrote: "I know of no economist of any standing from that time [Bentham's time] to this who has favored a legal limit on the rate of interest that borrowers could pay or lenders receive—though there must have been some." Paul A. Samuelson (1969, 32), whose views were less free market oriented than Friedman's, observed: "The concern for the consumer and for the less affluent is well taken. But often it has been expressed in a form that has done the consumer more harm than good. For fifty years the Russell Sage Foundation and others have demonstrated that setting too low ceilings on small loan interest rates will result in drying up legitimate funds to the poor who need it most and will send them into the hands of illegal loan sharks."

2. Discussion here of the history of regulation of interest rates in the United States and elsewhere draws on many sources, including Homer and Sylla's (1996) classic on the history of interest rates from antiquity to modern times. For further historical discussion of consumer credit and its institutions in the United States, see especially Michelman (1966), Rogers (1974), Olney (1991), Calder (1999), and Gelpi and Julien-Labruyere (2000). Gelpi and Julien-Labruyere also provide an extended discussion of the rationales for interest rate regulation through longer history.

Code permitted pledging of one's wife, concubines, children, and slaves as collateral for loans but limited personal slavery for nonpayment of debt to three years (see Homer and Sylla 1996). Later, ancient Athens eliminated both interest rate ceilings and personal slavery for debt, while Rome limited interest rates to 8.3 percent but permitted personal slavery for debt repayment. As these ancient examples suggest, there was often an implicit or explicit relationship between the imposition of limits on interest rate charges and the use of collateral (including barbarous practices such as slavery) to reduce nonpayment risk and cost of collection upon default.

These legal caps on interest rates often had little practical effect, however. When the legal limit was higher than the prevailing market rate, the ceiling was irrelevant, but when market rates were higher than the legal rate, the legal rate was usually simply ignored. For instance, the limits set by Hammurabi's Code generally were higher than prevailing market rates at the time, but when market rates exceeded the legally permitted rates, they were ignored (see Ackerman 1981). Roman interest rates were also sometimes below the legal cap, but when interest rates rose, the limits were not enforced.

Old Testament restrictions on taking interest (Exodus 22:25, Leviticus 25:35–37, and Deuteronomy 23:19–20) and an interpretation of a New Testament exhortation to benevolence (Luke 6:34–35) led the medieval Christian church to condemn any loan repayment in excess of the original principal. This effectively prohibited payment of any interest at all. Later, the church condemned only the taking of excessive interest. Interest prohibited by the church was commonly called usury.[3]

During these times, lenders employed a variety of measures to circumvent these de jure restrictions on the lending of money for interest. For instance, medieval merchants avoided religious prohibitions on usury by writing a note (IOU) in one currency and promising repayment later in another currency at an inflated exchange rate. This practice concealed the de facto charging of interest in the exchange rate (see de Roover 1967 and Ackerman 1981).

While the medieval Christian church prohibited the paying of interest on loans, church leaders made an exception, beginning in the fifteenth century, permitting payment of interest to Jews so as to spur commerce (see Horack 1941). Moreover, the church permitted lenders to collect a fine if the principal sum was not returned at the time of maturity. This gave rise to the practice of stipulating a short nominal loan period after which the borrower became liable to pay both the principal and also a "penalty" amount that strongly resembled an interest rate (Horack 1941, 37). Lenders could also impose penalty charges for purportedly late payment, even where payment was not actually late (see Rockoff 2003 and Jones 2008).

3. The origin of the word *usury* is from the Middle English *usurie*, itself from the medieval Latin *usuria*, alteration of the Latin *usura*, from *usus*, past participle of *uti*, "to use." The first known use of *usury* was in the fourteenth century. For a concise discussion of the church's views, see the entry on usury in the *Catholic Encyclopedia* (Vermeersch 2011 [1912]).

Bankers such as the Medici family in Florence often received "gifts" from grateful borrowers. Contracts might also include the "sale" of an overpriced good in connection with the loan or the inclusion of some other bogus risk term to give the appearance of something other than interest. By the mid-fifteenth century, some countries approved charging low rates of interest for loans issued by "poor men's banks" (Jones 2008). Permitting these lenders arose as an anti-Semitic countermeasure against the legal Jewish lenders who were not bound by the church's rules.

In the Reformation period, Martin Luther and Philipp Melanchthon continued to reject the lending of money for interest. John Calvin and some Catholic writers eventually accepted the practice of charging some interest on loans (as opposed to what was deemed exorbitant interest). New thinking slowly led to a change in Christian moral views on the propriety of interest generally (see Nelson 1969).

During the Enlightenment period, influential thinkers attacked usury laws for their counterproductive economic and commercial consequences. John Locke (1691) addressed the practical questions of where to set the rate and how to manage the adverse consequence of contractions in the supply of available funds if the rate ceiling were low. He also argued that experienced and clever individuals would find a way to evade the law, and only unsophisticated individuals would be bound by the legal rate.

In the following century, Adam Smith (1994 [1776]) further criticized the effects of usury laws in interfering with the free flow of credit. Nonetheless, he supported continued imposition of usury laws on the peculiar grounds that the restrictions would encourage productive investment and discourage consumptive spending by reducing costs for productive borrowers while making mainstream credit unavailable to consumptive borrowers. According to Smith, if interest rates were allowed to be high, only reckless and profligate borrowers would borrow. Keeping interest rates low, by contrast, would encourage lenders to lend only to sober and responsible borrowers who would make productive use of the funds. These latter arguments in support of interest rate ceilings would persist in some form for many years and were discussed here in chapters 3 and 5.[4]

In 1787, Jeremy Bentham published a hugely influential criticism of usury regulations in his *Defense of Usury*, which included a critique of Smith's views (see Bentham 2009 [1787]). Bentham's critique incorporated arguments that usury laws (1) restrict mutually beneficial trades between individuals, (2) are often evaded in ways that increase costs, and (3) cause some borrowers to resort to illegal lenders, whose rates are higher than unfettered market rates as a result of the added risk premium of nonpayment occasioned by the usury laws themselves. Bentham also addressed Smith's concern about reckless and profligate borrowers, arguing that prodigals are able to borrow at market rates as long as they are able

---

4. Chapter 3 discussed Seligman's (1927) critique of distinctions between credit used for productive and for consumption purposes. The idea that only reckless and profligate borrowers (that is, high-risk borrowers) apply when interest rates are high is basically an argument of adverse selection, which Stiglitz and Weiss (1981) analyzed more fully later (see chapter 5).

to provide collateral and that successful projectors rather than sober businessmen are responsible for much of economic progress.[5]

These arguments were later amplified in the nineteenth century by British economist and philosopher John Stuart Mill, whose views eventually led Parliament to abolish the British usury laws in 1854 (see Horack 1941 and Rockoff 2003). Over the next thirteen years, usury laws were repealed throughout much of western Europe, including Belgium, Denmark, Geneva, Holland, the North German Confederation, Norway, Prussia, Sardinia, Saxony, Spain, and Sweden (see Horack 1941). Rockoff (2003) argued that the rapid European repeal movement may have been spurred by a concern over a loss of local capital toward Britain and the other countries that had repealed usury laws.

Evolution of Interest Rate Ceilings in the United States

Usury laws in Britain served as the model for the American colonies in the eighteenth century. The colonies (and later the fledgling states) adopted a usury ceiling of 6 percent as a carryover of the prevailing 5 percent ceiling in Britain at the time, with an extra percentage point added to help raise capital. For the next century, ceilings on loan interest rates were the rule throughout the states, although with wide variance in levels. The western states, where capital was in great demand and scarce supply, generally adopted higher rate ceilings and weaker penalties for violation of the law than the eastern states, where capital was more plentiful.[6] A lack of hard (coin) money in the west also necessitated a greater reliance on credit, making the inevitable shortages that accompanied interest rate and other lending restrictions more painful (see Mandell 1990).

INTEREST RATE CEILINGS BEFORE THE CIVIL WAR

Legal limits in the colonial period and the early republic sometimes exceeded prevailing market rates and thus were not binding. When binding, interest rate ceilings were commonly evaded. Benjamin Franklin reported that during the colonial era, interest rates routinely exceeded legal limits. Efforts to enforce usury regulations were also largely ineffective (see Ackerman 1981, 85).

Bentham's ideas on usury were influential in both the United States and England, and most leading American economic thinkers in the early republic followed him in condemning usury regulations (see Dorfman 1946 and Horwitz 1977). Usury regulations were heavily criticized at the time on the grounds that they restricted credit access for many legitimate borrowers while sometimes permitting unscrupulous borrowers to invoke the law strategically to escape contractual obligations for repayment (see, e.g., Bryant 1981 [1836] and Bodenhorn

5. Persky (2007) reports that Bentham sought to gain Smith's support for his position but that evidence on Smith's views on Bentham is contradictory.

6. See Boyes (1982) and Rockoff (2003). For analyses of effects of regional differences in usury ceilings, see Eichengreen (1984) and Snowden (1988).

2007). These views suggest widespread tolerance of lending above rate ceilings in the nineteenth century and corresponding efforts to relax interest rate ceilings.[7]

When market rates of interest rose so that usury limitations were actually binding, states often moved to raise or abolish the ceilings so that they no longer placed a constraint on the market (see Benmelech and Moskowitz 2010). Many states loosened or eliminated their usury regulations in the first half of the nineteenth century, sometimes beginning by repealing interest rate ceilings on loans to businesses that were thought not to need the protection of usury ceilings. States sometimes retained an official ceiling but softened the penalty for noncompliance. Many states also eliminated the traditional practice of imprisonment for debt during this period. By 1880, thirteen states had repealed their interest rate ceilings (Horack 1941).

Credit that we think of today as consumer credit was not especially common in the first half of the nineteenth century, but it was not unknown. Merchants provided a large share of consumer credit in the nineteenth century through installment sales of consumer durable goods.[8] The buyer in an installment sale makes payments to the merchant over a period of time rather than a lump sum at the time of the sale.

Under the "time price" legal doctrine, the courts exempted such arrangements from usury laws. The courts held that merchants may offer a good at different prices, a cash price and a time price. With this approach, even if the interest rate implied by the difference between the cash price and the time price exceeded the usury ceiling, this was irrelevant. The courts, somewhat implausibly, deemed such an arrangement as a sale of a good at a higher price for time payment but not a loan. In this view, usury laws were intended to regulate compensation for the use of borrowed *money*, not for time sales (Collins 1941, 58). The "time price doctrine" became very important later in the nineteenth century and in the twentieth century in the development of consumer credit associated with the sale of goods on the installment plan.[9]

---

7. In a study of borrowing by Massachusetts textile mills between 1840 and 1860, Davis (1960) found that rates of interest tended to cluster around the legal limit (6 percent discount). In periods of tight credit, however, the textile mills borrowed at above ceiling rates from noninstitutional lenders (which paid less attention to legal limits than banks) and out-of-state lenders (which were subject to less restrictive laws).

An analysis of loans made between 1845 and 1859 by a New York bank found that a large share of the loans had interest rates that exceeded the statutory interest rate ceiling (Bodenhorn 2007). That detailed records of usurious transactions even exist suggests that such transactions were widely tolerated. Access to credit was apparently more important to borrowers than short-term gains that might arise from taking legal actions to seek relief from usurious loans.

8. The introduction of the installment sale for consumer durables has been attributed to the New York furniture seller Copperthwait and Sons in 1807 (see Seligman 1927 and Nugent 1939).

9. The leading US case involving the time price doctrine is *Hogg v. Ruffner*, 66 US (1 Black) 115 (1861).

Another exception to usury restrictions involved "salary buying" agreements. Under salary buying agreements, the salary buyer purchased an employee's next paycheck in advance at a discount (paying, for example, $22.50 for the worker's next $25.00 paycheck). Courts held that usury ceilings did not affect the right to purchase the salary or wages of another (or to sell one's salary or wages to another) and the right to agree to a discount that exceeded the legislated ceiling on interest payments. Similar to the reasoning regarding the time price doctrine, the courts, again implausibly, considered the outright purchase of the worker's future salary not to be an extension of credit for the use of future money today and hence not to be a loan subject to usury law. It was simply a salary purchase, not a loan (see Collins 1941, 62).

CONSUMER CREDIT IN THE SECOND HALF OF THE NINETEENTH CENTURY

As discussed in chapter 3, growth in the middle class and greater availability and affordability of consumer durable goods stimulated demand for consumer credit in the decades following the Civil War. Merchants were the major source of credit for middle-class consumers at this time. Relatively conservative lending by financial institutions limited availability of consumer credit from them. Pawnbrokers, small loan companies, and peddlers provided credit to working-class consumers (see Calder 1999). Working-class consumers were typically families of unskilled blue-collar workers living in industrial cities. They often lived from paycheck to paycheck and often had unpredictable employment and income. Many were immigrants.

Pawnbrokers, who lent small amounts on collateral items deposited with them, were common in working-class neighborhoods. Calder (1999) reported that working-class families sometimes resorted to multiple pawnbroker loans, especially in the winter when factories typically closed down. Small loan companies lent small amounts secured by either future wages ("wage assignments") or furniture and other household goods. These companies openly operated in violation of usury laws or relied on subterfuges to avoid or evade usury laws. Small loan companies were probably the largest source of cash loans for working-class families at this time (Rogers 1974, Calder 1999).[10]

Peddlers arranged a line of credit with a wholesale or retail merchant to finance a stock of goods that they sold door-to-door on an installment basis. Peddlers tended to sell goods on lenient credit terms, collected weekly payments through visits to their customers, and relied on personal relationships to help collect debts. Peddlers were often immigrants who sold goods to others in their own immigrant communities (Calder 1999).[11]

---

10. The exemption for salary buying discussed earlier in this section was one of the methods used to avoid usury laws. Collins (1941) discussed the various methods used to avoid or evade usury laws.

11. A similar industry, the weekly collected credit industry, emerged in the United Kingdom in the late nineteenth century and still exists today. See Rowlingson (1994) and O'Connell and Reid (2005) for discussions.

These various lenders charged (implicitly or explicitly) interest rates that exceeded usury rate ceilings, often by considerable margins. Pawnbrokers generally were regulated, but merchants and peddlers invoked the time price doctrine and avoided rate regulation. Small loan companies in the nineteenth century operated largely outside the law, and their interest charges included compensation for bearing risks of social condemnation and legal prosecution. Small loan companies also sometimes resorted to embarrassing and aggressive collection practices to enforce repayment of these illegal debts.[12]

Consumer Credit Reform

High rates of interest, abusive collection practices in some cases, and a perception that small loan cash lenders preyed on the poor gave rise in the 1880s to calls for stricter laws and more vigorous reform. Most of the states that had earlier repealed usury laws reinstated them over the next two decades. Many states prohibited or restricted wage assignments and use of household goods as collateral.[13] Generally, these reform efforts were ineffective and counterproductive. Lenders often changed the details of the transaction to place it outside the purview of the revised law; and borrowers, unwilling to risk losing access to credit, were often reluctant to complain to enforcement authorities (see Horack 1941 and Rogers 1974).

The ineffectiveness of restrictive laws in curbing illegal lending gradually led to an acceptance of the view that laws should regulate but not prohibit cash loans, either explicitly or through restrictions that make small, relatively short-term unsecured loans economically infeasible. Around the turn of the century and especially after 1910, states began passing specific legislation to create a regulated lending industry. Early efforts typically were viewed as consumer protection.

Among the earliest initiatives was legislation authorizing semi-philanthropic lending institutions known as remedial loan societies. Remedial loan societies were established primarily to provide credit to working-class borrowers at lower rates than those charged by illegal small loan companies. The legislation authorized higher charges for remedial loan societies than allowed by restrictive "usury" laws, but they were still limited. Remedial loan societies were not wholly philanthropic, in that suppliers of funds risked loss of principal, which, unlike a charity, they wanted to be repaid. They also were not wholly commercial, because they were willing to accept a low return on investment, with earned surplus being

12. As indicated, small loan companies were generally one of two types. One type made loans secured by wage assignments. The second type took chattel mortgages on household goods. Both types of lenders were called loan sharks at the time, but not all small loan companies imposed exploitative terms or used abusive collection practices. That some small loan companies provided a useful, albeit relatively costly, product was recognized. See, for example, Clark (1931, 32–34).

13. See Gallert, Hilborn, and May (1932) for an extensive discussion of efforts to reform the small loan business. Michelman (1966) and Calder (1999) also provide good discussions of reform efforts.

returned to borrowers through lower interest rates. By 1909, fifteen remedial loan societies had been established in the United States (Rogers 1974).

The first law authorizing credit unions in was passed 1909. Credit unions were cooperative organizations whose members were individuals having a common bond, which often was place of employment. Sponsors and members believed that the common bond mitigated information and incentive problems affecting the risk of repayment, since all borrowers were members of the group (see Clark 1931). The legislation allowed credit unions to charge rates of 12 percent per annum, higher than most usury ceilings. The cooperative structure of credit unions provided them with cost advantages over for-profit lenders. Credit unions were also exempt from taxation and typically enjoyed another cost advantage: the receipt of subsidized personnel and facilities from sponsoring organizations. The approach underlying both remedial loan societies and credit unions involved higher, specialized interest rate ceilings than allowed by usury laws.

An alternative approach involved complying with usury ceilings but tying the loan to a repayment method that raised the lender's yield. The classic example here was the Morris Plan, named after Arthur J. Morris, who initially conceived the idea. Under the Morris Plan, lenders would offer a loan at the legal rate allowed under the usury law. Interest was quoted on a discount basis. Discount loans collected interest in advance out of the loan principal. This practice reduced the lender's outlay, thereby increasing the revenue relative to other methods for quoting interest (see Mors 1965). More important, the Morris Plan also required a simultaneous purchase on installments by the borrower of a non-interest-bearing certificate of deposit from the bank in the same amount as the loan principal. When the certificate was fully paid for, it would be used to pay off the loan (see Michelman 1966 and Oeltjen 1975). This arrangement increased the yield to the bank by bringing its funds back before actual maturity of the loan contract but without violating usury ceilings.[14]

Morris implemented his idea through a chain of lending institutions beginning in 1910. They were known as Morris Plan banks or "industrial" banks, because their customers were primarily industrial workers.

As industrial banks became established by Morris and others, many states passed industrial loan laws sanctioning the arrangement. The laws typically authorized the bank discount method of charging interest whereby the interest was deducted in advance and sometimes set rate ceilings for industrial banks above the usury ceilings.

The Russell Sage Foundation developed a fourth approach to reforming consumer lending. The foundation chose credit reform as a major focus if its activities, which it undertook through research, investigations, publicity campaigns, legal activities, and lobbying. From 1910 through 1948, the Russell Sage Foundation played a central role in efforts to reform consumer lending.

---

14. To reduce costs associated with the risk of repayment, Morris Plan loans typically required the signatures of two co-makers.

The foundation first supported remedial loan societies, but over time, it concluded that semi-philanthropic and cooperative lending institutions would never be able to attract sufficient capital to satisfy the demand for small loans. Recognizing the relatively high cost of making small loans compared with the size of the loan, the foundation believed that legal interest rates had to be high enough to allow lenders to earn a competitive return on invested capital. In conjunction with sufficient interest rates, the foundation believed that the loan terms should be transparent to the borrower and that lenders should be licensed and regulated (see Ham 1912).

Between 1910 and 1916, the foundation worked with legislatures in several states to enact legislation to establish a system of regulated small loan lending based on these beliefs. Lenders licensed to operate under new small loan laws also formed state associations to promote their interests, and in 1916, the state associations formed the American Association of Small Loan Brokers (AASLB). The AASLB cooperated with the Russell Sage Foundation in 1916 to develop a model small loan act known as the Uniform Small Loan Law. The model became the basis for future state legislation authorizing small cash loans for consumers. By 1932, twenty-five states had adopted a version of the Uniform Small Loan Law. By the 1960s, almost all states had done so.

State small loan laws based on the Uniform Small Loan Law and enacted during this period allowed for the emergence of a regulated consumer finance company industry. The laws authorized a fixed percentage finance charge per month for loans not exceeding a specified limit, required lenders to be licensed by the state, included provisions for supervision and enforcement of the laws, and required lenders to provide borrowers with a record of the transaction. Many states at first adopted the ceiling specified in the model uniform law: a finance charge of 3.5 percent per month on unpaid balances without fees or additional charges for loans up to $300.[15]

Licensed cash lending grew rapidly after development of the Uniform Small Loan Law but did not entirely eliminate illegal lending by unlicensed small loan companies in some places.[16] Some states enacted rate ceilings lower than the

---

15. In order to be effective, a small loan law must provide for an exception to the general usury ceiling over the range of loan sizes that the small loan regulation is intended to permit. The uniform law's choice of a 3.5 percent rate was made with this intent and based on the studies of cost and experience of remedial loan companies and other small loan lenders (see Clark 1931, 46–47; Robinson and Nugent 1935, 115–117; and Carruthers, Guinnane, and Lee 2009, 13).

The Russell Sage Foundation recognized that most lending costs are fixed, so that a 3.5 percent ceiling made a $100 loan less profitable than a $300 loan. The foundation's position on transparency of the transaction prevented it at first from supporting any particular remedy for this problem, however, such as allowing the lender to charge a higher-percentage finance charge for smaller loans or a fixed fee per loan (see Carruthers, Guinnae, and Lee 2009). Either of these changes would complicate the transaction. Graduated rate ceilings, which allow higher rates on smaller loans, later became a common feature in state small loan laws and are discussed further below. See chapter 5 above for a discussion of the costs of consumer lending.

16. Small loan companies taking chattel mortgages on household goods were more receptive to the 3.5 percent ceiling and licensing than companies making loans secured by wage assignments.

3.5 percent ceiling or later reduced ceilings to below that level. In these states, licensed lending became inhibited, and illegal lenders were not always completely displaced, or they regained their market presence (Clark 1931; Robinson and Nugent 1935; Hubachek 1941, 126; Nugent 1941, 12).

As experience with regulated small lending accumulated, the foundation revised its draft of the uniform law several times between 1916 and 1942 (see Neifeld 1961). A notable revision was the introduction of a graduated rate ceiling, 3.5 percent on the first $100 of the loan amount and 2.5 percent on the part in excess of $100, in the sixth draft of the uniform law in 1935 (see Robinson and Nugent 1935). This revision reduced lenders' incentive to make only larger loans, which with a single rate ceiling were more profitable than smaller loans.[17] Apparently, reducing this distortion in incentives outweighed the foundation's concern about transparency in finance charges through having a single fixed-rate ceiling. In subsequent years, graduated rates became a common feature of state small loan laws.

The first quarter of the twentieth century also saw emergence of sales finance companies to provide third-party financing for retail transactions such as automobiles and consumer durable goods. The stimulus for the emergence of the sales finance industry was not the enactment of legislation, since the sales finance companies could invoke the time price doctrine to avoid usury laws. Instead, the stimulus was the growth of the automobile industry, which created a demand for financing not only consumers' purchases but also auto dealers' inventory and working capital. The sales finance companies established by the automobile manufacturers contributed substantially to the growth of consumer credit in the early twentieth century.[18]

States eventually applied interest rate ceilings to sales finance companies and merchants beginning in 1935, in effect overturning the time price doctrine through legislation. Some sales finance legislation applied only to motor vehicles. Other sales finance legislation covered all types of personal property and sometimes services associated with the installation and repair of such property (see Robinson 1960).

This outcome probably came about because the larger size of loans made by chattel mortgage lenders ($10 to $300 compared with $5 to $50 for wage assignment lenders) made licensed lending more profitable for the chattel mortgage lenders (see Nugent 1941). Clark (1931) reported that about 90 percent of licensed lending was done on a chattel mortgage basis.

17. An example of lenders' preference for larger loan sizes is Household Finance Corporation's decision to reduce the finance charge to its customers from the ceiling rate of 3 or 3.5 percent to 2.5 percent in 1928 and to discontinue making loans of less than $100 because such loans were not profitable. See Clark (1931, 55).

18. Merchants also operating under the time price doctrine continued to be an important source of credit for smaller-ticket consumer purchases in the first half of the twentieth century. Olney (1991) reported statistics from the 1930s indicating that the majority of sales of household furniture, appliances, radios, cameras, and jewelry and substantial shares of rugs, hardware, sporting goods, and encyclopedias and other book sets were installment sales (see Olney 1991, 100–101, table 4.4).

Commercial banks slowly became interested in consumer lending beginning in the mid-1920s. Until that time, commercial banks were often discouraged by the high cost of making small loans and the social stigma attached to making consumption loans. Between 1924 and 1929, however, the volume of personal loans by banks grew from less than $1 million per year to more than $30 million. This amount was still substantially below the amount of lending by regulated small loan companies, industrial banks, and pawnbrokers at the time (see Foster 1941).

Commercial banks tended to offer consumers discount method loans, often with a repayment plan like that used by industrial banks. Although a precedent was provided by industrial loan laws, the legality of these methods for commercial bank loans was uncertain at the time. This uncertainty prompted most states eventually to enact personal loan laws exempting commercial bank consumer lending from usury laws and designating their own set of procedures for these institutions. Most of the bank personal loan laws specified ceilings as discount rates, sometimes at levels higher than general usury ceilings.

Commercial banks rapidly became the largest single supplier of consumer credit. By January 1950, commercial banks supplied about 39 percent of total consumer credit (see Board of Governors of the Federal Reserve System 1976). Sales finance companies were the second largest supplier of consumer credit (26 percent). Consumer finance companies provided only 8 percent of total consumer credit at that time, and credit unions and all other consumer lenders each provided 4 percent. Retail stores and dealers continued to play a significant role in financing consumers in the mid-twentieth century, financing 19 percent of total consumer credit.

The expansion of legal credit choices reduced the market for illegal loan sharks but did not eliminate it entirely. Caplovitz (1963, 105) wrote that a number of the families he studied admitted to having borrowed from an illegal loan shark. Seidl (1970), drawing on his doctoral dissertation, described the operation of the loan sharking market in the early part of the second half of the twentieth century.

EMERGENCE OF MODERN CONSUMER CREDIT MARKETS

Consumer credit reforms in the first half of the twentieth century created the institutional structure for modern consumer credit markets, excluding three-party credit cards which also depend on more modern data processing and communications. Interest rate ceilings have profoundly influenced the development of the institutions.

As indicated, by the mid-twentieth century, most states had adopted regulations for the different kinds of consumer credit, and the various regulations contained differential rate ceilings and loan size limits by institutional class of lender and loan type (see examples in table 11.1 for selected states in 1969, 1989, and 2012). In many cases, these differences segmented the markets. Banks, for instance, commonly had lower interest rate ceilings and higher loan size limits than small loan finance companies. This meant that small cash loans became almost the exclusive province of consumer finance companies. Maximum loan sizes assigned to finance companies prevented them from competing with banks for larger loans, and rate ceilings assigned to banks made smaller loan sizes

Table 11.1 EXAMPLES OF STATE RATE CEILINGS ON CONSUMER LOANS, SELECTED STATES, 1969, 1989, 2012

Mississippi	
1969	
Consumer finance companies	2% per month add-on for loans of $100 or more
Bank small consumer loans	8% per year add-on for loans up to $1,000
Bank installment loans	6% per year add-on
Bank revolving credit	No law
Auto sales finance	7% per year add-on for new cars (higher rates for used cars)
Nonauto sales finance	No law
Usury law	8% per year
1989	
Consumer finance companies	36% per year to $1,000, 33% to $1,800, 24% to $5,000, 14% to $25,000, or 18% on entire balance
Bank small consumer loans	12% per year add-on up to $5,000
Bank installment loans	7% per year add-on
Bank revolving credit	21% per year, 18% if annual fee assessed
Auto sales finance	18% per year for new cars (higher rates for used cars)
Nonauto sales finance	24% to $2,500, 21% on balance over $2,500
Usury law	10% per year to $25,000
2012	
Consumer finance companies	36% per year to $1,000, 33% to $2,500, 24% to $5,000, 14% to $25,000, or 18% on entire balance
Bank small consumer loans	12% per year add-on up to $5,000
Bank installment loans	7% per year add-on
Bank revolving credit	18% per year
Auto sales finance	18% per year for new cars (higher rates for used cars)
Nonauto sales finance	24% per year to $2,500, 21% on balances over $2,500
Usury law	10% per year
Nevada	
1969	
Consumer finance companies	9% per year add-on to $1,000, 8% to $2,500
Commercial banks	8% per year discount to $500, 7% on larger loans

Table 11.1 (Continued)

Nevada (continued)	
Revolving credit	1.8% per month
Closed-end sales finance	12% per year add-on
Usury law	
1989	
Consumer finance companies	No limit
Commercial banks	No limit
Revolving credit	No limit
Closed-end sales finance	No limit
Usury law	No limit
2012	
Consumer finance companies	No limit
Commercial banks	No limit
Revolving credit	No limit
Closed-end sales finance	No limit
Usury law	No limit
New York	
1969	
Consumer finance companies	2.5% per month to $100, 2% to $300, 0.75% to $800
Commercial banks	6% per year discount
Bank revolving credit	1% per month
Auto sales finance	7% per year add-on plus annual fee add-on for new cars (higher rates for used)
Nonauto sales finance	10% add-on to $500, 8% add-on for amounts greater than $500
Usury law	7.25% per year
1989	
Consumer finance companies	25% per year
Commercial banks	25% per year
Bank revolving credit	25% per year
Auto sales finance	25% per year
Nonauto sales finance	10% add on to $500, 8% add on for amounts greater than $500
Usury law	16% per year
2012	
Consumer finance companies	No limit

Table 11.1 (CONTINUED)

New York (Continued)	
Commercial banks	No limit
Bank revolving credit	No limit
Auto sales finance	No limit
Nonauto sales finance	No limit
Usury law	16% per year

Many states also had specialized rates for savings banks, savings and loan associations, and credit unions.

Add-on and discount rates are calculating rates and not APRs. Add-on rates were used by multiplying the rate times the original balance times the relevant number of months and years and adding on the interest to the principal balance. Discount calculations were similar, except the interest was subtracted in advance, giving the rate different mathematical properties. For discussion of add-on and discount rate calculations, see Mors (1965). Truth in Lending required that calculating rates be transposed into APRs defined in the act and regulation for disclosure to consumers.

SOURCES: Barrett and Ulrich (1969), Jones (1989), and Financial Publishing Company (2012).

unprofitable for them. The effects of differential rate ceilings are discussed further below.

In addition, the maximum allowable interest rates on sales credit offered by merchants to finance the purchase of goods differed from those for cash loans (from either banks or consumer finance companies). Credit unions and industrial banks had their own rate ceiling laws. Moreover, interest rate ceilings on open-end credit such as department store accounts were different from permitted rates on closed-end installment loans. Using New York State as an example, Johnson aptly described the situation in the late 1960s:

> The result of this ad hoc development of legislation is clearly demonstrated, for example, in New York, where there are separate statutes regulating installment loans by commercial banks, loans by industrial banks, banks' check-credit plans, revolving charge accounts, motor vehicle installment sales financing, installment financing of other goods and services, insurance premium financing, loans by consumer finance companies, and loans by credit unions. In these nine statutes there are 14 different ceilings on consumer finance charges. (Johnson 1968, 305)

Early in the 1970s, reports by the President's Commission on Financial Structure and Regulation (1971, also called the Hunt Commission after its chairman, Reed O. Hunt) and the National Commission on Consumer Finance (1972) recommended easing of interest rate ceilings and relaxation of regulations that restricted competition within and across institutional classes of lenders. Both federal commissions sought to promote competition as a way to reduce prices and increase availability of financial services, including consumer credit. By recommending elimination of diverse interest rate ceilings as a way of increasing market competition and thereby greater availability of credit at still reasonable prices, the two commissions laid the intellectual groundwork for the interest rate deregulation that followed.

In another reform proposal at around the same time, the National Conference of Commissioners on Uniform State Laws approved in 1968 a new model consumer credit law, the Uniform Consumer Credit Code (UCCC). It proposed a standardized and simplified set of consumer finance laws, including deregulation and partial relaxation of rate ceilings. The intent was to remove market segmentation by institutional class and improve market competitiveness overall by specifying a single regulatory regime for all institutions. The new model act also attempted to foster a more transparent market for consumer credit through disclosures.

But while the UCCC proposed a greatly simplified approach to the regulation of loan rates, it did not propose removing ceilings altogether. The controversial UCCC (and a revised version in 1974) was eventually adopted by only nine states; an additional two states passed consumer finance laws that were somewhat similar. Although widely discussed at the time, it is safe to say that the proposal did not have a great deal of legislative success. Even where it did pass, ceilings remained in place because of the traditional fear that free market competition could generate exploitation of consumers, especially poor and uneducated consumers (see discussion by Johnson 1968).

Nonetheless, as financial markets continued to evolve to cope with periods of rapid inflation and high market interest rates during the 1970s and early 1980s, it became clear that rate ceilings (on both loans and deposits) were severely restricting the supply of loans to consumers, especially home mortgage loans (see Vandenbrink 1982 and 1985). In 1980, the Depository Institutions Deregulation and Monetary Control Act (DIDMCA) effectively eliminated usury ceilings on first-mortgage loans made by federally insured lenders, including state regulations on points and fees (see Pridgen 2006, 660).[19] During the 1980s, many states on their own initiative either also raised or eliminated many rate ceilings on mortgage and consumer credit.

Perhaps of more significance in relaxing the influence of interest rate ceilings on consumer credit during these years was the rise of interstate competition resulting from Supreme Court decisions. Despite relaxation of many state interest rate ceilings on nonmortgage credit, many states still retained interest rate

19. States were given an opportunity to opt out if they did so by April 1, 1983. Fifteen states did so, although some later repealed their opt-out legislation.

In 1982, the Depository Institutions Act, better known as the Garn-St. Germain Act, further preempted state restrictions on "creative home financing" (i.e., mortgages with adjustable interest rates, balloon payments, etc.). For discussion, see Alperin and Chase 1986, Vol. 2, 165).

restrictions on consumer credit. In 1978, the US Supreme Court in *Marquette National Bank v. First of Omaha Service Corporation* (439 US 299, 1978) ruled that national banks could charge interest rates permitted by the lending bank's home state regardless of the rate permitted by the borrower's state of residence.

This important court ruling probably had its greatest impact on the issuance of credit cards. Most major credit card lenders moved operations (along with their white-collar jobs) to states that did not limit interest rates, such as South Dakota, which removed its rate ceiling in 1979, and Delaware, which followed in 1981. A rapid expansion of bank card offers to customers nationwide soon followed (see Erdevig 1988).

Subsequent Supreme Court decisions reaffirmed the *Marquette* decision, extended the applicability of home state regulation to other fees and charges (such as late and over the limit fees), and subsequent cases have extended the principles articulated in these decisions to other types of credit (see White 2000). After centuries of usury ceilings, the dismantling of rate ceilings that took place in the credit card industry within a few years after 1978 was startling in its rapidity (see DeMuth 1986).

Between 1979 and mid-1985, eighteen states relaxed their rate ceilings on revolving credit, and another sixteen states removed ceilings altogether. This was on top of required elimination of ceilings on mortgage credit mandated by the federal legislation. Credit card receivables at bank card issuers in states without rate ceilings increased in real terms (price level adjusted terms) by 135 percent between 1980 and 1985, compared with a 58.4 percent in states with restrictive ceilings. Credit card issuers in the low-ceiling states continued to offer credit cards with low interest rates (as permitted by state law), but they rejected many more card applicants, charged higher annual fees, offered lower credit limits, and provided fewer card holder benefits than issuers in the high- and no-ceiling states (see Evans and Schmalensee 1993, 59; and Sinkey and Nash 1993).[20]

ECONOMIC EFFECTS OF INTEREST RATE REGULATION

Chapter 5 examined the general economic theory of the impact of interest rate ceilings and the important result that ceilings cause credit rationing when ceilings are set below the level required by marketplace demand and supply. Blitz and Long (1965) provided further detailed theoretical analysis of the effects of interest rate regulation in markets that differ in borrower risk. They recognized that administrative costs of lending also differ across markets but focused on differences arising from risk. Their work shows how ceilings can affect lending to different risk groups differently.

---

20. Another consequence of the *Marquette* and related decisions was that the credit operations of many large retail stores and consumer finance companies were acquired by or otherwise became affiliated with national banks and their subsidiaries. These actions further reduced the coverage of state interest rate ceilings.

Their analysis showed that interest rate ceilings may affect the distribution of credit across risk classes of borrowers in ways that are difficult to predict. Some risk classes of borrowers may benefit, notably the lower-risk groups, and others may be harmed. They were concerned with questions of competition versus monopoly in the marketplace, and their theoretical findings led them to argue that usury laws are unlikely to be an effective remedy to any monopoly power of lenders. Because their theoretical work is important, it is discussed here in some detail, even if a bit technical.

For their analysis, Blitz and Long specified the loan interest rate as consisting of a base rate plus a premium for risk. In this environment, imposition of a rate ceiling can prevent riskier borrowers from obtaining credit at an interest rate below the ceiling, thereby reducing effective demand for credit overall. They explored implications for both competitive and monopolistic markets.

In a *competitive* market, the reduction in effective demand resulting from rationing riskier borrowers out of the market would reduce the base rate for lower-risk borrowers. Thus, lower-risk borrowers would face lower interest rates than they otherwise would; consequently, they would borrow more.

But in a *monopolistic* market, results are more complicated, and Blitz and Long found that the outcome is uncertain for the lower-risk borrowers, although cutbacks in credit availability for higher-risk individuals remain. Under the monopolistic condition, they showed that the effect of an interest rate ceiling depends on three things: the distribution of risks, borrowers' elasticity of demand, and the lender's marginal cost curve and elasticity of supply. For their analysis of the monopolistic case, they assumed three types of borrowers whose demand is identical but who differ in risk: riskless, low-risk, and high-risk borrowers.

They first analyzed the effect when (1) the rate ceiling does not change the base rate to riskless borrowers or total amount of loans but (2) the rate ceiling is set at a level that makes lending to low-risk borrowers more profitable than lending to high-risk borrowers. In this situation, high-risk borrowers are rationed out of the market, and low-risk borrowers borrow more at a lower interest rate than the rate they would borrow in the absence of rate regulation. This is like the competitive case. If total amount of loans is unchanged, the additional amount borrowed by the low-risk borrowers is equal to the amount that high-risk borrowers would have borrowed in the absence of the rate ceiling.

Blitz and Long then considered the case in which the rate ceiling causes a decrease in the base rate paid by the riskless borrower. Under this condition, the supply and demand equilibrium would occur at a lower risk-free rate and quantity of credit for risk-free borrowers, but they could still borrow all they wanted based on their demand curve. In contrast, low-risk but not riskless borrowers would not be able to borrow as much as they desired at the regulated price. High-risk individuals again would not be able to borrow at all. The total amount of credit in the market would be lower than in the absence of regulation. Altogether, the regulated outcome would reduce the profit of the monopolist, but the reduction in profit would come at the cost of a lower volume of lending, notably to high-risk borrowers and others who are low-risk but not riskless.

They also examined a third monopolistic case that produced an increase in the total amount of loans, depending on the distribution of riskiness of borrowers and the various elasticities of demand and supply. In this situation, high-risk borrowers whose unregulated rate is higher than the rate ceiling might be able to pay a lower rate under regulation, but they would be unable to borrow as much as they would like. Risk-free borrowers, whose unregulated rate was below the rate ceiling, would now be forced to pay more. In this case, the low-risk borrowers in the middle would be main beneficiaries of the regulation. They would be able to borrow more and pay a lower rate. Overall, with higher loan volume in the market and lower average interest rates, this outcome would be closer to a competitive outcome than to the unregulated monopolistic case, but the regulation would make some borrowers better off and others worse off.

Blitz and Long were skeptical that authorities possessed the analytical capabilities to assess the supply and demand conditions, price elasticities, and cost conditions in credit markets in order to set ceiling rates in a way that would reduce monopolistic power and produce competitive outcomes. They noted also that a lender's experience with customers provides information for assessing risk that may not be available to the authorities. Furthermore, they pointed out that in many situations, credit is provided in conjunction with the sale of goods, making evasion of rate ceilings relatively easy. And so interest rate ceilings may not be very effective for controlling such sources of market power, and they suggested that other means have more promise.

Early Evidence of Effects of Ceilings in Small Loan Laws

In their theoretical context, Blitz and Long demonstrated convincingly the complicated nature of the theory of setting appropriate rates to produce favored social outcomes outside of the market context. Various government attempts over the years have demonstrated the practical difficulties, especially if one of the goals involves providing for credit availability at reasonable rates to all risk classes of borrowers.

As suggested above, the Russell Sage Foundation collected data to support its advocacy of higher rate ceilings in order to expand legal and supervised consumer lending. State lending supervisors later required licensees to report statistics on small loan lending. Over the years, these data provided considerable information on the effects of the small loan laws.

The Russell Sage Foundation determined that the original 3.5 percent per month rate ceiling made larger secured loans profitable but was not sufficiently high to cover the cost and return on capital required for smaller unsecured loans. Robinson and Nugent (1935, 174) noted that the Russell Sage Foundation was aware that small salary purchase loans were largely unprofitable at the rate ceilings in the uniform law but made no effort to address the issue. There was evidence that unsecured lenders shifted capital from regulated states (i.e., states with small loan laws) to unregulated states. Unsecured lenders that remained in regulated states attempted to reduce costs through reduced lending service and consolidation of lending offices.

Rate ceiling reductions in several states provided direct evidence on the restrictive effects of rate ceilings (see Nugent 1933, Robinson and Nugent 1935). In 1929, four states—Maine, Missouri, West Virginia, and New Jersey—reduced their maximum rates. Maine reduced its maximum monthly rate slightly from 3.5 to 3 percent. The number of licensees declined from 47 in 1929 to 33 (30 percent) in 1933, but the change in volume of loans outstanding was similar to changes in states in which no rate reduction occurred. This suggests that the decline in number of offices was not a result solely of the difficult macroeconomic situation during these years but probably was an attempt to reduce costs and maintain lending profitability through larger offices.

More aggressively, Missouri reduced its maximum rate from 3.5 to 2.5 percent. The number of offices there declined 49 percent from 174 to 89 at the end of 1932. Growth in loan volume stopped abruptly. Lenders specializing in larger loans secured by household goods continued to increase their lending. Most other licensed lenders stopped making smaller loans or took steps to liquidate their businesses. Unlicensed lenders stepped in to provide smaller loans, which were no longer available from licensed lenders.

Even larger rate ceiling reductions in West Virginia and New Jersey had more serious consequences still. West Virginia reduced its maximum rate from 3.5 to 2 percent. The number of offices declined 65 percent, from 62 to 22 at the end of 1933. Loan volume decreased 75 percent between 1929 and 1932. New Jersey reduced its maximum rate from 3 to 1.5 percent. The number of offices in New Jersey decreased 81 percent, from 437 to 83 in 1932, and all but 19 of the 83 were liquidating. Loan volume declined 73 percent in the first year the rate reduction was effective.

In both West Virginia and New Jersey, the remaining licensed lenders offered only larger secured loans. As in Missouri, unlicensed lenders entered the markets to provide smaller loans at rates that were considerably higher than permitted rates before rate reductions. Ultimately, the consequences of these legislated rate ceiling reductions were deemed undesirable. The New Jersey legislature increased the maximum monthly rate ceiling to 2.5 percent in 1932, and the West Virginia legislature increased the maximum rate ceiling to 3.5 in 1933.

Rate Ceilings, Market Segmentation, and Competition

In addition to the obvious direct impacts on borrowers and lenders of these attempts to manipulate marketplace rates, the differential ceilings according to institutional class of lender found in many states had the more subtle effect of reducing marketplace competition. Fragmented markets for consumer credit and the reduced competition they entailed encouraged higher, less competitive prices in each fragment. For unsecured personal loans, rate ceilings for finance companies typically were higher than those for banks, particularly for small loan sizes. Rate ceilings for credit unions were usually closer to rate ceilings for banks, although most credit unions enjoyed cost advantages over the other institutions. As a result, banks tended to make larger, lower-cost loans per loan dollar, and credit unions and especially finance companies tended to make smaller, higher-cost loans.

As discussed earlier, separate rate ceilings also commonly existed for other types of loans. In many states, sales finance laws specified different maximum rates for new automobiles, used automobiles, and other consumer durable goods, sometimes encouraging specialized institutions for each.

By segmenting the consumer loan market, these differential laws dampened competition in each segment and tended to foster less competitive markets overall (see Shay 1968 and 1970). Rogers concluded in his study of consumer banking in New York that rates charged by different types of lenders there "closely followed" the statutory ceilings provided by state law for the different types of lenders and that there was significant market segmentation in the size of loans offered by different types of lending institutions (Rogers 1974, 33).

A simplified example using loan sizes prevalent in the past illustrates how the structure of rate ceilings promotes market segmentation by lender type (see table 11.2). In the example, finance companies face a rate ceiling of 36 percent on loan amounts up to $500 and 18 percent on incremental loan amounts from $501 to a maximum loan amount of $1,200. Commercial banks face a rate ceiling of 18 percent to $1,000 and 9 percent on incremental amounts greater than $1,000 with no loan size limit.

Recall from chapter 5 that most of the costs of extending credit do not vary with loan amount. Assume that the fixed cost of loans at finance companies and banks is the same ($100) and that costs varying with loan amount are higher at finance companies than banks (3 percent and 2 percent, respectively). Higher variable costs at finance companies may be attributed to their higher cost of funds because they obtain funds from money markets rather than deposits.

Assuming a one-year term to maturity and abstracting from credit risk, these conditions produce the revenue ceilings and cost rates shown in table 11.2. Looking at $100 increments, finance company cost exceeds the revenue ceiling for loan sizes up to $600. Smaller loans are unprofitable, as cost exceeds revenue. Finance companies can then lend profitably up to the maximum loan size of $1,200.

Although bank costs are lower, they exceed legal bank revenue ceilings up to loan size $1,600. In effect, finance companies have a monopoly on loans from sizes $700 to $1,200, and banks have a monopoly for loans greater than $1,600. No one makes the smallest loans or loans of sizes between $1,200 and $1,600. The smallest loans are unprofitable for everyone, and loans between $1200 and $1,600 are unprofitable for banks and illegal for finance companies. Banks and finance companies conceivably could compete for larger loan sizes, but loan size limits for finance companies prevent this.

This type of rate structure can allow finance companies to lend to higher-risk consumers at some loan sizes without competition from banks. Higher collection costs and loan losses associated with higher-risk borrowers would shift cost curves upward. In this example, finance companies' higher rate ceiling provides them with greater ability than banks to lend to higher-risk borrowers in some loan sizes. Thus, the regulatory structure tended to segment consumer credit markets according to both borrower risk and size of loans.

Table 11.2 RATE CEILINGS AND MARKET SEGMENTATION EXAMPLE

Loan Size	Finance Companies				Banks			
	APR	Lending Revenue	Lend-ing Cost	Profit	APR	Lending Revenue	Lend-ing Cost	Profit
100	36.00	20.55	103	(82.45)	18.00	10.02	102	(91.98)
200	36.00	41.11	106	(64.89)	18.00	20.03	104	(83.97)
300	36.00	61.66	109	(47.34)	18.00	30.05	106	(75.95)
400	36.00	82,22	112	(29.78)	18.00	40.06	108	(67.94)
500	36.00	102.77	115	(12.23)	18.00	50.08	110	(59.92)
600	33.06	112.79	118	(5.21)	18.00	60.10	112	(51.90)
700	30.95	122.80	121	1.80	18.00	70.11	114	(43.89)
800	29.35	132.82	124	8.82	18.00	80.13	116	(35.87)
900	28.11	142.83	127	15.83	18.00	90.14	118	(27.86)
1,000	27.11	152.85	130	22.85	18.00	100.16	120	(18.84)
1,100	26.29	162.87	133	29.87	17.19	105.10	122	(16.90)
1,200	25.61	172.88	136	36.88	16.52	110.04	124	(13.96)
1,300					15.94	114.96	126	(11.01)
1,400					15.45	119.93	128	(8.07)
1,500					15.03	124.87	130	(5.13)
1,600					14.65	129.81	132	(2.19)
1,700					14.32	134.75	134	0.75
1,800					14.03	139.69	136	3.69
1,900					13.77	144.64	138	6.64
2,000					13.53	149.58	140	9.58

APRs are in percent; all other columns are in dollars.
Finance company rate ceiling is 36% APR to $500 and 18% for incremental amounts greater than $500 with a loan size limit of $1,200.
Finance company lending costs are $100 plus 3% of the loan amount.
Bank rate ceiling is 18% APR to $1,000 and 9% for incremental amounts greater than $100.
Bank lending costs are $100 plus 2% of the loan amount.

The National Commission on Consumer Finance

In 1971–1972, the National Commission on Consumer Finance (NCCF), a federal government study commission authorized by the Consumer Credit Protection Act, verified important facts about consumer lending markets at the time:

(1) Market rates did not always rise to ceilings as broadly believed.
(2) Differential rate ceilings by institutional class segmented markets and reduced competition.
(3) The degree of competition influenced both rate and credit availability.
(4) Rate ceilings promoted credit rationing.

The NCCF conducted extensive analyses of effects of rate ceilings and market segmentation in the markets for different types of consumer credit (see National Commission on Consumer Finance 1972). Its final report relied on staff studies published in six additional volumes. The staff conducted theoretical and econometric analyses of the effects of interest rate ceilings, competition, and creditors' remedies in markets for personal, automobile, other consumer goods, and mobile home credit.

Significantly, the NCCF found that loan rates did not rise always to ceilings, which was surprising to some observers. At the time, there was widespread belief that rates on consumer loans always rose to the ceilings, and so ceilings were needed to keep rates reasonable. The NCCF's analyses showed that interest rates did not generally rise to rate ceilings, at least in the lower-risk portion of the segmented markets generally catered to by banks. In fact, in states with relatively high rate ceilings, the ceilings had little influence on either bank or finance company average rates. The NCCF found that the average actual annual percentage rate (14.8 percent) for personal loans from commercial banks in the five states with the highest rate ceilings was only a little more than half the average rate ceiling at the time in those states (25.6 percent). In contrast, the NCCF found that in low-rate-ceiling states, market rates at commercial banks approximated the ceilings.

The finding for rates on personal loans at finance companies was broadly similar. The NCCF learned that as finance companies lent to higher-risk borrowers, the greater part of finance company loans was at rates near the ceiling in most states. But in regression analyses, the NCCF found that the average rate ceiling explained 80 percent of the variation in average APR in the low-ceiling states but only 11 percent of the variation in APR in high-ceiling states (National Commission on Consumer Finance 1972, 130). And in some states, finance companies made considerable proportions of loans at rates much lower than ceiling rates. All of this suggested to the NCCF that a degree of competition existed in the various individual compartments of consumer lending, even though rate ceilings and loan size limits tended to segment markets and stifle competitive influences, especially across classes of institutions.

Second, the NCCF determined that in the unsecured personal loan market, where banks and finance companies faced different rate ceilings, they segmented lending on the basis of both risk and loan size. The NCCF found that the higher rate ceilings generally available to finance companies allowed them to lend to consumers with higher credit risk than banks. Interestingly, segmentation was not only a result of differential rate ceilings. Specifically, in states with high *bank* rate ceilings or no bank rate ceilings, average bank rates were still lower, in many cases considerably lower, than average finance company rates.

This finding supported the widespread belief that banks specialized in lower-risk segments of the market partly on their own initiative, even when they legally could charge rates that allowed them to lend profitably to higher-risk consumers. Much of this difference likely arose from differences in the lending cost structures and availability of lending information that characterized the two kinds of institutions at the time. Banks simply did not have, or want to have, the level of staffing or the expertise among the staff that they did have, to engage in the higher-risk kinds of lending undertaken by the finance companies during those years, even if it could have been profitable. Apparently, they did not want to increase their costs, potentially interfering with their main business of lower-risk lending, in order to enter the other market (see chapter 5 for discussion of lending costs at these institutions). This cost structure differential tended to supplement legal rate ceilings in segmenting lending markets according to risk and loan size.

Third, the NCCF found that the degree of competition influenced credit availability and pricing. The NCCF regarded this finding as significant because of its view that even if some evidence suggested banks preferred lower-risk, lower-rate loans because of their lending cost structure, rate ceilings still limited competition across institutional classes, although it was unable to test this specific hypothesis empirically as completely as it would have preferred. For unsecured personal loans, the number and dollar amount from both finance companies and banks were greater in less concentrated markets than in more concentrated markets. The NCCF also found that the interest rates for new automobile and other consumer goods loans were higher in states with higher bank or finance company concentration, other things being equal, than in states with lower lender concentration. Again, this suggested the importance of competition in the marketplace and argued for minimizing constraints on competition, such as unequal rate ceilings by institutional class.[21]

Fourth, evidence from the NCCF's technical studies further suggested that low rate ceilings produced credit rationing. The number and dollar amount of personal loans from finance companies per family were lower and rejection rates were higher in states with low rate ceilings than in states with high rate ceilings. The NCCF also found evidence suggesting that rate ceilings may have impaired credit availability at banks. The number and dollar amount of unsecured personal loans from banks were lower in low-ceiling states than in high-ceiling states, but direct data on rejection rates at banks were not available.[22]

---

21. The NCCF and its staff measured concentration by the market share of the four largest finance companies or banks. Higher concentration is commonly associated with less competitive market structures, which may allow sellers to raise price above competitive price and thereby cause a reduction in quantity demanded. Lenders can exercise market power by raising price above the competitive price or by limiting extensions of credit to reduce risk (quality rationing). In the latter case, noncompetitive profit is achieved by reducing costs arising from loan losses.

22. In a further econometric analysis of the NCCF data, staff member Douglas Greer (1973 and 1975) found a significant negative association between the mean rate ceiling and the rejection rate at finance companies in low-ceiling states. In contrast, he found no statistically significant relationship between mean rate ceilings and rejection rates in states with high rate ceilings. Greer's analysis showed that larger proportions of the upper tail of the risk distribution of potential borrowers would be excluded from the market as the rate ceiling declines. Thus, increases in the rejection rate signify increasing risk-based credit rationing by finance companies.

The NCCF additionally reported that in by far most of the states, rate ceilings for new automobile direct loans were sufficiently high that they did not restrict credit availability to a significant extent at the time. For the small percentage of states that had relatively low rate ceilings for these types of credit, the evidence indicated that the rate ceilings restricted availability of credit for higher-risk borrowers, as might be expected.

Evidence of Interinstitutional Competition

The NCCF's report did not focus in detail specifically on competition across institutional boundaries, but several staff studies did consider the possibility. A few earlier statistical studies of effects of rate ceilings on credit availability at finance companies had included variables to account for bank or credit union participation in the personal loan market, a question that individual NCCF staff members decided to study more deeply.

Fand and Forbes (1968), Shay (1970), and Adie (1973) all had found in earlier work that variables reflecting bank personal lending activity influenced the volume of consumer loans at finance companies. Sartoris (1972) detected no significant effect of bank lending on consumer lending at finance companies, but he found greater credit union lending was associated with significantly less personal lending at finance companies.

The NCCF staff investigated this question further. Using data collected by the NCCF, Shay (1973) and Smith (1973) found statistically significant effects for bank activity on personal lending at finance companies. Greer (1973 and 1974b), however, using the same NCCF data but a different measure of bank activity in the marketplace, did not find evidence suggesting that bank activity influenced the volume of personal loans at finance companies. It seems that differences in the specific variables used to measure competition from banks and the structure of the statistical models used to estimate the effects likely influenced to some degree the findings on the effect of bank lending activity on availability of consumer credit at finance companies. However, considering this evidence together, it is reasonable to conclude that the variegated rate ceilings tended to segment the personal loan market on the basis of risk but that the segmentation may not have been perfect. Finance companies lent to high-risk borrowers but competed with commercial banks for some lower-risk borrowers.

Because of interest at the time in the question of degree of interinstitutional competition (especially between banks and finance companies), researchers at the time also applied other methodologies to the question. A few studies examining

---

Analyzing financial statement data collected by the NCCF for 1968 to 1970 from 124 consumer finance companies, Benston (1977b) later found that loan loss rates were positively related to average ceiling rates, a result consistent with lenders' accepting more risks when rate ceilings are higher. Most of the companies operated in a single state. For the companies operating in more than one state, the rate ceiling variable Benston used was a weighted average of rate ceilings of the states in which the companies operated.

characteristics of borrowers using different types of lenders provided evidence supporting the hypothesis of at least a degree of interinstitutional competition.

Eisenbeis and Murphy (1974) examined the borrowing experiences of finance company customers in Maine after restrictive legislation caused their lender to reject their requests for new loans. All of these customers would have been granted credit otherwise.[23]

Of the customers who subsequently sought credit, 53 percent were unable to find credit elsewhere. The remaining 47 percent were able to obtain credit at banks, credit unions, or other finance companies or, in a few cases, from friends or relatives. Examining a set of variables commonly used in application credit scoring models at the time, Eisenbeis and Murphy found that borrowers who successfully borrowed elsewhere were more likely to have been seeking a loan to finance a car (and thus could post collateral) and did business with more financial institutions than unsuccessful borrowers. Other variables (including weekly income, number of previous loans, and years of continuous borrowing) did not help distinguish between successful and unsuccessful borrowers.

Boczar (1978) used a statistical approach similar to Eisenbeis and Murphy's to examine profiles of personal loan customers at banks and finance companies using data from a 1970 Federal Reserve survey of consumers. Also using borrower characteristics commonly employed in application credit scoring, he estimated a statistical model to predict the probability that the consumer borrowed from a bank.

Boczar found that the distributions of predicted probabilities for bank and finance company borrowers differed significantly in some important ways. Few actual bank borrowers had low predicted probabilities of being bank borrowers, and few finance company borrowers had high probabilities of being bank borrowers. But there was a midrange, too: more than half of finance company borrowers had predicted probabilities of being a bank borrower of greater than 50 percent.

It seems that these finance company borrowers had risk-related characteristics similar to those of some bank borrowers and that they might have been able to borrow from banks. (Some of them also probably had poor credit histories and would have been high-risk and not "bankable," but Boczar did not have information on previous credit experience.) The influence of bank activity on personal loan volume at finance companies may arise from this middle segment of the risk distribution of borrowers.[24]

23. In 1967, Maine passed a law that limited the interest rate to 8 percent on the portion of any loan for which the term to maturity exceeded thirty-six months. Finance companies responded either by eliminating loans with terms longer than thirty-six months or by winding down their operations in the state. Finance companies provided a list of customers whose loan requests were turned down because the company did not make loans past thirty-six months or was closing operations. Eisenbeis and Murphy surveyed these customers about their subsequent borrowing experiences.

24. Lenders themselves apparently perceived other institutional types as competitors, at least to a degree. Analyzing lender survey data from the late 1970s, Peterson and Kidwell (1979) found that managers of bank and nonbank lenders reported sensing substantial competition from

Several subsequent studies examined distributions of profiles of borrowers using methods similar to Boczar's. Johnson and Sullivan (1981) used a proprietary credit scoring model of a large commercial bank to compare distributions of respondents to the Federal Reserve's 1977 Consumer Credit Survey whose most recent loan was from a bank or finance company. Like Boczar, they found considerable overlap in bank and finance company distributions but with few bank borrowers at the highest risk levels and few finance company borrowers at the lowest levels.[25]

Sullivan (1984) used a credit scoring model to compare risk distributions of bank and finance company borrowers in two local markets: Lake Charles, Louisiana, and Waukegan/North Chicago, Illinois. These areas differed substantially in terms of rate ceilings and were chosen for this reason. In Illinois, where rate ceilings for banks were lower than rate ceilings for finance companies, the risk distributions were highly unequal. Finance company borrowers were nearly two times more likely to be in the riskier half of the risk distribution than bank borrowers. In contrast, in Louisiana, where banks and finance companies operated under the same rate ceiling, the risk distributions for bank and finance company borrowers were much closer to each other. The model classified quite a large percentage of finance company borrowers as low-risk.

Durkin and Elliehausen (2000) replicated Boczar's analysis for respondents to the 1983 Survey of Consumer Finances who used bank or finance companies for a nonauto, closed-end loan. Their results were quite similar to Boczar's. Distributions of predicted probability of bank borrowing for bank and finance company borrowers differed, but a considerable percentage of finance company borrowers had a predicted probability of being a bank borrower of greater than 50 percent.

Durkin and Elliehausen then estimated statistical models to predict the probability of bank borrowing by respondents to the 1998 Survey of Consumer Finances, after the substantial deregulation of interest rate ceilings that took place during the 1980s and 1990s. They found little difference in the bank and finance company distributions of borrowers among the 1998 respondents. This suggested that risk segmentation for nonauto, closed-end credit by type of lender had largely disappeared by the end of the twentieth century. Many states had raised or eliminated rate ceilings during these years, allowed banks to charge the same rates as finance companies, and removed restrictions on expansion by the various competitors.

Technological changes that reduced costs of storing and evaluating lending information also contributed to the development of comprehensive credit reporting during this time. This development reduced the information advantage that

---

different types of lenders, though not as intense as competition from lenders of their own type. Much of the sense of competition involved nonprice terms such as speed, convenience, and payment flexibility but also differences in pricing terms.

25. Survey responses suggest that the lower-risk finance company borrowers' choice of a finance company was not because they were unaware of the cost. By far most finance company customers reported that finance companies were the most expensive type of lender.

individual lenders previously had over potential competitors in lending to their current or former customers.

Evidence on Rates and Availability

Using a theoretical framework similar to that of Blitz and Long, Villegas (1982 and 1989) developed empirical tests for the effects of rate ceilings on interest rates and the quantity of credit to different risk classes of borrowers. For his empirical work in the 1989 paper, Villegas employed household level data for quantity of credit, including nonmortgage credit from financial institutions, retail stores, and individuals, from the 1983 Survey of Consumer Finances.

Results of statistical estimation indicated that rate ceilings had a negative effect on the overall quantity of credit. More specifically, low- and middle-income households in states with a rate ceiling owed less debt than households in states with no rate ceilings. High-income households in low-rate states did not owe significantly less than households in states without rate ceilings.

Villegas also closely examined the effect of rate ceilings on auto loan interest rates on automobile credit using data from two surveys, the 1972–1973 Consumer Expenditure Survey (Villegas 1982) and the 1983 Survey of Consumer Finances (Villegas 1989).[26] He found that rate ceilings did not reduce interest rates paid by borrowers for automobile credit or increase the volume of lending overall, but low rate ceilings resulted in lower lending to lower- and middle-income households. Some analysts have claimed that this outcome is actually beneficial to them, but this is arguable at best.[27] These households did not pay lower interest rates on the credit that they did obtain, at least for automobiles, and they did not obtain all the

26. His underlying economic model statistically adjusted for the censoring of the upper end of the distribution of the dependent variables because of rationing and the unwillingness to pay high rates. In these cases, volumes and interest rates are not observed, because loans are not extended. In such situations, ordinary regression methods produce biased estimates. For the truncated dependent variables, Villegas used statistical methods that produce consistent estimates that concentrate around the true parameter value as the sample size increases.

In both studies, estimated coefficients of ceiling variables for models estimated without the adjustment for truncation of high-risk loans were negative. These results occurred because only loans to low-risk households were observed in low-ceiling states. Rates for higher-risk households that were rationed out of the market were not observed in the data.

27. These analysts have suggested that rationing credit to high-risk borrowers is a benefit because they use less credit. Avio (1973) and Posner (1995), for example, argued that rate ceilings reduce high-risk borrowers' ability to borrow amounts of credit that they quite likely may have difficulty repaying. Thus, social costs from adverse events such as unemployment or unexpected medical expenses, which may lead to provision of public assistance, may be reduced. In a different vein, Wallace (1976) proposed that high-risk borrowers may underestimate the likelihood and cost of default. This underestimation causes them to make mistakes in evaluating the desirability of credit. Although behavioral economists have also suggested similar hypotheses (see chapter 4), there is little statistical evidence to support any of these views. They rely mainly on anecdotal historical evidence and are intended to rationalize historical practice (see Hynes and Posner 2002).

credit they may have needed for emergencies or to invest in durable goods with a high rate of return (see chapter 3). Higher-income households were unaffected by rate ceilings. Higher-income borrowers in low-rate states did not receive less credit, nor did they obtain auto credit at a lower price. Any benefit from diverting funds away from higher-risk borrowers in states with low rate ceilings accrues to consumers in less regulated states or to borrowers in capital markets.[28]

In sum, evidence developed over many years suggests several conclusions about the effects of interest rate ceilings in personal loan markets:

(1) State interest rate ceilings restricted credit availability when set at levels that are lower than market rates for higher-risk borrowers. When rate ceilings were set at higher levels, higher-risk borrowers were less likely to experience reductions in credit availability.

(2) Different rate ceilings for different institutional types of lenders tended to segment consumer credit markets, with lenders that had higher ceilings (finance companies) lending to higher-risk borrowers than institution types that had lower ceilings (banks). Such restrictions tended to reinforce banks' preference to specialize in the low-risk segment of the market.

(3) Despite market segmentation, the risk distributions of bank and finance company borrowers overlapped. That many finance company borrowers had risk characteristics similar to those of bank borrowers suggests that these finance company customers may have been able to obtain loans from banks, although this would have been uncertain without better information on previous repayment experience. That the volume of finance company lending was influenced by bank activity suggests that banks and finance companies competed over at least some of the range of the risk distribution of borrowers.

(4) Interest rates did not generally rise to ceiling rates, unless ceiling rates were relatively low. Average interest rates charged by banks in high-ceiling states were not much different from average rates in low-ceiling states, and interest rates for considerable shares of finance company loans in some states were below rate ceilings.

More generally, it appears that the effect of a usury ceiling on the overall volume of credit, distribution of loans across risk classes, and specific interest rates paid by borrowers in different risk classes depends on the factors that Blitz and Long (1965) demonstrated were important theoretically: distribution of borrower risk in the marketplace, borrowers' elasticity of demand, and the available supply of

---

28. These findings vindicate Blitz and Long's skepticism that rate ceilings are an effective remedy for curbing monopoly power of lenders. Historical data also do not support the view that rate ceilings reduce monopoly power of lenders. Benmelech and Moskovitz's (2010) study of nineteenth-century usury laws in the United States did not find lower usury ceilings to be associated with lower bank concentration, a measure commonly used to assess competition in markets (less concentrated is regarded as more competitive).

loanable funds. As a result, completely predicting the specific effects of a given rate ceiling is difficult in advance, as they showed theoretically, although general tendencies toward credit restriction of riskier borrowers seems clear enough.

MARKET ADJUSTMENTS TO RATE CEILINGS

As might be guessed, lenders and consumers constrained in a market might enter into agreements that find ways around the restrictions. For interest rate ceilings, one way to evade the restriction is to enter into agreements that adjust other terms of the transaction, including price of associated purchases. Lenders and borrowers have employed this approach in lending transactions for millennia, as reviewed briefly earlier in this chapter. Not surprisingly, researchers have studied some specific reactions to state-based interest rate ceilings on consumer credit.

Joint Purchases: Arkansas and Low-Income Markets

As discussed here in chapter 3, credit use involves intertemporal shifting of receipt of services from a product and payment for the product. Properly allocating the total of the expenditure into its components (cost of the actual product and costs of the timing rearrangement) is not always simple or clear, especially when the same source supplies both the product and credit. Since product prices generally are not regulated, even when purchased with credit that is regulated, sellers may respond to limits on the credit price by increasing the price of products. An increase of this kind is easy enough to accomplish if the product is usually purchased using credit.

ARKANSAS
In earlier decades, the state of Arkansas was a favorite place to study the impacts of rate ceilings. For many years, the state strictly enforced a 10 percent usury ceiling without the kinds of exceptions for small loan companies, industrial banks, and other institutions that marked the laws of other states. In 1957, the Arkansas Supreme Court affirmed that all forms of credit in the state were subject to the 10 percent usury ceiling in the state constitution, regardless of actions the legislature might take (*Sloan v. Sears*, 228 Arkansas 464, 308 S.W., 2d 802 1957). This difference led to many studies of the effects of the usury law.

These studies provided evidence that sellers do respond to limitations to the price of credit by raising product prices. For instance, Lynch (1968) compared appliance prices in Arkansas and other states. At that time, most of the larger household appliances were typically purchased using closed-end credit.

Lynch found that prices on comparable appliances were several percentage points higher in Arkansas than in cities in surrounding states.[29] In border cities

---

29. Both retail stores and direct lenders could also increase the price of products ancillary to the credit component of the sale, including repair contracts and other closely related products.

such as Texarkana on the Arkansas-Texas border, Arkansas retail stores reported facing aggressive price competition from Texas retailers. Cash purchasers from the Arkansas side frequently crossed the state line into Texas to purchase appliances in order to avoid subsidizing below-market interest rates for credit purchasers in Arkansas through higher prices for goods.

Lynch also found relatively few consumer credit direct lenders in Arkansas. Those he did find concentrated mainly on automobile lending, which because of the larger loan size and the presence of collateral was more profitable than other types of consumer lending in the controlled environment. Even so, low loan losses on the automobile credit suggested that high-risk borrowers in Arkansas were rationed.

In subsequent research focusing on Texarkana and Fort Smith, on the border respectively with Texas and Oklahoma, Blades and Lynch (1976) examined the location choices of retail stores in the first sixteen years following the strict application of the 10 percent ceiling in Arkansas. They found that the numbers of credit-oriented retail institutions, such as automobile dealers, furniture and appliance dealers, and department stores, declined on the Arkansas side of the border at Texarkana and increased on the Texas side. This change included both the formation of new retail stores and the relocation of existing stores from Arkansas into Texas. In Fort Smith, on the border with Oklahoma but entirely in Arkansas, initially there had been little commercial development on the Oklahoma side, but this changed in the 1960s with the opening of many new retail establishments there. By the early 1970s, Fort Smith retail outlets reported facing substantial new competition from retailers in Oklahoma, which previously had not been a concern.

Blades and Lynch also found that Arkansas retail stores financing customer sales applied higher credit standards, required larger down payments, and offered shorter lending terms than Texas retailers. Arkansas retailers almost universally charged ceiling rates on purchases they financed. Texas and Oklahoma retailers charged rates higher than the Arkansas ceiling but generally lower than the Texas or Oklahoma ceiling. National retail chains, however, charged rates in compliance with customers' state of residency.

Texas retail dealers financed a greater proportion of their sales than Arkansas retailers in the years following strict application of the 10 percent ceiling in Arkansas. Greater credit availability in Texas certainly contributed to this outcome, although there may also have been other contributing factors, including potentially more favorable nonprice credit terms in Texas. Blades and Lynch also reported that Arkansas retail dealers perceived a reduction in the number of financial institutions willing to buy their installment sales contracts. Reduced

Comparing lending practices in Little Rock, Arkansas, to Champaign-Urbana, Illinois, which had less restrictive lending laws than Arkansas, the *Illinois Law Forum* (Board of Student Editors 1968) found that lenders in Arkansas were much more aggressive about efforts to sell credit insurance to borrowers and that credit insurance prices were substantially higher in Arkansas even though the covered risks were no higher. This finding suggests that lenders in Arkansas marked up credit insurance prices at that time to offset below-market interest rates.

competition among the remaining financial institutions on the Arkansas side resulted in the retailers receiving less favorable terms for sales financing.[30]

Somewhat later, Peterson and Falls (1981b) compared borrowers in Texarkana with borrowers in three local markets in other states with less restrictive rate ceilings. They found that despite restrictions on consumer credit from local sources, Texarkana borrowers did not owe less consumer debt overall. Their sources of credit merely differed. Arkansas borrowers obtained substantially larger shares of credit through retailers than the consumers in other markets, presumably paying higher prices for the goods in the process. They also obtained more credit from out-of-state sources. Whether Arkansas consumers not living in Texarkana and with less convenient access to out-of-state retail credit were able to obtain similar levels of debt is not known. That many Arkansas consumers living near the border chose Texas retailers suggests that the 10 percent Arkansas rate ceiling did not benefit these consumers. More recently, Arkansas has revised its state constitution and usury law, but the revised law remains relatively restrictive compared with most other states. Today, the ability of Arkansas residents to obtain revolving credit from out-of-state credit card companies vitiates in large part the state's restrictive usury law.

LOW-INCOME MARKETS

In the past, it also appeared that rate ceilings had the result of encouraging questionable sales tactics in a segment of the market for durable goods sometimes referred to as the low-income marketplace. In this case, rate ceilings discouraged competition and marketplace entry into areas with large concentrations of low-income residents by mainstream sellers of retail durable goods. This provided opportunities for other sellers freed from this competition to allocate part of the cost of credit to product prices. It seems that the ceilings, in effect, rationed riskier borrowers out of the mainstream credit markets but did not help them out of their difficult circumstances.

Caplovitz (1963) studied the credit market for families living in four low-income housing projects in New York City. He found that low-income retailers seldom charged a single price for a product. Consequently, product prices were not posted, and customers needed to ask a salesperson about the price. In this environment, consumers perceived to be poor credit risks, judged to be naive, or referred by another retailer (who sometimes received a commission for the referral) were quoted higher prices. Prices ranged from one to several times more than the wholesale price, depending on these considerations. Products typically were of poor quality.

New York law limited the maximum charge for retail credit, so the retail goods prices included part of the cost of credit. The installment sales contracts had weekly payment schedules, which provided retailers with several advantages.

---

30. Financial institutions eliminated the dealer spread, paid little or no interest on dealer reserves, and purchased paper only with full recourse (which requires the dealer to absorb any credit losses). See also Peterson and Falls (1981b).

Smaller, more frequent payments imposed greater budget discipline than the monthly payment schedule of mainstream credit products. The weekly payment schedule also gave the retailer frequent contact with customers, which allowed retailers to assess customers' payment performance more closely.

With this advantage, the retailers could learn when customers received paychecks or paid rent. When payments on the goods sold were missed, the seller knew whether the reason was legitimate (such as an illness or a job layoff) or not. Caplovitz found that the retailers expected customers to miss about one of every four payments and computed markups accordingly. Constant contact with the customers allowed the sellers to act quickly to bring customers back to making payments and increased chances of finding delinquent borrowers and repossessing goods before they disappeared. In addition, frequent contact provided retailers with the opportunity to sell other items to customers who demonstrated that they would make payments. This latter advantage has been criticized as leading to keeping customers continuously in debt.

In 1967, the Federal Trade Commission (FTC) Bureau of Economics conducted a study of the installment credit and retail sales practices in Washington, D.C. (see Federal Trade Commission 1968). The FTC study provided statistics that highlighted some of the differences between low-income and general market retailers. Nearly all (93 percent) of sales of the low-income market retailers studied involved use of credit, reflecting customers' need for credit from them and lack of alternative sources. In contrast, just 27 percent of general market retailers' sales involved use of credit at that time. Bad debt losses were nearly 7 percent of sales at low-income market retailers, compared with less than 1 percent at general market retailers. Despite the high credit risk, average finance charges at low-income market retailers in the District of Columbia (23 percent) were not much higher than finance charges at general market retailers (21 percent).[31] Low-income market retailers clearly included credit costs in product prices, however. Product markups averaged 2.55 times the wholesale price at low-income market retailers but only 0.59 times the wholesale price at general market retailers.

There is little systematic evidence on the role of low-income market retailers today. Most evidence on low-income market retailers is from the 1960s and 1970s (see Andreasen 1993). Much of the current literature on low-income markets involves groceries and financial services other than credit. However, in a more recent article, Fellowes (2007) mentioned lower-income consumers' reliance on rent-to-own stores for durable goods such as furniture, appliances, and electronics. Grow and Epstein (2007) provided anecdotal evidence on some newer forms of low-income market retailing. To some extent, rent-to-own stores have substituted for low-income market retailers (see chapter 8). The relaxation of rate ceilings in the 1980s, improvements in credit reporting, and advances in statistical methods of credit evaluation have expanded availability of credit to some but

---

31. Low-income market retailers also had higher salary and commission expense than general market retailers, which the study's authors attributed to the use of peddlers as a distribution channel.

certainly not all lower-income consumers, giving them access to general market retailers and competitive prices for goods.[32] It is likely that many consumers continue to rely on low-income market retailers and that customers' limited access to credit shield these retailers from competition from general market retailers.

Adjustments to Rate Ceilings through Nonrate Terms

Experience in Arkansas and in the low-income market showed that responses to rate ceilings included higher prices on goods purchased on credit and specific restrictions through tighter credit standards for users. Lenders in Arkansas also required larger down payments and offered shorter terms to maturity than lenders in states with less restrictive regulations. The latter kinds of adjustments, known as adjustments in nonprice credit terms, have also been common responses to restrictive rate ceilings elsewhere.

In a study of four local markets that varied in both rate ceilings and creditors' remedies, Peterson (1979) found that lenders in the two markets with more restrictive rate ceilings required larger down payments on automobile loans and had higher minimum loan sizes for personal loans than lenders in the other two states. Either effect could eliminate potential borrowers who would not qualify for loans with smaller down payments or larger loan size. The finding on minimum loan size is further noteworthy because even when it did not exclude borrowers, the higher minimum loan size may have forced some borrowers to obtain larger loans than they otherwise would have preferred. Either way, higher minimum loan size was likely accompanied by a change in the risk distribution of borrowers, with a resulting risk distribution skewed more toward lower-risk borrowers.

This was hardly a new result of rate ceilings. In a study of eighteenth-century loan transactions at a London bank, Temin and Voth (2008) found that the 1714 reduction in the usury ceiling from 6 percent to 5 percent resulted in nearly a doubling of the average loan size and an increase in the share of loans to the gentry and commercial or political elite. Nearly all of the loans were made at the ceiling rate both before and after the reduction in the usury ceiling. Bodenhorn's (2007) study of loans made between 1845 and 1859 by a New York bank found that average loan size increased substantially when market rates exceeded the state's 7 percent limit. In seeking larger, lower-risk loans, the bank reduced availability of smaller high-rate loans to riskier customers. Although the bank routinely made usurious loans, legal and default risk associated with high-rate loans likely made these loans less attractive in periods in which the usury ceiling was binding. Bodenhorn also found that the bank's loans had shorter terms to maturity when the rate ceiling was binding.

---

32. General market retailers are not always welcomed into these neighborhoods, often because of opposition of local businesses that fear competition from new entrants. For a recent example, see discussion by Mossburg (2010), Harris (2010), and Debusmann (2010).

Wheatley and Gordon (1971) showed that a 1969 reduction in interest rate ceilings in the state of Washington also stimulated adjustments in nonrate credit terms. Lenders there raised credit standards, required larger down payments, increased minimum loan size, and offered shorter terms to maturity following a reduction in rate ceilings from 18 percent to 12 percent on most types of consumer credit. Retailers made similar adjustments in nonrate credit terms. In addition, most retailers increased prices of products that were typically sold using credit and changed product offerings to include more items with higher markups.

Suppliers of credit card credit have also adjusted terms in response to constraints imposed by rate ceilings. Zywicki (2000a) reported that during the 1970s, bank card issuers responded to the inability to raise interest rates when market rates were high by restricting supply and by altering other terms of the credit card agreement. One such alteration was to attach annual fees to customers' accounts. Other alterations included changing the method for determining balances on which interest was calculated, shortening grace periods during which card users could pay in full without incurring a finance charge, selling ancillary products such as credit insurance, and bundling bank cards with other bank products.[33]

Zywicki also noted that higher ceilings allowed these effects to go the other way. In response to the *Marquette* decision by the Supreme Court, which allowed out-of-state national banks to charge (often higher) rates than allowed to local banks, a whole new class of card issuers entered the marketplace. In the 1980s, AT&T, General Motors, Discover, and others offered bank-type credit cards with no annual fees and shook up the structure of the industry. Bank-type cards with no annual fees spread rapidly. Some of these cards offered enhancements to users in the form of cash and merchandise rebates in the competitive environment that developed.

Product Substitution: High-APR and Informal Lending

Credit rationing does not necessarily prevent high-risk borrowers from obtaining credit. As described above, retailers may allocate credit costs in excess of the legal maximum to product prices, especially when there are few cash buyers. In addition, as discussed in chapter 8, a variety of high-APR lenders (such as pawnbrokers, payday lenders, and auto title lenders) and implied high-rate financing sources (such as rent-to-own and low-income market retailers) are available in many states. Rationed consumers can sometimes substitute these forms of credit for installment loans from banks, finance companies, or credit unions.

Such substitutions can entail substantial costs. Pawnbroker loans, for example, require the borrower to forgo use of the item pawned during the term of the loan. Payday loans are designed to be repaid when the borrower receives his or her next

---

33. For an interesting discussion of methods of determining balances for application of rates at the time, see McAlister and DeSpain 1974.

paycheck. Consequently, loan amounts are relatively small, and finance charges are quite high compared with loan size. Consumers desiring larger loans may obtain two or more payday loans simultaneously, "doubling up," but the cost of this practice is quite substantial.[34] Rent-to-own transactions are short-term leases, and the customer can return an item at any time without penalty. But this means that rent-to-own companies assume the risk of ownership, and monthly rents paid by consumers include the cost of bearing this risk, regardless of consumers' inclinations to exercise the return option. That high-APR lenders and implied high-rate financing sources such as renting to own are much more expensive than installment lenders suggests that the amount of credit obtained from these sources is less, quite likely much less, than the amount of normal installment credit forgone as a result of rationing.

Consumers also may obtain loans from various informal sources. One informal source of credit is family or friends. Loans from family or friends often do not involve a written contract, have flexible terms, and charge little or no interest. But these loans have several disadvantages. Funds are limited by the liquid assets of the lenders, lenders may be inquisitive about the need for credit, and lenders may expect the borrower to reciprocate in times of reverse need (Austin 2004). Often, individuals simply do not like to lend to family members (or to borrow from them).

Illegal lenders sometimes may be another source of informal credit for rationed consumers, even today. Passage of the small loan laws in the 1920s greatly reduced illegal lending, and the relaxation of rate ceilings in the 1980s and laws allowing various forms of high-APR lending likely reduced it further.[35]

Illegal lenders have never disappeared entirely, however (see Filkins 2001 and Venkatesh 2006). Illegal lenders reportedly lend to consumers that even the high-risk lenders reject and often are found in immigrant and low-income neighborhoods. Illegal lenders ask few questions and provide credit quickly, often at times and places in which other lenders would be unavailable. But rates charged by illegal lenders are quite high. Anecdotes about rates report that 10 percent or 20 percent a week is typical. Some illegal lenders, especially those associated with criminal activities, use threats of violence to enforce repayment and occasionally inflict physical harm. Other illegal lenders will

34. This practice is not new. It also occurred in consumer finance company personal lending when borrowers desired larger loans than maximum loan size limits allowed or sometimes when two smaller loans were arranged simultaneously from the same lender in place of a larger loan to evade lower ceilings for larger loan sizes. See discussion by Shay (1970), Kawaja (1971), and Greer (1974b).

35. See Robinson and Nugent (1935) for early-twentieth-century US evidence. Current US evidence is anecdotal, but contemporary statistical data on interest rate ceilings and use of illegal lenders are available for other countries. Policis, a London-based consultancy specializing in social and economic research for the public sector, reported greater illegal lending in France and Germany than in the United Kingdom, where legal credit options for high-risk borrowers exist (Policis 2004 and 2006). And Ellison and Forster (2008) found that in Japan, the use of illegal lenders doubled after a tightening of interest rate regulations in 2006.

take assets (such as cars, appliances, or electronic equipment) of defaulting borrowers.

Neither friends and family nor illegal lenders likely provide rationed consumers with amounts of credit equal to the amount of installment credit forgone as a result of rationing. The generally limited resources of friends and family in the former case and the high interest rates and potentially harsh creditors' remedies in the latter case suggest that these sources likely provide substantially less than forgone installment credit.

Conclusions on Rate Ceilings

Interest rate ceilings have been a feature of state regulation that has helped determine the institutional structure of consumer credit markets in the United States. Rate ceilings have in the past tended to segment consumer credit markets by institutional type of lenders, thereby reducing the ability of different lender types to compete with one another. Thus, interest rate regulation has tended to foster market power of lenders, one of the alleged problems that rate ceilings were intended to remedy.

Evidence suggests that low rate ceilings reduce the quantity of consumer credit and do not reduce its price. This result argues against rate ceilings producing more competitive outcomes than markets in which rates are not restricted. Evidence further suggests that competitive influences have always existed in consumer credit markets, both within lender type and across lender types, despite the adverse effects of market segmentation arising from rate ceilings in the past.

Interest rate ceilings have not affected all consumers equally. Higher-risk consumers are more likely to experience a reduction in credit availability than lower-risk consumers, with lower rate ceilings affecting greater percentages of the risk distribution of consumers than higher rate ceilings. Lenders may offer potentially rationed borrowers less risky loan contracts, such as contracts requiring larger down payments or with shorter maturities.

High-risk consumers also have obtained credit from sellers who reallocated part of the cost of credit to product prices. The presence of substantial numbers of cash customers (or lower-risk credit customers who can obtain credit elsewhere) limits mainstream sellers' ability to reallocate credit costs in this way. This has given rise to specialized retailers in certain areas without substantial numbers of cash customers or others with access to outside credit sources. Those sellers willing to specialize in credit sales to high-risk consumers face little competition from mainstream sellers and sometimes have been able to charge very high prices for the goods purchased.

Finally, high-risk consumers may obtain credit from friends or family, high-APR lenders, and illegal lenders. Limited financial resources and high-interest or non-interest prices for these sources suggest that high-risk borrowers will not obtain as much funds at a lower price from these sources as from forgone institutional installment credit. This outcome may prevent some perhaps excessive consumption, as some proponents of interest rate ceilings have argued, but it is likely that much investment in higher-quality household durable goods is also forgone. Since household investment can have high rates of return and be wealth-increasing, such rationing likely harms many rationed consumers (see discussion of household investment in chapter 3).

CREDITORS' REMEDIES AND COLLECTION PRACTICES

As part of the attempt to lower lending costs, creditors have used many means over the centuries to aid and simplify their collection efforts. In ancient times, creditors' "remedies" included barbaric practices such as selling the debtor into slavery to recover the balance. In more modern times, remedies have involved much more benign approaches, such as telephone call centers employed to remind debtors of their obligations if they miss a payment or payments.

To remedy cases of serious default, modern lenders have also inserted remedy clauses that operate through the legal system into loan contracts. Today some of these legal-system-based remedies are no longer common. For example, a "confession of judgment" is a contract provision, better known in the past, in which a borrower agrees in the event of default to let the creditor enter a legal judgment directly against him or her without a further court hearing. In the eighteenth century, this might have led to debtors' prison. Also more common in the twentieth century than now, a "wage assignment" is a contract provision in which a borrower agrees upon default to authorize an employer to transfer payments from a payroll directly to the lender.

A lender may also take a security interest in the borrower's property to secure the payment of a loan, which gives the lender the right to seize, and usually to sell, the property to discharge the debt. Security interest agreements like this are very common today in such secured lending as auto lending. Other creditors' remedies through the legal system also exist, and many will be discussed in this section.

Lenders also may use collection practices that do not operate through the intricacies of the legal system and so might be called extralegal collection methods (*extralegal* does not mean *illegal*). A common example is simply contacting the debtor with a reminder. Contact may be by telephone, mail, or electronic communication. Sometimes such collection efforts result in modifications in payment schedules to accommodate borrowers' financial difficulties. At other times, lenders may simply be relying on the general unpleasantness to debtors of being reminded of default and their awareness of potential adverse effects of default.

In earlier times, some lenders also contacted third parties about existing debts of defaulting borrowers and engaged in extralegal practices that are now illegal. In the nineteenth century, for instance, lenders sometimes sent an employee called a "bawler-out" to trap a borrower in front of coworkers, friends, or family and browbeat the borrower for failing to repay the loan. Another earlier type of contact was a call to the employer, especially if a defaulting borrower's employer was known to dismiss employees who obtained small loans or caused the employer any unpleasantness over collection activity. In these cases, a lender's threat to inform the borrower's employer of the defaulted debt often was quite effective in enforcing payment.[36]

Regulation of Creditors' Remedies and Collection Practices

Today regulations govern use of both creditors' legal-system remedies and other collection practices. In the former case, regulation limits or prohibits legal actions that are deemed to be coercive in consumer credit transactions. In the latter case, regulation distinguishes between legitimate contact and persuasion and harassing or intimidating behavior.

Historically, state laws governed which creditors' remedies were available to lenders on consumer credit transactions in their states. State legislatures determined what practices were acceptable in their jurisdictions, and they changed their credit codes from time to time as needed. Several states placed new limits on creditors' remedies when they adopted the Uniform Consumer Credit Code or similar consumer credit protection laws beginning in the late 1960s (Letsou 1995, 590).

In 1968, the federal government entered the field by restricting wage garnishments. Wage garnishments involved obtaining a court order to have a defaulting borrower's employer transfer payments from the borrower's paycheck directly to the lender. The federal law limited garnishment to a maximum of 25 percent of wages (with some exceptions, such as for the Internal Revenue Service). The wage garnishment limitation was contained in the Consumer Credit Protection Act that year, the same legislation that instituted federal Truth in Lending. Today some states limit wage garnishment still further than federal law or prohibit it altogether (see Hynes and Posner 2002, 178–179).

In the 1970s, the federal government continued the process of instituting new national restrictions on creditors' remedies, moving further into the province of what had been an area of state law. In particular, the Federal Trade Commission's Credit Practices Rule, finally promulgated officially in 1985 after long discussion, prohibited several traditional legal collection remedies that were formerly relatively widespread, including confessions of judgment, wage assignments, and waivers of statutory property exemptions. (Property exemptions under state law limit the kind and amount of property that can be seized by lenders to satisfy their claims for unpaid debts, covering items such as home equity, clothing, furniture, retirement accounts, medical aids, and others assets considered necessary to the ability to earn a living and provide for oneself and one's family.) The Credit Practices Rule also limited non-purchase-money security interests in household

---

36. As part of a project for the National Commission on Consumer Finance, Greer (1974a) found that while a considerable percentage of lenders at the time sometimes contacted delinquent customers at work or contacted customers' employers at least occasionally, those lenders used these collection practices only rarely. Greer's data were from 1971, when contacting employers was legal.

goods. Federal bankruptcy law provides additional protections from seizure of borrower assets or future income to settle debts in default (see chapter 13 of this book for further discussion of the Bankruptcy Code).

Concerning extralegal collection practices, the 1978 federal Fair Debt Collection Practices Act prohibits third-party contacts, limits the time of day that lenders can contact a borrower about a debt, and prohibits harassment, intimidation, and abusive language (see Hynes and Posner 2002, 182). Many state laws also cover extralegal collection activities.

Rationales for Regulation

There are three main rationales given for (state or federal) regulation of creditors' remedies: (1) redressing unequal bargaining power, which is alleged to enable lenders to force harsh remedies on consumers in need of credit; (2) protecting unsophisticated borrowers, who may be unaware of the remedies in their credit contracts and may tend to underestimate the likelihood and cost of default; and (3) adverse selection that causes lenders to offer only credit contracts with harsh remedies (for discussion of these rationales, see, for example, Leff 1970, Wallace 1973, and Whitford 1979 and 1986).

The adverse selection argument contends that contracts with weak remedies would be unprofitable, because consumers know their credit risk better than lenders, and only consumers who expect to default choose contracts with weaker creditors' remedies (therefore, lenders prefer stronger remedies in all cases). It is notable that this third rationale is inconsistent with the others. If, as this rational suggests, consumers are aware of both their own likelihood to default and the relative harshness of penalties in contracts, they hardly either are unsophisticated in these matters or have no bargaining power. If lenders can force harsh remedies on consumers or consumers are unaware of creditors' remedies, then adverse selection as the mechanism that drives weaker remedy contracts out of the market cannot occur.

All three rationales motivated the Federal Trade Commission (FTC) to promulgate the Credit Practices Rule, which became effective, after a long period of discussion and gestation lasting almost a decade, on March 1, 1985. In the staff memorandum recommending the rule, the Division of Special Projects of the FTC Bureau of Consumer Protection issued a study of particular credit collection practices. At the heart of the study was the conviction that consumer credit contracts were "contracts of adhesion," imposed on consumers in a "take it or leave it" fashion that exploited consumer ignorance and desperation and lender monopoly power (see Federal Trade Commission 1974, 30–43).

The FTC memorandum asserted that consumer creditors uniformly demanded that borrowers permit them to use all remedies available: "The contracts reflect each company's undeviating policy of laying claim to all possible contractual remedies. The industry's unitary approach to this matter precludes any consumer so disposed from shopping for a loan agreement which dispenses with the harsher remedies" (Federal Trade Commission 1974, 16–17).

Elsewhere, the memorandum asserted: "Each contract contains a complete catalogue of any and all contractual devices. The extent to which the creditor arms himself with collection tools depends in no way on any knowledge he may have gained concerning the particular circumstances of a given debtor; the complete inventory of remedies is recited in every contract, and they are completely nonnegotiable" (36). The memorandum also cited adverse selection as a reason. A lender offering a contract with less onerous remedies than those of its competitors "would become especially attractive to relatively high risk borrowers.. . . Thus, a company that promoted more lenient remedy terms might experience a higher rate of borrower default than its competitors. Unless its higher rate of interest could fully compensate it for this higher rate of default, the company would find these remedy provisions unprofitable, even if consumers would prefer the provisions."

The theoretical and empirical conclusions of the FTC memorandum were controversial at the time and stimulated considerable theoretical and empirical study (see discussion in Letsou 1995, 614–615). Actually, the availability of creditors' remedies varied considerably across states before promulgation of the Credit Practices Rule, and this facilitated analyses of the effects of remedies in consumer credit markets. The remainder of this chapter section on creditors' remedies reviews the theoretical and empirical evidence on the economics of creditors' remedies that this episode generated. The objective of the review is to examine how creditors' remedies affected the supply and demand for consumer credit at the time and not to evaluate any particular remedy or to judge the Credit Practices Rule per se. It is no doubt possible that restrictions on certain actions of creditors may be judged entirely appropriate by many or all observers, even if they have a demonstrably adverse impact on credit availability.

The Economics of Creditors' Remedies and Collection Practices

Creditors' legal remedies facilitate the collection of loans in default. They provide lenders with claims to the borrowers' assets or future income in default and thereby influence borrowers' decisions to default. Creditors' remedies also influence lenders' collection costs associated with the claims. Models by Barro (1976) and Benjamin (1978) on the effects of collateral and the model by Jaffee and Russell (1976) on asymmetric information and default costs provide a theoretical foundation for the analysis of creditors' remedies. Chapter 5 discusses these models in detail, and the following discussion examines applications to creditors' remedies.

AN ECONOMIC MODEL OF CREDITORS' REMEDIES
Barth et al. (1983) and Barth, Cordes, and Yezer (1986) adapted this theoretical foundation for their analyses of the effects of the FTC's Credit Practices Rule. From their theoretical analysis, it is not possible to demonstrate conclusively that

consumers are better off with elimination of creditors' legal remedies; some are better off, and some are not. To study the matter further, Barth et al. and others also engaged in extensive empirical studies on the likely economic effects of the Credit Practices Rule.

The Barth et al. theoretical model in the two papers is a two-period asymmetric information model. Borrowers know their second-period income, but lenders cannot observe borrowers' second-period income. The existing set of permissible creditors' remedies limit lenders' potential claims on second-period income in case of credit default and establish a floor for borrowers' second-period consumption.

In the model as presented by Barth, Cordes, and Yezer (1986), borrowers borrow in period one and repay principal and interest if their consumption *after repayment* is greater than the floor. Otherwise, borrowers default. Borrowers who value future consumption more highly than current consumption borrow small amounts relative to income and therefore do not default in period two. Borrowers who value current consumption more highly borrow more and default more often.

Limiting creditors' remedies raises the floor on period two consumption above what it would be otherwise. Under the circumstances, lenders' claim on defaulting borrowers' future income is smaller, and borrowers' incentive to default is greater than without the restriction on remedies. Thus, the overall expected profitability of lending declines. Lenders respond by increasing the required sacrifice by borrowers of period two consumption for each loan amount (that is, by requiring larger repayment of principal and interest through higher interest rates) for each loan amount.[37]

The effects of limiting creditors' remedies on borrowers are ambiguous, however. Some borrowers who previously would not default also would not default when creditors' remedies are restricted. With larger repayment amounts in period two (because the interest rate is higher), they would borrow less than previously. The larger sacrifice of period two income to increase period one income makes these consumers worse off.

Other borrowers who previously did not default (whose preference for current consumption is stronger than that of the first group) would default in the second period. This second group of borrowers would borrow more in the first period, promising to repay a larger amount in period two. In this case, however, the period two consumption after repayment of the loan is greater (because they default on repayment) than the floor on consumption, inducing these consumers to default. Since consumption in both periods is greater, the second group is better off when creditors' remedies are restricted.

The third group of consumers would default regardless of whether creditors' remedies are restricted or not. The effect of restricting creditors' remedies on the third

---

37. Conversely, providing new creditor remedies lowers the floor on period two consumption, increases lenders' claim on borrowers' future income, and reduces borrowers' incentive to default. This increases expected profit of lending and thereby reduces the necessary sacrifice of period two consumption for each loan amount.

group is ambiguous. As a result of the restriction of creditors' remedies, they would consume more in period two (because of the higher floor on consumption) but less in period one (because of the shift in lenders' supply).[38]

And so from the Barth et al. economic model, it is not possible to conclude that consumers are unambiguously better off from restriction of creditors' remedies; some are, but others are not. But consumption patterns in a competitive market are not the only theoretical matter studied at the time of discussion of the Credit Practices Rule. There is also the question of consumer information.

IMPERFECT INFORMATION ON CONTRACT TERMS

As mentioned earlier, one of the rationales for regulation of remedies is the belief that consumers are uninformed about the terms of their credit contracts and the underlying risk of the transaction. Furthermore, lenders are alleged to exploit consumer unawareness by including harsh terms in their credit contracts. Before examining the empirical evidence on creditors' remedies, it is useful to consider whether lack of information prevents consumers from choosing harmful contracts. Economic models of search behavior provide some guidance on this question.

Seldom is it the case either that nearly all consumers are well informed on an issue or that hardly any consumers are informed. Generally, a significant number of consumers are well informed, but substantial numbers of consumers are only moderately informed or are uninformed.[39] Schwartz and Wilde (1979 and 1983) showed theoretically that the presence of at least some consumer search creates the possibility of a pecuniary externality; that is, consumers who shop for price may protect consumers who do not shop.[40] This result occurs when firms cannot distinguish among extensive shoppers, moderate shoppers, and nonshoppers. Firms may lose sales when they offer inferior contracts to informed consumers. Thus, if enough consumers shop, firms will offer the same contracts to both shoppers and nonshoppers.[41] Schwartz and Wilde estimated that it may be necessary for only as little as one-third of consumers to be shoppers for the market to generate a competitive equilibrium. As long as the preferences of shoppers and nonshoppers are positively correlated, competition among firms for shoppers protects all consumers.

---

38. The effects here of providing new creditors' remedies would be the opposite. The first group would be better off, the second group would be worse off, and the effect on the third group would still be ambiguous, but period one consumption would be greater and period two consumption less. Lenders in a competitive market would not be worse off or better off with restrictions on creditor remedies because of the zero profit condition for equilibrium in a competitive market.

39. See Katona and Mueller (1954), Day and Brandt (1973), and Day (1976) for evidence on shopping behavior for durable goods and credit.

40. Other search models have also produced similar conclusions. See, for example, Salop and Stiglitz (1977), Rothschild (1973), and Wilde (1977).

41. Standard form contracts often are cited as evidence of lenders imposing unwanted contract terms. Schwartz and Wilde suggested that standard form contracts may promote efficiency by reducing origination costs, facilitating comparison of contracts, and making lender discrimination among potential customers more difficult.

Schwartz and Wilde argued that when a sufficient number of consumers shop to produce a competitive equilibrium price, enough of these shoppers likely would also be conscious of other terms also. Firms would then find it profitable to compete on the basis of both price and other terms. When consumers prefer certain terms, the market will provide the terms that consumers want (Schwartz and Wilde 1983).

Of course, it is plausible that consumers may not be as sensitive to creditors' remedies as they are to price, because remedies are legal terms and not as prominent. This means that remedies are costly for consumers to evaluate. Further, if consumers believe that they are not likely to default and thereby become subject to remedies, they may well not see much benefit in incurring the costs of shopping for remedies.

Schwartz and Wilde (1983) considered the possibility that consumers err in assessing their default risk. They pointed out that individual consumers generally have better information on their likelihood of default than lenders. This information includes their ability to manage their finances and their objective circumstances. An error is more likely to arise from consumers' analysis of the information than from the information itself. After considering potential sources of cognitive errors, Schwartz and Wilde concluded that any errors are probably random and unbiased. If consumers do not systematically underestimate the probability of default, and at least some of them are knowledgeable about remedies, then firms would be unable to impose harsher creditors' remedies than consumers would choose on their own.

EMPIRICAL EVIDENCE ON THE USE OF REMEDIES

Available empirical evidence on creditors' legal remedies and collection practices is largely from the years before formal adoption of the Credit Practices Rule in 1985. Almost a decade of discussion of the rule before adoption generated many studies. They covered patterns of use of specific remedies across different lenders and types of credit, reasons for differences in use of remedies, and effects of remedies on prices and availability of credit at that time.

The NCCF report undertook extensive studies of creditors' remedies (National Commission on Consumer Finance 1972, chapter 3). In one of the NCCF's technical studies, Greer (1974a) conducted an exhaustive investigation of lenders' collection practices and use of various creditors' remedies present in contracts in 1971, a few years before the FTC first publicly proposed the Credit Practices Rule. The Greer study covered several different types of credit and included more than one thousand banks, finance companies, and retail stores.

Greer found that lenders generally made substantial use of informal or extralegal debt collection procedures before initiating formal collection actions involving creditors' remedies. Lenders relied on the least expensive (and typically least intrusive) collection methods first, such as mailing delinquency notices to a borrower's home. This typically was followed by phone calls to the borrower's home. Lenders rarely contacted a borrower at work or attempted to contact a borrower's employer. Delinquency notices resolved most delinquencies, but lenders considered the telephone calls to be the most effective means of collection. Personal visits by collection personnel to the borrower's home were considered highly effective, but the high cost of personal visits limited their use.

Use of legal contract terms varied across lender type and credit type. For example, 15 percent to 17 percent of banks included confession of judgment provisions in their contracts, depending on the type of credit. Far fewer finance companies (5 percent to 7 percent) included confession of judgment provisions in their contracts.

Other remedies occurred more frequently. For instance, lenders generally included acceleration clauses, which make the entire debt due and payable upon default, in their credit contracts. Seventy-seven to 86 percent of banks and 90 to 95 percent of finance companies included acceleration clauses in their contracts, depending on the type of credit. There was wide variation by credit type at retail stores. Retailers included acceleration clauses in 68 percent of revolving credit contracts but just 4 percent of closed-end installment credit contracts.

Of the other remedies considered by Greer, some were included in most credit contracts, but others were included in only a minority of contracts. In the former category were provisions requiring a defaulting borrower to pay a fee to cover part of the lender's legal costs upon default and allowing the lender to repossess items taken as security without a judicial process. In the latter category were provisions taking security interest in household goods other than the items being financed and allowing wage assignments. Garnishment and deficiency judgments (obtaining a judgment against a borrower for any part of a debt not recovered by sale of the collateral) were also in the uncommon category.

The incidence of these remedies varied, sometimes substantially, by type of lender and credit product. But Greer found no evidence that credit contracts contained blanket provision making available to creditors every remedy available at all. Moreover, even when certain remedies were included in contracts, he found that lenders often did not use the remedies in actual collections. In his discussion, "use" included mentioning the remedies in letters or telephone calls to persuade borrowers to repay and in formal legal actions.

Peterson (1986) used a simple net present value rule to analyze empirically creditors' use of creditors' remedies. In Peterson's analysis, the net present value of collections arising from invoking a creditor remedy at a point in time consisted of the present value of recoveries made minus the present values of (1) costs associated with invoking a remedy, (2) forgone payments that would have been made if the remedy had not been invoked, and (3) the expected loss of goodwill. Forgone payments consisted of payments from borrowers who would have resumed payments anyway. Loss of goodwill referred to the loss of future business resulting from a reputation for using a (harsh) creditor remedy. Using this present value rule, Peterson found that lenders invoked the remedy having the highest net present value at the time they made the decision, certainly illustrative but not exactly startling. Lenders forbore if all remedies had a negative net present value.

Considering probable values for these remedies, Peterson proposed several hypotheses about lenders' use of collection practices and creditors' remedies:

1. Lenders are more likely to turn to third-party collectors or invoke legal actions in states with low interest rate ceilings than in states with high interest rate ceilings. This occurs because interest accrues more slowly on lower-rate contracts than on higher-rate contracts. Thus, if a remedy

is invoked, the expected present value of forgone future payments from the portion of borrowers who eventually resume payments voluntarily is lower in a low-rate state than in a high-rate state (assuming the level of the contract rate does not materially affect the percentage of borrowers who eventually resume payments).

2. Lenders are less likely to use a creditor remedy in states where the cost of invoking the remedy is high or the probable recovery is low than in states where the cost is low and the probable recovery is high.
3. Because of considerations of goodwill, lenders are more likely to use remedies that are acceptable to consumers than ones that are unacceptable.
4. Lenders will use a remedy that is unacceptable to consumers only if it is highly effective (that is, probable recoveries are high).

Peterson tested these hypotheses using survey data from lenders and consumers in four local markets in states that differed by the height of rate ceilings and the availability of creditors' remedies.[42]

Peterson's findings provided support for these hypotheses. Lenders were more likely to use third-party collectors or invoke legal remedies in the two low-rate-ceiling states than in the high-ceiling states. Lenders in the high-ceiling state with restricted remedies were least likely to resort to a third-party collector or invoke a legal remedy, since both higher expected present value of forgone future payments and high costs of invoking creditors' remedies restrained these actions.

Overall, lenders considered garnishment, late payment charges, fees to pay lenders' legal costs, repossession of collateral, and cosigner agreements to be the most effective remedies. In surveys, consumers viewed late payment fees, repossession, garnishment of savings accounts (but not wages), collection calls, and loan workouts as appropriate collection practices. Consumers especially disapproved of taking household goods not being purchased as collateral, contacting employers, and wage garnishment or wage assignment.

Peterson's list of creditors' remedies considered effective included those creditors' remedies that Greer (1974a) had found in most credit contracts: specifically, fees to pay lenders' legal costs and repossession of collateral. Consumers generally approved of these remedies. One difference was garnishment of wages, which many lenders found effective but used sparingly, possibly because of distaste among consumers.[43]

---

42. The markets were Little Rock-North Little Rock, Arkansas (low rate ceilings, remedies not restricted); Racine-Kenosha, Wisconsin (low rate ceilings, remedies restricted); Waukegan-North Chicago, Illinois (high rate ceilings, remedies not restricted); and Lake Charles, Louisiana (high rate ceilings, remedies restricted). Peterson and Falls (1981a) described the surveys that provided the data analyzed in this study and additional analyses of the data.

43. Greer (1974a) found that depending on the type of credit, garnishment was used 11 percent to 16 percent of the time by banks holding a defaulted contract, 21 percent to 44 percent of the time by finance companies, and 24 percent to 30 percent of the time by retail stores.

Remedies that lenders did not very often consider effective were, not surprisingly, among those Greer found to be uncommon in contracts: taking as collateral household goods not being purchased, wage assignments, and confession of judgment. That by far most consumers disapproved of these remedies provided another reason for not including the remedies in credit contracts.[44]

EFFECTS OF REMEDIES ON PRICES AND AVAILABILITY OF CREDIT

Other things being equal, restricting creditors' remedies reduces the expected profitability of lending. In the Barth et al. (1983 and 1986) theoretical model, this result occurs because the borrowers' incentive to default increases, causing some borrowers who previously did not default to do so. Lenders then respond by increasing the required repayment of principal and interest for each loan amount.

Restricting remedies also may increase the cost of collections, increase delays associated with recoveries, or reduce fees imposed to defray collection costs (late fees or attorneys' fees, for example). All of these considerations indicate that restricting creditors' remedies would shift lenders' supply curve to the left. In other words, they would be willing to supply the same amount of credit only at a higher price.

Changes in remedies may also affect credit demand. Barth et al. showed theoretically that restricting creditors' remedies may increase some consumers' demand for credit but reduce the demand of others. Thus, the effect of restricting creditors' remedies on consumers' demand is indeterminate from theory. The reasoning is that some consumers place a positive value on protection from creditor remedies, while others find no need for it. Falls and Worden (1988) found that the former group was willing to pay lenders some amount to obtain such protection. Since theory suggests two effects that operate in different directions, the overall impact of changes in remedies on price and availability of credit becomes an empirical question.

Greer (1973), Peterson and Frew (1977), and Shay (1973) empirically investigated the effects of state restrictions on creditors' remedies on the volume of lending and average interest rate. For their studies, all used the state level aggregate data collected by the National Commission on Consumer Finance.

Results of their work provided empirical evidence that restrictions on remedies reduce the volume of lending and increase interest rates overall, although the effects for specific individual remedies were sensitive to specific model specification.

Specifically, Greer (1973) found that for various lenders, estimated regression coefficients for prohibition of wage assignment, prohibition of garnishment, restriction of garnishment, prohibition of fees for lenders' legal costs, and prohibition of confession of judgment were consistently negatively related

---

44. Umbeck and Chatfield (1982, 513) noted that "the most significant cost of an additional remedy to the lender is the decline in the borrower's demand for a credit contract as the remedy shifts more of the risk to him. Wealth maximizing creditors will weigh the gains and costs of adding an extra remedy to a standardized contract and their resulting behavior is predictable through the use of an economic model."

to lending volume but often not statistically significantly different from zero. Using a similar model with a somewhat different set of explanatory variables, Peterson and Frew (1977) also obtained negative, often statistically insignificant coefficients. Shay (1973) included creditors' remedies as explanatory variables in his analysis of interest rate ceilings for small loans at finance companies. He found that the prohibition of wage assignments was significantly inversely related to the volume of lending in low-rate-ceiling states but not in high-rate-ceiling states.

These state level aggregate studies appear consistent with the prediction of the theoretical models that restricting creditors' remedies can reduce lending. The studies do not provide clear evidence on which specific restrictions matter. This limitation is at least in part a result of statistical considerations: the indicator (dummy) variables summarizing the various state laws suppress the heterogeneity in the laws; and because states that restricted one remedy often restricted others, the effects of individual restrictions are estimated imprecisely. These studies also do not provide information on the extent to which the estimated effects are influenced by changes in demand.

In addition to their theoretical work in a study mentioned previously, Barth et al. (1983) empirically examined account level data on personal loans originated by nine large consumer finance companies that accounted for about 40 percent of personal lending by finance companies at the time. They estimated reduced form models to explain the interest rate and loan amount. For the interest rate, they used a statistical model that corrected for truncation of interest rates at the rate ceiling. A further innovation was consideration of continuous variables to measure the dollar amount of late fee and wage assignment/garnishment remedies. These specifications recognize that state restrictions were not homogeneous.

They found that the coefficients of the continuous remedy variables were statistically significant and had the hypothesized signs: larger dollar amounts of late fee and wage assignment/garnishment remedies were associated with lower interest rates and larger loan amounts.[45]

Barth, Cordes, and Yezer (1986) later estimated supply and demand equations for the subset of loans from the Barth et al. (1983) data set that had interest rates below the legal interest rate ceiling. The dependent variable in their estimation was the interest rate. They employed the same continuous variables for the amount of late fee and wage assignment/garnishment remedy variables used in the earlier paper and also included indicator variables for several other restrictions on creditors' remedies.

---

45. In contrast, the coefficients for the indicator (dummy) variables often had implausible signs. For instance, estimated coefficients of the dummy variables for remedy restrictions were negative in the interest rate regressions. These results are implausible, because even if supply is unchanged (perhaps because the remedy is not useful to lenders), any increase in demand would result in a higher interest rate. A remedy restriction would have to reduce demand to produce a lower interest rate, which is clearly implausible.

Generally, the estimated coefficients for creditors' remedies in their *supply* equation were statistically significant and had the hypothesized sign: greater availability of a remedy was associated with a lower interest rate. The estimated effects of creditors' remedies were also economically significant (measurable size).

In contrast, most of the estimated coefficients for creditors' remedies in the *demand* equation were quite small and were statistically insignificant, with a few exceptions. For example, the statistical estimates showed that borrowers were willing to pay 1.8 percentage points in interest for a prohibition on taking security interest in household goods not being purchased. Also, borrowers apparently would pay 2.4 percentage points to revoke a wage assignment provision in a state that allows garnishment. They also would require a 2.3 percentage point reduction in the interest rate in a contract that contains a provision for a fee to require paying the lender's legal costs in the event of default. Overall, Barth, Cordes, and Yezer's results implied that state restrictions on creditors' remedies raised the cost of personal loans by more than borrowers valued the restrictions.

Villegas (1990) provided further evidence on the net effects of restricting creditors' remedies. Using the same theoretical model based on Blitz and Long (1965) that he had used for his rate ceiling studies (Villegas 1982 and 1989), he derived an empirical model of household borrowing for estimation. He used data from the Federal Reserve's 1983 Survey of Consumer Finances.

Results of his estimation indicated that restriction on taking security interest in household goods not being purchased produced both a greater probability of consumers' having credit and higher quantities of credit in use. This finding suggests that restricting security interests in household goods not being purchased has a net benefit. This is consistent with the finding of Barth, Cordes, and Yezer that borrowers are willing to pay for this restriction.

Villegas also found that restrictions on wage assignments were associated with lower borrowing, and restrictions on garnishment were associated with more borrowing. These findings appear to be contradictory, because invocation of both remedies involves attaching borrowers' wages. However, garnishment gives rise to legal expenses for both the lender and the borrower associated with a court judgment, but wage assignments do not. The legal costs for garnishment incurred by the lender and the borrower may explain why restricting garnishment might produce a positive net benefit, but restricting relatively low-cost wage assignments produces a negative net benefit.[46]

The consumer surveys in the four-market study analyzed by Peterson (1986) included questions that sought to elicit consumers' valuations of protection from late fees, repossession, fees to pay lenders' legal costs, and deficiency judgments. The survey questions described the remedy and included a dollar cost to the consumer if the remedy was invoked. The survey also included a question asking respondents to assess the likelihood that they would have trouble repaying debts

---

46. Johnson (1978) discussed additional considerations that differentiate garnishment and wage assignments. Villegas also found that some restrictions did not have statistically significant effects on household borrowing, including restrictions on deficiency judgments, fees for lenders' legal costs, late charges, and confessions of judgment.

in the next two years. Peterson and Falls (1981a) and Falls and Worden (1988) analyzed the responses to these questions.

Only a relatively small percentage of respondents said that they would be willing to pay something to avoid these remedies. Overall, 17 percent to 19 percent of respondents said that they would be willing to pay something, depending on the remedy. The percentages of self-assessed higher-risk respondents who said that they would be willing to pay something to avoid these remedies was significantly greater (29 percent to 39 percent).

About two-thirds of respondents who were willing to pay to avoid remedies provided dollar amounts of how much they were willing to pay. The mean amounts they were willing to pay were $47 (0.69 percentage point increase in the interest rate) for a reduction in the late payment amount from $5 to $1, $112 (1.70 percentage points) for avoiding a fee of up to $300 for the lender's legal costs, $132 (1.81 percentage points) to avoid repossession after paying half of the loan principal, and $93 (1.41 percentage points) to avoid a deficiency judgment of $500. Mean amounts for self-reported higher-risk respondents were greater than those for lower-risk respondents.

These responses were to hypothetical loan situations and may not, of course, reflect behavior that would be observed in actual loan transactions. Nevertheless, there is some reason to believe that the responses have some plausibility. First, the change in the expected present cost of default to a borrower from invoking a remedy is likely quite small in most cases. Expressed precisely, the expected present cost of default is $\sum_{t=1}^{n} p_t q_t L_t (1 + r)^{-t}$, where p_t is the probability of default in month t, q_t is the probability that the lender invokes the remedy when the consumer defaults, L_t is the loss incurred by the consumer when the lender invokes the remedy, n is the total number of monthly payments, and r is the consumer's discount rate. On any loan for most borrowers, the probability of defaulting is very small. Further, lenders may not invoke a remedy initially upon default (recall that some borrowers eventually resume making payments) or ever (some remedies are costly to lenders). Greer (1974a) noted that most delinquencies are resolved by reminder notices and other extralegal measures, without invoking creditors' remedies.

Johnson (1978) provided illustrative calculations suggesting that the value to the borrower of restricting creditors' remedies may be relatively small. He hypothetically considered a thirty-six-month loan of $1,300 at an APR of 21 percent with a creditor remedy that would cost the borrower $800 upon default, regardless of the month of default. Assuming a 4 percent probability of default, a borrower discount rate of 12 percent, and that default occurs sometime between the fourth and the thirtieth month, the expected present cost of default would be $27.10.

The expected present cost of default can be converted into a rate by subtracting the $27.10 from the loan amount and solving for the rate: The solution is r = 22.56 percent. The difference between the APR for the contract with the $800 creditor remedy and 22.56 percent (1.56 percentage points) is the maximum increase in the APR that that the borrower in this example would be willing to pay for a loan without the $800 remedy. [47]

That higher-risk respondents were more likely to be willing to pay something and were willing to pay larger dollar amounts to avoid a remedy than lower-risk respondents also gives some credibility to the data. Falls and Worden also estimated a multivariate model explaining respondents' willingness to pay to avoid a remedy. Respondents in the two markets with restrictions on allowable creditor remedies were less likely to be willing to pay to avoid remedies than respondents in the less restrictive markets, and respondents in low-rate-ceiling markets were more likely to be willing to pay to avoid remedies than those in high-rate-ceiling markets. These results seem reasonable. Borrowers in markets with restrictive regulation likely would perceive remedies to be less harsh than respondents in markets with less restrictive regulation. And, as evidence suggests, lenders in markets with low rate ceilings more frequently resort to permitted remedies than lenders in high-rate states (Peterson 1986).

Conclusions on Creditors' Remedies

Creditors' remedies make default costly to borrowers and facilitate collection of delinquent debts. Theoretical models indicate that restricting availability of creditors' remedies moves the credit supply curve to the left (raises prices for the same amount of credit). Theoretical effects of restricting remedies on credit demand are ambiguous, however.

Empirical evidence supports the theoretical predictions for supply. Restrictions on creditors' remedies generally produce significant increases in interest rates (Greer 1973; Peterson and Frew 1977; Barth et al. 1983; Barth, Cordes, and Yezer 1986).

Regression results of Barth, Cordes, and Yezer (1986) and Villegas (1990) suggest that state restrictions on creditors' remedies generally did not have much effect on consumers' demand for consumer credit. However, a few remedies did appear to matter, and consumers' different responses to contractual omissions and legal prohibitions of certain remedies suggest that at least some consumers are sensitive to the inclusion of remedies in contracts.

---

47. The loss in each period is $800, and the loss is assumed to be equally likely in each month between the fourth and the thirtieth month. Assume that the lender invokes the remedy immediately upon default ($q_t = 1$). Expected present cost of default is $\sum_{t=1}^{3} 0 \times 1.0 \times \$800 (1+0.12/12)^{-t} + \sum_{t=4}^{30} 0.037 \times 1.0 \times \$800 (1+0.12/12)^{-t} + \sum_{t=31}^{36} 0 \times 1.0 \times \$800 (1+0.12/12)^{-t}$.

The monthly payment is $48.98. To simplify calculation, Johnson assumed that potential default was expected in the last six months of the contract, but this assumption is not necessary.

Calculation of the rate without the default cost is as follows:

$$\$1,300 - \$27.10 = \sum_{t=1}^{36} -\$48.98 (1+r/12)^{-t}$$

Peterson (1986) found that lenders did not value remedies that consumers found offensive unless the remedies were highly effective. Greer's (1974a) examination of lender contracts indicated that they tended to include effective remedies that consumers found acceptable more frequently than ineffective or offensive remedies.

POLITICAL ECONOMY OF REGULATION OF INTEREST RATES AND CREDITORS' REMEDIES

If interest rate ceilings have a negative impact on credit availability and restrictions on creditors' remedies lead to higher prices, it is not too surprising that many economists have expressed skepticism about the efficacy of these kinds of restrictions. Consequently, the ongoing popularity of such policies over the decades and centuries, particularly usury ceilings, have stimulated several studies in recent years to search for motives for these regulations. Before ending this chapter, it seems worthwhile to raise this question briefly.

In a historical analysis, Ekelund, Hebert, and Tollison (1989) proposed a self-interest story about the medieval church's support for usury ceilings. Although they acknowledged the origins of the church's teaching as based in religious doctrine arising from the Bible and not from some sort of self-interest, Ekelund, Hebert, and Tollison documented a pattern of selective enforcement of the usury doctrine that was consistent with the church's self-interest. Lenders condemned as usurers but without identifiable victims were often required to forfeit some of their "ill gotten" gains to a "pious purpose," typically a local religious purpose such as building a church. In addition, the church sometimes ignored usurious lending practices by major church patrons. The church was often also a borrower. Some popes borrowed to finance the Crusades, for example, and other political and military activities. Because the church often could also pledge valuable collateral to support its borrowing activities, stringent interest rate restrictions may have made preferential access to loans possible.

Looking at more modern times, Boyes (1982) argued that political support for usury laws has come not from the purported beneficiaries of the laws (low-income consumers) but rather from middle-class borrowers who, Boyes argued, were the actual beneficiaries of the laws: Such laws enabled them to gain access to credit at below-market interest rates. In this view, because usury laws artificially dampen demand by making it economically infeasible to lend to higher-risk borrowers, they tend to divert lending capital away from markets serving higher-risk borrowers and (at least to some extent) toward lower-risk borrowers. This increase in capital supply in lower-risk markets could lead to a reduction in interest rates to those borrowers.

In a sense, Boyes's argument resembles Ekelund, Hebert, and Tollison's contention with middle-class constituents replacing state or church as the primary beneficiary of rationing relatively higher-risk borrowers out of the market. Villegas (1989) found, however, that although the presence of usury laws decreased access to credit by lower- and middle-income borrowers, there was no evidence that the presence of usury laws led to lower interest rates for well-to-do households. Thus, he concluded that even though usury regulations produced a capital outflow from markets serving lower-income individuals in a particular state, that capital did not necessarily increase credit supply to others within the same state. He speculated that the excess capital might instead flow into lending markets in other less tightly regulated states or into other capital markets.

Focusing on the nineteenth century, Benmelech and Moskowitz (2010) also argued that the primary beneficiaries and political supporters of usury regulations were upper-class individuals. They reported that usury laws led to allocation of credit on nonprice terms, such as reputation, repeat dealing, and connections. Because usury laws tended to favor established borrowers over riskier new entrants, they could be used to control entry of borrowers, hamper competition by them, and reduce the costs of capital for more established individuals. When such individuals sought credit for their businesses, usury laws could thus serve to erect barriers to entry for new firms by shutting off their access to capital. This could allow incumbent firms to earn economic rents.

In empirical tests, they found that states with stringent voting suffrage laws, and therefore a well-entrenched political elite, typically had tighter usury laws. States with wealth-based suffrage laws had maximum interest rate ceilings 1.32 percent lower on average than states with broader suffrage. States with a lower percentage of white males who actually voted in elections, therefore exhibiting a higher concentration of voting power, also had lower interest rate ceilings (a 10 percentage point increase in voting concentration translated into a 1.5 percentage point lower rate ceiling). As noted above, these findings contradict the standard hypothesis that usury laws benefit the poor. Benmelech and Moskowitz found, however, that this ability of elites to manipulate lending markets through rent seeking was constrained by the threat of competition from neighboring states to attract capital across borders.

Some commentators have argued that illegal lenders have in the past lobbied for unrealistically low rate ceilings, with the knowledge that this would tend to increase consumer demand for illegal loans. Samuelson (1969) and Kawaja (1971, 27) have made this point. Although illegal lenders can certainly benefit from the presence of usury laws, there is no direct evidence of lobbying efforts by illegal lenders in support of stricter laws. Nonetheless, the possibility of an unholy alliance between social reformers and loan sharks, like the "Baptists and bootleggers" phenomenon hypothesized as supporting Prohibition in the 1920s, certainly has been suggested historically (see Stearns and Zywicki 2009).

It thus appears that many regulations proposed for consumer finance over the decades and centuries run the risk of being welfare-reducing for borrowers who then cannot benefit from access to credit (see chapter 3). The possibility of such outcomes raises doubts about a purely public interest explanation for the regulation of both interest rates and consumer credit remedies.

Hynes and Posner (2002) observed that restrictions on creditors' remedies can have distributive consequences. If restrictions on rates or remedies have more severe impact on unsecured lending but those with assets can offset the cost of these restrictions by offering collateral instead, they may be able to avoid many of the costs of inefficient regulation more easily than others. Thus, it is plausible that the overall effect of usury and creditor remedy restrictions may be a net redistribution from lower- to higher-income borrowers.

Concerning creditors' remedies, Letsou (1995) has provided a political economy explanation for the prevalence of limits in this area. Applying the insights of public choice theory, he examined the dynamics of political organization and lobbying efforts by competing interest groups.

Letsou argued that there are several groups that can benefit from restrictions on creditor collection action: consumers who actually default, legal aid organizations that obtain subsidies or clubs to use for their clients against lenders, lenders operating in other parts of the market, and even regulators themselves. Although defaulting consumers are unlikely to be a potent lobbying force because of their difficulties in organizing for effective collective action, the other groups may well have both the incentive and the ability to organize for effective political action. Those with these narrow interests may well not focus on or may even overlook the negative impact that costly excessive protections might have on the much larger number of consumers who do not default but who face higher credit costs or reduced access to credit.

Letsou noted that legal aid organizations have tended to be very heavily involved in legislative lobbying and regulatory rule-writing activities, such as the FTC Credit Practices rule making. He also observed that banks and some other lenders may also benefit from restrictive creditors remedies. Regulation that bars some remedies but not others can have a disproportionately negative effect on creditors who previously used the now prohibited remedies and raise the cost for some types of creditors more than for others. Letsou pointed out, for example, that while personal finance lenders aggressively challenged the FTC's Credit Practices Rule at all stages of its enactment, banks were largely passive. This is consistent with Villegas's (1990) findings that the impact of the Credit Practices Rule was to reduce the market share for finance companies, to increase that of credit unions, and to leave banks unaffected. Finally, Letsou argued that regulatory expansion leads to increased power and budgets for regulators vested with the new responsibilities, benefits realized by regulators even if the regulations fail to advance consumer interests overall. Letsou also argued that there are few parties providing effective countervailing political pressure. The primary losers from inefficient restrictions on creditors' remedies, for instance, are nondefaulting borrowers who pay more for credit or are unable to gain access to credit. But, unlike defaulting borrowers, these groups have no effective proxy interest group lobbying on their behalf.

In contrast, Scott (1989) argued that the persistence of welfare-reducing policies may be consistent with a public interest view of regulation. Suppose that regulators systematically suffer from cognitive biases that lead them to overvalue concentrated and out-of-pocket losses, such as when a lender seizes the property or wages of a defaulting borrower. Suppose also that they undervalue more diffuse benefits, such as the marginally lower cost of credit and the marginal increase in access to credit for borrowers as a result of contracting for enhanced creditor protections upon default. Then their support may go to the former group rather than to the latter. Thus, Scott, unlike many of the proponents of enlarged use of behavioral economics, draws on many of the claimed biases of behavioral economics but applies them to regulators and policymakers rather than to other individuals. Moreover, unlike private market actors who have strong incentives to overcome such biases in their actual decision making (to the extent that such biases actually exist), regulators and legislators have little incentive to overcome such biases and provide information and incentives to correct them (Stearns and Zywicki 2009, chapter 6).[48]

The Consumer Financial Protection Bureau

THE CFPB: HISTORY AND STRUCTURE

The financial crisis that began in 2008 brought about a significant growth in the federal government's role in areas of consumer credit regulation formerly the province of the states through the establishment of the Consumer Financial Protection Bureau (CFPB), established as part of the Dodd-Frank Wall Street Reform and Consumer Protection Act in 2010. The new federal agency was given power to regulate virtually every aspect of every consumer credit product in America, including many products offered by nonbanks that traditionally had been regulated primarily by state and local authorities with only modest federal oversight. These products included payday lending, auto title lending, debt collection services, and mortgage brokerage. In particular, the Dodd-Frank Act provided the CFPB with broad regulatory, supervisory, and enforcement powers to carry out its mission. It also scaled back on federal preemption of state authority with respect to banks, thereby providing state officials with enlarged powers over institutions previously supervised almost exclusively by the federal government.

The idea of a new federal consumer financial protection agency was first introduced into the public discussion in 2007 in an article in *Democracy* magazine by then-Harvard Law Professor and subsequently United States Senator Elizabeth Warren (Warren 2007). The article, entitled *Unsafe At Any Rate* (alluding to Ralph Nader's famous 1960s tract *Unsafe At Any Speed*), called for a new consumer financial protection agency modeled on the Consumer Product Safety Commission. In a memorable analogy, Warren stated, "It is impossible to buy a toaster that has a

---

48. On the other hand, Scott's public interest explanation for the persistence of regulatory action seems incomplete. For example, it fails to explain the intellectual framework of the Federal Trade Commission (1974) memorandum that rested on broad theoretical assertions about the predominance of contracts of adhesion in consumer credit markets, which evidence previously collected from the National Commission on Consumer Finance indicated were not correct. These sorts of intellectual errors are difficult to explain as resulting wholly from unconscious bias. Moreover, Scott's implicit assumption that regulators are motivated solely or predominantly by the public interest is difficult to sustain in light of the development of the (public choice) economic theory of regulation and the influence of interest groups on the regulatory process (Letsou 1995, 626–627).

one-in-five chance of bursting into flames and burning down your house. But it is possible to refinance an existing home with a mortgage that has the same one-in-five chance of putting the family out on the street—and the mortgage won't even carry a disclosure of that fact to the homeowner." She asked, "Why are consumers safe when they purchase tangible consumer products with cash, but when they sign up for routine financial products like mortgages and credit cards they are left at the mercy of their creditors?" She answered, "The different between the two markets is regulation."

Housing foreclosures soared during 2007–2008 as the housing market bubble burst and prices collapsed, precipitating a global financial crisis. The election of Barack Obama as President 2008 and his call for comprehensive reform of the American financial and banking system catapulted Warren's idea from the periphery of the political debate to the center. In 2009 the new Administration's Treasury Department issued a report that provided the basis for the subsequent Dodd-Frank legislation, with the establishment of a new consumer financial protection agency as a centerpiece of the reform proposal (see United States Department of the Treasury 2009, the "Treasury Report"). The Treasury Report blamed the crisis in large part on inadequate consumer protection regulation at the federal level and federal interference with state consumer protection efforts through preemption of state laws.

Prior to the establishment of the CFPB, the federal government's institutional structure of consumer financial protection was highly fragmented. With respect to banks and other depository institutions, regulators had dual missions of consumer protection and safety and soundness of the banking system. The Treasury Department feared this could create a conflict of interest if certain profitable banking practices were actually harmful to consumers but were not adequately regulated in order to protect the banking system. In addition, the Treasury Department argued that the regulatory structure created further conflict of interest because of the ability of financial institutions to change the nature of their charter, such as by converting from a national bank to a state bank or a saving institution, thereby bringing them under the jurisdiction of a new, and possibly more friendly, regulator. And while other federal consumer protection regulators, most notably the Federal Trade Commission, were charged with the primary mission of consumer protection without the possible conflict of safety and soundness concerns, their jurisdiction was limited to nondepository institutions, which substantially limited their substantive reach. Finally, because of federal preemption of state laws by federal banking regulators claiming these were federal regulatory matters, many state regulations (such as so-called "anti-predatory lending" laws) were inapplicable to nationally chartered banks. According to the Treasury Report, this balkanized system of federal regulation allowed sharp and allegedly fraudulent lending practices to proliferate, "Most critically in the run-up to the financial crisis, mortgage companies and other firms outside of the purview of bank regulation exploited that lack of clear accountability by selling mortgages and other products that were overly complicated and unsuited to borrowers' financial situation. Banks and thrifts followed suit, with disastrous results for consumers and the financial system" (55).

As initially proposed and introduced in the House of Representatives, the new agency was modeled after the Consumer Products Safety Commission, a stand-alone agency administered by a multi-member commission structure. As the legislation progressed through Congress, however, the idea of a stand-alone agency headed by a multi-member board eventually was replaced by a new structure, a "bureau" of the Federal Reserve headed by a single Director, who would be nominated by the president and confirmed by the US Senate for a five-year term, removable only for cause, defined as "inefficiency, neglect of duty, or malfeasance in office" (12 U.S.C. 5491(c)(3)). The budget of the CFPB would not be subject to Congressional appropriations, but instead would be provided directly by the Federal Reserve to the CFPB in "the amount determined by the [CFPB] Director to be reasonably necessary" to carry out the CFPB's activities, subject to a 10 percent cap of the Fed's total operating expenses in 2011, an 11 percent cap in 2012, and a 12 percent cap in 2013 and each year thereafter (12 U.S.C 5497(a)). In 2013, the CFPB's operating budget was $597.6 million, almost double that of the Federal Trade Commission. The CFPB is permitted to request still further funds from Congress under certain circumstances.

Although technically characterized as a "bureau" of the Federal Reserve, the Federal Reserve has virtually no relationship with the CFPB other than providing its funding. For example, the Federal Reserve has no oversight authority over the CFPB or power to amend or veto proposed actions by the CFPB. In this sense, the status of the CFPB's relationship to the Federal Reserve differs from Bureaus in other agencies, such as the Consumer Protection Bureau of the Federal Trade Commission, which reports to and acts only through the agency. The only entity that can veto proposed acts of the CFPB is the Financial Stability Oversight Council (FSOC, also established by the Dodd-Frank Act) and only if "the regulation or provision would put the safety and soundness of the United States banking system or the stability of the financial system of the United States at risk." Moreover, any regulation can be set aside only upon a two-thirds vote of members of the FSOC under this high standard. Furthermore, the CFPB Director sits on the board of directors of the FDIC, which is a member of the FSOC—thus, the CFPB can influence the positions taken by the FSOC members with respect to their review of the CFPB's rules.

The CFPB was given two sources of substantive powers by Dodd-Frank Act. First, the administration of all existing federal consumer protection laws, including both rule-making and enforcement authority, was transferred to the CFPB from the various agencies and departments that previously administered them. Second, the CFPB was given new powers over entities traditionally not regulated by the federal government, including supervisory authority over entities such as large payday lenders, debt collectors, and credit reporting bureaus that did not have federal charters. The Dodd-Frank also specifically provides that in any situation in which the CFPB's interpretation of a statute conflicts with that of another agency, the CFPB's interpretation is to prevail (U.S.C. 5512(b)(4)(B).

The Dodd-Frank Act gives broad and loosely defined substantive powers to the CFPB to protect consumers. In particular, the CFPB is given the power to regulate and prosecute any "unfair, deceptive, or abusive act or product" (U.S.C.

5536(a)(1)(B). These three terms are vague and potentially expansive, but the terms "unfair" and "deceptive" incorporate, at least as an initial matter, the definitions of those terms built up over a long period of legal history of the FTC, an agency in existence for a century. Nonetheless, the CFPB also has the power to redefine those terms as it sees fit going forward, and so this initial clarity may not be permanent.

In contrast to the terms "unfair" and "deceptive," which draw on FTC practice, the term "abusive," as used in this context, appears to be an entirely novel term. There is no similar forerunner in any prior federal or state statute or regulation nor any legislative history to suggest what the term might mean. This suggests the likelihood of substantial future amounts of litigation until this matter is sufficiently clarified.

Thus, the CFPB thus combines broad, vaguely defined powers with a complete absence of effective oversight by any other branch of the government, even including Congress in the absence of new governing legislation. The president can appoint but cannot remove the Director, Congress cannot affect the CFPB's budget, the CFPB is headed by a single Director and thus lacks the internal checks and balances of a commission structure, and neither the Federal Reserve nor any other regulatory body has any authority to override the acts of the CFPB. Finally, although the CFPB is required to do its own cost–benefit analysis of proposed regulations, it is insulated from review by the Office of Information and Regulatory Affairs of the Office of Management and Budget. Consequently, it is immune from the standard cost–benefit analysis applied to other Executive departments. In short, the CFPB is arguably the combination of the most powerful and least accountable regulatory agency in American history.

While the clear purpose of Dodd-Frank Act in establishing the CFPB was to centralize consumer financial protection at the federal level, at the same time it also fragments consumer financial protection by increasing the authority of the states. One view of the financial crisis has argued that although the federal government was slow to respond to the growth of the subprime mortgage market, state legislatures and enforcement officials were actively moving in that area, only to be thwarted by federal preemption. As a result, the Dodd-Frank Act reduces the ability of the federal government to preempt state regulation of consumer credit and specifically preserves state laws that provide "greater protection" than those provided by federal law. In addition, the Act gives state officials the power to enforce rules issued by the CFPB. Finally, states are empowered to petition the CFPB formally to initiate a rulemaking process to establish or amend a new rule, which the CFPB shall do upon a petition by a majority of states.

In effect, much of Dodd-Frank's regulatory scheme turns existing law concepts on their head. Traditionally, the regulation of consumer financial services had reflected a compromise between state and national interests. National banks were traditionally regulated by the federal government and lenders whose effects were almost exclusively local were regulated under state and local law. Under Dodd-Frank, the CFPB will have authority to regulate entities whose effects are almost entirely local in effect, such as payday lenders and debt collectors, and which have virtually no link to any systemic or interstate effects. And state officials will now have heightened authority to enforce CFPB regulations and to regulate national banks which have substantial effects on interstate commerce and the national banking system.

The CFPB and the Financial Crisis

As noted, the original proposal for formation of a new federal consumer financial protection agency came before the financial crisis occurred. Nevertheless, once the financial crisis did occur, advocates for the new agency seized the political groundswell that arose in its wake and used it as an opportunity to promote the new agency. Although claimed as a justification for the agency's creation, the tie between the financial crisis and the CFPB's final creation is highly attenuated.

First, the need for a more coherent and consistent federal regulatory regime with respect to consumer financial products predated the onset of the financial crisis. The structural defects that were identified were real—multiple different agencies with different jurisdictions over different industries and the lack of coordination that created. But the need for a coordinated consumer protection regulatory regime within one agency did not necessarily mean that it was necessary to create a *new* agency. One obvious option would have been to combine all of the authority in the Federal Trade Commission, which had existing expertise in consumer protection generally and in many areas of financial protection specifically. In addition, the anomalous structure of the CFPB—an agency located within the Federal Reserve but not accountable to Federal Reserve or any other institution also did not necessarily follow.

Second, although the financial crisis was offered as the proximate cause for the creation of the CFPB, in fact the agency's jurisdiction reaches many areas of consumer financial protection that were irrelevant to the financial crisis, such as payday loans, prepaid cards, and debt collections, and for which there was no evidence that state governments were regulating inadequately or for which a stronger federal response was necessary.

Third, and perhaps most important, there is little tangible evidence that the financial crisis was substantially the result of a failure of consumer protection. To be sure, the onset of the financial crisis involved a mortgage loan foreclosure crisis on a scale not seen since the Great Depression. But there is scarce evidence that the foreclosure crisis resulted from fraudulent acts against consumers. The financial crisis had many causes including a housing price bubble that may have arisen at least in part from monetary and interest rate policies in prior years. There also was a deterioration of downpayment requirements and other innovations in mortgage lending that resulted in lower levels of accumulated equity by homeowners that increased the risk of falling into a negative equity position when housing prices fell. Further, there clearly were erroneous expectations of continued price housing appreciation on the part of both lenders and borrowers. While all of these factors contributed to the foreclosure crisis, none of them raise consumer protection issues, especially in localized consumer credit lending.

Intellectual Influences on the CFPB

The establishment of the CFPB is also important because it reflects a sea change in the intellectual foundation of the federal government's approach to consumer financial protection. In particular, the political case for the CFPB and the animating intellectual influence on the CFPB is heavily tied to the ideas of behavioral economics (see chapter 4). The embrace of behavioral economics by advocates for the CFPB was largely political at first, but the intellectual ascendancy of behavioral economics coincided in timing with the onset of the financial crisis and the two movements coalesced.

Previously, as Joshua Wright has shown, beginning in the 1980s, the dual evolution of antitrust law and consumer financial protection law reflected a growing influence of traditional economics over both areas of law (Wright 2012). Still older interventionist policies gave way at that time increasingly to policies based less on substantive restrictions on the terms and conditions of products and consumers' choices and more on disclosure-based obligations like Truth in Lending designed to further consumer welfare through the promotion of competition and consumer choice. These prescriptions were based largely on the ideas of widely accepted economic principles and the growing recognition of the unintended consequences in the financial area of government intervention through such traditional means as usury restrictions and other substantive restrictions on consumer credit products. The arrival of behavioral economics and its emphasis on cognitive biases among consumers seems to have ushered in another phase of interventionist policies of the old school. It remains to be seen where all this will lead.

Overall, the long-term benefits or costs of the CFPB for consumers and the economy are too early to tell. Economists David Evans and Joshua Wright estimated before the agency was created that the predicted long-term effect of the new agency would be to increase interest rates on consumer loans by 160 basis points (1.6 percentage points) and to reduce consumer borrowing by 2.1 percent and net new jobs created in the economy by 4.3 percent (Evans and Wright 2010). Although these precise estimates are subject to challenge, Evans and Wright estimate that the costs of the new agency could be substantial.

12

A Complement and a Supplement to Consumer Credit

Debt Protection and Automobile Leasing

Previous chapters have focused on consumer credit growth, credit demand, production costs and supply, policy issues, and regulation. This chapter first examines a complement to many consumer credit transactions known as debt protection and then looks at a substitute for automobile credit, namely, automobile leasing. Both of these product groups involve big markets themselves and deserve more than a passing mention in this book. Like so many other aspects of consumer credit use and choices, they have their own history, supporters, and critics to go along with their important market niches.

CREDIT INSURANCE AND OTHER DEBT PROTECTION

Debt protection products, including credit insurance and others, are relatively common complements to consumer credit arrangements. The term *debt protection* generically refers to a collection of insurance and other products that either pay off credit obligations in their entirety or continue or defer required payments on credit outstanding if unfortunate events such as death, disability, or involuntary unemployment occur to covered debtors. These products are, of course, only available in conjunction with credit arrangements, but they are "add-ons" and are by no means part of all consumer credit contracts.

Despite their long history, extending almost a century, debt protection products appear not to be especially well known among nonusers, and they have sometimes been controversial in policy discussions despite widespread popularity among users. In part because of past controversies, credit insurance is heavily regulated by the states. Other debt protection products are regulated by the federal banking agencies. The following subsections of this chapter examine the origin and kinds of debt protection commonly available with consumer credit and mortgage credit contracts, the controversies that have surrounded them historically, the costs of these products for consumers, and evidence of using consumers' favorable attitudes toward them.

Origins and Kinds of Debt Protection

Debt protection in the form of credit insurance has been around for decades, and its basic purpose and components are very simple. It arose from an identifiable market demand in the early twentieth century, as did consumer credit itself. The innovation underlying credit insurance was the simple idea of reducing risk for consumers through insuring them against inability to repay obligations when unforeseen personal disasters such as death, disability, or unemployment occur.

Even before consumer credit came into widespread use early in the last century, situations arose where individuals passed away or became sick or disabled and unable to satisfy the terms of their credit agreements. Repayments of consumer credit obligations typically depended on future wages, but insufficient family assets frequently meant that debts were not easily dischargeable upon occurrence of these unfortunate events. Death or disability of an employed debtor often promised significant financial unpleasantness for both the family and the creditors. Over the years, criticism and public policy concerns over debt protection have arisen not so much from the basic nature of the original product as financial protection but rather largely from questions over product delivery and pricing, discussed later.[1]

Such contingencies as death and disability quickly stoked a demand among borrowers and lenders for some sort of enhanced risk control for debtors. Borrowers entering into credit arrangements often felt uncomfortable about possible future inability to repay, and lenders found attractive the profit potential of providing insurance coverage that also would help with collections on their credit investments. The almost inevitable outcome was a new product called credit insurance directly covering the terms of specific consumer credit obligations. Today the potential inability to meet debt obligations still concerns many consumers entering credit arrangements, even if only to retain a good credit score with the credit reporting agency.

CREDIT INSURANCE
The oldest and probably still the best-known form of debt protection is credit life insurance, first offered in 1917 by the Morris Plan Insurance Society. In 2012, based on annual premium dollars, credit life insurance represented about one-eighth of credit-related insurance.[2] Credit life insurance is a form of term

---

1. There have never been many academic analyses of debt protection, but a paper by Belsky, Case, and Smith (2008) discusses it among other methods of reducing risk on credit transactions and provides a short bibliography in this area. For background discussions, see also Hubbard (1973), Fagg (1986), Barron and Staten (1996), Government Accountability Office (2011), and Consumer Credit Industry Association (2013).

2. Consumer Credit Industry Association (2013, 7). According to the American Council of Life Insurers (2013), at year end 2012, there was $94 billion of credit life insurance in force, less than 1 percent of the total of life insurance in force in the United States. The volume of credit life insurance in force peaked in 1989 at $260 billion, which represented about 3 percent of life insurance at that time.

life insurance that can accompany credit obligations and repays the debt if death occurs.

Credit disability insurance, often referred to as credit accident and health (A&H) insurance, is a credit-related form of A&H insurance that continues credit payments until the sick or disabled debtor recovers (up to the policy maximum). Credit involuntary unemployment insurance (credit IUI) is a form of casualty insurance that also continues to make payments until the unemployment situation is resolved (or the policy maximum is reached). Credit IUI is the only kind of insurance readily available to protect against involuntary unemployment. Credit property insurance involves collateral (such as automobiles) that underlies some credit obligations. Most individual credit insurance arrangements do not involve all these kinds of coverage.

In recent years, credit insurance purchased by consumers has been declining, in part as some of it is replaced by newer related debt protection products called debt cancellation contracts (DCCs) and debt suspension agreements (DSAs). Creditors offering these new versions of debt protection offer them directly to consumers as debt forgiveness or deferral by the lender and not as insurance. They typically offer them under their own brand monikers, such as "credit protector," and avoid any mention of insurance. Federal banking regulators and courts have declared that these newer forms of debt protection are not insurance under state laws, and so they are regulated differently from credit insurance, although they are basically the same in purpose and consumer use as traditional credit insurance. From the consumer's view, these new arrangements are functionally equivalent to credit insurance, in that they protect debtors against occurrence of the same personal disasters, and the legal and regulatory distinctions are probably largely transparent and uninteresting to purchasers. Because they are not actually counted as insurance for regulatory purposes, however, their volume is not included in state figures on insurance in force.

Most features of credit life insurance and the other kinds of credit insurance are similar to ordinary term insurance, but there are some special features that arise from their close association with a specific credit account. For instance, regulation has always constrained credit insurance (and other debt protection products) to following the terms of the associated credit contract closely, for instance, approximating the size of the credit contract. This requirement has maintained and fostered some continuing differences between credit insurance and other term insurance that remain features of these products today.

SOME DIFFERENTIATING FEATURES OF CREDIT INSURANCE
The association of credit insurance with a particular debt is the cause of an obvious first difference between credit insurance and other term insurance. The face amount of credit insurance in force is not fixed; rather, it declines over the life of the certificate of insurance as the credit is repaid.[3] In contrast, most ordinary

---

3. Credit insurance products usually are structured as certificates of insurance through a group policy in which the group is the insured customers of the creditor. In this case, the insured consumer receives a certificate of insurance coverage rather than an individual policy.

term insurance is sold in fixed amounts and remains at the same face amount for the specified period of time. For example, common group life insurance available to employees of a particular employer normally maintain the same insurance amount (or the same relationship to salary) throughout the period of employment, unless individual employees voluntarily purchase more insurance later or individuals drop the insurance amount when the premiums increase as the employee ages. Some insurance companies have on occasion attempted to compete with credit life insurance on mortgage credit by selling a decreasing-balance term insurance product through their life insurance agents, but declining-balance term insurance that is not specifically credit insurance is not common.

In the past, the conventional kind of declining-balance credit life insurance was gross indebtedness life insurance. This product insured the life of the debtor for the unpaid principal balance of the credit plus finance charges payable on the loan. The insurance in force declined in lock step with the scheduled progress of the payments of principal and interest on the credit account.

Because it included unearned finance charges in the insurance amount in force, gross indebtedness credit life insurance resulted in a face amount of insurance slightly larger than the net principal amount actually owed at any point during the indebtedness period, however. This product developed when typical amounts of consumer credit were small and maturities short, so that gross indebtedness normally did not exceed net indebtedness on an account by very much. Life insurance face amounts that at all times slightly exceeded net indebtedness outstanding had the advantage that this typically permitted repayment of an account in full upon death of the insured, even if the account were slightly delinquent. A claim arising from an account that was not delinquent resulted in a small payment to the estate of the insured individual.

Today, in large part because of criticism that gross indebtedness insurance is "overinsurance" because it includes unearned finance charges in the insured balance (particularly where large accounts such as mortgage loans are involved), some states have required net coverage on some or all loans. Insurance in force on a net indebtedness basis declines as the principal amount of the loan outstanding declines.[4]

Industry actuaries and experts say that virtually all credit life insurance associated with mortgage credit today is declining net indebtedness term life insurance, with monthly premiums (known as monthly outstanding balance, or MOB insurance). Industry sources also say that all remaining credit insurance on open-end credit, such as credit card credit and home equity lines of credit, is net indebtedness insurance with monthly premiums.

---

4. Because, unlike gross indebtedness, the principal amount of a loan does not decline linearly on credit accounts where payments are the same size each month, there is additional mathematical complexity in the pricing calculations on net indebtedness insurance for individualized certificates. This complexity has made development of net indebtedness insurance more dependent on the advent of electronic computer and communication systems. Many states specifically require that credit insurance on mortgage-related credit be on net basis. Many state laws also contain a maximum term for credit life that is shorter than the term of many mortgage loans.

Small contract size is a second differentiating feature between credit insurance and ordinary term insurance. Along with declining balance, small coverage amounts also reflect the heritage of credit insurance in the automobile credit, furniture and appliance credit, and small cash loan industries, rather than in the traditional insurance industry. The small size of credit contracts and related insurance also caused the revenue streams from the insurance product to be small. Small amounts of insurance producing only limited revenues led, in turn, to highly simplified underwriting, marketing, and paperwork procedures.

Underwriting

Historically, credit insurance has been presented to potential purchasers by lending personnel at the time of generation of the credit account, although in recent years, there has been a trend toward postapplication solicitation of credit insurance through mail and telemarketing, especially on credit card accounts. There never have been insurance agents specializing in credit insurance. Relatively small amounts of insurance generated at potentially thousands of geographically distinct locations (bank and credit union branches, auto dealerships, retail stores, and finance company offices) meant that insurers providing the policies were both unwilling and unable to invest the sums necessary to have them carefully underwritten consumer by consumer or sold by independent or ordinary licensed, full-time insurance agents.

Instead, the products developed without a differentiating set of actuarially variable characteristics for pricing, such as age, health, or smoking habits. Therefore, credit insurance has been variable only according to the size and maturity of the credit arrangements offered by the creditor and without consideration of these other underwriting factors. The states later adopted this approach as part of state requirements.[5]

Other things being equal, absence of underwriting differentiation means that at any price, credit life or disability insurance products become relatively more attractive for males, older consumers, those in poorer health, and those adopting certain lifestyle choices (such as smoking). This means that the insured pool of consumers purchasing credit insurance naturally tends to exhibit characteristics of adverse selection against the insurer compared with the population of all credit users. That is, a pool of credit insurance purchasers is likely to include a larger portion of older and riskier consumers than the population of credit users generally.

---

5. Today there may be a few eligibility questions concerning sales, such as age and a few simple health questions, but not for purposes of pricing. For example, credit life insurance is generally not available for sale to consumers older than sixty-five, although consumers of all eligible ages pay the same price. In general, state laws and regulations, in effect, now require the absence of underwriting differentiation, except that insurers may ask some questions about insurability for loan amounts greater than $15,000 if there is a downward rate adjustment (see National Association of Insurance Commissioners, Consumer Credit Insurance Model Regulation, section 6). State laws also generally require extensive consumer disclosures of the provisions of insurance certificates (see Consumer Credit Insurance Model Act, section 6).

Marketing

Although required by subsequent regulation to be available to any debtor meeting the age requirements, the simplified marketing of credit-related insurance through lending personnel rather than through experienced agents has been controversial. Sometimes lender personnel have been known to market the products quickly or aggressively, although the same complaint is sometimes also noted concerning ordinary insurance agents. Part of the contention has been that in the absence of any attempt to explore customers' insurance portfolio needs and their special risk characteristics, they receive no professional aid in the decision. This is one reason some observers have maintained that the marketing is so simplified that the product and its pricing are not even adequately explained. As a consequence, they contend, some consumers do not consider implications of the purchase adequately or sometimes even understand at all what they purchased or whether they purchased it.

Industry personnel have maintained that the product is so simple and straightforward that a discussion of the borrower's overall insurance needs is hardly called for. Under the circumstances, lenders may tout the insurance as good protection, and consumers must consider the implications for themselves. Lenders also note that the small size of the insurance amounts and associated revenues hardly permits full review of consumers' financial needs, the province of paid financial advisers.

Production and Paperwork Procedures

Further, to save on paperwork and record keeping expenses, production processes and associated paperwork have also been very simple. Because of the simple nature of the product and its distribution system, credit insurance typically was sold with a single premium for the whole term payable at the outset. This amount was forwarded to the insurer, and there was no subsequent need for the insurance sales agents (the lender's personnel who collect the monthly payments on the credit) to engage in any processing, subdividing, forwarding, or other insurance paperwork to send part of monthly loan payments to the insurer. Indeed, after the initial sale of the policy or certificate, the lending personnel needed only to be concerned with assisting the insured or survivors with filing appropriate forms on the minority of cases where a claim occurs and for calculating and crediting refunds of unearned premiums when an early loan payoff or refinancing takes place. There was no normal monthly record keeping or paperwork burden for the insurance company, either. This simplified set of procedures reduced the costs for both the lender and the insurer of distributing the product and of booking and recording the small transactions.

Typically, consumers paid the single premium for the insurance in advance by financing it as part of the proceeds of the credit. It is certainly possible to pay the premium in advance from another source of cash, but this is rarely done. Insurers and creditors have argued that this method of payment has the additional advantage that the insurance never lapses while the loan is outstanding because of failure of the consumer to meet a monthly payment obligation in a timely manner. The insurance never lapses to the detriment of the consumer, because it is prepaid.

Nonetheless, financing a single premium has also become controversial and is discussed further below. To some critics, the product and its regulation have not evolved sufficiently away from their roots in past small transactions, when single premiums may have made sense. To these critics, single-premium insurance is no longer appropriate in today's more robust marketplace for consumer financing in larger amounts.

Credit Disability Insurance

The other historically common form of credit insurance is credit disability insurance, sometimes called credit accident and health (A&H) insurance, and a related but separate newer product, credit involuntary unemployment insurance, frequently referred to as credit IUI. Taken together, these nonlife kinds of credit insurance have generated a bit more than half of annual premium dollars for nonproperty credit-related insurance in recent years.[6] Unlike credit life, which pays off the entire credit balance in the case of the insured event (death), credit A&H and IUI merely maintain the credit payments for a period of time until the end of the insured circumstances or until repayment of the debt in full or passage of the maximum benefit period, whichever is earlier. Thus, historically, these coverages have been gross coverages that include accrued finance charges but only for a limited time. For credits of longer maturities, these coverages tend to be more expensive than credit life insurance, so fewer consumers are prone to purchase them. Lower sales penetration, in turn, tends to produce even more adverse selection in the risk pool than would otherwise be the case.

Sales features of the A&H types of insurance are similar to credit life, and they have generated the same controversies. Historically, they also have been sold by loan officers in the process of granting credit. They also were for small amounts for limited terms with single premiums for the same reasons as credit life, and they also have been sold with little or no underwriting differentiation based on actuarial risk of the insured. There are some differences among coverages and associated premiums based on such things as waiting periods before a disability is considered sufficient to generate insurance payments (fourteen days is common, with benefits then retroactive). Maximum number of payments the insurer will make also may vary somewhat, but consumers typically do not have choices in these matters with an individual insurer or credit source. There also may be some exclusions for preexisting conditions treated during a short period before the opening of the credit arrangement and recurring within a specified short period after opening the account. Exclusions for normal pregnancy, self-inflicted injuries, war, and personal aviation also are common. Again, as with credit life

---

6. Consumer Credit Industry Association (2013, 5). The remaining portion of credit insurance is credit property and casualty insurance on credit collateral, a form of property insurance that is not discussed here. A large portion of credit property insurance is creditor-placed insurance that arises when debtors allow their normal property insurance on collateral such as houses to lapse, despite contracts not to do so, and creditors institute insurance on their own to cover their interest in the collateral. Because this is not normal credit insurance that consumers purchase on their own, this kind of insurance also is not discussed here.

insurance, the product is simplified to reduce costs, and a lifestyle-independent disability insurance product, now enshrined in regulation, generally prevails at a given creditor for a given type of credit.

DEBT CANCELLATION AND SUSPENSION PRODUCTS

As mentioned above, in recent years, changes in the market for debt protections have encouraged the growth of debt cancellation contracts (DCCs) and debt suspension agreements (DSAs) as substitutes for traditional kinds of credit insurance. These are contract clauses originally specifically allowed for credit contracts generated by national banks, savings and loan associations, and credit unions that were regulated by the federal Office of the Comptroller of the Currency, the Office of Thrift Supervision, or the National Credit Union Administration. In many cases, state laws that gave state-chartered banks regulatory parity with federally chartered institutions extended the authority to generate DCCs and DSAs to state-chartered institutions.

DCCs and DSAs are similar to credit insurance in that they provide financial benefits to covered individuals similar to credit life insurance (DCCs) and to credit A&H and IUI (DSAs). Concerning DCCs, in exchange for a fee a lender inserts into its lending contract a clause that the debt is canceled if a covered event (death) occurs. In the case of DSAs, another clause permits suspension of payments (with or without suspension of accruals of finance charges) if a covered event such as sickness, disability, or involuntary unemployment occurs. Thus, these clauses in a credit contract can directly substitute for credit insurance, and they may well represent a complete substitute from an individual consumer's viewpoint. They have had a substantial recent effect on the market for credit insurance and have substituted for credit insurance completely in the consumer lending arrangements of many lenders, especially credit card issuers.

DCCs and DSAs are not the same as credit insurance in some other ways, however, and they are not regulated in the same way. One important difference is that, strictly speaking, DCCs and DSAs are two-party arrangements between the creditor and the consumer, while in a credit insurance arrangement there is a third party, the insurance company, even if closely affiliated with or even controlled by the lender. For a consumer, this distinction may make little or no difference, but it is sometimes used as an argument for why state insurance regulation is not needed for DCCs and DSAs: there is no insurance company regulated by the state that might become insolvent. The argument is that insolvency of the "insurer" is of no concern to a consumer in the case of DCCs and DSAs, because there is no third-party insurance company that might have to make a claim payment in case of an insured event and must remain solvent to do so.[7] Rather, a DCC or DSA could be enforced if a covered event occurred even against an insolvent counterparty lender simply by not making the payments otherwise due the lender,

---

7. The bank may enter into an insurance contract with an insurance company to diversify the risks of its DCCs and DSAs, but the insurance company has no contact or contract directly with consumers.

as permitted under the DCC or DSA contract clause. It also follows that if there is no state-regulated insurance company entity involved, then the federal banking agencies, which are already concerned about and monitoring the solvency of banking institutions, are the appropriate regulators of this kind of contract.

A second difference is that the DCCs and DSAs, since they are not insurance for regulatory purposes, are not subject to state pricing regulations on insurance. There is not much publicly available information on the practical implications of this on pricing, but some observers claim that DCCs and DSAs are priced above comparable credit insurance. Others say that DCCs and DSAs closely follow the pricing of regulated credit insurance with which they compete. While it is not possible to comment definitively on this at present, if history is any guide it likely is going to be an ongoing issue between critics and supporters of credit insurance and its substitute products.[8]

Controversies over Debt Protection

As already indicated, marketing and sale of credit insurance and related products have sometimes been controversial. Although there has been a variety of kinds of criticism, most ultimately are based on the heritage from credit insurance already alluded to: the protection mostly comes in small packages, and its form, underwriting, sale, pricing, and regulation reflect this background.

CONTENTIONS OF CRITICS
To be sure, there also have been some other contentions. Using the credit insurance example, some observers have argued that the insurance merely protects the lender, even though the consumer pays for it. By itself, this kind of criticism hardly seems relevant. While credit insurance can simplify collections for lenders, in that they certainly are more likely to receive complete and timely repayment on covered loans if personal disasters strike certain borrowers, it is difficult to agree that only lenders and not also debtors and their families benefit from the protection. Debt protection is a risk diversification for borrowers, in that purchasers pool their risk of loss resulting from covered contingencies and pay a fee to make it go away from them (or their heirs). It is like arguing that only hospitals and doctors benefit from major medical health coverage and there is no benefit to the patient. At a minimum, credit insurance can help defend a consumer's credit score, if not his or her basic financial well-being and estate.

Beyond this sort of criticism, most of the controversy over credit insurance has arisen not from the concept and usefulness of the product but from the nature of the sales methods and pricing. Because of the relatively small size of credit insurance transactions, most of it historically has been sold as part of the origination

8. For further description and discussion of DCCs and DSAs on credit card credit, see Government Accountability Office (2011), a report actually more balanced and nuanced than its pejorative title suggests. See also Fagg and Nelson (2008).

(booking) of a credit account. The lending officer acts as the sales agent of the insurance company providing the insurance to consumers, and the lender receives a commission for each insurance sale.

Many observers have maintained that the lender should not profit from insurance sales that also benefit the lender, in large part because this sales channel can put too much pressure on prospective purchasers. The critics argue that consumers might feel that the insurance is a required part of the credit, or they might believe that buying the insurance will help their credit standing with the lender. According to this view, some consumers might be subtly (or unsubtly) coerced into taking the insurance when they do not need it, or unnecessary insurance might even be "packed" into the transaction without the consumer even knowing about it. Lenders and insurance companies dispute these claims and offer evidence of customer support from consumer surveys (discussed more fully below).

Further, some of the criticism of credit insurance goes even beyond questioning the good-faith nature of credit insurance sales. In this case, the criticism arises not so much from the marketing method as from the cost of the product. Some observers see the sale of small amounts of insurance as too costly per dollar of coverage. These critics believe that credit insurance is simply too expensive for the protection offered, which they feel many consumers do not need anyway. They assert that consumers should obtain other kinds of life and disability insurance if needed, and they contend that many lower-income or poorly educated consumers who may sometimes purchase credit insurance could better spend their money elsewhere.

Lenders and insurance companies also dispute the claims that credit insurance is too costly for the protection provided. In their view, any higher cost per dollar of insurance coverage reflects the small size of the insurance amount, much like the purchase of many commodities in small volumes. They also point out that the *total* cost of the insurance may well be less, even much less, than purchase of larger amounts of insurance than needed for the circumstances, even at a lower cost per dollar of coverage.

At a minimum, the critics maintain that consumers should not be permitted to finance the purchase of credit insurance premiums into the rest of the credit amount, as has been the typical practice in the past. Ability of consumers to finance the insurance premium has allowed insurance companies to sell coverage with the full premium paid in one payment at the outset (single-premium credit insurance) by making the insurance payment part of the monthly credit payment. Critics have argued that financing insurance makes it even more expensive because of finance charges on the insurance premium, and it hides the cost of an expensive insurance product by making the premium part of seemingly affordable monthly credit payments, even if the product provides the purchaser with substantial peace of mind.

CONTENTIONS OF SUPPORTERS

In contrast to these views, many lending and insurance industry personnel have long argued that credit insurance is a sensible and even almost essential protection for many consumers when they enter credit contracts, because they often are otherwise underinsured. These observers typically recall the origin of the product. They see it as protecting potentially underinsured individuals who enter into credit contracts, and their families, from financial uncertainty and resulting distress that easily could arise upon occurrence of a personal disaster such as death, disability, or involuntary unemployment.

Supporters also point out that premiums on credit insurance sales are regulated carefully by state insurance codes. They note that not all premiums paid by consumers are paid out in death and disability benefits, but there are still costs involved in producing the products, and states also have a clear interest in making sure that rates are sufficient so as not to jeopardize the solvency of the insurance companies that must have the reserves to manage the potential future claims of consumers.

Furthermore, these supporters defend the sales channel as the least costly approach for buying small amounts of insurance. They argue that financing the purchase of credit insurance makes it more affordable by lowering necessary payments for the many consumers who are otherwise underinsured, and might remain so to their detriment, if they were forced to pay for insurance in a single cash lump sum or through a small number of payments over too short a time period. They contend that the single premium ultimately reduces costs necessarily passed on to consumers, by minimizing underlying processing and paperwork that would otherwise raise these costs if the insurance were separately billed monthly. They argue that it also prevents lapses in insurance that might occur on monthly premium insurance if the debtor becomes delinquent for a period and does not meet the payment schedule.

CONTINUATION OF THE DEBATE

The debate over the merits of credit insurance has been ongoing for many decades, but it became recharged a decade or so ago because of some proposals at that time for federal regulatory changes. First, in late 2000, the Federal Reserve Board proposed to revise Truth in Lending disclosure regulations governing sale of credit insurance on certain subprime mortgage loans.[9] After a public comment period, in 2001, the agency made the proposed changes, requiring substantial additional disclosures on many mortgage loans with single-premium credit insurance. Second, in September 2002, the Office of the Comptroller of the Currency (OCC), the branch of the US Treasury Department that regulates national banks, reaffirmed its view that DCCs and DSAs that often substitute for credit insurance at national banks were part of bank lending products and not insurance. This contention placed the regulation of these substitute products for nationally chartered banking institutions solely within the purview of the OCC bank regulators and outside the province of insurance codes and regulators of the individual states.

Both federal regulatory issues provoked immediate reactions at the time. Certain critics contended that revisions to federal disclosure regulations were

---

9. See Federal Reserve Board, Notice of Proposed Rulemaking, Docket R-1090, December 13, 2000.

insufficient for credit insurance and that financed credit insurance should be banned completely on mortgage credit, if not on all credit used by consumers. This view led directly to a provision in the Dodd-Frank Act legislation in 2010 that banned single-premium credit insurance on mortgage loans. Critics of credit insurance and the OCC position that DCCs and DSAs are not insurance also maintained that state regulation of insurance-like products was important, because the state insurance departments at least had regulations and price ceilings already in place in this area. These advocates complained that the federal banking regulators did not immediately institute price ceilings and were not proposing to establish them.

In contrast, industry spokespersons generally continued to maintain that credit insurance for mortgage loans, including subprime mortgages, remained useful and valuable, as it had long been for other kinds of credit that consumers use. In this view, no regulatory changes that might interfere with its availability were needed or appropriate. Bank lenders also argued that banking institutions freed from state regulation by the position of the OCC could operate more efficiently in producing substitutes for credit insurance, because they did not have to comply with myriad separate regulations for each kind of insurance across all fifty states.

As these opposing views suggest, part of the debate about the merits of credit insurance concerns facts, such as whether some consumers are underinsured and whether they know what they are purchasing, but much of it centers on differing degrees of confidence that markets, even with price ceilings and disclosure requirements, will provide consumers with desirable products, meaningful choices, and sufficient information to enable them to make good decisions for themselves. This is just extension to credit-related insurance and risk sharing much of the old debate over the usefulness of consumer credit in the first place. No examination of theoretical or empirical information can completely and satisfactorily resolve a debate of this kind, as it has not done for consumer credit more generally.

Although economic evidence may not settle all aspects of the debate between detractors and supporters of debt protection, evidence may at least highlight and clarify the areas of disagreement. The next section provides some information on the pricing and loss ratios arising from credit insurance. This is followed by review of consumer cash flows on a typical automobile credit transaction and how the purchase of credit life insurance might change them. This latter exercise helps focus the philosophical controversies concerning the costs of this product. The final section examines available survey information on consumers' use of and attitudes toward debt protection.

Pricing and Loss Ratios

Originally, there were two basic pricing approaches to providing credit-related insurance, and both types still exist today. The first approach is the noncontributory group policy, which automatically covers all debtors of a particular creditor and in which the premiums are included as part of the cost of the credit. Historically, this type of arrangement has been especially common in credit union lending, but it is generally less common today than in the past, in part because it does not give consumers a choice.

The second type is the contributory group policy, in which the debtor chooses whether to purchase the insurance and the fee is itemized separately. As a general rule, this latter sort of coverage will be a bit more costly, because it is administratively more complicated than just charging everyone as part of the cost of the credit. It also generally produces a less favorable risk pool of insured consumers, other things being equal, and is also more costly for that reason. As indicated, both types of insurance are regulated at the state level through legislation or regulation that sets maximum rates and other terms and by insurance commissioners and departments that approve policy forms and are responsible for monitoring compliance.

Some examples can show the order of magnitude of premiums on credit insurance products. In 1917, when a $300 loan was common, the Morris Plan charged $1 per $100 of original indebtedness per year for gross indebtedness credit life insurance. This amounted to a $3 charge on a one-year loan of $300 (25 cents per month), hardly enough money even then to lead to establishment of an extensive agent network, careful underwriting, or monthly billing procedures. Common smaller credit amounts at the time produced even less revenue.

Today a purchaser of a $35,000 automobile or truck with a $5,000 trade-in and making a $5,000 down payment and financing the rest at a 4 percent APR on a five-year automobile financing contract would pay about $608 for net indebtedness credit life insurance (about $10.13 per month before finance charges) in a state with a mandatory rate ceiling of $0.49/$100 per year. While this may be a relatively high cost for a small amount of declining amount life insurance for a younger consumer, it is still not a large amount of money, and the consumer may not otherwise be able to obtain a small amount of insurance (and the buyer may not be young). Opinions diverge sharply on the value of the insurance, whether $608 over sixty months is a large or small amount of money, and whether the coverage is worth $608 to a (younger? older?) consumer with no other (or substantial other) coverage. Clearly, the outcome is in the eye of the beholder.

PRIMA FACIE RATES OF CHARGE

State laws concerning traditional credit insurance vary, but they generally follow guidelines in the form of model insurance codes published by the National Association of Insurance Commissioners (NAIC). Key elements of the regulation of credit-related insurance are the prima facie rates and the related loss ratio.

After extensive discussion and review over many years concerning appropriate rate levels and other regulations, the general position taken by most state law provisions on credit insurance is that the maximum permitted premium rate for the product in a state is the rate that will provide for sufficient benefits to purchasers while also considering the need to maintain solvency of the insurer so it can meet its obligations. States call this insurance premium pricing rate the prima facie rate. Although there has been considerable debate over the standard, and experience in some states does not always meet the standard set, a statewide loss ratio of 50 to 60 percent of written premiums for credit life insurance is generally believed to meet the needs of consumers, insurers, and states.[10] The prima facie rate, then, is the premium rate intended to produce the state-specified loss ratio.

Another, somewhat more complicated manner of determining both rates of charge for individual companies and prima facie rates for state regulatory purposes involves basing company rates of charge and state requirements on a wider range of expenses than just the loss ratio. A little thought immediately suggests a variety of cost components involved in pricing under what has become known as the component rating method. There are some differences in the formulas that actuaries use in developing rates for different classes of insurance business, but there is general agreement on the following components: claims costs, commissions to agents, general expenses, premium taxes, state licenses and fees, investment income, federal income taxes, and acceptable profit and contingency margins. Formulas and underlying assumptions can become quite complex, necessitating the mathematical skills of trained and certified actuaries, but including a broader list of components and applying relevant formulas to individual classes of business for individual companies suggest a greater likelihood of success in matching consumers' needs with those of insurance companies and states.

Mortality experience varies according to the insured risk pool among creditors and credit types and across states, but for typical contributory credit life insurance on consumer credit, the national average single-premium prima facie rate in recent years has been $0.49 per year per $100 of insurance initially in force, down from $0.62 in 1984 (Consumer Credit Industry Association 2013, 23). Some states have chosen higher or lower rates. Rates on mortgage-related insurance may be lower, and they may also be stated differently (reflecting its monthly pay or MOB basis, such as a monthly rate per thousand dollars of loan principal outstanding). Insurers who can demonstrate that the prima facie rate is actuarially insufficient for a given class of business in a particular state may request a higher rate for that business, called an upward deviation. Some states are more likely to grant such requests than others. Also, some states require downward deviations because of such things as insurer size, under the argument that scale economies should permit reduced production costs and a lower price to the consumer. Some states also specify discounts on single-premium plans, since reception of the full premium at the outset allows the issuer to earn investment income on it over the life of the insurance certificate.

Although insurance premiums are for the consumer an add-on to the cost of financing, they tend to be a small add-on relative to the finance charges, despite the controversies over the cost of the insurance. If voluntary and separately

---

10. See National Association of Insurance Commissioners, Model Regulation, 1994, section 4, which offers some alternative approaches in terms of suggested regulatory wording. Only a few states have adopted a loss ratio standard as high as 60 percent for credit life insurance. There is a state-by-state summary of loss rates and prima facie rates of charge in Consumer Credit Industry Association (2013, 10–11).

disclosed and signed for, the insurance premiums are not finance charges under Truth in Lending rules, but if they were finance charges, the automobile example above would add less than one percentage point to the financing APR. Nonetheless, prima facie rates have been subject to criticism over the years that they permit charges that are "too high." Typically, the criticism focuses on loss ratios that do not meet the 50 to 60 percent threshold for an acceptable level of consumer benefits, which leads to their contention that rates should be reduced enough to produce a loss ratio of 50 to 60 percent or more.[11]

It is difficult to determine in a meaningful sense whether prices for credit life insurance on particular credit products such as automobiles or subprime mortgages are "too high," especially when individuals purchase the products voluntarily.[12] It does appear, however, that states and state insurance departments are sensitive to the loss ratio issue. As mortality experience has improved over time, thirty-seven states lowered their basic prima facie rates for credit life insurance between 1984 and the end of 2012, while ten states and the District of Columbia stayed the same. Only two states increased their prima facie rates, both recently. The rates in effect in 2012 produced an overall national loss ratio of 46 percent for credit life insurance in that year.[13]

Insurers providing public comments in the Federal Reserve Board's December 2000 rule making proposal on Regulation Z concerning treatment of financed insurance premiums on mortgage credit (Federal Reserve Docket R-1090) argued that insurance loss ratios on subprime mortgage accounts were actually higher than the national 41 percent at that time. They contended that the 41 percent loss ratio reflected very favorable recent experience at that time on credit card related

11. See, for example, Griffin and Birnbaum (1999). It is important to note that a national average loss rate of 49 percent is just that, an average. It does not mean that all companies have that result in a given year or that an individual company has the same rate every year. In fact, loss rates can and do vary over time and over companies, and state insurance departments must keep in mind the impact of changes in prima facie rates on the solvency of companies with liabilities to consumers and whose loss experience varies.

12. It is not possible directly to compare loss ratios on credit life insurance with loss ratios on other insurance products that are competitive with credit life. One study attempted to calculate loss ratios on annual renewable term life insurance (sometimes called ART) from pricing information and mortality tables in order to compare the loss ratios on this product with credit life loss ratios. It concluded that the benefit-to-cost ratio may be higher for credit life than for ART, especially if the insurance certificate is held for shorter terms (see Smith and Cash 1993). Apparently using similar methodology, one company providing a public comment on the Federal Reserve Board's regulatory proposal on mortgage disclosures contended that the loss ratios on these two products are similar (see Federal Reserve Board Docket R-1090, comment 1938, Assurant Group, appendix chart).

13. On occasion, a state may make partial adjustments for one or more classes of business or for one or more insurers, or it may quote rates differently for one or more classes of business. The overall comparison reported here uses the chart and table in Consumer Credit Industry Association (2013, 10, 23).

accounts.[14] They also argued at the time that credit insurance loss ratios on subprime mortgage accounts actually are higher than the average, because the risk pool of home owners is older on average than the pool of typical consumer debtors overall.[15] The issue of loss ratios on credit insurance has long been controversial, and it remains so, even as loss rates have risen in recent years.

CONSUMERS' CASH FLOWS

Although it is not possible to analyze credit insurance loss ratios by lending product line, it is feasible to simulate the impact of different premium rates to examine the effect on the cash flows of a consumer debtor. As suggested by the automobile example above, it turns out that the cost impact of a large change in the prima facie insurance rate for credit life insurance has much less impact on the total consumer cost of a typical financing transaction than a relatively small change in the APR. Credit life insurance is the only kind of credit insurance that can be compared with ordinary term insurance. Small disability policies that are not credit insurance are simply not otherwise available in the marketplace.

Table 12.1 illustrates the terms and cash flow consequences associated with an automobile loan of $25,000 for five years at annual percentage (interest) rates of 4 percent (columns 1, 2, and 3) and 6 percent (columns 4, 5, and 6). (Four percent is a bit below the most recent estimate of the national average rate at auto finance companies in 2011, and 6 percent is a bit above the national average for forty-eight-month auto loans at commercial banks in 2011 reported in the February, 2014 consumer credit report from the Federal Reserve, monthly statistical release G19. The Federal Reserve is currently not publishing these terms while it refines the data collection methodology.)

Both the lower and the higher interest rates are further differentiated according to rates of charge for single-premium credit life insurance. Columns 1 and

14. The loss ratio on open-end credit, reported to be mostly credit card credit, was 33 percent in 1999 (see Fagg 2001, 11). Informal contacts with insurers suggest that much of the favorable experience in this area at the time arose from very favorable experience in one area: low claims experience on involuntary unemployment insurance (IUI) during the long economic upswing in the late 1990s. Apparently, in their view, claims experience on credit life and A&H coverage on open-end credit is normally more like experience on other forms of credit, although, again, no publicly available claims experience is available by credit type. Information in Government Accountability Office (2011) suggests that claims experience on DCCs and DSAs remained very favorable to card issuers in 2009 but that credit insurance generated by card issuers had declined dramatically to the point where new insurance coverage became almost zero by 2009.

15. See, for example, Federal Reserve Board Docket R-1090, comment 1938 (Assurant Group): "It usually takes a number of years to build equity in a home. As a consequence, the average of an insured in the home equity market is 4 to 10 years older than the typical credit life insured. Our single premium credit life book of business on home equity loans is only a couple of years old and already has a loss ratio of 50%. As the book of business matures and the insured individuals continue to get older, the loss ratio will rise because the rates of mortality and disability increase as people get older. We project the credit life loss ratio will level off at around 60%. Our single premium disability inception-to-date loss ratio for home equity loans is 116%."

Table 12.1 PRICES AND PAYMENTS FOR EXAMPLES OF AUTO LOANS WITH AND WITHOUT CREDIT INSURANCE

Loan and insurance rates and terms						
Principal	25,000	25,000	25,000	25,000	25,000	25,000
APR	4%	4%	4%	6%	6%	6%
Maturity (years)	5	5	5	5	5	5
Life insurance rate	None	.49/100	.65/100	None	.49/100	.65/100
(1) Credit life premium	0	608.04	813.04	0	617.86	826.28
(2) Finance charge	2,624.74	2.688.62	2,710.15	3,999.10	4,098.04	4,131.38
(3) Monthly payment[a]	460.42	471.61	475.39	483.33	495.26	499.29
(4) Total of payments	27,624.78	28,296.66	28,523.19	28,999.10	29,715.97	29,957.66

[a]In each case, the final payment is a few cents less than the others.

4 show the case of no insurance for comparison. Columns 2 and 5 designate as an "average rate" the 2012 national average rate of $0.49/$100 per year according to the 2013 *Fact Book of Credit-Related Insurance* (Consumer Credit Industry Association 2013, 23). Columns 4 and 6 employ a "high" premium rate of $0.65/$100, about one-third higher than the national average rate and higher than the prima facie rate in all but five states in 2010. The insurance calculations are for single-premium credit life insurance on a net indebtedness basis. The premium is financed at the annual percentage rate, and the payments amortize the account to zero at the maturity of the note. The calculations reflect that the final payment in each case is a few cents smaller than the others.

The table shows that amortizing the $25,000 auto loan over five years requires monthly payments of $460.42 without any insurance (column 1, line 3). This compares with monthly payments of $471.61 (column 2, line 3) for the same loan covered by credit life insurance for five years, calculated at the "average" premium rate and financed on a single-premium basis. The total insurance premium is $608.04, and the total of payments is $671.88 higher for the 4 percent loan with credit life insurance. This amount reflects a finance charge higher by $63.84 in addition to the insurance premium.

Whether $671.68 (including additional finance charge) is a large or small amount to pay for additional declining balance life insurance upon taking on a credit obligation of $25,000 to be repaid over five years ultimately is answerable only through the eyes of the beholder and depends on the beholder's circumstances. For some (maybe those with little or no life insurance in force), the purchase may well seem like a good idea, as evidenced by consumer surveys noted below. For others, maybe those with substantial other insurance, the product is less attractive, and they probably are less likely to buy it.

Column 3 of the table shows the same calculations for the "high" insurance premium rate. The "high" rate adds $205 to the insurance premium compared with the average premium case and $21.53 to the finance charge. This increases the monthly payment by $3.78 over the average rate case. The insurance costs $813.04 over five years, and total costs of the transaction, including finance charges on the single-premium arrangement, rise by an (undiscounted) $898.41, or $14.98 per month, over the no-insurance case. The increase is equal to a bit less than two more monthly payments but actually spread across the sixty payments of the transaction.

These amounts contrast with the loans at the higher annual percentage rates (columns 3 through 6). It is obvious from the table that the higher interest rates add much more to the cost of the transaction than higher insurance premium rates. And so for shopping purposes, it seems much more reasonable for consumers desiring credit life insurance and wanting to save money on the entirety of the transaction to shop for lower APRs than for lower credit insurance premiums.

COMPARISON WITH ORDINARY TERM INSURANCE

A recurring pricing issue concerning credit-related insurance is how the cost of credit life insurance compares with ordinary term life insurance. It appears that the cost of insurance alternatives to credit-related insurance is highly variable, enough so that credit-related insurance sometimes costs more and sometimes less. A few examples from typical mass mailings, sent presumably with the intent of being attractive to a wide audience, can illustrate this phenomenon; many more examples would be possible. The mailings demonstrate that finding the appropriate low-cost alternative to meet a given insurance need requires consumer understanding and probably some shopping effort.

A mailing in 2011 from AAA (American Automobile Association) Life Insurance Company provides a useful first example. The mailing promises: "Direct term is the kind of life insurance financial planners recommend. This is because you can get the most coverage for your money, and yet at rates more suited to a family's budget." The offering is especially interesting because it specifically contains rates for life insurance policies in amounts of $25,000 and $50,000, along with larger amounts of coverage. Term life insurance is not available from many sources in amounts less than $100,000.

Table 12.2 contains the premium calculated for $25,000 of term life insurance for five years of coverage from this source for consumers at successive age intervals beginning at eighteen and extending through sixty-four. The insurance product is not strictly comparable to credit-related insurance, because it makes some distinctions among customers. The first column is for male nonsmokers, and the second is for male smokers. The third column is for female nonsmokers and the fourth for female smokers. The back of the brochure indicates that "the answers that you provide to the health questions contained on the application may be used to determine your eligibility for coverage" and also that "If for some reason you do not qualify for this offer, we may recommend another product which may require

Example 1. Advertised Plan of AAA Life Insurance Company, $25,000 of Term Life Insurance for Five Years

Age	Male		Female	
	Nonnicotine	Nicotine User	Nonnicotine	Nicotine User
18–34	359.40	599.40	299.40	479.40
35–39	407.40	719.40	329.40	539.40
40–44	497.40	899.40	395.40	641.40
45–49	641.40	1,199.40	491.40	797.40
50–54	809.40	1,679.40	629.40	1,139.40
55–59	1,223.40	2,579.40	839.40	1,679.40
60–64	1,757.40	3,899.40	1,199.40	2,423.40

Example 2. Advertised Plan of Transamerica Life Insurance Company, $100,000 of Term Life Insurance for Five Years for "Trendsetter Super 10 Preferred Nonsmoker"

Age	Male	Female		
40	703.80	656.40		
41	735.00	687.60		
42	771.60	719.40		
43	813.60	756.00		
44	855.60	792.60		
45	908.40	829.80		
46	960.60	882.00		
47	1,013.40	939.60		
48	1,065.60	992.40		
49	1,118.40	1,039.80		
50	1,176.00	1,071.00		
51	1,254.60	1,134.00		
52	1,375.80	1,197.00		
53	1,491.00	1,260.00		
54	1,606.80	1,323.20		
55	1,743.00	1,386.00		
56	1,879.80	1,464.60		
57	2,031.60	1,554.00		
58	2,194.80	1,648.80		
59	2,357.40	1,753.80		
60	2,520.00	1,863.60		

Table 12.2 (CONTINUED)

Example 3. Advertised Plan of United of Omaha Life Insurance Company, $20,000 of Life Insurance for Five Years Also Building a Small (Undisclosed) Cash Value				
Age	Male	Female		
45–49	3,960.00	3,180.00		
50–54	4,600.20	3,720.00		
55–59	5,770.20	4,260.00		
60–64	7,060.20	5,160.00		

a medical exam." Also, the ordinary term product is not decreasing balance insurance like the credit insurance.

Although for these reasons, the products are not strictly comparable, examining the premiums in the upper panel of table 12.2 relative to the credit life premiums calculated in table 12.1 shows the cost relationship. Looking at the loan with the lower interest rate and the lower insurance rates (column 2 of table 12.1) shows that the (undiscounted) sum of the premiums for the ordinary term life example is lower than the credit insurance cost (including associated finance charges) only for nonsmoking males younger than forty-five and smokers younger than thirty-five. Females fare a bit better, but savings of more than $1 per monthly payment still are available only to female nonsmokers younger than fifty and smokers younger than forty.

Thus, in this example from a widely circulated source of a large life insurance company, credit insurance premiums are not uniformly higher or lower than the cost of ordinary term life insurance coverage. Choice between the ordinary term insurance in the specific example in table 12.2 and the credit-related insurance example in table 12.1 depends on age, sex, and smoking preference of the borrower and also on the premium rate on the credit-related insurance. For some consumers, there may also be some complications from the "few health questions" and the possibility of a health examination, which would not normally be a factor for the credit life insurance. Also, the ordinary term insurance is level balance insurance. But the cost also is higher for both sexes for higher age groups, in some cases much higher, especially for smokers. For male smokers ages sixty to sixty-four, the level balance term insurance costs more than five times as much as the average credit insurance cost for five years.

It seems likely that the risk pool in the AAA example probably could be characterized as "average," given the widespread dissemination of the marketing approach and the diversity of the membership of AAA. The risk pool on an insurance arrangement does not have to be average, of course. An early 2011 brochure from an agency distributing insurance for Transamerica Life Insurance promised lower rates for "Trendsetter Super 10 Preferred Nonsmoker" applicants (second panel of table 12.2). This marketing piece also notes: "Insurance eligibility and premiums are subject to underwriting in the form of a brief examination, at no cost to you." One noteworthy feature of the brochure is that it makes no mention of life insurance amounts less than $100,000.

Again comparing tables 12.1 and 12.2 reveals that the "Trendsetter Super 10 Preferred Nonsmokers" relative to the credit insurance premiums show much higher total costs. To be sure, the insurance amount is much higher and does not decline over the course of the term, but some, maybe many, consumers will not want to spend this much for life insurance protection coverage for a $25,000 declining debt. Some consumers also may not want a medical examination, and it might lead to higher price after underwriting. And there is no indication of a policy price for smokers. Apparently, under this program, there is no indication that insurance is even available for smokers. And those consumers who do qualify do not have the option of accepting any potential cost savings per dollar of insurance in cash. Instead, they must realize any advantage in the form of additional face amount of insurance, at higher total cost, rather than a lower net premium amount.

In contrast to this plan for relatively large amounts of term life insurance for healthy nonsmoking consumers, there are also widely available insurance plans of much smaller face amounts at much higher cost and apparently aimed at a much riskier group of consumers. For example, in early 2011, United of Omaha Life Insurance Company, a company of the Mutual of Omaha Group, offered in a mass mailing to customers of a large banking company much higher rates for small amounts of cash value insurance (third panel of table 12.2). The marketing literature specifically notes: "Your acceptance for this United of Omaha Life Insurance policy is guaranteed as long as you're between the ages of 45–85 (45–75 in MO)." The literature notes, however, that "in order to guarantee acceptance, the death benefits payable (for any cause other than accidental) are reduced during the first two years of the policy."

It appears that this third product has some of the characteristics of credit life insurance, in that it is not generally dependent on health status, and it does not otherwise differentiate between smokers and nonsmokers or among occupations and lifestyles. Coverage does not decline over time, but the face amount is only $20,000 on a single policy. Unlike credit insurance, this product does differentiate by age. The brochure indicates that this policy builds a cash value, but it does not explain this component of the package, and over five years, this would not be a large amount. The plan to be appears aimed at a risk pool even more adverse to the insurer than credit life purchasers, and this insurance is only available in very small amounts at substantial price (see panel 3 of table 12.2). As with the other examples, it demonstrates that the comparison with credit life insurance depends on the purchaser's conditions and needs.

Consumer Acceptance

As indicated earlier, it may not be possible with empirical information to settle to everyone's satisfaction the ongoing debates over the usefulness of credit insurance, but certainly, consumers' insurance needs and attitudes toward the product provide some relevant insights. As it turns out, many consumers do not have much other life insurance, and, maybe because of this fact, many users are generally favorably inclined to the credit insurance products.

OTHER LIFE INSURANCE

One relevant piece of information is that surveys of consumers show that a substantial fraction of the public does not otherwise have much life insurance. The 2010 Survey of Consumer Finances indicates that about 37 percent of families had little or no life insurance, totaling both term insurance and whole life (table 12.3). Another 33 percent of families had moderate amounts of life insurance within the range of $10,000 to $100,000 of face amount, and about one-fifth of families had life insurance in the amount of $100,000 to $500,000. The remaining 8 percent of families had life insurance of more than $500,000.

Not especially surprisingly, there appears to be a strong income effect in life insurance coverage. The median income of families with little or no life insurance was $27,000, and for those with moderate amounts, it was $40,000. Many of these families are credit users, however. Thirty percent of those with little or no life insurance in the 2010 survey were users of mortgage credit, and about 20 percent had automobile credit. About two-fifths (39 percent) of those with moderate amounts of life insurance had mortgage credit, and 28 percent had automobile

Table 12.3 LIFE INSURANCE HOLDING AMONG FAMILIES IN 2010

	Proportion of families	Median income of these families	Proportion of these families with mortage[a]	Proportion of these families with auto credit[a]
With life insurance amounts of				
$10,000 or less	37	$27,000	30	20
$10,001 to $100,000	33	$40,000	39	28
$100,001 to $500,000	21	$74,000	65	43
$500,001 or more	8	$141,000	80	39
Total	100			

[a]Proportion of families with this amount of life insurance who have credit of this type outstanding.

SOURCE: 2010 Survey of Consumer Finances

credit. Even without any further information about these individuals, it seems likely that some of them would at least think about credit insurance, if presented the opportunity, when entering into credit arrangements.

CREDIT INSURANCE SALES PENETRATION

Another piece of empirical information involves penetration rates of credit insurance sales in credit markets. Sometimes the contention is heard that high penetration rates for credit insurance are just indications of coercive sales or even "packing." Since from this viewpoint credit insurance is not needed, high penetration rates could be a bad sign.

If penetration rates are high, however, this does not necessarily indicate that sales are coercive. All purchasers could be purchasing the product voluntarily, even at 100 percent penetration, although high penetration would be more likely indicative of potential sales abuses than low penetration rate.[16] In contrast, if insurance penetration rates are not high, this must be an indication of available choice, at least for the proportion of consumers who make the choice not to purchase the insurance products.

Limited publicly available information on the question of credit insurance sales penetration rates for various kinds of consumer and mortgage credit information suggests that sales penetration rates for credit insurance are relatively low and have been declining for consumer credit, even before widespread availability of DCCs and DSAs. For example, a public comment in 2000 to the Federal Reserve Board concerning its proposed revision of Regulation Z said that its "placement" of credit insurance in the subprime mortgage area was 8 to 9 percent of "loan production" in calendar year 2000.[17] A public comment by a large writer of credit insurance policies suggested that the penetration rate in this market at that time was around 12 to 13 percent.[18]

---

16. High penetration rates of credit insurance sales on small cash loans at finance companies have been argued in the past as indicative of coercive sales. See *USLife Credit Corp v. Federal Trade Commission*, 559 F2d 1387 (Fifth Circuit, 1979). In this case, the administrative law judge and the US Court of Appeals decided that a high penetration ratio is not a per se indication of coercive sales. The US Supreme Court denied further consideration.

17. Docket R-1090, comment 1973 (Bank of America), speaking about subsidiary EquiCredit. Comment 1955 to the same docket reported the penetration in its prime mortgage business at about 3 to 5 percent (FleetBoston Financial).

18. Docket R-1090, comment 1938 (Assurant Group). A request to this company for further information concerning this penetration rate produced a reply about how its consulting actuary produced the estimate based on his knowledge of the portfolios of the large credit insurers, together with some analytical assumptions about the size and nature of the subprime mortgage market, which was not well known at the time. Because of the necessity of making assumptions in the analysis, it is difficult to conclude that the overall penetration rate in the subprime mortgage market was precisely the 12.6 percent stated in the comment; but based on the analysis of the actuary, it does seem reasonable to conclude, at a minimum, that the penetration rate among clients of this insurer was not very high.

Limited information from other sources indicates a somewhat higher penetration rate on subprime mortgage credit in the past, although it is still well less than a majority of loans. Informal contacts with selected creditors in the subprime mortgage market indicated penetration rates around 20 to 30 percent in 2001. Calculations using a data base of 1.4 million subprime mortgage loans indicated a penetration rate of about 28 percent on first-mortgage credits and 48 percent on junior lien loans at that time.[19] Still, this information suggests that there is choice in the matter of adding insurance to credit contracts. This, in turn, argues the likelihood that many purchasers affirmatively select the product.[20]

SURVEYS OF CONSUMERS

Additional empirical information about sales penetration arises from the results over the years of surveys of consumer attitudes about credit-related insurance. For the most part, survey data concerning consumer desire for or acceptance of credit-related insurance have focused on consumers who have purchased credit-related insurance on closed-end, nonmortgage consumer credit transactions; only fairly recently has there been any publicly available consumer survey data concerning credit-related insurance on mortgage credit and credit cards. Over the years, the surveys were undertaken in part specifically to explore the sales coercion issue. In each case, an underlying contention of the survey research was the view that if insurance packing or other abusive insurance sales practices were widespread, they should be visible in direct questioning of consumers and in their unfavorable post hoc attitudes toward the product and their overall experience with it.[21]

Attitude surveys have indicated, as might be expected, a wide range of opinions and circumstances among consumers concerning credit insurance and related forms of debt protection. On balance, however, consumer surveys of experience with these products over the years have consistently led to the conclusion that many consumers want to purchase them, and they mostly do not believe the products are expensive for the peace of mind they apparently produce. A monograph reporting on a new survey in 1993 summarized results of the earliest studies as follows:[22]

A common theme emerges from these four surveys of consumers. Respondents across all surveys viewed credit insurance products favorably. Among purchasers of credit insurance, the Ohio [University] study found that 90 percent would recommend credit life insurance to a friend, relative or neighbor. The 1977 FRB [Federal Reserve Board] study found that

19. Docket R-1090 (American Financial Services Association).

20. See also discussion in Government Accountability Office (2011), which indicates that sales penetration for DCCs and DSAs on credit card accounts was about 7 percent in 2009.

21. The survey results are found in the following sources: Hubbard (1973), Huber (1976), Durkin and Elliehausen (1978), Eisenbeis and Schweitzer (1979), Cyrnak and Canner (1986), Barron and Staten (1996), Durkin (2002), and Durkin and Elliehausen (2012).

22. Barron and Staten (1996, 9–10). This source also reviewed and compared methodologies employed in the earlier surveys (see their chapter 2).

85 percent of all borrowers (purchasers and non purchasers) viewed credit insurance as "good" or "good with qualifications." In the 1985 FRB survey, 93 percent of purchasers and 65 percent of non purchasers viewed credit insurance as "good" or "good with qualifications." In the 1976 CRC [Credit Research Center] survey, 54 percent of general respondents and 90 percent of credit insurance purchasers said it would be desirable if more retailers from whom they purchased would offer credit insurance products.

In early 2012, a nationwide population survey of consumers on these issues updated previous information on use of and attitudes toward credit insurance and related debt protection products (see Durkin and Elliehausen 2012). Where possible and appropriate, this survey employed identical lines of questioning and question wording to those used in earlier survey efforts.

The 2012 survey showed that the penetration rate on closed-end consumer installment credit apparently had stabilized at around one-quarter of users of this kind of credit after a steep fall between 1985 and 2001. From sales penetration exceeding three-fifths in 1977 and 1985, the ratio had fallen to between one-fifth and one-quarter in 2001 (table 12.4). The penetration rate on mortgage credit was similar to insurance penetration on installment credit in 2012, with penetration on credit card credit lower.

Although sales penetration appears to have fallen over recent decades, it seems that the attitudes of actual purchasers of the protection products among installment credit users have not changed over time. More than 85 percent of installment credit users with debt protection continue to maintain a favorable attitude in 2012, in the same high range as in 1977 and 1985 (table 12.5). Furthermore, about three in four purchasers of protection on installment credit in 2012 said that they would purchase again, down a bit from 2001 but still in a high range (table 12.6). Willingness to purchase again on mortgage credit was similar.

Table 12.4 DEBT PROTECTION PENETRATION RATES, 1977–2012 (PERCENTAGE DISTRIBUTIONS WITHIN GROUPS OF CREDIT USERS)

	1977	1985	2001	2012	2001	2012	2001	2012
	Install Credit	Install Credit	Install Credit	Install Credit	Mortgage Credit	Mortgage Credit	Credit Card	Credit Card
Have	63.9	64.7	21.9	26.7	32.1	23.9	20.1	14.0
Do not have	30.1	33.1	74.4	75.3	60.5	72.3	73.9	82.0
Do not know/ refuse	6.0	2.2	2.9	2.8	7.4	3.8	6.0	4.0
Total	100.0	100.0	100.0	100.0	100.0	100.0	100.0	100.0

Columns may not add to totals because of rounding.

Table 12.5 ATTITUDES TOWARD DEBT PROTECTION AMONG USERS OF INSTALLMENT CREDIT, 1977–2012 (PERCENTAGE DISTRIBUTIONS OF USERS OF INSTALLMENT CREDIT, WITH AND WITHOUT DEBT PROTECTION)

Attitude	1977		1985		2001		2012	
	Have	Do Not Have	Have	Do Not Have	Have	Do Not Have	Have	Do Not Have
Good	86.7	59.8	89.9	56.4	88.5	32.3	85.5	53.8
Good with qualifications	8.6	18.9	2.9	8.3	3.8	6.1	*	3.2
Neither good nor bad	2.1	9.1	1.9	6.4	3.2	13.9	3.1	1.8
Bad with qualifications	*	2.7	*	2.6	*	1.6	*	0.8
Bad	2.2	9.5	5.2	26.3	4.5	46.0	11.4	40.5
Total	100.0	100.0	100.0	100.0	100.0	100.0	100.0	100.0

* Less than one-half of one percent.
Columns may not add to totals because of rounding.

Table 12.6 WILLINGNESS TO PURCHASE DEBT PROTECTION AGAIN, 2001 AND 2012 (PERCENTAGE DISTRIBUTIONS WITHIN GROUPS OF CREDIT USERS)

Purchase again?	2001	2012	2001	2012
	Installment Credit	Installment Credit	Mortgage Credit	Mortgage Credit
Yes	94.2	74.6	71.0	71.2
No	5.8	24.4	24.2	28.0
Do not know/ refuse	*	1.0	4.8	0.8
Total	100.0	100.0	100.0	100.0

* Less than one-half of one percent.
Columns may not add exactly to totals because of rounding.

The consistently favorable attitudes among protection purchasers contrast sharply with the views of those who do not purchase the products. For the latter group, those reporting that the products are "good" or "good" with some qualification, fell from about three-quarters of respondents in 1977 to only a bit more than a third of respondents in 2001 and half in 2012, while unfavorable attitudes among nonpurchasers jumped sharply (table 12.5). Unfavorable attitude toward the products among this group of consumers likely is an important reason for not purchasing debt protection. Since the views of users and nonusers are so divergent with respect to these products, however, it seems care should be taken so

Table 12.7 RECOMMENDATIONS CONCERNING DEBT PROTECTION PURCHASE
AT POINT OF SALE ON INSTALLMENT CREDIT, 1977–2012 (PERCENTAGE
DISTRIBUTIONS WITHIN GROUPS OF USERS OF INSTALLMENT CREDIT, WITH
AND WITHOUT DEBT PROTECTION)

	1977		1985		2001		2012	
	Protection		Protection		Protection		Protection	
	Have	Do Not Have	Have	Do Not Have	Have	Do Not Have	Have	Do Not Have
Recommendation								
Never mentioned	10.6	52.2	14.8	45.2	15.4	53.3	18.7	62.7
Offered	15.0	22.6	44.7	35.5	53.2	33.9	43.5	29.5
Recommended	33.1	17.0	16.4	12.9	12.2	4.1	17.6	0.5
Strongly recommended/ required	39.3	2.3	20.1	2.6	16.6	3.4	20.1	0.9
Do not know/ refuse	2.1	5.9	3.9	3.9	2.6	5.3	*	6.5
Total	100.0	100.0	100.0	100.0	100.0	100.0	100.0	100.0

* Less than one-half of one percent.
Columns may not add to totals because of rounding.

that the views of users are given sufficient weight in developing regulatory and other public policies in this area, especially since nonusers have already clearly expressed their preference by not purchasing the products.

Another reason for not purchasing is that the products apparently are not offered to all credit users, or at least not vigorously enough for them to be aware of any sales effort. In each of the years studied, about half or more of nonpurchasers of debt protection on installment credit indicated that the product was never offered to them (table 12.7). Only a small (and declining) portion of nonusers said that the creditor recommended the product.

Not surprisingly, a somewhat higher portion of purchasers said that the creditor had offered and/or recommended debt protection. It appears that the portion of consumers who might feel pressured to purchase has declined over the years, however. In 1977, about two-fifths of purchasers indicated that the creditor had strongly recommended or even required purchase. By 2001, this proportion had declined to around one-fifth.

Survey results also reveal that favorable attitudes among purchasers of credit insurance and related products apparently are not limited to users of closed-end installment credit. About three-quarters of mortgage and bank card credit users with protection products also held a favorable attitude (table 12.8). In each case, those with the same kinds of credit outstanding but without debt protection held much different views, not especially surprising given that

Table 12.8 CONSUMER ATTITUDES TOWARD DEBT PROTECTION, 2012 (PERCENT
DISTRIBUTIONS WITHIN GROUPS OF CREDIT USERS WITH AND WITHOUT DEBT
PROTECTION)

	Installment Credit[a]		Mortgage Credit	
	Have Protection	**Do Not Have Protection**	**Have Protection**	**Do Not Have Protection**
Good	85.5	53.8	80.4	44.9
Good with qualifications	*	3.2	1.3	2.0
Neither good nor bad	3.1	1.8	*	2.7
Bad with qualifications	*	0.8	*	*
Bad	11.4	40.5	18.3	50.3
Total	100.0	100.0	100.0	100.0
	Bank Card		**No Closed-End Credit**	
	Have Protection	**Do Not Have Protection**	**No Protection**	
Good	77.1	43.7	45.8	
Good with qualifications	*	1.7	1.9	
Neither good nor bad	1.6	1.9	2.3	
Bad with qualifications	0.5	0.3	0.4	
Bad	20.8	52.3	49.5	
Total	100.0	100.0	100.0	

* Less than one-half of one percent.
Columns may not add to totals because of rounding.

they chose not to purchase. Again, the extreme divergence in views between
purchasers and nonpurchasers raises the question of who is best suited to recommended the public policy posture with respect to these products. About
80 percent of each group of credit users reported satisfaction with the debt
protection product (table 12.9).

All of this suggests that credit insurance and its close substitutes in the form
of DCCs and DSAs are going to continue to complement consumer credit, unless
industry opponents succeed in their long-standing campaign to drive these products from the marketplace through legislation or regulation. It appears that many
consumers would be disappointed with this outcome.

Table 12.9 SATISFACTION WITH PURCHASE OF DEBT PROTECTION, 2001 AND 2012 (PERCENTAGE DISTRIBUTIONS WITHIN GROUPS OF CREDIT USERS)

Satisfied with Purchase?	2001	2012	2001	2012
	Installment Credit	Installment Credit	Mortgage Credit	Mortgage Credit
Very	26.9	38.2	25.8	32.6
Somewhat	63.5	40.9	56.5	52.9
Neither satisfied nor dissatisfied	3.8	20.9	11.3	10.6
Somewhat dissatisfied	2.6	*	1.6	2.1
Very dissatisfied	*	*	*	1.9
Do not know/ refuse	3.2	*	4.8	*
Total	100.0	100.0	100.0	100.0

* Less than one-half of one percent.
Columns may not add exactly to totals because of rounding.

CONSUMER AUTOMOBILE LEASING

Automobile leasing is closely related to consumer credit but also distinct from it. Leasing of automobiles is offered by dealers and financing sources as an alternative to credit financing, and while not credit legally, it is an alternative from a consumer's viewpoint, albeit with somewhat different features.[23]

Acquiring and financing a substantial asset through purchase credit ranks among the most complicated financial transactions a typical consumer undertakes; in some ways, a lease is even more complicated. Since leases can provide convenient substitutes for credit purchases and frequently offer lower monthly payments, many vehicle acquisitions today involve a lease. In fundamental economic terms, a consumer's decision to lease rather than use more traditional forms of credit is relatively straightforward to a financial analyst, but it often is much less obvious to consumers. Stating the problem in its simplest form, a consumer should lease an asset rather than purchase it on credit if the risk-adjusted discounted present cost of all the lease payments and outflows (including down payments and any deferred payment for a residual value where relevant) is less

---

23. The discussion here draws on more extensive discussion of the disclosure issues in Durkin and Elliehausen (2011, appendix B).

than the comparable present cost of all outflows for the credit purchase over a comparable period of time.[24]

Kinds of Leases

As the leasing market has evolved over the years, the closed-end operating lease has become typical in consumer transactions, at least in the big market for automobiles and light trucks. An "operating lease" covers a period of time shorter than the whole economic life of an asset. There is an expectation that an asset will still have an economic value (its "residual value") at the end of an operating lease. With an operating lease, an asset user (lessee) agrees to pay for the expected depreciation of an asset during the lease period, plus a financing or lease charge to compensate the owner (lessor) for the use of the lessor's capital, including a profit. Common car rentals or apartment leases are examples of short-term operating leases.

Also very familiar today are longer-term operating leases (possibly up to four or five years or even longer) that auto dealers offer consumers through leasing companies and banks. These are the operating leases that have become important substitutes for purchase financing for consumers, and they are widely advertised by both automobile manufacturers and dealers. Like a car renter or apartment lessee, a vehicle lessee under these plans uses the asset for a term but must return it to the lessor at the end of the lease period (unless the parties make some other arrangement for disposition). An operating lease always assumes that the asset will have some remaining economic life and value at lease end. Consequently, transfer of ownership at lease end (to the lessee or another party) requires additional payment for the residual value.[25]

Among operating leases for consumers, the closed-end operating lease, a "walk-away" lease, has become the most common form of automobile lease agreement. On a closed-end operating lease, the lessee has no obligation concerning the market value of the lessor's asset at lease end. The agreement merely requires the consumer to return the asset at lease end and to pay then for any excess damage above normal expected wear and tear.[26] Common, long-term, closed-end lease agreements for automobiles and trucks typically contain an option for consumers

24. There is only very limited academic literature on the criteria for a consumer's decision to lease an automobile (see Patrick 1984, Nunnally and Plath 1989, and Miller 1995 for some discussion). Instead, most studies of consumers and their automobiles focus more on the car purchase decision (see, for example, studies cited in Mannering, Winston, and Starkey 1999). For a more general discussion of leases and leasing (not specifically in the consumer context), see Schallheim (1994). For extended discussion of the operating aspects of automobile leasing, see McCathren and Loshin (1991).

25. The alternative to an operating lease is a "full-payout" or "financial" lease, which finances the whole economic life of an asset by fully paying for (amortizing) the asset's capitalized cost, plus financing charges. Financial leases are not common in consumer leasing; they are more common in commercial leases and sale-leaseback transactions involving industrial buildings and equipment.

26. There may be a refundable security deposit to guarantee payment for damages. For automobiles, there may also be a relatively small "disposition" or "drop-off" charge specified in the

to purchase their vehicles at lease end at a price agreed upon at the outset, but there is no obligation to purchase.

The closed-end operating lease contrasts with the less common open-end operating lease, where the lessee still does not have a requirement to purchase but where there is an obligation at lease end to make up to the lessor any shortfall from expectations in the actual market value of the asset. In effect, the open-end lessee guarantees the residual value of the lessor's asset. Under typical open-end automobile lease contracts, lessees also may purchase their vehicles at lease end for a purchase price guaranteed at the outset, but open-end lessees cannot walk away. Rather, if they return their vehicles, they are liable for any differences between assumed residual values and actual, realized market values at lease end. The Consumer Leasing Act limits a consumer's liability for the difference between expected and actual market value on an open-end vehicle lease to no more than three times the amount of the monthly payment. This provision likely has encouraged the use of closed-end leases by making open-end leases less useful to lessors as a way of shifting risks to their customers.

From this brief description of the basic characteristics of leases, it is easy to see that closed-end operating leases offer consumers a different set of risks from open-end leases or credit purchases of assets; notably, closed-end lessees do not bear any risk of decline in the residual value of used assets below expectations over the lease period, but open-end lessees and purchasers do.[27] If at lease end the value of the asset is below the deferred purchase price set at the outset, the closed-end lessee may return the asset and walk away (except from excessive wear and tear). If, in contrast, the market value at lease end is *greater* than expected, the lessee may keep the asset by paying the deferred purchase price agreed upon at the signing of the lease and can retain it or sell it. For the closed-end lessee, this amounts to a "heads I win, tails you lose" proposition, at least with respect to the residual value of the asset. It seems reasonable to suppose that lessors will charge closed-end lessees for the purchase option feature that transfers the residual-value risk to the lessor as part of the lease cost. Purchasers and open-end lessees bear this risk themselves. Ultimately, it is this difference in risk bearing, together with differences in the size and timing of cash flows (discussed in the next section), that characterizes the distinction for consumers between closed-end leasing and purchase financing.[28]

contract. The typical automobile lease contract also specifies a yearly average mileage limit to avoid having charges for excessive usage, usually collected at lease end.

27. Losses from this source can be substantial (for discussion, see Gruber 1992).

28. This difference is stated here in terms of the advantage of a lease for which there likely is a charge. Many consumers who regularly lease automobiles rather than purchasing them probably analyze this decision in the reverse, but equivalent, form: there is a disadvantage to purchasing rather than leasing in the form of concern over eventual trade-in value.

Suppose that a consumer likes driving new or recent cars and contemplates acquiring a new car every three years. This consumer could purchase the car and trade it in every third year, or the consumer could lease a succession of vehicles. In the latter case, the consumer would know in advance the disposition terms for each car, and, assuming reasonable care and good condition at turn-in time, this consumer would be free of haggling with the dealer over the trade-in value

Cash Flows

Beyond risk differences, closed-end leases also present consumers with a different pattern of cash flows from purchase financing. Ultimately, it is comparison of the present values of the outflows that arise under the different financing schemes, together with the distinction in risks, that resolves the question of best choice for consumers.

In the long run, in a competitive, perfect capital market with full information and without transaction costs or taxes, the type of financing arrangement for retail purchase of automobiles by consumers would be a matter of indifference to both consumers and creditors/lessors: both costs to consumers and yields to creditors and lessors would be the same under the two financing alternatives. Clearly, capital markets are not perfect, however. First of all, there are transaction costs, including paperwork and legal costs, that may differ between leasing and debt financing. Also, taxes may differ between consumers and lessors, and between financing schemes, and, as noted, there may be risk differences among consumers and among types of transactions. On occasion, there also may be marketing promotions that encourage one transaction form over the other. Consequently, at different times, leasing may be more or less advantageous than purchase financing to either consumers or creditors/lessors, and both consumers and creditors/lessors have an interest in evaluating the alternatives.

Fundamentally, consumers should choose a closed-end operating lease instead of debt financing only if the risk-adjusted present value of all the costs (outflows) arising from the lease (including any down payment) is less than the present value of outflows resulting from the credit purchase over a comparable period of leasing or ownership.[29] The present value of the purchase option embedded in a closed-end operating lease, which the consumer also pays for as part of the lease payments, must be subtracted from the present value of the lease payments in order to maintain comparability between the packages of transportation-related services purchased. This presents the following decision criterion:

$$\text{If Sum PV(LP)} - \text{PV(Option)} < \text{Sum PV(FP), then lease,}$$
$$\text{where PV}(\cdot) = \text{Present Value (of quantity in parentheses),}$$
$$\text{LP} = \text{All payments on a lease,}$$
$$\text{FP} = \text{All payments on a financed purchase, and}$$
$$\text{Option} = \text{Value to lessee of purchase option.}$$
$$\text{That is,}$$
$$\text{If Sum PV(FP)} + \text{PV(Option)} - \text{Sum PV(LP)} > 0,$$
$$\text{then lease.} \tag{12.1}$$

or running the risk that the value is low. Some consumers are probably willing to pay something for this freedom.

29. Although the discussion here concerns comparing a lease with a purchase, comparing two leases or two purchases would proceed in fundamentally the same way.

To analyze the decision, a consumer should discount the leasing flows at the APR available on the credit purchase or loan. If the discounted present value of the credit flows (which equals the purchase price) plus the present value of the option is greater than the discounted present value of the leasing flows, then leasing is the better choice, and vice versa.[30]

Leaving aside the question of whether consumers understand present values and the discounting process, the difficult matter in analyzing the decision is to specify the flows properly for the two kinds of arrangements. Typically, they will differ in form, timing, and amount. Also, valuing the purchase option available on a closed-end lease might become an important aspect of the decision.[31]

Table 12.10 provides a listing of the four possible patterns of cash outflows arising from (1) a closed-end lease and (2) a purchase agreement for an automobile. For the lessee, there are two possibilities at lease end: the lessee may return the vehicle to the dealer or may exercise the purchase option and buy it. For the credit purchaser, there are also two possibilities at the end of the payment period: the owner can keep the vehicle or sell it. The table adopts the convention that outflows are positive and inflows are negative; thus, the table expresses net costs of the transactions.

Under this convention, the consumer receives from a lease or a financed purchase an inflow (negative cost) of transportation and other services from the vehicle during the period covered by the agreement.[32] Over comparable time periods, the transportation services are assumed to be independent of the financing

---

30. Because discounting the flows from a financed purchase at the APR paid for the credit equals the price of the asset, substituting the price of the asset for the discounted present value of the finance flows produces a standard net advantage of leasing (NAL) equation (see Myers, Dill, and Bautista 1976). For comparability to the lease maturity, purchase price must be adjusted to a net purchase price by subtracting the present value of the residual value, if any, after a comparable time period. Substituting into equation 12.1 produces the decision criterion:

If NAL = Net Purchase Price + PV (Option) − Sum PV (LP) > 0, then lease.

31. As a practical matter, the value of this option may not be very great, to the extent that lessors are reasonably competent in predicting values of used assets in the future and set residual values and optional purchase prices at lease end accordingly. Still, if absence of the haggle/hassle factor at lease end is important to potential lessees/purchasers, then its value can be positive and potentially substantial.

32. Services provided by the vehicle may also include psychological services such as pride of ownership or opportunity to drive a new or stylish automobile or truck, and in the past, these psychological services may have varied depending on whether the transaction was a purchase with financing or was a lease. For example, it is possible that at least some drivers felt better thinking they "owned" a vehicle rather than that they merely leased its services. Leasing has recently become such a common financing alternative, however, that it seems reasonable to assume that these psychological services are similar for purchase financing and leasing today and that they are of comparable value. Therefore, psychological differences that may have existed formerly may be ignored today.

Table 12.10 CASH OUTFLOWS ASSOCIATED WITH OBTAINING USE OF ASSETS THROUGH CLOSED-END OPERATING LEASES AND CREDIT PURCHASES (READ DOWN COLUMNS)

	Lease		Credit Purchase	
	Retain Auto at Lease End	Turn in Auto at Lease End	Retain Auto When Paid	Sell Auto When Paid
(1)	– Trans Serv	= –Trans Serv	= –Trans Serv	= –Trans Serv
(2)	+ Trade-in	= + Trade-in	= + Trade-in	= + Trade-in
(3)	+ CCR	+ CCR	+ Down Pay	+ Down Pay
(4)	+ Secur Dep	+ Secur Dep		
(5)	– PV (Dep Ref)	– PV (Dep Ref)		
(6)	+ Sum PV (LP)	+ Sum PV (LP)	+ Sum PV (FP)	+ Sum PV(FP)
(7)			+ Sum PV (PPT)	+ Sum PV (PPT)
(8)	+ PV (Pur Price)			
(9)		+ PV (Disp Charge)		
(10)				– PV (Sale)
(11)				+ PV (EL/S)
(12)	+ PV (EL/ET)	= + PV (EL/ET)	+ PV (EL/ET)	= + PV (EL/ET)

PV ( ), present value (of quantity in parentheses); Trans Serv, transportation services provided; CCR, (cash) capitalized cost reduction; Down Pay, (cash) down payment; Secur Dep, security deposit; Dep Ref, security deposit refund; LP, lease payments; FP, finance payments; PPT, personal property taxes; Pur Price, purchase price; Disp Charge, disposition or drop-off charge; Sale, sale price; EL/S, expected loss on sale of the vehicle; EL/ET, expected loss upon early termination of lease or credit arrangement.

method (line 1 of table 12.10). This is denoted in the table by equal signs between columns.[33]

Some of the initial outflows arising from the two alternative financing methods will also be the same between the alternatives, but some will differ. For both types of financing, the consumer agrees to a series of outflows to satisfy the payment

33. Transportation services may differ between the leasing and the purchase financing cases if the amount of yearly mileage permitted under a lease without an additional mileage charge (typically 12,000 or 15,000 miles per year, but with variations) constrains the potential purchaser. For illustrative purposes, this limitation is assumed not to be binding, so that transportation services provided by the leased and financed vehicles are the same for this example. If the constraint were binding because the potential lessee intends to drive more than the yearly maximum, then another term for the present value of the expected deferred excess mileage charge due at lease end would be added to column 2 of the table.

obligation. Frequently, the first of these is a trade-in of a vehicle already owned by the consumer (line 2 in the table). With the assumption that the consumer trades in the same vehicle under both financing schemes, the trade-in is the same under the two alternatives (again denoted by equal signs).

Often the trade-in is accompanied by a cash down payment (line 3). (On a lease, the down payment and the trade-in are often called the capitalized cost reduction. In table 12.10, this term applies to the cash component.) A lessee typically must also provide a security deposit, which often approximates one monthly payment on the lease obligation (line 4). Upon satisfaction of the lease agreement, this security deposit is refunded at lease end (line 5).

In addition to these initial outflows, the consumer is also obligated for a series of further cash payments over the agreement period, usually monthly (line 6). On a lease, the first payment typically is due at signing, while a credit purchase agreement normally defers the first payment for a month.

In many jurisdictions, vehicle owners are also subject to personal property taxes on their vehicles owned or "garaged" within tax districts such as counties or states (line 7). On a lease, in some jurisdictions, the lessor may be responsible for these taxes, which it recoups by upping the necessary periodic payments. Consequently, for lessees, the flows for personal property taxes may not appear as a separate, explicit outflow on a lease in many tax jurisdictions, even if personal property taxes are explicit for financed purchases. For comparability with a credit purchase, therefore, the taxes in these jurisdictions must be either subtracted from the lease payments or added to the finance payments.[34]

End-of-term outflows also differ between purchasing and leasing. In the credit purchase case, the consumer owns the vehicle at the end of the financing period and holds the right to continued transportation services over the additional expected life of the vehicle; with a lease, the consumer does not have this right. To compare a lease with purchase financing, it is necessary to account for the remaining transportation services at lease end.

One possibility, of course, is that the consumer purchases the leased vehicle at the end of the lease period, thereby obtaining the remaining transportation services. On a typical closed-end lease, the consumer obtains the vehicle and its remaining services by purchasing it at the optional purchase price disclosed in the original lease agreement or at some other price negotiated between the parties.

---

34. Identifiable personal property taxes may be deductible from adjusted gross income for federal and state income tax purposes for some consumers, which also should be properly taken into account by those eligible for the deduction. There also may be sales taxes associated with both the credit purchase and the lease. For comparing a purchase to a lease, both must be accounted for properly to avoid erroneous conclusions. For example, on a purchase, sales taxes may be financed as part of the gross purchase price and paid for through the down payment and periodic payment flows. On a lease, they may be collected monthly as part of the monthly payment, either explicitly or not. Each of these possibilities would require an adjustment in the table to account properly for the facts of individual situations.

This price becomes another outflow (line 8), this one deferred until the end of the lease period.[35]

Because the lessee does not have to make the decision whether or not to retain the vehicle until the end of the lease period, at the outset, the deferred decision amounts to a call option for the lessee, and as noted previously, this option has value because it transfers risks of residual price fluctuations to the lessor. In effect, when lessees contract for the services of vehicles, they obtain options to call the residual values of their vehicles at the end of the leases by paying at lease end a deferred optional purchase price agreed at the outset. This differentiates the lessee from the credit purchaser who owns the vehicle and bears all of the residual price risk. To maintain comparability with a purchase, the present value of this option must be subtracted from the present value of the lease costs or added to the present value of the purchase finance costs (see equation 12.1, above).

The other possibility is that the consumer returns the vehicle to the lessor at lease end, thereby giving up any claim to transportation services remaining in the vehicle. In this case, the lessee returns the vehicle and pays any drop-off or disposition charge in the contract (line 9) but not any optional purchase price (line 8 is zero in this case).[36]

Purchasers who sell their vehicles receive a wholesale selling price upon sale (line 10). Those who sell them privately and not to a dealer may receive an amount closer to the retail price (if the cars are in good condition), minus, of course, their costs of selling, including advertising expenses and the costs of personal time spent on the sale process (and subjective personal costs of any accompanying aggravations).

Two contingencies might lead to additional outflows at the end of the relevant time period. First, there is a chance that a vehicle may be worth more or less at the time of eventual disposition than the consumer expects at the outset, which may be important to the consumer in some cases. If the consumer expects to purchase the vehicle at lease end or plans to retain the vehicle at the end of the purchase finance period, however, planned disposition likely will take place far enough into the future that the consumer may well not have at the outset any expectation about the value many years hence. If so, this contingency probably need not enter into the present value calculations at the outset of the transaction (or into columns 1 or 3 of table 12.10).[37]

---

35. This purchase price may also be financed, in which case, the price becomes another stream of outflows. The lessor and the lessee may also agree to another lease or to a continuation of the old lease agreement. The examples in the table do not reflect these possibilities.

36. The lessee still acquires the purchase option, even if the ultimate decision is to return the vehicle at lease end, and so the present value of the option remains a term in equation 12.1.

37. Even if there is a recognized prior probability of deferred gain or loss, there is no reason to expect a difference if original acquisition is through a lease or purchase contract. If loss expectations are equal at the outset, they can be ignored in the calculations (and the table) when making comparisons.

In the other situation, that is, if the consumer does *not* intend to retain the vehicle at lease end or plans to sell the purchased auto, the time before expected disposition is shorter, and unexpected loss may become a factor in decision making. For the closed-end lessee, the lessor bears this risk; the value to the consumer of avoiding the loss is subsumed into the value of the call option on the vehicle's residual value. Thus, of the four cases, only the purchaser who plans to sell the vehicle upon completion of the payments is subject to this potential risk (line 11, column 4).[38]

The second contingency is the chance of a loss upon an early termination of the lease or upon a sale of the vehicle before the end of the credit purchase agreement period. A loss on early termination might occur following theft or an accident not fully covered by insurance or because the consumer desires to change vehicles before the end of the lease or purchase financing agreement. For both lessees and purchasers, this risk is independent of plans to retain the vehicle or not at the end of the payment period and can be assumed to be equal for all lessors or all purchasers (indicated by equals signs on line 12 of table 12.10). Since a loss (outflow) is more likely than an unexpected gain under these circumstances, however, the expected value is probably positive. To minimize the size of such losses for lessees in the cases of accident or theft (and the financial and legal difficulties that might arise), "gap insurance" often is available from lessors, typically included as part of the leasing transaction and charge. For most consumers, though, either the prior probability of unexpected early termination (and, consequently, the expected value of any associated loss) is probably small enough in the consumer's mind at the outset of the transaction or the expectation of a difference in loss size in this area between leasing and purchase financing is probably small enough that expectation of a loss on early termination is probably not much of a factor in the choice between leasing and financing.[39]

Now, the quantities in table 12.10 can be substituted into equation 12.1 to derive the net advantage of leasing, first, for the case where the consumer keeps the vehicle at the end of the payment period (equation 12.2, below); and, second, for the situation where the consumer does not retain the vehicle (equation 12.3).

To ease solution, a few simplifications of the equations are possible. First, because transportation services (line 1 of table 12.10) are assumed to be the same for comparable periods of ownership and lease holding, they may be ignored and omitted from the equations. Likewise, since the trade-in is the same (line 2), it may also be dismissed. Third, if the expected value of the loss from an early termination (line 12) either is not very large or does not differ much between a financed purchase and a lease, it also can drop from the equation, since it is the difference between these quantities for a financed purchase and a lease, which would enter

---

38. For such a purchaser who plans to sell, there is the real possibility of an unexpected loss upon disposition of the vehicle, but there may also be an unexpected gain. If the likelihood of the loss or gain is unknown at the outset of the lease arrangement, it might be argued that the expected value of the distribution of possibilities may well be zero, arguing for its dismissal from the calculations and the table. Because the risk of loss exists, however, an expected value of loss upon disposition is a potential outflow for a purchaser (column 4, line 11).

39. This is not an argument against required disclosure of the existence of such a risk, however.

the equation anyway. Thus, with these assumptions and recalling that leases but not purchases commonly require one monthly payment in advance, this leaves the following specifications for equations 12.2 and 12.3 for finance and lease periods of N months:

Equation 12.2: When vehicle is retained, if

$$\text{Down Pay}_0 \hspace{4cm} \text{(Initial)}$$

$$+\sum_{t=1}^{N}\left(FP_t + PPT_t\right)\left(1+\frac{i}{12}\right)^{-t} \hspace{2cm} \text{(Periodic)}$$

$$-[(CCR_0 + \text{Secur Dep}_0 + LP_0) \hspace{2cm} \text{(Initial)}$$

$$+\sum_{t=1}^{N-1}\left(LP_t\right)\left(1+\frac{i}{12}\right)^{-t} \hspace{2cm} \text{(Periodic)}$$

$$+\left(\text{Pur Price} - \text{Dep Ref}\right)\left(1+i\right)^{-N} \hspace{1.5cm} \text{(End of Term)}$$

$$-\left(\text{Pur Opt}\right)\left(1+i\right)^{-N}] > 0, \hspace{2cm} \text{then lease.}$$

Equation 12.3: When vehicle is not retained, if

$$\text{Down Pay}_0 \hspace{4cm} \text{(Initial)}$$

$$+\sum_{t=1}^{N}\left(FP_t + PPT_t\right)\left(1+\frac{i}{12}\right)^{-t} \hspace{2cm} \text{(Periodic)}$$

$$-\left(\text{Sale} - \frac{EL}{S}\right)\left(1-i\right)^{-N} \hspace{2cm} \text{(End of Term)}$$

$$-[(CCR_0 + \text{Secur Dep}_0 + LP_0) \hspace{2cm} \text{(Initial)}$$

$$+\sum_{t=1}^{N-1}\left(LP_t\right)\left(1+\frac{i}{12}\right)^{-t} \hspace{2cm} \text{(Periodic)}$$

$$+\left(\text{Disp Charge} - \text{Dep Ref}\right)\left(1+i\right)^{-N} \hspace{1.5cm} \text{(End of Term)}$$

$$-\left(\text{Pur Opt}\right)\left(1+i\right)^{-N}] > 0, \hspace{2cm} \text{then lease.}$$

These equations exhibit some features that should receive special mention. First, as discount rates move higher but other things are equal, leasing becomes relatively more attractive. Specifically, in the case where the vehicle is retained (equation 12.2), higher discount rates make leasing more attractive, because higher discount rates relatively reduce the discounted future purchase price of the leased vehicle. This decreases the second (subtracted) term in equation 12.2 (the term in square brackets), tending the equation toward a positive value favoring leasing. In contrast, where the vehicle is not retained at contract end (equation 12.3), higher discount rates favor leasing for a different reason. In this case, as the discount rate rises, it relatively decreases the present value of the sale price of the vehicle in the future. Since this is a subtracted item in the first part of the equation, higher discount rates again increase the likelihood that the equation will be positive, again tending to favor leasing relatively.

Second, the nonretention case (equation 12.3) requires a term, the future sale price of the vehicle, that is not known at the outset of the transaction. Even if an expected used car price sometime in the future is available from some guidebook, there is no certainty concerning this price, and there is no certainty about advertising, sales, and aggravation costs that properly should reduce the final sales price. Consequently, equation 12.3 requires some estimating and cannot serve as a definitive guide.

Third, both equations 12.2 and 12.3 contain a term for the discounted value of the purchase option available on a closed-end operating lease. Estimating the value of this option is not a simple matter, even if experienced automobile dealers are reasonably proficient at estimating the values of used vehicles sometime into the future.[40] As already discussed, its value to many consumers may be enhanced by absence of necessary haggling over used car values at time of trade-in.

In sum, a consumer's informed choice of whether to lease or purchase an asset such as a vehicle depends on the amount and pattern of the stream of outflows and on the discount rate that converts the stream of outflows to present values. Unfortunately, presence in a closed-end lease of a purchase option with unknown value and consumer uncertainty about future used car prices mean that the single-equation optimal decision criterion will always contain multiple unknowns and be insoluble mathematically, even if the discount rate is known. Whether this is a major concern depends on the value of the option to consumers and how it is priced by producers. If the option has no value because residual values are easy to predict, then its value presumably can be ignored. Because this seems unlikely, however, the equation cannot easily be solved by consumers, even if they understand the concepts and can outline all the cash flows. Thus, the search is not for the perfect set of disclosures but rather for the set that enables most consumers to make good decisions most of the time.

---

40. The value of an option is a function of the value of the underlying asset, the variability in the asset's value, the price at which the option can be exercised, the length of time until the option can be exercised, and the rate of interest. Extended discussion and formulas can be found in textbooks of finance, such as Brealey, Myers, and Allen (2010).

Required Disclosures

As with the main body of Truth in Lending, it seems that the Consumer Leasing Act requires disclosure of virtually anything that might be useful to someone, sometime. Arising from a scheduled periodic review of Regulation M, which implements the act, the Federal Reserve promulgated a new disclosure regime in 1996 (effective in early 1998) that mandated a mathematical progression of the components of the disclosures in a manner designed to aid understanding. The redrafted regulation required that lessors make substantial changes in the format and content of required disclosures, but it seems that the new approach improved the quality and accessibility of useful information to consumers.

Not surprisingly, however, it does not provide all the information necessary to solve equation 12.2 or 12.3. For a variety of reasons, it does not even seem possible that any leasing disclosure scheme could provide all of the information required for consumers to solve equation 12.2 or 12.3 for the theoretically correct choice between a lease and a financed purchase. First of all, leasing disclosures cannot reasonably be expected to provide information about the purchase financing alternative to a lease, which is necessary to solve either equation. Consumers would have to obtain this information themselves by shopping, even if this merely means obtaining the necessary information from the same dealer. Second, some information such as personal property taxes and an individual's personal tax situation are idiosyncratic to each shopper and must be factored into the purchase or lease decision by that person. Third, as already mentioned, both equations 12.2 and 12.3 require some information, such as future prices of used vehicles and the present value of the purchase option, that is not readily available to either party to the transaction except by crude estimation.

Nonetheless, most of the information that consumers might need to characterize a lease is available from the required disclosures. Moreover, the revised disclosure scheme seems to make this information easier for consumers to comprehend and use. This is visible more clearly from a rapid tour of the revised disclosure regime.

Regulation M

Revised Regulation M requires segregation of a group of key disclosures in a highlighted "federal box" and, as mentioned, disclosure of elements that go into making up the monthly payment in a mathematical progression that is intended to be intuitive and easy to understand. Although a segregated "federal box" of disclosures and a mathematical progression are not strictly required by the statute, they follow the general approach for credit disclosures that became part of Regulation Z under the Truth in Lending Act amendments of 1980. They include for leases disclosure of gross capitalized cost, adjusted capitalized cost, residual value, rent charge, and total of payments. These new disclosures arise as components of a mathematical progression leading to the monthly payment. Gross capitalized cost is analogous to gross purchase price, including lease acquisition charges, carried-over balances on any previous transactions, initial taxes owed, registration fees, delivery charges, and any after-market products such as extended warranties. Adjusted capitalized cost is gross capitalized cost minus "capitalized cost reductions," including trade-in allowances, cash down payments, rebates, and any other reductions. The residual value of the lease is the estimated value of the asset at lease end. The rent charge is the lessor's designated added-on charge to cover transaction costs and the charge for capital use, including any profit from financing.

There are also requirements for calculating and disclosing certain subtotals. Lessors determine periodic payments by subtracting the capitalized cost reductions and lease residual from the gross capitalized cost and adding the rent charge. They then divide the resulting quantity by the number of periods to determine the size of the base periodic payments, excluding any added amounts for taxes and insurance. Thus, each of these new disclosure requirements in 1998 (gross capitalized cost, adjusted capitalized cost, rent charge, and lease residual) is an amount that lessors had readily available to make their calculations, although there previously was no requirement for their disclosure. Likewise, newly required subtotals such as total capitalized cost reduction (including cash component, trade-in, and rebate or other noncash component) and amount to be depreciated and amortized (adjusted capitalized cost minus lease residual) are directly derived from amounts already calculated and did not represent dramatic departures into a new disclosure scheme.

The revised regulation also requires itemization of the amounts due from the consumer at inception of the lease in two columns, one listing amounts due at signing and the other designating means of paying the itemized costs. Taken together with the mathematical progression leading to the monthly payment, these requirements include all of the cash flows for a lease that would be necessary to solve equation 12.2 or 12.3, even if the corresponding figures for a purchase (also necessary to solve the equations) would have to be supplied independently by the consumer.

It seems that Regulation M, as revised and effective in 1998, is a reasonable basis to make consumers aware of important terms without searching through the contract. Before revision, Regulation M contained no placement requirement for the key disclosures except that they be clear, conspicuous, in meaningful sequence, and on the same page and above the lessee's signature. Otherwise, lessors could spread the disclosures through the contract document. For disclosing monthly payments, the previous requirement had been disclosure of the total amount required plus identification of the components; the regulation did not require disclosure of the amounts of the individual components, although some lessors had disclosed amounts of components, and there had been some confusion concerning exactly what was required. It seems that the requirement for presentation of a mathematical progression for calculating both the amounts of monthly payments and amounts due at lease signing likely has should helped interested consumers understand the intricacies of their transactions.[41]

---

41. This does not mean that compliance is automatically easy for lessors. Rather, as seems to be the case with any new regulation, the new Regulation M has raised its own set of technical questions for interpretation and resolution. For discussion of these issues, see Huber and Hudson (1998).

Troubled Consumers

Bankruptcy and Credit Counseling

When an individual or business borrows money, there is some possibility in every case, and certainty in the aggregate, that some borrowers will be unable to pay their debts when they come due. Implicit in any system of debt and credit, therefore, is the need for some system for resolving financial distress as it occurs. This need arises since it is also implicit in any individual contract to lend pursuant to a legally enforceable contractual agreement that the creditor has the right to enforce the contract in the event that the debtor does not pay according to its terms. Chapter 11 examined the primary legal types of creditor collection methods against nonpaying borrowers: a system of legal actions known as creditors' remedies. These remedies include instances where debtors voluntarily provide the creditor with a security interest in identifiable property, which the debtor consents the creditor can repossess in the event of the debtor's nonpayment. There also are involuntary processes, such as lawsuits, to collect from nonpaying debtors. If debtors lack sufficient cash resources to pay debts, the creditors are entitled in these situations, assuming proper judicial procedures are followed, to seize property of the debtor in satisfaction of the claim pursuant to a "judicial lien" or a "judgment."

But what of a debtor who lacks sufficient funds *and* property to pay all of the debts owed? For example, an individual might borrow in good faith using credit cards and later experience job loss causing inability to pay the debts as contracted. This calls forth a need to devise systems for dealing with insolvent debtors, the subject of this chapter. Because any such system is going to function in its way as a type of social insurance for financially strapped consumers, benefits of the system, as with any system of insurance, must be balanced against creating concerns of moral hazard and adverse selection. This chapter examines two such systems for resolving consumers' financial distress: consumer bankruptcy and consumer credit counseling.

BANKRUPTCY

Spurred by high unemployment, massive wealth destruction in the residential real estate and stock market, and record levels of home mortgage foreclosures,

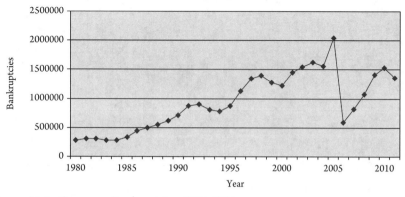

Figure 13.1 Consumer Bankruptcies, 1980–2011.

there were 1.1 million to 1.5 million consumer bankruptcy filings in the United States in 2010–2012, according to the Administrative Office of the US Courts (figure 13.1). These filings continued a long-term generally rising trend, temporarily with some interruptions but more significantly interrupted after 2004 by enactment of the Bankruptcy Abuse Prevention and Consumer Protection Act of 2005 (BAPCPA). This law partially tempered a century-long movement in the United States toward increasingly generous bankruptcy filing rules for consumers. The filing rates from 2009 to 2012 returned to the high bankruptcy filing rates preceding them, although exceeded by the record 2 million in 2005, a figure that was artificially inflated that year by a "rush to the courthouse" to file in the period immediately preceding the effective date of the new law.

History of Consumer Bankruptcy

Historically, insolvency for both business and consumer debtors has been treated harshly, but insolvency for consumer debtors has been treated more harshly by law than bankruptcy for business debtors. Business insolvency has often been attenuated by the recognition that debt and the risk of nonpayment are inherent in engaging in a commercial enterprise, such as making capital investments in productive facilities, borrowing to finance the purchase of inventory, or smoothing revenues and expenditures. In contrast, consumer debt traditionally has been viewed as largely zero-sum in nature, borrowing not to fund productive investment that can increase wealth but simply to consume immediately rather than postponing gratification. Chapter 3 discussed how consumer debt also largely supports productive investment, but observers have not typically viewed it this way. As a result, consumer insolvency historically has been much more likely to be conceived of as simply fraudulent, borrowing against the future with no obvious means to repay. The view of consumer credit as largely productive is relatively recent in financial history.

Consequently, bankruptcy laws worldwide have tended to be very harsh, and they generally remain so, although the United States and many European countries have liberalized their laws in recent decades. The extremely liberal bankruptcy laws that prevail in the United States today, even after the modest tightening in 2005, remain unique when compared with the rest of the world or even with the United States itself for much of its history.[1] The concept of bankruptcy originated primarily as a creditor protection mechanism to enable creditors to seize a debtor's property in order to prevent the debtor from absconding or concealing property from rightful creditors.

The origins of the term *bankruptcy* itself suggest a punitive nature. One theory is that the word derives from the Latin terms *bancus*, meaning "table" or "counter," and *ruptus*, meaning "broken," signifying the right of creditors to break the trading table of a nonpaying merchant in order to signal that the merchant was out of business (see Tabb 1997). Roman creditors were also empowered to divide physically the body of a bankrupt, although there is little evidence that this right was used often (see White 1977). In ancient Greece, a debtor who was unable to pay was taken into slavery by the creditor, along with the debtor's family and servants. (Some city-states limited debt slavery to a period of five years and provided protections for debt slaves, who previously were citizens, that standard Greek slaves lacked.) Through the Middle Ages, bankruptcy rules generally remained very harsh.

Bankruptcy law in the United States derives from English law, which focused on protecting creditors from misbehavior by debtors, not debtor protection. Imprisonment for debt was recognized in England beginning in 1285 with the Statute of Merchants and remained in effect for some types of debtors until the nineteenth century, both in England and in the United States (see Tabb 1997, 30). In the sixteenth century, England toughened its laws, increasing the power of creditors to reach a bankrupt debtor's assets. In 1604, law provided that a bankrupt debtor could be pilloried or have an ear cut off (Tabb 1997, 31).

The enactment in 1705 of the Statute of Anne marked a sea change in the English philosophy of bankruptcy. While it introduced the death penalty for fraudulent debtors, the Statute of Anne also introduced the concept of a discharge of debts for a debtor who was who cooperative and acted in good faith. Rather than the "stick"-based approach of earlier laws, which increased the authority of creditors to track down the debtor's property, the idea of a discharge introduced a "carrot"-based approach to bankruptcy by providing the debtor with an incentive to cooperate with creditors. A cooperative debtor could be discharged of debts, relieving further legal obligation to pay. In 1732, the Statute of George II further developed this carrot-and-stick approach to debtor relief. These changes in the early eighteenth century primarily affected merchant debtors, however. Nonmerchant debtors were still subject to insolvency laws that primarily concerned conditions for imposing and releasing individuals from debtors' prison (see Zywicki 2005a).

In the United States, under the Articles of Confederation, the states alone governed debtor and creditor relations. This led to diverse and contradictory state

---

1. For example, Sweden had no provision for bankruptcy discharge until 2005 (see Chatterjee and Gordon 2011).

laws at the time. It was unclear, for instance, whether a state law that purported to discharge a debtor of a debt prohibited the creditor from trying to collect the same debt in another state. Pro-debtor state laws also interfered with the reliability of contracts, and creditors confronted still further obstructions in trying to use state courts to collect their judgments when debtors absconded to other states to avoid collection.

Ultimately, Article I, section 8, of the Constitution vested sole authority for bankruptcy laws in the federal government in an effort to constrain populist pro-debtor legislation enacted by state legislatures that might imperil the national economy and undermine the enforceability of contracts. Writing in *The Federalist* (no. 42), James Madison observed: "The power of establishing uniform laws of bankruptcy is so intimately connected with the regulation of commerce, and will prevent so many frauds where the parties or their property may lie or be removed into different States, that the expediency of it [i.e., Congress's power to regulate bankruptcy] seems not likely to be drawn into question."[2] By contrast, there was little evidence that the purpose of the Bankruptcy Clause was to guarantee discharge for debtors.

Following ratification of the Constitution, the mercantile northeastern states spearheaded the movement for a national bankruptcy law. The first bankruptcy law was passed under the Federalists in 1800, but it lasted only until 1803. Other bankruptcy laws existed from 1841 to 1843 and from 1867 to 1878. Each followed in the wake of major financial crises. During the periods when there was no

---

2. Other constitutional provisions such as the Contracts Clause, the Full Faith and Credit Clause, and restraints on the power of states to print money arose from similar motivations. In the case of bankruptcy law, the northeastern states sought a national bankruptcy law to protect their merchant traders from business losses, because they believed that a consistent bankruptcy regime for merchants was necessary for the United States to flourish as a commercial republic. The Bankruptcy Clause helped to further the goals of uniformity and predictability within the federalist system.

Less clear, however, is whether the Constitution's grant of power to enact laws governing "bankruptcies" was intended to cover both merchants and nonmerchants (consumers). As noted, into the eighteenth century, English law distinguished between "bankruptcy," which referred to the discharge of merchants and traders, and "insolvency," which governed release from debtor's prison but did not provide a discharge. Some scholars have credibly argued that this usage of "bankruptcy" in the Constitution was deliberate and that the Constitution's grant of power to Congress to regulate "bankruptcies" created federal power to regulate only with respect to merchants and traders (see Plank 1996). The 1800 bankruptcy law notably applied only to merchants, not to individuals.

In this view, "insolvency" laws, remained under state control. In fact, notwithstanding this grant of power to Congress, many states retained debtors' prisons into the nineteenth century, until they were finally phased out. Others have argued that this traditional distinction between bankruptcy and insolvency had disappeared by the time of the Constitution, and the terms had become interchangeable so as to give Congress the power to regulate all insolvent debtors. Regardless, in 1819, the Supreme Court held in *Sturges v. Crowninshield* (17 US 4 Wheat. 122, 1819) that the use of the term *bankruptcy* in the Constitution did not limit Congress's jurisdiction, thereby permitting Congress to regulate both of these realms.

national bankruptcy law, debt collection was based on state debt collection law. Congress enacted the first permanent bankruptcy law in 1898, and it remained in effect, with amendments, until it was replaced with a comprehensive new law in 1978, the essential structure of which continues today.

The 1978 federal Bankruptcy Code dramatically liberalized the ability of both individuals and businesses to file for bankruptcy. The framers of the 1978 law viewed the new, more liberal law as a necessary response to the growing use of consumer credit in the American economy (see Stanley and Girth 1971). Apparently, it was not fully appreciated at the time that the new law might not just provide a safety valve for a response to rising debt and consumer distress but might also create new risks of moral hazard and adverse selection. Since 1978, there has been a tremendous increase in nonbusiness (consumer) bankruptcy filings (figure 13.1).

The Structure of American Consumer Bankruptcy Law

For most of history, bankruptcy was an involuntary proceeding. As noted, bankruptcy was a creditor protection device, initiated by creditors in order to seize debtors' property. With the development and growth of the discharge as a core principle of modern consumer bankruptcy law, however, the debtor has become the primary beneficiary of a bankruptcy filing. Besides the discharge, another important benefit under US law is that today filing for bankruptcy creates an "automatic stay" against all further collection actions by creditors, whether formal (such as initiating a collection action in court) or informal (for example, making phone calls to the debtor's house). According to surveys of bankruptcy filers, while the ability to gain a discharge from overwhelming debt is the main reason an individual chooses to file for bankruptcy, the fact that bankruptcy stops collection efforts and harassment is identified as a close second (see Mann and Porter 2010). Moreover, bankruptcy law today highly circumscribes the right of creditors to initiate an involuntary bankruptcy filing against an individual debtor. As a result, virtually all consumer bankruptcy filings today are initiated voluntarily by debtors.

An individual debtor can seek bankruptcy relief under two different chapters of the Bankruptcy Code: Chapter 7 or Chapter 13.[3] In a typical year, about 70 percent of bankruptcy petitioners file under Chapter 7, and about 30 percent file under Chapter 13. As a basic matter, in a Chapter 7 filing, the debtor surrenders all nonexempt property to creditors and in exchange receives a discharge of all debts. Under Chapter 13, a debtor keeps all property and enters into a repayment plan

---

3. In theory, debtors can also seek relief under chapter 11 and have a plan of reorganization. chapter 11, however, is generally intended for businesses. In some unusual cases, high-income individual debtors with complicated financial affairs in which their business and personal finances are highly tangled with large amounts of debt may choose to file chapter 11. For example, National Football League quarterback Michael Vick filed chapter 11 bankruptcy to reorganize his financial affairs after being sent to prison following conviction for association with illegal dog fighting.

of three to five years. During this period, the Chapter 13 filer dedicates to debt repayment all "disposable income," that is, income left over after paying living expenses for self and dependents. As might be expected, a debtor with substantial assets but not much disposable income might prefer Chapter 13, while a debtor with income but not many assets might prefer Chapter 7.

CHAPTER 7

Under Chapter 7, often referred to as "straight" bankruptcy, the filing of bankruptcy creates an "estate" that includes all of the debtor's property no matter where and by whom it is held. In a Chapter 7 filing, a debtor surrenders all *nonexempt* assets to creditors and in exchange receives a discharge of debts at the conclusion of the case. What constitutes *exempt* property is typically established by state law. Exemption of some property as off limits to creditors under the law is to prevent pauperization as a result of an unlucky financial setback. Thus, exemptions generally include some accumulated home equity, a car, medical aids, tools of a trade necessary to earn a living, and the like. Despite this stated purpose, some states have extremely generous exemptions. Texas and Florida, for example, permit a debtor to protect an unlimited amount of home equity, and other states have generous homestead exemptions or protection for certain other property, such as retirement accounts.

Actual distribution of property from the estate is according to the rules of the Bankruptcy Code. First in line are creditors with valid security interests in specific property. Common examples include a mortgage on real estate or a lien on a specific car through a car loan to purchase it. These creditors are known as *secured* creditors, and their claims on the specific property of the security interest are preserved in bankruptcy. This status arises because while bankruptcy discharges a borrower's *personal* obligation on a debt, it does not discharge a creditor's right to look to property in which the creditor has a valid security interest to collect the debt.

For example, if a debtor owes $4,000 on a car now worth $3,000, outside bankruptcy, a creditor would be entitled to repossess the car and sue for the remaining amount on the $1,000 still owed (an amount known as a deficiency and subject to a possible deficiency judgment). In bankruptcy, as a general rule, the lender can still repossess the car and sell it for its full value, but the lender cannot sue the debtor for the remaining $1,000. Instead, the creditor must collect the remaining debt through the bankruptcy case as an unsecured creditor.[4] Because security interests are consensual, not involuntary, they are not subject to the debtor's exemptions, either, essentially serving for secured loans as a waiver of the debtor's exemptions.

---

4. The debtor can choose to retain the car, by reaffirming the debt (promising to pay the full amount still owed on the loan according to its terms), by redeeming the collateral (paying to the creditor the full remaining value of the debt), or, in some instances, by filing chapter 13 and engaging in a "cram-down" of the loan to no more than the value of its collateral.

In the second place in the lineup of those who receive property (after secured creditors) are the debtors themselves. Debtors are permitted to set aside property for themselves that is classified as exempt under state law. Exemption laws apply both inside and outside bankruptcy proceedings and often vary significantly from state to state in the amount and types of property that debtors can protect from their creditors. As mentioned, Texas, Florida, and few other states recognize unlimited homestead exemptions, meaning that bankruptcy filers can protect the entire equity in their homestead, even if that is a multi-million-dollar ranch or beachfront home. Other states recognize only a very modest homestead exemption, such as $5000 or $10,000 in equity. Similar disparities exist for many other types of property, including motor vehicles and retirement accounts. Property exemptions are defined with reference to particular types of property, such as home equity, motor vehicles, retirement accounts, or personal possessions, rather than being simply a generally applicable dollar amount.

The importance of state law on the amount of exemptions comes about in two ways. Even though bankruptcy law is federal in nature and the Bankruptcy Code provides a menu of federal exemptions, the code also provides that states can "opt out" of the federal menu of exemptions and require debtors to use the same schedule of exemptions in bankruptcy that apply outside bankruptcy under state law. Thirty-five states have elected to opt out, thereby requiring bankruptcy filers to elect their state property exemptions.[5] Alternatively, in those states that have not opted out, the debtor can select at the time of bankruptcy filing whether to apply state's exemptions or instead use the federal menu of exemptions. Some property, such as qualified pension plans and certain trusts, are *excepted* from the bankruptcy estate, meaning that they never become property of the bankruptcy estate in the first place.

If there is any property remaining in the bankruptcy estate after (1) distribution of property to secured creditors that hold a security interest and (2) the debtor's exempt property is given to the debtor, then any remaining assets are distributed to unsecured creditors pro rata. This means that each receives a percentage of its claim based on the percentage of its claim to the overall amount of claims in the case. Thus, for example, if a creditor's claim amounts to 10 percent of the overall amount of claims in the case, and there is $2,000 in nonexempt assets available to pay creditors, then that creditor would receive a distribution of $200 in the case. At the end of the case, the debtor is granted a discharge.

While unsecured creditors can reach to all of the debtor's nonexempt assets, in practice, unsecured creditors recover very little or nothing in the typical Chapter 7 case; in other words, there typically are very few or no assets outside secured loans and exemptions. One recent study of bankruptcy filings found that 93 percent of Chapter 7 cases were no-asset cases, meaning that no nonexempt assets were available to distribute to creditors once property subject to a creditor's lien or security interest and the debtor's exemptions were accounted for, regardless of the income of the debtor (see Jimenez 2009). In the minority of cases where

---

5. See http://www.realworldlaw.com/stateoptout.html.

distributions were made to general unsecured creditors, the median distribution was approximately eight cents on the dollar of claims.

The paucity of distribution to unsecured creditors in the typical consumer bankruptcy case is a result of several factors. First, much of the debtor's valuable property (home, car, boat, etc.) in a typical case will be subject to security interests.

Second, the property exemptions of many states are quite generous for the average debtor and are made more generous as an effective matter because of the ability of the debtor to engage in prebankruptcy planning before filing. Such methods include building up exempt equity in a home by prepaying the mortgage or by increasing assets in exempt retirement savings. White (1998) estimated that at least 15 percent of the population would benefit financially from filing for bankruptcy and that with modest prebankruptcy planning efforts, the numbers would be much higher, especially in states such as Texas and Florida with large property exemptions.

Third, a debtor can simply consume some nonexempt assets, often by timing the purchase of discretionary goods and services before bankruptcy. Such spending might include home repairs, car repairs, or the like, which otherwise might have been postponed until later, absent upcoming bankruptcy.

Fourth, within the general category of unsecured creditors, some creditors are treated as having higher "priority" than others and are thus paid in full before any distribution is made to general unsecured creditors. This category of priority creditors includes recipients of domestic support obligations (such as alimony and child support), attorneys who file the bankruptcy cases, and certain taxes.

Finally, although it is unclear how widespread bankruptcy fraud is, in some instances, debtors will simply conceal assets, such as cash, that otherwise would have to be surrendered to creditors. Therefore, although Chapter 7 in theory permits creditors to reach all of a debtor's nonexempt assets, in practice that right will often be of little or no value to unsecured creditors.

CHAPTER 13

In Chapter 13, a debtor retains assets and instead dedicates future disposable income to repayment of debt to the extent possible, in contrast to Chapter 7, which allows debtors to protect their future income but surrender their current (nonexempt) assets. This makes Chapter 13 more appealing to debtors with substantial nonexempt assets relative to income that would need to be surrendered. As in Chapter 7, secured debt and priority debt are paid ahead of general unsecured debt in Chapter 13.

Chapter 13 also provides a debtor with certain kinds of flexibility that are lacking in Chapter 7. For example, a debtor who is in arrears on a home mortgage payment at the time of filing for bankruptcy can use Chapter 13 to make the missed payments and protect the property from foreclosure and repossession. (This is known as "curing" the missed payments with the lender and reinstating the mortgage to performing status.) In such situations, it is not uncommon for a debtor after curing to convert the case to Chapter 7 and discharge all remaining unsecured debt. This tactic is sufficiently common to be referred to facetiously as a "Chapter 20" proceeding (i.e., Chapter 13 plus Chapter 7). Only a minority of bankruptcy filers typically complete the full three to five years of their Chapter 13 plan (see Norberg and Velkey 2006), a proportion of them because of a later switch to Chapter 7.

In general, the debtor has discretion to choose whether to file under Chapter 7 or Chapter 13. Under the 2005 Bankruptcy Code revision (BAPCPA), however, debtors who earn above the state median income adjusted by family size and have the ability to repay a substantial portion of their debt by filing Chapter 13 are now required to file Chapter 13 unless they can demonstrate the presence of "special circumstances" that excuse them. Moreover, BAPCPA includes a number of provisions designed to reduce bankruptcy fraud, such as concealing assets. BAPCPA requires filing of tax returns and pay advices along with the debtor's bankruptcy schedules. It also attempts to prevent other forms of abuse, such as abuse of the automatic stay by repeat filings designed solely to stave off legitimate foreclosure actions.

The immediate result of BAPCPA was a dramatic plunge in the number of bankruptcy filings after the surge to beat the effective date of the new law. Nonbusiness filings fell from 1.6 million in 2004 and 2.0 million in 2005 to less than 0.6 million in 2006 (figure 13.1). Even if the reduction in 2006 was partially a result of the aftermath of the rush in late 2005, filings that year undoubtedly were fewer than would have occurred without the new law. After a gradual rise in 2007, filings started upward again in 2008 as the economy began to tilt toward recession and the banking crisis dried up credit for many. In response to high unemployment and a massive destruction of household wealth, filings finally reached almost their 2004 level again in 2010. The difference was that the previous high occurred in a period of economic prosperity, but the new high was the result of economic difficulties. This difference is consistent with the intent of the backers of bankruptcy reform to restore bankruptcy as a safety valve for economic downturn rather than a financial planning tool.

Economic Theory of Bankruptcy and the Fresh Start

Bankruptcy law serves three basic purposes: (1) to solve a collective action problem among creditors in dealing with an insolvent debtor, (2) to provide a "fresh start" for individual debtors overburdened by debt, and (3) to save and preserve the going concern value of firms in financial distress through reorganizing rather than liquidating. The first purpose applies to both individuals and businesses, the second applies only to individuals, and the third applies only to firms and, consequently, will be set aside from the discussion here.

The first purpose of bankruptcy law is to solve a collective action problem among creditors: who is going to get what and in what order. In contrast, nonbankruptcy debt collection law is an individualized process grounded in bilateral transactions between debtors and individual creditors. As noted above and in chapter 11 of this book, this process of creditors' remedies is governed primarily by state law, which identifies the rights of creditors to collect against debtors and also the debtor's property exemptions and other protections. When a debtor is insolvent and there are not enough assets to satisfy all creditors, however, a common pool problem arises. Each creditor has an incentive to try to seize assets of the debtor, even if this prematurely depletes the common pool of assets for creditors as a group. Although creditors as a group may be better off by cooperating and working together to liquidate the debtor's assets in an orderly fashion, each individual creditor has an incentive to race to grab its share right away. Bankruptcy's automatic stay, in addition to other provisions such as the ability to undo payments made in the prebankruptcy period, is designed to halt this race and create an orderly liquidation of assets and distribution of proceeds.

The second bankruptcy policy relevant to consumers is the provision of a fresh start through discharge of prebankruptcy debts. Although many rationales are offered for the fresh start, none is wholly persuasive, and none provides for all cases a compelling rationale for the current American rule that the debtor's right to a discharge is mandatory and not subject to any waiver. As a result, the right of a debtor to file for bankruptcy and discharge debts becomes an implicit term in every consumer credit contract. This required term increases the risk of lending and, of course, increases the risk of lending most to those debtors who are most likely to file for bankruptcy. The increase in risk, in turn, raises the cost of lending, other things being equal, resulting in higher interest rates, higher down payments, and other term repricing behavior, especially to potential borrowers deemed associated with such risk, and it encourages product substitution to greater use of secured credit and other types of credit that are less susceptible to modification or discharge in bankruptcy. It also can cause credit rationing, especially to higher-risk borrowers, including those unable to provide collateral for secured loans easily. Given these compensating adjustments, it is possible that rather than treating bankruptcy as a mandatory contract term, it might be more efficient to allow it to be waivable by some borrowers, at least under some circumstances.

As indicated, observers have offered a variety of rationales for the fresh start policy. One theory argues that the fresh start is a response to our inherently limited foresight, namely, that at the time we enter into a contract to borrow money, we are unable to anticipate future events (see Jackson 1985). A loan that seemed like a good idea for all parties at the outset might turn out to be otherwise because of unforeseen circumstances such as job loss. In this case, the higher price that all borrowers pay for credit may fund a form of insurance to deal with this lack of foresight.

An alternative rationale is communitarian in nature: when a borrower is overburdened with debt, the impact is borne not just by the borrower but also by family. Thus, there are externalities from the debtor's behavior. In this view, where the obligation to repay debt conflicts with the obligation to maintain one's dependents, a fresh start is appropriate in order to protect those who did not consent to the initial borrowing in the first place but who nevertheless are harmed by its weight.

A third rationale involves a charitable motivation: in effect, members of American society are willing to make a moral judgment to permit overburdened consumers to escape their debt obligations in order to avoid the shame and the psychological and physical distress of becoming pauperized. This is a modern reflection of the biblical provision for a "Jubilee" every seven years that would relieve all debts (for discussion, see Zywicki 2000b).

Fourth, the fresh start is seen as a vehicle for providing incentives for productivity and thereby through addressing the problem of "debt overhang." In this context, debt overhang refers to the possibility that if an individual believes that all earnings for the foreseeable future will be allocated to repayment of prior debts rather than current and future consumption, demoralization may lead to unwillingness to work. In this case, allowing an individual to escape debt overhang through the bankruptcy discharge may be a way of restoring incentives to engage in productive activity.

Although each of these theories provides a reasonable rationale for a fresh start, none suggests a wholly satisfactory general justification for the extremely liberal American fresh start policy, as opposed to a more tempered version of relief. There also are obvious economic advantages to a system in which debtors actually repay debts and unwillingness to undertake lending risks does not stifle productive endeavors by lenders and borrowers.

Each of the less general rationales for the fresh start listed above must be qualified by offsetting factors that suggest that limits on the fresh start at will can sometimes be appropriate. For instance, while the fresh start might serve as a type of insurance against limited foresight or to encourage productivity, at the same time, it can create problems of moral hazard and adverse selection. For example, too easy access to bankruptcy as a form of insurance can tend to discourage other forms of insurance that might reduce the need to file for bankruptcy, such as precautionary savings, or may reduce work effort to gain more income (Athreya and Simpson 2006). In addition, a discharge of debt in bankruptcy can have both a wealth effect and an income effect. Thus, while debt overhang may deter work effort because of the substitution effect (of having to pay some income to creditors, thereby reducing the effective marginal value of each hour worked), the elimination of debt may cause a debtor to work less because of the ability to maintain the same standard of living at lower income. Han and Li (2007) found no evidence that bankruptcy discharge leads to an increase in work effort and in fact found a 9 percent reduction in hours worked in the period following a Chapter 7 bankruptcy filing (albeit statistically insignificant), not suggesting a strong role for an income effect of the bankruptcy discharge. Chen (2011), however, found that work effort does increase following a bankruptcy discharge. Reductions in precautionary savings will also tend to reduce the overall supply of investment capital in the economy, resulting at the margin in higher interest rates and reduced credit access.

Second, to the extent that asymmetric information about a particular debtor's willingness to file for bankruptcy leads lenders to be unable to distinguish high-risk from low-risk borrowers perfectly, they will price default risk at an average price rather than at a price idiosyncratic to the specific transaction. This allows higher-risk borrowers to externalize some of the cost of their own riskiness onto lower-risk borrowers, which forces lower-risk borrowers to subsidize higher-risk borrowers. Making bankruptcy protection always nonwaivable thus interferes with the ability of borrowers to signal their private information about their likelihood of filing for bankruptcy. This would create a separating rather than a pooling equilibrium.

In this context, Athreya (2002) concluded that although access to bankruptcy can improve welfare by providing consumption insurance, on net, the current system is welfare-reducing, because the costs of moral hazard, adverse selection, and risk externalities exceed benefits. This means that systemic limits designed to reduce strategic use of bankruptcy, such as means testing eligibility for bankruptcy, can mitigate overall social costs.[6] Chatterjee and Gordon (2011) estimated that eliminating bankruptcy completely would reduce interest rates sufficiently for most households that there would be an overall welfare gain of 1 percent of consumption in perpetuity and that 90 percent of households would benefit, especially lower-income households that currently pay higher credit costs as a result of the bankruptcy system. Reviewing the literature on the welfare effects of bankruptcy, Athreya (2005) concluded theoretically that access to bankruptcy can be welfare-improving only if certain specified conditions are met and where large shocks to net worth can occur that exceed the ability to self-insure efficiently through precautionary savings. Others investigated further conditions where bankruptcy availability might not improve welfare.[7]

Moreover, while bankruptcy policy may be animated by communitarian concerns and externalities, these rationales do not justify a largely unfettered right of borrowers to file for bankruptcy with no showing of undue hardship from being forced to pay their debts. As discussed later, a new provision added by BAPCPA requires a potential bankruptcy filer first to seek counseling from a nonprofit debt counseling service before filing for bankruptcy, a provision designed to encourage borrowers to seek resolution of their financial situation outside of bankruptcy. Similarly, notions of charity are usually qualified and reserved for those who are in most need. Even in the Bible, the Jubilee was highly qualified and created a moral obligation to forgive debts only when the failure to do so would cause

6. Athreya argued that even with restrictions on strategic bankruptcy similar to those eventually enacted in 2005 in BAPCPA (such as means testing eligibility for chapter 7), the overall cost of the consumer bankruptcy system still generally exceeds the benefits. This suggests, in turn, that abolishing bankruptcy might, on net, be welfare-improving for consumers, although the reforms that took place likely produced an improvement.

7. For instance, Livshits, MacGee, and Tertilt (2010) constructed an economic model where moral hazard can be restrained and where lenders can observe personal risk characteristics with some degree of accuracy. Edelberg (2003) argued that over time, lenders have improved their ability to differentiate among the riskiness of borrowers according to personal characteristics and to price risk accordingly, which would reduce the pricing externalities of bankruptcy. In addition, if exemptions are defined to protect productive capital, they may also be welfare-enhancing (see Li and Sarte 2006). In practice, however, exemptions are usually defined to protect consumption goods rather than productive capital goods. Pavan (2008) expanded this analysis to treat consumer durable goods as capital goods providing a flow of services and thus having both a productive and a consumption function.

extreme hardship for a debtor and family (see Zywicki 2000b). Further, if a debt was forgiven as part of the Jubilee, forgiveness resulted in the discharge of only the legal obligation to repay, not the moral obligation. Thus, if a debtor received a discharge because of hardship, if that same debtor later came into money, there would be a continuing moral obligation to repay the debt to the creditor. Nor is the Judeo-Christian tradition unique on this point; every major religion and culture has treated default toward one's creditors as a highly shameful and socially disapproved act (see Efrat 1998).

This discussion of theory suggests that the optimal level of the bankruptcy discharge is ambiguous as an a priori matter. In general, the fresh start provides insurance for borrowers, but this insurance brings with it some degree of concern about moral hazard and adverse selection. As becomes clear from empirical studies discussed further below, increasing the generosity of the fresh start does, in fact, raise the risk of lending. This, in turn, leads to an increase in prices and less access to credit at the margin, especially unsecured credit. Where legislators choose to draw the line for the fresh start at any given time, therefore, is a matter of judgment regarding the trade-off between the benefits of the fresh start and its costs in terms of moral hazard and adverse selection. Fundamentally, this is an empirical question involving the number of bankruptcies and the circumstances under which bankruptcy relief might be made available.

Perhaps a more satisfactory general theory should begin with an analogy to limited liability for corporations and how limited liability controls certain kinds of risks. The purpose of limited liability for corporations is to provide incentives for those running the corporation to act in a risk neutral manner, not taking too much risk in the business or too little. This will tend to encourage growth (including job production) and maximize economic wealth for society. The purpose of limited liability for corporations, therefore, is to soften the cost of business failure ex post, not as an end in itself but rather as a means for encouraging optimal levels of risk taking ex ante.

Bankruptcy similarly provides a form of limited liability for consumers that may be useful to encourage them to act in a risk-neutral fashion. For example, consider an individual who has a choice between two courses of action: first, to continue working at a job with a salary of $40,000 per year or, second, to start a new business that has a 50 percent likelihood of producing $120,000 and a 50 percent likelihood of producing nothing, for an expected value of $60,000. Meanwhile, of course, the individual must still make mortgage payments and car payments, pay living expenses, and so on. Thus, even though the latter investment is most useful from a social perspective, the possibility of total loss and the consequences thereof (foreclosure, repossession, etc.) might well cause the debtor to act in a risk-averse manner and pursue the safer option. Here, if the investment fails, it is not the investment itself that pushes the debtor into insolvency but rather the necessary living expenses incurred while pursuing the investment option. The ability to file for bankruptcy and discharge the living expenses might, in this scenario, provide the incentives for the individual to engage in the socially beneficial, risk-neutral investment.

Why Do People File for Bankruptcy?

The question of why people file for bankruptcy can be subdivided into two sub-questions. First, one can ask why, in general, people file for bankruptcy. Clearly, the answer involves too much debt, but the question concerns specifically what it is that causes debt levels to become devastating enough to set off such a drastic response. Second, one can ask why bankruptcy filings have risen over time. Do the fundamental reasons consumers file for bankruptcy also explain the apparent increase in the willingness of consumers to file for bankruptcy over time? As part of this question, do these reasons explain the dramatic decline in bankruptcy filings in the aftermath of BAPCPA in 2005 and the subsequent increase?

The traditional explanation for the causes of bankruptcy filings might be characterized as the "distress theory." (Hynes 2006 distinguishes between the "distress" and "economic" models of bankruptcy. Zywicki 2005c makes the same distinction but refers to the distress model as the "traditional" model. We will use the terms *distress model* and *traditional model* interchangeably.) This view suggests that bankruptcy arises primarily from financial distress caused by some exogenous factor. Such factors might be some expense or income shock, such as an unexpected liability (e.g., large uninsured medical bills) or job loss. There might be a combination of factors, such as increased debt leverage that increases vulnerability to income or expense shocks.

The distress theory of bankruptcy dominated both intellectual inquiry and bankruptcy policymaking for much of American history (see Zywicki 2005b). As noted, during the nineteenth century, temporary bankruptcy laws were enacted in response to national economic crises and were repealed when economic conditions stabilized. This era of temporary bankruptcy lawmaking ended in 1898 with the enactment of the first permanent bankruptcy law in America (see Skeel 2001 and Tabb 1991). The primary focus of the 1898 act was business bankruptcy rather than individual bankruptcy, but the 1898 act did also create a new permanent structure for consumer bankruptcies.

The 1898 act did not substantially change the justification for consumer bankruptcy or the observed use of bankruptcy. The justification for bankruptcy continued to be providing relief for the "honest but unfortunate debtor" who stumbled into financial catastrophe through job loss, illness, or other major financial setback (Zywicki 2005b). It recognized implicitly that large-scale changes in the nature of the American economy had increased the vulnerability of Americans to such economic setbacks. The general migration from rural farms to urban industrial jobs brought with it a greater and more regular exposure to chronic business cycles and involuntary unemployment. There was a belief at the time that some degree of individual and business financial distress was a permanent part of a capitalist economy, thereby implying the need for a permanent bankruptcy law to ameliorate these recurrent economic difficulties (see Warren 1935). At the same time, the increasing national structure of the American economy suggested the need for a bankruptcy law of national scope to avoid the temptation of debtors to favor local creditors over distant ones. Even in the best of times, it was expected that there would be some level of individual and business financial failure and that one way to deal with this was to make available a permanent federal bankruptcy law.

Consumer bankruptcy filings for most of the twentieth century remained generally consistent with the distress model of bankruptcy. During the era of the Great Depression, for example, bankruptcy filings peaked in the early 1930s at just less than 60 per 100,000 population. As the economy recovered, however, bankruptcy filings fell to less than 10 per 100,000 by 1945. The post–World War II recession increased bankruptcy filings modestly, to 20 per 100,000, before trailing off again. For the next decade, consumer bankruptcy filings followed a pattern of rising during recessions but then tailing back off afterward during subsequent economic recovery.

By the mid-1950s, however, the underlying level of bankruptcy filings began a steady upward creep. In large part, this increase resulted from the rapid growth in access to consumer credit in the post–World War II period. An influential Brookings Institution study by Stanley and Girth (1971) claimed that this increased access to consumer credit was increasing the financial vulnerability of American households, making them more susceptible to other financial stresses. This study heavily influenced the Bankruptcy Commission of the 1970s, which drafted the 1978 Bankruptcy Code substantially liberalizing American bankruptcy laws. Their concern about the stresses of increasing household debt levels was echoed by other leading scholars and analysts of the era (see, e.g., Countryman 1975 and discussion by Skeel 2000). The distress theory explicitly or implicitly argued that households using more credit were becoming increasingly susceptible to exogenous budget shocks, such as job loss, divorce, or health problems, that increased the frequency of bankruptcy filings.

The distress model sees the causes of bankruptcy as being largely involuntary and exogenous. But it is also possible to be more expansive about the economics involved. Some modern economic models of bankruptcy see bankruptcy filings as not only caused by exogenous factors but also reflecting the underlying incentives created by the bankruptcy system itself. In this broader economic view, bankruptcy filings are at least to some extent a response to incentives.

Drawing on the theory of New Institutional Economics, Zywicki (2005b, 2005c, 2011) has provided the most extensive discussion of the broader economic model of the bankruptcy filing process. Zywicki argued that the decision to file for bankruptcy should be understood as a two-step process. The first step involves the cause of the debtor's financial distress, but then second is the decision of the debtor whether to file for bankruptcy or pursue some alternative path to resolving that financial distress. The debtor will often choose bankruptcy as the best course for dealing with financial distress, but not necessarily. Zywicki argued that the decision to file for bankruptcy depends not just on debt levels and the external shocks that generate bankruptcy filings but also on the set of incentives and constraints that debtors face at the time of deciding whether to file for bankruptcy, including the financial and other benefits and costs of filing for bankruptcy.

Further, although this economic model, like the distress model, sees the propensity for distress ex ante and the likelihood of distress ex post as interrelated, the causal link is at least partly the opposite of that postulated by the unadulterated distress model. While the distress model contends that rising debt, and especially credit card debt, along with factors such as job losses and unexpected emergencies, exogenously determines levels of bankruptcy, the economic model notes that one predictable consequence of easy bankruptcy relief would be to encourage consumers to take on increased debt levels. Of special concern is the period immediately preceding bankruptcy when debtors can strategically "load up" on debt, especially credit card debt. Consequently, a component of the economic model is a "strategic" component of bankruptcy filing, which focuses more specifically on moral hazard and adverse selection involved in the bankruptcy approach to dealing with financial distress. Let us look at these theories in more detail.

DISTRESS THEORIES OF BANKRUPTCY

As outlined, the distress theories of bankruptcy rest on the idea that bankruptcy is largely caused by exogenous factors that are largely unrelated to the set of incentives created to file for bankruptcy. These exogenous factors include levels of indebtedness, unemployment, health expenses, and others. To some extent, the distress theories can be read to argue that the consumer propensity for economic distress and demand for bankruptcy are largely unresponsive to the incentives created by the consumer bankruptcy regime.

Many researchers have shown a correlation between consumer debt and bankruptcy filings (see Congressional Budget Office 2000 for a literature review). Stanley and Girth's (1971) influential Brookings study focused on the role of household debt levels as a leading cause of bankruptcy filings. They found that bankruptcy filing trends followed the pattern of changes in the overall debt-to-income ratio and concluded : "We have seen that the growth of the personal bankruptcy rate since the end of World War II has been due primarily to a marked increase in personal indebtedness" (Stanley and Girth 1971, 32). Examining data from 1950 to 1970, Yeager (1974) found a statistically significant relationship between the per capita level of bankruptcy filings and the ratio of consumer credit to disposable personal income lagged by six months. Apilado, Dauten, and Smith (1978) also noted that higher debt levels were associated with higher bankruptcy filing rates.[8]

The most thorough attempt to claim a causal relationship between debt and bankruptcy was by David A. Moss and Gibbs A. Johnson (1999). They attributed the sharp rise in bankruptcy filings toward the end of the twentieth century to changes in the distribution of consumer credit. According to Moss and Johnson, by the mid-1980s, consumer lending began to move sharply down the

---

8. More recently. Baird (1998, 575, n. 7) has written, "Bankruptcy filings. . . are affected most by the amount of debt individuals carry relative to their annual income.. . .. The higher this ratio, the more likely individuals will be unable to pay their debts if they encounter economic misfortune.". Warren (1998, 1081, 1084) has similarly stated: "The macrodata are unambiguous about the best predictor for consumer bankruptcy. Consumer bankruptcy filings rise and fall with the levels of consumer debt. . . .. The simple explanation of the rise in filings—bankruptcies rise as household debt rises—is undeniable." Despite the definitive nature of these latter statements, the authors do not report multivariate statistical analysis concerning this relationship.

income distribution, especially through the expansion of credit card lending. As lower-income households assumed an even higher proportion of the nation's consumer debt load, filing rates increased.

But the relationship between debt and bankruptcy is more complicated as a causal matter than such simple correlations might make it appear at first glance. While higher debt levels would be expected to lead to higher bankruptcy filing rates, a more generous bankruptcy system that permits borrowers to discharge debt easily will lead to increased demand for credit by consumers. This means that debt levels are not necessarily exogenous causes of bankruptcy. Rather, the debt levels will in part simultaneously be "endogenous" to the bankruptcy system; that is, although consumer debt is a cause of bankruptcy, the debt level itself is a function of the bankruptcy system (see Jones and Zywicki 1999, Gross and Souleles 2002, and Zywicki 2005b).[9] This economic causal explanation for the correlation between debt levels and bankruptcy is complicated in an additional way: higher levels of debt increase the financial benefit from filing for bankruptcy and thus provides a stronger incentive for the borrower to file for bankruptcy.[10]

In general, the studies that have examined the relationship between debt and bankruptcy have not adequately addressed this problem of endogeneity. Indeed, it is not even clear that they always even recognize it. Those who offer the simple distress argument appear to assume a unidirectional model of causation from debt levels to bankruptcy filing rates. As a result, while the link between debt and bankruptcy seems intuitive, empirical support for the hypothesis and for the contribution of increased debt to rising bankruptcy filing rates is not convincing.

In addition to these theoretical problems, there are several empirical issues. Specifically, those who argue for a strong debt-to-bankruptcy link typically use as their measure of debt the aggregate household debt-to-income ratio as a measure of financial distress. This measurement of household financial condition is not very useful for this purpose, however, because it compares income (a short-term flow measure) to total debt (a long-term stock measure of financial liabilities). The latter is not a good measure of distress, because it includes principal balances that are not payable in lump sums or intended to be repaid with a month's income. Consumer credit is almost always payable in a series of monthly installments, not in a lump sum.[11]

9. To illustrate the point with an extreme example, assume that Congress chose to reinstate debtors' prisons in place of the current bankruptcy system upon a debtor's insolvency. It is quite likely that such a punitive bankruptcy system would reduce demand for debt and lead individuals more to steer clear of possible financial distress than would otherwise be the case. For instance, they might hold larger precautionary balances or choose employment opportunities with lower levels of potential volatility.

10. One exogenous force that may have contributed to increased financial distress among lower-income and risky borrowers could be regulatory policies that require increased lending to those groups, such as the Community Reinvestment Act. Gramlich (1999) claimed that 3 to 4 percent of bankruptcy filings were the result of loans required by the Community Reinvestment Act. In general, the potential impact of such laws on bankruptcy filings has been little studied.

11. Likewise, it would be misleading to compare current debt obligations with total assets (home equity, retirement assets, etc.) without further discussion such as taking account of whether

The use of the aggregate debt-to-income ratio also takes no account of interest rates or term maturities on consumer credit. As the maturity term lengthens or the interest rate on a loan falls, consumers can borrow a larger principal amount without any effective change in their propensity for immediate financial distress. For consumer loans, maturities have lengthened and interest rates have generally fallen over the past three decades on average. This has tended to increase overall debt loads relative to payments (the latter representing actual stress), other things being equal.

The debt-to-income ratio also fails to account for increases in household net wealth over time. Over the post–World War II period, household wealth, especially financial wealth (such as stocks and bonds) and residential real estate (homes), has generally increased more rapidly than income, at least until 2007. While some of these wealth gains were lost in the financial crisis beginning in 2008, on average, during the whole period, household wealth grew more rapidly than household income.[12]

Even those studies that have claimed a link between household debt (as measured by debt-to-income ratio) and consumer bankruptcy filings have observed that the link has weakened in recent decades, as filings increased more rapidly than debt. Over time, as bankruptcy filings have risen proportionately more than indebtedness, household debt levels explain *less* of the propensity to file for bankruptcy than in the past. Moreover, because the authors use questionable measure of the debt-to-income ratio as their measure of debt distress, the direct impact of debt on bankruptcy filings may be even more attenuated than their findings suggest. Finally, as indicated, they make no effort to control for the endogeneity problem of the manner in which the rules established by the bankruptcy system affect the incentives of borrowers to take on debt in the first instance. Thus, while intuition suggests that there is likely some relationship between debt levels and bankruptcy filings, clear and complete demonstration of the existence and strength of that relationship remains an open question as an empirical matter.

CREDIT CARDS AND BANKRUPTCY

A variation on the consumer overindebtedness argument is that credit cards cause overindebtedness, which then causes increased bankruptcy filings, or are

---

those assets are liquid or illiquid. chapter 2 above discusses such measures in more detail and reviews some of the studies that have discussed them further. See, for example, Luckett and August (1985).

12. Chapter 2 above discusses long-term trends in consumer debt and wealth and associated studies in more detail. In general, the long-term trends, especially concerning the relationship of consumer credit and various measures of income and wealth, appear much more benign than generally believed or often reported in the press. For this reason, in isolation, bankruptcy filings should have remained much more stable than they have. Instead, bankruptcy filings rose rapidly from 1980 to 1990, rose still more rapidly from 1990 until the enactment of bankruptcy reform legislation in 2005, and then plummeted in 2006 and 2007, notwithstanding an absence of any corresponding decrease in household debt levels.

a unique form of debt that for some reason consumers are especially prone to misuse, therefore ending up in bankruptcy (see Warren 1998; Sullivan, Warren, and Westbrook 2000; Mann 2006; and White 2007). Surveys have found that consumers frequently attribute their financial troubles and bankruptcy filing to overuse of credit cards (see White 2007). The argument is that credit cards combine high rates of interest with an insidious form of gradual and subconscious debt accumulation through many routine purchases (see Sullivan, Warren, and Westbrook 2000, 108–140; and Schor 2001).

As discussed in chapters 1, 2, and 7, credit card use has increased dramatically over the past several decades, but most credit card debt appears to be a substitute for other kinds of consumer credit, such as various forms of retail store credit and installment loans. Much of the growth in revolving credit arises from technological change in computerized record keeping and instantaneous communications that have made extensive revolving credit operations feasible. Consumers seem to prefer revolving credit for its convenience, price, and variety. Although it is frequently asserted that credit cards are unique contributors to consumer indebtedness, there is no evidence that credit card debt is more "insidious" than the installment loans they replaced, which offered the same appeal of "easy payments" stretched out over long periods of time. Those who claim that credit cards have been important in causing the increase in bankruptcies in recent decades generally do not mention the substitution effect that has arisen from technological change.

Even many statistical studies in this area do not mention the substitution effect (see Ausubel 1997; Ellis 1998; Moss and Johnson 1999; Domowitz and Sartain 1999a; Stavins 2000; Sullivan, Warren, and Westbrook 2000; Livshits, MacGee, and Tertilt 2010; and White 2007). It is true that both credit card debt and bankruptcies have risen, and so statistics will demonstrate a positive correlation, but without also investigating the substitution effect, this does mean that there is a causal relationship. These studies assert but do not explore fully the found correlation between credit card debt (or credit card defaults) and bankruptcy or whether increased credit card debt represents increased financial distress. The underlying problem is that these studies do not account for the substitution effect of credit cards for other types of credit, and thus they make an implicit assumption that credit card debt has actually produced higher levels of indebtedness and financial distress.

Moreover, overcoming the endogeneity problems in order to establish a causal direction is especially difficult with respect to credit cards. Not only is the standard endogeneity problem outlined above present (that individuals base their borrowing decisions in part on the nature of the bankruptcy regime), but credit cards offer a particularly vexing form of endogeneity: because credit cards provide a borrower with a prearranged, open, unsecured line of credit, they are particularly susceptible to moral hazard and adverse selection with respect to borrowing when conditions go south. For many bankruptcy filers, increasing credit card debt may not *cause* bankruptcy; it may simply be associated with a gradual slide into bankruptcy. Aggressive use of open credit lines on credit cards may in many cases be a last resort effort to try to stave off bankruptcy that was actually caused by other difficulties.[13] It is not at all clear that these studies convincingly demonstrate a causal relationship between credit card use and bankruptcy.[14]

Beyond the economic endogeneity problem and the substitution effect, some credit card use in the period preceding bankruptcy may actually be strategic. Debtors anticipating a bankruptcy filing may actually increase their use of credit cards, or "load up" in the vernacular, in the prebankruptcy period in the knowledge that they will be able to discharge that debt in bankruptcy. Thus, instead of increased credit card debt subsequently leading to an increased likelihood of bankruptcy, a debtor who has made a determination to file for bankruptcy might load up on use of credit cards immediately before filing for bankruptcy. This possibility should also be taken into account in any comprehensive study.

While the Bankruptcy Code places some limit on egregious types of prebankruptcy loading up, the code's limits are not very rigorous.[15] The code places almost no limit on a debtor's use of a credit card for purchases that do not qualify as luxury goods and services but are nonetheless discretionary in nature and could otherwise be postponed until after bankruptcy (for example, car repairs, home repairs, or purchases of professional and other services). Moreover, while the code prevents debtors from preferring one unsecured creditor over another during the ninety days preceding bankruptcy, it does not restrict the ability to pay secured debts instead of credit cards or a preference for one unsecured creditor over another outside of ninety days before bankruptcy (such as favoring creditors with nondischargeable claims) or accumulation of property that is exempt in bankruptcy.[16] Thus, while a disproportionate level of unpaid credit card debt might appear to be the proximate cause of bankruptcy, this appearance may actually reflect the debtor's own strategic behavior.

13. Consider, for example, a consumer who has a steady job and a credit card credit line of $25,000, but pays off the card balance each month in full. A job loss or some unexpected financial setback could suddenly turn this card holder from a low-risk user into a high-risk revolver drawing against the full credit line. If this individual later ends up in bankruptcy, it may appear that the sizable credit card debt was the proximate cause of the bankruptcy filing, both in timing and in amount. But this would mistake cause and effect. The large credit card balance was an effect of the exogenous shock, and so the use of the card was merely associated with the downward descent into a bankruptcy caused by other factors.

14. Mann (2006) acknowledges the endogeneity problem and the substitution effect and claims to find a strong causal relationship between credit card debt and personal bankruptcy at the macroeconomic level, thereby supposedly demonstrating the validity of the distress model. His analysis contains some significant unsolved econometric difficulties concerning use of lagged variables necessitating additional work, however. For further discussion, see Zywicki (2011).

15. 11 U.S.C. §523(a)(3) creates a presumption of nondischargeability of debt incurred for the purchase of "luxury goods and services" above a certain threshold within a certain number of days preceding a bankruptcy filing. Debts incurred for nonluxury goods and services are unaffected, as are even those charges incurred for luxury goods outside of the ninety-day window (seventy days for cash advances).

16. See Lehnert and Maki (2002). Conversion of nonexempt assets to exempt assets is generally permissible under the Bankruptcy Code.

Evidence is consistent with the hypothesis that some debtors engage in strategic behavior with respect to credit before bankruptcy filing. Gross and Souleles (2002) found in their large sample of credit card account use data that in the year before bankruptcy, borrowers significantly increased the use of their credit cards versus earlier periods, running up their balances rapidly in the period leading to bankruptcy. This finding that the rise in credit card debt is rapid and concentrated in the period immediately preceding bankruptcy suggests that credit card indebtedness does not cause bankruptcy in all cases but that the debtor may be already on the way toward bankruptcy when the credit card borrowing increases and is either tapping the credit line as last resort or acting strategically.

Lehnert and Maki (2002) also found evidence that supports the hypothesis of strategic behavior. They determined that generous bankruptcy exemptions at the state level tended to lead to increased bankruptcy filing rates in the state but also to a greater tendency of households to hold simultaneously both more low-return liquid assets and more high-cost unsecured debt, such as credit card debts. This suggests that these households *could* have paid some of their credit card debt but chose not to do so. Absent the bankruptcy option, it would be rational to use some of the low-return savings to reduce their high-cost debt obligations. With bankruptcy as an option, however, consumers can retain their assets through exemptions while discharging their unsecured debt. This provides an incentive to make the strategic decision to carry both more assets and more unsecured debt simultaneously.

Domowitz and Eovaldi (1993) found that Chapter 7 bankruptcy filers in states with larger exemption levels have larger asset holdings at the time of bankruptcy than households in low-exemption states and that Chapter 13 filers have higher than predicted indebtedness levels at the time of bankruptcy. Both of these findings are consistent with strategic models of bankruptcy. Lopes (2003) similarly found that some consumers borrow strategically with the intention of defaulting in the near future and that their likelihood of strategic borrowing depends on the relative generosity of exemptions. All of these concerns cast considerable doubt on the unadulterated theory of distress caused by credit cards as the sole or overarching cause of consumer bankruptcy.

Adverse Shocks and Bankruptcy

The other part of the distress theory of bankruptcy connection points to the role of adverse shocks that unexpectedly increase household liabilities or reduce income or assets, such as unemployment, divorce, and health problems. Many studies have found that bankruptcy filings are driven in part by adverse events that either increase costs or decrease income, although this fails to explain the unprecedented increase in bankruptcy filings during the 1990s and 2000s or the dramatic drop in bankruptcy filings following the passage of bankruptcy reform legislation in 2005. Furthermore, specifics of the evidence is mixed, depending in part on the question asked and the methodology engaged (for example, comparing to a control group or not in sociological studies or use or not of multivariate techniques in statistical studies).[17]

17. For discussion of the sociological studies, see Shuchman 1990 and White 1991.

Unemployment

Unemployment has been a linchpin of the distress model, under the argument that increased bankruptcy filings reflect underlying negative macroeconomic conditions, especially high unemployment, but evidence is mixed. Stanley and Girth (1971) found that the bankruptcy filing rate was sensitive in the short run to changes in the unemployment rate, but Apilado, Dauten, and Smith (1978) did not. Shepard (1984a) found that unemployment was a leading factor in the post–World War II growth in consumer bankruptcy filings, but Shiers and Williamson (1987), examining cross-state data from 1980, found that changes in the unemployment rate were significant only in explaining variations in the Chapter 7 filing rate but not for Chapter 13. Braucher (1998) and Sullivan, Warren, and Westbrook (2000) concluded that job-related difficulties were the most important cause of severe financial distress and bankruptcy, but a study by Visa (1996) suggested that it was not the level of unemployment that was important in predicting bankruptcy but changes in the level.

Some controlled studies have questioned the importance of unemployment to bankruptcy, finding that job disruption by the head of the household is *not* a statistically significant predictor of bankruptcy. Buckley and Brinig (1998) found little support in their study for the hypothesis that job loss was a significant factor in bankruptcy filings after controlling for other relevant economic variables. Fay, Hurst, and White (2002) also found that unemployment by a head of household or spouse was not a statistically significant predictor of bankruptcy filings.

More recently, Garrett and Wall (2010) found evidence of a "personal bankruptcy cycle" that is related to the business cycle, with bankruptcy rates significantly higher than normal during recessions and rising as recessions persist. They also found, however, that while recession and unemployment explain some of the variation in bankruptcy filing rates over time, they explained little of the larger trends in bankruptcy filing rates over time.[18]

More generally, while unemployment may account for variations in bankruptcy filings around the base level trend line, there is little evidence that unemployment or changes in the unemployment rate can explain the dramatic increase in bankruptcy filings over the past thirty years (Zywicki 2005b). During the 1990s and early 2000s, for example, the unemployment rate was low and steady, but bankruptcies rose dramatically. On the other hand, following the passage of bankruptcy reform legislation in 2005, the relationship between unemployment and bankruptcy filings appeared to reestablish itself as economic recession beginning in 2008 was accompanied by a rising bankruptcy filing rate.

18. Various studies have also found that local or regional recessions that create unusually high unemployment rates can explain higher bankruptcy rates in those local regions (see Brown 1998; Bishop 1998; Weiss, Bhandari, and Robins 2001; Barron, Elliehausen, and Staten 2000; and Cohen-Cole 2009). Others have found that the net effect of recessions on bankruptcy filing rates is insignificant (see Garrett 2007).

Divorce

Divorce also can be a precipitating cause of bankruptcy by creating simultaneous expense and income shocks (see Sullivan, Warren, and Westbrook 2000; Fay, Hurst, and White 2002). First, divorce increases costs, because when one household becomes two, divorce reduces the economies of scale of living in a single household. Rather than living in one housing arrangement with its associated set of expenses, it becomes necessary to maintain two households, with two sets of housing, food, and other expenses, including possibly new arrangements for child care. Second, divorce results in a drop in household income, especially if one spouse has less valuable market skills or has been out of the labor market for several years. Then that individual will have to support a new household on proportionately lower income than previously. Thus, divorce would be expected to be a significant cause of bankruptcy filings.

Again, however, evidence is mixed on the effect of divorce on bankruptcy filings. Shepard (1984a) found that the divorce rate was a factor explaining the post–World War II growth in consumer bankruptcy filings, and Buckley and Brinig (1998) and Barron, Staten, and Wilshusen (2002) found that divorce rates are correlated with regional differences in bankruptcy filing rates. Several econometric studies failed to find a significant relationship between divorce and bankruptcy filings, however (see Domowitz and Eovaldi 1993; Domowitz and Sartain 1999a; and Fay, Hurst, and White 2002). Shiers and Williamson (1987) found changes in the divorce rate to be a significant predictor of variation in Chapter 7 filing rates but not Chapter 13. It is also plausible that at least some of the observed correlation runs in the reverse direction, as bankruptcy may be a proxy for underlying financial problems that lead to divorce. Moreover, it is highly unlikely that divorce can provide a causal explanation for changes in the bankruptcy filing rate over the past several decades. The national divorce rate peaked in 1981 at 5.3 divorces per 1,000 population and has trended steadily downward over the past several decades.

Health Problems, Medical Debt, and Insurance

It is also reasonable to expect that health problems could precipitate a bankruptcy filing, possibly through a whipsaw effect that combines several adversities. First, health problems can create a shock to household income through inability to work. Second, health problems also can create a shock to household expenses through large, unanticipated expense and resultant debt, especially if the debtor does not have adequate health insurance. The combination of these two factors contributes to many bankruptcy filings (see Domowitz and Sartain 1999a; Sullivan, Warren, and Westbrook 2000; and Jacoby, Sullivan, and Warren 2001). Himmelstein et al. (2005) reported that 20 percent of bankruptcy filers stated that health problems had caused them to miss two weeks or more of work in the two-year period preceding bankruptcy. Follow-up telephone interviews with those who reported that they had missed two weeks or more of work as a result of health problems found that 71.6 percent said that income troubles from missed work contributed "very much" to their bankruptcy filing, and 8.6 percent said that their health problems had contributed "somewhat" (see Jacoby and Warren 2006).

Although health problems and missed work clearly can contribute to increased bankruptcy filings, it is unlikely that this factor can explain the increased bankruptcy filings that occurred between 1980 and 2005, however, or the dramatic reduction in bankruptcy filings following enactment of BAPCPA in 2005. There is no evidence that Americans have somehow become more intrinsically unhealthy over the past several decades or that they miss more work or suffer greater income reductions as a result of health problems. Instead, improvements in medical technology appear to have made rehabilitation after injury or illness more rapid and complete than in earlier eras. Moreover, to the extent that these authors classify as a precipitating event two weeks of missed work over the two-year period preceding bankruptcy as a causal factor in bankruptcy filings, this seems like a potentially overly expansive definition of the phenomenon.

Empirically, Fay, Hurst, and White (2002) found that health problems of the head of a household or spouse that cause missed work are *not* a statistically significant factor in bankruptcy filings. Mathur (2005) similarly found that poor health of the head of a household is not a statistically significant predictor of bankruptcy filings. She noted that only 6 percent of participants in the Panel Study of Income Dynamics survey self-reported that illness or injury caused their bankruptcy filing, and statistical analysis found no significant correlation between bankruptcy filings and individuals in poor health.

Rather than through increased income loss from health problems, it seems more likely that medical problems could increase bankruptcy filings if the out-of-pocket cost of medical treatment has increased or if access to health insurance has decreased, leading to an increase in uncovered adverse health events.

A comprehensive review by Gruber and Levy (2009) found, however, that although overall spending on health care in the United States had increased since 1980, there was no evidence of increased out-of-pocket health expenses for the nonelderly population during this period. Neither has there been a substantial increase in health cost risk for various subgroups, such as families with children. Gruber and Levy found that for families with lower education levels and with children, median household spending on health actually *declined* significantly after 1980, as many of these families shifted from private to public medical coverage.

Clearly, lack of health insurance also can contribute to bankruptcy filings, but there is no evidence that during the past three decades health insurance coverage decreased anything like the way bankruptcy filing rates increased, especially after government provision of insurance is taken into account. In fact, between 1993 and 2007, overall insurance rates were rising for native-born Americans and falling only for immigrants, especially noncitizens (see Zywicki 2007).

Empirical research has found little relationship between lack of health insurance and the large rise in bankruptcy filing. Gross and Souleles (2002) found that a lack of health insurance was not a statistically significant predictor of bankruptcy.[19] Stavins (2000, 22) similarly found in the Federal Reserve's 1998 Survey

---

19. Although they did not find lack of health insurance to be a predictor of bankruptcy, they did find it to be a predictor of credit card default.

of Consumer Finances "no notable difference" between the percentage of bankruptcy filers with health insurance and the percentage of nonfilers with health insurance.[20] Jacoby, Sullivan, and Warren (2001, 377) found that 80 percent of those who attributed their bankruptcy filing to health problems actually had health insurance during the relevant period.[21]

Medical problems can also precipitate bankruptcy from the expense side through an adverse debt shock if a debtor is confronted with large unpaid medical bills. Debt owed to medical providers is typically unsecured debt, and medical care is often provided regardless of a patient's demonstrated ability to pay. As a result, debtors can compile large medical debts that can subsequently precipitate a bankruptcy filing.

Early studies failed to identify medical debt as a major contributor to bankruptcy filings. A study by Sittner et al. (1967) concluded that medical debts were not an important factor in most bankruptcy filings. Gold and Donahue (1982) also found that medical debts were not a major cause of bankruptcy. An early study by Shuchman (1983) found medical debt present in half of bankruptcies but relatively low median levels of medical debt ($567). In a later paper, Shuchman (1985) similarly found that the average amount of medical bills expressed as a percentage of total unsecured debt was relatively small (about 5 percent of total unsecured debt). Evaluating data collected from bankruptcy cases filed in 1981 in ten federal districts, Sullivan, Warren, and Westbrook (1989) also concluded that medical debt played a minor role in overall bankruptcy filings. They found that about half of bankruptcy filers listed medical debt in their files and that medical debt accounted for about 11 percent of unsecured debt. But they concluded that "at most only 1 percent to 2 percent of the debtors in bankruptcy are demonstrably there because of catastrophic medical losses," and their central finding was "that crushing medical debt is not the widespread bankruptcy phenomenon that many have supposed" (Sullivan, Warren, and Westbrook 1989, 173).

Later research projects undertaken in the period before passage of BAPCPA and using data from bankruptcy filings in 2001 purported to find a large increase in the importance of medical debt in bankruptcy filings (see Himmelstein et al. 2005 and 2009). Both studies, however, have been criticized by health scholars, economists, and law professors (see Fleming 2005, Heriot 2005, Lemieux 2005, Mathur 2005, Zywicki 2005b, and Dranove and Millenson 2006). Criticisms

20. Stavins found that those who filed for bankruptcy in the past were *more* likely to have health insurance than those who did not, although they may have acquired health insurance after the filing. Although it is unlikely that bankruptcy filers are more likely to be insured at the time of filing than nonfilers, Stavins's findings certainly cast doubt on the claim that they are substantially more likely to lack insurance.

21. Having health insurance could even lead to offsetting behaviors that could tend to create new vulnerability to bankruptcy, such as reduction in precautionary savings (see Hubbard, Skinner, and Zeldes 1995 and Gruber and Yelowitz 1999). To the extent that health insurance allows an increase in consumption at the expense of saving for precautionary and other purposes, overall financial well-being may not improve as much as availability of the insurance suggests.

focus on an overly broad and controversial definition of "medical bankruptcies," use of means rather than medians in statistical discussions in ways that could skew findings, and incomplete discussion in the papers about other debts and failure to compare adequately with medical debts.

Most other studies have concluded that medical debt and health problems play a much smaller role in bankruptcy filings than Himmelstein et al. estimated. For instance, the Department of Justice's Executive Office for US Trustees (EOUST) reviewed the files of 5,023 no-asset Chapter 7 cases closed between 2000 and 2002 in the most thorough study of the problem to date of those who actually filed for bankruptcy (see US Department of Justice, Executive Office for US Trustees 2005). It reported that 54 percent of the cases in the sample listed no medical debt, meaning that the median amount of medical debt in the study was zero. Medical debt accounted for 5.5 percent of total general unsecured debt, and 90.1 percent of cases reported medical debts of less than $5,000. There were a few cases where extremely high medical debt likely explained the subsequent filing; 1 percent of cases accounted for 36.5 percent of medical debt, and less than 10 percent of all cases represented 80 percent of all reported medical debt. Of the minority of cases in the sample with medical debt, the average medical debt was $4,978 per case, 78.4 percent reported medical debts of less than $5,000 (an average of $1,212 for this group), and medical debts accounted for 13 percent of the total general unsecured debt for those reporting medical debt. Thus, even among those who reported medical debt, few reported medical debt levels sufficiently high to conclude that they were a primary cause of bankruptcy. Flynn and Bermant (2001) and Mathur (2005) reached broadly similar conclusions that while medical debt was important in a minority of cases, it was not important in most.

In conclusion, it is possible that the estimates of medical bankruptcies may either overstate or underestimate the true number of filings attributable to this cause. For example, those studies that look only at medical debt listed on a debtor's bankruptcy schedules may tend to underestimate the true incidence of medical debt if, for example, medical debt was paid off using a credit card or home equity line of credit and thus was not revealed as medical debt on the debtor's schedules. On the other hand, it is possible that the contribution of medical debt to bankruptcy may be overstated. Because medical bills are unsecured debt that can be discharged in bankruptcy and debtors suffer few consequences from the failure to pay medical bills (because future treatment rarely will be denied from failure to pay past medical bills), the frequency of unpaid medical bills in bankruptcy may reflect strategic behavior by debtors facing insolvency in choosing which bills to pay in the period preceding bankruptcy. Consequently, debtors disproportionately may choose not to pay medical debt, as opposed to secured debts (such as mortgages or car loans) or debts that are nondischargeable in bankruptcy (such as student loan debt). In addition, when survey evidence is used, bankruptcy filers may be more willing to attribute their difficulties to health problems or medical debt than to some factor that might be seen as more morally blameworthy or embarrassing, such as overborrowing on credit cards to support unrealistic consumption habits or general financial irresponsibility.[22]

---

22. In addition, methodology in specific surveys can skew results. For example, even though bankruptcy filers when asked often report that tax debts were an important factor in their

Scholars have identified additional factors that might contribute to rising bankruptcy filings. Gambling may have also contributed to rising bankruptcy filing rates in parts of the country where it has been legalized but likely has a very small impact on national bankruptcy filing rates. Barron, Staten, and Wilshusen (2002) found that bankruptcy rates would have been 2.6 percent lower in 1998 in counties that hosted or were adjacent to casinos but concluded that this would only have decreased nationwide filings by 0.5 percent, because the effects were geographically localized. Garrett and Nichols (2008) also found a modest effect of casinos on increased bankruptcy filings, but the effect was geographically concentrated in the South. In contrast, Thalheimer and Ali (2004) found no effect.

Tax obligations have also likely contributed to personal bankruptcy filings, both directly (because of unpaid tax arrearages, which generally cannot be discharged in bankruptcy) and indirectly by reducing household disposable income. Although systematic research is lacking, some evidence suggests that tax obligations may play a role in a significant number of bankruptcies. In a 1997 Gallup poll, for example, 10 percent of respondents indicated that taxes played a role in their filing, a number that exceeded those naming college expenses or a death in the family and five times higher than those identifying gambling as a cause (see McKinley 1997, 34). Efrat (2008) also found that taxes played a substantial role in small business bankruptcies, many of which also entangle personal assets and liabilities. Warren and Tyagi (2003) indicate that a rising tax burden may also play an important indirect role in prompting bankruptcy filings by reducing household disposable income, although they do not discuss this point in their analysis.

LEGAL FACTORS

Researchers have also explored the incentives provided by the Bankruptcy Code itself for bankruptcy filing. As a first-order proposition, the link seems obvious: more lenient bankruptcy laws should lead to higher levels of bankruptcy filings. If, for example, debtors' prisons were revived, one would expect bankruptcy filing rates to be much lower than today. But, as introduced earlier, there is an endogeneity problem here as a theoretical matter, and the effect may be more ambiguous. While easier access to bankruptcy might provide incentives for higher bankruptcy filing rates ex post, these incentives will factor into decisions made by debtors and creditors ex ante. Under a regime of strict bankruptcy laws, for example, debtors will desire to borrow less (thereby reducing their risk of insolvency), but lenders may be willing to lend more and to lend to riskier borrowers than in a regime of laxer bankruptcy laws, other things being equal. By contrast, lax bankruptcy laws will encourage borrowers to borrow more and lenders to lend

bankruptcy filing, many surveys nonetheless omit taxes as a potential answer for the cause of the bankruptcy filing, potentially implicitly steering debtors to alternative explanations.

less than would otherwise be the case. How these factors offset one another will be ambiguous theoretically.

Changes over Time

Researchers have examined the impact of bankruptcy laws on bankruptcy filing rates empirically. One purpose animating the enactment of the 1978 Bankruptcy Code was to liberalize access to bankruptcy. The enactment of the code, therefore, provided a natural experiment to measure both the short-term and the long-term response of bankruptcy filing rates to changes in the bankruptcy laws. In turn, the substantial tightening of the incentives to file for bankruptcy with the enactment of BAPCPA in 2005 provided a natural experiment with the response of bankruptcy filing rates in the opposite direction.

Researchers generally found that the more generous terms of the 1978 Bankruptcy Code led to an increase in the bankruptcy filing rate. For example, an early study by Carter (1982) compared the annual trend in bankruptcy filings for 1959 to 1979 with that for 1980 to 1981 and concluded that, adjusting for recessions, as much as three-fourths of the increased filings under the new code were because of the new law. Using regression analysis, Kowalewski (1982) estimated that the Bankruptcy Code was responsible for 13 to 47 percent of the increase in personal bankruptcy filings, depending on the specification. Boyes and Faith (1986) examined monthly bankruptcy petitions filed in the US District Court in Phoenix, Arizona, between January 1976 and December 1981, inclusive of 1978, when the code was enacted, and estimated that the enactment led to an increase of 21.6 percent over the prior trend. Nelson (2000) estimated that the passage of the 1978 Bankruptcy Code increased bankruptcies by approximately 36 percent relative to the pre-code period.

Peterson and Aoki (1984) found that bankruptcy filings rose sharply in most states after the Bankruptcy Reform Act came into effect. They concluded that the significant increase in filing rates from 1978 to 1980 could not be accounted for by changes in state laws or employment conditions and that the act was primarily responsible for the increase. Similarly, Shepard (1984b) found that additional bankruptcy filings would not have occurred in the absence of the 1978 act. Domowitz and Eovaldi (1993) examined quarterly data from 1960 to 1985 and estimated a range of findings for the impact of the 1978 Bankruptcy Code on filings, controlling for a number of other potentially relevant variables (including unemployment, debt-to-income ratios, interest rates, inflation, public transfer payments, and divorce rates). They found that at the low end of their estimated range, the revised Bankruptcy Act increased bankruptcy filings by 22 percent but that this estimate is not statistically significant until higher in the estimated range. And so their estimate is that the impact was greater than 22 percent.

In contrast, Bhandari and Weiss (1993) found, using annual data for the period 1947 to 1987 that controlled for debt-to-income ratio, unemployment, and divorce, that the impact of the enactment of the Bankruptcy Code was statistically insignificant. Nelson (2000) questioned this finding, because Bhandari and Weiss did not adjust the data for reporting changes resulting from joint petitions and did not test for stationarity of the data series. In any case, the bulk of evidence supported the hypothesis that consumers respond to incentives to file for bankruptcy and that the loosening of the bankruptcy laws under the 1978 code produced an increase in bankruptcy filings.

Further, the dramatic decline in the number of bankruptcy filings after the legal tightening caused by passage of BAPCPA in 2005 is consistent with the views of those who predicted an economic response to an increase in the price of bankruptcy (see, for example, Jones and Zywicki 1999 and Zywicki 2005b). The decline is not consistent with the views of those who contended that the bankruptcy rise in recent decades has been solely or largely caused by exogenous increases in indebtedness and various adverse economic shocks rather than legal factors, although it seems that resumption of the rise in bankruptcy filings after 2007 is consistent with this hypothesis.[23]

Some circumstantial evidence of the effect of legal incentives on bankruptcy filings is provided by comparisons of bankruptcy filings across countries with different legal regimes. Duygan-Bump and Grant (2008) examined the effects of a variety of different legal and economic variables across different European countries. They began by noting that while a particular adverse shock, such as unemployment, is the same in every country, the impact of the shock should have substantially different results on the likelihood of defaulting on debts in different countries, depending on the legal rules and other institutions in those countries.

Counterintuitively, they found that making it more difficult to collect debts using formal legal procedures was associated with a *decrease* in the default rate, a result that they attributed to lenders offsetting the increased risk of collecting by reducing their lending volume.[24] They also found that increasing the amount of adverse credit information reported to lenders reduced delinquency rates,

---

23. As immediate evidence of the impact of legal factors and the incentives that they provide for filing for bankruptcy, the filing rate rose dramatically before the more restrictive BAPCPA went into effect in 2005. Before BAPCPA, national consumer bankruptcy filings were about 1.5 million per year, or approximately 30,000 per week. In the two weeks preceding the effective date of BAPCPA, 500,000 individuals filed for bankruptcy, including 350,000 in the week immediately preceding its effective date. By contrast, when the 1978 Bankruptcy Code was enacted, which liberalized the bankruptcy laws, no filing rush occurred, suggesting that consumers were responding to an anticipated change in the incentives for filing for bankruptcy, not merely uncertainty. Similarly, when Congress considered repealing the post–Civil War bankruptcy law in 1878, it was reported that "debtors were rushing into bankruptcy in anticipation of repeal" (US Senate 1931, 53).

Some individuals who opposed passage of BAPCPA quickly mounted a study to show the impact of the new law on actual and potential bankruptcy filers, a different question from whether legal changes have an impact on filing trends. The study has some methodological difficulties and will not be discussed further here. See Lawless et al. (2008). Discussion of the methodology of this report may be found in Pardo (2009a). Lawless et al. (2009) then replied, and Pardo (2009b) replied again.

24. Note that this might also be consistent with the possibility that consumers may be electing "informal bankruptcy" at different rates in different countries (that is, countries with weaker creditor collection powers may lead consumers to be more likely simply to default without consequence), an explanation that the authors did not consider.

consistent with the prediction that consumers will be less willing to default where the consequences to their credit reputation are more severe (or alternatively, that more information about borrowers' risk characteristics leads to greater exclusion of poor risks from markets). The authors observed that their findings supported the hypothesis that adverse shocks are mediated through institutions and that the decision of whether to default is in part strategic, since the debtor's decision of whether to default is in part a response to the structure of the incentives faced.

Exemption Laws and Incentives

Researchers have also examined the incentives for bankruptcy filing created by particular elements of the bankruptcy laws. Most notable are the incentive effects created by property exemption law, which define the types and amounts of property that debtors are entitled to protect from creditors in bankruptcy. Although bankruptcy law is federal in nature, exemption laws have long been a creature of state law, and the Bankruptcy Code effectively incorporates those state law property exemptions for purposes of identifying the property that the debtor may protect in bankruptcy. As noted above, allowable exemptions vary among states.

This state-by-state variation provides a natural laboratory for testing the effect of the incentives provided by different exemption levels on bankruptcy filing rates through cross-section analyses. As with the generosity of bankruptcy laws generally, however, the theoretical impact of higher homestead exemptions is ambiguous. On one hand, larger exemptions provide incentives for a troubled borrower to file for bankruptcy because of the ability to shield more property in bankruptcy. This would tend to increase the demand for credit in addition to the demand for bankruptcy. In contrast, larger exemptions make lending more risky, which predicts that lenders will reduce the supply of credit to borrowers in that state and charge higher interest rates. Both of the latter factors would reduce the amount of credit generated, especially to riskier borrowers, and may well then reduce the demand for bankruptcy.

This theoretical ambiguity may well be the reason the results of studies in this area have been mixed. It is also possible that the effects have changed over time (see Hynes and Posner 2002). Total household wealth and housing wealth grew during the 1990s and into the 2000s, at least until the bursting of the residential real estate bubble beginning in 2007. Because the homestead exemption is usually the largest exemption allowed in bankruptcy, this growth in housing wealth implied a growing number of consumers over time with substantial housing wealth to protect in bankruptcy via homestead exemptions should financial difficulties arise.

In the late 1970s, Apilado, Dauten, and Smith (1978) found a nonlinear relationship between exemption levels and bankruptcy filings. They found that the number of bankruptcies was lower in states with low exemptions relative to states with high exemptions but that states with medium exemptions had higher bankruptcy filing rates than states with either low or high exemptions. They attributed the particular shape of this curve to two offsetting factors. In states with low exemptions, the incentive to file for bankruptcy is low, but in states with high exemptions, creditors are willing to lend less. Thus, states with medium exemptions have the highest filing rate. White (1987) also reported that the generosity of a state's exemptions had a positive and statistically significant effect on bankruptcy filing rates. Fay, Hurst, and White (2002) and Agarwal, Liu, and Mielnicki (2003) similarly found the effect of homestead exemptions to be positive and significant.[25]

Shiers and Williamson (1987), however, found an *inverse* relationship between exemption levels and bankruptcy, finding that filing rates for both Chapter 7 and Chapter 13 bankruptcies were higher in low-exemption states. They attributed this result to reduced risk screening in the low-exemption states caused by creditors' confidence that they could recover more money from debtors there if the loan soured. Because exemptions apply both inside and outside bankruptcy, debtors may also have less need of actually filing for bankruptcy to protect themselves from collection efforts in high-exemption states, making informal bankruptcy more attractive.

Using both cross-section and time series data from 1984 to 1995, Gan and Sabarwal (2005) found that factors such as financial benefit, the amount of unsecured debt, and the amount of nonexempt assets are exogenous to the bankruptcy filing decision, suggesting that bankruptcy filings are triggered by adverse events rather than incentives.

Overall, empirical studies have shown a somewhat ambiguous relationship between the liberality of a state's exemption laws and the propensity of individuals to file for bankruptcy. In part, this is because borrowers in states with larger exemptions may gain less access to credit in the first place or may create incentives for informal bankruptcy to default with the knowledge that creditors may be unable to reach certain property and thus might not sue the debtor at all. Moreover, measuring the marginal impact of more generous exemption levels may be difficult, because most bankruptcy debtors are in dire financial straits at the time of filing and thus have few nonexempt assets under almost any state's exemption regime. Thus, the incentive effect will be weak or nonexistent for many filers. Nevertheless, more recent studies suggest at least a weak relationship between exemption levels and bankruptcy filings, an effect that economic theory predicts would be largest for higher-income and higher-wealth debtors.

Concerning impact on credit demand and supply, Gropp, Scholz, and White (1997) found that more generous exemptions simultaneously increase demand by consumers for credit (by reducing the negative consequences of default) and reduce supply of credit by lenders (because of the higher risk of lending). Both of these impacts lead to higher credit prices, and they found higher interest rates in states with unlimited exemptions. As a theoretical matter, the overall consequence on the amount of credit generated is ambiguous, because the demand and

25. State-by-state variation in exemptions may also prompt debtors to relocate on the eve of bankruptcy to avail themselves of another state's exemptions. Elul and Subramanian (2002) found, however, that this propensity is small. The 2005 reforms placed several new restraints on the ability to engage in this sort of forum shopping, such as by imposing waiting periods on the ability of bankruptcy filers to avail themselves of the new state's exemptions.

supply factors push in opposite directions. Empirically, they found that the market effect varied according to the income of the borrower: high-income debtors borrowed more in states with high asset exemptions, suggesting that the demand factors predominated with them, but low-income borrowers had less access to credit, suggesting that supply factors predominated with them. Lin and White (2001) found that applicants were more likely to be rejected for home improvement loans in states with high asset exemptions. Berkowitz and White (2004) found that small businesses had less access to credit and paid higher interest rates in states with high asset exemptions.[26]

State laws other than those setting levels of allowed exemptions may also influence the propensity of troubled consumers to file for bankruptcy. For example, state wage garnishment rules have been shown to be a factor in bankruptcy filings. Where creditors can aggressively garnish a debtor's wages in satisfaction of judgments, the debtor will experience a reduction in effective income and greater incentives to file for bankruptcy to discharge the debt. Where garnishment laws are weak, by contrast, debtors can essentially file an "informal" bankruptcy simply by choosing to default, while the weak remedies available to creditors make collection difficult. Stanley and Girth (1971, 29–30), for example, found a positive relationship between the ability of creditors to garnish debtors' wages and the bankruptcy filing rate. Apilado, Dauten, and Smith (1978) also found that restrictions on creditors' garnishment rights reduced bankruptcy filing rates. More recently, Dawsey and Ausubel (2004) and Lefgren and McIntyre (2009) found similar relationships between tough wage garnishment laws and bankruptcy filing rates.

Over the past several decades, federal law has placed restrictions on state garnishment laws, however, making those laws more uniform and less severe for debtors. Hynes (2006) found that although bankruptcy filing rates rose from the 1980s to the early 2000s, there was no rise in the frequency of wage garnishments over that time. As a result, although wage garnishment laws likely contribute to the propensity to file for bankruptcy, changes in wage garnishment laws almost certainly cannot explain changes in the bankruptcy filing rate over the past several decades. Shiers and Williamson (1987) found the wage garnishment level to be insignificant in predicting bankruptcy filing rates in a cross-state comparison.

Institutional Economics of Bankruptcy

Why *have* bankruptcy rates increased so dramatically over time? Legal incentives and constraints are just a portion of those confronting debtors deciding

---

26. Although exemptions increase the cost of credit, they may nevertheless be welfare-improving under certain circumstances by providing a form of insurance against consumption fluctuations (see Athreya 2006 and Grant 2003). Grant and Koeniger (2009) found that states with more pro-debtor bankruptcy exemptions exhibit less variation in their aggregate consumption levels over time, which is consistent with the hypothesis that exemptions provide welfare-improving consumption insurance.

whether to borrow, how much risk to take, and eventually whether to file for bankruptcy. There also is a range of social and other factors that affect a debtor's decision on whether to file for bankruptcy. They include information and transaction costs of filing for bankruptcy, social norms, and relationships of trust and reciprocity with lenders. It is important also to note how some of these factors may have contributed to the decades-long increase in bankruptcy filings.

CHANGES IN THE COST AND BENEFITS OF FILING FOR BANKRUPTCY

First, a number of societal developments have altered the cost-benefit analysis that borrowers face when deciding whether to file for bankruptcy. On the benefit side, as noted above, there have been changes in bankruptcy laws over time that have tended to provide stronger incentives to file for bankruptcy than in the past. But there are also other factors that have reduced the search and transaction costs of filing for bankruptcy.

Before a debtor can file for bankruptcy, there must first be awareness that it is an option. Developing the awareness of options and alternatives involves "search costs." There is good reason to believe that the search costs of filing for bankruptcy have fallen in recent years (see Zywicki 2005c). First, attorney advertising is much more prevalent than in the past, and it appears that a substantial portion of the advertising refers to bankruptcy services. There is some evidence of a correlation between the amount of attorney advertising of bankruptcy services and the number of bankruptcy filings in the relevant community, although, again, the direction of causation is ambiguous (attorneys may advertise bankruptcy services more aggressively where the number of bankruptcy filings is high). According to a Visa survey of bankruptcy filers, 19 percent reported that they learned about bankruptcy through attorney advertising (see McKinley 1997). Braucher (1993) noted that bankruptcy lawyers also indicated that they rely heavily on advertising to recruit new clients, especially in the Yellow Pages but also in newspapers, on radio, and on television. Braucher also reported that one of the most difficult tasks confronted by bankruptcy lawyers is to persuade their new clients that bankruptcy is as easy and beneficial as it actually is. An additional source of information about bankruptcy in recent decades may be the substantial number of celebrities who have filed for bankruptcy, a type of celebrity endorsement of the system. In fact, lawyers have reported that they often have referred to these celebrity bankruptcy filers to persuade their less famous clients to file for bankruptcy (Braucher 1993).

Perhaps the most important factor in reducing the search costs of bankruptcy, however, is simply the high number of bankruptcies. As bankruptcy filings become more commonplace, this may create a "contagion" or "herding" effect (or, less formally, a "water cooler" effect), as knowledge of bankruptcy flows through social networks and simple word of mouth. Surveys of bankruptcy filers reveal that friends and family are the single most important source of information about bankruptcy and that a majority of bankruptcy filers knew a friend or family member who had filed for bankruptcy (see Jones and Zywicki 1999, 212–213, summarizing studies). It also appears that the number of people who learn about bankruptcy from friends and family has risen over time (Duncan 1998).

The transaction costs of filing for bankruptcy have also fallen over time. In particular, the growth in bankruptcy filings over time has enabled increased legal specialization in bankruptcy practice by high-volume bankruptcy firms. This has enabled the firms to make capital investments in computer software and specialized paralegal personnel that drive down the cost of producing bankruptcy filings for consumers. When combined with the ability to advertise to further enlarge their client base, these high-volume practices can produce large numbers of standardized bankruptcy filings at low cost.

Another factor that has changed the cost-benefit basis of filing for bankruptcy involves changes in consumer credit markets that have made it easier for bankrupt filers to obtain credit after bankruptcy. It has generally been believed that filing for bankruptcy makes it more difficult for borrowers to gain access to subsequent credit. Stanley and Girth (1971) found that 35 percent of those surveyed in their study said that it was harder to get credit following bankruptcy, and only 8 percent reported that it was easier. Nevertheless, 35 percent said that it was the "same" in terms of the difficulty of obtaining credit, suggesting that the long-held assumption that filing for bankruptcy would destroy one's access to credit may have been overstated.

This disqualification of bankruptcy filers from credit markets has weakened over time. In some ways, those who file for bankruptcy may be a better credit risk following bankruptcy than before, both because their existing debt burden is largely wiped clean (eliminating competition for payment from other creditors) and because receiving a discharge in a Chapter 7 bankruptcy case bars the debtor from receiving another discharge for eight years.

Staten (1993) found that at that time, 16 percent of bankruptcy filers were able to receive unsecured credit within one year after filing for bankruptcy, and 55 percent received access to unsecured credit within five years. Credit sources encompassed a broad cross section of lenders, including bank credit cards, department stores, gasoline companies, sales finance companies, and installment lenders. A later study by Visa (1997) found that three-quarters of bankruptcy filers have at least one credit card within a year after filing.

Musto (2004) found, however, some continued negative effect of filing for bankruptcy. In particular, he noted that removal of a Chapter 7 bankruptcy record from an individual's credit report leads to a substantial increase in the number and aggregate credit limit of bank cards offered, suggesting that having a bankruptcy on one's credit report continues to result in some reduced access to credit. Han and Li (2011) also found lingering effects from filing for bankruptcy. Those who file for bankruptcy have less access to unsecured debt, pay higher interest rates, and use more secured debt than those who have never filed for bankruptcy, although the negative effects decline over time. Still, it seems likely that improved risk analysis and more complete consumer credit markets, including the expansion of subprime lending markets for credit cards, auto loans, and mortgages over the decades, have tended to increase the ability of bankruptcy filers to access credit markets following bankruptcy.

CHANGES IN SOCIAL NORMS REGARDING BANKRUPTCY

There also have been changes in social factors over time that have contributed to increased bankruptcy filings. One important one is changing social norms over filing for bankruptcy. There is a widespread belief that the "stigma" associated with filing for bankruptcy has fallen in recent years, although this view is not universal (on the latter point, see Sullivan, Warren, and Westbrook 2006). This factor was widely mentioned by supporters of bankruptcy reform during the congressional debates over BAPCPA.

Measuring the impact of changing social norms on bankruptcy filing rates is difficult, because it is impossible to measure these psychological attitudes directly. Moreover, simply asking those who file for bankruptcy whether they feel ashamed will not resolve the issue, because the relevance of stigma to bankruptcy filings does not involve whether a debtor feels ashamed *after* filing for bankruptcy but rather whether the sense of shame is sufficiently strong to deter the debtor from actually filing for bankruptcy. To determine fully the impact of social norms in deterring bankruptcy, it would be necessary to establish whether the sense of anticipated shame from filing for bankruptcy is sufficiently strong to lead the debtor to avoid financial habits that may cause vulnerability to financial shocks in the first place. This effect may be especially important for the behavior of middle- and upper-class debtors, since they will have the strongest financial incentives to file for bankruptcy. They generally will have higher debt levels, more property to protect through bankruptcy exemptions, and often higher future income than lower-income borrowers.

Several researchers have attempted to test indirectly the potential effect of changing social norms regarding bankruptcy (see Bermant 2003, Athreya 2004, and Zywicki 2005c for summaries). Scholars have attempted to measure the influence of social norms on bankruptcy filing rates by using as a proxy the statistical residual of unexplained variation in bankruptcy filing rates after controlling for other factors in a regression analysis. Empirical studies have found large, unexplained statistical residuals on bankruptcy filings after controlling for multiple other variables. Although these residuals could be explained by a variety of factors, including information costs, decline of social stigma is a plausible partial explanation. Moreover, these unexplained residuals appear to have grown larger over time, suggesting a change in certain unobserved variables, possibly including social stigma (see Moss and Johnson 1999).

Fay, Hurst, and White (1998) found that after controlling for other relevant variables, there are systematic patterns of higher bankruptcy filing rates in particular districts, possibly because either the higher level of filings increases the available information about bankruptcy or the prevalence of bankruptcy in the community reduces the stigma attached to filing. Miller (2012) found that geographic and social networks also contribute to the bankruptcy filing decision through information or norms-generating channels. Gross and Souleles (2002) created a multivariate model to predict bankruptcy filings and found that after controlling for economic risk variables, the probability that a given individual will file for bankruptcy is, in part, a function of the number of people who filed for bankruptcy in the recent past in that community. This correlation in filing rates, which is not explained by economic risk variables, is consistent with the presence of either a stigma or information effect that varies among local communities.

The effect of stigma on bankruptcy filings may also be measured by examining quantifiable variables that might provide a proxy for the strength of social norms. For example, social norms tend to be stronger in smaller, more stable and homogenous communities than in larger, more anonymous urban communities. Consistent with the hypothesis, cities with higher population densities tend to have higher bankruptcy filing rates than smaller communities, holding other factors constant (see Barron, Staten, and Wilshusen 2002 and Luckett 2002). Cities with more transient populations also exhibit higher bankruptcy filing rates, perhaps because of weaker social ties and less concern about social reputation in cities than in more stable communities (see Buckley and Brinig 1998).

Agarwal, Chomsisengphet, and Liu (2011) examined loan level panel data for more than 170,000 credit card holders to test the effects of various social and economic factors on bankruptcy filings. They found that a borrower who migrated 190 miles from his state of birth was 17 percent more likely to default and 15 percent more likely to file for bankruptcy than average. In contrast, a borrower who remained in his or her home state was 14 percent less likely to default and 10 percent less likely to file for bankruptcy. They also found that a borrower who moved to a rural area was less likely to file for bankruptcy.

Efrat (2006) measured changing social norms regarding bankruptcy through an examination of media characterizations of the bankruptcy system and bankruptcy filers from 1864 to the present. He identified a dramatic change in the media characterization of bankruptcy filers beginning in the 1960s, from dishonest cheats to unlucky victims of factors beyond their control or honest but irresponsible borrowers. Efrat argued that this media characterization has both reflected and shaped public opinion about the morality of personal bankruptcy and that it is consistent with the general perception that the stigma of bankruptcy has declined over time.

If it is true that the stigma associated with personal bankruptcy has weakened over time, it still remains to be explained why that evolution occurred. Moss and Johnson (1999) noted that the claim that bankruptcy has "lost its stigma" has been a recurrent theme in American history for generations. Why might social stigma and personal shame about bankruptcy have declined?

Zywicki (2005c) identified several possible explanations for changing social norms during this period. Broad social change associated with the rise of the baby-boom generation may provide part of the answer (see Putnam 2000, who analyzed the disruptive effect of the baby-boom generation on traditional social norms). Baby-boomers have been dramatically overrepresented in bankruptcy filings relative to their percentage of the population at every stage of their life span and have exhibited higher filing rates than preceding and succeeding generations of Americans (see Sullivan, Warren, and Westbrook 2000). Generation X, which followed the baby-boomers, has experienced a decline in bankruptcy filing rates relative to the baby-boomers (although not a full reversion to the lower rates of the past). This suggests some sort of unique baby-boomer effect as that generation passed through the economy.

Other factors that might have contributed to the erosion of stigma about bankruptcy include the role of bankruptcy attorneys in normalizing the idea of bankruptcy as a purely financial rather than moral decision. The commonplace nature of bankruptcy filings by celebrities and leading corporations may also have contributed to the normalization of bankruptcy. Moreover, the 1978 Bankruptcy Code itself sought to eliminate some of the traditional stigma of filing for bankruptcy, for example, by purging the traditional pejorative reference to bankruptcy filers as *bankrupts* (replacing it with the more neutral term *debtors*) and prohibiting governmental discrimination and discrimination in employment against those who file for bankruptcy. Finally, the sheer number of bankruptcy filers alone may have contributed to the normalization of bankruptcy, as social norms against behavior previously widely regarded as questionable tend to become increasingly difficult to maintain when large numbers of otherwise respectable people engage in it.

CHANGES IN THE NATURE OF CONSUMER CREDIT
The evolution of the nature of consumer credit in the economy may be another factor potentially contributing to the growth in bankruptcy filings in recent decades (Zywicki 2005b and 2005c). The substitution of impersonal credit cards offered in a national market for installment credit often tied to local banks or merchants likely has brought about a variety of changes in credit relations. For example, in earlier decades, department store financing of credit purchases typically was secured credit, because department stores retained a security interest in the items purchased. In this case, bankruptcy may discharge the debt, but the creditor could still repossess the property. Thus, the consequences of default and bankruptcy often are less severe for default today on purchases such as household goods than in the past.

Also, consumer credit markets today are also more nationalized than in the past. Traditionally, consumer credit was embedded in local commercial relations, such as a local bank or store. As a result, borrowers were subject to potential constraints such as need for repeat dealing, reputation in the local community, and trusting commercial relationships. Today, by contrast, debtors receive credit from large institutional lenders in South Dakota and elsewhere, potentially eliminating many of the traditional constraints on postcontractual opportunism. This tends to reduce the psychological and reputational costs to borrowers from defaulting. Thus, even if credit cards have only substituted for other types of credit, they might still contribute to a rising bankruptcy filing rate by changing the institutional constraints and incentives for debtors to default.

Chapter Choice in Bankruptcy Filings

Related to the question of why households file for bankruptcy in the first place is the issue of consumer choice between filing straight bankruptcy under Chapter 7 or entering a rehabilitation payment plan in Chapter 13. Unless the debtor is a higher-income debtor who triggers the means testing provisions of the code as revised under BAPCPA, in most cases, the bankruptcy filer has broad discretion to choose whether to file under Chapter 7 or Chapter 13. As noted, Chapter 7 requires the debtor to surrender all nonexempt assets to creditors, but in exchange, there is a debt discharge that protects future income from seizure by creditors. Chapter 13, by contrast, permits the debtor to retain assets but requires contribution to a repayment plan of disposable income over living expenses for a three-to-five-year period. In general, about 70 percent of cases are filed under Chapter 7, a ratio that has remained largely constant for many years (except for a few years in the immediate aftermath of the enactment of BAPCPA, when the percentage of Chapter 13 filings was significantly higher, at about 45 percent).

These disparate rules between the two Chapters suggest certain predictions about patterns of debtor choice.

- Where state law provides for generous exemptions (thereby allowing a debtor to retain a larger amount of property as exempt), relatively higher proportion of Chapter 7 filings is predictable.
- Where debtors have large amounts of wealth, they would be more likely to elect to file Chapter 13 to protect assets.
- Where a debtor wants flexibility through a Chapter 13 plan to accomplish certain results not possible in a Chapter 7 proceeding, such as curing a mortgage default, then Chapter 13 is preferable (maybe followed by a refiling under Chapter 7 at a later time).
- Where the filer owns a business, Chapter 13 provides certain rules that enable the debtor to continue operating the business.

Domowitz and Sartain (1999b) found that consumers generally chose between different Chapters as predicted but that the effects tended to be relevant only where the incentives were large. Thus, they found that the propensity to file Chapter 13 increased as the amount of a home owner's equity increased (making it more likely that equity levels would exceed allowable exemption levels). Merely owning a home did not predict Chapter choice. Debtors in states with high exemption levels were more likely to file Chapter 7. Debtors with higher levels of unsecured debt also were more likely to file Chapter 7. Business debtors with relatively low levels of debt were more likely to file Chapter 13, whereas those with high debt (and perhaps less interested in trying to maintain the business) were not.

In another paper, Domowitz and Sartain (1999a) found that home ownership, higher levels of home equity, higher levels of equity in large assets (such as consumer durables), and higher income all predicted an increased propensity to file Chapter 13 rather than Chapter 7. Higher levels of student loan debt, which was more easily dischargeable in Chapter 13 at the time than in Chapter 7, also increased the likelihood of filing Chapter 13. Larger medical debts, by contrast, predicted an increased likelihood of filing Chapter 7 instead of Chapter 13, as did higher exemption levels under state law, higher levels of mortgage debt (possibly suggesting earlier use of Chapter 13 in order to cure arrearages in at least some cases), and higher levels of (unsecured) credit card debt.

Interestingly, researchers have found also that the choice between Chapter 7 and Chapter 13 cannot be explained solely by these rational economic reasons.

Instead, it appears that the choice is often at least partly determined by elements of what might be called local legal culture, that is, norms of practice by attorneys and judges in the area that promote disproportionate use of one Chapter rather than the other (Braucher 1993).

Researchers have found that the choice between the two Chapters may also be affected by other factors. For example, Agarwal, Chomsisengphet, McMenamin, and Skiba (2010) discussed some possible social factors, for instance, that white attorneys are more likely to recommend Chapter 13 to Hispanic debtors. They also reported that white judges were more likely to dismiss a petition of an African American debtor.[27]

Political Economy of Bankruptcy Law

One of the striking characteristics of American consumer bankruptcy law is its highly pro-debtor orientation, especially dating to enactment of the 1978 Bankruptcy Code. Even after modest reforms introduced by BAPCPA, American bankruptcy law today remains highly pro-debtor in its orientation by both historical and global standards.

To some extent, the debtor-friendliness is a reflection of America's unique history. Many early immigrants were fleeing financial hardship in their homelands and brought with them debtor-friendly attitudes. The vast and rugged frontier often made it relatively easy to escape debts by disappearing and making a fresh start. Nevertheless, as noted above, many states retained stringent debtor creditor laws into the nineteenth century, and the use of the bankruptcy power by the national government in the nineteenth century was sporadic until the first permanent bankruptcy law was enacted in 1898.

The 1898 Bankruptcy Act arose from pressures exerted by the growth of the national economy during the post–Civil War era and particularly by tensions experienced by creditors that expressed frustration that debtors preferred to pay local creditors rather than out-of-state merchants (see Skeel 2001). The period after the Civil War was a time of declining prices and pressure on debtors generally. Although the impetus for a new bankruptcy law came from creditors, the final product turned out to be much more pro-debtor than originally expected. Moreover, the law that emerged ended up providing a central role for lawyers in the process, rather than a more administrative system. Skeel (2001) has argued that this basic structure, pro-debtor and pro-lawyer, has characterized American bankruptcy law ever since.

Skeel has contended that the structure of bankruptcy has evolved out of the interaction of three different political forces: creditors, lawyers, and a long-standing populist, pro-debtor ideological strain in American history. Although creditors as

---

27. The authors also purported to find an impact of a judge's political party on their behavior, but the variable that they use (partisan majority of the circuit court that appointed a given bankruptcy judge) is a poor proxy for the party of bankruptcy judges.

a group would seem to be a formidable lobbying force, Skeel notes that creditors are beset by collective action problems that limit their lobbying effectiveness. In particular, because bankruptcy cases rarely involve enough resources to pay all creditors in full, there is an inherent conflict between secured creditors and unsecured creditors over their respective shares of the bankruptcy estate. Moreover, secured creditors as a group may not even be very concerned about the bankruptcy threat, preferring to protect themselves by raising interest rates as needed and requiring larger down payments so as to match collateral value more closely to credit amount.

Unsecured creditors also confront collective action problems even within their own ranks. First, unsecured creditors include a large variety of creditors, including wholesalers, services providers, and tort claimants, and they may not be easy to organize. Second, any single unsecured creditor may suffer only modest losses in any given year to bankruptcy and then may have little incentive to invest substantially in lobbying for changes. Skeel contended that as a result of all these issues, creditors' lobbying often is not as strong in practice as it might appear in theory.

Bankruptcy lawyers, by contrast, are well organized and highly politically influential. The role of bankruptcy attorneys in the political process is especially important. The class of future bankruptcy filers is likely to be underrepresented in the political process (because they are virtually impossible to identify and organize as an effective lobbying force), but the interests of bankruptcy lawyers are closely aligned with the interests of potential bankruptcy filers. Bankruptcy lawyers earn their income from bankruptcies, and they have self-interest in supporting laws that result in a larger number of bankruptcy filings. As a result, they will tend to prefer more debtor-friendly bankruptcy laws that lead to increased bankruptcy filings, easy access to bankruptcy, and more expensive processes and to resist reforms that reduce bankruptcy filings. Moreover, the influence of bankruptcy professionals has been magnified, because bankruptcy traditionally has been considered to be a technical, nonideological area of law, leading politicians to provide substantial deference to the opinions of supposedly disinterested bankruptcy professionals, especially with respect to the details of legislation (see Carruthers and Halliday 1998).

Bankruptcy lawyers also are able to overcome their collective action problems more easily than creditors to be an effective lobbying body. The influence of bankruptcy lawyers is heightened still further by the historical fact that jurisdiction over bankruptcy law in Congress traditionally has resided with the Judiciary Committee, rather than the Banking Committee or the Commerce Committee. Because the Judiciary Committee deals with lawyers and legal matters much more frequently than other committees, this jurisdictional allocation heightens the influence of bankruptcy lawyers relative to other interests in the legislative process. Skeel (2001, 81) has observed that "of all these groups, bankruptcy professionals are the ones who have most strongly influenced the shape of U.S. bankruptcy law in the century since its enactment in 1898." Skeel also noted the long-standing ideological strain in American politics of distrust of banks.

Zywicki (2003) has noted that Skeel's three-factor model of bankruptcy politics also helps explain BAPCPA's reforms, which made the bankruptcy laws somewhat less pro-debtor in 2005. In particular, he pointed out that the influence of all three of the forces identified by Skeel had shifted somewhat at the time when comprehensive bankruptcy reform was first proposed in 1998. First, the takeover of Congress by the Republican Party in the 1994 elections reduced the influence of bankruptcy professionals in the political process. Lawyers tend to be overwhelmingly Democratic in their political and financial support, and Democratic politicians tend to be more responsive to the interests of lawyers. Republicans, by contrast, are less concerned about meeting the lobbying concerns of lawyers.

Second, at this time, creditors were able to overcome their collective action problems effectively to present a united front on many of the reforms. In particular, the perception of widespread fraud and abuse of the bankruptcy system presented all creditors (both secured and unsecured) with a slate of reforms that could benefit all creditors by improving the integrity and efficiency of the bankruptcy system. Rather than focusing on a zero-sum set of reforms that simply altered the distribution of assets between secured and unsecured creditors, BAPCPA's proposed reforms increased the overall value of the bankruptcy system for all creditors, secured and unsecured alike. But examining the voting patterns of members of Congress on the 2001 floor vote on bankruptcy reform, Nunez and Rosenthal (2004) estimated that only about fifteen votes (out of 306 cast in favor of the legislation) could arguably be attributed to the influence of creditor lobbying and campaign donations.

Instead, the Republican takeover of Congress in 1994 brought with it a new ideological orientation in Congress away from the traditional populist, pro-debtor ideology to one centered on personal responsibility. This change in political control also reduced the influence of groups such as law professors and consumer activists on the political process. BAPCPA passed with approximately 75 percent support in both houses of Congress, including all Republicans and centrist Democrats. By contrast, opposition was limited to a mere 25 percent of Congress, concentrated only among its most liberal members.

Finally, another interesting area of political economy has involved the decisions of some states to opt out of permitting their residents to elect the federal menu of exemptions under paragraph 522(d) of the Bankruptcy Code, thereby requiring them to use state exemptions. Approximately three-quarters of states have chosen to opt out. Examining the pattern of states that chose to opt out, Shiers and Williamson (1987) found that states most likely to do so were those with low exemption levels but relatively high levels of bankruptcy filings. These states may have been concerned that they already suffered high bankruptcy filings and that allowing the higher federal exemptions would only make this bad situation worse. Hynes, Malani, and Posner (2004) reviewed exemption laws in all fifty states over a twenty-two-year period and also found that states were more likely to opt out if their state exemption was lower than the federal exemption and that states were more likely to opt out if they had a high bankruptcy filing rate.

NONBANKRUPTCY ALTERNATIVES FOR FINANCIALLY DISTRESSED CONSUMERS

Bankruptcy is not the only alternative for financially distressed consumers. While more than 1 million households file for bankruptcy every year, approximately 8 million to 10 million consumers are reported as being seriously delinquent (120 days or more) on at least one credit account at any point in time (Wilshusen 2011). This disparity between delinquency and formal bankruptcy filings suggests that many delinquent consumers avail themselves of other means to change their situations. These other approaches range from complete repayment of debts to a variety of informal means to avoid repayment of certain debts.

As discussed earlier, some consumers simply elect self-help measures, such as "informal" bankruptcy. This means they simply default on the payment of some or all debts with the hope that creditors will be unable or unwilling to collect on those debts. For much of American history, the ability to uproot and move to the western frontier served as a sort of informal bankruptcy system. Distressed borrowers could simply disappear to escape creditors, starting anew with a blank slate. Today, as noted, the propensity of borrowers to file for bankruptcy is in part a function of the inability of consumers always to engage in informal bankruptcy, especially where creditors' remedies are strong (such as strong garnishment laws). Borrowers today show a greater demand for bankruptcy as a means of escaping debt in those states where creditors' remedies are strong, other things being equal.

A second alternative is for a distressed borrowers to enter into a private loan workout plan with a specific creditor. In such cases, the consumer negotiates a voluntary agreement with a particular creditor to repay a past due sum in full or in part according to an agreed-upon repayment schedule. These repayment plans are negotiated one-on-one between individual borrowers and lenders. Agarwal, Chomsisengphet, and Mielnicki (2008) examined 241,452 individual credit card accounts and found that 78 percent of accounts reinstated pursuant to such an agreement remained current afterward, and only 22 percent redefaulted. This suggests that such agreements can be a successful strategy for creditors to minimize losses. On the other hand, these agreements can be quite time- and labor-intensive to negotiate. Borrowers often are unsophisticated in such negotiations, meaning that the plans can take substantial time and effort to arrange and can fail to anticipate all of the issues that might arise in structuring a successful one. Also, because negotiations take place only on a one-to-one basis between consumers and specific credit issuers, they are limited in their ability to resolve problems of more general financial distress from liabilities owed to multiple creditors.

Not surprisingly, institutions that can serve as a more systematic alternative to bankruptcy by enabling distressed consumers to resolve debts with multiple creditors have arisen. Because they specialize in this function and typically have contacts with many creditors, they potentially can negotiate more rapidly and effectively than borrowers can do individually with several different creditors.

Two basic types of intermediaries have evolved: credit counseling agencies and, more recently, debt settlement companies. The primary difference is that credit counseling agencies intermediate between borrowers and creditors to develop, when possible, a plan for at least partial repayment over time. The plans are known as debt management plans, or DMPs. The counseling agency attempts to arrange concessions on finance charges and repayment terms with the creditors to permit a significant amount of repayment. The counseling agencies typically also offer some financial management education. Up to 9 million people sought advice and assistance from a credit counseling organization in 2003 (Loonin and Plunkett 2003).

Debt settlement companies, by contrast, attempt to negotiate a one-time lump-sum discounted principal payment between the borrower and the creditor. Although debt settlement is of relatively recent vintage, testimony from a debt settlement industry trade association estimated that the number of debt settlement companies in the United States had increased from three hundred in 2006 to one thousand by 2008 (see 74 *Federal Register*, August 19, 2009, 42013).

In both cases, the intermediary is paid for its services, through a share of the amounts recovered for the creditor in a payment plan (in the case of a counseling agency) or by the borrower based on the amount of debt erased (for debt settlement companies). Historically, creditors paid counseling agencies a "fair share" contribution of about 15 percent of the amounts recovered pursuant to a DMP, but heightened competition in recent years has driven down that percentage. Debt settlement companies charge commissions of as much as 15 to 30 percent of the amount of debt erased.

Voluntary repayment plans, whether private or through an intermediary, can be useful and efficient for both debtors and creditors, especially as an alternative to bankruptcy. For borrowers, a consensual repayment plan can eliminate social stigma and cost of bankruptcy and also benefit credit score and access to future credit. For creditors, especially unsecured creditors, a debt repayment plan can avert the costly process of bankruptcy, which, as noted above, often results in little or no payment of unsecured debt by a borrower. On the other hand, relying on third-party intermediaries can create agency cost problems for both debtors and creditors. In particular, creditors face the risk that credit counseling agencies will steer lower-risk, potentially high-repayment borrowers to a DMP, even if they might otherwise have been able to pay the debt directly or work out a private arrangement with the creditor without the concessions embedded in the DMP. Similarly, debtors might end up paying debt settlement companies a substantial fee to settle a debt that the debtor could have resolved voluntarily or that might have been uncollectible as a legal or practical matter.

But DMPs can be a valuable alternative to bankruptcy. According to Furletti (2003a) and Brown, Link, and Staten (2012), in 2002, approximately $17 billion in outstanding balances from the ten largest US bank credit card issuers were being serviced through credit counseling DMPs. By comparison, total industry-wide credit card charge-offs amounted to $35 billion that year. These figures indicate the size and importance of the counseling industry.

Historical Origins and Growth of Credit Counseling

The modern-day version of the counseling agency DMP had its origins in the first half of the twentieth century, when financially troubled consumers with difficulty making payments to multiple creditors would turn to commercial debt poolers for assistance (see Hunt 2005 and Staten 2006 for comprehensive discussion). A debt pooler of the time was typically a for-profit company that would act as an intermediary between borrowers and creditors. The primary objective of the debt pooler was to negotiate a repayment arrangement acceptable to most or all of the creditors. The repayment plans would generally entail either a reduction of the outstanding balance and interest charges or a longer payout period or both. The debtor would make regular payments to the debt pooler, who would then distribute the proceeds to the creditors according to the plan. For this service, the debt pooler typically received a fee from the borrower. When these plans worked well, debtors were able to utilize the creditor concessions to resolve their debts and avoid bankruptcy. On the other hand, debt poolers were criticized for a variety of abuses that sometimes crept in, including charging exorbitant fees, diverting consumers' payments to the pooler's fees rather than to creditors, and approving plans that were not feasible (see Milstein and Ratner 1981).

Legislative steps to curtail deceptive practices and exploitation of borrowers by debt poolers began as early as 1935, when Minnesota and Wisconsin established licensing requirements for poolers (Milstein and Ratner 1981). The pace of legislation accelerated during the 1950s, as states either prohibited for-profit debt pooling or regulated its operation. By 1980, twenty-nine states and the District of Columbia had prohibited commercial debt pooling. An additional sixteen states allowed commercial debt pooling but imposed a variety of regulations to curtail abusive practices. These measures included licensing requirements, the posting of a bond or cash deposit by debt pooling companies, establishing ceilings on fees charged to consumers, and maximum time limits for forwarding consumer payments to creditor accounts. At the same time, many of these regulations exempted categories of institutions that provided debt pooling services, presumably because they were structured to operate in the consumer's best interest. Exempted institutions included (1) the debtor's attorney or other agent working on the debtor's behalf and (2) organizations or parties whose loyalty to creditor interests was clearly disclosed, including representatives of one or more creditors. Some states specifically exempted nonprofit debt poolers, presumably based on the belief that nonprofits lacked commercial motives that spawned abusive practices.

Perhaps in response both to the rising numbers of delinquent accounts and to an increasingly constrained "pooling" industry, in the late 1960s, the credit granting industry supported a reconstitution of the existing National Foundation for Consumer Credit (NFCC). The NFCC was originally established in 1951 to promote borrower education about how to handle credit wisely. In 1967, the organization's mission was redirected so as to establish and promote nonprofit credit counseling agencies across the country. Over the next fifteen years, a national network of nonprofit credit counseling agencies evolved under the sponsoring and licensing umbrella of the NFCC. (Eventually, the umbrella organization changed its name to the National Foundation for Credit Counseling.) By 1980, NFCC member agencies operated in more than two hundred cities in forty-seven states, generally under the trademarked name Consumer Credit Counseling Service.

Credit counseling was increasingly touted as an alternative to rising bankruptcy filings (Milstein and Ratner 1981). Unlike the earlier commercial debt pooling business, in which debtors directly bore the cost of hiring intermediaries to negotiate on their behalf, credit counseling evolved as an alternative to bankruptcy funded mostly by creditors. The DMP method offered by the credit counseling agencies became a voluntary agreement between a consumer and creditors that resembles earlier debt pooling arrangements but without the fee payments by the consumers. Creditors recognized that through mutual forbearance, they could collect more as a group if they suspended their individual collection efforts and avoided pushing consumers into the bankruptcy court.

The incentive to participate in a DMP is greatest for unsecured creditors, who would typically collect nothing (or close to it) in a Chapter 7 bankruptcy liquidation.[28] Mortgage holders and auto lenders worry less about recovery of principal, given that they can repossess the underlying collateral (house or automobile), so they have been less likely to participate in DMPs. Consequently, the concept of the DMP administered by a credit counseling agency historically had the strongest early backing from retail store creditors and later from bank credit card issuers as general-purpose credit card debt expanded rapidly through the 1980s.

The rapid expansion in unsecured credit and the number of serious account delinquencies during the 1990s caused demand for counseling services to soar. This produced entry into the industry of hundreds of new competitors, many of them not affiliated with NFCC. The number of credit counseling agencies mushroomed during these years, well beyond the original NFCC member agencies, from fewer than 250 agencies operating about 800 offices in 1992 to more than 900 agencies operating as many as 2,000 offices by the end of 2003 (US Senate, 2005). NFCC member agencies alone returned $2.3 billion to creditors in 2002 through DMPs and continued to return between $1.5 billion and $2.0 billion to creditors through 2010.

Increased competition combined with technological change transformed the industry dramatically. The growth in electronic technology use by the counseling agencies, especially telephones, computers, and the Internet, reduced the costs of administering plans, since counseling via telephone or Internet is less

---

28. The vice president of the American Association of Creditor Attorneys said in an interview: "Most of my clients take the position that we'd rather have the debtor go into consumer credit counseling and accept the proposed repayment plan than have the debtor go into chapter 7" (see Daly 1993, 46).

expensive to provide on average than in-person counseling (Clancy and Carroll 2007). Electronic approaches increased efficiency and at the same time removed geographic constraints on competition. Whereas credit counseling was traditionally highly localized and face-to-face, now debtors, creditors, and intermediaries began to interact on a much broader geographic scale, thereby further reducing the cost of negotiating and servicing DMPs.

Examining counseling by telephone or Internet versus traditional face-to-face methods, Barron and Staten (2011) found no reduction in the efficacy of the programs compared with the traditional model. Sometimes performance even improved, suggesting that the greater use of technology was beneficial to consumers.[29] At the same time, computers increased the efficiency of payment processing and accounting, reducing administrative costs.

The combination of increased competition, greater efficiency, and lower costs put pressure on the traditional 15 percent fair share commission paid by the creditors to the credit counseling agencies. But the downward pressure on fees, combined with the traditional creditor-pays model of debt relief, had some unintended consequences. In particular, creditors increasingly were willing to pay for only the services for which they saw a tangible financial reward, namely, the negotiation and effectuation of a DMP. They became less willing to support other traditional services of credit counseling agencies, such as financial education programs.[30] Some regulators also expressed concern about the practices of some credit counseling agencies (see Federal Trade Commission 2004).

Impact of Counseling

Empirical evidence on the impact of the counseling experience on consumers has been sparse. Hunt (2005) noted that completion rates on DMPs were not much higher than the 33 percent rate experienced in Chapter 13 bankruptcy repayment plans. DMP completion translates into much higher proportion of debt recovery than the 35 percent recovery typical for Chapter 13 cases, however (see Norberg 1999 and Eraslan, Li, and Sarte 2007). But there have been few large-scale empirical studies on consumer outcomes other than the amount of debt recovered. Kim, Garman, and Sorhaindo (2005) found that clients who stayed on counseling agency debt repayment plans for more than eighteen months reported improved financial management behaviors and fewer stressful events. Hunt (2005) cited results on borrower outcomes from survey studies conducted by Visa USA of borrowers who either sought credit counseling and DMPs or filed for bankruptcy.

---

29. Although perhaps counterintuitive, this finding that the delivery channel selection of electronic versus in-person does not matter, or could even improve performance, might be explained by self-selection. Some financially distressed borrowers might be embarrassed to go to an in-person counseling session but might be willing to participate via telephone or Internet.

30. BAPCPA now requires completion of a financial education program as a condition for a debtor's final discharge in bankruptcy; see 11 USC. §111(d)(1)(C).

Compared with borrowers who filed for bankruptcy, participants in DMPs appeared to have better subsequent access to both secured and unsecured credit. Those who successfully completed a DMP were more likely to hold a credit card and purchase a home, relative to those who did not complete a DMP.

Elliehausen, Lundquist, and Staten (2007) examined eight thousand consumers who received counseling during 1997 but did not qualify for a DMP. For these consumers, the counseling intervention provided education in the form of budget review and advice but no debt payment product. The authors then used credit bureau data (with care and appropriate privacy safeguards) to construct objective (as opposed to self-reported) measures of postcounseling credit performance. They looked at the sample of consumers during the three years following counseling relative to a comparison group of observationally similar borrowers who were not counseled.

They found that receipt of counseling was associated with a positive change in borrower credit profiles. Statistical techniques to account for self-selection revealed that much of the improved performance in the counseled group was attributable to characteristics unique to those consumers who sought counseling, but the counseling treatment itself was also associated with significant reductions in debt use later. Counseling appeared to provide the greatest benefit to those borrowers who had the least ability to handle credit before counseling.[31]

Brown, Link, and Staten (2012) examined the records of more than seventeen thousand consumers who were counseled and recommended for a DMP by a large nonprofit credit counseling agency in 2003 to determine the effectiveness of DMPs and the factors that affect credit use success rates later. They found that the higher the interest rate on the original loan, the greater the repayment amount under completed DMPs. They suggested that this indicated debtors' desire to complete the plan, which includes concessions on finance charges, thereby avoiding reversion to the original loan terms. On the other hand, a higher interest rate reduced the attractiveness of completing the DMP rather than filing for bankruptcy.

Not surprisingly, higher levels of assets and higher income also predicted higher repayment, while higher levels of liabilities and monthly expenses predicted lower repayment. In addition, the authors found that DMPs produced higher levels of repayment when the cause of the debtor's distress was habitual (poor financial management) than when it was the result of a financial shock, such as divorce or job loss. This finding may reflect how Chapter 7 bankruptcy relief may be particularly attractive for a debtor to recover from a one-time financial shock through a discharge of debt rather than trying to repair a chronic budgeting problem. Moreover, the authors found that the potential agency costs problems were not a major concern in practice, as credit counseling organizations appeared to recommend DMPs to their clients in an objective manner.

---

31. In the context of prepurchase home ownership counseling, Hirad and Zorn (2002) and Hartarska and Gonzalez-Vega (2005) found that counseling helps to reduce future repayment problems for debtors.

As indicated, recent years have also seen the development of debt settlement companies that have provided an additional competitive threat to traditional counseling. Debt settlement companies operating mostly as for-profit enterprises offer, for a fee, debt relief services in the form of negotiated agreements with creditors to settle the debt for some fraction of the full balance owed. These negotiation attempts at settlement for less than full balance are heavily advertised on television, radio, and the Internet.

In a typical debt settlement arrangement, the consumer makes payments, including the fees, to the settlement company (instead of the creditor) for a series of months. This builds up sufficient resources for the settlement company to approach the creditor with a lump-sum payment offer. Unlike the credit counseling DMP in which the creditor agrees to the repayment plan from the outset (and receives regular monthly payments while the consumer is on the plan), the debt settlement product is necessarily a more adversarial arrangement for everyone. The settlement company promises (but may not deliver) a successful negotiation of a settlement. In the meantime, the consumer who has paid fees to the settlement company has an increasingly delinquent account with the creditor or creditors and is subject to the full range of creditor collection actions. Not surprisingly, creditors prefer the traditional credit counseling plan arrangement, which typically calls for full payment of the outstanding balance over time (as opposed to a discounted payment). In addition, this 100 percent payment serves a regulatory purpose for banks by permitting them to avoid writing off the uncollected portion of the debt against required capital.

Of course, many counseling clients have insufficient income to qualify for a DMP that results in 100 percent amortization of debt. An internal study conducted in 2007 by two credit counseling industry associations examined the outcomes of 380,000 counseling sessions across fifteen member agencies during 2006–2007.[32] About 30 percent of clients interviewed were declined for a DMP because of insufficient income but had enough income to make some payment though not all. Ultimately, it seems these individuals are prime candidates for some version of a settlement at less than full payment. Bankruptcy is another option, but for consumers who wish to avoid the stigma of bankruptcy, the debt settlement companies offer a third way.

Typical of other segments of the debt relief industry, data on debt settlement activity is scarce. Wilshusen (2011) offered a glimpse as reflected in the account status codes maintained by the major credit bureaus. As of May 2011, Trans Union credit bureau files indicated that 10 million consumers had at least one account in their credit report with a code indicating that the account was settled for less than the full balance. Many of these settlements could have been negotiated, of course, by the consumer directly with the lender, without the debt settlement company as intermediary. By comparison, only 1.6 million consumers had at least one account with a DMP indicator in the file.

---

32. The associations were the National Foundation for Credit Counseling (NFCC) and the Association of Independent Consumer Credit Counseling Agencies (AICCCA).

Consumer Credit Counseling and the Bankruptcy Code

The role for credit counseling and DMPs has grown as a result of enactment of BAPCPA amending the Bankruptcy Code in 2005. Section 109(h) of the code now requires that in order to be eligible to file for bankruptcy, a debtor must first seek consumer credit counseling from an approved nonprofit counseling agency to investigate nonbankruptcy alternatives. Specifically, a consumer must obtain a certificate from the counseling agency that a DMP is not a realistic alternative. If the counseling agency recommends a DMP instead of bankruptcy, then the code requires creditors to accept the DMP if reasonable, under pain of a financial penalty of reduction of the creditor's allowed claim in bankruptcy by 20 percent. As discussed earlier in this chapter, BAPCPA also generally tightened access to chapter 7 bankruptcy, especially for high-income debtors with high repayment capacity, and placed new limits on serial bankruptcy filings. By limiting the incentives to file for bankruptcy for some individuals, BAPCPA also may indirectly have pushed many debtors toward a voluntary repayment plan rather than bankruptcy, especially those with substantial repayment capacity.

The purpose of these requirements was twofold. First, they recognized the potential value of DMPs to creditors, debtors, and the economy over the expensive process of bankruptcy. Thus, they sought to affirm that bankruptcy should be a last resort for financially distressed debtors. Second, they recognized the potential for self-interested behavior by bankruptcy lawyers who have a financial interest in steering debtors toward bankruptcy (for which the lawyer generates fees) rather than to a DMP (which does not generate legal fees). Because many financially distressed debtors first evaluate their options in consultation with a bankruptcy lawyer (often in response to an advertisement), the view was that this self-interest can lead to unnecessary bankruptcy filings. Requiring the debtor to seek an independent assessment from a third-party credit counseling agency before filing for bankruptcy can mitigate any distorting effects of the lawyer's self-interest and asymmetric information advantage over debtors about the need for bankruptcy.

Analyses conducted in the period relatively soon after the requirements went into effect suggested that the costs of these requirements were minimal but that benefits in redirecting debtors away from bankruptcy to a DMP were also limited (see Government Accountability Office 2007). A survey by the NFCC of its member agencies found that about 3 percent of clients who signed up for prefiling counseling from October 2005 to August 2006 enrolled in a DMP (see Government Accounting Office 2007, 22). Also, a review by the Department of Justice's Executive Office for the US Trustees, in the period after BAPCPA became effective, found that approximately 10 percent of the certificates that were granted by consumer credit counseling agencies were not used within six months of their issuance. This suggested that many eligible debtors had found alternatives to bankruptcy (US Senate 2006).

Debtors referred to credit counseling as a prerequisite for filing for bankruptcy also appear to differ substantially from debtors who typically enter credit counseling, notably by being in worse financial shape. According to a survey by the

NFCC (reported by Clancy and Carroll 2007), those referred to credit counseling before filing for bankruptcy had average income of $26,873 and average unsecured debt of $38,472. Typical nonbankruptcy consumers, by contrast, had average income of $31,143 and average unsecured debt of $22,597. In addition, those who sought counseling before bankruptcy were far more likely to use telephone or Internet-based counseling than traditional counseling clients.

The 2005 bankruptcy reform legislation also added a new requirement for bankruptcy filers to complete a postbankruptcy mandatory financial education program to receive a discharge in bankruptcy.[33] This mandatory predischarge counseling provides education in topics such as household budgeting and money management. At the time, the requirement was supported by a wide cross section of consumer groups, bankruptcy trustees, and bankruptcy lawyers as a useful requirement (Government Accountability Office 2007). Studies of the effectiveness of debtor education programs have generally found positive, albeit somewhat small, effects on financial outcomes over time (see Collins and O'Rourke 2010 for a comprehensive survey and assessment of the studies).[34]

Canada adopted mandatory counseling for bankrupt debtors in 1992. The Canadian system is a blend of the counseling and education components adopted later in the United States under BAPCPA. The sessions are one-on-one with debtors, and they convey advice about money management, spending habits, and budgeting skills (see Ramsay 2002).

Schwartz (2003) used credit report data to study the impact of the Canadian requirement. The author compared the credit histories, measured six to ten years after bankruptcy, for two groups of borrowers. One group filed for bankruptcy in 1992 just before implementation of mandatory counseling, with some in the group having received counseling on a voluntary basis. The other group filed in 1996 after the mandatory counseling was well established.

Comparing credit report variables for both groups as of 2002, the author concluded that "on balance, the evidence presented in this paper does not strongly support the idea that bankruptcy counseling leads to any appreciable improvement in future creditworthiness. . ... In general, there are few substantive differences between the counseled and uncounseled bankrupts" (Schwartz 2003, 277).

There also are a few studies of debtor education in the United States from the period before BAPCPA. Braucher (2001) studied the impact of a Chapter 13 debtor education program administered by the Trustees Education Network (TEN), a group of US Chapter 13 trustees who were running educational programs in the early 1990s. Specifically, the author examined eight thousand debtors who filed for Chapter 13 in 1994 in five cities. In three cities, the Chapter 13 trustees mandated that debtors attend an educational course before the start of their Chapter 13

---

33. 11 USC §111(d)(1)(C).

34. One problem with self-identified levels of financial knowledge is that people tend to overestimate their financial knowledge relative to their actual knowledge. See Agnew and Szykman (2005).

repayment plan, but there was no such requirement in the other two cities. Braucher compared plan completion rates as of 2000 and found that debtors in the three cities where education was required had a 41.9 percent completion rate, as opposed to 29.6 percent for debtors in cities where it was not. However, the lack of controls for varied local legal practices and regional differences in debtors made the results inconclusive regarding the overall effectiveness of the education.

Wiener et al. (2005) conducted a study on a debtor education program developed by the Coalition for Debtor Education and piloted in the US Bankruptcy Court's Eastern District of New York. The study compared the knowledge gains and changes in financial habits of bankruptcy filers that received financial education after bankruptcy filing with a control group of filers who did not receive financial management training and a group of participants in the program who did not file for bankruptcy. Using pretests and posttests, the authors found that participants in the debtor education course experienced positive gains in financial knowledge and improvements in financial behaviors (such as attitudes toward unnecessary spending and behaviors regarding credit cards, bill paying, and use of high-cost lenders) when compared with bankruptcy filers who did not participate in the course.

There has only been one study to date of the effectiveness of BAPCPA's mandate for counseling before final bankruptcy discharge. While it is much too early to assess longer-term effects of either program on debtor financial stability, there is some early evidence of positive impact. Lyons, White, and Howard (2008) conducted a survey study in 2006 of forty-three hundred clients who received bankruptcy counseling from Money Management International (MMI), a large nonprofit credit counseling agency. The authors also surveyed thirty-five hundred MMI clients who completed the predischarge debtor education program.

The authors conducted pretests and posttests for both groups. They found statistically significant net knowledge gains, on average, of 11 percent among counseling clients and 5 percent among clients of the education program. Although the surveys found little change in actual financial behavior (such as setting financial goals, comparison shopping, reviewing bills for accuracy, tracking income and expenses, saving money regularly), debtors exhibited significant change in planned behaviors, especially those that were not directly dependent on the stage of the bankruptcy process at the time of the survey. The authors also found that nearly all debtors surveyed held a favorable view of the counseling and educational experience. More than 94 percent of debtors said their overall ability to manage their finances had improved as a result of the counseling, and 98 percent indicated the same regarding the financial education program.[35] Borrowers at the teachable moment presented by the bankruptcy experience seem to appreciate the education.

---

35. Interestingly, this finding echoes results from interviews with Canadian borrowers who experienced bankruptcy counseling (Ramsay 2002, 536–541) and was also generally reported by Braucher (2001).

Federal and State Regulation of Credit Counseling Agencies

Historically, the debt relief industry was primarily regulated at the state level in a relatively unsystematic fashion and at the federal level by the Federal Trade Commission (Wilshusen 2011). But the advent of the Consumer Financial Protection Bureau as part of the Dodd-Frank legislation will change this traditional relationship. Dodd-Frank provides the CFPB with rule-making, examination, and enforcement authority over bank and nonbank providers of consumer credit, along with debt collection firms, credit counseling agencies, and debt settlement firms. Beginning in 2012, the CFPB and the FTC share enforcement authority over for-profit debt relief organizations.[36]

In addition, because the Internal Revenue Service determines the federal nonprofit, tax-exempt status of organizations, it has some limited oversight authority over the operations of nonprofit credit counseling organizations. As a result of concerns discussed above regarding quality of service and deceptive practices of some counseling agencies and settlement firms, in 2006, the IRS substantially tightened its requirements for credit counseling agencies seeking tax-exempt status.[37]

---

36. In July 2010, the FTC amended its Telemarketing Sales Rule to address deceptive practices in the debt settlement industry. In particular, the new rules require more disclosures to consumers about the benefits and consequences of the debt settlement option.

37. Following the Pension Protection Act of 2006, the IRS established new rules and guidance under section 501(q) of the Internal Revenue Code and developed its Core Analysis Tool (CAT) to provide guidelines for operations that would qualify for continued tax exemption. The CAT requires that the business focus of a nonprofit credit counseling agency must be financial counseling and education, not something else. Counseling sessions must incorporate a detailed review of the client's budget and financial position and include an evaluation of options tailored to the client's own circumstances. Advertising is permitted, but the emphasis must be on counseling and debt management services. The CAT rules extend to limits on fees and ancillary activities (e.g., making loans on behalf of clients and paying or receiving referral fees) and placing a cap on the amount of revenue an agency can receive from creditors in the form of fair share payments from debts paid through DMPs (50 percent cap as of 2011). Together with fee caps and other operational rules imposed by various state regulatory agencies, these regulations combine to constrain sharply the business models of nonprofit counseling agencies.

Conclusions

Because government decrees have regulated personal use of credit for almost four thousand years, we know that people have sought the benefits of personal credit use and paid its costs for at least that long and probably much longer. Personal borrowing and lending likely extend at least to Neolithic times, when debtors found themselves in need of or actually using resources prepared by or belonging to someone else and a transferal bargain or a dispute ensued. Centralized regulation of such borrowing probably extends to the same time, when some tribal chieftain became tired of arbitrating such matters and set up rules for their orderly undertaking and resolution.

In any case, the economics of such arrangements have remained basically the same over the millennia, even if much updated in terms of actual mechanics. As the simple fish net example of chapter 3 shows, credit use can be productive for individuals, in that it is wealth-increasing when there is a positive net present value to the transaction, and it can change the timing of consumption to a preferred pattern. Individuals intuitively realize this, even though they hardly undertake the specifics of financial calculations inherent in the economics of finance pioneered by Irving Fisher (1907 and 1930) and in the consumer area by Edwin R. A. Seligman (1927). Survey evidence suggests that most uses of consumer credit involve productive purposes such as purchase of assets that provide a positive flow of services over time. These assets include vehicles, education, home repairs and modernization, furniture and appliances, and large recreation and hobby items. Although, to be sure, some uses of consumer credit may on occasion be less productive, even to the point of involving some sort of underlying irrational decision making, irrationality is by no means the expectation or the norm (chapter 4).

Today borrowing arrangements typically do not involve a direct resource transfer between two interested individuals, as they might have in the time before written history, but they rather involve the participation of one or more intermediaries known today as financial institutions. Existence of such "middlemen" does not mean that the transaction becomes more expensive because of their existence and participation (chapter 5).

Costs of lending arise ultimately from the concerns of those providing the resources that they must give up use of them now and that there is the possibility that they may not get them back. Even in Neolithic times, lenders likely basically understood that resources in hand were worth more to them than a promise by someone else to repay a loan of those same resources at some time in the future. The delay in receiving the resources back, plus the good chance that they may not come back at all, gives rise to the concept of interest as an inducement to make the loan. At some level, the inducement becomes sufficient to make the lender willing to supply a loan, even a risky one (at least, up to some degree of risk). Throughout history, there have been lenders willing to make loans at zero interest, either for altruistic purposes (simply to be helpful) or based on charitable motivations (helping those in true need), but it seems there never are sufficient resources available at zero interest to satisfy the demand for risky loans at such a rate. We know from historical sources that interest existed in ancient Babylon, Greece, and Rome and among the Israelites who wrote the initial books of the Bible. Regulation of the amount of interest extends at least to this period, and this ancient legacy of centralized controls continues (chapter 11).

Skipping forward four thousand years in one jump, the term *consumer credit* today refers to all kinds of household and personal borrowing employed by individuals but not collateralized by real estate (that is, not home loans and home equity credit, which make up "mortgage credit") or by specific financial assets such as stocks and bonds and not used for business purposes. Although such borrowing apparently has existed for millennia, its real domestic growth began early in the twentieth century with development of a large middle class and simultaneously of new products such as automobiles that did not fit conveniently into the common schedule of monthly paychecks (chapter 1). In the period between the two world wars, new kinds of consumer credit arose, with new institutions to provide it. Automobile credit and personal loans from retail sellers and finance companies became commonplace, and credit unions and consumer credit departments of banks developed as important forces in the marketplace. In the decades since World War II, credit for appliances, home repair and modernization, recreational goods such as campers and boats, mobile homes, and student loans have become important, although overall growth of consumer credit has not been as rapid as is sometimes believed (chapter 2).

The resources for consumer credit are provided ultimately by consumers themselves, who invest their reserves in the form of pension assets, life insurance premiums, stocks, bonds, and bank accounts with financial institutions. Many of these intermediary institutions also make loans to businesses and governments. Return on the consumers' assets invested with these institutions arises from the wants and needs of those (including businesses and governments) who borrow the resources now. Consumers as lenders may well be unwilling to make these loans themselves, which highlights the role of financial institutions in the transfer process (chapter 5). If they were willing to do so, we would see more supply of direct lending by individuals in the marketplace.

Financial intermediaries perform several functions that facilitate the transfer of funds from savers to borrowers, none of which individuals likely want to, or are able to, provide for themselves. The concern that resources may not be returned in full (risk) suggests the usefulness of risk intermediation through diversification that institutional lenders can undertake. Paraphrasing the old saying, diversification means that all eggs need not be in one basket or even in a small number of baskets.

Knowing how to lend effectively in a modern economy goes beyond merely hanging out a shingle saying that loans are available. Lending institutions must determine information about the needs, capabilities, and progress of those on the borrowing side of the equation if they hope to receive repayments as agreed. Financial information processing and monitoring is an intense and costly business (chapter 5). It is pretty clear that individuals supplying resources will not often want to undertake such cost-causing activities themselves or that they can perform such functions as efficiently as institutions that operate full-time in the lending business. Lenders that make many loans can also more easily provide temporal intermediation (alteration of maturities of obligations from those preferred by ultimate consumer lenders to those preferred by borrowers) and size intermediation (transfer of small collections of resources into larger loans or conversion of large pools of capital into small loans).

Observation suggests that there are fixed costs associated with the lending process as a result of establishment and maintenance of the information and monitoring lending infrastructure. Existence of these costs suggests, and statistical examination shows, that this means that lending cost per loan dollar becomes inversely related to loan size. In other words, recapturing lending costs means that small loans must carry a higher interest rate than large loans, unless there is a cross subsidy by loan size (large loans subsidizing the small ones). Necessity of such cross subsidies if rates are not higher on smaller loans argues, in turn, that in a competitive marketplace, new lenders will enter the marketplace to compete in the (overpriced) large loan segment. The result is that large loans will not be able to provide such cross subsidies and, therefore, that small loans will disappear from the marketplace unless interest rates on such loans are sufficient to allow them to stand on their own.

The attempt to keep lending costs under control and actually reduce them in a competitive marketplace has encouraged a variety of innovations in lending procedures and processing in recent decades. There is a variety of such changes that range from aspects of office automation and improved personnel education and training to financial market innovations such as securitizations. The latter have experienced some difficulties in recent years because of unfortunate experience with certain mortgage credit securitizations during the financial crisis of 2008–2009, but there is little doubt that the financial innovation of securitization has enhanced the ability of consumer-oriented lending intermediaries to raise pools of funds worldwide and direct them into existing and new kinds of consumer lending.

There are also important innovations intended ultimately to reduce lending costs, including the costs of making smaller loans. Some are highly visible to consumers and now so ubiquitous that they spend little time thinking about them as any sort of change from the experience of consumers in the past. Such innovations include statistical methodologies for evaluating consumers' credit history and capacity, automated credit record keeping, and the advent of prearranged lines of credit evidenced by pieces of plastic known as credit cards.

Research into statistical methods for evaluating a consumer's past credit experience and repayment capacity began only in the 1940s, and lenders had to await development of inexpensive computing capability before they became useful to them. Known widely now as credit scoring, the computerized and today almost completely automated statistical approaches have proven themselves to be worthwhile tools for reducing costs (final section of chapter 5).

A related innovation in recent decades is the automated credit reporting agency (CRA, or popularly the "credit bureau"). CRAs provide the raw material of information on past credit experience necessary for employment of credit scoring (chapter 6). Domestic credit reporting agencies arose in the twentieth century, along with the development of consumer credit itself, as a means for lenders to evaluate evidence on potential borrowers' willingness and ability to repay potential loans. What is new recently is the movement away from localized record keeping in favor of truly national CRAs. Today national automated CRAs enable consumers to take their credit record with them as they move around the country, for better or worse.

Credit reporting agencies provide obvious benefits to lenders, in that both past credit experience and available current capacity are predictive of repayment probability. But CRAs also directly benefit potential borrowers by allowing them to signal their creditworthiness and therefore to obtain the lower interest rates that creditworthiness entails. They also help prevent those who might not willingly reveal all other obligations from obtaining amounts of credit that might amplify potential for default.

Possibly the best-known and maybe the most controversial cost-reducing innovation of recent decades is the credit card (chapter 7). Although there were some forerunners in the form of "charge plates" issued by department stores, the plastic credit card did not exist until the 1950s. By the 1960s, commercial banks had become major issuers of card credit, and today the lion's share of consumer credit generated by banks is offered in the credit card format.

The convenience of credit cards has meant that they are now the major source of consumer credit for medium-ticket consumer purchases such as appliances, automobile and home repair, and sizable hobby items. The innovation of credit cards is that they are evidence of an existing credit arrangement that is approved in advance and available to the consumers carrying the cards instantaneously worldwide. No longer is it necessary to visit the retail outlet's credit department or one's own bank or the neighborhood finance company to purchase a new refrigerator or water heater and extend the payments over a few months. Today credit cards are accepted by most retail outlets and even by service professionals such as doctors, lawyers, plumbers, and car repair shops practically anywhere. Furthermore, credit card credit is open-end credit and does not require periodic payments in fixed amounts or even payments sufficient in amount to liquidate the debt within a reasonably short time. After approval of an initial credit line, consumers with credit cards are on their own concerning the amount of use and speed of repayment, as long as use does not exceed the prearranged credit line and the monthly payment meets some small contractual minimum.

The instantaneous availability of card credit and its unsecured nature (no collateral) are what surround credit cards with controversy. Supporters note that the consumer convenience of instantaneous credit availability and flexible payment requirements of open-end credit are what make credit cards important to consumers. In contrast, opponents argue that these same features can lead to irrational credit use by some consumers, who then can get into debt over their heads, with all the personal difficulties such experiences involve. Similarly, supporters of cards note that this sort of credit is unsecured, meaning that users do not have to offer acceptable collateral, which some of them may not have readily available. Card opponents again maintain that the unsecured nature of card credit and the greater risk such lending entails mean that interest rates will be higher on card credit than on other credit, to consumers' detriment. Supporters counter that no one forces anyone to use card credit and that the generally small amounts of card credit outstanding for most individual consumers do not lead to exorbitant finance charges anyway, even if the credit is unsecured. They also point to the automated communications and record keeping that have made possible the instantaneous credit availability worldwide while also keeping costs to a minimum for the quality of the service offered.

It is probably never going to be possible to solve such controversies through observation and discussion. Controversies over benefits and costs of credit use by individuals have existed for decades and indeed for centuries, as already noted. These controversies have led to the credit industry being one of the most heavily regulated of all lines of business. Historically, in the United States, domestic regulation of credit for consumers was only at the state level. This changed in 1968, with passage of the Truth in Lending Act, the initial federal regulation of credit for consumer protection purposes (that is, excluding wartime federal control for economic stabilization purposes).

The methods and underlying purposes of state and federal consumer credit regulation have differed. The classic approach of most state regulation arose from the ancient and medieval heritage of controlling credit pricing and permitted entry of lenders into the marketplace (chapter 11). Such laws came to be described broadly as usury laws, ceilings, or controls, and they were widespread until recent decades. There still are usury constraints on some types of credit in some places and continual discussion of imposing more such regulation. In contrast, federal regulation has been more directed toward issues of perceived unfairness in credit granting (the Equal Credit Opportunity Act, chapter 9) and concerns about insufficient information availability for participants in the marketplace (disclosure such as Truth in Lending, chapter 10).

Two other sometimes controversial areas of the marketplace for deferred payment products (credit) involve close relatives that are not actually credit. Credit insurance and other debt protection products are a complement to consumer credit arrangements that consumers can decide for themselves whether they need, depending on their individual situations and aversion to risk (first part of chapter 12). Automobile leasing is a substitute for automobile credit in some situations, again depending on consumer preferences (second part of chapter 12). In many ways, automobile leasing is like automobile credit, but in other ways, it is different, and in some ways, the underlying consumer decision is different.

And then there is the possibility that despite the care and quality of decisions that might have accompanied (or not) the consumer and lender decisions that established the credit account in the first place, something still might go terribly wrong. For whatever reason, the consumer might not be able to (or even want to) repay the obligation as agreed. This can lead to creditor remedies (discussed in chapter 11) but also to default and individual bankruptcy at the individual level (chapter 13). The concept of bankruptcy has its own lengthy history, and even the reasons consumers sometimes become bankrupt have been controversial for a long time. Although discussion of remedies and bankruptcy is less than pleasant, they, too, are components of the credit system and the experience of some borrowers.

But probably the most noticeable feature of consumer credit, its institutions, its complements, and its substitutes is its ubiquitous nature that can only arise from its underlying inherent usefulness in many situations. It still seems that no one loves creditors, however, although few want them to disappear from the marketplace. Like the vast majority of consumer products or services ever invented, consumer credit clearly has its place in civilized society, even if something can go wrong after the fact of an account opening. Probably no amount of controversy, discussion, or regulation can ever solve these concerns completely. The authors merely hope that the discussion here can put this ubiquitous product into better and more useful perspective.

Ackerman, James M. 1981. Interest Rates and the Law: A History of Usury. *Arizona State Law Journal.*

Adelson, Mark. 2004. *Home Equity ABS Basics.* New York: Nomura Fixed Income Research.

———. 2008. The Credit Market Dislocation: Putting the Key Factors in Perspective. *Standard and Poors Ratings Direct* (September 3).

Adie, Douglas. 1973. Competition in the Consumer Credit Market. In *Consumer Credit Life and Disability Insurance,* edited by C. L. Hubbard. Athens: Ohio University.

Adler, Jane. 2002. Two Faces of the Card Market. *Collections and Credit Risk* (October).

Afshar, Anna. 2005. Use of Alternative Credit Data Offers Promise, Raises Issues. Federal Reserve Bank of Boston. *New England Community Developments* (Third Quarter).

Agarwal, Sumit, Jaqueline Barrett, Crystal Cun, and Mariacristina De Nardi. 2010. The Asset-Backed Securities Markets, the Crisis, and TALF. *Federal Reserve Bank of Chicago Economic Perspectives* (Fourth Quarter).

Agarwal, Sumit, Souphala Chomsisengphet, and Chunlin Liu. 2010. The Importance of Adverse Selection in the Credit Card Market: Evidence from Randomized Trials of Credit Card Solicitations. *Journal of Money, Credit and Banking* (June).

———. 2011. Consumer Bankruptcy and Default: The Role of Individual Social Capital. *Journal of Economic Psychology* (August).

Agarwal, Sumit, Souphala Chomsisengphet, Chunlin Liu, and Nicholas S. Souleles. 2005. Do Consumers Choose the Right Credit Contracts? Federal Reserve Bank of Chicago, Working Paper (December 18).

Agarwal, Sumit, Souphala Chomsisengphet, Robert McMenamin, and Paige Marta Skiba. 2010. Dismissal with Prejudice? Race and Politics in Personal Bankruptcy. Vanderbilt Law and Economics Research Paper 10-08 (August 25).

Agarwal, Sumit, Souphala Chomsisengphet, and Lawrence Mielnicki. 2008. Do Forbearance Plans Help Mitigate Credit Card Losses? *Journal of Family Economic Issues* (March 25).

Agarwal, Sumit, John C. Driscoll, Xavier Gabaix, and David Laibson. 2008. Learning in the Credit Card Market. Cambridge, MA: National Bureau of Economic Research, Working Paper 13822 (February).

Agarwal, Sumit, Chunlin Liu, and Lawrence Mielnicki. 2003. Exemption Laws and Consumer Delinquency and Bankruptcy Behavior: An Empirical Analysis of Credit Card Data. *Quarterly Review of Economics and Finance* (Summer).

Agnew, Julie, and Lisa R. Szykman. 2005. Asset Allocation and Information Overload: The Influence of Information Display, Asset Choice and Investor Experience. *Journal of Behavioral Finance* 6, no. 2.

Aizcorbe, Ana M., Arthur B. Kennickell, and Kevin B. Moore. 2003. Recent Changes in U.S. Family Finances: Evidence from the 1998 and 2001 Survey of Consumer Finances. *Federal Reserve Bulletin* (January).

Akerlof, George. 1970. The Market for Lemons: Qualitative Uncertainty and the Market Mechanism. *Quarterly Journal of Economics* (August).

Alchian, Armen A., and Reuben A. Kessel. 1962. Competition, Monopoly, and the Pursuit of Money. In *Aspects of Labor Economics*, National Bureau of Economic Research. Princeton, NJ: Princeton University Press.

Alperin, Howard D., and Roland F. Chase. 1986. *Consumer Law: Sales Practice and Credit Regulation.* St. Paul, MN: West.

Altman, Edward I. 1968. Financial Ratios, Discriminant Analysis, and the Prediction of Corporate Bankruptcy. *Journal of Finance* (September).

Altman, Edward I., Robert B. Avery, Robert A. Eisenbeis, and Joseph F. Sinkey. 1981. *Application of Classification Techniques in Business, Banking, and Finance.* Greenwich, CT: JAI.

Amel, Dean F., Arthur B. Kennickell, and Kevin B. Moore. 2008. Banking Market Definition: Evidence from the Survey of Consumer Finances. Board of Governors of the Federal Reserve System, Finance and Economics Discussion Series, Number 2008-35.

American Council of Life Insurers. 2013. *Life Insurance Fact Book 2013.* Washington, DC: American Council of Life Insurers.

Amromin, Gene, Jennifer C. Huang, Clemens Sialm, and Edward Zhong. 2012. Complex Mortgages. Paper presented at the American Finance Association Annual Meeting, Chicago. Available at http://papers.ssrn.com/sol3/papers.cfm?abstract_id=1714605.

Anderson, Michael H., and Sanjiv Jaggia. 2009. Rent-to-Own Agreements: Customer Characteristics and Contract Outcomes. *Journal of Economics and Business* (January–February).

———. 2012. Return, Purchase, or Skip? Outcome Duration and Consumer Behavior in the Rent-to-Own Market. *Empirical Economics* (August).

Andreasen, Alan R. 1993. Revisiting the Disadvantaged: Old Lessons and New Problems. *Journal of Public Policy and Marketing* (Fall).

Andriotis, Annamaria. 2011. Subprime Credit-Card Offers Pick Up. *Smart Money* (January 12).

Apilado, Vincent P., Joel J. Dauten, and Douglas E. Smith. 1978. Personal Bankruptcies. *Journal of Legal Studies* (June).

Apilado, Vincent P., Don C. Warner, and Joel J. Dauten. 1974. Evaluative Techniques in Consumer Finance: Experimental Results and Policy Implications for Financial Institutions. *Journal of Financial and Quantitative Analysis* (March).

Ariely, Dan, and Klaus Wertenbach. 2002. Procrastination, Deadlines, and Performance: Self-Control by Precommitment. *Psychological Science* (May).

Arrow, Kenneth J. 1972. Models of Job Discrimination. In *Racial Discrimination in Economic Life*, edited by A. H. Pascal. Lexington, MA: Lexington Books.

Arshadi, Nasser, and Gordon V. Karels. 1997. *Modern Financial Intermediaries and Markets.* Upper Saddle River, NJ: Prentice Hall.

Ashcroft, Adam B., and Til Scheuermann. 2008. *Understanding Securitization of Subprime Mortgage Credit*. Federal Reserve Bank of New York, Staff Report No. 318.

Aspan, Maria. 2011. H&R Block, Under Pressure, Kills Tax Refund Loans. *American Banker* (September 15).

Associated Press. 2009. 22 Held in Staten Island Betting and Loan Sharking Raids (November 18).

Athreya, Kartik. 2002. Welfare Implications of the Bankruptcy Reform Act of 1999. *Journal of Monetary Economics* (November).

——. 2004. Shame As It Ever Was: Stigma and Personal Bankruptcy. *Federal Reserve Bank of Richmond Economic Quarterly* (Spring).

——. 2005. Equilibrium Models of Personal Bankruptcy: A Survey. *Federal Reserve Bank of Richmond Economic Quarterly* (Spring).

——. 2006. Fresh Start or Head Start? Uniform Bankruptcy Exemptions and Welfare. *Journal of Economic Dynamics and Control* (November).

Athreya, Kartik, and Nicole B. Simpson. 2006. Unsecured Debt with Public Insurance: From Bad to Worse. *Journal of Monetary Economics* (May).

Attanasio, Orazio. 1994. The Intertemporal Allocation of Consumption: Theory and Evidence. National Bureau of Economic Research, Working Paper 4811 (July).

Attanasio, Orazio, Pinelopi K. Goldberg, and Ekaterini Kyriazidou. 2000. Credit Constraints in the Market for Consumer Durables: Evidence from Micro Data on Car Loans. *International Economic Review* (May).

Austin, M. Jill, and Melodie R. Phillips. 2001. Educating Students: An Ethics Responsibility of Credit Card Companies. *Journal of Services Marketing* (December).

Austin, Regina. 2004. Of Predatory Lending and the Democratization of Credit: Preserving the Social Safety Net of Informality in Small Loan Transactions. *American University Law Review* (August).

Ausubel, Lawrence M. 1991. The Failure of Competition in the Credit Card Market. *American Economic Review* (March).

——. 1997. Credit Card Defaults, Credit Card Profits, and Bankruptcy. *American Bankruptcy Law Journal* (Spring).

——. 1999. Adverse Selection in the Credit Card Market. University of Maryland, Working Paper (June 17).

Avery, Robert B. 1981a. Estimating Credit Constraints by Switching Regressions. In *Structural Analysis of Discrete Data with Econometric Applications*, edited by C. F. Manski and D. McFadden. Cambridge, MA: MIT Press.

——. 1981b. Indirect Screening and the Equal Credit Opportunity Act. Washington, DC: Board of Governors of the Federal Reserve System, Research Papers in Banking and Financial Economics.

——. 1982. Discrimination in Consumer Credit Markets. Washington, DC: Board of Governors of the Federal Reserve System, Research Papers in Banking and Financial Economics.

Avery, Robert B., Raphael W. Bostic, Paul S. Calem, and Glenn B. Canner. 1996. Credit Risk, Credit Scoring, and the Performance of Home Mortgages. *Federal Reserve Bulletin* (July).

——. 2000. Credit Scoring: Statistical Issues and Evidence from Credit-Bureau Files. *Real Estate Economics* (September).

——. 2003. An Overview of Consumer Data and Credit Reporting. *Federal Reserve Bulletin* (February).

Avery, Robert B., Paul S. Calem, and Glenn B. Canner. 2004. Credit Report Accuracy and Access to Credit. *Federal Reserve Bulletin* (Summer).

Avery, Robert A., Gregory Elliehausen, Glenn B. Canner, and Thomas A. Gustafson. 1984. Survey of Consumer Finances, 1983. *Federal Reserve Bulletin* (September).

Avio, Kenneth L. 1973. An Economic Rationale for Statutory Interest Rate Ceilings. *Quarterly Review of Economics and Business* (Autumn).

Awh, R. Y., and D. Waters. 1974. A Discriminant Analysis of Economic, Demographic, and Attitudinal Characteristics of Bank Charge-Card Holders: A Case Study. *Journal of Finance* (June).

Azzi, Corry F., and James C. Cox. 1976. A Theory and Test of Credit Rationing: Comment. *American Economic Review* (December).

Bacchetta, Phillipe, and Stefan Gerlach. 1997. Consumption and Credit Constraints: International Evidence. *Journal of Monetary Economics* (October).

Baird, Douglas G. 1998. Bankruptcy's Uncontested Axioms. *Yale Law Journal* (December).

Baltensperger, Ernst. 1976. The Borrower-Lender Relationship, Competitive Equilibrium, and the Theory of Hedonic Prices. *American Economic Review* (June).

——. 1978. Credit Rationing: Issues and Questions. *Journal of Money, Credit and Banking* (May).

Barba, Robert. 2011. Republic Bankcorp in Kentucky Exiting Tax Refund Lending. *American Banker* (December 9).

——. 2012a. Another Tax Preparer Severs Ties with Republic of Kentucky. *American Banker* (September 19).

——. 2012b. Republic Bankcorp Parts Ways with Tax-Servicing Partner (August 30).

Barr, Michael S. 2012. *No Slack: The Financial Lives of Low-Income Americans.* Washington, DC: Brookings Institution.

Barrett, Roger S., and Charles C. Ulrich. 1969. *Summary of State Consumer Credit Laws and Rates.* Chicago: Household Finance Corporation.

Barro, Robert J. 1976. The Loan Market, Collateral, and Rates of Interest. *Journal of Money, Credit and Banking* (November).

Barron, John M., Gregory Elliehausen, and Michael E. Staten. 2000. Monitoring the Household Sector with Aggregate Credit Bureau Data. *Business Economics* (January).

Barron, John M., and Michael E. Staten. 1996. *Consumer Attitudes toward Credit Insurance.* Norwell, MA: Kluwer Academic.

——. 2003. The Value of Comprehensive Credit Reports: Lessons from the US Experience. In *Credit Reporting Systems and the International Economy*, edited by Margaret Miller. Cambridge, MA: MIT Press.

——. 2011. Is Technology-Enhanced Credit Counseling as Effective as In Person Delivery? Federal Reserve Bank of Philadelphia, Working Paper 11-11.

Barron, John M., Michael E. Staten, and Stephanie M. Wilshusen. 2002. The Impact of Casino Gambling on Personal Bankruptcy Filing Rates. *Contemporary Economic Policy* (October).

Barth, James R., Joseph J. Cordes, and Anthony M. J. Yezer. 1986. Benefits and Costs of Legal Restrictions on Personal Loan Markets. *Journal of Law and Economics* (October).

Barth, James R., Padma Gotur, Neela Manage, and Anthony M. J. Yezer. 1983. The Effect of Government Regulation of Personal Loan Markets: A Tobit Estimation of a Microeconomic Model. *Journal of Finance* (September).

Baumol, William J. 1952. The Transactions Demand for Cash: An Inventory Theoretic Approach. *Quarterly Journal of Economics* (November).

Beacom, Miles. 2008. Letter from Premier Bankcard to Board of Governors of the Federal Reserve System Regarding Proposed Revisions to Regulation AA. Federal Reserve Docket No. R-1314 (July 31).

Beales, J. Howard, Jeffrey A. Eisenach, and Robert E. Litan. 2012. Consumer Welfare Implications of Rent-to-Own Transactions. Navigant Economics, Working Paper (May).

Becker, Gary S. 1965. A Theory of the Allocation of Time. *Economic Journal* (September).

———. 1971. *The Economics of Discrimination.* Chicago: University of Chicago Press.

Becker, Gary S., and Casey B. Mulligan. 1997. The Endogenous Determination of Time Preference. *Quarterly Journal of Economics* (August).

Bell, Frederick W., and Neil B. Murphy. 1968. *Costs in Commercial Banking: A Quantitative Analysis of Bank Behavior and Its Relation to Bank Regulation.* Federal Reserve Bank of Boston, Research Report Number 41.

Belsky, Eric S., Karl E. Case, and Susan J. Smith. 2008. Identifying, Managing, and Mitigating Risks to Borrowers in Changing Mortgage and Consumer Credit Markets. Cambridge, MA: Harvard University Joint Center for Housing Studies, Working Paper.

Belsky, Eric S., and Ren S. Essene. 2007. Consumer and Mortgage Credit at a Crossroads: Preserving Expanded Access While Informing Choices and Protecting Consumers. Paper presented at Harvard University Joint Center for Housing Studies Conference, Understanding Consumer Credit (November 28–29).

Bendor, Jonathan Brodie, Sunil Kumar, and David A. Siegel. 2009. Satisficing: A "Pretty Good" Heuristic. *B.E. Journal of Theoretical Economics* 9, no. 1.

Benhabib, Jess, and Alberto Bisin. 2005. Modeling Internal Commitment Mechanisms and Self-Control: A Neuroeconomic Approach to Consumption-Saving Decisions. *Games and Economic Behavior* (August).

Benjamin, Daniel K. 1978. The Use of Collateral to Enforce Debt Contracts. *Economic Inquiry* (July).

Benmelech, Efraim, and Tobias J. Moskowitz. 2010. The Political Economy of Financial Regulation: Evidence from U.S. State Usury Laws in the 19th Century. *Journal of Finance* (June).

Benston, George J. 1965. Scale Economies and Marginal Costs in Banking Operations. *National Banking Review* (June).

———. 1972. Economies of Scale of Financial Institutions. *Journal of Money, Credit and Banking* (May).

———. 1975. The Costs to Consumer Finance Companies of Extending Consumer Credit. In *National Commission on Consumer Finance, Technical Studies,* Vol. 2. Washington, DC: Government Printing Office.

———. 1977a. Rate Ceiling Implications of the Cost Structure of Consumer Finance Companies. *Journal of Finance* (September).

———. 1977b. Risk on Consumer Finance Company Personal Loans. *Journal of Finance* (May).

Benston, George J., Gerald A. Hanweck, and David B. Humphrey. 1982. Scale Economies in Banking: A Restructuring and Reassessment. *Journal of Money, Credit and Banking* (November).

Benston, George J., and Clifford W. Smith, Jr. 1976. A Transitions Cost Approach to the Theory of Financial Intermediation. *Journal of Finance* (May).

Bentham, Jeremy. 2009 [1787]. *Defense of Usury.* Newcastle, UK: Cambridge Scholars Publishing.

Berger, Allen N., W. Scott Frame, and Nathan H. Miller. 2005. Credit Scoring and Availability, Price and Risk of Small Business Credit. *Journal of Money, Credit and Banking* (April).

Berger, Allen N., Philip Molyneux, and John O. S. Wilson, eds. 2010. *Oxford Handbook of Banking.* Oxford: Oxford University Press.

Berger, Allen N., and Gregory F. Udell. 2002. Small Business Credit Availability and Relationship Lending: The Importance of Bank Organizational Structure. *Economic Journal* (February).

Berkovec, James A., Glenn B. Canner, Stuart A. Gabriel, and Timothy H. Hannan. 1998. Discrimination, Competition, and Loan Performance in FHA Lending. *Review of Economics and Statistics* (May).

Berkowitz, Jeremy, and Michelle J. White. 2004. Bankruptcy and Small Firms' Access to Credit. *RAND Journal of Economics* (Spring).

Bermant, Gordon. 2003. What's Stigma Got to Do with It? *American Bankruptcy Institute Journal* (July–August).

Bertrand, Marianne and Adair Morse. 2011. Information Disclosure, Cognitive Biases, and Payday Borrowing. *Journal of Finance* (December).

Bettman, James R. 1979. *An Information Processing Theory of Consumer Choice.* Reading, MA: Addison-Wesley.

Bhandari, Jagdeep S., and Lawrence A. Weiss. 1993. The Increasing Bankruptcy Filing Rate: An Historical Analysis. *American Bankruptcy Law Journal* (Winter).

Bhutta, Neil. 2012. Payday Credit Access and Household Financial Health: Evidence from Consumer Credit Records. Working Paper, Federal Reserve Board (June).

Bhutta, Neil, Paige Marta Skiba, and Jeremy Tobacman. 2012. Payday Loan Choices and Consequences. Working Paper, Federal Reserve Board (December 6).

Bishop, Paul C. 1998. A Time Series Model of the US Personal Bankruptcy Rate. *Bank Trends* (February).

Bizer, David S., and Peter M. DeMarzo. 1992. Sequential Banking. *Journal of Political Economy* (February).

Black, Sandra E., and Donald P. Morgan. 1999. Meet the New Borrowers. *Federal Reserve Bank of New York Current Issues in Economics and Finance* (February).

Blackwell, Roger D., Paul W. Miniard, and James F. Engel. 2006. *Consumer Behavior,* 10th ed. Stamford, CT: Thomson South-Western.

Blades, Holland C., and Gene C. Lynch. 1976. *Credit Policies and Store Locations in Arkansas Border Cities: Merchant Reactions to a 109 Percent Finance Charge Ceiling.* West Lafayette, IN: Purdue University Credit Research Center, Monograph Number 2.

Blitz, Rudolph C., and Millard F. Long. 1965. The Economics of Usury Regulation. *Journal of Political Economy* (December).

Board of Governors of the Federal Reserve System. 1957. *Consumer Installment Credit,* 6 vols. Washington, DC: Board of Governors of the Federal Reserve System.

——. 1976. *Banking and Monetary Statistics, 1941–1970.* Washington, DC: Board of Governors of the Federal Reserve System.

——. 1977. Equal Credit Opportunity. *Federal Reserve Bulletin* (February).

——. 1987. *Annual Percentage Rate Demonstration Project.* Washington, DC: Board of Governors of the Federal Reserve System.

——. 2007. *Report to the Congress on Credit Scoring and Its Effects on the Availability and Affordability of Credit*. Washington, DC: Board of Governors of the Federal Reserve System.

——. 2013. *Report to the Congress on the Profitability of Credit Card Operations of Depository Institutions*. Washington, DC: Board of Governors of the Federal Reserve System.

Board of Governors of the Federal Reserve System and Department of Housing and Urban Development. 1998. *Joint Report to the Congress concerning Reform to the Truth in Lending Act and the Real Estate Settlement Procedures Act*. Washington, DC: Board of Governors of the Federal Reserve System and Department of Housing and Urban Development.

Board of Student Editors. 1968. An Empirical Study of the Arkansas Usury Law: With Friends Like That... *Illinois Law Forum* (Winter).

Boczar, Gregory E. 1978. Competition between Banks and Finance Companies: A Cross Section Study of Personal Loan Debtors. *Journal of Finance* (March).

Bodenhorn, Howard. 2003. *State Banking in Early America*. Oxford and New York: Oxford University Press.

——. 2007. Usury Ceilings and Bank Lending Behavior: Evidence from Nineteenth Century New York. *Explorations in Economic History* (April).

Boggess, William P. 1967. Screen Test Your Credit Risks. *Harvard Business Review* (November–December).

Borges, B., Daniel G. Goldstein, A. Ortmann, and Gerd Gigerenzer. 1999. Can Ignorance Beat the Stock Market? In *Simple Heuristics That Make Us Smart*, edited by Gerd Gigerenzer and Peter M. Todd. New York: Oxford University Press.

Bostic, Raphael W., Kathleen C. Engel, Patricia A. McCoy, Anthony Pennington-Cross, and Susan M. Wachter. 2008. State and Local Anti-Predatory Lending Laws: The Effect of Legal Enforcement Mechanisms. *Journal of Economics and Business* (January–February).

Boyes, William J. 1982. In Defense of the Downtrodden: Usury Laws? *Public Choice* 39, no. 2.

Boyes, William J., and Roger L. Faith. 1986. Some Effects of the Bankruptcy Reform Act of 1978. *Journal of Law and Economics* (April).

Boyes, William J., D. Hoffman, and S. Low. 1986. Lender Reactions to Information Restrictions: The Case of Banks and the ECOA. *Journal of Money, Credit and Banking* (July).

Braucher, Jean. 1993. Lawyers and Consumer Bankruptcy: One Code, Many Cultures. *American Bankruptcy Law Journal*: 501.

——. 1998. Increasing Uniformity in Consumer Bankruptcy: Means Testing as a Distraction and the National Bankruptcy Review Commission's Proposals as a Starting Point. *American Bankruptcy Institute Law Review*, no. 1.

——. 2001. An Empirical Study of Debtor Education in Bankruptcy: Impact on Chapter 13 Completion Not Shown. *American Bankruptcy Institute Law Review* 9.

Brealey, Richard A., Stewert C. Myers, and Franklin Allen. 2010. *Principles of Corporate Finance*, 10th ed. New York: McGraw-Hill.

Bricker, Jesse, Arthur Kennickell, Kevin B. Moore, and John Sabelhaus. 2012. Changes in US Family Finances from 2007 to 2010: Evidence from the Survey of Consumer Finances. *Federal Reserve Bulletin* (June).

Brito, Dagobert L., and Peter R. Hartley. 1995. Consumer Rationality and Credit Cards. *Journal of Political Economy* (April).

Brobeck, Stephen. 2003. Testimony at Hearing on H.R. 2622, the Fair and Accurate Credit Transactions Act of 2003, before the US House of Representatives, Committee on Financial Services, July 9.

Brown, Daniel T., Charles R. Link, and Michael E. Staten. 2012. The Success and Failure of Counseling Agency Debt Repayment Plans. *Eastern Economic Journal* (March 21).

Brown, Richard A. 1998. Time Series Analysis of State-Level Personal Bankruptcy Rates, 1970–1996. *Bank Trends* (March).

Brueckner, J. K. 2000. Mortgage Default with Asymmetric Information. *Journal of Real Estate Finance and Economics* (May).

Bryant, William Cullen. 1981 [1836]. On Usury Laws. *The Freeman* (January).

Buckley, Frank H., and Margaret F. Brinig. 1998. The Bankruptcy Puzzle. *Journal of Legal Studies* (January).

Bucks, Brian K., Arthur B. Kennickell, Traci L. Mach, and Kevin B. Moore. 2009. Changes in U.S. Family Finances from 2004 to 2007: Evidence from the Survey of Consumer Finances. *Federal Reserve Bulletin* (February).

Bucks, Brian K., Arthur B. Kennickell, and Kevin B. Moore. 2006. Recent Changes in U.S. Family Finances: Evidence from the 2001 and 2004 Survey of Consumer Finances. *Federal Reserve Bulletin* (January).

Burck, Gilbert, and Sanford Parker. 1956. The Coming Turn in Consumer Credit. *Fortune* (March).

Burnett, Kimberly, Meryl Finkel, and Bulbul Kaul. 2004 Mortgage Lending in North Carolina after the Anti-Predatory Lending Law. Cambridge, MA: ABT.

Burstein, Nancy R. 1978. A Comment on Consumer Preferences for Alternative Retail Credit Plans. *Journal of Marketing Research* (November).

Business Week. 1978. Consumers Using IOUs to Fight Inflation (October 16).

Calder, Lendol C. 1999. *Financing the American Dream: A Cultural History of Consumer Credit*. Princeton, NJ: Princeton University Press.

Calem, Paul S., Michael B. Gordy, and Loretta J. Mester. 2005. Switching Costs and Adverse Selection in the Market for Credit Cards: New Evidence. Federal Reserve Bank of Philadelphia, Research Department, Working Paper No. 05-16 (July).

Calem, Paul S., and Stanley D. Longhofer. 2000. Anatomy of a Fair Lending Exam: The Uses and Limitations of Statistics. Washington, DC: Board of Governors of the Federal Reserve System, Working Paper (March).

Calem, Paul S., and Loretta J. Mester. 1995. Consumer Behavior and the Stickiness of Credit-Card Interest Rates. *American Economic Review* (December).

Camerer, Colin, George Loewenstein, and Drazen Prelec. 2005. Neuroeconomics: How Neuroscience Can Inform Economics. *Journal of Economic Literature* (March).

Canner, Glenn B., Thomas A. Durkin, and Charles A. Luckett. 1994. Home Equity Lending: Evidence from Recent Surveys. *Federal Reserve Bulletin* (July).

——. 1998. Recent Developments in Home Equity Lending. *Federal Reserve Bulletin* (April).

Canner, Glenn B., and Gregory Elliehausen. 2013. Consumer Experiences with Credit Cards. *Federal Reserve Bulletin* (December).

Canner, Glenn B., and James T. Fergus. 1987. The Economic Effects of Proposed Ceilings on Credit Card Interest Rates. *Federal Reserve Bulletin* (January).

Canner, Glenn B., Arthur B. Kennickell, and Charles A. Luckett. 1995. Household Sector Borrowing and the Burden of Debt. *Federal Reserve Bulletin* (April).

Caplovitz, David. 1963. *The Poor Pay More: Consumer Practices of Low Income Families*. New York: Free Press of Glencoe.

Capon, Noel. 1982. Credit Scoring Systems: A Critical Analysis. *Journal of Marketing* (Spring).

Cargill, Thomas F., and Jeanne Wendel. 1996. Bank Credit Cards: Consumer Irrationality versus Market Forces. *Journal of Consumer Affairs* (Winter).

Carrell, Scott E., and Jonathan Zinman. 2008. In Harm's Way? Payday Loan Access and Military Personnel Performance. Federal Reserve Bank of Philadelphia, Working Paper 08-18 (August).

Carroll, Christopher D. 2001. A Theory of the Consumption Function with and without Liquidity Constraints. *Journal of Economic Perspectives* (Summer).

Carruthers, Bruce G., Timothy W. Guinnane, and Yoonseok Lee. 2009. Bringing "Honest Capital" to Poor Borrowers: The Passage of the Uniform Small Loan Law, 1907–1930. New Haven, CT: Yale University, Economic Growth Center, Center Discussion Paper No. 971 (May).

Carruthers, Bruce G., and Terence C. Halliday. 1998. *Rescuing Business: The Making of Corporate Bankruptcy Law in England and the United States.* (Oxford: Clarendon).

Carter, Charlie. 1982. The Surge in Bankruptcies: Is the New Law Responsible? *Federal Reserve Bank of Atlanta Economic Review* (January).

Caskey, John P. 1991. Pawnbroking in America: The Economics of a Forgotten Credit Market. *Journal of Money, Credit and Banking* (February).

——. 1994. *Fringe Banking.* New York: Russell Sage Foundation.

——. 2005. Fringe Banking and the Rise of Payday Lending. In *Credit Markets for the Poor,* edited by P. Bolton and H. Rosenthal. New York: Russell Sage Foundation.

——. 2010. Payday Lending: New Research and the Big Question. Federal Reserve Bank of Philadelphia, Working Paper 10-32 (October).

Castronova, Edward, and Paul Hagstrom. 2004. The Demand for Credit Cards: Evidence from the Survey of Consumer Finances. *Economic Inquiry* (April).

Chandler, Gary G. 2004. Generic and Customized Scoring Models: A Comparison. In *Credit Scoring for Risk Managers: The Handbook for Lenders,* edited by Elizabeth Mays. Mason, OH: Thomson/Southwestern.

Chandler, Gary G., and John Y. Coffman. 1979. A Comparative Analysis of Empirical vs. Judgmental Credit Evaluation. *Journal of Retail Banking* (September).

Chandler, Gary C., and David C. Ewert. 1976. Discrimination on the Basis of Sex under the Equal Credit Opportunity Act. West Lafayette, IN: Purdue University Credit Research Center, Working Paper 8.

Chandler, Gary G., and Lee E. Parker. 1989. Predictive Value of Credit Bureau Reports. *Journal of Retail Banking* (Winter).

Chang, Yu-Chun, and Sherman Hanna. 1991. Consumer Credit: An Exploratory Study of Search Behavior. Paper presented at the Annual Conference of the American Council on Consumer Interests.

Chapman, John M., and Robert P. Shay, eds. *The Consumer Finance Industry: Its Costs and Regulation.* New York: Columbia University Press.

Chatterjee, Samprit, and Seymour Barcun. 1970. A Nonparametric Approach to Credit Screening. *Journal of the American Statistical Association* (March).

Chatterjee, Satyajit, and Grey Gordon. 2011. Dealing with Consumer Default: Bankruptcy vs. Garnishment. Federal Reserve Bank of Philadelphia, Working Paper 11-35 (August 29).

Chen, Daphne. 2011. The Impact of Personal Bankruptcy on Labor Supply Decisions, Florida State University, Working Paper (October 9).

Chien, Yi-Wen, and Sharon A. Devaney. 2001. The Effects of Credit Attitude and Socioeconomic Factors on Credit Card and Installment Debt. *Journal of Consumer Affairs* (Summer).

Choy, Susan P., and Xiaojie Li. 2005. *Debt Burden: A Comparison of 1992–93 and 1999–2000 Bachelor's Degree Recipients a Year after Graduating.* US Department of Education, National Center for Education Statistics. Washington, DC: Government Printing Office.

——. 2006. *Dealing with Debt: 1992–93 Bachelor's Degree Recipients 10 Years Later.* Washington, DC: US Department of Education, Center for Education Statistics.

Clancy, Noreen, and Stephen J. Carroll. 2007. *Prebankruptcy Credit Counseling.* Arlington, VA: RAND Corporation.

Clark, Evans. 1931. *Financing the Consumer.* New York and London: Harper.

Cochran, William G. 1963. *Sampling Techniques*, 2nd ed. New York: John Wiley.

Cohen-Cole, Ethan. 2009. The Option Value of Consumer Bankruptcy. Federal Reserve Bank of Boston, Working Paper QAU09-1 (February 23).

College Board. 2013. Trends in Student Aid. New York: College Board.

Collins, J. Michael, and Collin M. O'Rourke. 2010. Financial Education and Counseling—Still Holding Promise. *Journal of Consumer Affairs* (Fall).

Collins, Jackson R. 1941. Evasion and Avoidance of Usury Laws *Law and Contemporary Problems* (Winter).

Congressional Budget Office. 2000. *Personal Bankruptcy: A Literature Review.* Washington, DC: Congressional Budget Office.

Congressional Record. 1969. Washington, DC: Government Printing Office.

Consumer Bankers Association. 2002. *CBA Automobile Finance Study.* Arlington, VA: Consumer Bankers Association.

Consumer Credit Industry Association. 2013. *The 2012 Fact Book of Credit-Related Insurance.* Atlanta: Consumer Credit Industry Association.

Consumer Federation of America and National Credit Reporting Association. 2002. *Credit Score Accuracy and Implications for Consumers.* Washington, DC: Consumer Federation of America.

Consumer Financial Protection Bureau. 2012. *Key Dimensions and Processes in the U.S. Credit Reporting System.* Washington, DC: Consumer Financial Protection Bureau.

Cosmides, Leda, and Tooby, J. 1996. Are Humans Good Intuitive Statisticians After All? Rethinking Some Conclusions from the Literature on Judgment under Uncertainty. *Cognition* (January).

Countryman, Vern. 1975. Improvident Credit Extension: A New Legal Concept Aborning? *Maine Law Review*, no. 1.

Cox, Donald, and Tullio Jappelli. 1993. The Effect of Borrowing Constraints on Consumer Liabilities. *Journal of Money, Credit and Banking* (May).

Crook, Jonathan. 1996. Credit Constraints and US Households. *Applied Financial Economics*, no. 6.

——. 2001. The Demand for Household Debt in the USA: Evidence from the 1995 Survey of Consumer Finance. *Applied Financial Economics*, no. 1.

——. 2002. Adverse Selection and Search in the Bank Credit Card Market. Edinburgh: University of Edinburgh, Department of Business Studies, Credit Research Centre, Working Paper 02/1 (March).

——. 2003. The Demand and Supply for Household Debt: A Cross Country Comparison. Credit Research Centre, University of Edinburgh, Working Paper 03/01.

Curran, Barbara A. 1965. *Trends in Consumer Credit Legislation*. Chicago: University of Chicago Press.

Cyrnak, Anthony W., and Glenn B. Canner. 1986. Consumer Experiences with Credit Insurance: Some New Evidence. *Federal Reserve Bank of San Francisco Economic Review* (Summer).

Daly, James J. 1993. The Boom in Credit Counseling. *Credit Card Management* (July).

Danes, Sharon M., and Tahira K. Hira. 1990. Knowledge, Beliefs, and Practices in the Use of Credit Cards. *Home Economics Research Journal* (March).

Danielian, N. R. 1929. Theory of Consumer Credit. *American Economic Review* (September).

Davidson, Andrew S., Anthony Sanders, Lan-Ling Wolff, and Anne Ching. 2003. *Securitization: Structuring and Investment Analysis*. New York: John Wiley.

Davis, Lance E. 1960. The New England Textile Mills and the Capital Markets: A Study of Industrial Borrowing 1840–1860. *Journal of Economic History* 20, no. 1(March): 1–30.

Dawsey, Amanda E., and Lawrence M. Ausubel. 2004. Informal Bankruptcy. Unpublished manuscript (April 12). Available at http://www.ausubel.com/creditcard-papers/informal-bankruptcy.pdf.

Day, George S. 1976. Assessing the Effects of Information Disclosure Requirements. *Journal of Marketing* (April).

Day, George S., and William K. Brandt. 1973. A Study of Consumer Credit Decisions: Implications for Present and Prospective Legislation. In *National Commission on Consumer Finance: Technical Studies*, Vol. 1. Washington, DC: Government Printing Office.

——. 1974. Consumer Research and the Evaluation of Information Disclosure Requirements: The Case of Truth in Lending. *Journal of Consumer Research* (June).

Debusmann, Bernd. 2010. Walmart Faces Opposition in New York City—Again. Reuters (December 16, 2010).

Dell'Ariccia, Giovanni, Ezra Friedman, and Robert Marquez. 1999. Adverse Selection as a Barrier to Entry in the Banking Industry. *RAND Journal of Economics* (Autumn).

Demery, Paul. 1998. How Technology Boosted Plastic. *Credit Card Management*, 10th anniversary ed. (May).

DeMiguel, Victor, Lorenzo Garlappi, and Raman Uppal. 2009. Optimal versus Naïve Diversification: How Inefficient Is the 1/N Portfolio Strategy? *Review of Financial Studies* (May).

DeMuth, Christopher C. 1986. The Case against Credit Card Interest Rate Regulation. *Yale Journal on Regulation* (Spring).

Dennis, Warren L. 1995. Fair Lending and Credit Scoring. *Mortgage Banking* (November).

De Roover, Raymond. 1967. The Scholastics, Usury, and Foreign Exchange. *Business History Review* (Autumn).

Deutscher, Terry. 1973. Credit Legislation Two Years Out: Awareness Changes and Behavioral Effects of Differential Awareness Levels. In *Technical Studies of the National Commission on Consumer Finance*, Vol. 1, no. 4. Washington, DC: Government Printing Office.

Dickson, Martin. 1992. Record Take-Up for GM Card. *Financial Times* (November 17).

Dietrich, Jason, and Hannes Johannsson, 2005. Searching for Age and Gender Discrimination in Mortgage Lending. Washington, DC: Office of the Comptroller of the Currency, Working Paper 2005-2 (August).

Dodwell, William J. 2010. Will Private Label Securitization Return? The Enabling Conditions and What Is in Store. Working paper available at SSRN, http://ssrn.com/abstract=1624043.

Dole, Kate, and Rob Levy. 2012. *Building Consumer Credit: A Winning Strategy for Financial Institutions and Consumers.* Chicago: Center for Financial Services Innovation.

Domowitz, Ian, and Thomas Eovaldi. 1993. The Impact of the Bankruptcy Reform Act of 1978 on Consumer Bankruptcy. *Journal of Law and Economics* (October).

Domowitz, Ian, and Robert L. Sartain, 1999a. Determinants of the Consumer Bankruptcy Decision. *Journal of Finance* (February).

——. 1999b. Incentives and Bankruptcy Chapter Choice: Evidence from the Reform Act of 1978. *Journal of Legal Studies* (June).

Dorfman, Joseph. 1946. *The Economic Mind in American Civilization,* Vol. 2, 1606–1865. New York: Viking.

Dranove, David, and Michael L. Millenson. 2006. Medical Bankruptcy: Myth versus Fact. *Health Affairs* (February).

Duca, John V., and Stuart S. Rosenthal. 1993. Borrowing Constraints, Household Debt, and Racial Discrimination in Loan Markets. *Journal of Financial Intermediation* (October).

Due, Jean Mann. 1955. Consumer Knowledge of Installment Credit Charges. *Journal of Marketing* (October).

Dugas, Christine, 2001. Debt Smothers America's Youth. *USA Today* (February 13).

Duncan, Greg J. 1986. *Years of Poverty, Years of Plenty: The Changing Economic Fortunes of American Workers and Families.* Ann Arbor: Survey Research Center, University of Michigan.

Duncan, Mallory B. 1998. Testimony on Bankruptcy Law Revision before the Subcommittee on Commercial and Administrative Law of the House Committee on the Judiciary. 105th Congress (March 18).

Dunkelberg, William C. 1989. Analyzing Consumer Spending and Debt. *Business Economics* (July).

Dunkelberg, William C., and James Stephenson. 1975. Durable Goods Ownership and the Rate of Return. In *Technical Studies of the National Commission on Consumer Finance,* Vol. 4. Washington, DC: Government Printing Office.

Durand, David. 1941. *Risk Elements in Consumer Installment Financing.* New York: National Bureau of Economic Research, Study Number 8.

Durkin, Thomas A. 1975. A High Rate Market for Consumer Loans: The Small Loan Industry in Texas. In *National Commission on Consumer Finance, Technical Studies,* Vol. 2. Washington, DC: Government Printing Office.

——. 2000. Credit Cards: Use and Consumer Attitudes 1970–2000. *Federal Reserve Bulletin* (September).

——. 2002. Consumers and Credit Disclosures: Credit Cards and Credit Insurance. *Federal Reserve Bulletin* (April).

——. 2006. Credit Card Disclosures, Solicitations, and Privacy Notices: Survey Results of Consumer Knowledge and Behavior. *Federal Reserve Bulletin* (August).

Durkin, Thomas A., and Gregory E. Elliehausen. 1978. *The 1977 Consumer Credit Survey.* Washington, DC: Board of Governors of the Federal Reserve System.

——. 1998. The Cost Structure of the Consumer Finance Industry. *Journal of Financial Services Research* (February).

——. 2000. Interinstitutional Competition for Consumer Credit at the End of the Twentieth Century. Working Paper (June).

——. 2011. *Truth in Lending: Theory, History, and a Way Forward*. New York: Oxford University Press.

——. 2012. Consumers and Debt Protection Products: Results of a New Consumer Survey. *Federal Reserve Bulletin* (December).

——. 2013. Assessing the Price of Short Term Credit. Board of Governors of the Federal Reserve System, Division of Research and Statistics, Working Paper (November 6).

Durkin, Thomas A., Gregory Elliehausen, and Todd J. Zywicki. 2014. The Behavioral Law and Economics of Credit Cards. *Supreme Court Economic Review* (Forthcoming).

Durkin, Thomas A., and Zachariah Jonasson. 2002. *An Empirical Evaluation of the Content and Cycle of Financial Reporting: The Case of Consumer Credit*. Washington, DC: Georgetown University Credit Research Center.

Durkin, Thomas A., and E. Ray McAlister. 1977. *An Economic Report on Consumer Lending in Texas*. Monograph No. 4. West Lafayette, IN: Purdue University, Credit Research Center, Krannert Graduate School of Management.

Durkin, Thomas A., Keith Ord, and David A. Walker. 2010. Long-Run Credit Growth in the US. *Journal of Economics and Business* (September–October).

Durkin, Thomas A., and Michael E. Staten. 2002. Introduction. In *The Impact of Public Policy on Consumer Credit*, edited by Thomas A. Durkin and Michael E. Staten. Boston: Kluwer Academic.

Duygan-Bump, Burcu, and Charles Grant. 2008. Household Debt Repayment Behavior: What Role Do Institutions Play? Federal Reserve Bank of Boston, Working Paper QAU08-3.

Dynan, Karen, Kathleen Johnson, and Karen Pence. 2003. Recent Changes to a Measure of U.S. Household Debt Service. *Federal Reserve Bulletin* (October).

Dynan, Karen, and Donald L. Kohn. 2007. The Rise in U.S. Household Indebtedness: Causes and Consequences. Federal Reserve Finance and Economics Discussion Paper 2007-37.

Eastwood, David B., and Cynthia A. Sencindiver. 1984. A Reexamination of Consumer Credit Growth. University of Tennessee, Working Paper.

Edelberg, Wendy. 2003. Risk-Based Pricing of Interest Rates in Household Loan Markets. Federal Reserve Board, Working Paper 2003-62.

——. 2006. Risk-Based Pricing of Interest Rates on Consumer Loans. *Journal of Monetary Economics* (November).

Edelberg, Wendy M., and Jonas D. M. Fisher. 1997. Household Debt. *Chicago Fed Letter* (November).

Efrat, Rafael. 1998. The Moral Appeal of Personal Bankruptcy. *Whittier Law Review* (Fall).

——. 2006. The Evolution of Bankruptcy Stigma. *Theoretical Inquiries in Law*, no. 2.

——. 2008. The Tax Burden and the Propensity of Small-Business Entrepreneurs to File for Bankruptcy. *Hastings Business Law Journal* (Spring).

Eichengreen, Barry. 1984. Mortgage Interest Rates in the Populist Era. *American Economic Review* (December).

Einhorn, Hillel J., and Robin M. Hogarth. 1981. Behavioral Decision Theory: Processes of Judgment and Choice. *Annual Review of Psychology* 32.

Eisenbeis, Robert A. 1978. Problems in Applying Discriminant Analysis in Credit Scoring Models. *Journal of Banking and Finance* (October).

——. 1980. Selection and Disclosure of Reasons for Adverse Action in Credit-Granting Systems. *Federal Reserve Bulletin* (September).

Eisenbeis, Robert A., and Neil B. Murphy. 1974. Interest Rate Ceilings and Consumer Credit Rationing: A Multivariate Analysis of a Survey of Borrowers. *Southern Economic Journal* (July).

Eisenbeis, Robert A., and Paul R. Schweitzer. 1979. *Tie Ins between the Granting of Credit and Sales of Insurance by Bank Holding Companies and Other Lenders.* Washington, DC: Board of Governors of the Federal Reserve System, Staff Study 101.

Ekelund, Robert B., Jr., Robert F. Hebert, and Robert D. Tollison. 1989. An Economic Model of the Medieval Church: Usury as a Form of Rent Seeking. *Journal of Law, Economics, and Organization* (Autumn).

Elliehausen, Gregory. 2005 *Consumer Use of Tax Refund Anticipation Loans.* Washington, DC: Georgetown University, McDonough School of Business, Credit Research Center, Monograph No. 37.

——. 2006. Consumers' Use of High-Price Credit Products: Do They Know What They Are Doing? Indiana State University, Networks Financial Institute, Working Paper 2006-02 (May).

——. 2009. *An Analysis of Consumers' Use of Payday Loans.* Washington, DC: George Washington University, Financial Services Research Program, Monograph No. 41.

Elliehausen, Gregory, and Thomas A. Durkin. 1989. *Theory and Evidence of the Impact of the Equal Credit Opportunity Act: An Agnostic Review of the Literature.* West Lafayette, IN: Purdue University Credit Research Center Monograph Number 28.

Elliehausen, Gregory, and Robert D. Kurtz. 1988. Scale Economies and Compliance Costs for Federal Consumer Credit Regulations. *Journal of Financial Services Research* (January).

Elliehausen, Gregory E., and Edward C. Lawrence. 1990. Discrimination in Consumer Lending. *Review of Economics and Statistics* (February).

——. 2001. *Payday Advance Credit in America: An Analysis of Customer Demand.* Washington, DC: Georgetown University Credit Research Center Monograph Number 35.

Elliehausen, Gregory E., Christopher Lundquist, and Michael E. Staten. 2007. The Impact of Credit Counseling on Subsequent Borrower Behavior. *Journal of Consumer Affairs* (Summer).

Elliehausen, Gregory, and Michael E. Staten. 2004. Regulation of Subprime Mortgage Products: An Analysis of North Carolina's Predatory Lending Law. *Journal of Real Estate Finance and Economics* (December).

Ellis, Dianne. 1998. The Effect of Consumer Interest Rate Deregulation on Credit Card Volumes, Charge-Offs, and the Personal Bankruptcy Rate. *Bank Trends* (March).

Ellison, Ann, and Robert Forster. 2008. The Impact of Interest Rate Ceilings: The Evidence from International Experience and the Implications for Regulation and Consumer Protection in the Credit Market in Australia. London: Policis. Available at http://www.policis.com/pdf/International/Australia%20The%20impact%20of%20interest%20rate%20ceilings%20FINAL%2020080326.pdf, accessed April 18, 2011.

Elul, Ronel, and Narayanan Subramanian. 2002. Forum-Shopping and Personal Bankruptcy. *Journal of Financial Services Research* (June).

Engel, James F., David T. Kollat, and Roger D. Blackwell. 1968. *Consumer Behavior,* 1st ed. New York: Holt, Rinehart and Winston.

Enthoven, Alain. 1957. The Growth of Installment Credit and the Future of Prosperity. *American Economic Review* (December).

Eraslan, Hulya, Wenli Li, and Pierre-Daniel Sarte. 2007. The Anatomy of US Personal Bankruptcy under Chapter 13. Federal Reserve Bank of Philadelphia, Working Paper 07-31.

Erdevig, Eleanor H. 1988. Small States Teach Big Banking Lesson. *Chicago Fed Letter* (June).

Ernst, Keith, John Farris, and Eric Stein. 2002. North Carolina's Subprime Home Loan Market after Predatory Lending Reform. Durham, NC: Center for Responsible Lending.

Eugeni, Francesca. 1993. Consumer Debt and Home Equity Borrowing. *Federal Reserve Bank of Chicago Economic Perspectives* (March–April).

Evans, David S., Robert E. Litan, and Richard Schmalensee. 2011. Economic Analysis of the Effects of the Federal Reserve Board's Proposed Debit Card Interchange Fee Regulations on Consumers and Small Businesses. Boston: Market Platform Dynamics.

Evans, David S., and Richard L. Schmalensee. 1993. *The Economics of the Payment Card Industry*. Cambridge, MA: National Economic Research Associates.

———. 2005. *Paying with Plastic: The Digital Revolution in Buying and Borrowing*, 2nd ed. Cambridge, MA: MIT Press.

Evans, David S. and Joshua D. Wright. 2010. The Effect of the Consumer Financial Protection Agency Act of 2009 on Consumer Credit. *Loyola Consumer Law Review* 22, no. 3.

Fagg, Gary. 1986. *Credit Life and Disability Insurance*. Springfield, OH: CLICO Management.

———. 2001. *The 2001 Fact Book of Credit-Related Insurance*. Chicago: Consumer Credit Insurance Association.

Fagg, Gary, and Keith Nelson. 2008. *Debt Protection Products: A Practical Guide for Lenders*. Dallas: CreditRe Corporation, 2008.

Fair Isaac Companies. 1990. *The Associated Credit Bureaus, Inc., Study on Adverse Information Obsolescence, Phase 1*. San Rafael, CA: Fair Isaac.

Falls, Gregory A., and Debra Drecnik Worden. 1988. Consumer Valuation of Protection from Creditors' Remedies. *Journal of Consumer Affairs* (Summer).

Fama, Eugene F. 1998. Market Efficiency, Long-Term Returns, and Behavioral Finance. *Journal of Financial Economics* (September).

Fama, Eugene F., and Merton K. Miller. 1972. *The Theory of Finance*. New York: Holt, Rinehart, and Winston.

Fand, David I., and Ronald W. Forbes. 1968. On Supply Conditions in Consumer Credit Markets. In *Papers in Quantitative Economics*, edited by J. P. Quirk and A. M. Zarley. Lawrence: University of Kansas Press.

Fay, Scott A., Erik Hurst, and Michelle J. White. 1998. The Bankruptcy Decision: Does Stigma Matter? University of Michigan, Working Paper 98-01, 1998. Available at http://papers.ssrn.com/sol3/papers.cfm?abstract_id=70915.

———. 2002. The Household Bankruptcy Decision. *American Economic Review* (May).

Federal Deposit Insurance Corporation. 2008. *FDIC Study of Bank Overdraft Programs*. Washington, DC: Federal Deposit Insurance Corporation.

Federal Reserve Bank of New York. 1953. The Problem of Consumer Credit. *Monthly Review* (April).

Federal Reserve System. 2008. *The 2007 Federal Reserve Payments Study*. Washington, DC: Federal Reserve System.

———. 2011. *The 2010 Federal Reserve Payments Study*. Washington, DC: Federal Reserve System.

———. 2013. *The 2012 Federal Reserve Payments Study*. Washington, DC: Federal Reserve System.

Federal Trade Commission. 1968. *Economic Report on Installment Credit and Retail Sales Practices of District of Columbia Retailers*. Washington, DC: Government Printing Office.

———. 1974. Unpublished Memorandum to Commissioners from the Division of Special Projects, Bureau of Consumer Protection, in Support of a Trade Regulation Rule to Limit Creditors' Remedies. Washington, DC: Federal Trade Commission Staff.

———. 2004. Consumer Protection Issues in the Credit Counseling Industry. Testimony before the Permanent Subcommittee on Investigations, US Senate Committee on Governmental Affairs.

———. 2010. Keeping Score on Credit Scores: An Overview of Credit Scores, Credit Reports and Their Impact on Consumers, Prepared Statement of the Federal Trade Commission. US House of Representatives, Subcommittee on Financial Institutions and Consumer Credit, Committee on Financial Services (March 24).

———. 2012. Report to Congress under Section 319 of the Fair and Accurate Credit Transactions Act of 2003. Washington, DC: Federal Trade Commission (December).

Fellowes, Matt. 2006. Credit Scores, Reports and Getting Ahead in America. *Survey Series, Metropolitan Policy Program*. Washington, DC: Brookings Institution.

———. 2007. Making Markets an Asset for the Poor. *Harvard Law and Policy Review* 1, no. 2.

Ferguson, C. E. 1969. *Microeconomic Theory*. Homewood, IL: Richard D. Irwin.

Fickenscher, Lisa. 1999. Credit Bureaus Move against Lenders That Withhold Information. *American Banker* (December 30).

Fiedler, Klaus. 1988. The Dependence of the Conjunction Fallacy on Subtle Linguistic Factors. *Psychological Research* (September).

Filkins, Dexter. 2001. In Some Immigrant Enclaves, Loan Shark Is the Local Bank. *New York Times* (April 23).

Financial Publishing. 2012. *Cost of Personal Borrowing in the United States*. Boston: Financial Publishing.

Finley, M. I. 1981. *Economy and Society in Ancient Greece*. London: Chatto & Windus.

Fischer, Gerald C. 1968. *American Banking Structure*. New York: Columbia University Press.

Fishelson-Holstine, Hollis. 2005. Credit Scoring's Role in Increasing Homeownership for Underserved Populations. In *Building Assets, Building Credit*, edited by Nicolas P. Retsinas and Eric S. Belsky. Washington, DC: Brookings Institution.

Fisher, Irving. 1907. *The Rate of Interest: Its Nature, Determination, and Relation to Economic Phenomena*. New York: Macmillan .

———. 1930. *The Theory of Interest*. New York: Macmillan.

Fissel, Gary S., and Tullio Jappelli. 1990. Do Liquidity Constraints Vary over Time? Evidence from Survey and Panel Data: Note. *Journal of Money, Credit and Banking* (May).

Fitch IBCA. 1998. ABCs of Credit Card ABS, Structured Finance Special Report (July 17).

Flannery, Mark, and Katherine Samolyk. 2005. Payday Lending: Do the Costs Justify the Price? Federal Deposit Insurance Corporation, Center for Financial Research, Working Paper 2005-09.

Fleming, Kevin C. 2005. Author's Conclusions Not Supported by Study Results. *Health Affairs eLetters* (February 16).

Flynn, E., and G. Bermant. 2001. The Class of 2000. *American Bankruptcy Law Institute Journal* (October).

Foster, William Trufact. 1941. The Personal Finance Business under Regulation. *Law and Contemporary Problems* (Winter).

Frederick, Shane, George Loewenstein, and Ted O'Donoghue. 2002. Time Discounting and Time Preference: A Critical Review. *Journal of Economic Literature* (June).

Freimer, Marshall, and Myron J. Gordon. 1965. Why Bankers Ration Credit. *Quarterly Journal of Economics* (August).

Friedman, Milton. 1957. Consumer Credit Control as an Instrument of Stabilization Policy. In *Consumer Installment Credit*, Part II, Vol. 2, Board of Governors of the Federal Reserve System. Washington, DC: Board of Governors of the Federal Reserve System.

———. 1970. Defense of Usury. *Newsweek* (April 6).

Friedman, Milton, and Anna Jacobson Schwartz. 1963. *A Monetary History of the United States 1867–1960*. Princeton, NJ: Princeton University Press for the National Bureau of Economic Research.

Furletti, Mark. 2002. An Overview of Credit Card Asset-Backed Securities. Discussion Paper, Federal Reserve Bank of Philadelphia, Payment Cards Center.

———. 2003a. Consumer Credit Counseling: Credit Card Issuers' Perspectives. Discussion Paper, Payment Cards Center, Federal Reserve Bank of Philadelphia.

———. 2003b. Credit Card Pricing Developments and Their Disclosure. Payment Cards Center, Federal Reserve Bank of Philadelphia, Discussion Paper.

Gallert, David J., Walter S. Hilborn, and Geoffrey May. 1932. *Small Loan Legislation: A History of the Regulation of the Business of Lending Small Sums*. New York: Russell Sage Foundation.

Gan, Li, and Tarun Sabarwal. 2005. A Simple Test of Adverse Events and Strategic Timing Theories of Consumer Bankruptcy. National Bureau of Economic Research, Working Paper 11763 (November).

Garcia, Rene, Annamaria Lusardi, and Serena Ng. 1997. Excess Sensitivity and Asymmetries in Consumption: An Empirical Investigation. *Journal of Money, Credit and Banking* (May).

Garner, C. Alan. 1996. Can Measures of the Consumer Debt Burden Reliably Predict an Economic Slowdown? *Federal Reserve Bank of Kansas City Economic Review* (Fourth Quarter).

Garrett, Thomas A. 2007. The Rise in Personal Bankruptcies: The Eighth Federal Reserve District and Beyond. *Federal Reserve Bank of St. Louis Review* (January–February).

Garrett, Thomas A., and Mark W. Nichols. 2008. Do Casinos Export Bankruptcy? *Journal of Socio-Economics* (August).

Garrett, Thomas A., and Howard J. Wall. 2010. Personal-Bankruptcy Cycles. Federal Reserve Bank of St. Louis, Working Paper 2010-010A (March).

Gelpi, Rosa-Maria, and Francois Julien-Labruyere. 2000. *The History of Consumer Credit*. New York: St. Martin's.

General Accounting Office. 2001. *Consumer Finance: College Students and Credit Cards*. Washington, DC: General Accounting Office.

——. 2003. *Consumer Credit: Limited Information Exists on Extent of Credit Report Errors and Their Implication for Consumers*. Washington, DC: General Accounting Office.

Gigerenzer, Gerd. 1994. Why the Distinction between Single-Event Probabilities and Frequencies Is Important for Psychology (and Vice Versa). In *Subjective Probability*, edited by G. Wright and P. Ayton. New York: John Wiley.

——. 1996. On Narrow Norms and Vague Heuristics: A Reply to Kahneman and Tversky. *Psychological Review* (July).

Gigerenzer, Gerd, and Henry Brighton. 2009. Homo Heuristicus: Why Biased Minds Make Better Inferences. *Topics in Cognitive Science* (January).

Gigerenzer, Gerd, and Wolfgang Gaissmaier. 2011. Heuristic Decision Making. *Annual Review of Psychology* (January).

Gigerenzer, Gerd, and Daniel G. Goldstein. 1999. Betting on One Good Reason: The Take the Best Heuristic. In *Simple Heuristics That Make Us Smart*, edited by Gerd Gigerenzer and Peter M. Todd. New York: Oxford University Press.

——. 2011. The Recognition Heuristic: A Decade of Research. *Judgment and Decision Making* (January).

Gigerenzer, Gerd, Wolfgang Hell, and Hartmut Blank. 1988. Presentation and Content: The Use of Base Rates as a Continuous Variable. *Journal of Experimental Psychology: Human Perception and Performance* (August).

Gigerenzer, Gerd, and Ulrich Hoffrage. 1995. How to Improve Bayesian Reasoning without Instruction: Frequency Formats. *Psychological Review* (October).

Gigerenzer, Gerd, and Thomas Sturm. 2012. How (Far) Can Rationality Be Naturalized? *Synthese* (July).

Godwin, Deborah. 1997. Dynamics of Households' Income, Debt, and Attitudes toward Credit. *Journal of Consumer Affairs* (Winter).

Golann, Dwight, et al. 1998. Re-examining Truth in Lending: Do Borrowers Actually Use Consumer Disclosures? *Personal Finance Law Quarterly.Report* (Winter).

Gold, Barry A., and Elizabeth A. Donahue. 1982. Health Care Costs and Personal Bankruptcy. *Journal of Health Politics, Policy, and Law* (Fall).

Goldstein, Daniel G., and Gerd Gigerenzer. 1999. The Recognition Heuristic: How Ignorance Makes Us Smart. In *Simple Heuristics That Make Us Smart*, edited by Gerd Gigerenzer and Peter M Todd. New York: Oxford University Press.

Government Accountability Office. 2006. *Credit Cards Increased Complexity in Rates and Fees Heightens Need for More Effective Disclosures to Consumers, Report to the Ranking Minority Member, Permanent Subcommittee on Investigations, Committee on Homeland Security and Governmental Affairs, US Senate*. Washington, DC: Government Accountability Office.

——. 2007. *Bankruptcy Reform: Value of Credit Counseling Requirement Is Not Clear*. Washington, DC: Government Accountability Office Report 07-203 (April).

——. 2011. *Credit Cards: Consumer Costs for Debt Protection Products Can Be Substantial Relative to Benefits but Are Not a Focus of Regulatory Oversight*. Washington, DC: Government Accountability Office.

Gramlich, Edward M. 1999. A Policy in Lampman's Tradition: The Community Reinvestment Act. Remarks at the Second Annual Robert J. Lampman Memorial Lecture, University of Wisconsin, Madison (June 16). Available at http://www.federalreserve.gov/boarddocs/speeches/1999/19990616.htm.

Grant, Charles. 2003. Evidence on the Effect of US Consumer Bankruptcy Exemption. European University Institute, Working Paper 2003/19.

Grant, Charles, and Winfried Koeniger. 2009. Redistributive Taxation and Personal Bankruptcy in U.S. States. *Journal of Law and Economics* (August).

Green, Leonard, and Joel Myerson. 1996. Exponential versus Hyperbolic Discounting of Delayed Outcomes: Risk and Waiting Time. *American Zoologist* (September).

Greenspan, Alan. 2004. Understanding Household Debt Obligations. Remarks at the Credit Union National Association 2004 Governmental Affairs Conference, Washington, DC.

Greer, Douglas F. 1973. An Empirical Analysis of the Personal Loan Market. In *Technical Studies of the National Commission on Consumer Finance*, Vol. 4. Washington, DC: Government Printing Office.

———. 1974a. *Creditors' Remedies and Contract Provisions: An Economic and Legal Analysis of Consumer Credit Collection.* Technical Studies, Vol. V. Washington DC: National Commission on Consumer Finance.

———. 1974b. Rate Ceilings, Market Structure, and the Supply of Finance Company Personal Loans. *Journal of Finance* (December).

———. 1975. Rate Ceilings and Loan Turndowns. *Journal of Finance* (December).

Griffin, Mary, and Birny Birnbaum. 1999. *Credit Insurance: The $2 Billion a Year Rip Off.* Washington, DC: Consumers Union.

Griffiths, Thomas L., and Joshua B. Tenenbaum. 2006. Optimal Predictions in Everyday Cognition. *Psychological Science* (September).

Groenfeldt, Tom. 2000. Customer Data, Right Here, Right Now. *U.S. Banker* (May).

Gropp, Reint, John Karl Scholz, and Michelle J. White. 1997. Personal Bankruptcy and Credit Supply and Demand. *Quarterly Journal of Economics* (February).

Gross, David B., and Nicholas S. Souleles. 2002. Do Liquidity Constraints and Interest Rates Matter for Consumer Behavior? Evidence from Credit Card Data. *Quarterly Journal of Economics* (February).

Grow, Brian, and Keith Epstein. 2007. The Poverty Business. *Business Week* (May 21).

Gruber, Gerald H. 1992. Recovering Hidden Values in Retail Lease Portfolios. *Journal of Retail Banking* (Fall).

Gruber, Jonathan, and Helen Levy. 2009. The Evolution of Medical Spending Risk. *Journal of Economic Perspectives* (Fall).

Gruber, Jonathan, and Aaron Yelowitz. 1999. Public Health Insurance and Private Savings. *Journal of Political Economy* 107 (December).

Gurley, John G. and Edward S. Shaw. 1960. *Money in a Theory of Finance.* Washington: Brookings Institution.

Gust, Christopher and Jaime Marquez. 2004. International Comparisons of Productivity Growth: The Role of Information Technology and Regulatory Practices. *Labor Economics* (February).

Haberler, Gottfried. 1942. *Consumer Installment Credit and Economic Fluctuations.* New York: National Bureau of Economic Research.

Hall, Robert E., and Frederic S. Mishkin. 1982. The Sensitivity of Consumption to Transitory Income: Estimates from Panel Data on Households. *Econometrica* (March).

Haller, Mark H., and John V. Alviti. 1977. Loansharking in American Cities: Historical Analysis of a Marginal Enterprise. *American Journal of Legal History* (April).

Ham, Arthur. 1912. *The Campaign against the Loan Shark.* New York: Russell Sage Foundation, Division of Remedial Loans.

Hammond, Bray. 1957. *Banks and Politics in America from the Revolution to the Civil War.* Princeton, NJ: Princeton University Press.

Han, Song, B. Keys, and Geng Li. 2012. Unsecured Credit Supply over the Credit Cycle. Federal Reserve Board, Working Paper (July).

Han, Song, and Geng Li. 2011. Household Borrowing after Personal Bankruptcy. *Journal of Money, Credit and Banking* (March–April).

Han, Song, and Wenli Li. 2007. Fresh Start or Head Start? The Effects of Filing for Personal Bankruptcy on Work Effort. *Journal of Financial Services Research* (June).

Hand, David J., and W. E. Henley, 1997. Statistical Classification Methods in Consumer Credit. *Journal of the Royal Statistical Society*, Series A.

Harris, Elizabeth A. 2010. Walmart Tries Again for New York City Store. *New York Times* (December 12).

Harris, Maury, and Karen Bradley. 1977. Are Households Financially Overextended? *Federal Reserve Bank of New York Quarterly Review* (Autumn).

Harvey, Keith D., and Peter J. Nigro. 2004. Do Predatory Lending Laws Influence Mortgage Lending? An Analysis of the North Carolina Predatory Lending Law. *Journal of Real Estate Finance and Economics* (December).

Hartarska, Valentina, and Claudio Gonzalez-Vega. 2005. Credit Counseling and Mortgage Termination by Low-Income Households. *Journal of Real Estate Finance and Economics* 30, no. 3.

Hayhoe, Celia Ray. 2002. Comparison of Affective Credit Attitude Scores and Credit Use of College Students at Two Points in Time. *Journal of Family and Consumer Sciences* (January).

Hayhoe, Celia Ray, Lauren Leach, and Pamela R. Turner. 1999. Discriminating the Number of Credit Cards Held by College Students Using Credit and Money Attitudes. *Journal of Economic Psychology* (December).

Hayhoe, Celia Ray, Lauren Leach, Pamela R. Turner, Marilyn J. Bruin, and Frances C. Lawrence. 2000. Differences in Spending Habits and Credit Use of College Students. *Journal of Consumer Affairs* (Summer).

Heckman, James J. 1979. Sample Selection Bias as Specification Error. *Econometrica* (January).

———. 1998. Detecting Discrimination. *Journal of Economic Perspectives* (Spring).

Heriot, Gail L. 2005. Misdiagnosis: A Comment on Illness and Injury as Contributors to Bankruptcy and the Media Publicity Surrounding It. *Texas Review of Law and Politics* 10, no. 1 (Fall).

Hertwig, Ralph, and Gerd Gigerenzer. 1993. Frequency and Single-Event Judgments. Unpublished manuscript.

———. 1999. The "Conjunction Fallacy" Revisited: How Intelligent Inferences Look Like Reasoning Errors. *Journal of Behavioral Decision Making* (December).

Hilder, David B., and Peter Pae. 1991. Rivalry Rages among Big Credit Cards, *Wall Street Journal* (May 3): B1.

Himmelstein, David U., Elizabeth Warren, Deborah Thorne, and Steffie J. Woolhandler. 2005. Illness and Injury as Contributors to Bankruptcy. *Health Affairs* (February 8).

Himmelstein, David U., Deborah Thorne, Elizabeth Warren, and Steffie Woolhandler. 2009. Medical Bankruptcy in the United States, 2007: Results of a National Study. *American Journal of Medicine* (August).

Hirad, Abdighani, and Peter M. Zorn. 2002. Pre-Purchase Homeownership Counseling: A Little Knowledge Is a Good Thing. In *Low-Income Homeownership: Examining the Unexamined Goal*, edited by Nicolas P. Retsinas and Eric S. Belsky. Washington: Brookings Institution.

Hirshleifer, Jack. 1958. On the Optimal Investment Decision. *Journal of Political Economy* (August).

Ho, Giang, and Anthony Pennington-Cross. 2005. The Impact of Local Predatory Lending Laws. Federal Reserve Bank of St. Louis, Working Paper 2005-049B.

——. 2006. The Impact of Local Predatory Lending Laws on the Flow of Subprime Credit. *Journal of Urban Economics* (September).

Hochstein, Marc. 2012. Blog of the Day: Tax-Preparation Lending Lives On, as Does Regulatory Arbritrage. *American Banker* (December 16).

Hodgman, Donald R. 1960. Credit Risk and Credit Rationing. *Quarterly Journal of Economics* (May).

Homer, Sidney, and Richard E. Sylla. 1996. *A History of Interest Rates*, 3rd ed. New Brunswick, NJ: Rutgers University Press.

Horack, Benjamin. S. 1941. A Survey of the General Usury Laws. *Law and Contemporary Problems* (Winter).

Horwitz, Jeff. 2012. Regulators Hasten Demise of Tax Refund Loans. *American Banker* (December 28).

Horwitz, Morton. 1977. *The Transformation of American Law: 1780–1860*. Cambridge, MA: Harvard University Press.

Howard, John A., and Jagdish N. Sheth. 1969. *The Theory of Buyer Behavior*. New York: John Wiley.

Hsia, David C. 1977. The Effects Test: New Directions. *Santa Clara Law Review* (Fall).

Hubachek, F. B. 1941. The Development of Regulatory Small Loan Laws. *Law & Contemporary Problems* (Winter).

Hubbard, Charles L., ed. 1973. *Consumer Credit Life and Disability Insurance*. Athens: Ohio University College of Business Administration.

Hubbard, R. Glenn, Jonathan Skinner, and Stephen P. Zeldes. 1995. Precautionary Saving and Social Insurance, *Journal of Political Economy* 103 (April).

Huber, Elizabeth A., and Thomas B. Hudson. 1998. Road Testing the New Regulation M. *Business Lawyer* (May).

Huber, Joel. 1976. *Consumer Perceptions of Credit Insurance on Retail Purchases*. West Lafayette, IN: Purdue University Credit Research Center.

Hunt, Robert M. 2005. Whither Consumer Credit Counseling? *Federal Reserve Bank of Philadelphia Business Review* (Quarter 4).

——. 2006. Development and Regulations of Consumer Credit Reporting in the United States. In *The Economics of Consumer Credit*, edited by Guiseppe Bertola, Richard Disney, and Charles Grant. Cambridge MA: MIT Press.

Hunter, Helen Manning. 1966. A Behavioral Model of the Long Run Growth of Aggregate Consumer Credit in the United States. *Review of Economics and Statistics* (May).

Hynes, Richard M. 2006. Bankruptcy and State Collections: The Case of the Missing Garnishments. *Cornell Law Review* (March).

Hynes, Richard M., Anup Malani, and Eric A. Posner. 2004. The Political Economy of Property Exemption Laws. *Journal of Law and Economics* (April).

Hynes, Richard, and Eric A. Posner. 2002. The Law and Economics of Consumer Finance. *American Law and Economics Review* (Spring).

Jackson, Thomas H. 1985. The Fresh-Start Policy in Bankruptcy Law. *Harvard Law Review* (May).

Jacoby, Melissa B., Teresa A. Sullivan, and Elizabeth Warren. 2001. Rethinking the Debates over Health Care Financing: Evidence from the Bankruptcy Courts. *New York University Law Review* (May).

Jacoby, Melissa B., and Elizabeth Warren. 2006. Beyond Hospital Misbehavior: An Alternative Account of Medical-Related Financial Distress. *Northwestern University Law Review* (Winter).

Jaffee, Dwight M. 1972. A Theory and Test of Credit Rationing: Further Notes. *American Economic Review* (June).

Jaffee, Dwight M., and Franco Modigliani. 1969. A Theory and Test of Credit Rationing. *American Economic Review* (December).

——. 1976. A Theory and Test of Credit Rationing: Reply. *American Economic Review* (December).

Jaffee, Dwight M., and Thomas Russell. 1976. Imperfect Information, Uncertainty, and Credit Rationing. *Quarterly Journal of Economics* (November).

Jappelli, Tullio, and Marco Pagano. 1989. Consumption and Capital Market Imperfections: An International Comparison. *American Economic Review* (December).

——. 2002. Information Sharing, Lending and Defaults: Cross-Country Evidence. *Journal of Banking and Finance* (October).

——. 2006. The Role and Effects of Credit Information Sharing. In *The Economics of Consumer Credit*, edited by Guiseppe Bertola, Richard Disney, and Charles Grant. Cambridge MA: MIT Press.

Jimenez, Dalie. 2009. The Distribution of Assets in Consumer Chapter 7 Bankruptcy Cases. *American Bankruptcy Law Journal* (Fall).

Jobst, Andreas A. 2005. Asset Securitization as a Risk Management and Funding Tool: What Does It Hold in Store for SMES? Unpublished paper, available at http:// ssrn.com/abstract=700262.

Johnson, Andrew. 2010. Reg. Order Forces HSBC, H&R Block to Stop Offering Refund Anticipation Loans. *American Banker* (December 27).

Johnson, Kathleen W. 2002. Consumer Loan Securitization. In *The Impact of Public Policy on Consumer Credit*, edited by Thomas A. Durkin and Michael E. Staten. Boston: Kluwer Academic.

——. 2005. Recent Developments in the Credit Card Market and the Financial Obligations Ratio. *Federal Reserve Bulletin* (Autumn).

Johnson, Kathleen W., and Geng Li. 2007. Do High Debt Payments Hinder Household Consumption Smoothing? Federal Reserve Finance and Economics Discussion Paper 2007-52.

——. 2008. The Debt to Income Ratio as an Indicator of Borrowing Constraints: Evidence from Household Surveys. Board of Governors of the Federal Reserve System, Working Paper.

Johnson, Robert W. 1968. Economic Rationale of the Uniform Consumer Credit Code. *Journal of Finance* (May).

——. 1978. *Cost/Benefit Analysis of Creditors' Remedies: An Evaluation of the Memorandum Prepared by the Division of Special Projects, Bureau of Consumer Protection, Federal Trade Commission, in Support of a Trade Regulation Rule to Limit Creditors' Remedies.* West Lafayette, IN: Purdue University Credit Research Center, Monograph No. 12.

Johnson, Robert W., and Dixie P. Johnson. 1998. *Pawnbroking in the U.S.: A Profile of Customers.* Georgetown University Credit Research Center, Monograph No. 34.

Johnson, Robert W., and A. Charlene Sullivan. 1981. Segmentation of the Consumer Loan Market. *Journal of Retail Banking* (September).

Johnston, Jack. 1972. *Econometric Methods*, 2nd ed. New York: McGraw-Hill.

Jones, Christian T. 1989. *Summary of Consumer Credit Laws and Rates*. Washington, DC: American Financial Services Association.

Jones, Edith H., and Todd J. Zywicki. 1999. It's Time for Means-Testing. *Brigham Young University Law Review*, no. 1.

Jones, Norman. 2008. Usury. In EH.Net Encyclopedia, edited by Robert Whaples (February 10). Available at http://eh.net/encyclopedia/article/jones.usury, accessed April 18, 2011.

Juster, F. Thomas. 1966. *Household Capital Formation 1897–1962*. New York: National Bureau of Economic Research.

Juster, F. Thomas, and Robert P. Shay. 1964. *Consumer Sensitivity to Finance Rates: An Empirical and Analytical Investigation*. New York: National Bureau of Economic Research, Occasional Paper 88.

Kahneman, Daniel, Jack L. Knetsch, and Richard H. Thaler. 1990. Experimental Tests of the Endowment Effect and the Coase Theorem. *Journal of Political Economy* (December).

———. 1991. Anomolies: The Endowment Effect, Loss Aversion, and Status Quo Bias. *Journal of Economic Perspectives* (Winter).

Kahneman, Daniel, and Amos Tversky. 1973. Psychology of Prediction. *Psychological Review* (July).

———. 1979. Prospect Theory: An Analysis of Decision under Uncertainty. *Econometrica* (March).

———. 1982. Evidential Impact of Base Rates. In *Judgment under Uncertainty: Heuristics and Biases*, edited by Daniel Kahneman, Paul Slovic, and Amos Tversky. Cambridge, UK: Cambridge University Press.

Karst, Kenneth L. 1966. The Files: Legal Controls over the Accuracy and Accessibility of Stored Personal Data. *Law and Contemporary Problems* (Spring).

Karlan, Dean S., and Jonathan Zinman. 2010. Expanding Credit Access: Using Randomized Supply Decisions to Estimate Impacts. *Review of Financial Studies* (January).

Katona, George. 1975. *Psychological Economics*. New York: Elsevier Scientific.

Katona, George, et al. 1960–1970. *The 1961 [or other year] Survey of Consumer Finances*. Ann Arbor, MI: Survey Research Center.

Katona, George, and Eva Mueller. 1954. A Study in Purchase Decisions. In *Consumer Behavior*, edited by L. Clark. New York: New York University Press, 1954.

Kawaja, Michael. 1971. *The Regulation of the Consumer Finance Industry: A Case Study of Rate Ceilings and Loan Limits in New York State*. New York: Columbia University Graduate School of Business, Studies in Consumer Credit, No. 3.

Kennickell, Arthur B., and Janice Shack-Marquez. 1992. Changes in Family Finances from 1983 to 1989: Evidence from the Survey of Consumer Finances. *Federal Reserve Bulletin* (January).

Kennickell, Arthur B., and Martha Starr-McCluer. 1994. Changes in Family Finances from 1989 to 1992: Evidence from the Survey of Consumer Finances. *Federal Reserve Bulletin* (October).

Kennickell, Arthur B., Martha Starr-McCluer, and Annika E. Sunden. 1997. Family Finances in the U.S.: Recent Evidence from the Survey of Consumer Finances. *Federal Reserve Bulletin* (January).

Kennickell, Arthur B., Martha Starr-McCluer, and Brian J. Surette. 2000. Recent Changes in U.S. Family Finances: Results from the 1998 Survey of Consumer Finances. *Federal Reserve Bulletin* (January).

Kim, Jinhee, E. Thomas Garman, and Benoit Sorhaindo. 2005. Study Finds Positive Financial Behaviors Increased: Credit Counseling and Debt Management Effective. *Journal of Family and Consumer Sciences* 97, no. 2: 35–39.

Kisselgoff, Avram. 1952. *Factors Affecting Demand for Consumer Installment Sales Credit.* New York: National Bureau of Economic Research, Technical Paper 7.

Klein, Daniel B. 1992. Promise Keeping in the Great Society: A Model of Credit Information Sharing. *Economics and Politics* (July).

Kleiner, Morris M., and Richard M. Todd. 2009. Mortgage Broker Regulations That Matter: Analyzing Earnings, Employment, and Outcomes for Consumers. In *Studies of Labor Market Intermediation,* edited by David H. Autor. Chicago: University of Chicago Press.

Knittel, Christopher R., and Victor Stango. 2003. Price Ceilings as Focal Points for Tacit Collusion: Evidence from Credit Cards. *American Economic Review* (December).

Kosobud, Richard F., and James N. Morgan. 1964. *Consumer Behavior of Individual Families over Two and Three Years.* Ann Arbor: University of Michigan Survey Research Center Monograph 36.

Kowalewski, Kim J. 1982. Personal Bankruptcy: Theory and Evidence. *Federal Reserve Bank of Cleveland Economic Review* (Spring).

Krueger, Dirk, and Fabrizio Perri. 2002. Does Income Inequality Lead to Consumption Inequality? National Bureau of Economic Research, Working Paper 9292.

Krynski, Tevye R., and Joshua B. Tenenbaum. 2003. The Role of Causal Models in Reasoning under Uncertainty. In *Proceedings of the 25th Annual Conference of the Cognitive Science Society.* Boston.

Kwast, Myron L., Martha Starr-McCluer, and John D. Wolken. 1997. Market Definition and the Analysis of Antitrust in Banking. *Antitrust Bulletin* (Winter).

Lacko, James M., Signe-Mary McKernan, and Manoj Hastak. 2000. *Survey of Rent to Own Customers.* Washington, DC: Federal Trade Commission.

LaCour-Little, Michael. 2001. A Note on Identification of Discrimination in Mortgage Lending. *Real Estate Economics* (Summer).

Laibson, David. 1997. Golden Eggs and Hyperbolic Discounting. *Quarterly Journal of Economics* (May).

Lampe, Donald C., Fred H. Miller, and Alvin C. Harrell. 2009. Introduction to the 2009 Annual Survey of Consumer Financial Services Law. *Business Lawyer* (February).

Lancaster, Kelvin J. 1966. A New Approach to Consumer Theory. *Journal of Political Economy* (April).

Landers, Jonathan M., and Ralph J. Rohner. 1979. A Functional Analysis of Truth in Lending. *UCLA Law Review* (April).

Lansing, John B., E. Scott Maynes, and Mordechai Kreinin. 1957. Factors Associated with the Use of Consumer Credit. In *Consumer Installment Credit,* Board of Governors of the Federal Reserve System, Vol. I, Part II. Washington, DC: Government Printing Office.

Lawless, Robert M., Angela K. Littwin, Katherine M. Porter, John A. E. Pottow, Deborah K. Thorne, and Elizabeth Warren. 2008. Did Bankruptcy Reform Fail? An Empirical Study of Consumer Debtors. *American Bankruptcy Law Journal* (Summer).

——. 2009. Interpreting Data: A Reply to Professor Pardo. *American Bankruptcy Law Journal* (Winter).

Lawrence, Edward C., and Gregory Elliehausen. 2008. A Comparative Analysis of Payday Loan Customers. *Contemporary Economic Policy* (April).

Lehnert, Andreas, and Dean Maki. 2002. Consumption, Debt, and Portfolio Choice: Testing the Effect of Bankruptcy Law. Federal Reserve Board, Working Paper 2002-14.

Lee, Alyssa Stewart, Ann Schnare, Michael A. Turner, Patrick D. Walker, and Robin Varghese. 2006. *Give Credit Where Credit Is Due: Increasing Access to Affordable Mainstream Credit Using Alternative Data.* Washington, DC: Political and Economic Research Council and Brookings Institution Urban Markets Initiative.

Lee, Donghoon, and Wilbert van der Klaauw. 2010. An Introduction to the FRBNY Consumer Credit Panel. Federal Reserve Bank of New York Staff Report No. 479.

Leff, Arthur A. 1970. Injury, Ignorance and Spite—The Dynamics of Coercive Collection. *Yale Law Journal* (November).

Lefgren, Lars, and Frank McIntyre. 2009. Explaining the Puzzle of Cross-State Differences in Bankruptcy Rates. *Journal of Law and Economics* (May).

Lemieux, Jeff. 2005. A Cautionary Note on the Number of Health-Related Bankruptcies. *Health Affairs eLetters* (April 13).

Letsou, Peter V. 1995. The Political Economy of Consumer Credit Regulation. *Emory Law Journal* (Spring).

Lewis, Edward M. 1992. *An Introduction to Credit Scoring.* San Rafael, CA: Fair Isaac.

Lexis Nexis Risk Solutions. 2012. Successfully Lend to the Underbanked Consumer. Available at http://insights.lexisnexis.com/creditrisk/wp-content/uploads/2012/04/Successfully-Lend-to-the-Underbanked.pdf

Li, Wenli, and Pierre-Daniel G. Sarte. 2006. U.S. Consumer Bankruptcy Choice: The Importance of General Equilibrium Effects. *Journal of Monetary Economics* (April).

Lin, Emily Y., and Michelle J. White. 2001. Bankruptcy and the Market for Mortgage and Home Improvement Loans. *Journal of Urban Economics* (July).

Lindley, J. T., P. Rudolph, and E. B. Selby. 1989. Credit Card Possession and Use: Changes over Time. *Journal of Economics and Business* (May).

Lindley, J. T., E. B. Selby, and J. D. Jackson. 1984. Racial Discrimination in the Provision of Financial Services. *American Economic Review* (September).

Livshits, Igor, James MacGee, and Michele Tertilt. 2010. Accounting for the Rise in Consumer Bankruptcies. *American Economic Journal* (April).

Lochner, Lance, and Alexander Monge-Naranjo. 2011. Credit Constraints in Education. National Bureau of Economic Research, Working Paper (September).

Locke, John. 1691. *Some Considerations of the Consequences of the Lowering of Interest, and Raising the Value of Money.* London: Awnsham and John Churchill.

Long, Michael S., and John J. McConnell. 1977. Credit Scoring System Aids Second Mortgage Makers. *Mortgage Banker* (July).

Loomes, Graham, Chris Starmer, and Robert Sugden. 2003. Do Anomalies Disappear in Repeated Markets? *Economic Journal* (March).

Loonin, Deanne, and Travis Plunkett. 2003. *Credit Counseling in Crisis: The Impact on Consumers of Funding Cuts, Higher Fees and Aggressive New Market Entrants.* Washington, DC: Consumer Federation of America.

Lopes, Paula. 2003. Credit Card Debt and Default over the Life Cycle. Financial Markets Group, London School of Economics, Working Paper.

Lucas, Peter. 2002. Score Updates. *Collections and Credit Risk* (October).

Luckett, Charles A. 1990. Consumer Debt and the Household Balance Sheet. Unpublished paper presented to the Annual Meeting of the National Association of Business Economists (September).

———. 1994. Consumer Credit Measurement Issues. Unpublished discussion memorandum, Board of Governors of the Federal Reserve System, Division of Research and Statistics (April).

———. 2002. Personal Bankruptcies. In *The Impact of Public Policy on Consumer Credit*, edited by Thomas A. Durkin and Michael E. Staten. Boston: Kluwer Academic.

Luckett, Charles A., and James D. August. 1985. The Growth of Consumer Debt. *Federal Reserve Bulletin* (May).

Luther, J. Wade. 1999. Overview of Asset-Backed Securities. Atlanta: Munich American Reassurance Company.

Lynch, Gene C. 1968. Consumer Credit at Ten Per Cent Simple: The Arkansas Case. *Illinois Law Forum* (Winter).

Lyons, Angela C., Tommye White, and Shawn Howard. 2008. *The Effect of Bankruptcy Counseling and Education on Debtors' Financial Well-Being: Evidence from the Front Lines*. Houston: Money Management International.

Lyons, Fran, and Lee Allen. 1990. Importance of Aged Public Record Derogatory Information. *Management Decision Systems Group Dialogue* (Fall).

Maddala, G. S. 1983. *Limited Dependent and Qualitative Variables in Econometrics*. New York: Cambridge University Press.

Maki, Dean. 2002. The Growth of Consumer Credit and the Household Sector Debt Burden. In *The Impact of Public Policy on Consumer Credit*, edited by Thomas A. Durkin and Michael E. Staten. Boston: Kluwer Academic.

Malkiel, Burton G. 2003. The Efficient Market Hypothesis and Its Critics. *Journal of Economic Perspectives* (Winter).

Mandell, Lewis. 1990. *The Credit Card Industry: A History*. Boston: Twayne.

Mann, Ronald J. 2006. *Charging Ahead: The Growth and Regulation of Payment Card Markets*. New York: Cambridge University Press.

———. 2013. Assessing the Optimism of Payday Loan Borrowers. Columbia University School of Law, Center for Law and Economic Studies, Working Paper 443 (March 12).

Mann, Ronald J., and Katherine Porter. 2010. Saving Up for Bankruptcy. *Georgetown Law Journal* (January).

Mannering, Fred, Clifford Winston, and William Starkey. 1999. An Exploratory Analysis of Automobile Leasing in the United States. University of Washington, Working Paper (January).

Markowitz, Harry. 1952. Portfolio Selection. *Journal of Finance* (March).

Marshall, Alfred. 1920. *Principles of Economics*, 8th ed. London: Macmillan.

Marshall, J. 1979. Discrimination in Consumer Credit. In *The Costs and Benefits of Public Regulation of Consumer Financial Services*, edited by Arnold A. Heggestad and John J. Mingo. Cambridge, MA: ABT.

Mathur, Aparna. 2005. Medical Bills and Bankruptcy Filings. American Enterprise Institute, Working Paper (July 19).

Mayer, Robert. 2004. Payday Lending and Personal Bankruptcy. *Consumer Interests Annual*.

Mays, Elizabeth. 2004. *Credit Scoring for Risk Managers: The Handbook for Lenders*. Mason, OH: Thomson/Southwestern.

McAlister. E. Ray and Edward DeSpain. 1974. *An Empirical Analysis of Retail Revolving Credit*. West Lafayette, IN: Purdue University Credit Research Center, Monograph 1.

McCathren, Randall R., and Ronald S. Loshin. 1991. *Automobile Lending and Leasing Manual*. Boston: Warren, Gorham, and Lamont.

McKinley, Vern. 1997. Ballooning Bankruptcies: Issuing Blame for the Explosive Growth. *Regulation* (Fall).

McNamara, Robert M., Jr. 1973. The Fair Credit Reporting Act: A Legislative Overview. *Journal of Public Law* (Fall).

Melzer, Brian T. 2011. The Real Costs of Credit Access: Evidence from the Payday Loan Market. *Quarterly Journal of Economics* (February).

Mester, Loretta J. 1987. A Multiproduct Cost Study of Savings and Loans. *Journal of Finance* (June).

———. 1997. What's the Point of Scoring? *Federal Reserve Bank of Philadelphia Business Review* (September–October).

Michelman, Irving S. 1966. *Consumer Finance: A Case Study in American Business*. New York: Frederick Fell.

Milde, H. 1974. Informationskosten, Anpassungkosten und die Theorie des Kreditmarktes. *Kredit und Kapital*, no. 7.

Mill, John Stuart. *Principles of Political Economy*. 1909. London: Longmans, Green.

Miller, Earl K., and Jonathan D. Cohen. 2001. An Integrative Theory of Prefrontal Cortex Function. *Annual Review of Neuroscience*.

Miller, Margaret J. 2003. Credit Reporting Systems around the Globe: The State of the Art in Public Credit Registries and Private Credit Reporting Firms. In *Credit Reporting Systems and the International Economy*, edited by Margaret J. Miller. Cambridge, MA: MIT Press.

Miller, Merton H. 1962. Credit Risk and Credit Rationing: Further Comment. *Quarterly Journal of Economics* (August).

Miller, Michelle M. 2012. Social Networks and Personal Bankruptcy. Paper presented at Seventh Annual Conference on Empirical Legal Studies Paper, Palo Alto, CA (June 20) http://papers.ssrn.com/sol3/papers.cfm?abstract_id=2088192.

Miller, Rae-Ann, Susan Burhouse, Luke Reynolds, and Aileen G. Sampson. 2010. A Template for Success: The FDIC's Small Dollar Loan Pilot Program. *FDIC Quarterly* 2, no. 2.

Miller, Stephen E. 1995. Economics of Automobile Leasing: The Call Option Value. *Journal of Consumer Affairs* (Summer).

Milstein, Abby Sniderman, and Bruce C. Ratner. 1981. Consumer Credit Counseling Service: A Consumer-Oriented View. *New York University Law Review* (November–December).

Miner, Jerry. 1960. Consumer Debt: An Inter Temporal Cross Section Analysis. In *Consumption and Saving*, Vol. II, edited by Irwin Friend and R. Jones. Philadelphia: University of Pennsylvania Press.

Morgan, Donald R., and Michael R. Strain. 2008. Payday Holiday: How Households Fare after Payday Credit Bans. Federal Reserve Bank of New York, Staff Report no. 309 (February).

Morgan, Donald R., Michael R. Strain, and Ihab Seblani. 2012. How Payday Credit Access Affects Overdrafts and Other Outcomes. *Journal of Money, Credit, and Banking* (March–April).

Mors, Wallace. 1965. *Consumer Credit Finance Charges*. New York: National Bureau of Economic Research.

Morse, Adair. 2011. Payday Lenders: Heroes or Villains? *Journal of Financial Economics* (October).

Moss, David A., and Gibbs A. Johnson. 1999. The Rise of Consumer Bankruptcy: Evolution, Revolution, or Both? *American Bankruptcy Law Journal* (Spring).

Mossburg, Marta H. 2010. New York Should Learn to Love Walmart: The Low Cost Retailer Is Good for the Nation's Priciest City. *New York Daily News* (May 2).

Muolo, Paul, and Mathew Padilla. 2008. *Chain of Blame*. New York: John Wiley.

Murphy, Neil B. 1980. Economies of Scale in the Cost of Compliance with Consumer Protection Laws: The Case of the Implementation of the Equal Credit Opportunity Act. *Journal of Bank Research* (Winter).

Murray, Alan P. 1997. Debt and "The" Consumer. *Business Economics* (April).

Musto, David K. 2004. What Happens When Information Leaves a Market? Evidence from Post-Bankruptcy Consumers. *Journal of Business* (October).

Myers, James H., and Warren Cordner. 1957. Increase Credit Operation Profits. *Credit World* (February).

Myers, James H., and Edward W. Forgy. 1963. The Development of Numerical Credit Evaluation Systems. *American Statistical Association Journal* (September).

Myers, Stewart C., David A. Dill, and Alberto J. Bautista. 1976. Valuation of Financial Lease Contracts. *Journal of Finance* (June).

Nadler, Marcus. 1957. For Standby Consumer Credit Control. In *Consumer Installment Credit*, Part II, Vol. 2, Board of Governors of the Federal Reserve System. Washington, DC: Board of Governors of the Federal Reserve System.

National Association of State Public Interest Research Groups. 2004. *Mistakes Do Happen: A Look at Errors in Consumer Credit Reports*. Washington, DC: National Association of State Public Interest Research Groups.

National Commission on Consumer Finance. 1972. *Consumer Credit in the United States: The Report of the National Commission on Consumer Finance*. Washington, DC: Government Printing Office.

National Foundation for Credit Counseling. 2012. The 2012 Consumer Financial Literacy Survey. Prepared by Harris Interactive.

National Pawnbrokers Association. 2013. *Pawn Industry Overview*. Keller, TX: National Pawnbrokers Association.

Navarro-Martinez, Daniel, Linda Court Salisbury, Katherine N. Lemon, Neil Stewart, William J. Matthews, and Adam J. L. Harris. 2011. Minimum Required Payment and Supplemental Information Disclosure Effects on Consumer Debt Repayment Decisions. *Journal of Marketing Research* 48, special issue.

Neifeld, M. R. 1961. *Neifeld's Manual on Consumer Credit*. Easton, PA: Mack.

Nellie Mae. 2005. *Undergraduate Students and Credit Cards in 2004*. Braintree, MA: Nellie Mae.

Nelson, Benjamin. 1969. *The Idea of Usury: From Tribal Brotherhood to Universal Otherhood*. Chicago: University of Chicago Press.

Nelson, Jon P. 2000. Consumer Bankruptcies and the Bankruptcy Reform Act: A Time-Series Intervention Analysis, 1960–1997. *Journal of Financial Services Research* (August).

Nevin, J. R., and G. A. Churchill, Jr. 1979. The Equal Credit Opportunity Act: An Evaluation. *Journal of Marketing* (Spring).

New America Foundation. 2011. Federal Student Loan Programs—History (May 10). Available at http://febp.newamerica.net/background-analysis/federal-student-loan-programs-history.

Newlyn, W. T. 1962. *Theory of Money*. Oxford: Clarendon.

Nicosia, Francesco M. 1966. *Consumer Decision Processes*, Englewood Cliffs, NJ: Prentice Hall.

Nocera, Joseph. 1994. *A Piece of the Action*. New York: Simon & Schuster.

Noonan, Jeanne. 1991. Testimony of Associated Director for Credit Practices, Federal Trade Commission, at a Hearing before the Subcommittee on Consumer Affairs and Coinage of the Committee on Banking, Finance and Urban Affairs. US House of Representatives, June 6.

Norberg, Scott F. 1999. Consumer Bankruptcy's New Clothes: An Empirical Study of Discharge and Debt Collection in Chapter 13. *American Bankruptcy Institute Law Review* 7: 415.

Norberg, Scott F., and Andrew J. Velkey. 2006. Debtor Discharge and Creditor Repayment in Chapter 13. *Creighton Law Review* (April).

Nugent, Rolf. 1933. Three Experiments with Small Loan Interest Rates. *Harvard Business Review* (October).

———. 1939. *Consumer Credit and Economic Stability*. New York: Russell Sage Foundation.

———. 1941. The Loan Shark Problem. *Law and Contemporary Problems* (Winter).

Nunez, Stephen, and Howard Rosenthal. 2004. Bankruptcy "Reform" in Congress: Creditors, Committees, Ideology, and Floor Voting in the Legislative Process. *Journal of Law, Economics, and Organization* (October).

Nunnally, Bennie H., Jr., and D. Anthony Plath. 1989. Leasing versus Borrowing: Evaluating Alternative Forms of Consumer Credit. *Journal of Consumer Affairs* (Winter).

Oaksford, Mike, and Nick Chater. 1996. Rational Explanation of the Selection Task. *Psychological Review* (April).

O'Connell, Sean, and Chris Reid. 2005. Working Class Consumer Credit in the UK, 1925–60: The Role of the Check Trader. *Economic History Review* (May).

O'Donoghue, Ted, and Matthew Rabin. 1999. Doing It Now or Doing It Later. *American Economic Review* (March).

———. 2000. The Economics of Immediate Gratification. *Journal of Behavioral Decision Making*, special issue (April/June).

Oeltjen, Jarret C. 1975. Usury: Utilitarian or Useless? *Florida State Law Review* (Spring).

Olney, Martha L. 1991. *Buy Now, Pay Later: Advertising, Credit, and Consumer Durables in the 1920s*. Chapel Hill: University of North Carolina Press.

Ornstein, Stephen E. J. 1996. Examining the Effect of New Legislation on Consumer Protection for "High Cost" Mortgages. *Real Estate Law Journal* (Summer).

Ors, Evren. 2004. Postmortem on the Federal Reserve's Functional Cost Analysis Program: How Useful Was the FCA? *Review of Financial Economics*, nos. 1–2.

Padilla, Jorge A., and Marco Pagano. 1997. Endogenous Communication among Lenders and Entrepreneurial Incentives. *Review of Financial Studies* (Spring).

———. 2000. Sharing Default Information as a Borrower Discipline Device. *European Economic Review* (December).

Pae, Peter. 1992. Success of AT&T's Universal Card Puts Pressure on Big Banks to Reduce Rates. *Wall Street Journal* (February 4).

Pagano, Marco, ed. 2001. *Defusing Default: Incentives and Institutions*. Washington, DC: Development Centre of the Organization for the Economic Inter-American Development Bank.

Pagano, Marco, and Tullio Jappelli. 1993. Information Sharing in Credit Markets. *Journal of Finance* (December).

Palash, Carl J. 1979. Household Debt Burden: How Heavy Is It? *Federal Reserve Bank of New York Quarterly Review* (Summer).

Paquette, Lynn. 1986. Estimating Household Debt Service Payments. *Federal Reserve Bank of New York Quarterly Review* (Summer).

Pardo, Rafael I. 2009a. Failing to Answer Whether Bankruptcy Reform Failed: A Critique of the First Report from the 2007 Consumer Bankruptcy Project. *American Bankruptcy Law Journal* (Winter).

——. 2009b. Setting the Record Straight: A Sur-Reply to Professors Lawless et Al. *Seattle University Law Review* (Fall).

Park, Sangkyun. 1993. The Determinants of Consumer Installment Credit. *Federal Reserve Bank of St. Louis Review* (November–December).

Patrick, Thomas M. 1984. A Proposed Procedure for Facilitating the Analysis of Lease-Purchase Decisions by Consumers." *Journal of Consumer Affairs* (Winter).

Pavan, Marina. 2008. Consumer Durables and Risky Borrowing: The Effects of Bankruptcy Protection. *Journal of Monetary Economics* (November).

Pearce, Douglas K. 1985. Rising Household Debt in Perspective. *Federal Reserve Bank of Kansas City Economic Review* (July–August).

Pennington-Cross, Anthony, and Giang Ho. 2008. Predatory Lending Laws and the Cost of Credit. *Real Estate Economics* (Summer).

Persky, Joseph. 2007. From Usury to Interest. *Journal of Economic Perspectives* (Winter).

Peterson, Richard L. 1979. An Investigation of Sex Discrimination in Commercial Banks. West Lafayette, IN: Purdue University Credit Research Center, Working Paper 28.

——. 1981. An Investigation of Sex Discrimination in Commercial Banks' Direct Consumer Lending. *Bell Journal of Economics* (Autumn).

——. 1986. Creditors' Use of Collection Remedies. *Journal of Financial Research* (Spring).

Peterson, Richard L., and Kyomi Aoki. 1984. Bankruptcy Filings before and after Implementation of the Bankruptcy Reform Act. Journal of Economics and Business (February).

Peterson, Richard L., and Gregory D. Falls. 1981a. *Costs and Benefits of Restrictions on Creditors' Remedies.* West Lafayette, IN: Purdue University Credit Research Center, Working Paper 41.

——. 1981b. Impact of a Ten Percent Usury Ceiling: Empirical Evidence. West Lafayette, IN: Purdue University Credit Research Center, Working Paper 40.

Peterson, Richard L., and James R. Frew. 1977. Creditor Remedy Restrictions and Interstate Differences in Personal Loan Rates and Availability: A Supplementary Analysis. West Lafayette, IN: Purdue University Credit Research Center, Working Paper 14.

Peterson, Richard L., and David K. Kidwell. 1979. Bank and Non Bank Competition in Consumer Loan Markets. *Journal of Retail Banking* (December).

Peterson, Richard L., and Carol M. Peterson. 1978. Testing for Sex Discrimination in Commercial Bank Consumer Lending. West Lafayette, IN: Purdue University Credit Research Center, Working Paper 10.

Pew Charitable Trusts, 2012. *Payday Lending in America: Who Borrows, Where They Borrow, and Why?* Philadelphia, PA: Pew Charitable Trusts.

Phelps, Edmund S. 1972. The Statistical Theory of Racism and Sexism. *American Economic Review* (September).

Phillips, Lynn W., and Bobby J. Calder. 1979. Evaluating Consumer Protection Programs: Part I, Weak but Commonly Used Research Designs. *Journal of Consumer Affairs* (Winter).

——. 1980. Evaluating Consumer Protection Laws II: Promising Methods. *Journal of Consumer Affairs* (Summer).

Phillips, Robert F., and Anthony M. Yezer. 1996. Self-Selection and Tests for Bias and Risk in Mortgage Lending: Can You Price the Mortgage If You Don't Know the Process? *Journal of Real Estate Research*, no. 1.

Plank, Thomas E. 1996. The Constitutional Limits of Bankruptcy. *Tennessee Law Review* (Spring).

Plott, Charles R. 1996. Rational Individual Behavior in Markets and Social Choice Processes: The Discovered Preference Hypothesis. In *The Rational Foundations of Economic Behavior*, edited by Kenneth J. Arrow, Enrico Colombatto, Mark Perlman, and Christian Schmidt. London: Macmillan, IEA Conference Vol. 114.

Plott, Charles R., and Kathryn Zeiler. 2005. The Willingness to Pay–Willingness to Accept Gap, the "Endowment Effect," Subject Misconceptions, and Experimental Procedures for Eliciting Valuations. *American Economic Review* (June).

Plummer, Wilbur C. 1927. The Social and Economic Consequences of Buying on the Installment Plan. *Annals of the American Academy of Political and Social Science* 129, suppl.

Poapst, J. V., and W. R. Waters. 1964. Rates of Return on Consumer Durables. *Journal of Finance* (December).

Policis. 2004. *The Effect of Interest Rate Controls in Other Countries*. London: Policis. Available at www.policis.com/pdf/credit/Effect%20of%20interest%20rate%20controls.pdf.

——. 2006. Economic and Social Risks of Consumer Credit Market Regulation: A Comparative Analysis of the Regulatory and Consumer Protection Frameworks for Consumer Credit in France, Germany and the UK. London: Policis. Available at www.policis.com/pdf/credit/Economic%20and%20Social%20Risks%20of%20Consumer%20Credit%20Market%20Regulation.pdf.

Political and Economic Research Council. 2011. General Response to Criticisms of Recent PERC Report. Durham, NC: Political and Economic Research Council. Available at www.credit.com/blog/2011/06/new-study-examines-reliability-of-credit-reports.

Politser, Peter. 2008. *Neuroeconomics: A Guide to the New Science of Making Choices*. New York: Oxford University Press.

Posner, Eric A. 1995. Contract Law in the Welfare State: A Defense of the Unconscionability Doctrine, Usury Laws, and Related Limitations on the Freedom to Contract. *Journal of Legal Studies* (June).

Powell, Andrew P., Nataliya Mylenko, Margaret Miller, and Giovanni Majnoni. 2004. Improving Credit Information, Bank Regulation, and Supervision: On the Role and Design of Public Credit Registries. Washington, DC: World Bank Policy Research Working Paper 3443 (November 2).

Prager, Robin A., Mark D. Manuszak, Beth K. Kiser, and Ron Borzekowski. 2009. Interchange Fees and Payment Card Networks: Economics, Industry Developments, and Policy Issues. Federal Reserve Board Finance and Economics Discussion Series 2009-23.

Pratt, R. J. A., and W. P. McGhee. 1967. An Application of Multivariate Statistical Techniques as an Aid in Decision Making with Regard to Applications for Credit.

Investigations of Corporate Credit and Risk Policies, University of Pittsburgh, Working Paper 2.

Prelec, Drazen, and George Loewenstein. 1998. The Red and the Black: Mental Accounting of Savings and Debt. *Marketing Science* (Winter).

Prell, Michael J. 1973. The Long Run Growth of Consumer Installment Credit—Some Observations. *Federal Reserve Bank of Kansas City Monthly Review* (September).

President's Commission on Financial Structure and Regulation. 1971. *Report of the President's Commission on Financial Structure and Regulation.* Washington, DC: Government Printing Office.

Pridgen, Dee. 2006. *Consumer Credit and the Law.* Eagan, MN: Thomson/West.

Protecting the Subjects of Credit Reports. 1971. *Yale Law Journal* (April).

Putnam, Robert D. 2000. *Bowling Alone: The Collapse and Revival of American Community.* New York: Touchstone.

Quercia, Roberto G., Michael A. Stegman, and Walter R. Davis. 2004. Assessing the Impact of North Carolina's Predatory Lending Law. *Housing Policy Debate*, no. 3.

Ramsay, Iain. 2002. Mandatory Bankruptcy Counseling: The Canadian Experience. *Fordham Journal of Corporate and Financial Law* 7: 525.

Rasor, Paul B. 1993. Biblical Roots of Modern Consumer Credit Law. *Journal of Law and Religion* 10, no. 1.

Ratcliff, Paul. 2000. Managing Deeper Relationships. *Mortgage Banking* (March).

Real, Leslie, and Thomas Caraco. 1986. Risk and Foraging in Stochastic Environments. *Annual Review of Ecology and Systematics.*

Redlich, Fritz. 1947. *The Molding of American Banking.* New York: Hafner.

Robinson, Louis N., and Rolf Nugent. 1935. *The Regulation of the Small Loan Business.* New York: Russell Sage Foundation.

Robinson, W. F. 1960. Legal Aspects. In Sales and Consumer Finance Companies: A Lecture Series, presentation by Bank of New York and Pacific Finance Corporation. New York: New York Society of Security Analysts.

Rockoff, Hugh. 2003. Prodigals and Projectors: An Economic History of Usury Laws in the United States from Colonial Times to 1900. Cambridge, MA: National Bureau of Economic Research, Working Paper 9742 (May).

Roebuck, J. 2014. In Court, 'Frankie the Fixer' Describes Collecting Loan-Sharking Debts. *McClatchy Tribune Information Services* (January 2).

Roever, W. Alexander, John N. McElravey, and Glenn M. Schultz. 2000. Home Equity Line of Credit (HELOC) Securitizations. In *Handbook of Nonagency Mortgage Backed Securities*, 2nd ed., edited by J. Fabozzi, Chuck Ramsey, and Michael Marz. New Hope, PA: Frank J. Fabozzi Associates.

Rogers, David H. 1974. *Consumer Banking in New York.* New York: Columbia University Press.

Rosen, Sherwin. 1974. Hedonic Prices and Implicit Markets: Product Differentiation in Pure Competition. *Journal of Political Economy* (January/February).

Rosenberg, Eric, and Alan Gleit. 1994. Quantitative Methods in Credit Management: A Survey. *Operations Research* (July–August).

Rothschild, Michael. 1973. Models of Market Organization with Imperfect Information: A Survey. *Journal of Political Economy* (November–December).

Rothschild, Michael, and Joseph E. Stiglitz. 1970. Increasing Risk: I. A Definition. *Journal of Economic Theory* (September 1970).

Rothstein, Jesse, and Cecilia Elena Rouse. 2011. Student Loans and Early-Career Occupational Choices. Journal of Public Economics (February).

Rowlingson, Karen. 1994. *Money Lenders and Their Customers.* London: Policy Studies Institute.

Rubin, Edward L. 1991. Legislative Methodology: Some Lessons from the Truth in Lending Act. *Georgetown University Law Review* (December).

Rubinstein, Ariel. 2003. Economics and Psychology? The Case of Hyperbolic Discounting. *International Economic Review* (November).

Runkle, David E. 1991. Liquidity Constraints and the Permanent Income Hypothesis: Evidence from Panel Data. *Journal of Monetary Economics* (February).

Sallie Mae. 2009. *How Undergraduate Students Use Credit Cards: Sallie Mae's National Study of Usage Rates and Trends 2009* (April). Newark, DE: Sallie Mae.

Salop, Stenen, and Joseph Stiglitz. 1977. Bargains and Ripoffs: A Model of Monopolistically Competitive Price Dispersion. *Review of Economic Studies* (October).

Samuels, Richard, Stephen Stich, and Michael Bishop. 2002. Ending the Rationality Wars: How to Make Disputes about Human Rationality Disappear. In *Common Sense, Reasoning, and Rationality,* edited by Renee Elio. New York: Oxford University Press.

Samuels, Richard, Stephen Stich, and Luc Faucher. 2004. Reason and Rationality. In *Handbook of Epistemology,* edited by I. Niiniluoto, M. Sintonen, and J. Wolenski. Dordrecht: Kluwer.

Samuelson, Paul A. 1937. A Note on Measurement of Utility. *Review of Economic Studies* (February).

———. 1969. Statement by Dr. Paul A. Samuelson before the Committee of the Judiciary of the General Court of Massachusetts in Support of the Uniform Consumer Credit Code, January 29, 1969. Chicago: National Conference of Commissioners on Uniform State Laws.

Santomero, Anthony M. 2001. Perspectives on Research Issues in Consumer Behavior. *Federal Reserve Bank of Philadelphia Business Review* (Third Quarter).

Sartoris, William L. 1972. The Effects of Regulation, Population Characteristics, and Competition on the Market for Personal Cash Loans. *Journal of Financial and Quantitative Analysis* (September).

Saunders, Anthony. 2000. *Financial Institutions Management,* 3rd ed. Boston: Irwin McGraw Hill.

Schallheim, James S. 1994. *Lease or Buy?* Cambridge, MA: Harvard University Press.

Schoemaker, Paul J. H. 1982. The Expected Utility Model: Its Variants, Purposes, Evidence and Limitations. *Journal of Economic Literature* (June).

Schor, Juliet B. 2001. Who's Going Bankrupt and Why? *Texas Law Review* (April).

Schwartz, Alan, and Louis L. Wilde. 1979. Intervening in Markets on the Basis of Imperfect Information: A Legal and Economic Analysis. *University of Pennsylvania Law Review* (January).

———. 1983. Imperfect Information in Markets for Contracts Terms: The Examples of Warranties and Security Interests. *Virginia Law Review* 69 (November).

Schwartz, Saul. 2003. The Effect of Bankruptcy Counseling on Future Creditworthiness: Evidence from a Natural Experiment. *American Bankruptcy Law Journal* 77: 257.

Scott, Robert E. 1989. "Rethinking the Regulation of Coercive Creditors' Remedies." *Columbia Law Review* (May).

Seidel, Joseph L. 1998. The Consumer Credit Reporting Reform Act: Information Sharing and Preemption. *North Carolina Banking Institute* (April).

Seidl, John M. 1968. *Upon the Hip—A Study of the Criminal Loan Shark Industry.* Unpublished Ph.D. dissertation, Harvard University.

——. 1970. Let's Compete with Loan Sharks. *Harvard Business Review* (May–June).

Seligman, Edwin Robert Anderson. 1927. *The Economics of Installment Selling: A Study in Consumers' Credit,* 2 vols. New York: Harper.

Sexton, Donald E. 1977. Determining Good and Bad Credit Risks among High and Low Income Families. *Journal of Business* (April).

Shay, Robert P. 1953. *Regulation W: Experiment in Credit Control.* University of Maine Studies, Second Series, No. 67. Orono: University of Maine Press.

——. 1957. Consumer Credit Control as an Instrument of Monetary Policy for Economic Stability. In *Consumer Installment Credit,* Part II, Vol. 2, Board of Governors of the Federal Reserve System. Washington, DC: Board of Governors of the Federal Reserve System.

——. 1968. The Impact of the Uniform Consumer Credit Code upon the Market for Consumer Installment Credit. *Law and Contemporary Problems* (Autumn).

——. 1970. Factors Affecting Price, Volume, and Credit Risk in the Consumer Finance Industry. *Journal of Finance* (May).

——. 1973. The Impact of State Legal Rate Ceilings upon the Availability and Price of Consumer Installment Credit. In *Technical Studies of the National Commission on Consumer Finance,* Vol. 4. Washington, DC: Government Printing Office.

——. 1974. The Econometric Analysis of the National Commission on Consumer Finance. Paper presented at the Annual Meeting of the American Finance Association.

Shay, Robert P., and William K. Brandt. 1979. Consumer Credit Protection Legislation and Consumer Credit Shopping: Truth in Lending and Equal Credit Opportunity Acts. In *The Costs and Benefits of Public Regulation of Consumer Financial Services,* edited by Arnold A. Heggestad and Ruth Brannon. Cambridge MA: ABT.

Shay, Robert P., and William C. Dunkelberg. 1975. *Retail Store Credit Card Use in New York.* New York: Columbia University Press.

Shay, Robert P., and Donald E. Sexton. 1979. Anti-Discrimination Laws in Consumer Credit Markets: Their Impact on Creditors' Approval of Applications. In *The Costs and Benefits of Public Regulation of Consumer Financial Services,* edited by Arnold A. Heggestad and John J. Mingo. Cambridge, MA: ABT.

Shepard, Lawrence. 1984a. Accounting for the Rise in Consumer Bankruptcy Rates in the United States: A Preliminary Analysis of Aggregate Data (1945–1981). *Journal of Consumer Affairs* (Winter).

——. 1984b. Personal Failures and the Bankruptcy Reform Act of 1978. *Journal of Law and Economics* (October).

Sherer, Paul M. 2000. A Circle of Debt: Many Borrowers Are Also Lenders. *Wall Street Journal* (July 5): C1.

Shiers, Alden F., and Daniel P. Williamson. 1987. Nonbusiness Bankruptcies and the Law: Some Empirical Results. *Journal of Consumer Affairs* (Winter).

Shinkel, Bernard A. 1980. The Effects of Equal Credit Opportunity Legislation in Consumer Finance Lending. *Journal of Business Research* (March).

Shuchman, Philip. 1983. The Average Bankrupt: A Description and Analysis of 753 Personal Bankruptcy Filings in Nine States. *Commercial Law Journal* (June–July).

——. 1985. New Jersey Debtors, 1982–83: An Empirical Study. *Seton Hall Law Review,* no. 3.

——. 1990. Social Science Research on Bankruptcy. *Rutgers Law Review* (Fall).

Simmons, Edward C. 1957. Consumer Credit Control and Central Banking. In *Consumer Installment Credit*, Part II, Vol. 2, Board of Governors of the Federal Reserve System. Washington, DC: Board of Governors of the Federal Reserve System.

Simon, Herbert A. 1986. Rationality in Psychology and Economics. *Journal of Business* (October).

——. 1990. Invariants of Human Behavior. *Annual Review of Psychology*.

Simon, Ruth. 2010. Credit Card Rates Climb. *Wall Street Journal* (August 23): 1.

Sinkey, Joseph F., Jr., and Robert C. Nash. 1993. Assessing the Riskiness and Profitability of Credit-Card Banks. *Journal of Financial Services Research* (June).

Sittner, Larry, S. Grummert, C. J. Potthoff, and E. D. Lyman. 1967. Medical Expense as a Factor in Bankruptcy. *Nebraska State Medical Journal* (September).

Skeel, David A., Jr. 2000. Vern Countryman and the Path of Progressive (and Populist) Bankruptcy Scholarship. *Harvard Law Review* (February).

——. 2001. *Debt's Dominion: A History of Bankruptcy Law in America*. Princeton, NJ: Princeton University Press.

Skiba, Paige Marta, and Jeremy Tobacman. 2011. Do Payday Loans Cause Bankruptcy? Vanderbilt University Law and Economics Research Paper No. 11-13.

Smith, Adam. 1994 [1776]. *The Wealth of Nations*. New York: Modern Library.

Smith, James F. 1977. The Equal Credit Opportunity Act of 1974: A Cost Benefit Analysis. *Journal of Finance* (May).

Smith, Michael L., and James F. Cash 1993. Adverse Selection, Regulated Prices and Returns to Holders of Credit Life Insurance. *Journal of Insurance Regulation* (Winter).

Smith, Paul F. 1964. *Consumer Credit Costs, 1949–59*. National Bureau of Economic Research, Studies in Consumer Installment Financing No. 11. Princeton, NJ: Princeton University Press.

——. 1967. Recent Trends in the Financial Position of Nine Major Consumer Finance Companies. In *The Consumer Finance Industry: Its Costs and Regulation*, edited by John M. Chapman and Robert P. Shay. New York: Columbia University Press.

——. 1973. The Status of Competition in Consumer Credit Markets. In *Technical Studies of the National Commission on Consumer Finance*, Vol. 6. Washington: Government Printing Office.

Smith, Vernon L. 1972. A Theory and Test of Credit Rationing: Some Generalizations. *American Economic Review* (June).

——. 1991. Rational Choice: The Contrast between Economics and Psychology. *Journal of Political Economy* (August).

——. 2005. Behavioral Economics Research and the Foundations of Economics. *Journal of Socio-Economics* (March).

Smith, Warren L. 1967. Is the Growth of Private Debt a Cause for Concern? In *Monetary Process and Policy: A Symposium*, edited by George Horwich. Homewood, IL: Irwin.

Snowden, Kenneth A. 1988. Mortgage Lending and American Urbanization, 1880–1890. *Journal of Economic History* (June).

Soman, Dilip. 2001. Effects of Payment Mechanism on Spending Behavior: The Role of Rehearsal and Immediacy of Payments. *Journal of Consumer Research* (March).

——. 2003. The Effect of Payment Transparency on Consumption: Quasi-Experiments from the Field. *Marketing Letters* (October).

Soman, Dilip, and John T. Gourville. 2001. Transaction Decoupling: How Price Bundling Affects the Decision to Consume. *Journal of Marketing Research* (February).

Sonntag, Janet. 1995. The Debate about Credit Scoring. *Mortgage Banking* (November).

SourceMedia. 2008. *Card Industry Directory*, 20th ed. New York: SourceMedia.

Sowell, Thomas. 2009. *The Housing Boom and Bust*. New York: Basic Books.

Spence, A. Michael. 1973. Job Market Signaling. *Quarterly Journal of Economics* (August).

———. 1974. *Market Signaling: Informational Transferring in Hiring and Related Screening Processes*. Cambridge, MA: Harvard University Press.

Spiro, Leah Nathans. 1991. How AT&T Skimmed the Cream Off the Credit-Card Market, *Business Week* (December 16).

St. John, Cheri. 2003. What the CFA Got Right—and Wrong—about Credit Score Accuracy. In *Fair Isaac Viewpoints* (January–February).

Stango, Victor. 2000. Competition and Pricing in the Credit Card Market. *Review of Economics and Statistics* (August).

Stango, Victor, and Jonathan Zinman. 2011. Borrowing High vs. Borrowing Higher: Sources and Consequences of Dispersion in Individual Borrowing Costs. University of California, Davis, and Dartmouth College, Working Paper (November).

Stanley, David T., and Marjorie Girth. 1971. *Bankruptcy: Problem, Process, Reform*. Washington, DC: Brookings Institute.

Staten, Michael E. 1993. The Impact of Post-Bankruptcy Credit on the Number of Personal Bankruptcies. Purdue University Credit Research Center, Working Paper 58.

———. 2006. The Evolution of the Credit Counseling Industry in the United States. In *The Economics of Consumer Credit*, edited by Giuseppe Bertola, Richard Disney, and Charles B. Grant. Cambridge, MA: MIT Press.

Staten, Michael E., and John M. Barron. 2002. College Student Credit Card Usage. Washington, DC: Georgetown University, Credit Research Center, Working Paper 65.

Staten, Michael E., and Fred H. Cate. 2003. The Impact of Opt-In Privacy Rules on Retail Credit Markets: A Case Study of MBNA. *Duke Law Journal* (February).

———. 2005. Accuracy in Credit Reporting. In *Building Assets, Building Credit*, edited by Nicolas P. Retsinas and Eric S. Belsky. Washington, DC: Brookings Institution.

Staten, Michael E., John R. Umbeck, and Otis W. Gilley. 1990. A Theory of Indirect Lending. *Economic Inquiry* (July).

Stavins, Joanna. 2000. Credit Card Borrowing, Delinquency, and Personal Bankruptcy. *New England Economics Review* (July–August).

Stearns, Maxwell, and Todd J. Zywicki. 2009. *Public Choice Concepts and Applications in Law*. St. Paul, MN: West.

Steinbuks, Jevgenijs. 2008. Essays on Regulation and Imperfections in Financial Markets. Unpublished Ph.D. dissertation, George Washington University.

Steinbuks, Jevgenijs, and Gregory Elliehausen. 2014. The Economic Effects of Legal Restrictions on High-Cost Mortgages. *Journal of Real Estate Finance and Economics* (forthcoming).

Stigler, George. 1961. The Economics of Information. *Journal of Political Economy* (June).

Stiglitz, Joseph E., and Andrew Weiss. 1981. Credit Rationing in Markets with Imperfect Information. *American Economic Review* (June).

Straka, John W. 2000. A Shift in the Mortgage Landscape: The 1990s Move to Automated Credit Evaluations. *Journal of Housing Research* 11, no. 2.

Strotz, R. H. 1955–1956. Myopia and Inconsistency in Dynamic Utility Maximization. *Review of Economic Studies* 23, no. 3.

Student Monitor. 2000, 2005. *Student Monitor: Financial Services*. Ridgewood, NJ: Student Monitor. Available at www.studentmonitor.com.

Suits, Daniel. B. 1958. The Demand for New Automobiles in the United States, 1929–1956. *Review of Economics and Statistics* (August).

Sullivan, A. Charlene. 1984. *Prices of Consumer Credit in the Absence of Rate Ceilings: An Update*. West Lafayette, IN: Purdue University Credit Research Center, Monograph 27.

Sullivan, Teresa A., Elizabeth Warren, and Jay Lawrence Westbrook. 1989. *As We Forgive Our Debtors*. New York: Oxford University Press.

———. 2000. *The Fragile Middle Class: Americans in Debt*. New Haven, CT: Yale University Press.

———. 2006. Less Stigma or More Financial Distress: An Empirical Analysis of the Extraordinary Increase in Bankruptcy Filings. *Stanford Law Review* (November).

Tabb, Charles Jordan. 1991. The Historical Evolution of the Bankruptcy Discharge. *American Bankruptcy Law Journal* (Spring).

———. 1997. *The Law of Bankruptcy*. Westbury, NY: Foundation.

Tapscott, Tracy R. 1985. Consumer Installment Credit 1980–1985. *Survey of Current Business* (August).

Temin, Peter, and Hans-Joachim Voth. 2008. Financial Repression in a Natural Experiment: Loan Allocation and Change in the Usury Laws in 1714. *Economic Journal* (April).

TERI. 1998. *Credit Risk or Credit Worthy? College Students and Credit Cards*. Boston: Education Resources Institute.

Thaler, Richard H. 1980. Toward a Positive Theory of Consumer Choice. *Journal of Economic Behavior and Organization* (March).

———. 1981. Some Empirical Evidence on Dynamic Inconsistency. *Economics Letters* 8, no. 3.

———. 1985. Mental Accounting and Consumer Choice. *Marketing Science* (Summer).

Thaler, Richard H., and Eric J. Johnson. 1990. Gambling with House Money and Trying to Break Even: The Effects of Prior Outcomes on Risky Choice. *Management Science* (June).

Thalheimer, Richard, and Mukhtar M. Ali. 2004. The Relationship of Pari-Mutuel Wagering and Casino Gaming to Personal Bankruptcy. *Contemporary Economic Policy* (July).

Theodos, Brett, Rachel Brash, Jessica F. Compton, Karen Masken, Nancy Pindus, and C. Eugene Steuerle. 2010. *Who Needs Credit at Tax Time and Why: A Look at Refund Anticipation Loans and Refund Anticipation Checks*. Washington, DC: Urban Institute.

Thomas, Lyn C. 2000. A Survey of Credit and Behavioural Scoring: Forecasting Financial Risk of Lending to Consumers. *International Journal of Forecasting* (April–June).

Thomas, Lyn C., David B. Edelman, and Jonathan N. Crook. 2002. *Credit Scoring and Its Applications*. Philadelphia: Society for Industrial and Applied Mathematics.

Timmons, Heather. 2000. Putting Borrowers in a Bind: Fearful of Competition, Lenders Won't Divulge Credit Records. *Business Week* (March 20).

Tobin, James. 1956. The Interest Elasticity of the Transactions Demand for Cash. *Review of Economics and Statistics* (August).

Touche, Ross, and Company. 1969. *Economic Characteristics of Department Store Credit*. New York: National Retail Merchants Association.

Turner, Michael A. 2003. *The Fair Credit Reporting Act: Access, Efficiency and Opportunity*. Washington, DC: National Chamber Foundation.

Turner, Michael A., and Robin Varghese. 2007. Economic Impacts of Payment Participation in Latin America. Chapel Hill, NC: Political and Economic Research Council.

Turner, Michael A, Alyssa Stewart Lee, Ann Schanave, Robin Varghese, and Patrick D. Walker. 2006. *Give Credit Where Credit is Due: Increasing Access to Affordable Mainstream Credit Using Alternative Data*. Washington, DC: Brookings Institution and Political and Economic Research Council.

Turner, Michael A., Robin Varghese, and Patrick D. Walker. 2011. *U.S. Consumer Credit Reports: Measuring Accuracy and Dispute Impacts*. Durham, NC: Political and Economic Research Council.

Turner, Michael A., and Patrick D. Walker. 2008. *Impact of Proposed Fee Cap on the Subprime Card Industry*. Chapel Hill, NC: Political and Economic Research Council, Center for Competitive Credit (September).

Turner, Michael A., Patrick D. Walker, Sukanya Chaudhuri, and Robin Varghese. 2012. *A New Pathway to Financial Inclusion: Alternative Data, Credit Building, and Responsible Lending in the Wake of the Great Recession*. Durham NC: Policy and Economics Research Council.

Tversky, Amos, and Daniel Kahneman. 1974. Judgment under Uncertainty: Heuristics and Biases. *Science*, new series (September).

———. 1981. The Framing of Decisions and the Rationality of Choice. *Science*, new series (January).

———. 1983. Extensional versus Intuitive Reasoning: The Conjunction Fallacy in Probability Learning. *Psychological Review* 90 (October).

Umbeck, John, and Robert E. Chatfield, 1982. The Structure of Contracts and Transaction Costs. *Journal of Money, Credit and Banking* (November).

US Department of Justice, Executive Office for US Trustees. 2005. Bankruptcy Abuse Prevention and Consumer Protection Act of 2005. Washington, DC: US Department of Justice.

US Department of the Treasury. 2009. *Financial Regulatory Reform, A New Foundation: Rebuilding Financial Supervision and Regulation*. Washington: Department of the Treasury (June 17).

US House of Representatives. 1968. Hearings on Commercial Credit Bureaus before a Subcommittee on Invasion of Privacy of the House Committee on Government Operations. 90th Congress, 2nd session.

———. 1975. *Equal Credit Opportunity Act Amendments of 1975: Report Together with Additional Views, House Report 94-210*. Washington, DC: Government Printing Office.

US Senate. 1931. *Report to the President on the Bankruptcy Act and Its Administration in the Courts of the United States*. Washington, DC: Government Printing Office (December 5).

———. 1973. *Report of the Committee on Banking, Housing, and Urban Affairs to Accompany S. 2101 Together with Additional Views*, Senate Report 93-278. Washington, DC: Government Printing Office.

———. 1976. *Report of the Committee on Banking, Housing, and Urban Affairs to Accompany S. 6516 Together with Additional Views*, Senate Report 94-589. Washington, DC: Government Printing Office.

——. 2005. Profiteering in a Nonprofit Industry: Abusive Practices in Credit Counseling. Senate Report 109-55, prepared by the Permanent Subcommittee on Investigations of the Committee on Homeland Security and Government Affairs, 109th Congress, 1st Session.

——. 2006. Hearing before the Subcommittee on Administrative Oversight and the Courts of the Committee on the Judiciary. December. Available at: http://www.gpo.gov/fdsys/pkg/CHRG-109shrg34119/pdf/CHRG-109shrg34119.pdf.

Vandenbrink, Donna C. 1982. The Effects of Usury Ceilings. *Federal Reserve Bank of Chicago Economic Perspectives* (Midyear).

——. 1985. Usury Ceilings and DIDMCA. *Federal Reserve Bank of Chicago Economic Perspectives* (September–October).

Venkatesh, Sudhir Alladi. 2006. *Off the Books: The Underground Economy of the Urban Poor.* Cambridge, MA: Harvard University Press.

Verant, William J. 2000. *Consumer Lending Study Committee Report for the Forty-Fourth Session of the New Mexico State Legislature Submitted by the Financial Institutions Division Director.* Santa Fe: New Mexico Regulation and Licensing Department, Financial Institutions Division.

Vercammen, James A. 1995. Credit Bureau Policy and Sustainable Reputation Effects in Credit Markets. *Economica* (November).

Vermeersch, Arthur, 2011 [1912]. *The Catholic Encyclopedia,* Vol. 15. New York: Robert Appleton.

Villegas, Daniel J. 1982. An Analysis of the Impact of Interest Rate Ceilings. *Journal of Finance* (September).

——. 1989. The Impact of Usury Ceilings on Consumer Credit. *Southern Economic Journal* (July).

——. 1990. Regulation of Creditor Practices: An Evaluation of the FTC's Credit Practice Rule. *Journal of Economics and Business* (February).

Visa USA. 1995. *1995 Credit Card Functional Cost Study.* San Mateo, CA: Visa US. Business Research and Reporting Department.

——. 1996. Consumer Bankruptcy: Causes and Implications. *Visa Consumer Bankruptcy Reports* (July).

——. 1997. *Consumer Bankruptcy: Annual Bankruptcy Debtor Survey.* San Rafael, CA: Visa.

Wack, Kevin. 2014. Do Banks Have a Future in Small-Dollar Credit? *American Banker* (February 20).

Walker, Orville C., Jr., and Richard F. Sauter. 1974. Consumer Preferences for Alternative Retail Credit Terms: A Concept Test of the Effects of Consumer Legislation. *Journal of Marketing Research* (February).

Wallace, George J. 1973. The Logic of Consumer Credit Reform. *Yale Law Journal* (January).

——. 1976. The Uses of Usury: Low Rate Ceilings Reexamined. *Boston University Law Review* (April).

Warner, Dave. 2011. Authorities Accuse 13 in Philadelphia of Mob Charges. Reuters (May 13).

Warren, Charles. 1935. *Bankruptcy in United States History.* Washington, DC: Beard Books.

Warren, Elizabeth. 1998. The Bankruptcy Crisis. *Indiana Law Journal* (Fall).

Warren, Elizabeth. 2007. Unsafe At Any Rate. *Democracy* (Summer).

Warren, Elizabeth, and Amelia Warren Tyagi. 2003. *The Two-Income Trap: Why Middle-Class Mothers and Fathers Are Going Broke.* New York: Basic Books.

Warwick, Jacquelyn, and Phylis Mansfield. 2000. Credit Card Consumers: College Students' Knowledge and Attitude. *Journal of Consumer Marketing* (December).

Weiss, Lawrence A., Jagdeep S. Bhandari, and Russell Robins. 2001. An Analysis of State-Wide Variation in Bankruptcy Rates in the United States. *Emory Bankruptcy Developments Journal*, no. 2.

Wells, Beverly. 1999. At Wachovia, Customer Focus Means Information-Driven Continuous Relationship Management. *Journal of Retail Banking Services* (Summer).

Wheatley, John J., and Guy G. Gordon. 1971. Regulating the Price of Consumer Credit. *Journal of Marketing* (October).

White, James J. 2000. The Usury Trompe l'Oeil. *South Carolina Law Review* (Spring).

White, James J., and Frank W. Munger, Jr. 1971. Consumer Sensitivity to Interest Rates: An Empirical Study of New Car Buyers and Auto Loans. *Michigan Law Review* (June).

White, Lawrence H. 1977. Bankruptcy as an Economic Intervention. *Journal of Libertarian Studies* (Fall).

White, Michelle J. 1987. Personal Bankruptcy under the 1978 Bankruptcy Code: An Economic Analysis. *Indiana Law Journal*, no. 1.

——. 1991. Economic versus Sociological Approaches to Legal Research: The Case of Bankruptcy. *Law and Society Review.*

——. 1998. Why Don't More Households File for Bankruptcy? *Journal of Law, Economics, and Organization* (October).

——. 2007. Bankruptcy Reform and Credit Cards. *Journal of Economic Perspectives* (Fall).

Whitford, William C. 1979. A Critique of the Consumer Credit Collection System. *Wisconsin Law Review.*

——. 1986. The Appropriate Role of Security Interests in Consumer Transactions. *Cardozo Law Review* (Summer).

Wiener, Richard L., Corinne Baron-Donovan, Karen Gross, and Susan Block-Lieb. 2005. Debtor Education, Financial Literacy, and Pending Bankruptcy Legislation. *Behavioral Sciences and the Law* (May–June).

Wilde, Lewis L. 1977. Labor Market Equilibrium under Nonsequential Search. *Journal of Economic Theory* (December).

Wilshusen, Stephanie M. 2011. Meeting the Demand for Debt Relief. Discussion Paper, Payment Cards Center, Federal Reserve Bank of Philadelphia.

Wilson, Bart J., David W. Findlay, James W. Meehan, Jr., Charissa P. Wellford, and Karl Schurter. 2010. An Experimental Analysis of the Demand for Payday Loans. *B.E. Journal of Economic Analysis & Policy* 10, no. 1.

Wolbers, H. L. 1949. The Use of the Biographical Data Bank in Predicting Good and Potentially Poor Credit Risks. Unpublished M.A. thesis, University of Southern California.

Wright, Joshua D. 2012. The Antitrust/Consumer Protection Paradox: Two Policies at War with Each Other. *Yale Law Journal* 12.

Yang, Lien-Sheng. 1950. Buddhist Monasteries and Four Money-Raising Institutions in Chinese History. *Harvard Journal of Asiatic Studies* (June).

Yeager, Frederick C. 1974. Personal Bankruptcy and Economic Stability. *Southern Economic Journal* (July).

Yezer, Anthony M. J. 2010. *Review of Statistical Problems in the Measurement of Mortgage Market Discrimination and Credit Risk*. Washington, DC: Mortgage Bankers Association, Research Institute for Housing America.

Yezer, Anthony M., Robert F. Phillips, and Robert P. Trost. 1994. Bias in Estimates of Discrimination and Default in Mortgage Lending: The Effects of Simultaneity and Self-Selection. *Journal of Real Estate Finance and Economics*, no. 3.

Yieh, Kaili. 1996. Who Has a Negative Attitude toward Installment Debt in the U.S.?" *Consumer Interests Annual*.

Yoo, Peter S. 1997. Charging Up a Mountain of Debt: Accounting for the Growth of Credit Card Debt. *Federal Reserve Bank of St. Louis Review* (March–April).

——. 1998. Still Charging: The Growth of Credit Card Debt between 1992 and 1995. *Federal Reserve Bank of St. Louis Review* (January–February).

Zandi, Mark. 2009. *Financial Shock*. Upper Saddle River, NJ: FT.

Zeldes, Stephen P. 1989. Consumption and Liquidity Constraints: An Empirical Investigation. *Journal of Political Economy* (April).

Zhang, Yan. 2010. Fair Lending Analysis of Mortgage Pricing: Does Underwriting Matter? Washington, DC: Office of the Comptroller of the Currency, Working Paper 2010-1.

Zinman, Jonathan. 2010. Restricting Consumer Credit Access: Household Survey Evidence on Effects around the Oregon Rate Cap. *Journal of Banking and Finance* (March).

Zywicki, Todd J. 2000a. The Economics of Credit Cards. *Chapman Law Review* (Spring).

——. 2000b. With Apologies to Screwtape: A Response to Professor Alexander. *Bankruptcy Law and Practice* (September–October).

——. 2003. The Past, Present, and Future of Bankruptcy Law in America. *Michigan Law Review* 101.

——. 2005a. The Bankruptcy Clause. In *The Heritage Guide to the Constitution*, edited by Edwin Meese. Washington, DC: Heritage Foundation.

——. 2005b. An Economic Analysis of the Consumer Bankruptcy Crisis. *Northwestern University Law Review*, no. 4.

——. 2005c. Institutions, Incentives, and Consumer Bankruptcy Reform. *Washington and Lee Law Review* (Summer).

——. 2007. Testimony before the US House of Representatives, Committee on the Judiciary, Subcommittee on Commercial and Administrative Law. Hearing on Working Families in Financial Crisis: Medical Debt and Bankruptcy (July 17).

——. 2010a. Consumer Use and Government Regulation of Title Pledge Lending. *Loyola Consumer Law Review* (April).

——. 2010b. The Economics of Payment Card Interchange Fees and the Limits of Regulation. International Center for Law and Economics, Working Paper.

——. 2011. Credit Cards and Bankruptcy. George Mason School of Law, Working Paper (March).

——. 2013. The Consumer Financial Protection Bureau: Savior or Menace? George Mason University School of Law, Working Paper.